Piaget: With Feeling

Piaget: With Feeling

Cognitive, Social, and Emotional Dimensions

PHILIP A. COWAN
University of California, Berkeley

HOLT, RINEHART AND WINSTON

*New York Chicago San Francisco Dallas
Montreal Toronto London Sydney*

**For Carolyn
and for Joanna, Dena, and Jonathan**

Library of Congress Cataloging in Publication Data

Cowan, Philip A
Piaget : with feeling.

1. Child psychology. 2. Cognition in children.
3. Knowledge, Theory of. 4. Piaget, Jean, 1896–
BF721.C666 155.4'13'0924 78-993
ISBN 0-03-039856-8

Printed in the United States of America

8 9 0 1 090 9 8 7 6 5 4 3 2 1

Preface

Over the past fifty years, Jean Piaget and his co-workers have created a rich theory of intellectual development. Best known for its description of stages and changes in how children think, Piaget's theory has begun to stimulate investigation of how children feel and how they relate to others. These extensions of cognitive theory give promise of providing a new and comprehensive view of children from birth through adolescence. Parents and teachers are finding that this view leads to exciting ideas about the creation of more optimal environments for cognitive, social, and emotional growth.

Piaget lives and works in Geneva, Switzerland; in 1978 he is a vigorous eighty-two years old. Having written nearly one hundred volumes alone or in collaboration with his colleagues, he has established a pre-eminent reputation as a developmental psychologist. In his own eyes, however, he has made his primary contribution as a philosopher who has established genetic epistemology as a theory to explain the development of scientific knowledge.

As a developmental and clinical psychologist, and as a parent of three children, I have been intrigued and challenged by the possibility of bringing together the various aspects of Piaget's work. During fifteen years of teaching about Piaget to undergraduate and graduate students, and of consulting to teachers and families, I have become very sympathetic to the "so what" questions—so what difference will this theory make to our understanding of children at home and in the classroom? I have also begun to take Piaget's own philosophical endeavors more seriously. I have found that Piaget's theory of intelligence can be understood more clearly if it is viewed as a set of answers to questions which have troubled philosophers for centuries.

Traversing the range of Piaget's interests from theory to practice and from psychology to philosophy, I have organized this book with six specific goals in mind:

1. To show how Piaget's cognitive approach can serve as a framework for understanding social and emotional development. I want to provide an account of Piaget, and the child, *with feeling*.
2. To explore the implications of Piaget's psychological theory for educational practices from preschool through high school. Eleven of the fourteen chapters include a section on the educational implications of Piaget's approach.
3. To balance Piaget's usual emphasis on regularities and similarities in the develop-

ment of children with a discussion of factors which lead to normal individual differences and factors which may lead to serious disturbances in development.
4. To set Piaget's psychological theory within the broader context of genetic epistemology.
5. To present a description of Piaget's work that does justice to the theory's complexity, but does not presume that the reader has an extensive background in biology, psychology, physics, logic, mathematics, and epistemology.
6. To provide an up-to-date account of researchers outside Geneva who are making important contributions within Piaget's cognitive developmental framework.

No single volume can describe in complete detail all of the work by Piaget and the Piagetians on cognitive, social, emotional, educational, and philosophical topics. In writing this book for students, teachers, and parents with some knowledge of child development, my intention is to create a guide to the territory in which these important areas come together.

Plan of the book

Piaget: With Feeling contains four major sections. Part I begins with a brief biography of Piaget and continues with an introductory presentation of his general conceptual framework. It concludes with a description of Piaget's clinical method of research, showing how it differs from standardized intelligence testing and how it provides a useful approach to understanding the world of the child.

In Part II, each of the seven chapters describes the child at a single stage or substage of cognitive, social, and emotional development. Previous accounts have focused on infancy (birth to two), the primary grades of elementary school (around six to eight), and early adolescence (twelve to fourteen). I have included an equivalent depth of detail about the in-between years and stages, especially the preschool ages (two to five), intermediate schoolers (ten to twelve), and high schoolers (fourteen, plus). So that the reader can begin to go beyond the catalogue of specific achievements at each level, I have presented Piaget's general model of the changing logic structures presumed to underlie cognitive organization in the child and adolescent.

Part III is composed of two chapters which focus on individual differences in development. The first investigates variations that occur naturally in different social settings, and those that occur in the laboratory when we attempt to accelerate children's progress through the stages. (Piaget calls this "the American question.") The second chapter provides a beginning Piagetian model of diagnosis and treatment of developmental disturbances (schizophrenia, retardation, learning disabilities, neurosis). Understanding the so-called exceptional child raises a number of important issues for the understanding of all children.

Part IV contains a single chapter describing Piaget's genetic epistemology. Although philosophical questions come before psychological answers, I have found that the questions are usually understood better after readers have more familiarity with a psychological picture of the developing child.

Acknowledgments

The idea of writing this book was first suggested by Ted Sarbin, then at Berkeley, then and still a valued friend. As an editor at Holt, Roger Williams understood what I was trying to do with this book and offered concrete assistance with that task. Kathleen Nevils, the project editor, I know only as a voice on the telephone. She has managed to hold me to impossible deadlines while at the same time sounding supportive and sympathetic.

The first draft of the manuscript received many friendly criticisms and illuminating suggestions from Michael Maratsos and from John Watson; their thoughtful efforts helped me to make important additions and revisions of the book. Additional comments and welcome encouragement came from Paul Mussen, Dan Slobin, and Jonas Langer. I acknowledge with pleasure Jonas Langer's influence during my early years at Berkeley, when I came to see the importance of understanding the philosophical underpinnings of Piaget's approach. I have also benefited from a great many comments and interchanges with students at Berkeley—in particular, Lenny Breslow, Steve Schultz, Carol Slotnick, and Linda Kastelowitz. I am especially grateful to Linda Kastelowitz for her untiring search of the Piagetian research literature. Various parts of the final manuscript were typed by Sue Eicher, Kathaleen Pearce, and Norma Partridge-Wallace, with the major portion deciphered from my unreadable handwriting by Carolyn Bennett.

Carolyn Cowan has collaborated with me as a partner in this project. Her experience as a teacher has been invaluable in helping me to spell out the implications of Piaget for the classroom. By sharing ideas, improving clarity and style on every page, and just being the kind of person she is, she has played a crucial role in the creation of this book—and in my own development as well. Joanna Cowan, Dena Cowan, and Jonathan Cowan have worked on the bibliography, various versions of the title, and some of the ideas presented here. More important, each one has taught me different things about what it is like to see the world through the eyes of children and adolescents.

In the exchange of viewpoints with my family, colleagues, and students, I have discovered how much the writing of a book is a cognitive, social, *and* emotional process.

P.A.C.

Berkeley, California
January 1978

Contents

PART I

Biography, General Concepts, and Clinical Method

CHAPTER 1

Biographical Sketch

A recurring theme in Piaget's work is that ideas and theories are interpretations made by theorists, shaped by their particular frame of reference. As a first step in understanding Piaget's own theory, I have found it helpful to take a look at the man and the life experiences which have strongly influenced his point of view.

Most brief descriptions of Piaget's life, including this one, have been drawn from his autobiographical chapters in the series *A History of Psychology in Autobiography* (1952). Some additional details have been taken from two later books: *Insights and Illusions in Philosophy* (Piaget, 1965)[1], and *Psychologie et Épistémologie Génétiques* (Bresson and Montmollin, 1966).

THE MAN

As Piaget sits quietly, tamping his pipe, listening courteously to a speaker at a conference, he appears to be in complete repose. His appearance at these times belies the restless, active mind and the physically active person who at seventy often made the three-mile daily trip between home and office on a bicycle. On a visit to Berkeley in 1968 (at the age of seventy-two) he emerged from a long cross-country airplane trip one evening, ready to go hiking in the hills. Piaget is a physically substantial man, but he does not convey that impression, perhaps because one's gaze is immediately drawn to his face. One is almost forced to

[1]In the text, English titles will be used wherever translations exist, but the dates refer to the original publications in French.

smile in response to the constant twinkle in his eye and the snowy white hair that is often topped with a jaunty beret. The meerschaum pipe, which is also a part of his face, punctuates his speech or his thoughtful silence with unspoken comment. I have met Piaget briefly and I have read others' accounts of meeting him on public occasions during his visits to the United States (e.g., Elkind, 1970; Gardener, 1974). The impression is of a man of charm, wit, playfulness, and intellectual excitement. But others who have visited Piaget in Geneva also describe his role as "le patron"—a demanding "boss" who is accustomed to having things run just the way he wants them.

Piaget's prodigious work output is simply not explicable. Strictly speaking, of course, I should not refer to Piaget's theory, but to the point of view of the Genevan school. His chief colleague and coauthor has been Mlle. Bärbel Inhelder, who originally came to study child psychology with Piaget and has remained to share the leadership in many of his projects. Pierre Greco, Vinh-Bang, Guy Cellerier, Aline Szeminska, and Magali Bovet, who are also developmental psychologists, J. B. Grize and L. Apostel, who are logicians, S. Papert, a mathematician, along with Hermine Sinclair de Zwart, a psycholinguist, and many others, have been centrally involved in the creation of the theory. Despite the shared effort, all of them turn often to *le patron* for leadership, stimulation, and the organized written material which transmits much of their thinking to the rest of the world. Almost every day Piaget delivers to his secretary twelve long pages of a new text or monograph. He can be seen writing on planes, on trains, at conferences, in restaurants, and especially throughout most of his summer vacations in the mountains. He has recently remarked that one reason he is able to produce so much is that he does not have to spend his time reading Piaget.

EARLY EDUCATION

Jean Piaget was born on August 9, 1896, in Neuchatel, Switzerland, a small, French-speaking "college town." A precocious child with an early interest in biological science, he published his first scientific paper at the age of ten. He soon volunteered as a laboratory assistant to the director of a natural history museum, a man who studied molluscs (invertebrate soft- and hard-shelled animals such as snails, slugs, cuttlefish, and squids). When the director died, Piaget began publishing his own account of the experiments. On the basis of these papers he was offered a position as curator of a museum of natural history in Geneva. Only eleven years old, he reluctantly declined the invitation.

In adolescence and early adulthood Piaget became immersed in the philosophical controversies of his time. When he was fourteen, he was introduced to the epistemology of Henri Bergson, who regarded mathematics and logic as static systems inadequate for the understanding of time concepts and biological life forces. Piaget comments that this view supported his unwillingness, at that time, to study mathematics and logic. Later, he was exposed to Professor Reymond, a modern follower of Aristotle, who insisted that logic was the initial key to unlocking the secrets of the universe. Piaget felt pulled between these two apparently antithetical approaches to knowledge, logic versus intuition—the study of concepts versus the study of life. After hearing a lecture by William James, the famous American philosopher-psychologist, Piaget wrote an essay on neopragmatism in an attempt to show that there exists a logic of behavior and action distinct from rational logic. One gets the feeling, from reading Piaget's account of this period of his life, that this controversy between the static, timeless rules of logic and the dynamic changeability of living matter was not merely an abstract game; it was a deeply felt conflict. Perhaps, as he has speculated, it reflected an attempt to deal with the difference between the cold reason and logic shown by his historian father, and the intuitive emotionality of his mother.

By the time Piaget was twenty-two he had obtained his B.A. and Ph.D. from the University of Neuchatel and had published about twenty papers in the field of mallacology. He had also written one philosophical novel containing some of the themes which today still occupy the center of his attention. Perhaps the most general of Piaget's principles was part of his thinking even then—the notion of examining child and adult thought in terms of structure or organization rather than in terms of content.

SEARCH FOR A LIFEWORK

Having finished his "formal education" in 1918, Piaget was not at all certain what he wanted to do in his professional life. He had always been excited by the cosmic questions asked by philosophers, especially those questions having to do with the ways in which people can know about the world. However, he despaired at the fact that there were so many controversies in philosophy with no clear methods available to resolve them. Piaget admired the methods evolved in the natural sciences for delimiting problems, for making precise observations, and for choosing between alternative interpretations. The problems investigated by the natural sciences, however, seemed to him to be too narrow and uninteresting. On the one hand, then, good questions with no answers; on the other, an exciting method directed toward uninviting problems. Piaget began searching for a way to bridge the gap by synthesizing the two approaches. It is interesting that in Piaget's theory, and in his life, many issues are described as conflicts between polar opposites which he proposes to bring together in a new synthesis.

During the three years following his degree, Piaget's search led to jobs in a variety of settings. In 1918 he studied in Zurich, becoming acquainted with experimental psychology in the laboratories of G. E. Lipps and Wreschner. He also worked in Bleuler's psychiatric clinic, reading Freud and listening to lectures on psychoanalysis by Pfister and Jung.[2] He found experimental psychology to be scientific but dull, while psychoanalysis he regarded as interesting but highly speculative and nonscientific. In a quandary, he went back to Valais, the site of his dissertation research, to investigate the interaction of nature and nurture on the development of molluscs. However, his contact with the study of human behavior, unsatisfactory as it was, evidently altered his outlook; thereafter he returned to his biological research only as a diversion or hobby.

In 1919, after World War I, Piaget went to Paris. At the Sorbonne, he studied psychopathology, learning to interview patients in mental hospitals. He also kept up his passionate interest in philosophy by attending lectures in logic and philosophy of science given by Lalande and Bunschvicg.

In 1920, quite unexpectedly, he found his career direction. Henri Simon, Binet's original co-worker in the creation of the IQ test, hired Piaget to standardize some verbal reasoning items originally developed by Cyril Burt in England. Piaget was becoming bored with the task when he began to notice some consistencies in the incorrect answers given by the Parisian children. The errors did not seem to be random; the answers often made sense given the premises of the child. In the standardized question/answer/next-question format of the IQ test, all that was revealed was the content of the child's response, to be scored right or wrong. In his psychiatric studies, Piaget had used a clinical interview method, unstandardized, but systematic, with extensive probes designed to reveal the structure of thought and personality underlying the content of behavior. He began to use this clinical method in an attempt to understand more clearly the general intellectual organization behind specific verbal responses. Today, in addition to interviews, the clinical method includes observation of spontaneous play and nonverbal behavior and also includes specially constructed tasks in which children both manipulate materials and discuss with the experimenter their understanding of what they are doing. The clinical method, combining standardized testing with psychiatric interviewing, allowed Piaget to pull together the strands of his previously disparate interests. In his psychological studies of developmental changes in children's conceptions of the world, he could examine a biological organism on the way toward the creation of adult philosophical theories.

Although Simon was not fully aware of what Piaget was up to, Piaget continued his own research along with the standardization of tests. One of the articles based on this work brought him to the attention of E. Claparede, the head of the Institute Jean Jacques Rousseau, a center for scientific child study and for teacher training. Claparede invited Piaget to be the Director of Studies in the Institute. So, in 1921, at the age of twenty-five, Piaget arrived in Geneva to begin his major life's work.

[2]By that time, both Bleuler and Jung had departed from the orthodox Freudian point of view.

EARLY FAME AND ITS AFTERMATH

Piaget immediately began a number of studies of language, concepts, and reasoning processes in children from four to twelve years of age. The first outcome of these studies was that he met and married one of his assistants—Valentine Châtenay. The second was the series of five books based on this research and quickly translated into English, which made Piaget world-famous before he was thirty years old.

In retrospect, there was a critical omission in the presentation of this early research. Partly because he had not completely worked out his theoretical position, and partly because he believed the books would not be widely read, he postponed a systematic presentation of the guiding theoretical principles which made the data meaningful from his point of view. Many readers assumed that Piaget was simply interested in examining changes in content of behavior as a function of age. His philosophical interests, his concern with the underlying organization of intelligence, and the reasons for his stage theory of intellectual development were not clearly presented. Misunderstanding his methods and measures, researchers who attempted to replicate the results often failed, and the approach was soon rejected.

The fact that between 1935 and 1955 Piaget's writings were virtually ignored in English-speaking countries is not solely due to these initial misunderstandings. British and American psychology came to be dominated by behaviorism, psychoanalysis, and standardized IQ testing. The behaviorists reacted strongly against Piaget's clinical method and the absence of what they regarded as rigorous experimental methodology. Psychoanalysts welcomed the clinical method but were uninterested in a theory which focused on intelligence and paid relatively less attention to emotional, social, and personality aspects of the developing child.[3] And the IQ test movement tended to adopt a maturational view of intelligence as a fixed characteristic of *how much* a child knows relative to his or her peers; Piaget's interest in qualitative stages of intellectual understanding was discounted. Piaget's ideas were not incompatible with all aspects of these approaches to child development, but, taken together, they constituted too hostile an environment for his theory to take hold.

Meanwhile, he continued to work. In 1929 he was appointed director of the Bureau International Office de l'Education. This Bureau, which has since become affiliated with UNESCO, has been devoted to international cooperation in the field of education, to the improvement of teaching methods, and to the adoption of techniques better adapted to the mind of a child. While Piaget the theorist has not written a great deal about practical applications, Piaget the man takes great interest and pride in his contribution to education.

[3]These aspects will be featured in Parts II and III of this book.

In the 1930s, Piaget became codirector of the Institut Jean Jacques Rousseau and guided its affiliation with the University of Geneva. Over the span of a decade he published, among many other works, three books devoted to a detailed description of the early development of his own three children, Jacqueline, Lucienne and Laurent (*The Origins of Intelligence in Children*, 1936; *The Construction of Reality in the Child*, 1937; *Play Dreams and Imitation in Childhood*, 1946a). The general principles derived from this research have since been replicated, and also questioned, by other investigators using much larger samples of children, but the original work stands unsurpassed as an organized naturalistic record of thousands of observations proceeding, both by induction and deduction, to general laws. This trilogy was largely responsible for the gradual reawakening of interest in Piaget in the English-speaking world.

MAJOR THEMES—1930 TO THE PRESENT

During the 1930s Piaget began to teach a course on the history of scientific thought. He found striking parallels between people's changing view of the world over the course of history and developmental changes in the child's understanding. The testing of the same hypothesis both by historical analysis and by developmental analysis is central to Piaget's philosophical theory of knowledge.

In the past thirty-five years Piaget's thinking has been dominated by four major concerns. First, in the early 1940s he published a book on logic which presented, for the first time, a language to describe the structures of intelligence. While Piaget has never argued that children or adults always think logically, he has been evolving a logical model of the regularities characterizing each new intellectual stage. Second, Piaget has developed a theory of perception. The extensive series of experiments devoted to this topic are quite unlike the research on intelligence, much more laboratory-oriented, quantitative, and "rigorous." The difference in method from the clinical approach used in his studies of intelligence reflects his assumption that there are fundamental differences in the nature of perception and cognition and in the course of their development. Third, beginning in the 1940s and continuing to the present, Piaget, along with Mlle. Bärbel Inhelder, has headed a veritable task force of senior and junior collaborators, investigating the development of various scientific and intellectual concepts (e.g., space, time, number, geometry). Each year a particular problem is tackled. Researchers fan out in all directions and collect data which are coordinated by the senior collaborators into a book, monograph, or journal article. In the European tradition, almost all research emerging from a laboratory bears the senior professor's name as well as those who perform the studies, so it is hard to tell precisely to what extent Piaget is directly involved in every project.

Finally, Piaget has returned to the original philosophical questions that started him on his long and productive career. He has often told how in 1921 he expected his child development research to last four or five years at most, after which he would proceed to write his philosophical theory of knowledge. In fact that developmental research took thirty years; it was not until 1950 that Piaget explicitly returned to the field of philosophy, with the publication of his three-volume work on genetic (developmental) epistemology.[4] This is Piaget's attempt to create a new philosophical discipline, in which different theories of knowledge are weighed against the facts of historical change and child development. Instead of asking, as traditional epistemologists do, "What is knowledge and how can we attain it?" Piaget's genetic epistemology attempts to explain how knowledge changes and develops over time—both historical time and the lifetime of each individual.

Piaget's interest in epistemology has taken on more than literary reality. In 1955, financed by funds from the Rockefeller Foundation, he set up the Center International d'Épistémologie Génétique in Geneva. Each year he invites a number of scholars from various fields of psychology, philosophy, mathematics, and logic to consider problems relevant to each of their disciplines, in an attempt to extend the usefulness of the genetic epistemological approach. A monograph series resulting from these collaborations now includes more than thirty book-length essays and the flow of monographs appears to be increasing.

To an outside observer, at least, Piaget has more than achieved his intellectual goals first stated in idealistic terms during his adolescence. He has created genetic epistemology in an attempt to provide a unified approach to the philosophy and psychology of knowledge. His contributions to philosophy are more recent and less well known than his psychological investigations, so we do not yet have a systematic assessment of his work by philosophers, mathematicians, and logicians. As a developmental psychologist, Piaget's eminence is secure. The scope of his painstaking investigation of intellectual development from birth to maturity has not been equalled. It has provided leadership for the cognitive developmental approach to intelligence, ranking with Freud's contribution to psychoanalytic theories of personality development and with Pavlov's and Skinner's contributions to behaviorist theories of learning.

Piaget's name is involved and his ideas used daily in the creation of new ideas for the classroom, some of which involve national projects with the expenditure of millions of dollars (e.g., the Nuffield Mathematics project in England; the Science Curriculum Improvement Study in the United States). But for Piaget and for his theory, the quest for knowledge is more important than the attainment of specific goals. This book chronicles the attempts by Piaget, and others in the cognitive developmental tradition, to understand that quest.

[4] *Introduction à l'épistémologie génétique*, Vols. 1–3, 1950.

CHAPTER 2

The World through Children's Eyes

Stages and Changes

Children are always trying to make sense of things. Like detectives, they investigate, reason, question, fantasize, and experiment in an attempt to understand what people do and how things work. From our point of view as classroom teachers, or parents, or developmental psychologists, children are often puzzling because what makes sense to them does not always make sense to us. The world through children's eyes appears to be quite different from our own. Many of us act as if the distance from childhood to intellectual adulthood is measured only in terms of quantity—children acquire more experience, greater information, and broader knowledge as they grow older. Piaget begins with another assumption. The most significant intellectual differences between children and adults lie in the nature and *quality* of their understanding. As children develop, they pass through a series of cognitive stages; each stage represents a different organization of experience, information, and knowledge, and each leads to a very different view of the world.

This chapter describes Piaget's general approach to stages of intelligence and the principles which account for changes from one cognitive stage to another. Cognition and intelligence will be defined more precisely in the following two chapters. For now, I am using both terms in the sense of thinking, understanding, interpreting, relating, inferring, and symbolizing.

DEVELOPMENTAL STAGE-STRUCTURES

Contrasts between children and adults

A few examples illustrate what happens when children and adults try to understand the same events.

EXAMPLE 1: PHYSICAL CAUSALITY

> A four-year-old child and his father are watching the setting sun. "Look, Daddy. It's hiding behind the mountain. Why is it going away? Is it angry?" The father grasps the opportunity to explain to his son how the world works. "Well, Mark, the sun doesn't really feel things. And it doesn't really move. It's the earth that's moving. It turns on its axis so that the mountain moves in front of the sun. . . ." The father goes on to other explanations of relative motion, interplanetary bodies and such. The boy, escaping from the cascade of words, firmly and definitely responds, "But *we're* not moving. *It* is. Look, it's going down."

The child has made an important inference based on evidence; he is convinced that the way he sees things corresponds to the way they are. He attributes intention and feelings to the sun, assuming that it operates like him and other people he knows. By contrast, the father distinguishes between appearance and reality and between physical and psychological principles in living and nonliving matter. Their different assumptions lead them to very different conclusions concerning the meaning of what they have seen.

EXAMPLE 2: QUANTITY CONSERVATION AND IDENTITY JUDGMENTS

> Mark and his father return home for dinner. On the table are two identical glasses, each with the same amount of juice to drink; one is for Mark and one is for his ten-year-old sister Debbie. Before the family begins dinner, Debbie goes to get her favorite glass and pours her juice into it. Mark eyes the result and then protests, "Hey, now she's got more than me." "No, Mark," his mother responds, "Debbie's glass is higher, but it's thinner, so it comes out the same." "But there's *more*, see." Mark places the glasses side by side and points to the line in Debbie's glass.

Here is a living example of one of Piaget's famous conservation experiments. Again, Mark's judgment depends upon how things look. The ability to conserve liquid quantity—to realize that the amount stays the same despite transformations in appearance—is an important cognitive developmental milestone which Mark will probably attain by the time he is seven or eight. A little before that time, he will be able to conserve number (to realize that, for example, five things stay the same number of things no matter how they are arranged and rearranged). And slightly earlier, he will achieve for the first time a stable view of his own identity—believing that he is the same person as he was yesterday or even when he was born. Without these conservation and identity judgments, the young child's world has an Alice-in-Wonderland quality in which everything is always changing into something else.

EXAMPLE 3: MORAL JUDGMENT

While Father is clearing the table, he trips and drops a tray with four plates on it. Mother is sympathetic and helps him to tidy up. Mark is outraged, "But last week you got mad at *me*. I only broke one plate. Why don't you yell at *him?*" His mother replies, "Well, you were up in the cupboard trying to take a cookie that I told you was to be saved for tomorrow's snack." Mark says, "Yeah, but Dad broke a whole lot more stuff." Father replies, "That was an accident; you were in the cupboard on purpose." Mark mutters, "But I didn't smash all those plates."

Young children understand intention, but in judging what is good and bad, they tend to disregard statements of intent and focus on the consequences. They may behave in what adults regard as a moral fashion but they interpret the moral issues differently. Even though Mark can be taught to stay out of the cupboard, he will have a great deal of difficulty with attempts to provide a rationale for moral behavior based upon abstract, adult-level principles.

EXAMPLE 4: EGOCENTRISM IN COMMUNICATION

The children have cleared the table and have gone to watch TV. The parents are washing the dishes in the kitchen. Mark bursts in, "He shot him!" "Who shot whom?" "The guy on the TV, he shot him." "Is that a made-up program or is it real?" "It's my favorite one—it's not real. But oh boy, he really got shot. And then she came and got him." "Who came dear?" The parents want to be attentive but know it will take forever to elicit the details of the story so that they can understand it.

At four years of age Mark often has a difficult time of it in communication, especially when he and a listener are not able to view the same events. The problem is not simply a lack of appropriate language and concepts. The problem resides, in part, in children's egocentrism—the inability to differentiate and coordinate two or more points of view. Even when young children are quite clear that they are physically separate from someone else, it is difficult and sometimes impossible for them to be aware of their psychological separation from others. Often children tell their parents about secret misdeeds on the assumption that the parents already know. As a speaker, Mark cannot yet simultaneously have his own point of view and also adopt the point of view of the listener. Since adults may be unaware of the nature of the child's difficulty, both participants in the conversation may contribute to the garbled exchange.

EXAMPLE 5: SOCIAL CAUSALITY

> The children have turned off the TV. They are discussing something of concern to them. Their mother is visibly pregnant, and is due to give birth in a month. There has been much talk about it in the house. Both parents have explained the whole process, bought appropriate books, and read them to each child. Mark has wondered how the baby is going to get out. Debbie replies with another question: "Do you know how the baby got there?" "Sure," said Mark, "Mommy got a duck." "A duck?" "Yeah, they just get a duck or rabbit and it grows a little more and it turns into a baby." "A duck will turn into a baby?" Mark says, "Sure, they give them some food, people food, and they grow into a baby." Debbie is skeptical, "Where did you get that idea?" "I saw it in a book and Mommy and Daddy told me." "They told you that ducks turn into babies?" "Yeah." (Adapted from Bernstein and Cowan, 1975.)

It is likely that Mark's parents, in their efforts to provide clear and concrete analogies between animal and human reproduction, have provided him with more information than he knows how to integrate in adult terms. Sex education is only one of many areas in which adult teachings are not taken in directly, but are transformed by the child's cognitive apparatus.

At four, Mark is certainly a long way from infancy. His theories about birth or the sun's motion represent important conceptual achievements. He has managed to make mysterious events meaningful—to arrive at his own conclusion based on generalizations from what he has observed. And he maintains his own ideas despite counter-examples in his family and despite their explicit attempts to persuade him to change his mind.

While Mark's view of the world is advanced when compared with his understanding in infancy, it is a long distance from what we have come to accept as adult-level understanding. Mark believes that the sun moves across the sky, quantity changes with alterations in appearance, morality is defined by consequences, animals can easily be changed into human infants. For Piaget, the cognitive generation gap between children and adults is not defined solely by the content of these ideas. He reminds us that before the fourteenth century, almost all adults shared Mark's belief that the sun moves around a stationary earth. Many adults today define morality in terms of consequences and they communicate egocentrically. Yet, most adults from then and now are capable of understanding the world in a far more complex and sophisticated manner than present-day four-year-olds. In contrast with adults, children of Mark's age deal with events one variable at a time. How things look, and how they look now, tend to determine how they are understood. Past and present events, intentions and consequences, speaker and listener roles are not yet coordinated. Mark may know less than his sister and parents, but he also knows different things and he knows things differently.

The first general principle to be derived from Piaget's work is that children and adults understand the world in different ways. Communicating with children, then, and planning educational settings for them, require that we find out how our world appears through their eyes.

Regularities in children's conceptions of the world

If children below the age of about seven are asked to respond to a series of test questions about the sun's apparent motion, conservation of number, the birth of a baby, and so on, their answers would all be incorrect, as judged from an adult point of view. Almost sixty years ago, as Piaget worked at standardizing IQ test items, he began to realize that an analysis of these "wrong answers" might help us to understand more about the way in which children's conceptions of the world are organized. He noted two facts about children's responses which called for an explanation: (1) Within a two- to three-year age range, many children give *the same* kinds of wrong answers to questions asked by adults or by the children themselves; and (2) as children grow up, there is a sequence of changes in which one view of the world is replaced by more sophisticated views, only to be replaced again by adult-level conceptions.

Content. The beliefs attributed to four-year-old Mark in the examples above are shared by many of his age-mates. Children who have advanced beyond his level would have given almost identical responses only a short time ago. Piaget's books document many other similarities in the conceptions of the world of a child who is approximately four years old.

> Mark believes that changing the shape of the juice container increases the amount available for drinking. For young children, this belief is generalized to alterations in the appearance of most objects and materials. If a row of objects is rearranged, children think that the number of objects is increased or decreased. Flattening a ball of clay into a sausage shape leads young children to believe that the amount of clay is now different ("it's less because it's thinner" or "it's more because it's longer").
>
> Examples of similarities in "wrong answers" extend across many different content areas. Young children assume that word names are inseparably attached to objects; a table cannot arbitrarily be called a chair because "you're not supposed to sit on a table." Concepts tend to be limited to absolutes rather than relational meanings even when words are used correctly; four-year-old boys who know that they have an older brother, vigorously deny that *they* are a brother to their older sibling. Young children tend to assume that when two events occur simultaneously, one causes the other; because the moon appears to move when they walk along the street, they believe that their activity is the cause of the moon's apparent motion.

Specific wording varies greatly, but there is remarkable similarity in young children's beliefs about common events and in their justification or reasons for their beliefs. This conclusion applies to children in Western cultures; and while there has not been enough research to conclude that the trends are universal, there is impressive evidence that it applies to other cultures as well (see Chapter 12).

At the time when Piaget began his work, many theorists attributed the child's intellectual advances to adult teaching or to "experience." Piaget's explorations raised a question which was difficult for those holding this point of view to deal with: if adult teachings or experience are the major sources of children's ideas, how do we account for the pervasively incorrect but similiar beliefs of very young children? It is unlikely that parents tell all children the same wrong answers when they are young, only to change their instruction at a later age. This does happen for example when the fables of the stork or the cabbage patch are used as a first explanation of where babies come from. However, adults do not systematically misinform children about the sun's rotation or the relation between words and things. It is also unlikely that a "lack of experience" could lead so many children to the same incorrect conclusions. Piaget believes that these regularities in young children's conceptions of the world are natural and systematic outgrowths of the way in which their thinking is organized or structured.

Sequence. In the examples focusing on Mark and his parents, his ten-year-old sister Debbie was left in the background. If we were to turn our attention her way, we would find that she and her age-mates have rejected many of Mark's ideas as childish, but they have not yet adopted adult versions of reality.

> Debbie does not believe that a change in shape alters the amount of clay, but as far as she and her peers are concerned, it *will* change the volume of the clay. Ten-year-olds may be giving up their emphasis on consequences as a basis for judgments of morality, but they still translate abstract moral principles into their own language; their most common understanding of the "golden rule" (Do unto others as you would have them do unto you) is "do to others what they do to you." Ten-year-olds have abandoned the idea that they can make the moon move when they walk along the street, but almost all of them search for causes of events randomly rather than systematically. They have not yet developed the strategy of holding conditions or variables constant and investigating each variable separately, testing all possible combinations. As many high school science teachers can attest, the hypothetico-deductive method, and the complex reasoning that it implies, may not be part of the child's intellectual equipment until mid- or late adolescence, if at all.

Cognitive generation gaps exist not only between children and adults, but also among children at different points in their development. There appears to be a sequence in which the widely shared "wrong answers" of younger children are replaced by widely shared beliefs of older children, only to be replaced again by adult views. This sequence makes it even more difficult to attribute children's ideas directly to adult teaching or to the gradual effects of experience.

Logic and stage in developmental regularity

Piaget, like Freud and all other developmental stage theorists, attempted to find an organizing principle to account for communalities in children's approach to the world during a given period of time and regularities in the sequence of development. Piaget was familiar with Freud's developmental theory in which the stages (oral, anal, phallic, latency, genital) are defined by the bodily locus of the most salient area of sensual pleasure (mouth, anus, genitals). Freudian stages are concerned with people's motivations and feelings. Each stage provides an explanation for the dominant content or theme of the child's most important types of satisfactions at a given time.

Piaget, in attempting to explain similarities and sequences in conceptions of the world, created another kind of stage theory. He began to wonder whether common trends in children's beliefs could result from a general cognitive organizational structure through which adult teachings and experience must always be filtered. A series of changes in this cognitive structure might account for the regular developmental shifts in point of view. In his search for a conceptual framework or model to describe this cognitive organization more precisely, Piaget turned to the field of logic.

In its most general usage, logic is a set of rules for relating symbols and making inferences. Any time we are trying to make sense of the world we must classify or categorize objects, events, or symbols. In our attempts to classify particular instances and to relate them to past and future events or statements, we make inferences going beyond the information immediately given (Bruner, 1964). Logic is obviously employed in deducing what must necessarily follow from a set of premises, but it is also involved, for example, in understanding the power relationships among people in a group—if A dominates B and B dominates C, does A dominate C? Whether the answer is yes or no, logic models can be used to understand the relations among events. The painter arranging space and color on canvas is manipulating symbols in relation to certain rules. Understanding what we feel and why we feel it, finding meaning in an event that makes us afraid or ecstatic, all of these activities require adults and children to manipulate symbols in systematic ways. Human reason, then, is utilized not only in rational, intellectual pursuits; it is also required to make sense of artistic, social, and emotional aspects of our existence.

The precise rules described in academic theories of formal logic are not always followed by adults in the course of their daily lives. Children's thinking seems even further away from logicians' rules for classifying and ordering concepts and relating statements to each other. Piaget searched for a way of relating formal logic and human reasoning so that he could use the precision of formal logic to describe the cognitive structures underlying children's ideas. He began to focus on the fact that children's reasoning, even when departing noticeably from the assumptions of adult logic, has a regularity and a rule-following quality of its own.

Piaget often describes charming examples of "incorrect" reasoning in the two- to four-year-old. He cites the familiar tendency of young children to call all four-legged animals "doggies" or "bow-wows." In another illustration (1946a) he describes his younger daughter Lucienne at three years and three months. As they were walking, they passed a man. Lucienne inquired "Is that man a daddy?" Piaget, ever on the alert, asked "What *is* a daddy?" Lucienne responded "It is a man. He has lots of

Luciennes and lots of Jacquelines." (She has an older sister Jacqueline.) "What are Luciennes?" "They're little girls, and Jacquelines are big girls."

In each case, the young child generalizes that if this thing is called *X*, then all things having that one characteristic are called *X*; all four-legged animals are called dogs, all adult men are called daddies, all daddies have Luciennes, all big girls are Jacquelines. The point here is that this reasoning represents a regular rule-following form; there is a logic to the child's apparent illogic, even when reasoning is incorrect or inconsistent by adult standards.

While academic logicians are primarily concerned with rules which lead us to true statements, Piaget as a developmental psychologist also reconstructs the rules which lead us into error. It is important to keep in mind the fact that the child, or even the adult, is not aware of following an explicit logical system, just as the young child talks grammatically, without awareness of grammatical rules. Rather, the observer concludes from regularities in behavior that a person is acting as if a particular set of rules are in use.

It is assumed, then, that a general set of logic rules describes the cognitive organization underlying the specific content of children's reasoning. As we watch a child mature from birth to adulthood, we can see four major changes in the organization of these logic rules: there is a Sensorimotor logic (from birth to about two years), a Preoperational logic (from about two to seven years), a Concrete operational logic (from about seven to twelve years), and a Formal operational logic (from about twelve on). Each new set of rules integrates the one before into a more differentiated and flexible cognitive structure. And each new cognitive structure defines a new stage of intellectual development, with corresponding changes in the quality of the child's understanding of the world.

The ages associated with each logic-structure-stage are only approximate in two senses. First, there is considerable stage variation among children of the same chronological age. Inherited characteristics, environmental circumstances, motivation, and social-emotional factors combine in various ways so that there are children at two or three different cognitive stage levels in every grade of elementary and secondary school. Second, no child is entirely consistent in the application of a particular stage level of reasoning across all situations. In fact, we shall see that there is more within-individual variation and fluctuation than Piaget's presentation of this theory suggests (Part III). What does seem to be invariant is the structural sequence in which children develop specific ideas and concepts.

In sum, Piaget uses logic rules as stage-structural principles to account for regularities in the content and sequence of children's correct and incorrect conceptions of the world. Logic rules provide the blueprints by which adults can construct a model of the world as it is interpreted through children's eyes.

Establishing the logic and sequence of stages represents only one aspect of Piaget's contribution to developmental theory and educational practice. None of this information can really be useful until we know how the child changes from one stage to another.

HOW STAGES CHANGE

Underlying assumptions

This section begins with a brief account of three approaches to educating children, each one based on a different set of assumptions about the nature of intellectual growth. In one view, the basic impetus for intellectual growth and organization comes from sources external to the child (people, events, books); children are regarded as clean slates upon which knowledge must be written. In a second approach, the major source of motivation and intellectual growth is believed to be a flowering from within. In a third alternative, the one adopted by Piaget, we find a synthesis of these opposing points of view.[1]

Children as clean slates. The clean-slate approach to education was prevalent in Piaget's student days but has by no means vanished from our own (e.g., Skinner, 1968; programmed learning, Markle, 1969; Bereiter and Engelman's approach to early childhood education, 1966, later developed into the DISTAR program, Osborn, 1971).

> In a geography lesson within this framework, a fifth-grade teacher may bring a map of Africa into the classroom. He or she points out the principal countries, cities, and topographical features, and describes their salient characteristics. Teachers may supplement their lectures with books, pictures and movies, or programmed learning texts in which each complex idea is divided into a series of simple frames to which children respond and then immediately check their answer. Teachers may raise questions or have discussions to stimulate student involvement, but the basic organization of the ideas to be learned (they believe) rests with the teacher and with the materials.

The clean-slate approach has come under fire in recent years, but it is based upon a general principle which has not received much criticism: we learn "by experience." The phrase is usually interpreted as meaning that ideas come from our contacts with the physical world or with the spoken or written ideas of other people. "Where did you get that idea?" we ask, as if it had to come from somewhere outside of a person. There seems to be an organized external environment "out there" which impresses itself on us and leads to the organization of ideas "in here." When the assumption is made that ideas come *only* from experience, the child's mind is treated as a clean slate to be written upon or an empty vessel into which knowledge must be poured. The philosophical roots of these metaphors go back to John Locke and the British Empiricists in the seventeenth century (see Part IV). They believed that while knowledge goes far

[1]Kohlberg and Mayer (1972) define a similar tripartite division of educational ideologies, which they label "cultural transmission, romanticism, and progressivism." They note the relationship of each ideology to a basic metaphor of development described by Langer (1969a). The labels here were chosen to emphasize each theory's conceptions of sources of developmental change.

beyond the confines of daily experience, meaningful ideas ultimately rest on impressions received through the physical senses. It is a belief still held by many people today.

In the clean-slate approach it is usually assumed that there are mental mechanisms which function something like present day videotape recorders; despite frequent distortions they can provide and store reasonably faithful copies of events occurring in front of the camera. The clean-slate approach to education leads to a reliance on teacher-structured experience for students as the major road to knowledge. It places a great deal of responsibility for the students' success or failure on the teacher, and assumes that students are passive consumers, who must be externally motivated in order to become involved in learning.

Children as flowering seeds. In the past two decades a "new" educational approach has grown almost to the status of a social movement. A number of influential writers (Goodman, 1960; Featherstone, 1971; Holt, 1964; Kohl, 1967; Neill, 1964; Silberman, 1973) have championed "open classrooms," a "Summerhill approach," British infant schools, alternative education, and other radical departures from teacher-centered education. Their basic argument against the clean-slate approach appears to have roots in Rousseau's philosophical contention that the child is basically good until corrupted by adult society. The teacher is likened to the gardener who must feed and water the plant and then stands back, allowing it to grow. The gardener has no influence upon what kind of flower will emerge; that is determined by the nature of the seed. While ideas may arise in experience (external), these educators contend that active, curious children can be entrusted to make sense of the world on their own (i.e., both the motivation and the ability to organize are internal).

> A teacher advocating this theoretical view may never "teach" about Africa at all. He or she would provide maps, books, visual aids in the classroom, and if anyone became interested in Africa, the teacher would function as a helpful resource person.

In this view the student plays the most active role in learning; the teacher's role is to provide an environment in which students follow their intellectual pursuits with as few restrictions as possible. In some versions of this position, formal academic schooling may not even be required. A quote from Paul Goodman:

> We see that infants learn to speak in their own way in an environment where there is speaking and where they are addressed and take part. If we tried to teach children to speak according to our own theories and methods and schedules, as we try to teach reading, there would be as many stammerers as there are bad readers. Besides, it has been shown that whatever is useful in the present eight-year elementary curriculum can be learned in four months by a normal child of twelve. If let alone in fact, he will have learned most of it by himself. (Goodman, *Saturday Review*, May 18, 1968, p. 73.)

Children as interactive generator-transformers.[2] There is a third explanation of the fact that children come to show increasingly organized perceptions and conceptions of their world. It may be, argues Piaget, that this organization arises in interaction between the structured characteristics of the environment and the active imposition of order by the child. It is too easy to agree quickly that "both are involved." A more precise meaning of interaction is that one factor can *never* be evaluated without knowing the other. It is not possible to account for a particular idea or cognitive organization without specifying a particular environmental condition, and it is not possible to assess the impact of any environmental event without knowing something about the child's intellectual organization. Intelligence, metaphorically, acts as a generator which transforms raw input into usable power. Curriculum approaches based on this metaphor have been described for children in preschools (Kamii, 1972), elementary schools (Nuffield, 1967; Karplus and Thier, 1967), and high schools (Renner & Stafford, 1972).

> The geography lesson based on this point of view might proceed as did one outlined by Bruner (1968). The teacher enters the classroom carrying a topographical map of Africa (with the continent unlabelled) indicating rivers, forests, mountains, and other features. The teacher then says, "All right, class, where shall we put the cities, towns, and villages?" The children may be stunned momentarily, but soon are busy arguing, discussing, and deciding the pros and cons of each location. In the course of their discussion the children find out for themselves the reasons why people come to live in certain locales, what the principal products may be, and so on. The teacher here is directly active in providing a challenge and raising questions, but the children combine past notions and emerging ideas into their own new synthesis.

The view of children as clean slates, flowering seeds, or generator-transformers is not limited to educational development within classrooms. Both formal and informal theories of parenting and child-rearing tend to adopt the same metaphors: some look to parent treatment and example as the major factors determining child characteristics; others believe that children will develop best if allowed to actualize their own potential; and still others look to the interaction between parental treatment and child characteristics to account for the kind of adult each person eventually becomes.

The assumptions underlying each of the three major approaches to developmental change are summarized in Table 1. Treating the child as a clean slate implies that the mind is organized primarily by external forces and that knowledge represents a more or less accurate copy of external reality. The flowering-seed theory assumes a maturational process of unfolding in which knowledge is an invention, springing forth from internal sources. Piaget's generator-transformer picture of the child presents a view of education in which knowledge is a construction, arising as a product of interaction between external

[2]Piaget does not use this metaphor, but he conveys this impression.

stimulation and the nature of the child's cognitive stage-structures. The distinction between knowledge as invention and construction is subtle, but the implications are far reaching. Inventions, in this restricted definition, are created primarily from inside, while constructions represent a balanced synthesis of internal organization and external materials or stimulation. It makes a difference in a classroom whether teachers assume that knowledge will unfold from within, or whether it can only be created in the process of active interaction with external events. When we select certain curriculum approaches, then, we are not simply deciding what and how to teach. The choices we make force us to adopt, at least implicitly, a comprehensive point of view about what knowledge is, where it originates, how we come to know things, and how knowledge changes (Piaget, 1971, 1976).

TABLE 1 Assumptions Underlying Three Approaches to Developmental Change

The Nature of the Child	*Source of Organization*	*The Nature of Knowledge*
Clean slate	External	Copy
Flowering seed	Internal	Invention
Generator-transformer	Interaction	Construction

Piaget's equilibration model

Having made a general argument for an interactive generator-transformer conception of intellectual functioning, Piaget went on to create a detailed model of how the interaction occurs (1936, 1967). His synthesis of clean-slate and flowering-seed approaches is based upon extensions of principles used by organismic biologists to explain how living things interact with their physical environments.

Piaget assumes that intelligence, like any property of living things, is useful in adapting the organism to its environment. Adaptation does not simply mean conformity to external pressure. Rather, it is a shorthand summary of the only two possible ways in which an organism can function in relation to an environment; it can modify the environment to fit its needs and structures (assimilation), or it can modify itself in response to environmental demands (accommodation). Extending these physical principles to the area of psychological functioning, Piaget constructed a model of intelligence in which the two opposing functions of assimilation and accommodation create a dynamic tension of balance (equilibration) or imbalance (disequilibration). I will describe each of these terms in turn; if you are not already familiar with them, it will probably take some time to remember which is which.

Assimilation. In biological terms, assimilation is the process of taking additional elements into an existing structure. In this process, new elements are not simply added, but rather transformed in some important ways. Food is the most familiar example; we take in and alter some elements for our body's use, reject other elements (e.g., hard shells), and eliminate still others as waste.

Piaget suggests that the biological concept of assimilation can profitably be applied to behavior and thought. No new stimulus or behavior is taken in *as is;* some aspects are always transformed by the existing cognitive organization. The assimilative function of intelligence can be seen at every age or stage level.

> A young infant is holding a rattle when her arm shakes and the rattle makes a pleasing sound. In succeeding days, every new object is shaken in the same way—hands, combs, rattles, beads, spoons full of food. Not all of these objects have rattle-qualities, but the child is cognitively transforming the objects by assimilating them (fitting them) into the shaking-an-object activity. In the process some aspects of the new stimuli are incorporated while others are ignored (e.g., size, color, shape).
>
> A four- to six-year-old usually fits the activity of counting into his or her ideas about quantity. For example, a row of six red checkers is placed in one-to-one-correspondence with a row of six black checkers. The child agrees that there is the same number of checkers in each row. The six red checkers are then spread out and the child is asked whether that row has more, less, or the same number of checkers as the black row. The child answers that there are more checkers in the red row, an example of failure to conserve quantity. When some children are asked how they know that the red row has more, they first begin to count one row, placing a finger on each checker "one, two, three, four, five (they count a space in between) six, *seven.*" Counting has been assimilated (molded) to the child's conception of quantity.
>
> Eight-year-olds, still conceptually egocentric, assimilate the world to their own point of view. Asked to draw a picture of a scene as it would be viewed by someone at a different location, they draw the scene as they themselves view it. Others' viewpoints are transformed to be identical with one's own.
>
> Adults assimilate too, of course. We travel to different countries interpreting "strange customs" through our own eyes. We listen to lectures and to conversations, extracting our own meanings, often failing to check whether that is the meaning intended by the speaker.

The above examples focus on assimilation of events to internal structures. Piaget makes the point that in biology and psychology we must also examine the function of assimilation when one internal process interacts with another. In *Origins of Intelligence in Children* (1936) Piaget's observations of his young children provide many examples of inner assimilation.

> At first, the infant's vision is uncoordinated with grasping. When the coordination is established it is apparent that seeing has assimilated grasping; the organization of vision directs and alters grasping behavior. Grasping also assimilates seeing; the grasping movements often shape the child's visual attention. This internal assimilation is not observed directly, of course, but is inferred from overt behavior.

Assimilation is a process which actively transforms what it incorporates. By fitting new elements into existing structures it preserves continuity and provides meaning. Imagine how the world would appear if every event were literally new, without any previous structural organization or past experience to provide a context. Without the function of assimilation (or something which does the same job) every new event would be unintelligible.[3]

The role of assimilation in providing a structure to incoming information emphasizes the active organizing properties of the child's intelligence. This aspect of Piaget's theory echoes, in part, the concern of the flowering-seed approach with the child's contribution to the learning process. However, if assimilation were the only process of incorporating events, then everything would be molded to fit what we already know and nothing would be new (unless we add a maturational principle which provides new ideas). For an explanation of how we are shaped and changed in the process of learning, we must turn to the concept of accommodation as the other pole of the equilibration process.

Accommodation. In describing the assimilation of food, I was focusing on what happens to the external element as it becomes transformed by the organism's digestive structure. However, it is also possible to focus on what happens to the structure. As the food is eaten, muscles contract, chemicals are released, energy is consumed; the body adjusts. The structure is accommodating or bending itself to the requirements of the food.

Extending the concept of accommodation to behavior and thought, Piaget shows how existing structures, as they attempt to transform and incorporate new information, are also becoming transformed in the process.

> The infant develops a behavioral pattern partly based on reflex sucking at the breast or bottle. When the infant attempts to assimilate a thumb to the sucking pattern, at first the hand motions are random and the sucking is not coordinated with them. Soon, however, the hand moves directly to the mouth, and the mouth moves to incorporate the thumb. In this case, hand movements accommodate to the location of the mouth, while the mouth accommodates to the movement of the hand.
>
> The four-year-old who assimilated counting to his or her concept of numbers, was also involved in some accommodation, most noticeably when modifying judgments of "the same" number of checkers because of a change in physical arrangement. The conceptual judgment accommodated to the perceptual data; this example illustrates that accommodative changes do not always produce more correct or adaptive responses.
>
> Accommodation at older levels can be seen in the fact that hypotheses (hunches, expectations) are often modified by feedback from observations and experiments. In fact, without direct feedback in a learning situation it is often difficult to produce any change.

As with assimilation, there are both internal and external aspects of accommodation. Internal structures are constantly in the process of transformation as

[3]It is possible that assimilation does not work well for some disturbed and developmentally disabled children and that they do experience most events as surprising or novel (see Chapter 13).

they coordinate with each other (e.g., seeing is modified by hearing and vice versa). We actively seek to modify our ideas in order to meet environmental challenges.

The accommodation of the individual to the environment, as described in Piaget's theory, echoes the concern of the clean-slate approach with providing an account of how the child's intellect can be affected by external events. However, in Piaget's view, we should not focus on accommodation alone; we must also pay attention to flowering seedlike transformations as the child assimilates new events and new changes to his or her already-existing cognitive structures. In the interaction between person and environment, accommodation is the changing, discriminating side of intelligence while assimilation is the more stable generalizing side. Taken by itself, each process is inadequate to account for intellectual growth. Together they function to create a more differentiated and integrated logical structure.

Equilibration as a self-regulating process. Piaget often uses the word "equilibrium" to describe both the process and outcome of balanced assimilation and accommodation. However, the term too often has the connotation that the system has returned to a resting state or has eliminated tension. The word "equilibration" stresses the idea that the system is always in some sort of controlled tension. When the balance is disturbed (disequilibration) there is a possibility of advancement to a new level of balanced tension, not necessarily a return to a state of imbalance or a state of rest. While most of us attempt to resist situations of tension and conflict, one of Piaget's central theses is that *only* through the tension and conflict of imbalanced assimilation and accommodation does intellectual growth occur (see below).

Consistent with the above analysis of internal and external aspects of assimilation and accommodation, there are two interrelated aspects of equilibration (Langer, 1969b; Turiel, 1974). The first refers to a tendency toward balance in the interaction between an individual and his or her environment. The second refers to a wholeness or balance within the individual's cognitive structure so that both stable and changing aspects of situations can be understood.

a) Balance between the individual and the environment. The most obvious challenge to an existing balance occurs whenever we are presented with something new, like an unfamiliar object or an unexpected sensation. Assimilation, the application of old patterns, may not help us to understand and cope; accommodative changes may not yet have developed. At the moment, our existing cognitive structure is inadequate. "The resulting state of heightened disequilibrium (manifested in conflict and confusion) could lead to compensatory activity. In such a case, the feedback of new information could result in transition to a new stage" (Turiel, 1974, p. 15). In another part of his discussion, Turiel makes it clear that the disequilibration is usually long-lasting, and the new stage will not occur for some time.

A less obvious challenge to the equilibrative balance between persons and environment may occur in the *absence* of environmental change, surprise, or novelty. Faced with monotony, most people engage in activities which create complexity and avoid boredom (changing tasks or locations, daydreaming, self-stimulations, etc.). Environmental events, then, evoke both assimilative and accommodative actions which may eventually lead to a more adaptive interaction between individuals and environments.

b) Balance within the structural organization. A child who has achieved conservation is demonstrating one version of an equilibrated cognitive structure.

> An experimenter places two identical glasses of water in front of an eight-year-old child. The child is asked to make certain that there is the same amount of water to drink in each glass. The experimenter then pours the water from one of the glasses into a taller, narrower container and asks whether there is still the same amount to drink, or more, or less.
>
> The child firmly maintains that there is still the same amount of water and implies that the experimenter is asking a stupid question. The answer is justified by stating that the water in the third glass is higher, but the glass is narrower, or that none was added or taken away during pouring, or that if the water were poured back into the second container it would still be the same amount.

These answers demonstrate that the child's concept of amount of water (at least in this task) is embedded in a balanced conceptual system. The child conceptualizes the experiment in either temporal direction—from before to after the pouring and back again. Perceived changes in height can be offset (mentally) by alterations in width of the glass. The observed changes are evaluated in light of a rule which states that pouring is a transformation which does not affect the amount of water.[4] Further evidence of an equilibrated cognitive structure would come from the fact that the system could be applied across many (but not necessarily all) tasks involving water conservation, and across other concepts of quantity.

The environment-individual and internal structural balances stem from the same source—the process of equilibration between assimilation and accommodation. Piaget's assumption about how this process achieves a balance' is difficult to accept for most of us raised in a different intellectual tradition. He believes that the function of intelligence has *self-regulating* properties—something like a steam governor which shuts down the engine temporarily when the steam pressure builds up, and then allows the engine to switch on again. In an equilibration model, the governor does not hold the pressure always at the same level, but enables the structure to become more differentiated and integrated.

[4]Actually it does: pouring transforms some water into energy and some water remains on the sides of the second glass. However, these fine points are not considered relevant to conservation at the Concrete operational level (ages seven to twelve).

With great effort and persistent practice a young baby learns to reach for a rattle and grasp it with one thumb and finger. She tries the same thing successfully in reaching for a block, a doll, and a small blanket. However, the more she assimilates (generalizes) her new grasping skill, the more she encounters objects which do not fit the initial grasping structure. She reaches for a ball and it rolls away. She reaches for a large toy and fails to move it. The external pressure from objects points toward accommodation. The internal pressure from disequilibration points the same way, so that the child soon takes actions which change the response (e.g., using two hands), bringing the process of interaction with objects and the organization of behavior back into balance.

A similar sequence may begin with accommodation. A young child is quickly moved from one environment to another—different rooms with different objects and different people. After a short time in which there is a great deal of responsiveness to each new situation, the child may "tune out" or play repetitively with a favorite toy; now it is assimilation which tends to bring the child's interaction with the world back into balance.

Why doesn't the child simply give up? What keeps him or her working away at one side or the other of the intellectual functions? Again, our intellectual tradition (mostly of a "clean-slate approach) makes us wonder what *external* forces keep the child active. We look for events which "motivate" intellectual activity, implying that without some motivation, either external or internal, intellectual activity would not occur. Piaget, as a biologist, takes the position that living things by definition require active interaction with the environment, or they will die. In the case of human beings, one essential aspect of interaction is the processing of information; it is as necessary to human beings as eating.[5] The child, then, is kept in intellectual interaction with the environment in order to survive, and in the process, the self-regulating balance between assimilation and accommodation produces intellectual growth.[6]

Disequilibration. While there is always a self-regulating pressure toward equilibration, in fact both children and adults spend a great deal of time in a disequilibrated or imbalanced state—sometimes in short-term bursts and sometimes over long periods of time.

(a) Early failure to separate assimilation and accommodation. When babies are born and for some months afterward, assimilation and accommodation are not yet differentiated enough for cognitive balances to occur.

[5]Later research on stimulus change or deprivation (Heron, Scott, Bexton, 1954) and on infant deprivation (Bowlby, 1969) tends to support the view that some kind of processing of changes in stimulation is necessary for normal human functioning.

[6]Because Piaget as a philosopher is trying to account for the presence of adult formal thought, it often sounds in his writings as if growth were inevitable. In Chapter 13 I will present some examples in which assimilation and accommodation do not inevitably lead to developmental progress.

According to Piaget, newborns and young infants function in a continuous present; they do not yet have a symbol system that enables them to think about, imagine, or represent situations which are not being perceived. Once people or objects disappear from sight, sound, or touch, they are gone. (This idea disturbs some parents who believe that their babies are crying for *them.*) Because there is no conceptual notion of a permanent object, every time newborns interact with the world they transform events and are themselves transformed at the same time. For example, three-month-olds often attempt to grasp (assimilate) a toy. As they move toward it, they change body position (accommodate) and this gives them a new view of the toy. Since they are unable to retrieve the image of the previous perception of the toy, the new view creates (conceptually) a new object to assimilate. Further attempts to assimilate result in further accommodations, and so on. Not until the age of about six to eight months[7] does the infant establish a symbolic representation of a permanent object. Then the child is not always changed by events and he or she does not always transform events in some way.

Cognitive disequilibration seems to be the permanent state of the infant until the development of symbolic representation, some time during the middle of the first year of life.

(b) Short-term imbalance: assimilation predominates. The clearest examples of temporary imbalance between the two functions of intelligence occur in the Preconceptual stage (approximately two to four years of age). Children who are assimilating more than accommodating are often engaged in symbolic play. They bend the world to their fantasies. Things or actions are treated as symbols; children use them as *they* wish, to represent meanings which *they* choose. Dolls are treated as babies, and pieces of cloth become pillows. Children pretend with objects and with their own actions.

> A little girl who while on vacation had asked various questions about the mechanics of the bells observed on an old village church steeple, now stood stiff as a ramrod beside her father's desk, making a deafening noise. "You're bothering me, you know. Can't you see I'm working?" "Don't talk to me," replied the little girl, "I'm a church." Similarly, the child was deeply impressed by a plucked duck she'd seen on the butcher table, and that evening was found lying on the sofa, so still that she was thought to be sick. At first she did not answer questions; then in a faraway voice she said, "I'm the dead duck!" (Piaget and Inhelder, 1966a, p. 59.)

(c) Short-term imbalance: accommodation predominates. When children are temporarily accommodating more than assimilating, they may be engaged in imitation—shaping and changing their actions and structures to match what they see and hear in their environment.

[7]Piaget usually mentions eight months as the age at which object permanence is achieved, but many of his examples show that his six-month-olds could do it. Also, newer research suggests an even earlier age (Bower, 1974).

> Imitation in the very young child is easy to see and delightful to watch. At around eight or nine months, the child begins to mimic adults (making faces, trying to copy sounds) and even objects (being a car, opening and closing the mouth in imitation of a matchbox opening, etc.). In the last half of the second year, the child demonstrates an ability to imitate when the event is no longer present. For example, Piaget's daughter had a visit from a little friend who flew into a tantrum in a playpen—something Piaget states she had never seen before. "The next day, she herself screamed in her playpen and tried to move it. The imitation of the whole scene was most striking." (Piaget and Inhelder, p. 63).

Parents and teachers sometimes worry about their children's use of fantasy and their tendency to imitate undesirable behavior. While some particular examples may provide cause for concern, Piaget's approach stresses the healthy, necessary, growth-producing function of temporary imbalances in favor of assimilation (e.g., play) and accommodation (e.g., imitation).

(d) Long-term disequilibration and growth. The assimilation and accommodation functions of intelligence always operate together, but they only achieve a balanced state or process with respect to given kinds of tasks at a given period in a person's life. The child may demonstrate an equilibrated logic of sensorimotor action, in which physical movements are coordinated in three-dimensional space, and yet he or she may be far away from an equilibrated structure of symbolic thought.

> If four-year-old Mark were to be given the conservation of water task, and he observed water poured into a taller, narrower container, he would conclude that there is now more water. He would accommodate, change his answer depending upon the visual appearance of the water level. He would also assimilate—for example, he would assimilate the concept of "more" to the concept of "higher." But neither the accommodation nor the assimilation would result in a conceptual compensation for the perceived changes.[8]

Disequilibration in the area of conservation of liquid and many other conceptual tasks will help to keep Mark and his peers actively engaged in attempting to understand a puzzling world, and in several years, a new level of equilibration may be reached (Concrete operations, about ages seven to twelve). In turn, this new level contains its own long-term disequilibrations, ultimately stimulating activity leading to yet a new cognitive level (Formal operations).

This discussion helps us to tie together the two parts of this chapter—stages and changes. It seems likely that cognitive stage-structures place limits on the extent to which assimilation and accommodation can be equilibrated, and thus

[8]Compensation and balance are difficult to define here. With respect to the quantity of water, the child will eventually compensate for the perceived changes in physical arrangement. But surface area of the water and pressure at the bottom of the glass *do* change with the pouring into a third glass, and so the child must eventually distinguish between those changes which fit the conservation rules and those which do not.

stage-structures help to create disequilibrations leading to change. At four, Mark cannot simultaneously assimilate and accommodate present and past events without distorting them. In several years, after experience in physical environments, much intellectual work, and the achievement of a new cognitive stage, this will be a relatively easy task.

At every stage, disequilibration inevitably occurs. It often arises naturally and spontaneously when we come upon something unexpected or when we try something that doesn't work. It is usually an essential aspect of the questions we keep asking ourselves, the ones that we are truly interested in answering. And of course disequilibration results from questions, puzzles, and problems posed by other people and events. Those events which exactly fit our current structures presumably lead to little or no disequilibration. Events very far outside our experience or level of understanding may also fail to create disequilibration; they may not even be perceived. Hunt (1961) describes disequilibration as a process that occurs when there is an optimal degree of mismatch between the child's present structures and the structure of new internal or external events. It will probably take some time before we are clear about which events are neither too close nor too far away. What is more certain, according to Piaget, is that disequilibration is absolutely necessary for significant cognitive growth.

I have presented Piaget's general argument that equilibration is a self-regulating process and that disequilibration is central in stimulating intellectual development. Unfortunately, it is still very difficult to pin down these concepts in a specific child or adult. Many tasks or measures can be used to assess stage or structure, though these measures are not without controversy (Chapter 12). But there is no precise way to measure functional balance—to decide when a child is equilibrated and when not. Too often, Piaget's examples imply that correct answers are more equilibrated (e.g., conservation), but surely it is possible to arrive at incorrect answers through an equilibrated process (Formal reasoning), and correct answers may be obtained in a state of cognitive disequilibration (e.g., through imitation).

A related difficulty is that neither Piaget nor others have been able to specify what will and what will not produce disequilibration. We can present tasks which raise issues at a structural level near that of the child. But while we can estimate discrepancies between the structure of the task and the structure of the child, we have no direct way of assessing the extent of the child's disequilibration. It must be inferred from careful, but as yet incomplete, sets of observations (e.g., Langer, 1969b).

Although we do not have measures of equilibration and disequilibration, Piaget's conceptions do lead to a new and interesting way of looking at developmental change. In sum, Piaget's equilibration theory suggests that the maintenance of life requires physical and mental interaction within the child's cognitive structures and between the child and the environment. The process of interaction is a self-regulating, equilibrating, coordination of two forces—assimilation transforms incoming stimulation and aspects of internal structures, while accommodation alters the existing structures and overt behavior in order to cope with new events. The functions of assimilation and accommodation remain unchanged over the life span (Piaget calls them the "functional invariants"), but they produce changes in intellectual structure. The child's intelligence shapes his or her conception of the world, while at the same time the world shapes the child's understanding. In the process, the child is an interactive generator of knowledge.

SOME GENERAL EDUCATIONAL IMPLICATIONS

In this and other chapters in Part I, I will present a few general implications of the major points in each chapter. In Part II the implications will be more specific to children at a particular cognitive stage.

Implications of stage theory

Going beyond correct and incorrect answers. For Piaget, what is important in assessing children's intellectual development is not only the answer to a question, but also the reasons for choosing that particular response.

> As a consultant to a second-grade teacher, I was introduced to an eight-year-old boy having great difficulty with arithmetic. The teacher showed me his math paper, which looked like this:
>
> 9−1 = (child's answer) 9
> 8−1 = 8
> 7−1 = 7
>
> The teacher was somewhat exasperated. I asked the child what he was doing. "I'm doing take-aways," he said. "Nine take away one is nine, eight take away one is eight, seven take away one is seven." All incorrect. I asked him to tell me a bit more about how he was doing the work. "Sure" he said, covering the −1 with his finger, leaving the page like this:
>
> 9 ( ) = 9
>
> "You just go, nine, *take away the one,* equals nine!"
>
> Piaget's way of thinking about wrong answers is also important in thinking about correct answers. Suppose we ask a nine-year-old, "What makes this pencil fall when I drop it?" If the child answers, "gravity," it is tempting to stop the questioning. But if we probe a little, we might find that the child believes that gravity is a set of tiny invisible buglike things which hook onto the pencil and pull it down to the floor.

In both of these examples, further questioning revealed not only that the child's answer had a different meaning from what the adult initially thought, but that the child was, in effect, responding to a different question from the one the teacher intended to ask. The second example goes beyond the simple recognition of differences between children and adults to highlight an issue at the core of Piaget's stage theory. Underlying the child's definition of gravity, I expect that we would find some principles of causal explanation based in part on a specific logic system. Teachers and students often operate at different stages in the logic they use to make sense of the same events. For Piaget the focus of assessment and education is not on right answers, but rather on the quality of understanding shown by both teacher and child.

Structural differences in the classroom. In addition to the cognitive generation gap between teachers and students, there will inevitably be qualitative differences among students in their predominant intellectual stage. Especially in the older grades, it is possible that some students may use Formal logic, some may be at the Concrete operational level, and a few may still use Preoperational logic most of the time. Even when students are grouped homogeneously on the basis of IQ or achievement scores, it is likely that at least two stage-levels will be represented. Like a speaker at the United Nations General Assembly, the teacher talks in one language, but the speech is immediately translated by listeners with different "languages," from different "cultures."

The issue of multiple stages exists for students as well as teachers. On one hand, as we shall see, discrepancies between peers in their level of understanding can have a positive effect on communication and cognitive growth. On the other hand, children who sit side by side may be living in two different cognitive worlds and may have difficulty in exchanging points of view.

It is truly difficult for everyone to contend with the structural differences between teachers and their students and among students of different intellectual levels, *given the way most classrooms are organized.* I will discuss this problem and describe alternative classroom organizations in other chapters. At this point I simply want to focus on the implications of Piaget's approach for individualizing our approach to education.

It is certainly a fact that some children develop faster than others, but Piaget does not see intellectual development as a race in which the swiftest child reaps the rewards. Rather, Piaget helps to direct our attention toward the necessary sequence of stages through which all children must proceed, though some never reach the final stages. If we know a child's place in that sequence, we may understand how he or she interprets events. Our concern should not be to compare students' progress with that of their peers, but rather (a) to design instruction so that it will be interpreted appropriately and meaningfully by each child, and (b) to attempt to provide an optimal level of mismatch to provoke activity in the direction of higher stage-structure-logic.

Piaget's emphasis on the child's view does not imply that we must limit what is taught because children aren't "ready" to learn. Instead he stresses the idea that children, and adults too, will transform what is taught in a way that fits their rules for making sense of the world. His stage theory helps us to overcome our egocentrism by viewing what is happening in the classroom through the eyes of our students. From this standpoint it becomes both possible and necessary to rethink the criteria by which we evaluate both student progress and teacher success.

Implications of the equilibration model

The search for optimal strategies of educating children has often been obscured by endless rhetoric and sloganeering. In the United States and Canada, for some decades, debate has tended to polarize around two extremes, either the "traditional," "three-R," teacher-centered classroom consistent with the clean-slate approach, or the "progressive," "open classroom," child-centered environment consistent with the flowering-seed assumptions about knowledge and how we know things. While most classrooms are not at either extreme, there is a tendency for one or the other ideology to hold sway. Piaget's theory of equilibration suggests that the choice between clean slates and flowering seeds, or even the adoption of a bit of both, is oversimplification.

We sometimes forget that the effectiveness of any strategy must be evaluated not only in terms of assumptions about learning, but also in terms of our educational goals. When it is important to know the exact location of cities in Africa, for instance, or to add numbers correctly, or to describe precisely what happened in historical or scientific events, the accommodative aspect of a clean-slate approach may be useful. It certainly pays much-needed attention to specific external factors affecting learning. Sometimes, to induce disequilibration or to fit in with the child's short-term disequilibration, teachers can provide highly structured material to which children can accommodate. Piaget's principle objection to the clean slate as the sole approach to education is that it ignores the assimilative function of the child.

Because Piaget has emphasized the child's active assimilative role in learning, a number of writers advocating open classrooms have quoted him in support of their views. Like any other approach, the open classroom is actually a summary of a variety of practices, all reacting against the clean-slate view by focusing on the child as the prime mover in education. Children are usually allowed to change freely from one activity to another within classrooms and sometimes between classrooms. Some plans for open classrooms include fairly precise teacher-student contracts concerning the amount and type of work to be done; the child determines the sequence and the timing (Featherstone's description of British Infant Schools, 1971). Other approaches make little or no explicit demand that children learn, or even that they attend classes at all (e.g., Neill, 1964). They have in common the optimistic view that motivation and knowledge flower from within. As we have seen, Piaget questions the flowering seed as the sole factor in developmental change because it minimizes accommodation, just as strongly as he criticizes the clean slate for minimizing assimilation.

A number of teachers in alternative schools and open classrooms have used the flowering-seed assumption as a justification for a very passive teacher role. It is interesting that in anecdotal examples used by some of the more visible writers who describe their open classrooms (e.g., Holt, Kohl), teachers often take very active roles as challengers, stimulators, questioners, and sometimes as traditional presenters of material. While the theory favors a flowering-seed view of children, the practice generally reflects interactive generator assumptions about intelligence.[9]

Piaget's approach goes beyond suggesting that clean-slate and flowering-seed teaching strategies have their place in the classroom. He encourages us to design situations in which optimal disequilibration between assimilation and accommodation can lead to the construction of new concepts. A lovely example, from the Science Curriculum Improvement Study, designed by Robert Karplus and his associates (Karplus and Thier, 1967):

> Professor Robert Karplus, a bespectacled University of California physicist is showing that second and third graders can engage in original inquiry concerning physical systems, equilibrium, interaction, and simple relativity. . . . Karplus trains regular public school teachers to start a typical lesson by showing the class two drawings. The first, labeled "Before," shows a beaker half-full of colorless fluid, with a small cube resting at the bottom. Bubbles are rising from the cube. The second picture, labeled "After" shows the beaker, still half-filled with fluid, but minus the cube and the bubbles. Question: What has happened? The following responses were given by different children in one class:
> Pupil: "It's sugar. It's a sugar cube. A sugar cube breaks up in the water."
> Pupil: "It's ice and the ice melts in water."
> Pupil: "No, if it was ice you'd have more water."
> Pupil: "It's not ice. Ice would float at the top."
> Pupil: "It looks like sugar. It's a sugar cube because it's square."
> Teacher: "Could the ice be square?"
> Pupil: "Yes, but not all the time, so it's probably sugar."
> Teacher: "Will sugar float at the top?"
> The children say no, sugar will not float at the top, but they do not seem entirely ready to accept the idea.
> Pupil: "It's a dice."
> Pupil: "No, dice doesn't melt."
> Pupil: "Somebody might have taken it out of the water."
> Pupil: "It's soap, because the bubbles come off."
> Pupil: "It's not soap. Soap takes too long a time to dissolve, and anyhow it forms lots of bubbles and lather."
> Pupil: "I measured, the height of water in both is the same—about 16 inches."
> The teacher writes down on the board all the things the class thought might be in the jar. The next day she places three jars of water before the children and has them try out each of the possibilities. One of the children who thought the object in the jar was ice obtains a piece from the school cafeteria for the experiment. Others bring a cube

[9]Or as John Watson suggests (personal communication) it might simply reflect the inability of a good teacher to remain relatively passive.

of sugar and a piece of soap. After observing and discussing the experiments, the class decides for sugar. Apparently the telling clue is the fact that the sugar cube in their own experiment gives off bubbles like those shown in the picture the day before.

The teacher could, of course, have given the children the relevant facts at the outset. Instead, 30 third-graders spent a considerable time observing, analyzing their observations and using them to defend or modify their conclusions. This type of lesson is sometimes called "How to take Half an Hour to Teach What You Could Tell in One Minute."

Professor Karplus' Science Curriculum Improvement Study, like most of the curriculum revision programs, combines this kind of "learning discovery" with conventional expository teaching. Basic scientific concepts are introduced by the teacher, but the children are then encouraged to discover interrelations and applications (Gross, 1964).

Piaget's equilibration theory suggests that the most important role of teachers is to serve as disequilibrators of their students. By their challenges, their questions, their provision of materials and physical arrangements of the classroom, they can help to provide optimal amounts of match and mismatch between the material and the students' present level. Even when the subject matter to be taught is determined by state guidelines or boards of education, the teacher can help students to formulate their own questions. Because it is unlikely that the same events will raise the same question for each child in the class, multiple opportunities for evoking temporary disequilibration must be arranged; at a given time, some students will find that assimilative activities lead to disequilibration and some will become disequilibrated in accommodative activities. Fortunately, according to Piaget, the teacher does not have total control of the learning environment. Equilibration theory suggests that overaccommodative demands may result in assimilative activity by the child, while overassimilative "freedom" may trigger a quest for more structure and direction.

Students, by the challenges, questions, and materials which they bring to the classroom, will also function as disequilibrators of themselves, their peers, and their teachers. Everyone in the classroom at his or her own level can provide the occasion for disequilibrating events. Learning involves an interactive coordination of viewpoints in which questions, rather than answers, provide the impetus for intellectual growth.

While this chapter has emphasized the cognitive implications of stage and equilibration theory for education, other chapters will explore social and emotional implications as well. Briefly stated, we will see that by affecting social perception and the ability to adopt others' points of view, cognitive structures play a major role in communication and other forms of social interaction. And by shaping the child's interpretation of events, logic-structure-stages have a great impact on how children feel about specific external events and about themselves.

Finally, the discussion in this and other chapters will focus on classrooms, but I hope that readers will keep in mind the potentially rich applications of

Piaget to parenting and the raising of children at home. Certainly it is no less important for parents than for teachers to understand the world through the eyes of their children and to find out whether childrearing proceeds best under clean-slate, flowering-seed or interactive generator-transformer assumptions about how children change.

CHAPTER 3

Symbolic Thought

Perception, Cognition, Action, and Emotion

Imagine yourself in the following predicament:

> Stimulation is bombarding your senses. Your eyes, ears, nose, mouth and skin are deluged by a chaotic array of sights, sounds, smells, tastes, and kinesthetic vibrations. You have no categories for classifying events or arranging them in order, no ability to compare these stimuli with past events or to plan for the future. You are limited to perceiving the world and acting on it in the present. Every time the environment changes, your reality changes with it; each recurring situation presents a new and unexpected problem. While you have a few inborn adaptive reflexes, you are unable to alter your behavior on the basis of experience or to plan manipulations of the environment in order to satisfy your needs.

As an adult, you may have felt something like this on an extremely bad day, but Piaget describes this situation as the constant condition of the newborn infant.

Newborns have two mechanisms—perception and Sensorimotor actions—which keep them in touch with stimulation at a particular moment in the present. The most important thing that newborns are missing in their task of making sense of the world, is a symbolic function. They retain no images which enable them to recall details of events gone by or to imagine what might be in the future. They have no pictures, words, gestures, or drawings which they can use to bring back—re-present—persons or objects, so that they can think about or communicate about events in the immediate present. According to Piaget, this symbolic function is the essence of human intelligence.

If we think of it at all, most of us do not have much of a problem accounting for the existence of symbols in the mind or explaining the fact that symbols are meaningful. It seems self-evident that the mind operates a kind of camera which stores pictures for later review. When we examine the shapes and shadows at a later time, they provide a faithful copy of the original events and so we can say, "I wonder what happened to Uncle Charles?" or "Remember when we skied down that mountain and almost got buried by an avalanche?" Piaget questions the common assumption that cognitive symbols are created from picture-copies. Differentiating clearly between perception and cognition, he combines both of these mechanisms along with action *and emotion* in a new theory of meaningful symbolic thought.

THE ROLE OF PERCEPTION IN SYMBOLIC MEANING

"Picture theory"

In classes I have taught, students tend to have a consistent, usually implicit, picture theory of how we come to be able to think about events which we are no longer able to perceive. An example of adult symbolic function:

> You are looking at a red object which is round, but not perfectly round. You attempt to bounce it and there is a thud as it smashes to pulp at your feet. Taking another similar object, you smell it (it smells good), you bite it (it yields, you can taste it), you feel its fleshy skin stretching over a softer interior. How is information transmitted from the object into your mind? Most people believe that somehow, like a camera or videotape recorder, the eyes, ears, nose, tongue, and fingers take pictures of events and transmit these pictures to the brain.
>
> Now the experience is over. You close your eyes and bring it back in imagination. Or, as a reader, you try to imagine these events as I have written them, whether or not you have experienced them in the same way. How did you do it? Most people are able to re-create experienced perceptions by forming mental images of sights, sounds, and so on. Can you imagine the event as vividly as you could perceive it? Usually, images are believed to be somewhat less vivid and detailed copies of the initial perceptions.
>
> Assume for the moment that you have never seen round red objects quite like the two you have experimented with. You attempt to make sense of your experience. They are not balls. They appear to be food, perhaps fruit. They have a color, size, shape, and texture similar to an apple but the taste is quite different. From particular past events you have selected and combined images to arrive at some ideas about these objects. In contrast with the specificity of images, symbolic ideas usually seem to be more general and less vivid abstractions.

Symbolic ideas are meaningful, it is assumed, because they can be traced to images, which in turn can be traced to perception-copies of external events. If this description fits with your own answers to the question of how symbols become meaningful, you are probably a believer in some version of picture theory.

In slightly altered forms, picture theory dominates many psychological models of perception and cognition (cf. Furth's analysis, 1969). It is also the view of symbols consistent with the clean-slate approach to learning; the direct link between meaningful symbols and external events enables knowledge to be a copy of external reality. Probably because it is so difficult to think of an alternative to the hypothesis that perception leads to mental symbols, many people who reject the role of the teacher as a writer on slates still hold firm to a picture theory of symbolic development.

Piaget's general equilibration model of intellectual function assumes that there *is* no mechanism which provides copies of external events, and therefore, that the picture theory of symbolic meaning is inaccurate. Why did he write three books summarizing hundreds of observations and experiments in refutation? (*Play, Dreams and Imitation in Childhood,* 1946; *The Mechanisms of Perception,* 1961; *Mental Imagery in the Child* [with Inhelder], 1966b.) Because almost everything about our understanding of thinking and learning rests on assumptions about the nature of symbols. If symbolic meaning is based on picture-copies, then intellectual development can be facilitated simply by exposure to perceptual experience. The clean slate is there to be written upon by increasingly complex environmental events. But if, as Piaget argues, symbolic meaning is based upon a combination of perception, action, and emotion, structuring and transforming events, then other approaches to educational enrichment must be designed to give the generator-transformer of symbols a chance to develop its power.

Relation between perception and cognitive understanding

The central claim of picture theory is that perception provides a foundation for cognitive understanding. Piaget demonstrates in many ways that perception and cognition are very different mechanisms: they are defined differently; they function differently; they follow different laws; they show different developmental patterns; and neither one provides exact copies of external events. So, a theory of symbolic thought cannot be based entirely on a perceptual approach to meaning.

Different definitions and functions. Perception is the mechanism that operates in the present to organize information about the current state of a stimulus. For instance, in the familiar Müller-Lyer perceptual illusion (Figure 1), subjects are asked to compare the length of lines 1 and 2, and to judge which is

longer. Almost all subjects from about five years of age to adulthood state that line 1 is longer, even though the lines are actually the same length.

In contrast with the present-orientation of perception, the mechanisms of cognition allow us to think about events which are not present to the senses and to coordinate memories of the past with present perceptions.

Piaget has constructed a cognitive version of the Müller-Lyer perceptual task. He makes lines 1 and 2 into identical sticks and shows them, at first without arrows, to subjects who are asked to compare lengths. While the subjects watch, stick 1 is placed on a card between arrows pointing inward and stick 2 is placed between arrows pointing outward. Five- and six-year-olds who initially judged the sticks equal in length, now claim that stick 1 is longer than stick 2, just like the Müller-Lyer illusion. Children at about the age of seven and older, maintain their judgment that the length of the sticks remains the same.

In the Müller-Lyer perceptual task, people at all ages are subject to illusion when no information is given about the initial length of lines or their transformations.[1] In Piaget's variation, young children are given this information but cannot seem to make use of it; they judge the final state of the sticks as a perceptual comparison in the present. However, older children and adults are able to re-present past states and transformations and to coordinate them with present perceptions. Their ability to go beyond immediately perceived events and to make inferences based on symbolic re-presentations is a cognitive rather than a perceptual skill. Thus, perception and cognition are defined differently; in contrast with younger children, the two mechanisms function differently in older children and adults.

Different laws of adult functioning. We tend both to trust and to distrust the evidence from our senses. On the one hand, "seeing is believing"; on the other, "don't believe any of what you read and only half of what you see." Piaget suggests that the issue is not simply one of right or wrong, correct or incorrect. Rather, the mechanism of perception in an adult follows different rules and leads to different conclusions about the world from the cognitive aspects of symbolic function. Examples can be found in many areas. Here are illustrative laws of part-whole relations and reversibility characteristics.

(a) Part-whole relations. One of the best-known maxims of Gestalt psychology is that "the whole is different from the sum of its parts." Four lines arranged this way | | | | will have a different meaning from the same lines arranged this way □. This axiom applies to many perceptual events, but Piaget points out that it does not apply to all conceptual problems. In mathematics, for example, no matter how the elements are combined and recombined, they must still retain their identity: a "1" cannot change its meaning when included in a "7"; 2 + 2 equals 4 no matter how the parts are arranged (under the usual assumptions of mathematical values). Similarly, it must be possible to retrieve the exact meaning of a logical class (e.g., boys) when it is included in a large class

[1]Packagers take advantage of this principle to make containers appear larger than they really are. Adults can avoid the perceptual illusion only if they see a smaller-appearing package transformed before their eyes to a new shape, with nothing added or taken away from the contents. Or they can use cognitive information by reading containers and finding that the smaller-appearing package has more product inside; then they can ignore perceptual illusion in favor of what they know (believe) to be true.

(e.g., children = girls + boys). The Gestalt perceptual principle that the whole is different from the sum of its parts does not apply to some important topics in cognition.

(b) Reversibility. Perceptual judgments are not always reversible; the order in which events are perceived often affects the outcome. If a person goes from a warm room to a cold one and back to a warm room, the room at the end of the sequence will feel warmer than at the beginning. However, numbers or ideas may be combined in any order and it is possible to return without distorting the starting place.

$$1 + 2 = 3$$
$$3 - 2 = 1$$

The quantity "1" at the end of this operation is identical to the quantity "1" at the beginning. This ability to reverse direction without distortion in conceptual thought is a major source of the power and mobility of adult cognition.

Differences in developmental patterns. The fact that adult perception is so different from cognition makes it difficult to accept the hypothesis of picture theory, that perception is the primary mechanism of symbolic meaning. Perhaps, though, there is a developmental priority, with perceptions or images always emerging before the corresponding ideas. According to Piaget, this alternative is not supported by the evidence.

(a) Perception and concepts.

> Groups of children averaging 6, 8, and 10 years of age were asked to compare the length of rod A placed 1 m. away with rod B placed 4 m. away. All ages made many errors in judging the relative size. In one part of the study, the children were shown rod M, equal in length to both A and B. First the rod was placed beside A, then B. It was now possible to *infer* rather than perceive the relative size of A and B by applying the transitive rule "A = M, M = B, therefore, A = B." Six-year-olds, not able to use the rule, made a substantial number of errors. Ten-year-olds, aware of the rule, made few errors. But eight-year-olds, who were quite able to use the logical transitivity rule, continued to respond that B, the far rod, was smaller than A, the near rod. (Piaget and Lambercier, 1946)

In this and other examples, Piaget showed that sensory-perceptual judgments do not always precede conceptual understanding. Sometimes concepts develop earlier, and after some delay, begin to regulate perceptual judgments.

(b) Images and concepts. As adults we can entertain the picture-theory hypothesis that external objects lead to images, which lead to ideas. Newborns can see objects in front of their eyes, but for the first six to eight months, once the objects are gone, they disappear from awareness. The ability to create a re-presentational image, argues Piaget, does not emerge until there is a conceptual object permanence. Conceptual development, then, may play a major role in the emergence of images, rather than vice versa.

In addition, the structural development of image memories follows closely the growth of cognitive stages; it does not at all resemble the development of perception.

In a cognitive task focusing on concepts of serial order, children are given ten sticks and asked to arrange them from smallest to largest. Four- and five-year-olds generally place the sticks in random order or pairs. Six- and seven-year-olds partially order the series and sometimes complete the task correctly by laborious trial and error. Seven- and eight-year-olds, in the stage of Concrete operations, systematically select the shortest, then the next shortest, and so on. In an intriguing experiment on memory images (Inhelder and Piaget, 1968), the same children were shown the ten sticks already arranged in order. A week later, and again six months later, they were not shown the sticks, but they were asked to draw what they remembered. They consistently produced drawings corresponding to their cognitive level. Five-year-olds drew pairs or short series, six-year-olds drew longer series, and the eight-year-olds in the Concrete stage tended to recall and draw the display correctly. Children who advanced in cognitive level over the six months actually improved the accuracy of the drawn images.

This is an intriguing experiment and there is still controversy about its design and interpretation. The authors focus on the change in performance accompanying a change in cognitive structures. But the original encoding of the events must have been accurate; improvement in performance probably lies somewhere in the ability to retrieve and decode the original images.

Perceptions cannot provide copies. Most theories accept the notion that images and ideas distort, transform, and otherwise alter reality. Their emphasis on perception in knowledge is one optimistic way of searching for a mechanism which can provide an accurate or true picture of the external world. The above analyses suggest that perception is neither logically nor developmentally prior to conception and imaging. But does perception have prior claim to understanding the physical world because it can provide exact copies of objects and events? In a number of experiments with adults, Piaget provides evidence that the perceptual mechanism is always and inherently distorting. For example, if identical objects or vertical lines of the same size are within our field of vision, the one which we center on (focus on) appears to be larger. The basic perceptual activity of sensory centering misinforms us about the nature of the stimulus. While perception is absolutely essential as a mechanism for keeping us in contact with the physical and social world, it is never free from distortion.

The above examples are selected from many apparently simple experiments with sticks, lines, and enclosed figures. Perception is concerned with present events, while cognition is the mechanism for past and future symbolic representation. These two mechanisms operate differently in both adults and children, following different laws and different paths of development. Images, which have usually been treated as extensions of perception, appear to accompany, rather than precede, cognitive development. From all these findings, Piaget drew the important conclusion that symbols are not merely abstractions from sensory-perceptual experience; the cognitive organizing apparatus has an equally important role in the development of symbolic thought.

The investigations by Piaget and his coworkers of the role of perception in symbolic thought support the assumptions underlying the general equilibration model of intelligence. To the extent that perception is oriented to specific events in the present, it involves the accommodative, bending-our-structures-to-fit-the-world aspects of symbols, even though it can never produce exact copies. But the development of meaningful images and ideas seems to require an assimilative function which coordinates specific perceptions into a general system of concepts, relationships, and rules.

PIAGET'S TWO-FACTOR COGNITIVE THEORY OF SYMBOLIC MEANING

> A mother says to her eighteen-month-old daughter: "Where's your ball?" The daughter who is just beginning to talk, stops and thinks for a moment, her eyes looking up as though to visualize the ball somewhere above her head. Suddenly she grins, turns around and points to the next room at a location neither of them can see.

During the past year and a half, before many major developments of spoken language, the daughter has accomplished two essential tasks in the development of meaningful symbols. She can extend the "here-and-now-ness" of immediate perception by creating images of objects that are not in view, and she can conceive of a thing as a permanent object which exists even when she doesn't see it.

We have explored the general assumption of picture theory that these two tasks are accomplished by a single mechanism (see Figure 2a) which transmits and stores a copy of external events and also conveys their conceptual meaning. In Piaget's model, each task is accomplished by a separate mechanism (see

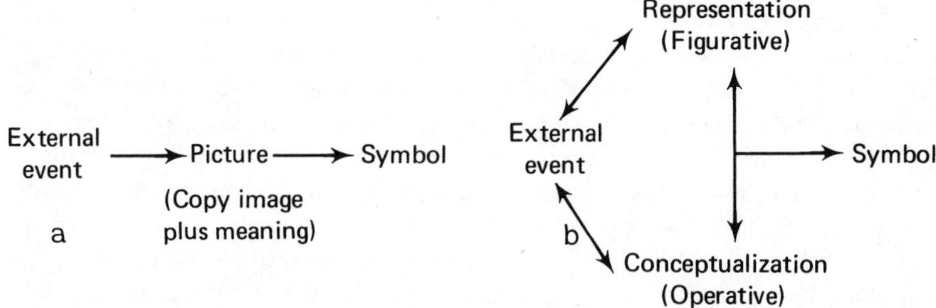

Figure 2b). The representation mechanism brings back images of sights, sounds, tastes, smells, and kinesthetic movements, but these images are not

meaningful until they are structured by a conceptualization mechanism. In the interaction between the two mechanisms, symbolic meaning is constructed, not simply copied.

Representation—the figurative aspect of symbols

The function of representation is to encode, store, and retrieve accurate images of specific events. According to Piaget, the representation mechanism constructs schematic maps or diagrams. Maps are accurate, not because they are photographic copies, but because the arrangement of points on a map corresponds with the configuration of a territory in the real world. Representations are *schemas* corresponding to the essential features of a particular set of objects or events. They are *figurative* schemas because in some way they match the *configuration* of the events they represent.

Although the map metaphor refers primarily to visual schemas, representational images occur in all sensory modalities. And sense-based images are not the only way in which we can represent events. When a child or adult imitates the actions of someone in the past, imitation represents the essential features of what was initially perceived. Drawings are another example of a medium of representation. Even the most realistic portraits are not exact copies, but they still evoke the essential features of the object or person portrayed.

In all the examples of representation cited so far, there is a direct correspondence between the form or shape of the symbol and the external event. By contrast, the meaning of written or spoken language symbols has no such direct connection. In most languages, letters are arbitrary representations of sounds, and most word sounds are arbitrarily related to events. But even here, there are figurative aspects of language symbols. The letters you are reading now can be used for communication only if they correspond with some standard shapes. If you read the text aloud, no one can understand it unless the spoken words are similar in sound to the words spoken by others.

Figurative schemas (in whatever symbolic medium) represent configurative aspects of specific events: map points correspond with geographical features; imitations match past actions; the lines in realistic drawings are arranged to evoke previously observed objects; letters are shaped and words are sounded to mimic specific linguistic models. In each case, *figurative schemas are primarily accommodative*—they are formed in such a way as to repeat aspects of a specific event.

If the analysis stopped here, we would have a symbolic mechanism not much different from picture theory, with schemas instead of copies as the single mechanism of meaning. It would be compatible with most psychological learning theories in which Pavlovian conditioning and Skinnerian reinforcement are conceptualized as stimulus events responsible for producing changes in the organism's response. Newer social learning theories (e.g., Bandura and Walters, 1963; Bandura 1969a) go beyond conditioning and reinforcement principles to explore how the child learns from watching adults and other children. Here, learning is still attributed primarily to external cues, and the mechanisms of learning are observation and imitation, both of which emphasize accommodation to the environment. As we have seen in Piaget's analysis of the clean-slate approach, this accommodative learning constitutes only one of the two necessary aspects of intellectual functioning. It does not take into account the assimilative aspects of learning in general, or symbol formation in particular.

Conceptualization—the operative aspects of symbols

Back to the eighteen-month-old and her ball. When she pointed to another room, the location of the ball may have been represented by a visual image, but the understanding that this red round thing (the word mother mentioned) is a *ball,* came in part from a system of classification which included some objects as balls and excluded some others.

Thus, before it becomes meaningful, a specific representational image or drawing or imitation must be incorporated in a general conceptual structure. Piaget calls this structure an operative *scheme.* Until recently, the distinction between schema and scheme was rarely made in English translations of Piaget's work. It is worth devoting some effort to understanding the distinction because very different learning experiences and very different cognitive processes are thought to be involved in the development of these two aspects of symbolic thought.

Schemes. A scheme is an organized system of actions—a structural unit which is repeatable and generalizable across situations. One specific grasping motion would not be considered a scheme, but the structure enabling the child to pick up many different objects would be referred to as a grasping scheme. A single fixation of an object by the eye would not be a scheme, but the ability to follow objects visually would be called a looking scheme. The static image of a specific red round object is a schem*a*. The general conceptual notion that an object exists even when it is out of sight is a permanent object schem*e*.

I have stated that schemas are primarily accommodative in their matching of representations to the external world. Schemes, by contrast, are primarily assimilative. For example, the four- or five-month-old attempts to put every new object in his or her mouth—to assimilate objects to a general set of organized actions. From the point of view of the adult, each object has many attributes and meanings. From the point of view of the child, the scheme gives meaning to the objects by creating, in effect, two classes—those-things-that-I-can-pick-up-and-put-in-my-mouth and those-things-that-I-can't-pick-up-and-put-in-my-mouth. Similarly, at a higher level, the eighteen-month-old wondering where the ball is creates a figurative schema of a specific round red thing; but it is only possible to represent this schema because she also has a general scheme of a permanent object that exists where she doesn't see it and a general scheme of classification (round things, things that bounce) which helps her to differentiate between balls and other objects. A meaningful symbol is a product of figurative schemas assimilated to conceptual schemes.

Schemes are considered to be part of the child's repertoire even when they are not in use; for instance, infants who are not engaged at the moment in visually tracking objects still have the use of a visual tracking scheme. Schemes are potential actions. Like plans or blueprints they exist in a state ready to be used whenever the environment can be assimilated to an existing structure.

Why doesn't Piaget simply adopt the notion of conditioned reflexes or learned habits to explain the generality of even the earliest infant behaviors? He provides an analysis of his reasons in the *Origins of Intelligence in Children* (1950, pp. 123–124). Starting with animal research, associative learning theorists tend to assume that habits emerge when new stimuli are paired with existing stimulus-response reflexes (e.g., a bell is paired with the dog's food-salivation reflex) or when reinforcement follows a particular action (e.g., food is given when the rat presses a bar). The concept of habit conveys a passive connection between an external stimulus and a response—in the manner of a clean slate. Piaget argues that reinforcement is not simply a property of the stimulus; an event becomes reinforcing only when it becomes significant or meaningful to the child. He also argues that the incredibly quick growth of understanding in the infant cannot reasonably be explained on the basis of one-by-one associations between stimulus and response. The infant's cognitive schemes play an active organizing and selecting role in making connections among events. While Piaget emphasizes the primarily assimilative nature of schemes, he does acknowledge that the environment has an important impact and that schemes do accommodate to external events; the associative learning theorists are in error, he believes, mainly in their neglect of assimilation, not in their claim that responses can be altered.

One of the problems in describing schemes precisely is that their size and complexity change qualitatively as the child develops. From birth to two years there is an impressive shift from schemes of rooting, looking, searching, and so on, to schemes of permanent objects, causality, space, and time. During this Sensorimotor stage, all schemes are coordinations of perceptions and external actions. In the Pre-operational stage (ages two to seven), the child develops symbolic schemes, which will later be coordinated in Concrete (ages seven to twelve) and Formal (ages twelve and on) schemes of thinking (e.g., abstract reasoning and hypothesis testing). The fact that the infant's rooting for the nipple and adolescent's scientific reasoning are both described in terms of schemes, can be confusing. The connecting theme is the organized, coordinated, generalized, and transformational nature of the child's conceptual approach.

Operations and actions. Schemas are particular, primarily accommodative, and figurative (matching an external configuration). Schemes are general, primarily assimilative, and *operative.* The term "operation" comes from the language of mathematics and logic; operations are the rules for combining symbols. In mathematics, +, −, ×, ÷, stand for rules of operating on numbers (adding, subtracting, multiplying, dividing). There are similar rules for combining classes; boys + girls = children; small toys × red toys = small red toys. All forms of mathematical and logical reasoning require operations on numbers or classes (concepts) and on relations among numbers or classes.

The ability of adults and older children to combine classes mentally is traced back in time through the younger child's ability to combine objects in the real world; and even farther back, Piaget sees the roots of operative intelligence in the infant's Sensorimotor combination of action achemes. Ultimately, these action roots nourish the growth of operative aspects of symbols in a manner quite different from the perception-dominated figurative aspects of symbolic thought.

I believe that when Piaget discusses Sensorimotor schemes, he is thinking primarily of voluntary muscle activities in which the body or parts of the body are in motion, such as in grasping, manipulating objects, kicking, walking. These activities show four clear contrasts with perception. First, they are easily visible, not only to the observing adult, but also to the child. For example, the one-year-old child who sits quietly observing a tower of blocks on the floor is unaware of the activity required to focus her perceptions. But when she reaches out to pick up the bottom block, her own activity may be more salient. Second, as the consequence of the visibility of sensorimotor action, children can observe the transformations of the external world which follow from their actions. They can see or feel what happens when objects are assimilated (picked up, turned over, banged, thrown) and also see at least part of what happens when they accommodate to objects (the changes in hand position, body orientation, etc.) The whole cause-and-effect sequence has external manifestations. Third, muscle actions may be inherently more generalizable than perceptual action. Perception, by definition, is an accommodation to specific characteristics of objects. But the muscle actions of opening and closing fingers, moving of arms, and walking, may be more independent of specific environmental circumstances. Fourth, and perhaps most important, muscle actions have built-in reversible properties; open-close; flex-relax; come-go. A particular body notion is easily undone, but perception cannot be unmade. All these properties of Sensorimotor schemes, taken together, imply that a young infant can combine and transform things in action, can observe the results of transformations, and can reverse the process. In the overt action of Sensorimotor schemes, then, are the basic properties of later logical or mathematical operations.

Symbols and development

In Piaget's two-factor approach to meaningful symbolic thought, picture theory is inadequate at every point in Figure 2a. First, perception cannot provide exact picture copies of external events; what is encoded and stored is a schematic map or blueprint, matching the essential configurative features of the external situation. Second, perception does not lead directly to re-presentational images; these images emerge only with the development of conceptual schemes. Third, picture-images cannot carry their own meaning; symbols become meaningful when specific representational schemas are assimilated to general operational schemes.

A summary of the complex vocabulary of Piaget's two-factor theory of symbolic meaning is as follows. The representation mechanism arises from figurative schemas within the general accommodation function. The conceptualization mechanism arises from operative schemes within the general assimilation function. In the process of equilibration, as accommodation and assimilation interact, meaningful symbols are formed. Piaget lists the symbolic modes in order of developmental complexity: acting out past events ("deferred imitation"); using objects and actions to stand for other objects and actions ("symbolic play"); drawing ("graphic representation"); imagination ("mental imagery"); spoken or written language. These modes are grouped together in what Piaget calls the semiotic function.[2]

Each symbol has both a figurative and an operative aspect, though one aspect may more often predominate. For example, images are primarily figurative schemas, but they become meaningful in their integration with permanent object schemes, classification schemes, and so on. Drawings can be representational (realistic, figurative schemas) or conceptual (abstract, operative schemes). Symbolic play has been described as primarily assimilative (operative schemes), but it can also be used to re-enact a specific set of traumatic events. In each of these examples, operative assimilative schemes enable the child to *construct* general symbols out of specific figural representations of events. It is as if the child says, "I will now let this box be a bed and this doll will be my child." The choices are determined in part by figural resemblances, but symbol constructions depend in part on a conceptual transformation mechanism which allows the child to use a representation of one thing to stand for something else.

We have seen at the beginning of this chapter that the newborn is not equipped with the capacity to use meaningful representational symbols. In a sense, Piaget's theory has only two major cognitive stages, one before and one after the emergence of the semiotic function (before and after about eighteen months to two years of age). His other well-known stages describe qualitative

[2]Piaget's terminology in discussing representation and symbols is quite confusing. The semiotic function was initially called the symbolic function. The name was changed because Piaget wanted to reserve the term "symbol" for representations which the child creates and which show some resemblance to the things represented, like images. The term "sign" is reserved for arbitrary and conventional representation such as language. Despite this distinction, "symbolic function" and "representation" are sometimes used to refer to the whole process of understanding. Sometimes there is a narrower definition in which representations are the schematic pictures of real events, which only become meaningful when transformed by cognitive operations. I am indebted to Furth's discussion (1969) for clarifying some of these issues, but I have adopted what I hope will be a more consistent terminology still faithful to Piaget's approach.

changes in the way that symbols are organized and transformed (operative logic systems). Since the semiotic function does not even begin until late in the first year of life, a complete account of the two-factor theory of symbolic meaning must include an explanation of how overt actions come to function internally as mechanisms of representation and conceptualization. Piaget has different explanations for the development of each mechanism. He points to two different kinds of activities and two different kinds of abstraction from experience, which are necessary for the development of symbolic thought.

Representation through internalization. All representational images, according to Piaget, are created in a process by which imitative actions are internalized. At about three months of age, Piaget's daughter Jacqueline first sees a doll on a string wiggle when her bassinette moves; her subsequent kicking is, in some sense, an imitation of (accommodation to) the doll's actions. Piaget describes how at first the kicking, accompanied by a smile, occurs at great intensity. Gradually the overt response grows smaller—fewer kicks, then just a slight leg motion—until, several months later, only the smile remains as an overt response. It is as if the outlines of the overt reaction have been "taken inside."

Like picture theory, Piaget describes an accommodative taking in of external events, but unlike picture theory, what is taken in is a short-circuited imitative schema, not an exact perceptual copy. Thus, a two-year-old who is sitting quietly and thinking of a day in the park, is re-evoking a set of imitative actions in internal, representational form. As the child grows older, it is less and less necessary to act out the situation in observable behavior; the images, however, never lose their basic tie with imitative actions.

As the child develops, imitations and images become more accurate representations of specific events; the correspondence between a particular object and a particular image becomes stronger. According to Piaget, the accuracy increases as the child becomes more adept at *abstracting* the essential configurative aspects of objects and events. Images, then, become more sophisticated blueprints (in the sense of construction outlines) not more detailed photographs.

Conceptualization through interiorization. At the same time as the link between figurative images and objects becomes more specific, the relation between operative concepts and objects becomes more general. In play, young children resist accommodation. They come to ignore many figurative aspects of objects; instead the objects are assimilated to present structures; for instance, anything that can be grasped gets shaken as if it were a rattle. Assimilative play results in generalization of schemes to many situations, and all objects that fit into the same scheme constitute sensorimotor examples of concepts or classes. Schemes, then, become increasingly detached from the particulars of events in a process which Piaget calls interiorization.

In contrast with internalization, which involves an abstraction from objects, interiorization is an abstraction from the child's own actions. The distinction may be easier to see in older children.

> Conservation is a conceptual scheme applied to specific events. A seven-year-old observes two sets of six checkers and *knows* immediately that there will be the same number in each set, no matter whether they are arranged in lines, circles, crosses, or piles. But how does the child come to know that the number stays the same despite rearrangements? This information is not given in any single, static, perception, or figurative schema. Rather, the child arrives at a conservation scheme only after repeated attempts at arranging and rearranging checkers and many other sets of objects. The conservation schemes emerges when a general principle abstracted from the child's actions (changing the arrangement) can be coordinated with the figurative information abstracted from the objects ("there are still six").

In describing the development of interiorization, Piaget emphasizes the increasing coordination inside the child, in which one action scheme is assimilated to another. While figurative schemas are enriched from a feedback loop with external objects, operative schemes are enriched from playful exercise and coordination of actions already in the child's repertoire. Even though there has been contact with external objects, the focus is on the feedback among interior schemes. It is this interior coordination which permits a flexible detachment of schemes from the particulars of events.

Symbols, then, are constructed mentally from two kinds of overt behaviors which have been transformed into internal activities by different processes. Representations are developed from internalized (accommodative) imitations and perceptions, while conceptualizations are developed from interiorized (assimilative) activities such as play. In the case of representation, developmental progress will occur in the direction of accuracy and specificity; in the case of conceptualization, progress will occur in the direction of comprehensiveness and generality. Knowledge in the form of symbolic thought is not simply taken in from experience, but is actively constructed by the child, beginning with the earliest Sensorimotor substages.

EMOTION IN SYMBOLIC DEVELOPMENT

When Piaget summarizes his model of the symbolic function (1948; Piaget and Inhelder, 1966a) or when others summarize it (Flavell, 1963; Furth, 1969), the emphasis is primarily on the cognitive, rational processes of thought. There seems to be little or no room for what are usually described as emotions, or feelings. However, from his first major treatment in *Play Dreams and Imitation in Childhood* (1946a), Piaget is clear that symbols always carry both cognitive and affective meanings. Unfortunately, his subsequent thoughts about emotions appear as incidental comments in many writings on other topics. I am aware of only one extended presentation of his theory of emotional development, given in a course at the Sorbonne (1954). The lack of availability of sources is typified by the fact that a xeroxed English translation of some of the lecture notes from that course has been passed from one American university to another. Despite Piaget's statements about the importance of emotion in symbolic function, his views must be pieced together from different fragments.

A brief introduction is necessary to place Piaget's discussion in the general context of theories of emotion and motivation, a topic which is probably one of the most controversial and confused in the fields of psychology and philosophy. Ancient Greeks divided psychological functions into cognition, emotion, and conation (will). Once the functions were separated, there followed countless attempts to understand the relationships among them. Like the king's men, philosophers and psychologists have been trying to put Humpty Dumpty back together, with about the same degree of success as that nursery rhyme described.

A major difficulty in the psychological study of emotion is that there are four quite distinct definitions of the term. Emotion is conceptualized by some as a general level of arousal—a quantity which provides an amount of energy or intensity behind behavior. Sometimes emotion or motivation is thought to be an explanatory concept which accounts for the selection of a specific goal (hunger leads to eating), or a specific set of goal-directed actions (fearful, angry, or loving behavior). Emotions are also considered to be the expressive styles that accompany other behavior, but are not necessarily goal-directed (laughter, tears, etc.). And finally, emotion has been described as experienced feeling states (anxiety, joy, anger) which seem to have qualities different from thoughts. Unfortunately, there tends to be a circularity in the use of emotions as explanatory constructs, because the emotions are often inferred from the same behavior they are called upon to explain. Why is he crying? He's sad. How do you know he's sad? He's crying.

Piaget notes that many theories of development treat cognition and emotion as separate but interlocked systems; Freudian theory is probably the best known example. Affect, in the form of instinctual drives, is dominant and exists prior to the development of cognition. In very young infants these drives lead to hallucinated images of objects. The failure of hallucinations to satisfy the drives promotes the development of ego (more cognitive) functions, placing the child in contact with the real world. Other theories, not mentioned by Piaget, also treat cognition and affect as interlocked systems but tend to view cognition as dominant (e.g., Festinger's theory of cognitive dissonance, 1957; Lazarus' appraisal theory, 1966).

Inseparability of cognition and emotion

While it is possible for purposes of analysis to distinguish between cognitive and affective aspects of any behavior or mental symbol, Piaget advises that it is a mistake to assume that there are two separate systems. For him they represent "two sides of the same coin." (1964)

No cognition without emotion. Perceptions are never merely organizations of information. What is selected for attention from a complex field is an index of our interest or curiosity. In Sensorimotor functions, the infant's choice of activities is accompanied by interests, needs, pleasure, or pain. Even in the most abstract mathematical operations of adults there is always curiosity or boredom, success or failure, aesthetic sentiments, and other elements. Cognitive acts are never affectively neutral. Piaget is not arguing here that there may be great depth of feeling involved every time we say the alphabet, but rather that whenever we cognize anything, we are making choices among things to think about; therefore the act of cognition always implies some movement toward or away, some interest or lack of interest, and so on, even if the intensity is very low.

No emotion without cognition. Piaget also claims that drives, feelings, emotions always occur in a cognitive framework. He cites Lorenz's ethological work (Tanner and Inhelder, 1954) to indicate that animal instinctual drives are released only when certain stimuli are perceived. Pavlovian conditioning only occurs when connections are established between stimulus and response. And, the statement of the most profound feeling, for example, "I love you," presupposes a highly developed conceptual organization in which there is an "I" and a "you" and some notion of a relation between the two.

Feelings as essential aspects of symbols. One implication of Piaget's claim that cognition and emotion are inseparable brings him to a discussion of emotions as feelings. He suggests that the exploration of feelings is a central function of symbolic play.

> . . . the essential instrument of social adaptation is language, which is not invented by the child but transmitted to him in ready-made, compulsory and collective forms. These are not suited to expressing the child's needs or his living experience of himself. The child, therefore, needs a means of self-expression, a system of signifiers constructed by him and capable of being bent to his wishes. Such is the system of symbols characteristic of symbolic play. (Piaget and Inhelder, 1966a, p. 58).

In a brief flirtation with psychoanalytic theory, Piaget illustrates how play symbols appear to contain more than the child consciously puts into them.

> (At five years and eight months) . . . , being for the moment on bad terms with her father, X charged one of her imaginary characters with the task of avenging her: *"Zoubab cut off her daddy's head. But she has some very strong glue and partly stuck it on again. But it's not very firm now."* (Piaget 1946a, p. 174).

Since the child must ultimately accommodate to adult language, assimilative play becomes the symbolic medium for expression of private, personal, and interpersonal feelings. But beyond the function of emotional expression, the exploration of feelings in play becomes part of the very construction of the symbol. Just as manipulation of objects enriches symbolic knowledge of the physical world, so exploration of feelings and relationships enriches symbolic knowledge of the self and the world of interpersonal relationships.

Emotion as motivation in cognitive development. The most general source of intellectual energy for both children and adults is the state of disequilibration when assimilation and accommodation are out of balance. We cannot say that the child acts *in order to* redress this imbalance, but over time the child engages in a number of activities which have that effect. In this case, disequilibration acts as a general energizer, not a specific selector among many possible activities the child could choose in the search for knowledge. Piaget does see a role for emotion in the choice of specific goals. In combination with cognition, emotion helps to determine interest—in the people, objects, and activities with which children and adults prefer to spend time and exert effort.

In both the general sense of disequilibration and the specific sense of interest or value, emotional factors affect cognitive development by influencing the child's or adult's tendency to become involved in the active manipulative experiences necessary for cognitive growth. If we are interested, we may explore objects and build up figurative schemas, or we may engage in transformational activities and enrich our operative schemes. If we are not interested, or we actively avoid certain situations, there will be less opportunity to construct meaningful symbols. Thus, emotional factors may play an important role in cognitive growth and in the development of individual differences which make some of us more skilled in math, some in science, some in art, even when we are at the same general level of intellectual development.

Issues in Piaget's view of emotion

At first glance there appears to be little difference between Freud's view that emotion and cognition are separate systems and Piaget's that they are different aspects of one system. The distinction does make an important difference in accounting for the early phases of development. For Freud, affect develops first, and there is always some unstructured affective energy in the system; the *primacy* of affect tends to account for the widespread tendency toward irrationality, even in (or especially in) the most rational adults. For Piaget, the systems are coequal; one can and does dominate the other at any time. But, Piaget stresses the complementary rather than the conflictful relation between cognition and emotion, with each supplying a necessary part of human symbolic functioning.

Where Piaget's approach becomes most controversial, and is based on the least amount of evidence, is his hypothesis that cognition and emotion each supply a very different symbolic ingredient; according to him, emotion constitutes the "energetics" of thought while cognition provides the structure. And, except for instances of conflict when concept-feelings at one cognitive level disagree with concept-feelings at another, we should expect complementarity and parallelism between feeling and thinking.

For example, Piaget speculates that there may be a correspondence between the developing structure of logic and the structure of values (feelings about what is good, right, important, etc.). By the time children reach Concrete operations (at about ages seven or eight), they are able to reason about logical class inclusion hierarchies. If A includes B, and B includes C, then A will necessarily include C. At about the same time, Piaget asserts, values and moral sentiments are also beginning to be structured in hierarchies. The child maintains a clear, ordered "list" which extends beyond the whim of the moment; clear preferences exist, and if the first choice cannot be granted, a second is forthcoming.

There are a number of links missing in Piaget's argument here which will have to be filled in by future research and theoretical analysis. First, there is no systematic evidence about the joint emergence of logical class hierarchies and value hierarchies. Second, there is some question whether values inevitably display hierarchical properties: if I value A more than B, and B more than C, do I necessarily value A more than C? Third, Piaget's claim that cognition provides the structure for emotion is supposed to apply in all affective areas. But there may be other important instances in which the logic of cognitive structures may not apply to what we describe as feelings.

In logical classification, polar opposites are mutually exclusive. Given two objects to compare, we can say that one is: taller or shorter, but not both; larger or smaller, but not both; newer or older, but not both. However, feelings with polar-opposite valences frequently occur together—love-hate, pleasure-pain, admiration-hostility. Perhaps the reason that adults have such difficulty with ambivalence stems from this discrepancy between cognitive logic and the "logic of feelings." Ambivalence might not be a problem for a younger child who does not expect opposites to be mutually exclusive.

These counter examples do not suggest that feelings and values are without logic or structure, but they do question the expectation that there will *generally* be correspondence between more cognitive and more affective schemes. My own impression is that Piaget is on much safer ground when he points to the presence of both cognition and emotion in symbolic thought than when he clearly divides their roles into structure and energetics and when he expects complementary development in both cognitive and affect domains. Since there is as yet almost no research on developmental theories of emotion, by Piaget or anyone else, the field is wide open for further inquiry.

EDUCATIONAL IMPLICATIONS

Facts as symbolic constructions

As teachers, we want our students to be creative, to invent new strategies, to play with ideas. However, most of us also feel some obligation to make certain that they are in command of scientific, mathematical, historical, linguistic, and other facts. Student grades on report cards and achievement tests often reflect their ability to produce certain facts on demand.

Facts are statements or ideas *about* something. Although they are usually conveyed in spoken or written language, they can also occur as drawings, actions, imitations, and images. Facts about events in the physical and social world are remembered and expressed in the form of representational-conceptual symbols.[3] What makes a fact different from other symbolic statements is that a fact is supposed to be true, to refer to something which "really happened" in contrast with opinions, beliefs, theories, and fantasies.

The definition of "fact" implies that it is possible for symbols to be accurate picture-copies of reality, uninfluenced by the prejudice or point of view of the person making the statements. Piaget's model of symbols with its combination of figurative schemas, operative schemes, and emotions, leads to a very different view of facts.

> In psychology as in physics there are not pure "facts" if by "facts" are meant phenomena presented nakedly to the mind by nature itself, independent respectively of hypotheses by means of which the mind examines them, of principles governing the interpretation of experience, and of the systematic framework of existing judgments into which the observer pigeon-holes every new observation. (Piaget, 1926, p. 9)

There are no facts independent of the observer; all statements about reality are interpretations, or constructions—products of the interaction between figurative representations of external events and operative conceptualizations. Even the "facts" presented by scientists, the supposed champions of objectivity, are constructions. Although scientists build complex instruments and do controlled and replicated experiments to eliminate experimenter bias, *they* still decide what to measure, determine the units of measurement, build the apparatus, read the dials, and interpret the results.[4]

Nowhere is the fact treated more reverentially than in school textbooks. Most of us do not believe that texts contain clean-slate picture-copy facts independent of the author's interpretations, but we sometimes expect children to treat the author's statements of facts as eternal verities carved on tablets of stone. In social studies or history texts it is usually presented as a fact that Columbus discovered America and yet it is easy to wonder who actually "dis-

[3]There are some facts about topics such as language which may not be encoded and expressed in the sensory representational modes Piaget has described above. Psycholinguists talk about a-modal symbols which allow a language user to distinguish between past and future tenses, or among logical ideas such as possibility-probability-impossibility. Piaget would probably argue that even these symbols can still be traced to figurative schemas and operative schemes.

[4]Piaget's view strongly rejects the kind of seventeenth-century model of physics which psychologists have used as a scientific ideal long after its abandonment by physicists themselves. Those of us brought up in the "hard science" approach to psychology and education may have trouble believing in the possibility of a systematic science which follows a different model (see Part IV).

covered America" when everyone who sailed from Europe found the continent already inhabited. How do writers know about events that happened more than 500 years ago? A few texts are beginning to present historical events and ideas explicitly as interpretations, sometimes offering more than one alternative and encouraging students to decide for themselves; in the process they learn both history and historiography.

In a subject like history, it may be easy to agree with Piaget that facts are interpretations. But what about mathematics, where 2 + 2 seems always and inevitably to equal 4? We shall see in Chapters 7 and 8 that the concept of number must be constructed anew by each child, after a long period of experimentation with operational schemes of classifications and serial ordering. Even in the area of simple arithmetic the child does not copy external reality, but rather constructs representational-conceptual symbols.

Even though information is assimilated to the child's point of view, facts have an accommodative emphasis in their function of representing the "true" state of affairs in the real world. Science, mathematics, and history are important fields in which facts can be investigated and understood. But facts are not the only important ingredients of symbolic development. Poetry, fine arts, physical education, exploration of feelings and relationships are important in developing the assimilative side of intelligence.[5] In educational practice we tend to draw clear distinction between fact and theory or fact and fantasy in what we define as knowledge. Piaget's model leads to the conclusion that there are no absolute distinctions between them and both are central to the development of symbolic thought.

The blurring of absolute distinctions between fact and fantasy does not mean that any casual observation must be accorded as much status as a carefully worked out set of conclusions. While it is not possible, according to Piaget, to achieve objectivity in the sense of transcending one's own (necessarily limited) point of view, it is possible to achieve more sophisticated knowledge by *coordinating* points of view. Optimal intellectual development tends to occur when events and issues are examined from the perspective of more than one historical period, more than one academic discipline, more than one theory, by more than one person. Useful facts, then, represent a synthesis of interpretations rather than a report of one person's idiosyncratic notions. Many teachers stress that students should "work on their own," get "their own answers." Based on his conception of objectivity as a coordination of viewpoints, Piaget suggests that the sharing of points of view (sometimes regarded as chattering or even cheating) is one essential part of the process of developing meaningful symbols.

> In most classrooms that I have visited, from preschool through university, teachers encourage discussion among students in hopes of eliciting a correct or better answer. Responses which are considered off the track are bluntly or deftly shoved

[5]They are not exclusively assimilative activities, but the emphasis is usually more on the individual's action in coordinating and structuring the world.

aside. However, if facts are to be considered points of view rather than picture-copies of truth, and if symbolic development can be facilitated by exchanges in point of view, then the process of interaction and not just the end point may begin to receive the kind of attention that it deserves.

The importance of action in symbolic thought

In the service of educational enrichment, audio-visual aids, field trips, and live demonstrations have been brought into the curriculum to augment the verbal rule-learning of many traditional schools. Often this enrichment is of a sensory-perceptual kind in which children are shown and told how the world functions. Of course, this added exposure brings children in contact with events which they might never see, hear, or touch. However, Piaget's view of symbolic development suggests that enrichment requires more than show and be told. Passive looking or other forms of figural accommodation are not enough. "To know is to transform reality in order to understand how a state is brought about" (Piaget and Inhelder, 1966b).

"What are you doing?" we ask a friend, and he replies: "I'm not doing anything—just thinking . . ." Thought seems quite different from action. It seems as if the natural sequence is mental planning, followed by overt behavior. However, as Furth (1969, p. 60) succinctly describes Piaget's approach, "thinking *is* action, and not merely *for* action." Mental symbols are created from coordinations of sensorimotor behavior. Even when the behavior becomes internal and unobservable to others, thinking retains its active, transformational character. When Piaget uses the term "operations" to describe mental combinations, the operative aspect of thought never loses its functional analogy with the combination of real objects. Adding 1 + 1 derives part of its meaning from the possibility of putting together one object with another in the physical world.

Once the child has been involved in enough activity that mental symbols are formed, he or she becomes capable of thinking about and communicating about events without always becoming involved in overt action. But the idea that symbolic meaning always involves active transformation is characteristic of every stage of intelligence. Richard Le Blanc, a teacher of twelve-year-old junior high school students passed on this example:

> One question math teachers are fond of asking is how many points there are on a line segment. I will call my two classes A and B. Class A I taught in my usual semi-discovery manner. Class B taught itself, grouped as they wished; usually with friends, but occasionally alone. The question I asked was, "How many points can you fit on a six-inch line segment?" Both classes had a firm knowledge of line segment and point. Since I expected Class B to get the material better, I tried the material out on them first so they would not get "answers" from the earlier Class A.
>
> Class B started drawing line segments and started putting points on them. I told them I would only look. I'd answer no questions. Some people worked diligently for 15 or 20 minutes, but as many worked while watching what their friends did.

> Whenever a new idea came up, they seized it and spread it around to other friends. After putting dots on for a while, one fellow figured out how many dots filled up an inch, with a dull pencil, and got his answer. A person working with him told him to sharpen his pencil. This idea could have solved it, but it died there, much to my dismay. Another group got this idea later and came to the conclusion that there could be as many dots as were wanted. All that was necessary was a sharp enough pencil. That *is* the idea of an infinite number. An infinite number is bigger than any number you can name. A few other groups filled out the line methodically, putting the first point in the middle of the line, the next two points in the middle of the remaining line, etc. One person filled in the line methodically, this way: one half of the line and then half of one piece toward the right, etc. Again, he found that there are as many points as one could name.
>
> As time went by, the noise became greater because some said there is an infinite number, some said there are more than you could name, but not necessarily infinite. I stopped work at this point and said, "Infinite means more than any number," so they were all right and most understood.
>
> In Class A, I tried all the methods used above, but I could not make them see what Class B saw easily. They understood, but never felt it. Weeks later, I had to remind Class A of the tests that I tried in order to get them to remember how many points were on a line, but Class B's knowledge was solid.

This example was chosen to illustrate the idea that active involvement in manipulating materials should not be reserved for very young children. While older children and adults are able to learn from verbal lectures and reading, they still require extensive experience with transforming objects, so that figurative schemas can be internalized, and they need experience in coordinating their own actions to facilitate the interiorization of operative schemes.

Emotions in learning

Piaget's equilibration model of functioning indicates that from the moment of birth, if not before, there is a need to process information, to become actively engaged with changing stimulation. Within the child, there is always an intrinsic motivation to learn, even though children do not always want to learn what we teach, in the way that we are teaching it.

Hunt's (1961) notion of optimal mismatch suggests that there is an optimal level of disequilibration at a given time. This suggests the (apparently not obvious) possibility that children and adults usually place a positive value on working at tasks which have a reasonable level of difficulty. They may avoid working when the task is too difficult, *or too easy,* but they will generally rise to appropriate challenge. One of the teacher's tasks, then, is to help stimulate student involvement in learning via cognitive perturbation—presenting tasks, ideas, and questions which are slightly mismatched with the present structures of the child.

No one would deny that education is an emotional as well as an intellectual endeavor. The role of teachers as disequilibrators, while not conceptualized in Piaget's terms, has long been acknowledged. So too has the need to capitalize on the child's natural interests, or to present material in a way which will lead to new interest. What Piaget brings to a discussion of emotional factors in learning is a sense that feelings are natural accompaniments, not foreign intruders in the intellectual endeavor. Rather than suggesting that teachers find ways of motivating children from the outside, or making certain that feelings do not interfere, Piaget's approach indicates that working and playing with feelings is part and parcel of symbolic development.

Specific implications of this point of view will be discussed in other chapters. One general implication is this: activities in schools which emphasize fantasies, feelings, and social interactions are not to be reserved for "breaks" between periods of work. Teachers need not adopt sensitivity training, touching, and trust games, and other exercises advocated by some educators as part of the human potential movement. Rather, in allowing children some time for daydreams, sharing conversations, drawing, and expressing some of their feelings about what they are learning, the teachers will still be working toward their goal of actively enriching student understanding. Piaget's view of the inseparable tie between emotion and cognition suggests that both are absolutely necessary for intellectual development in the widest sense.

CHAPTER 4
Clinical Method and the Assessment of Intelligence

Chapters 2 and 3 focused on children in the process of constructing interpretations of the world. If Piaget is correct in his view of symbolic thought and intelligence, shouldn't his model apply to himself and his coworkers—and really to all scientific investigators? Aren't they also constructors of theories and interpreters of data, rather than videotape camera operators, recording sound pictures of the facts of human existence? If all facts are shaped by the point of view of the observer, how are you, the reader, to know whether the ideas which you have been reading about so far represent an accurate account of child development? This chapter shifts from a description of children to a consideration of methods for learning about them. The general topic can be described in one complex question: how should we go about the task of gathering and interpreting data so that we can construct a comprehensive and useful theory of child development? In the search for an answer we will consider traditional views of scientific method and standardized measurement, and how Piaget and the members of the Genevan school came to develop a new clinical method for scientific investigation. This topic, important for researchers and theorists, is equally important for all those interested in assessing the current developmental status of a child and understanding how children make sense of the world. Near the end of the chapter, the discussion of methods of assessment leads to a summary-presentation of similarities and differences between Piaget's conception of intelligence and the conceptions underlying IQ or achievement tests and measurements of intellectual ability.

THE NEED FOR A NEW METHOD OF GATHERING AND INTERPRETING DATA

In his search for scientific methods of studying intellectual development in children, Piaget was faced with two especially difficult problems. First, his assumptions about human intelligence seriously questioned the possibility that anyone has access to facts which are independent of the observer's point of view. But in the early decades of this century, the prevailing logical positivist–behaviorist conception of scientific psychology insisted that it was possible and necessary for scientists to avoid observer bias in the gathering and interpreting of data. Second, Piaget's primary theoretical interests lay in understanding an individual's logical structures, equilibration processes, and symbolic functions—concepts which refer to unobservable events occurring inside the child's mind and body. But, in order to maintain scientific objectivity, behaviorists claimed that only observable events are open to scientific study; what happens in the mind is to be ignored. In response to these issues, over the course of fifteen years, Piaget and the Genevan school evolved a new clinical method which accepted some of the positivist–behaviorist notions about science but rejected their conception of the role of the scientist-observer. Details of the argument for this new method may call into question some long-held assumptions about what it means to provide an objective assessment of the child.

The ideology of behaviorism and the Scientific method

Behaviorism shares with all scientific approaches an insistence that scientific tests, observations, and experiments be: systematic rather than random; public and communicable rather than private and idiosyncratic; repeatable over time and across situation by different testers–observers–experimenters. Piaget accepts wholeheartedly the behaviorists' requirements that scientific observation be systematic, public, and replicable, but he does not accept the behaviorist assumption about how these goals are to be attained.

In an analysis of behaviorism and science, Breger (1969) argues that it is necessary to distinguish between specific behaviorist theories and a general behaviorist ideology concerning scientific method in psychology. This ideology risks being scientistic rather than scientific when it attempts to establish the observer as an objective fact-gatherer and when it attempts to rule out speculation about internal cognitive processes which may affect human behavior.

Behaviorists and others who adopt their view of science tend to rely on three methods to establish the objectivity of the observer—tests, naturalistic observations, and experiments, used singly or in combination. The test method presents the same stimulus to each subject in a standardized procedure and carefully records the subject's response; in this category are, for example, IQ and achievement tests, tests for ability to discriminate shapes, or tests which require the subject to push a bar when a colored light appears. Subjects can also be observed in their natural environments, without any specific presentation of stimuli by the observer, but great care must be taken to avoid observer influence on the results. Preferably, mechanical or electric data-gathering and recording devices are used. At the very least, data are required to be presented in the form of quantitative measurements rather than qualitative description. In a third method, scientists manipulate stimuli by performing experiments, again with standardized procedures, examining changes in an individual's response, or looking for differences between groups of subjects who have been treated differently.

All three methods are designed to study human beings in the same manner as any other natural phenomena—the observer simply records the relation between observable stimuli and observable responses or reactions. References to events occurring inside the organism are to be avoided or treated as mere speculation. Is there any way of knowing what goes on in the mind of another person? Many philosophers had created theories of mind by introspecting on their own thought processes, but this did not satisfy the demand of science for public and repeatable observations. In 1874, Wilhelm Wundt, the father of modern experimental psychology, proposed a new, "controlled," introspective method. The observer and his observations could be separated if an experimenter systematically manipulated stimuli and recorded the introspections reported by other trained observers. Forty years later, when American behavioristic psychology was first formulated (Watson, 1914), even the controlled method of introspection was bitterly denounced. In Watson's eyes, it had not produced a substantial body of knowledge. It had not even produced reliable agreement among highly trained introspectionists. The new behaviorism did not deny the existence of consciousness, but imperiously ruled it out as a proper object of psychological investigation.

In sum, behaviorists make every effort to avoid the influence of the observer on the gathering and interpreting of data, and they eliminate questions about the function of mind from the realm of scientific investigation. Both strategies are adopted in the hope of placing scientists in direct touch with the facts of human behavior. The behaviorist ideology, it appears, has adopted the clean-slate, picture theory of facts as potential copies of observable events.[1]

Piaget did not wish to eliminate tests, naturalistic observations, or experiments from scientific method. Rather, he questioned whether they could produce objective factual knowledge and he argued for the importance of including the child's interpretation of the stimulus, along with the experimenter's, in any exploration of intellectual development.

[1]It is not merely a coincidence that behaviorism adopts a clean-slate view of science. The philosophical roots of behaviorism can be traced in part to John Locke and the British Empiricist theories of knowledge (seventeenth and eighteenth centuries). In turn, these theories idealized Newtonian physics as the most important example of human understanding.

Is it possible to gather and interpret data objectively?

Tests. One of the highlights of the emergence of psychology as a science in the late nineteenth and early twentieth centuries was Binet's and Galton's work on the psychometric measurement of intelligence. These investigators were primarily interested in assessing individual differences in intellectual ability by administering a battery of tests to different people and comparing the number of correct responses. With age held constant, the greater number of correct responses, the higher the intellectual ability was assumed to be. The following discussion of the test method applies not only to psychometric IQ tests, but also to any standardized administration of a stimulus to a subject.

It has been an unquestioned assumption of individual difference theorists that intellectual tests must be standardized. How can we say that one child is more or less intelligent than another unless we give them the same items, administered and scored in the same ways? Following the model of the physical sciences, the test method attempts to rule out the possibility that the data are influenced by the unsystematic manner in which the tester presents the stimuli or evaluates the response.

Piaget acknowledges that the test method is valuable for the assessment of individual differences, for classifying individuals into already-established categories, and for exploring the effects of environmental manipulations on the subject's responses. However, he argues that this method should not be introduced too early in the process of constructing or verifying theories. The procedures by which items are selected, and the standardized manner in which tests are administered and scored, contain assumptions which may distort our understanding of intelligence and intellectual growth.

(*a*) Item selection

i. Theoretical bias. In the construction of an intellectual test, there are always explicit or implicit theoretical biases in the choice of items. For example, in the Binet, the Wechsler intelligence scale for children (WISC), and most other IQ tests, an item from the initial test pool is usually excluded unless a gradually increasing percentage of children pass as they grow older; if most five-year-olds fail an item which most six-year-olds pass, the item will probably not be included in the final version of the test. A theorist interested in exploring the hypothesis that intelligence develops in a series of discontinuous stagelike "jumps," would be unlikely to find support for that hypothesis using the Binet or WISC. Similarly, despite an endless number of studies actually done, it is not legitimate to use these tests to explore sex differences in the development of intelligence, because items have been chosen to equalize boys' and girls' scores at each age.

ii. Cultural bias

This is not the place for a detailed examination of the important and heated controversy about class and race bias in the construction of IQ tests. A simple reading of the language of most items, as well as a sampling of item content leaves no doubt that the most popular American IQ tests are slanted toward a racial majority middle class point of view. Questions from the WISC (1949, 1974):

1. What is the color of rubies? (This item was eliminated in the 1974 revision.)
2. What are some reasons we need policemen?
3. Why are criminals locked up? (An argument against locking them up would be given no credit.)
4. Why is it usually better to give money to a well-known charity than to a street beggar? (Again, an argument for giving money to a beggar receives no credit.)
5. In the general information subtest, children are asked about the location of countries bordering the United States, the continent in which Chile is located, and the capital of Greece, but no mention is made of Asian or African countries.

Some writers point to examples of theoretical and cultural bias and advocate greater effort devoted to the creation of an unbiased psychometric test. The argument in this section is that any test, by virtue of the fact that some items are selected and some rejected, involves the test constructor in shaping the conclusions derived from subsequent research on intellectual development.

(*b*) Standardized administration. Piaget's most important general criticism of tests is that when items are administered in one predetermined and standardized procedure, they falsify, or risk falsifying, the "natural mental inclination of the subject."

> For example, in trying to find out how a child conceives the movement of the sun and moon, the question may be asked, What makes the sun move? The child perhaps answers, "God makes it move," or "The wind blows it," etc. . . . It may well be that a child would never put the question to itself [sic] in such a form or even that it would never have asked such a question at all. The child quite possibly may imagine the sun to be a living being moving of its own accord. In asking "What makes the sun move?" the suggestion of an outside agent occurs at once, thus provoking the creation of a myth. . . . The only way to avoid such difficulties is to vary the questions, to make countersuggestions; in short, to give up all ideas of a fixed questionnaire [for the purpose of investigating the nature of intelligence, rather than the measurement of individual differences] (Piaget, 1926, pp. 3, 4).

In his early work for Henri Simon in the standardization of IQ tests, Piaget found that when he administered such items as "Define the following words" or "Name the months of the year in order," he obtained data concerning the content of the child's knowledge, but no information concerning the reasoning process behind correct or even incorrect answers. Since this information depended to some extent on what the individual child's answer had been, it could only come from individually tailored, and therefore unstandardized, interviews or experimental explorations. Unless an extremely careful investigation occurs, the test method loses in interpretive context what it gains in "objectivity." This loss is not great in later stages of theory construction when norms are needed, or when the theorist wants to assess the effects of certain variables on the behavior of large groups. However, in the early stages of theory construction, we risk misinterpreting children's responses unless we become more familiar with how *they* interpret the stimulus. One corollary of this argument is that standardization of stimuli and test administration exists only from the experimenter's point of view. The same stimuli or the same questions posed to a group of children may have very different meanings for each child.

So far, the examples illustrate that the tests as constructed do not allow for unbiased gathering and interpreting of data. In addition, there has been solid evidence that subjects' performance may be influenced by the personal characteristics and expectations of the experimenter, regardless of how carefully the standardized procedures are followed (Rosenthal and Jacobson, 1968[2]; Sattler and Theye, 1967).

All of these examples lead to the same major conclusion. The test method can be useful, but despite standardization of items and administration procedures, there is no guarantee that the use of tests facilitates the gathering of facts uninfluenced by the observer's point of view. Piaget and the members of the Genevan school adopt what initially seems to be a heretical position—that it is possible to be systematic without using standardized tests. At this point, it may be necessary to reassure the reader who may assume that "unstandardized" means "unscientific." Psychological researchers have been attracted to standardization in hopes of finding replicable results. Yet, Piaget's unstandardized clinical approach has yielded some of the most replicable results in the field.

Naturalistic observation. The test method may be contrasted with the method of "pure observations" (Piaget, 1926) derived from early work in the biological sciences, and now called nonparticipant or naturalistic observation. At first glance it would seem that there may be even less impact of the scientist on the observation than in the test method. No artificial stimuli are introduced. Instead, the observer records phenomena as they occur spontaneously in children's behavior, without any attempt to interact or to alter the stimulus conditions. For Piaget, this is where the theorist ought to begin.

> In the case of the present research, it is the observation of the spontaneous questions of children which furnishes data of the highest importance. The detailed study of the contents of these questions reveals the interests of children at different ages and reveals to us those questions which the child is resolving in its own mind and which might never have occurred to us, or which we should never have framed in such terms. Further, a study of the exact form of the questions indicates the child's implicit solutions, for almost every question contains its solution in the manner in which it is asked. For example, when a child asks "Who made the sun?" it is clear that he thinks of the sun as a product of an act of creation. . . . (Piaget, 1926, p. 4).

[2]Extensive and warranted criticisms of this study of how teachers' expectations affect IQ test performance, usually fail to acknowledge the general body of research support for the hypothesis that experimenter expectations do affect results.

Piaget's discussion applies to all situations in which data can be obtained. For example, selecting the game of marbles as an example because it was obviously of spontaneous interest to most of his prospective subjects, he investigated children's use and conception of rules (1932). He did not begin any systematic interviews or experiments until he had become an expert on the terminology, procedures, and variations in marble games as they occurred in playgrounds and streets in the districts surrounding Geneva. A long and serious discussion of the results of Piaget's naturalistic observations precedes his research report (pp. 15–24).

Despite Piaget's enthusiasm for pure observation, he clearly recognizes that it cannot be the sole method for gathering data. Comparability of results from child to child is difficult because situations vary in an unstandardized fashion (i.e., standardization is desirable as long as it is not the only approach to gathering data). It is extremely tedious to watch and wait for the child to say or dc something which is relevant to the experimenter's specific interests. Because of the time involved, it is impossible to amass data on large numbers of subjects.[3] More important, naturalistic observations, like tests, always run the risk of biasing the results by selection of what to observe and by omission of information inaccessible to the observer's eyes or recording apparatus. For example, especially in the case of young children, it is difficult to learn how they make sense of a great many events because they neither seek to communicate nor are able to communicate much of what they are thinking. Further, the nonparticipant observer can rarely distinguish between children's make-believe and their firmly held concepts. A child, who thinks no one is watching, says to a toy hammer "Please pound in some nails." Is the child pretending or does he or she attribute understanding to the toy? Only some kind of intervention by the tester–observer–experimenter can clarify the interpretation.

Experiments. Both tests and pure observations are ways of systematically recording the relations among variables. But it is not always easy to tell whether two variables just happen to occur together or whether there is a causal relation between them. One important way of approaching this question, though not always conclusive, is to do an experiment. The minimal conditions are: test or observe; manipulate one variable systematically, leaving all else (including a "control") as unchanged as possible; test or observe again.

Psychological experiments are often thought of in terms of large numbers of subjects, divided into experimental and control groups, with statistical tests for significant differences between groups. In fact, some of the most powerful experiments are single case studies in which the subject is his or her own control. One popular strategy is an on–off–on design.

> Increasing the amount of reward (on) makes it more probable that the child will obey a command. Withdrawing the reward (off) after a time results in disobedience.

[3]There is a mistaken impression that Piaget's studies are all performed on a very small sample. Vinh Bang (1966) gives some contrary information, especially for the early work in which Piaget failed to report the number of subjects.

Increasing the reward again reinstates the effect, and so on. The conclusion can be drawn that obedience is affected by the presence of rewards.

Experimentation is usually described as a method for testing hypotheses. In a broader sense, experimental manipulations are procedures for validating an interpretation. If I believe that disequilibration produces change, I can design an experiment which demonstrates such a change, and at the same time the experimental and control conditions help to rule out other possible explanations of the results.

In an experiment, the scientist plays an active role in manipulating the variables, but once the experiment is set in motion, tests and observations are used to gather data, as described above. The same question, then, can be raised about objectivity in experiments that has been raised by the heading at the beginning of this section, "Is it possible to gather and interpret data objectively?" (i.e., uninfluenced by the point of view of the scientist). In contrast with the ideology of behaviorism, Piaget's answer is an emphatic "No." His answer does not mean that any observation, however biased, is acceptable in a scientific approach, but it does mean that most of us must re-examine our assumptions about scientific facts.

The need for a triangulation approach

A method which assumes that the observer does *not* structure and shape observations, in effect makes a decision in favor of the clean-slate view of the child. An observer who acts as a recorder of the relation between external stimuli and observable responses will tend to conclude that the child's intelligence is organized by external rather than internal events. The scientist's conception of the experimenter as a passive observer will almost invariably lead him or her to ignore the hypothesis that children actively contribute to the making of meaning.

In search of an alternative method, Piaget created a triangulation strategy which was open to the possibility that in any scientific investigation, both experimenter and child are attempting to understand the same events. The metaphor of triangulation[4] is drawn from the activities of land-surveying and map-making. A surveyor at point B focuses on a mountain at point A (see Figure 3a). The height and location of the mountain cannot be specified until it has also

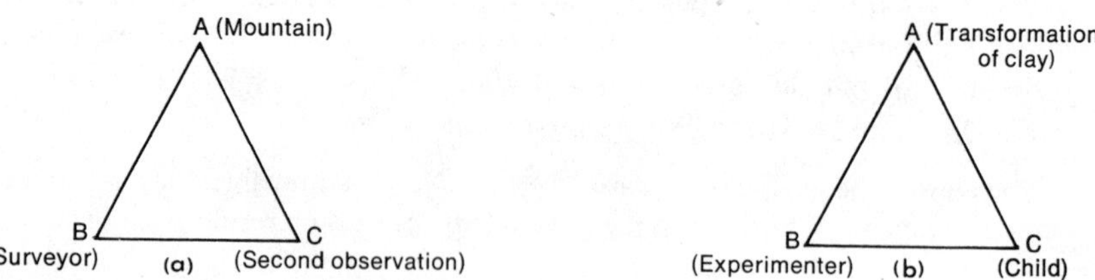

[4]The principle is Piaget's, but I have supplied the metaphor.

been sighted from a second observation point (C). Then, by a calculation of the distance between the two observation points B and C, and the angles formed with A, the surveyor can identify some important characteristics of the mountain without coming into direct contact with it.

In a psychological application of the triangulation metaphor (see Figure 3b), an experimenter (at B) asks a seven-year-old (at C) about an event (at A). The event is the transformation of one of two equal clay balls into a sausage shape. The behaviorist ideology would limit the experimenter to the AC side of the triangle, describing the clay at A and the child's response at C. However, Figure 3b makes clear that the description would involve primarily the *experimenter's* version of the event (BA) and the *experimenter's* version of the child's response (BC).

As we will see, the clinical method uses an extensive and unstandardized set of probes and manipulations of the material to explore the child's version of the event (CA) and the child's version of the experimenter's questions (CB). Then, the experimenter compares his or her own interpretation with the subject's interpretation, to arrive at a coordination of views concerning the meaning of events at A, B, and C. Of course, since the final synthesis is still in the control of the experimenter, bias inevitably creeps in, but for Piaget, assimilative transformation is part of the intrinsic nature of symbolic thought.

This analysis leads to a somewhat paradoxical conclusion. The behaviorists attempt to create an objective scientist–observer using standardized tests, observations, and experiments focusing on observable behavior. Yet their methods often *introduce* unseen bias into their observations and conclusions. In Piaget's approach, the explicit and active involvement of the experimenter, especially in coordinating points of view with the child, may result in less egocentric interpretations of the data by an adult. There is no claim in this contrast between methods that Piaget's approach is always and inevitably less egocentric; it would be clear by now that no method provides the scientist with direct access to picture-copy realities and objective truths.

THE CLINICAL METHOD

Having described the Piagetian critique of behaviorist ideology and sketched the general outlines of a triangulation approach, I will now describe in some detail how the clinical method operates in the assessment of a child. The active role of the observer, as well as the unstandardized procedures, make the method difficult to learn, but I believe that the results fully justify the effort.

". . . it is our opinion that in child psychology as in pathological psychology, at least a year of daily practice is necessary before passing beyond the inevitable fumbling stage of the beginner. It is so hard not to talk too much when questioning a child, especially for a pedagogue! It is so hard not to be suggestive! And above all, it is so hard to find the middle course between systemization due to preconceived ideas and incoherent due to the absence of any directing hypothesis! The good experimenter must, in fact, unite two often incompatible qualities; he must know what to observe, that is to say, to let the child talk freely, and later, manipulate objects freely, without even checking or sidetracking his utterances, and at the same time he must constantly be alert for something definitive. At every moment he may have some working hypothesis, some theory, true or false which he is seeking to check. To appreciate the real difficulty of the clinical method one must have taught it. When students begin they either suggest to the child all they hope to find, or they suggest nothing at all, because they are not on the lookout for anything, in which case, to be sure, they will never find anything. (Piaget, 1926, pp. 8–9)

Piaget's approach to gathering data can be systematically presented in a six-step sequence. It should be noted that the actual investigations do not always follow the sequence rigidly.

Step 1: formulating questions

From Piaget's historical analysis of traditional philosophical theories of knowledge (Chapter 14) and from his previous research, come the specific questions he wishes to investigate, the alternative hypotheses, and the kinds of data he believes to be most relevant.

Step 2: finding naturalistic examples

Next there is an extensive period of naturalistic observation of children in order to find experimental situations as relevant as possible to the child's spontaneous interests.[5] The aim is to present the kinds of problems and questions children pose to themselves, with the experimenter adopting the children's own language and concepts in the instructions and interviews.

Step 3: application of clinical method

Third comes the synthesis of pure observation, tests, and experimental methods. Based on the conclusions from steps one and two, Piaget and his coworkers developed a range of stimuli or tasks to be presented to each child. While the general problems, the materials, the initial procedures, and the first questions are now virtually standardized for many problems, further investigation in each session is determined by the child's initial verbal or sensorimotor responses.

Here are three rather detailed examples of the combinations of test observational and experimental methods. The first illustrates a purely nonverbal approach used with young infants, the second, a primarily nonverbal approach with older children, and the third, the by-now familiar combination of tasks-plus-clinical-interview.

[5]This was more often true in Piaget's early work. Later his own theoretical interests began to dominate the type of tasks and questions presented to the child.

Sensorimotor clinical method. In Chapter 5, I will summarize Piaget's description of the sequence of Sensorimotor development from reflex actions at birth to the highly coordinated but primarily nonverbal intellectual activity of the two-year-old. The method can be seen in hundreds of examples throughout the *Origins of Intelligence in Children* (1936). After an initial section concerning the automatic reflex responses of newborns and their subsequent modification into intentional goal-directed activity, Piaget focuses on the description of how isolated responses in different sensory modalities become coordinated into Sensorimotor schemes, that is how complex behavioral structures are formed. As one instance of this general problem, he describes the early interrelationship of vision and hearing (pp. 81–83).

> A 0;1 (8)[6] Laurent reveals an incipient localization of sound. He lies on his back without seeing me and looks at the roof of the cradle while moving his mouth and arms. Then I call him softly, "Aha, aha." His expression immediately changes, he listens, motionless, and seems to try to locate the sound by looking. His head oscillates slightly from right to left without yet finding the right location and his glance, instead of remaining fixed as previously, also searches. The following day Laurent better directs his head toward the sound and of course he then looks in the right direction, but it is impossible to decide whether the child tries to see the source of the sound or whether his looking simply accompanies pure auditory accommodation.

Piaget was looking for something specific. His theory and previous research led him to ask how two sensory modalities coordinate with each other. A search back through the developmental sequence located a time period *before* they are coordinated. Then comes an instance, spontaneously occurring, which may or may not represent coordination.

These passages are usually read as descriptions, but note what happens now. Piaget begins to use spontaneously occurring events and some of his own interventions to perform a controlled, single-case experiment.

> At 0;1 (15) On the other hand, it seems that on hearing my voice Laurent tries to see the face that goes with it but with two conditions which we shall try to specify. That morning Laurent smiled for the first time, three times, and, as we have seen, it is probable that the smile was started by a global impression, auditory as well as visual. That afternoon I stand at Laurent's left while he is lying in his cradle and looks to the right. I call, "Aha, aha." Laurent then slowly turns his head to the left and suddenly sees me after I have stopped singing. He looks at me at length. Then I move to his right (without his being able to follow me with his eyes) and I call. Laurent again turns in my direction and his eyes seem to search. He sees me and looks at me but this time without an expression of understanding (I am immobile at this moment). I move back to the left, call, and he turns back again. As a counterproof I repeat the same experiment but I tap the window panes with my hand (the cradle is between the two leaves of a French window). Each time Laurent turns to the correct side and looks in the direction of my face which, however, he perceives in passing. It appears

[6]Piaget generally gives the child's age in years; months (days). and so Laurent at 0;1 (8) is "no years," one month, and eight days old.

therefore that he associates the sound of the voice with the visual image of the human face and that he tries to see something else upon hearing a new sound.

The tap on the window pane, which Laurent ignores, shows that Laurent's eyes are now used in the service of locating a particular vocal sound, not just any noise. Piaget rarely stops his investigation once the child has begun to achieve a new level of organization. He goes on to examine its strengths and weaknesses—the conditions under which the new stage will or will not operate. In this way he points the direction toward future development.

But the rest of the observation shows that two conditions are still necessary for Laurent to look at a face when he has heard a voice: he must have seen this face shortly beforehand and it must be in motion. For example at 0;1 (20) I enter unobserved by Laurent and say, "Aha." He looks and searches most attentively (his arm movements stop completely) but limits himself to exploring the visual field exposed to him through his initial position (he examines the hood of the bassinet, the ceiling of the room, etc.). A moment later I appear in front of Laurent, then disappear and call him sometimes at the left sometimes at the right of the bassinet. Henceforth he searches in the right direction every time. The next day, same experiment and same result; furthermore I note that if I remain immobile he looks at me without interest and without even recognizing me, whereas if I move he looks at me and his searching ends as though he knew it was I who sang. At 0;1 (22) in the same way he searches anywhere at all although manifesting much attention to my voice; then he perceives me while I am immobile and continues searching without attributing importance to my visual image; after this I shake my head and thereafter he turns toward me wherever I call and seems satisfied as soon as he has discovered me. The following days, same phenomenon.

We see here that Piaget knows what he is looking for and seizes events perceived in the course of naturalistic observation to engage in systematic experiments attempting to verify his interpretive hypotheses.

A primarily nonverbal method at later stages. Using what has come to be called the Three Mountains Task (Piaget and Inhelder, 1948), an experimenter examines the child's ability to conceptualize spatial relations among objects, not only to study the emergence of a *system* of relationships, but also to gain more information concerning the distinction between the child's own viewpoint and that of other observers.

A three-dimensional display consisting of different colored mountains is placed on a table (see Figure 4). The child (between four and twelve years of age) is seated at position A and is given three different tasks, each of which represents a different method of ascertaining the same information. First, the child is shown separate pictures of mountains similar to those in the display and asked to recreate the scene as a doll or another person might see it from other compass points around the table (e.g. directly opposite the child, on the left, on the right, etc.). He or she is also asked to explain the response. In method 2 the child is asked to choose from among ten pictures of the total landscape, the one most likely to be seen by the doll at the various positions. Finally, the child is asked to select one of the pictures and to decide what position the doll would have to occupy in order to take a similar picture.

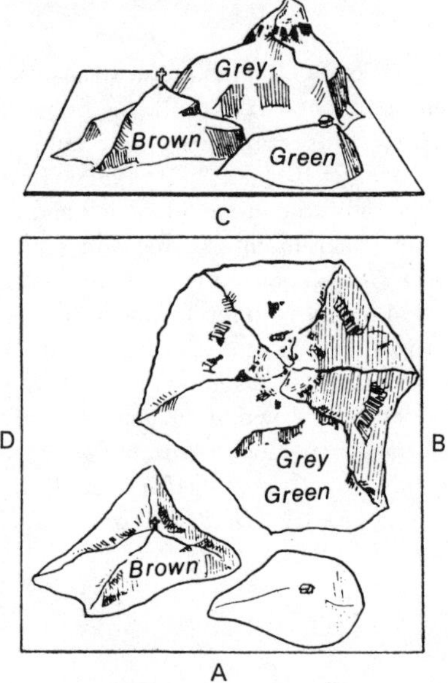

Figure 4. The Three Mountains Task. From Piaget and Inhelder, 1948.

The combination of methods, varying the kinds of response required, enables an experimenter to clarify his or her interpretations and helps to establish them as general principles rather than findings specific to one methodological approach (quotations from pp. 214–221).

METHOD 1

Luc (6;3) is seated at A and constructs an exact reproduction of what he can see, placing the green card on the right, the brown on the left and the grey in the center, its lower edges being hidden by the green and brown mountains as in the original. The doll is now placed opposite the child at C and he is asked to reproduce what the doll will see (the existing reproduction being moved far enough away from him not to keep looking at it). Luc takes the brown card and brings it close to the brown mountain as if to help himself think, then puts it down in front of it. He next takes the grey card and moves it about slowly, looking at the mountains the while. Then he puts it down under the brown card so that part is hidden, with its apex to the right of the brown card. Finally he places the green card partly in front of the grey one but somewhat to the right of it, thus reproducing exactly the previous construction (Position A, his own).

Tell me what you've done. Which is that photo there (his first construction)?—*That's when you're here* (position A)—And that one (the second)?—*That's when the little man is over there* (at C). *When he is here (at A) we have the green, then the brown and then the grey, and that's when he's over there (C) and we have the brown and green and the grey.*—Are the mountains really arranged as he sees them from there?—*Yes, it's right.*

The doll is put at B, to the right of the table; Luc dismantles his previous productions and replaces the green mountain on the right, the brown on the left and the grey in the middle, set back a little, thus reproducing not B but perspective A once more. He is then asked to seat himself at B to check his model. In the correct fashion he puts the grey mountain on the right, the green on the left and the brown in the centre and in the background. Can you remember what you saw from here (position A)?—*Yes.*—Was it the same?—*No.*—Try to copy it.—(He thinks, looking up at the ceiling, and produces the original model without looking at the mountains. He is thus working purely from memory).—Very good. Now show me the kind of photo the little man could take from there (position C). Luc now proceeds to place the grey card on the right, the green on the left, the brown in the centre, partly hidden by the other two. He has thus produced the perspective corresponding precisely with the position he actually occupies (B) and not with perspective C at all! Repeated with the doll at B (opposite B), the resulting construction again corresponds with B while Luc firmly believes he is reproducing a picture taken from D!

METHOD 2

Zan (6;6) is now seated at A and asked to select from among ten pictures one corresponding to a position near D (grey mountain on the left, brown on the right, green in the centre background). He searches for the right one, eventually choosing pictures I (position A: green right, brown left, grey centre) and VIII (somewhat to the left of A but very similar in appearance). Why do you choose these two?—*I saw they were both the same because the grey one is at the back and the other two in front.* The doll is then placed at B (from left to right: green, brown, grey). Again Zan picks out the picture corresponding to his own position and says, *It's this one because the green one is here* (points to his right) *and so is the little man* (points to the doll, also on his right).

METHOD 3

What will the child's response be to the question which is the converse of the previous one; namely, given a picture, find the relevant position of the doll? The results of such a study are in complete conformity with those already obtained. The child rests content with bringing the doll close to the main elements shown in the picture, but instead of putting it where it could see them from the outside and corresponding to some perspective, he simply puts it down among the mountains shown in the picture, in the perspective as he, not the doll, sees it.

Piaget and Inhelder go on to give representative examples of older children's responses to the same stimulus situation, finding a sequence from complete egocentrism, to recognition of different points of view, to a simultaneous coordination of perspectives. The data are then used to buttress their general conclusions concerning the changing nature of the child's underlying intellectual structures.

Task-plus-clinical-interview. There are many examples of the task-plus clinical-interview approach since 1940. One is a barns-and-fields problem designed to examine conservation of area (Piaget, Inhelder and Szeminska, 1948). Equal numbers of barns are placed in different spatial arrangements on two identical green "fields" (B_1 and B_2). If the child conserves area, the spatial arrangement of the barns will not affect the child's judgment of the equal area of the fields.

> The experimenter is interviewing six-year-old Vin (p. 268). With two bricks (barns) close together on B_1 and one brick at each end of B_2, Vin is asked whether the cows in B_2 have more, less, or the same amount of grass to eat. Vin replies: *There's more green left here* [B_1—the barns are close together and it looks as if there is more space. The experimenter then changes the task to its easiest possible form, with one brick in the same relative position on each card]. *Now there's the same left.*—and like this (moving brick on B_2)?—*It' the same. You've put it that way that's all.* [As the experimenter increases the number of barns, the child again fails to conserve area.]

When the first answer is incorrect, the experimenter reconstitutes the problem, testing whether the child has any verbal or conceptual understanding of area. As the difficulty increases, the point where the perceptual cues begin to dominate the conceptual judgment is located. The experimenter is not simply administering a test, but rather testing the limits of the child's understanding.

> At one point the problem is put aside and Vin is interviewed about some other conservation and measurement of area tasks. When he returns to the original barns and fields problem, he now answers differently. Seeing three blocks together at the bottom of B_1 and three at the side of B_2, he says: *There's the same amount of green left.* [The experimenter moves them in different arrangements and Vin maintains his answer until the three bricks are spaced widely on B_2.]—*There's more green here* (B_2).—What makes the green less?—*The houses. Oh, it's the same?*—Why? *Because it's always three houses. You just put them that way.* [Now Piaget puts four bricks on each.]—*It's less here* (B_2). *Oh no. It's the same because there's four houses on both.*—And like this (spacing them even more)?—*This time there's less green. Oh no! It's the same.*—But I'm talking about the green that's left over. Is that the same space for both?—*It's a little less. Oh no! . . . Yes. . . .*

Observation, test, experiment. Constantly varying the conditions, rephrasing the questions, rearranging the materials. In another context, Ausubel (1968) comments on how ironic it is that most educational assessments of learning focus only on what has already been acquired; the tester never actually sees the child involved in the process of gaining new understandings. By contrast, these examples illustrate the role of the tester as teacher, not aloof and waiting to evaluate answers, but providing experiences and asking questions designed to stretch the child's thinking. Many times in the course of a clinical interview children's stages appear to change before one's eyes.

Other strategies which Piaget uses to test the strength of children's beliefs are: countersuggestions ("A boy told me last week that there was *more* grass in this field."); shifts to related tasks in order to assess the generality of conceptual understanding; encouragement to verify answers and test out predictions; suggestions of helpful strategies. The clinical method is designed to give the child the widest possible latitude to display, verbally and nonverbally, what he or she knows; the procedures in the clinical method for poking and probing are designed to elicit the highest level of thought of which the child is capable, not to assess the child's typical or usual level of performance. The approach is consistent with Piaget's aim of describing and exploring the sequential structures by which children come to arrive at adult scientific thought.

A comment is in order concerning Piaget's presentation of clinical data. Rarely are there graphs, charts, or statistical tables. From extensive tests and interviews he selects a few typical, concrete examples representative of each developmental level he is discussing. When he states that a particular structure emerges at a given age, he means that 75 percent of the children in his sample give correct answers *and a specified level of explanation of their answers.* However, the size of the sample and its exact characteristics are not usually stated. This apparently casual method of data presentation has contributed to Piaget's North American image as lacking in "scientific" sophistication.

Step 4: further triangulations

Consistent with the behaviorist and other scientific approaches, specific tasks are first repeated with other subjects and other experimenters. Second, the experiment is repeated with children at different ages to add a developmental perspective.[7] Third, the data are examined from the theoretical perspectives relevant to the question asked (back to step 1); these perspectives include psychological theory, the history of ideas, and philosophical theories of knowledge. The data are discussed by representatives from different academic fields in an attempt to arrive at a new synthesis of points of view. The Centre Internationale d'Épistémologie Génétique is not only an exciting place where intellectual cross-fertilization can occur. It is a logically necessary extension of the clinical method to what has been called the clinical-critical method of studying the development of human thought.

Step 5: wider, more standardized testing

The fifth step in the process of gathering data involves increased standardization of tasks (e.g., Inhelder, Sinclair, and Bovet, 1974). Once the clinical method has established certain interpretable and replicable findings, Piaget and his coworkers may then use a much more standardized approach in their presentation of materials, allowing enough flexibility to enable the experi-

[7]There are also some longitudinal studies, referred to by Inhelder (1962), but not published, as far as I know.

menter to follow up on interesting responses. Despite the flexibility[8] of the interviewer's role, different observers in many countries have essentially repeated Piaget's results (see Chapter 12).

Step 6: Naturalistic verification

As a last step, at least in the early work, there was some effort made to recheck conclusions using naturalistic observation. The question here is, once the general conclusions have been established in a laboratory setting, can they be verified in terms of child behavior in a real-life situation? Again the clinical method emphasizes the use of converging lines of evidence and coordinations of points of view in order to understand the child and to verify theoretical hypotheses.

The clinical method is not entirely different from the methods advocated in the behaviorist ideology, but rather it reflects a different research strategy in the synthesis of tests, observation, and experiments.[9] While common usage contrasts scientific and clinical approaches, Piaget intends the clinical method to support a fully scientific study of the child: it is public and repeatable across situations and over time, yielding similar results when employed by different observers. The key word describing the clinical method is "systematic," replacing previous emphasis on "objectivity." The method provides a key to understanding the world through children's eyes, even though it does not provide picture-copy facts.

PSYCHOMETRIC AND CLINICAL APPROACHES TO INTELLIGENCE

"Piagetian," psychometric IQ tests

Just as any new idea is assimilated to existing cognitive schemes, so Piaget's clinical method has sometimes been assimilated to a psychometric, standardized, individual difference approach to the assessment of intelligence. For the past two decades, investigators have mined Piaget's materials for tasks which can be converted into IQ-type measures of cognitive performance. There is something natural and yet regrettable about this trend. It is natural that researchers would turn to Piaget's important investigations as a new and exciting source of information about cognitive development. It is regrettable,

[8]Piaget would say that replicability is impressive *because* of this flexibility.

[9]It resembles psychoanalytic clinical method in some respects, especially in the probing for underlying structures. However, it provides for a very active role of the experimenter, in contrast with the relatively passive therapist–investigator, and it places more emphasis on the provision of tasks and the observation of overt behavior, in addition to verbal reports from subjects concerning their interpretations of the world.

though, that they would attempt to transform an approach which was created to overcome the deficiencies of standardized psychometric testing, back into a standardized psychometric measure of intellectual performance.

The best justification that I have seen for the creation of Piagetian psychometric IQ tests is contained in a presentation by Tuddenham (1971) to a conference on *Measurement and Piaget* (Green, Ford, and Flamer, 1971). In contrast with the usual practice of selecting IQ test items empirically on the basis of increasing scores with increasing age, Tuddenham argues for the creation of an IQ test with items chosen on the basis of theoretically defined (Piagetian) criteria. Also, he carefully notes Piaget's own distinctions concerning the use of clinical and psychometric methods. As a vehicle for exploring the nature of intelligence, the clinical method of data gathering is necessary at the outset. Later, however, once concepts have been identified, sequences established, and theoretical contexts explored, it is possible to use Piaget's ideas about intelligence in a more standardized psychometric investigation of individual differences (step 5).

I will cite only a few of the many attempts to create standardized intellectual development tests for children based on Piagetian tasks. Uzgiris and Hunt (1975) have published an excellent infant scale. Among others, Goldschmidt and Bentler (1968), Tuddenham (1971), and Smedslund (1964) have developed sets of tasks for assessing the cognitive level of children in the Intuitive and Concrete operations stages (four-to-twelve years). Siegelman and Block (1969) have submitted Smedslund's tasks to a scalogram analysis which validates the sequential order of difficulty and also creates two parallel forms for test–retest purposes. A similar analysis of a set of tasks for Concrete and Formal operations was done by Bart and Airasian (1974). These have all been individually administered standardized scales. Paper-and-pencil tests of Formal operations have also begun to appear (Tisher, 1971; Rowell and Hoffman, 1975).

Over the years, attempts have been made to create nonverbal versions of Piaget tests, usually in hopes of demonstrating that children "get" concepts earlier than Piaget suggests, once the verbal complexities are removed. The problem with this approach is that there is usually a question about whether the nonverbal tasks are in fact assessing the same concept as their verbal counterparts. In an excellent review of these nonverbal assessments, Miller (1976) concludes:

> In many cases performance on the revised test proved no better than on standard Piagetian tests, and in many others a high level of performance was rendered suspect by methodological problems. Some studies, however, provided suggestive (although seldom conclusive) evidence that an understanding of concepts such as conservation and transitivity might emerge earlier than Piaget indicated.

Correlations and factor analysis of Piaget-based and IQ subtests indicate a moderate intercorrelation, averaging about .6 (Kaufman and Kaufman, 1972; Stephens, McLaughlin, Miller and Glass, 1972; De Vries, 1974). This means that about 36 percent of the variance in Piaget test scores can be accounted for by variation in IQ scores (and vice versa). Kuhn (1976a) qualifies this relationship between Piagetian and IQ intelligence in an important way. Her results suggest that the relation between the two kinds of items diminishes as children advance in age and stage level. While a high correlation was found at the early Concrete operational stage (six-to-eight years), almost no correlation was found at the late end of that stage (ten-to-twelve years).

The existing correlation between Piaget-type and other IQ tests may be artificially high, because the clinical method usually used in Piaget tasks has been converted into a standardized psychometric procedure. I am aware of no studies which compare a clinical and a psychometric assessment approach using the same kinds of items.

Does the moderate correlation between Piaget and individual-difference IQ intelligence mean that the Piagetian approach is not a good measure of intelligence as it is usually assessed in the schools (i.e., with IQ tests)? The usual interpretation of this moderate correlation is that the two approaches show some overlap but also measure different areas of cognitive function. While children as a group tend to perform well or poorly on both measures, there are many exceptions to the general trend because the tests do not tap exactly the same abilities. In my opinion, there are so many conceptual and methodological differences between Piagetian and IQ intelligence that we simply should not expect a higher level of correlation between them.

Contrasts in methods of assessment and conceptions of intelligence—a summary

Psychometric approach	*Piaget's approach*
IQ intelligence is measured by standardized psychometric tests.	Intelligence is assessed by the unstandardized but still systematic clinical method.
IQ is expressed as a quantitative measure, based on the number of correct responses to items of differing content.	Intelligence is treated as a quality of understanding. The child's level of intelligence is described in terms of stages, based on logical structures presumed to underlie the specific content of responses.
The IQ number is an index of the rate of intellectual development shown by an individual in relation to his or her age peers. With an IQ of 100 usually selected as average, people with scores considerably less than 100 may be described as retarded, and those with scores considerably above 100 may be described as accelerated or gifted.	Individual differences in rate of development are not central to theory; rather interest centers on universalities and regularities in developmental sequence. Comparisons are not made with age peers. Stage levels describe the kinds of interpretations the child will tend to make, as compared with the hypothetical high point of cognitive development (the structural model underlying Formal operations).
IQ levels do not specify specific cognitive skills. (A two-year-old and a twenty-two year-old, each with an IQ of 100, display very different intellectual abilities.)	Stage levels do specify a particular organization of cognitive skills.

Psychometric approach	Piaget's approach
The focus of IQ tests on correct answers tends to suggest a picture-copy view in which intelligence becomes more accurate with age.	The essence of intelligence is the child's symbolic representation function which constructs more complex meanings at higher stages.
In IQ tests there is little explicit distinction between perceptual and cognitive tests.	The emphasis in Piaget's study of intelligence is primarily on cognitive rather than perceptual development.
The IQ is a score which represents the average of abilities demonstrated by a child over many items and subtests.	In the Piagetian approach, children are categorized at the highest levels which they display during assessment.
With the exception of Wechsler's definition of intelligence (1958), psychometric approaches tend to separate cognitive and motivational aspects of test performance.	Piaget's model of symbols includes emotion and motivation as intrinsic aspects of cognitive functioning. The clinical method of assessment attempts to make certain that the child's answers are related to questions in which he or she has developed some interest.
There is a pervasive assumption that IQ intelligence should remain constant over time. Four-year-olds at the middle of their age group (IQ = 100) are expected on the average to have IQ's near 100 when they are 14 and 24 years old. (This expectation has not generally been supported; the younger the children tested and the longer between test and retest, the greater the change in IQ score, e.g., Achenbach's summary, 1974, p. 212.) While IQ is expected to remain relatively constant, mental age changes over time as a gradually increasing function of age, at least until early adulthood.	The organization of the symbolic function develops over time; development is defined as an increase in differentiation and integration of structures.
While there is now great dispute about this matter, IQ intelligence tends to be interpreted as an inner-determined trait or ability.[10]	Intellectual functioning and development is always a result of person-environment interaction.

In sum, the psychometric approach to IQ deals with quantitative aspects of intelligence, correct answers, and individual differences in the rate of development in comparison with one's peers. Intelligence tends to be conceptualized as a relatively stable, possibly inherited set of perceptual and cognitive characteristics of the person. By contrast, Piaget examines the qualitative aspects of intelligence, reasons for correct answers, and universalities in the

[10]There has been a tendency to confuse arguments about stability with arguments about heritability, with the assumption that if IQ is stable, then it is inherited. In fact, there is no necessary relation between the two; inherited traits may change over the lifespan (e.g., hair color) while environmentally influenced abilities may be relatively stable.

sequence of stages. Intelligence tends to be conceptualized as an interactively changing organization of structural, functional, and emotional aspects of cognitive symbolic schemes.

It is not necessary to choose between the psychometric approach to intelligence and Piaget's views. Each began with different questions and methods, and their answers necessarily led in different directions. Teachers and parents interested in their children's intellectual development can follow both roads. For example, it is often important to know how well a child is progressing in quantitative comparison with others of the same age and *also* to know about the characteristics of his or her qualitative understanding of the world. What is important to keep in mind is that the same word—intelligence—can refer to different aspects of the child, assessed in different ways.

IMPLICATIONS FOR EDUCATION

In this section I will present two related implications of Piaget's analysis of the test method and then briefly discuss the application of clinical method to understanding children in the classroom.

The test method

Test bias. The argument concerning theoretical and cultural bias in the selection of test items can be extended to what may be called the "knowledge bias" inherent in all tests, including those based on Piaget's theory. Especially when the assessment of achievement emphasizes correct answers, the content of the test tends to define what is important to know.

> IQ and achievement tests usually assess children's memory ability by presenting them with prose passages or a series of random numbers. The same child who is unable to remember this material may be quite able to memorize the lyrics of the Top Forty songs and to remember new songs every week, but he or she is rarely given a chance to demonstrate this talent in the classroom.

Because standardized tests of children are often used to evaluate specific educational programs and entire educational systems,[11] what the tests define as important to know tends to become what is important to teach.

To me, an even more serious bias arises from the scoring of most standardized tests. IQ and achievement scores would be useless if they varied with idiosyncrasies of the scorer. Individual difference theorists have tended to

[11] Every year in the communities around Berkeley, the average achievement test performance of first, sixth, and tenth graders compared to state and national norms are published in the local papers, with a discussion of "how our schools are doing."

assume that such idiosyncracies can be avoided by standardizing the scoring system. Further, they have assumed that scorer variability will be reduced by having items with clearly correct and incorrect answers. But this procedural decision restricts the measurement of IQ and achievement to the ability to produce correct answers. What about questions or problems which do not have "correct" answers—are they to be excluded from the realm of intelligence?

> We spend much energy in our lives trying to understand, negotiate, and make satisfying our personal relationships with others—our parents, friends, lovers, employers, children, colleagues, and others. Yet, partly because there are no clear-cut "right" ways of relating, schools do not include interpersonal relations as part of the curriculum and interpersonal items are rarely created for standardized tests.

Piaget has stated that the sophistication of the quest for knowledge, rather than the correctness of the response, should be used to define the child's intellectual level. The omission of interpersonal relations and many other items which have no apparently correct solutions removes from the measurement of intelligence important aspects of intellectual functioning. This criticism applies equally to IQ and to most Piagetian applications in classrooms.

Prediction of grades. Whether or not IQ and achievement tests can be considered as objective measures of intelligence, they have been used to establish expectations about the level of classroom performance that a teacher can legitimately expect.[12] For example, when children are having difficulty in learning, tests are used to assess their potential; this practice is based upon an assumed high correlation between IQ tests and academic grades. In fact, correlations range widely with an average around .6 (e.g., Lavin, 1965). There is a 36 percent overlap between the way in which schools measure achievement and the way in which IQ tests measure cognitive development. So far, evidence suggests that Piaget-based psychometric tests do about equally well (or poorly) as IQ tests at predicting academic performance in schools from elementary to university levels (Dudek, Lester, Goldberg, and Dyer, 1969; Kaufman and Kaufman, 1972; Lawson, Nordland, and DeVito, 1975; Sayre and Ball, 1975; Wheatley, 1967).

The fact that the overlap between tests and grades is far from perfect poses a potential problem for the evaluation of new curricula based on Piagetian concepts. In the development of other new curricula (e.g., the "new math") there has been a tendency to assess the effectiveness of new programs using the old tests. As a result, the new math curriculum has been severely criticized because it does not produce accurate computation skills, as assessed in traditional tests, even though this has not been an immediate goal of the program. I am

[12]Rosenthal and Jacobson (1968) claim that these tests tend to limit what teachers expect and that this can be especially detrimental to children receiving low test scores.

concerned that similar difficulties will arise in the evaluation of programs based on Piaget's theory; the evaluation instruments will have to contain both items and methods central to his approach.

The clinical method in the classroom

A specific set of assessment procedures. In Parts II and III you will see that Piaget's clinical method, as extended by many other investigators, provides a set of tasks and procedures for assessing child development in a wide variety of areas, in both cognitive and social–emotional domains: objects, space, time, causality, quantity, number, logic, experimental method, communication, interpersonal interaction, moral values, and so on.

The most noticeable difference between the usual psychometric approach and the clinical method in the classroom is that IQ achievement tests are usually administered to a whole group, while the clinical method requires one-to-one contact between tester and child. Clinical assessments as described by Piaget are usually formal, with the tester sitting down alone with the child, but it is possible to use the clinical method as part of the ongoing activities of the class.

> One does not have to wait for a defined test to find out about children's concepts of number. In preschools and kindergarten, there is often snack or juice time, and the dividing of amounts into glasses provides a good opportunity for questions or observations of individual children. The ability of children to adopt another point of view can be inferred from their tendency to convey details when the events are not in view of the listener. Anything unexpected or puzzling can provide an opportunity to explore such concepts as causality.

I have indicated in Chapter 2 that teachers tend to listen to a child's answer and stop after perfunctory questioning. If the answer is incorrect, the teacher asks someone else; if the answer is apparently correct, the teacher moves on to a new question. In both cases, further exploration may reveal the thinking behind the answer and avoid the teacher's egocentric assumption that he or she understands what is being said.

I will return to the issue of time required to do individual assessments. Here I will simply mention that not all children must be assessed on every concept every week. A few minutes spent with each individual can reveal a great deal about the structure of the child's intelligence on a particular topic of interest to the teacher.

Piaget has stated that the clinical method is difficult to learn. I can certainly testify from my own experience and that of my students that he is correct. The first tendency of a budding tester is to create a standardized test; most workshops for teachers that I have seen also attempt to convert the clinical method into a more simplified psychometric procedure. However, the essence of

Piaget's method is not only the choice of tasks but also the approach to gathering information. The method cannot be learned from a book.

> The best way that I have found is simply to try it out at first with one or two children. A tape recorder can be very helpful; it will cut down on the amount of necessary writing and you can listen later to the results, go over what you missed, and decide what you may want to do next time. In addition to the tape recorder and consistent with Piaget's general point of view, it is invaluable to have another adult watching and listening so that you can discuss the procedure after the testing is over. Then try it again with more children.
>
> In my experience, the beginning tester is so concerned with the materials and with "doing it right," that it is hard to listen to the child and follow up with the tests, observations, and experiments required to interpret the responses. With experience and feedback about the assessment, along with increasing knowledge of what it is that you are looking for, the clinical method becomes easier to apply in both formal and informal situations.

I am sympathetic with protests by teachers and others that the clinical method is complicated and takes time to master. However, I believe that it is essential to have a method that deals adequately with the real complexity of the child's intelligence.

A way of thinking about assessment. Long before the clinical method is mastered it begins to affect our general outlook on the process of coming to understand children. First, it helps us to reconceptualize what a test should be. Not simply an evaluation of student successes and failures, a test should be a procedure for finding and stimulating the child's highest level of understanding. The tester remains in the role of teacher, attempting to raise questions and present new material in order to examine how the child responds to disequilibration and how he or she transforms the input. Second, the clinical interview tends to be a validating experience for children. The tester conveys a sincere interest in finding out what the child really thinks; for some this seems to be a novel experience to have with an adult. Third, as teachers and parents demonstrate the clinical method in the classroom or at home (not all the time, of course), they provide a model of communication which may eventually have impact on children's interaction with each other. Adults who make great effort to understand each child are demonstrating that right-or-wrong evaluations are secondary to the process of exchanging points of view. Assessment, then, is an intrinsic aspect of good communication.

This presentation of clinical method completes the outline of general concepts in Piaget's approach to the study of intellectual development. Now we turn to a stage by stage account of children's cognitive and social–emotional growth from birth through late adolescence.

PART II

Stages of Cognitive, Social, and Emotional Development

CHAPTER 5

The Sensorimotor Stage

During the first two years of life, infants coordinate single reflex schemas and schemes into a system of Sensorimotor symbols. Beginning at birth with reactions to immediately present events, they become able to hold in mind complex cognitive maps, solve problems mentally before trying out the solutions in behavior, engage in imitation of past events, and participate in symbolic play. From an egocentric perspective which fails to differentiate between self and objects or self and others, two-year-olds can picture themselves as one object among others in the universe, subject to physical laws. This Copernican revolution in perspective occurs gradually in a succession of six Sensorimotor substages.

Several themes dominate this and every succession of substages in Piaget's theory. Beginning with schemes which organize perception and action, each substage involves repetition, variation, and coordination. Each new substage repeats a theme of coordination at a more differentiated and integrated level. With increased coordination of schemes, comes increased separation of means and ends, more focused and intentional strategies to reach goals, and eventually, more internalized symbolic schemes (e.g., of object permanence). Accompanying the growing equilibration of sensorimotor coordinations are more sophisticated accommodations (in the form of imitations) and assimilations (in the form of play). Also accompanying this development within the Sensorimotor stage is a more complex organization of emotional and social behavior (especially social attachment) and a resulting differentiation between the self and others as social beings.

SIX SENSORIMOTOR SUBSTAGES

The names used by Piaget and other writers for each substage vary somewhat with the focus of the discussion. What is consistent in each description is the list of characteristics ascribed to each substage and the sequence in which the substages occur. Within these general guidelines, there are variations in the ages ascribed by Piaget to the general substage and to each specific achievement (Piaget, 1937); there is also considerable individual variation in the speed with which infants develop through the sequence.

Substage 1—The emergence of directed behavior: Birth to one-and-a-half months

Coordination. Right from the first few hours after birth, the "ready-made schemes" (reflex reactions) begin to work in a more organized flexible fashion. However, for the first month or so, the newborn functions as if each sense modality is independent of every other. Sights are unrelated to sounds, sounds to kinesthetic sensations, muscle movements to visual cues, and so on. The perceived world is something like a living movie being shown without synchronization of events in space and time.[1]

In apparent contrast with the fragmentation of reflex schemes is the *lack* of separation of intellectual functions. As newborns search for intellectual nourishment for schemas and schemes, they repeat responses (assimilate) and also create new variations (accommodate). However, there is no evidence that assimilation and accommodation function independently, so every attempt to preserve stability by assimilation results in an accommodative change as well.

> The movements involved in grasping a rattle place the newborn in a new position, from which the rattle appears to be a different object. The next assimilative grasping leads to more accommodative variation in body positions, which in turn makes for new differences in the object from the newborn's point of view.

Goal direction. The major development of the first substage is a shift from relatively passive responsiveness to active utilization or search in each separate modality. Some reflexes, especially sucking and grasping, undergo rapid transformation into flexible schemes. At first an infant sucks only when his or her mouth is stimulated. Soon one can see a "rooting"—an active search when the face is stimulated by the nipple of breast or bottle. Later, infants may also suck

[1]Some new research which questions the details of Piaget's account of the early Sensorimotor substages will be briefly described toward the end of this chapter (e.g., Bower, 1974; Melzoff and Moore, 1977). The research does not call into question Piaget's general approach to stage theory or his emphasis on the active organization capacity of the child. In fact, it asserts that infant perception and cognition is even more organized, at an earlier point, than Piaget implies.

when stimulated by any bodily contact or with no apparent stimulation at all. Piaget documents a similar shift in the organization of each sensory modality. Initially sights, sounds, and physical contact release single, fleeting reactions. But soon the infant is able to sustain attention to a stimulus as long as it remains in the field of vision or hearing or touch. Passive seeing becomes active looking; generalized bodily reactions become directed search.

In an important sense, the directed activity of the first substage cannot be considered *goal* directed from the point of view of the child. To be sure, infants can move in a consistent direction, but their movements transform objects perceptually and cognitively, and they have no mechanism for keeping the initial goal in mind. Further, they have no way of coordinating a distinct set of schemes serving as a means to an end (e.g., grasping) with a set of schemes representing the end or goal itself.

Symbolic schemes

(*a*) Permanent objects. Piaget's model of symbolic development suggests that the scheme of a permanent object is quite complex. It requires the coordination of two mechanisms, representation and conceptualization, based on two separate intellectual functions, assimilation and accommodation. As we have just seen, the two functions are not yet separated; the qualities of the object are transformed by the newborn's activity. And so, the notion of the permanent object is outside the capacity of the child during Substage 1.

(*b*) Imitation and play. Imitation, the accommodative aspect of intellectual function, at this substage can be no more than momentary. Piaget speculates that there may be some imitation involved in the contagious crying often heard in hospital nurseries. There may also be some aspects of (assimilative) play in the repetitive exercise of reflexes. These examples are early forms of later, more clearly differentiated behavior.

Emotional–social aspects. Some of the newborn's reflexes form the basis of primary emotions. For example, the reflex startle reaction to sudden disequilibrium is probably the forerunner of the fear response. Generally, though, emotional reactions of the infant are seen in diffuse excitement rather than in specific, focused responses to stimulation.

As part of the shift from passive elicitation of reflexes to active search, schemes develop in connection with the so-called biological drives (hunger, thirst, elimination, breathing). In Piaget's view, these are no different in form or function from schemes developed in search of intellectual stimulation.

While the newborn infant is certainly a social object from the point of view of parents and relatives, the parents are not, for quite a long period, social objects for their children. In fact, the absence of permanent schemes indicates that once parents leave the perceived field they are gone. The crying that may follow is not a cry for their return, but simply an indicator of discomfort.

Substage 2—Scheme coordination and early goal direction: One-and-a-half to four months

Coordination. The major achievement of Substage 2 is a beginning coordination of different sensorimotor schemes. A lovely example of the emerging coordination of visual and motor schemes can be seen in one of Piaget's descriptions of his young son (Piaget, 1936).

> Observation 62. At 0;2(4)[2] Laurent by chance discovers his right index finger and looks at it briefly. At 0;2(11) he inspects for a moment his open right hand, perceived by chance. At 0;2(17) he follows its spontaneous movement for a moment, then examines it several times while it searches for his nose or rubs his eye. . . . At 0;2(21) he holds his two fists in the air and looks at the left one, after which he slowly brings it toward his face and rubs his nose with it, then his eye. A moment later the left hand again approaches his face; he looks at it and touches his nose. [Note the shift from passive to active.] He recommences and laughs five or six times in succession while moving the left hand to his face. He seems to laugh before the hand moves, but looking has no influence on its movement. He laughs beforehand but begins to smile again on seeing the hand. Then he rubs his nose. At a given moment he turns his head to the left but looking has no effect on the direction. The next day, same reaction. At 0;2(23) he looks at his right hand, then at his clasped hands (at length). At 0;2(24) at last it may be stated that looking acts on the orientation of the hands which tend to remain in the visual field (pp. 96–97).

In this and many other coordinations amongst sensory modalities, schemes are preserved even though they assimilate each other and accommodate to each other. Because assimilation and accommodation no longer inevitably alter schemes, Piaget concludes that the two equilibration functions are beginning to be differentiated.

Goal direction. The coordination of schemes, facilitated by the beginning separation of assimilation and accommodation, reinforces the infant's goal directedness. It is now possible to look *in order to see*, or to move *in order to look*. Assimilative repetition serves to prolong the activity of the scheme. And when the activity stops, the infant's accommodative groping creates new variations in the course of starting the activity again.

The coordination of schemes from different sense modalities makes possible the first general schemes of goal-directed behavior—the "primary circular reactions."

> Examples of these reactions are very common in young infants. Seemingly by chance they come upon a new activity and then they repeat it endlessly—scratching a sheet, moving a hand, fixating a sunbeam. The activity stops and then starts all over again as long as the infant is in contact with the stimulus.

[2]"No years," two months, four days

Circular reactions (schemes) are series of repetitive events which prolong new states of affairs. They can be viewed as the earliest form of what will later be called identity judgments, preserving sameness in the face of flux and chaos. The directed efforts involved in repeating new schemes, and in starting the activity once it has stopped, give primary circular reactions their goal-directed quality. The goal seems to be the activity itself; there is no evidence of conscious intention to reach some external goal. This focus on the infant's own activities is what leads Piaget to label the circular reactions "primary."

Symbolic schemes

a) Permanent object. The separation between assimilation and accommodation does not extend to a coordination between internal means and external goals outside the child's present activity. As in Substage 1, perceptions and understandings of objects are still tied to the infant's actions and are not represented when they disappear from view.

b) Imitation and play. Between the ages of one-and-a-half and four months, the infant begins to imitate an adult model. According to Piaget, the restriction on this imitation is that it occurs only when the adult first copies an action just made by the child. Like circular reactions, imitations are tied to the present and focused on the infant's own behavior.

The primary circular reactions, in their endless assimilative repetitions, have many qualities of play. Often they are accompanied by the infant's facial or vocal signs of pleasure. Possibly, in this early association of play and pleasure are the roots of the later use of play for expression of feelings and coping with conflicts.

Emotional–social aspects. The energy or motivation in the circular schemes can be described by a concept borrowed by Piaget from Buhler (1931)—function pleasure—the pleasurable effort involved in repeating actions for their own sake. In other words, there is both a biological and psychological need to function, independent of the need to satisfy primary drives of hunger, thirst, and the rest. Repetition in itself "nourishes" new schemes and temporarily reduces stimulus hunger. However, just as the stomach expands after a large meal, the repetitive exercise of schemes creates an increased need for functioning. "It is fruitless to ask if it is the need [for functioning] that explains the repetition, or the reverse; together they form an inseparable unity" (Piaget, 1936, p. 170). Despite the metaphorical allusion to food, few of the many activities described by Piaget as critical to intellectual growth are related directly to food and hunger in the physical sense.

The concept of function pleasure implies that there are also times of non-pleasure (boredom) or even displeasure (irritation). The first real differentiation of emotions has occurred. These emotions, like the "goals" of circular reactions, are still linked directly to the infant's behavior; there are as yet no emotional states specifically directed to people or to objects themselves.

It is consistent with this view that the focus of sensation and feelings centers on the infant's own body and actions. From the outside, it seems as if the infant is preoccupied with, and emotionally attached to, the self. Freud's observations of these same phenomena led him to assume that there is a narcissistic phase which occurs before emotional attachment to others. Piaget points out that in Substage 2 there is, as yet, no cognitive separation of self from physical or social objects. The infant's preoccupation with his or her body, is a "narcissism without a Narcissus."

In Substage 2 infants react responsively to people as interesting objects, but there is as yet no truly *social* interaction. There is a smile of recognition which warms the parents' hearts, but infants are just as likely to give the same smile to a stranger or to the furry panda in the corner of the crib.

Substage 3—Intention; beginning independence of actions and thought: Four to six months

Coordination. In previous substages, accommodation functioned simply to differentiate or bend to whatever stimulus came along. In this substage, the infant can actively search for and select certain movements which have given rise to an interesting effect. Accommodation now becomes a voluntary and systematic selector of interesting consequences once they have occurred by chance.

> Observation 105—Laurent, from 0;4(19) as has been seen (Obs. 103) knows how to strike hanging objects intentionally with his hand. At 0;4(22) he holds a stick; he does not know what to do with it and slowly passes it from hand to hand. The stick then happens to strike a toy hanging from the bassinet hood. Laurent, immediately interested by this unexpected result, keeps the stick raised in the same position, then brings it noticeably nearer to the toy. He strikes it a second time. Then he draws the stick back but moving it as little as possible as though trying to conserve the favorable position, then he brings it nearer to the toy, and so on, more and more rapidly.
>
> The dual character of this accommodation may be seen. On the one hand, the new phenomenon makes its appearance by simple fortuitous insertion in an already formed schema and hence differentiates it. But, on the other hand, the child, intentionally and systematically, applies himself to rediscovering the conditions which led him to this unexpected result (1936, p. 176).

Goal direction. A marvellous new achievement— the beginning of *intentional* goal-directed activity on the world. From the function pleasure repetition in Substage 2, the infant now moves on to repeat actions in order to prolong interesting events. This form of repetition is called a secondary circular reaction.

Observation 94—At 0;3(5)[3] Lucienne shakes her bassinet by moving her legs violently (bending and unbending them, etc.), which makes the cloth dolls swing from the hood. Lucienne looks at them, smiling, and recommences at once. These movements are simply the concommitants of joy. When she experiences great pleasure Lucienne externalizes it in a total reaction including leg movements. As she often smiles at her knick-knacks she caused them to swing. But does she keep this up through consciously coordinated circular reaction or is it pleasure constantly springing up again that explains her behavior?

That evening, when Lucienne is quiet, I gently swing her dolls. The morning's reaction starts up again, but both interpretations remain possible.

The next day, at 0;3(6) I present the dolls; Lucienne immediately moves, shakes her legs, but this time without smiling. Her interest is intense and sustained and there also seems to be an intentional circular reaction. . . .

At 0;3(8) I again find Lucienne swinging her dolls. An hour later I make them move slightly; Lucienne looks at them, smiles, stirs a little, then resumes looking at her hands as she was doing shortly before. A chance movement disturbs the dolls: Lucienne again looks at them and this time shakes herself with regularity. She stares at the dolls, barely smiles and moves her legs vigorously and thoroughly. At each moment she is distracted by her hands which pass again into the visual field: She examines them for a moment and then returns to the dolls. This time there is definite circular reaction.

At 0;4(4) in a new bassinet, she moves her loins violently in order to shake the hood. At 0;4(13) she moves her legs very rapidly while looking at the festoons on the bassinet hood; as soon as she sees them again, after a pause, she begins once more. Same reaction with regard to the hood in general. At 0;4(19) she recommences by examining each part of the hood in detail. At 0;4(21) she does the same in her carriage (and no longer in the bassinet): she studies the result of her shaking most attentively [i.e., the reaction was generalized to new stimuli] (1936, pp. 157–159).

Two clearly defined elements are part of this series of events. There are schemes which function as means (Lucienne's actions) and others which function as goals (prolonging the interesting spectacle). The increased independence of means and ends can be seen in the fact that Lucienne modifies her kicking and generalizes it to new situations, all the while maintaining her goal. The focus has shifted from her own actions to consequences in the world, which Lucienne can apparently produce intentionally and repetitively in a secondary circular reaction. While parents tend to describe what their infant is *trying* to do almost from the moment of birth, Piaget's evidence suggests that behavior directed by a conscious goal does not usually emerge until about four months at the earliest.[4]

[3]This is one of many instances in which Piaget chooses an example from a subject outside the age range given for the stage or substage. In any case, sequence and not age is the issue here.

[4]The relation of these observations to operant conditioning experiments with infants will be discussed below.

Symbolic schemes

a) Permanent object. The infant in Substage 3 must be able to maintain some scheme of the goal while engaged in strategies to reach it, but the ability to "keep the goal in mind" is quite limited.

> Lucienne as a five-month-old reaches across the crib to pick up a toy. Piaget places a hand in her path which obscures her view. She pushes the hand aside, but in the process becomes involved in playing with the hand or with new objects coming into view as a result of her actions.

In Substage 3 the infant follows the trajectory of an object as it disappears from view, but once it disappears, the search is abandoned. Despite the increased separation of means and ends, infants have not constructed mental symbols representing events which are independent of their actions. The separate goal schemes are maintained only when the stimuli remain in view and when there are no major detours in the path to the goal.

Failure to represent an absent object indicates that recall memory has not yet developed. However, Substage 3 infants do demonstrate a recognition memory for familiar events when they see them again. For example, when Lucienne responded to her favorite doll in the carriage with the kicking action previously made in the bassinet (Observation 94, above), it is as if she were thinking "Oh yes, here-is-the-thing-that-jiggles-when-I-kick-it."

b) Imitation and play. Along with the general emergence of goal-directed behavior, the four-to-six-month-old deliberately imitates actions and sounds made by others. However, the reproductions are limited to responses which are already in their repertoires.

By prolonging interesting spectacles, secondary circular reactions are useful for knowledge gathering, but they also have a playful quality of actions performed for their own sake. Piaget (1946a) notes that this function pleasure is augmented in Substage 3 by the infant's pleasure in being the cause of observable events.

Emotional–social aspects. The new ability of infants to initiate imitation of others is accompanied by an increased energy directed to careful observations of adults. This increased interest stimulates additional imitation, which, in the fashion described above, leads to expanded interest in adults as fascinating social objects.

Just as infants in Substage 3 will follow a moving object up to the point where it disappears, so they may now cry when parents leave the room. But again, once completely gone there is no thought of the parent (picture, sound, touch, etc.) actually retained in the child's memory. As Décarie indicates (1965), Piaget's view is quite different from that of Freud who assumed that powerful wish-fulfilling fantasies are present in infants at this stage. Piaget keeps pointing out that most psychoanalytic formulations of infancy are retrospective, while his views are based on observation as well as theoretical formulations. Now that newer methods of infant research have emerged, the details of Piaget's observations are also being questioned.

Substage 4—The first permanent object: six to twelve months

Coordinated goal direction. At about six months of age there is a dramatic change in the function of intelligence, which has special implications for cognitive structure. For the first time, assimilation and accommodation begin to operate independently. One important consequence of this independence can be seen in the goal-directed activity of the infant. In the third Sensorimotor stage, Lucienne would push away Piaget's hand but become distracted in the process and forget about the toy she was heading for. By the fourth Sensorimotor stage, she usually removed his hand firmly and returned to her goal.

This example illustrates the fact that schemes of means (moving, reaching, grasping) have now become differentiated from schemes of ends (the toy). Piaget also interprets this and other similar examples as demonstrating the first real differentiation between assimilation and accommodation. Lucienne's accommodation to the barrier was *not* assimilated to her activities of reaching the goal; she remained undistracted. Conversely, her assimilative focus on obtaining the object did not prevent her from accommodating adaptively to the barrier.

Symbolic schemes

a) Permanent objects. Piaget's description of the Sensorimotor stage was completed before his more recent emphasis on the distinction between schemas and schemes. My impression is that the fourth Sensorimotor stage is the time when schemas and schemes are first clearly differentiated from each other and coordinated with each other. As Lucienne turns to deal with her father's interruption, she is able to maintain a schematic image of this particular toy (figurative schema). She also has a general notion that there are objects that exist even when they are not in view (operative scheme). The coordination between figurative and operative mechanisms creates the first internalized symbol—a meaningful representation of a permanent object. This achievement stems directly from the new differentiation and coordination of assimilation and accommodation; it is the first equilibrated cognition.

Despite the new intellectual power implied by the infant's entrance into a world of permanent objects, Piaget shows that the infant's difficulty with object concepts is not over. The permanence is still relatively shaky.

> At 0;10 (10) Jacqueline is seated on a mattress without anything to disturb or distract her (no coverlet, etc.). I take her [toy] parrot from her hands and hide it twice in succession under the mattress on her left, in A. Both times Jacqueline looks for the object immediately and grabs it. Then I take it from her hands and move it very

slowly before her eyes to the corresponding place on her right, under the mattress in B. Jacqueline watches this movement very attentively, but at the moment when the parrot disappears in B, she turns to her left and looks where it was before, in A.

During the next four attempts, I hide the parrot in B every time without having first placed it in A. Every time Jacqueline watches me attentively. Nevertheless, each time she immediately tried to rediscover the object in A; she turns the mattress over and examines it conscientiously. During the last two attempts, however, the search tapers off (1937, p. 56).

Jacqueline has already demonstrated her ability to find a hidden object at A. Why doesn't she apply that strategy at B, or search where the parrot was hidden most recently? Piaget suggests that there are three interrelated reasons. First, infants in Substage 4 are unable to recall sequences of events. Second, although they can represent static schemas (i.e., the stationary object hidden at A), they are not able to represent a series of spatial transformations in location. Third, the object may have conceptual permanence, but it is still not conceived as a thing that can be moved, independent of the motions themselves. For all these reasons the hiding-action-and-the-object-at-A is not the same hiding-action-and-the-object-at-B. From Jacqueline's point of view, *the* parrot is the one hidden at A and that is where she returns to search, regardless of subsequent hidings.

b) Causality. The emergence of the permanent object concept, even its first fragile appearance, has important implications for the infant's interpretation of causal relationships (Piaget, 1937, provides an account of causality at all Sensorimotor substages). Before Substage 4, the infant himself or herself was the only perceived causal agent. Now, the notion that objects exist even when they are not being acted upon allows the infant to begin discovering external causes of observed events.

c) Imitation and play. For Piaget, this is the substage of the first "real" imitation. Simultaneous with the development of object permanence, infants develop two important skills. First, they imitate movements which they have previously made but never seen.

Piaget's daughter, in the last half of her first year, is sitting quietly, when he approaches and sticks out his tongue. She laughs and immediately imitates the action.

This imitation is deceptively complex. While infants often stick out their own tongues, they cannot observe themselves directly, and yet they are able to match their actions to behavior observed in others. A second new imitative skill occurs when infants copy sounds and gestures which are new to them, and which previously had been ignored. These imitations greatly expand the young child's range of responding to or coping with the world.

With the achievement of object permanence, play also changes radically. Because there can now be assimilations which do not alter objects, play becomes a medium for trying out and mastering actions which will later be used for more serious, goal-directed purposes. Rather than a single repetitive function, play takes on the function of preparation, practice, and coping. One example of the tendency to transform new cognitive achievements into play is the child's endless fascination with peek-a-boo games. The discovery of the permanent object, verified every time the child opens his or her eyes or looks behind a screen, is a source of never-ending delight; the repeated activity not only increases the infant's mastery of symbolic representation, but also provides useful knowledge about the objects themselves.

Emotional–social–personal aspects. Prior to Substage 4, infants may demonstrate contentment and happiness when fed and cared for, but they do not consistently display different emotional responses to different people.[5] Smiles are bestowed equally on parents (or caretakers) and strangers as they enter the room. Even prolonged separations from primary caretakers have no lasting effects, as long as adequate substitutes are provided. Then, around the middle of the first year, infants develop a strong attachment to a primary person or persons (Ainsworth and Bell, 1970; Bowlby, 1969, 1973; Schaffer and Emerson, 1964).

Attachment is usually discussed in terms of a special bond between mother and child. It is difficult to tell from research over the years whether fathers really tend to be uninvolved in parenting or whether researchers have chosen to investigate only mothering. It has been traditional to think of one primary caretaker; as far as I know, it is possible for the infant to develop multiple primary attachments to human beings *if* there are equally intimate involvements of two or more caretaking adults.

The emergence of attachment has profound implications for both emotional and social development. In contrast with the infant's reaction to strangers or to other members of the family, more intense pleasure and more intense frustration are now directed at the caretaker. The spontaneous sunny smiles previously distributed with such generosity on initial glance, now tend to be reserved for specific circumstances. The infant's first response, even to a parent returning after some hours away, may be solemn exploration, uncertainty, even occasional fear, before he or she warms up again. Parents often interpret this new behavior as rejection for having been away. More likely, at this substage it is not personal at all, but reflects the new salience of the infant's ability to distinguish between the familiar and unfamiliar.

Short separations can produce temporary anxiety and mild depression in the infant (Bowlby, 1960). At the extreme, Bowlby and some earlier investigators (Ribble, 1944; Spitz, 1946) claim that the disappearance of the primary caretaker for extended periods of time may have serious negative consequences for emotional and social development. These dire warnings do an injustice to

[5]There is some evidence that younger infants may react differently when held by different people (Ainsworth, 1964), but we do not know whether this is a reaction to the person or to the physical conditions.

families in which both parents work, provide adequate child care, and are intimately involved with their infants when they are home; the impact on attachment in this situation, much less extreme than the long-term separation studies of institutionalized children by Bowlby *et al.*, has not been systematically studied.

Freud suggested that attachment ("object" cathexis) emerges when the narcissistic focus on self and body is shifted and centered on another person. For him, this change represented a shift in the object of pleasure from self to mother—the major external source of physical and psychological gratification. For Piaget, the development of attachment is not simply a change in the direction of affective energy. It represents, instead, a restructuring of the whole cognitive and affective universe. As objects become permanent, people take on permanent existence in the child's mind. As objects are recognized despite changes in color or size (small or large bottles, toys), so caretakers are recognized no matter how they are dressed. When causality becomes independent of the infant's action and objects are conceived as causes of events, people begin to be perceived as causal agents. With the infant's distinction between known and unknown comes the possibility of anxiety at separation and the fear of strangers. Just as narcissism was correlated with the lack of differentiation between the external world and the self, so attachment becomes possible when there is a new differentiation between the two. The construction of attachment to caretakers, then, grows out of a matrix of changes in which there is reciprocal development in conceptions of the physical world, the social world, and the self.

Several corollaries follow from Piaget's view. First, the development of a relationship between infant and caretaker is exceedingly important, but so is the relation between infants and physical objects. Piaget and others from different theoretical points of view (e.g., Pinneau, 1955; Thompson and Grusec, 1970) reinterpret the early warnings of Bowlby, Spitz, and Ribble that maternal deprivation can produce serious negative effects, by pointing out that these infants (primarily in institutions) were deprived of physical stimulus interaction as well. Recent research on infancy (e.g., Bower, 1974; Watson, 1972) has begun to pay close attention to the specific influence of physical environments on cognitive development. Second, Piaget's general approach suggests that it is not the caretaker alone who is the independent variable affecting infant development. Rather, it is the *interaction* between caretaker and child. And, in this interaction the adult responses depend on the type of infant, just as the infant's responses are affected by the kind of parenting (Main, 1976). Third, Piaget's description of the interrelated advances of physical world, social world, and self raises a point which personality theorists tend to forget. In their investigations of self-concept and personality, theorists usually focus on self-esteem. Piaget's ideas suggest that from the child's point of view, not only the value, but also the structure of the self changes throughout the course of development. Here in the fourth Sensorimotor stage, the conceptual self emerges as a very important permanent object.

Substage 5—The search for knowledge through trial and error: twelve to eighteen months

Goal direction. From a focus on repetitive behavior in its own right (Substage 2) to a prolonging of the effects of that behavior (Substage 3), the young child shifts to an investigation of causes of events. The tertiary circular reactions describe the child's endless fascination and active search for variations in how things happen. Piaget characterizes the child in this substage as a miniature scientist–epistemologist. In one vignette, he describes his son Laurent:

> Observation 142. At 0;10 (29)[6] Laurent examines a watch chain hanging from his index finger. At first he touches it very lightly simply "exploring" it without grasping it. He then starts it swinging a little and at once continues this. . . . But, instead of stopping there, he grasps the chain with his right hand and swings it with his left while trying some new combinations (here the "tertiary reaction" begins); in particular he slides it along the back of his left hand and sees it fall off when it reaches the end. Then he holds the end of the chain (with his right index finger and thumb) and lets it slide slowly between the fingers of his left hand (the chain is now horizontal and no longer oblique as before). He studies it carefully at the moment when the chain falls from his left hand and repeats this ten times. Afterward, still holding the end of the chain in his right hand, he shakes it violently which makes it describe a series of varied trajectories in the air. He then slows these movements in order to see how the chain slides along the quilt when he merely pulls it. Finally he drops it from different heights and so rediscovers the schema acquired in the preceding observation.
>
> From his twelfth month Laurent has repeated this kind of experiment with everything that his hand came upon: my notebook, "plugs," ribbons, etc. He entertains himself either by making them slide or fall or by letting them go in different positions and from different heights in order to study their trajectory (1936, p. 269).

Children in the fifth Sensorimotor substage seem to be on a never-ending voyage of scientific discovery. Random trial-and-error groping is coming under the control of their already-established schemes, as if knowledge of the physical world has become a spontaneous, conscious goal.

Symbolic schemes

a) Problem solving. Piaget's interest in the symbolic problem solving qualities of this substage led him to pose some "insight" problems to his children. Similar to the famous studies of chimpanzees by the Gestalt psychologist Köhler (1925), they demonstrate the active trial-and-error behavior which comes before the emergence of sudden insight.

> In one experiment, a stick was placed outside the bars of Jacqueline's playpen, too long to fit horizontally through the wooden bars. Piaget described her exertions which, after several days, resulted in her systematically turning the stick vertically and slipping it through the bars. In another experiment, a toy was placed outside the

[6] Again, the age of the example is lower than the general range for this substage.

playpen, beyond arm's reach, with a stick placed closer to the child. After much effort, some directed and some random, Jacqueline was able to use the stick to reach the toy. This process of overt trial and error contrasts with Substage 6 behavior in which there appears to be a sudden mental solution to the problem (Piaget, 1936, pp. 305–320).

b) Permanent object. The new coordination of schemes in Substage 5 is still limited to sensorimotor rather than mental combinations. Overt activity on objects is the way problems are "thought out." There is an advance in the area of object permanence—one-year-olds can keep track of visible displacements of objects—but they get lost when they cannot see the displacements.

In this substage, when Jacqueline's toy parrot is hidden at A and then moved beyond a screen at B, she correctly looks for her toy parrot at B. However, when Piaget puts a ring in his hand and places his hand behind a screen, leaving the ring there, Jacqueline actively searches the hand and does not think of looking behind the screen (1937, p. 79).

Quite sophisticated inferences are being made about events which can be seen, but unless there is some direct contact with a transformation, it is beyond the realm of inference at this substage.

In the examples quoted above, and throughout Piaget's investigations of the Sensorimotor stage, it is remarkable how little reference there is to language—the chief symbolic medium of most adults. The child of one year may begin to use words and the eighteen-month-old may have some two-word phrases to communicate wants and needs beyond simply naming things or people. But for Piaget, the entire Sensorimotor period represents a rich foundation for all conceptual and symbolic thought, with crucial developments in object conceptions occurring before the development of the spoken word.

c) Imitation and play. During Substage 5, the general experimental quality of behavior can also be seen in imitation. The child tries out many ways of copying and attempts to copy many different models. Sometimes it almost seems as if there is a mime living in the house. The scientific attitude of this stage is reflected in the child's attempt to be more precise in imitation—to shake his or her head or make a sound *exactly* like the model.

While the fourth Sensorimotor substage infant delights in games of peek-a-boo initiated by adults, children at this substage initiate their own games—peek-a-boo, hide-and-seek, hiding objects. As always, in Piaget's theory, play constitutes important preparatory "work" for young children, especially in the service of developing mental symbols.

In this substage, play begins to be combined with imitation in the form of rituals.

For example, one morning a sixteen-month-old child sees a stuffed animal which he usually takes to bed with him; he lies down immediately, sucks his thumb and closes his eyes. In the fifth Sensorimotor stage, any schemes discovered in the course of an "experiment" may become part of a ritual, repeated every time the child approaches the object.

Rituals are self-imitations, accommodative repetitions of actions which the child has performed at another time. They are also assimilative and playful in that they repeat the action in a context different from the original, often with a quality of pretend. They have not yet become *symbolic* play because the child is merely following a cycle of events and does not appear to be aware of the make-believe. Extremely ritualized behavior is often interpreted as a pathological symptom (e.g., the ritualized repetitiveness of autistic children). Like many symptoms evaluated as pathological in older children, it is a necessary and adaptive aspect of normal development at an earlier stage.

Emotional–social–personal aspects. In the process of becoming active experimenters, children become increasingly aware of themselves as causal agents in a realistic rather than imaginal sense. Successes and failures in exploring the world begin to be reflected in evaluative feelings about the self.

Socially, the child is continuing to develop attachment, strengthening the investment in the caretaker(s), but extending involvement to close relatives and friends, and other young children.[7] Along with the multiplication of social relationships, there is a new spurt in the area of both verbal and nonverbal communication. Children begin to respond to verbal requests and prohibitions, sometimes with compliance, sometimes with defiance. Part of the "resistance" may reflect the overwhelming attractiveness of novel objects which stimulate greater interest than parents' verbal commands. The child may also have an experimental attitude toward what will happen when parents say "no." At this stage, parental prohibitions are not fully internal symbols, but often occur in the form of imitations. It is very common to see a fourteen-month-old come up to an electrical outlet, touch it, and shake his or her head from side to side.

Substage 6—Mental combinations of symbolic schemes: fifteen months to two years

Symbolic schemes. This substage is both a culmination of Sensorimotor development and a transition to the mental coordinations characteristic of the next stage. As a culmination, this substage is marked by a clear distinction between action and representation. It is a transitional substage in the sense that symbols are internalized in sensorimotor form and do not have the flexibility and rever-

[7]Piaget marks the first interest in other children emerging at this substage. It is only recently that people have become interested in the social interaction of children at even younger ages. The emergence at one year may simply reflect a lack of prior opportunity (Becker, 1977).

sibility of the conceptual, operational symbols which come later. Piaget documents four major achievements in symbolic development during Substage 6: mental trial and error in problem solutions; the capacity for mental detours; deferred imitation; symbolic play.

a) Mental trial and error. Returning to the playpen with stick and toys, Piaget describes what happens when insight problems are presented to two of his children for the first time.

> The problems earlier presented to Jacqueline in Substage 5 were posed to Lucienne and Laurent for the first time at 18 months of age. Both children solved them with a minimum of physical activity. After sitting and staring for a few moments, they turned the stick and drew it through the bars of the playpen or used the stick to reach for a toy without any overt trial and error (1936, pp. 333–340).

Piaget draws two conclusions from his results. Agreeing with Gestalt psychologists, he interprets problem solutions at this stage as an example of *mental* trial and error. This interpretation implies that the child now has the use of a coordinated system in which representational schemas of sticks and toys can be transformed by conceptual schemes of means and ends without distortion. Also, Piaget takes pains to point out that the apparently insightful solutions shown by his children were anything but sudden from a developmental point of view. Drawing on his extensive knowledge of his "subjects," accumulated over eighteen months of daily living, he describes the children's prior active experience with components of the problem—manipulating sticks, using things to reach for other things, and so on. He believes that insights do not occur until previous sensorimotor experience is made relevant by a new stage of cognitive organization.

b) Object permanence. The capacity for mental detours is demonstrated in anecdotes like this:

> At 1;6(8) Jacqueline throws a ball under a sofa. But instead of bending down at once and searching for it on the floor she looks at the place, realizes that the ball must have crossed under the sofa, and sets out to go behind it. But there is a table at her right, and the sofa is backed against a bed on the left; therefore she begins by turning her back on the place where the ball disappeared . . . goes around the table, and finally arrives behind the sofa at the right place (1937, p. 23).

This example illustrates a number of new developments. First, Jacqueline is now able to cope with invisible displacements; she represents the probable course of the ball without being able to follow its path visually. While previous cognitive developments have focused a great deal on the coordination between past and present, the ability to represent invisible displacements helps to project the child into the future. Second, children at this substage are able to construct cognitive maps (Tolman, 1932) which help them to locate objects in space. Mental travel to one location on the map does not distort the memory-image of another. The ability to make maps implies that figurative schemas are now encased in operative schemes; Jacqueline not only remembers where to look for *this* ball, she also has a general strategy of storing and remembering sensory information. Third, the capacity for mental detours implies a beginning conceptual reversibility. Previously, in Substage 5, Jacqueline for the first time was able to move toward a goal and return by the same or alternate paths (e.g., to know her way around a small maze for people in a public garden). Now between eighteen months and two years of age, Jacqueline shows the same skill in coordinating mental schemes. The use of the cognitive map allows children to consider the starting place, the goal, and the plan of the trip, going from start to finish or from finish to start. Finally, the ability to form a cognitive map in which she takes some mental "trips" implies that Jacqueline represents herself and her own displacements as if seen from the outside.

> When Jacqueline, following a path, no longer sees her mountain chalet or her house she nevertheless knows that they are behind her. Without having seen her grandfather for three days, she knows in what direction he went. In short, the displacements of her own body do not prevent her from constantly placing herself in a universe which has become stationary and which includes herself (1937, p. 234).

c) Deferred imitation and symbolization. In Chapter 3, I described the deferred imitations of Substage 6 children. At around eighteen months of age, they begin to do vivid imitations of people and events in the past; the events may have been forgotten by the parents, who may not realize what their child is doing. These combinations of visual image memories and overt actions are the first representations which include transformations of past events.

Piaget also describes a more assimilative use of imitation in this stage—the use of imitations to symbolize or stand for a plan of action.

> [Piaget has placed a watch chain in a match box, and left the lid with a small opening. Lucienne has not seen the preparation and is not familiar with the opening and closing of matchboxes. At first, she puts her finger inside, but cannot reach the chain. A pause follows . . .] She looks at the slit with great attention: then several times in succession she opens and shuts her mouth, at first slightly, then wider and wider! Apparently Lucienne understands the existence of a cavity subjacent to the slit and wishes to enlarge that cavity. The attempt at representation which she thus furnishes is expressed plastically, that is to say, due to inability to think out the situation in words or clear visual images she uses a simple motor indication as "signifier" or symbol . . . the motor reaction which presents itself for filling this role is not other than imitation, that is to say, representation by acts. . . . Lucienne, by opening her mouth, thus expresses, or even reflects her desire to enlarge the opening of the box. This schema of imitation, with which she is familiar, constitutes for her the means of thinking out the situation (1936, p. 338).

d) Symbolic play. Like imitation, symbolic play now has both accommodative and assimilative characteristics. It is accommodative in that it tends to use images and actions observed in the past. However, it is the assimilative quality which is stressed by Piaget.

> Symbolic play is the apogee of children's play. Even more than the two or three other forms of play which we shall discuss [games with rules; problem solving games] it corresponds to the essential function that play fulfills in the life of the child. Obliged to adapt himself constantly to a social world of elders whose interests and rules remain external to him and to a physical world which he understands only slightly, the child does not succeed as we adults do, in satisfying the affective and even intellectual needs of his personality through these adaptations. It is indispensable to his affective and intellectual equilibrium, therefore, that he have available to him an area of activity whose motivation is not adaptation to reality but, on the contrary, assimilation of reality to the self, without coercions or sanctions (Piaget and Inhelder, 1966a).

Emotional–social–personal aspects. The above quotation and the discussion in Chapter 3 emphasizes Piaget's view that emotions are central in symbolic development and that play provides an essential medium of emotional expression, understanding, and conflict resolution. Continuing the quotation:

> It is primarily affective conflicts that reappear in symbolic play. If there is a scene at lunch, for example, one can be sure that an hour or two afterward it will be re-created with dolls and will be brought to a happier conclusion. Either the child disciplines her doll more intelligently than her parents did her, or in play she accepts what she had not accepted at lunch (such as finishing a bowl of soup she does not like, especially if here it is the doll who finishes it symbolically). Similarly, if the child has been frightened by a big dog, in a symbolic game things will be arranged so that dogs will no longer be mean or else children will become brave. Generally speaking, symbolic play helps in the resolution of conflicts and also in the compensation of unsatisfied needs, the inversion of roles (such as obedience and authority), the liberation and extension of the self, etc. (ibid, pp. 57–60).[8]

Symbolic play and deferred imitation extend children's mental trial and error investigations to the emotional and social arena. In play it is possible to experiment with how it feels to be angry, or how to get back at an older brother, or to discover what will happen if parents are disobeyed. Dolls and furry animals are also ideal companions for exploring closeness and love. Mental trial and error converts play into a relatively safe medium for making discoveries about feelings and relationships.

When Jacqueline and other children in Substage 6 construct maps in which they locate their own positions, they have begun to adopt more than one point of view. From this new observation platform, children begin to examine themselves as physical objects among other objects, subject to physical laws. For the first time, a true self-concept has emerged. The fact that this self is conceived of as subject to physical laws helps to reduce the sense of omnipotence and invulnerability earlier attached to the self as a causal agent. In some sense, most two-year-olds *know* that if they step out of windows, they will fall, and if they

[8]This account resembles psychoanalyst Erik Erikson's description of play (1950).

stick their hand in flames, the fire will burn them. This knowledge, makes it easier for parents to impose some kind of protective social controls, but it does not guarantee that controls will be effective.

The emergence of a separate physical self, and the child's splendid advances in symbolic development, strengthen the child's interest in communicating with others. At the same time, sensorimotor symbols are limited in their ability to convey meaning from person to person. Langer's (1969a) discussion of Piaget points clearly to the constraints of the most flexible sensorimotor representations. Sensorimotor schemes of action and memory, even in their internal form, are tied directly to concrete events which have been experienced; children at this stage cannot yet think about hypothetical events or possibilities. The direct link to concrete experiences means that sensorimotor acts and thinking occur in the "slow motion" tempo of real events. Image-memories have the quality of taking as long to "play back" as they originally did to observe. Furthermore, sensorimotor symbols are private. Things have meaning for the child in terms of what he or she has done with them. Arbitrary signs, such as the word meanings of adult language, are not part of the eighteen-month-old's repertoire even when the child uses single words or phrases. The tie to experience, the slow motion, and the privacy of sensorimotor symbols all give testimony to the young child's egocentrism, which is just beginning to be overcome. Like Copernicus, who discovered that the earth's motion was responsible for the movement of the sun, Jacqueline becomes aware of her physical point of view. But there is still a profound psychological–social egocentrism in which she is not aware of the privacy and idiosyncrasy of her own communicative symbols (gestures, words, drawings). Thus, the Sensorimotor stage gives rise to representations and conceptions which form limited sensorimotor symbols. The complete transformation to mental symbols and the explosion of spoken language come with the next (Pre-operational) stage.

SOME RECENT RESEARCH ON SENSORIMOTOR DEVELOPMENT

Issues in ages and stages

Piaget locates the beginning of object permanence and "real" imitation in the fourth Sensorimotor substage (about six to twelve months). Some investigators find these cognitive skills in younger infants.

Object permanence. Bower (1974) summarizes a set of intriguing experiments, by him and others, to show that young infants establish object permanence in the *third* Sensorimotor substage (four to six months). He argues that these infants do not search for objects hidden under a cloth only because they do not have the motor skills necessary to grasp and lift it. In one type of study, a surprise response is examined instead.

> An object is hidden behind a screen. For one group of five-month-olds, the object reappears when the screen is raised, while for a second group, the object has vanished. This second group gives evidence of surprise, suggesting that five-month-old infants expected it to be there, and thus held a concept of the object while it was not being perceived (Bower, 1966; Charlesworth, 1966).

Other experiments indicate that the object permanence scheme is not all-or-none achievement. It is particularly difficult for infants to represent one object as inside or contained by another, but under some conditions, absent objects *are* re-presented.

> Bower and Wishart (1972). studied the behavior of infants who had failed the standard object-permanence test in a somewhat different hiding test. These infants were shown an object; but, before they could reach for the object, the room lights were extinguished so that object and everything else vanished. The infant's behavior was recorded by means of an infrared-sensitive vidicon camera. All of the infants were able to reach out and grasp the object they had observed but could no longer see. . . . In other words, out of sight was not out of mind as long as the transition to "out of sight" was accomplished by plunging the entire room into darkness (Bower, 1974, p. 207).

Bower argues that it is the nature of the transition from "in sight" to "out of sight" that facilitates or prevents successful hand and arm search. I believe that another factor may be involved. When the light goes out, the infant no longer must coordinate present visual perceptions (object gone) with past representations (object present), and this absence of conflict facilitates the representation of the object. Regardless of the specific details of interpretation, Bower's studies demonstrate that with different response criteria than Piaget used, and a more differentiated specification of object permanence task, we may arrive at a more differentiated view of object permanence and an earlier specification of the ages at which some kinds of object permanence emerge.

Imitation. In contrast with Piaget's claim that imitations of an adult sticking out his tongue do not occur until about six months of age, Melzoff and Moore (1977) in an excellent experiment demonstrated this imitation by infants *12 to 21 days old.* They controlled for the possibility that the infants were simply reacting with generalized arousal, by comparing infant responses to different adult gestures. They also controlled for possible scorer bias by videotaping responses and having them scored by observers unaware of which adult gesture had been made. Their results clearly indicate that these young infants matched one of four specific adult acts (lip protrusion, mouth opening, tongue protrusion and sequential finger movement). Agreeing with Piaget that these imitations require symbolic representation, Melzoff and Moore argue that symbolic representation is present very soon after birth.

This study poses a more serious challenge to Piaget than the Bower experiments, because it uses a stimulus just as Piaget described it and evaluates a similar response. One possibility is that Piaget is in error in his claim that symbolic representation arises in a sequence from initially uncoordinated to coordinated schemes. Another possibility is that Piaget, and Melzoff and Moore, are wrong in their assumption that this kind of imitation requires representation; other imitative responses will have to be investigated so that we know more about the range of imitative skills at this early age.

What Bower and Melzoff and Moore have accomplished is to reopen the question of when and how symbolic representation arises in infants. It should be noted that these investigators still assume that there are necessary stage-sequences in cognitive development and that disequilibration is an important developmental mechanism. In questioning some of Piaget's hypotheses, they are not rejecting the theory; in fact, their work should ultimately provide a more detailed and differentiated view of infancy, whether or not Piaget's theory is ultimately upheld.

Piaget-based infant tests

Using some Piaget-type items, Corman and Escalona (1969) and Décarie (1965) independently developed brief standardized measures of Sensorimotor development. Test results strongly supported the above-described sequence of substages.

A very comprehensive and significant new Piaget-based infant assessment instrument has been developed by Uzgiris and Hunt (1975). Items have been grouped into six scales: object permanence; the use of objects as means to obtain environmental events; vocal and gestural imitation; causality concepts; spatial relations among objects; coordination of schemes for relating to objects. In constructing the scales, Uzgiris and Hunt found more than six ordered landmarks in each area (i.e., more than one for each of six substages); the scales contain as many as fifteen items. Uzgiris (1973) examined twelve infants regularly from four weeks to two years of age. Despite the fact that the scales contain more than six Piagetian items, there were very few reversals of order from the theoretically determined stage sequence. Intercorrelaticns among scales were very high (around .8), confirming the notion that individuals develop as unitary wholes (Hunt, 1976, p. 38). The permanent object scheme appears to be central to all the scales, because advances on other scales seem to follow advances in the level of the permanent object concept.

Beginning evidence suggests that the Uzgiris-Hunt scales correlate significantly with the Bayley Mental Scale (black male infants assessed at 17, 18, and 22 months by King and Seegmiller, 1973) and the Stanford-Binet (Wachs, 1975). In this latter study, white infants were assessed at 12, 15, 18, 21, and 24 months, and their Uzgiris-Hunt scores correlated with a Binet test administered at 31 months. In the twelve-month-olds, only object permanence was correlated with Binet scores nineteen months later; over time, increasing numbers of scales showed a significant relation with Binet IQ. In all cases, the correlations between Hunt-Uzgiris and other tests were statistically significant but low to moderate. The two approaches show both overlap and divergence in the aspects of intellectual development which they assess.

In sum, Piaget's description of substage sequence seems to be supported by subsequent research on Sensorimotor development. Taken together, the findings are typical of other investigations at other cognitive stages, following up the Genevan approach. While the broad outline is replicated, it is possible to make more fine-grained distinctions than those offered in the initial formulation. There may be more than six substages. Some responses and skills occur much earlier than Piaget suggests, though the tasks and the method of measurement are usually changed. And, intercorrelations among Piaget subscales are high but never perfect; there are, inevitably, variations in the patterns of stage levels shown by each individual child.

Environmental influences on development

Two strategies have been adopted, both using the Uzgiris-Hunt scales, to investigate the effects of environmental circumstances on early cognitive development. The first approach selects infants from obviously different, generally specified environments. For example, Paraskevopoulos and Hunt (1971) studied Greek infants in an orphanage (caretaker ratio of ten infants for one caretaker), a baby care center (caretaker ratio of 3:1), and homes of working-class families. At the orphanage, the mean age for achieving the highest level of object permanence was 195 weeks; the baby care center infants averaged 154 weeks and home-reared infants averaged 130 weeks—a variation of one year and thirteen weeks among the three samples. Other examples are summarized by Hunt (1976).

A second research approach focuses on the specific characteristics of infant environments. An in-progress report by Wachs (1976) describes a study of 39 American infants from a wide socioeconomic range, who were observed twice a month in their homes, between 12 and 24 months. Data from a new instrument, the Purdue Home Stimulation Inventory, were correlated with Uzgiris-Hunt scales.

There were four general sets of findings:

1. The regularity and predictability of the child's environment was positively correlated with the rate of progress through cognitive stages.
2. The adequacy of stimulation was also positively correlated with sensorimotor development. Adequacy was defined by amount of visual and audiovisual stimulation, variety of change in stimulation, lack of physical or visual restraints (allowing child to explore), and the presence of toys which produce visual or sound feedback when they are manipulated.
3. While a certain minimum of stimulation and variation seems to be necessary, too

intense physical stimulation and too many people surrounding the child without space for him or her to escape, are associated with relative delays in cognitive development.

4. Verbal stimulation (only a few items assessed) was positively related to scores in Uzgiris-Hunt scales.

Again, correlations were significant but moderate. Not all infants with optimal stimulation did well and not all optimally stimulating environments produced higher scores on the Uzgiris-Hunt scales. I believe that scales and other assessments will have to include qualities of caretaker interactions with children and caretaker relationships with each other, in order to account more fully for the rates of Sensorimotor development in children.

Hunt (1976) suggests as he did earlier (1961) that an additional variable must be considered in studies of environmental impact on infant cognitive development—the mismatch between infant stage and environmental demands. In several examples he illustrates a potentially testable hypothesis: continuing stimulation at levels which the infant has already mastered lead to boredom, apathy, and potential slowing down of progress; however, adult demands for performance too far above the infant's level results in emotional distress and also leads to withdrawal. Presumably there is an optimal level of mismatch which facilitates developmental growth.

From different directions, Wachs and Hunt come to the same general conclusions. The physical environment can have a powerful impact on Sensorimotor development. Hunt comments:

> How Piaget should be expected to react to evidence of such great plasticity in the development of object construction is not at all clear. Were he to react in terms of the empirical findings that he has reported, he would be highly surprised. On the other hand, were he to react in terms of the implication of his theoretical constructs accommodation, assimilation, and equilibration, such findings need not surprise him at all (Hunt, 1976, pp. 32–38).

IMPLICATIONS FOR EDUCATION AT ALL STAGE LEVELS

Caring for infants

Caretaker understandings and expectations. Piaget's meticulous research on his own three children has been buttressed by subsequent accounts of stage sequences. This research yields some conclusions which are not obvious to casual observation, especially as it documents the late emergence of intention and object permanence.[9] Adults have tended to attribute too much to infants'

[9]Bower's research locates it in Substage 3, but even here infants are about four to six months old.

mental processes during the first six months. Paradoxically, they often attribute too little to symbolic development between six and twelve months, placing too much emphasis on language as a major indicator of symbolic function.

Caretakers can use Piaget's interpretation of sequence, though not his age norms, to understand the world of infants better and to interpret infant behaviors more realistically. Specifically, it may be easier to relax and comfort a four-month-old in the middle of the night, if we do not interpret the infant's crying as having been directed at us for having left them. Or, we may become more aware of the cognitive growth activities that children engage in while playing peek-a-boo, indulging in rituals, or shaking and banging the coffeepot in the cupboard under the sink. The way we interpret infant behavior is one important determinant of how we react to it.

The development of attachment. The construction of object permanence and social attachment requires both regularity and change in the child's environment. Radical long-term interruptions of caretaking after the first six months of life may be accompanied by adverse effects on cognitive development, but it is not clear whether such adverse effects are irreversible in later development. Other important questions have not been answered. Must there be *one* primary caretaker at first? Research evidence is not clear. If Piaget is correct, the most powerful influences on attachment should be the quality rather than the quantity of interaction between parent and child, but we will need to know much more about the details of what kinds of interactions produce what kinds of outcomes. It is likely that many different patterns may be optimal, depending on the characteristics of both caretaker(s) and child.

Characteristics of the child's environment. Systematic, severe deprivation of stimulus change may be detrimental to infant cognitive development. But the nature and the extent of deprivation makes a difference. In a famous study, Dennis (1940) found that a group of Hopi children who were bound on a cradle board for most of their first year learned to walk at about the same age as the children of Hopi mothers who had given up the practice of binding children on the board. Studies like this were used to support Gesell's maturational view of development. Nevertheless, Piaget's approach, focusing more on cognitive coordination and less on large muscle coordination, has led to a concern for the provision of challenging physical activity for infants. During the past decade, this interest may be responsible for a boom in toy sales directed at stimulation during the early months of a baby's life: the common butterfly and bird mobiles above infant cribs are advertised as providing important stimulus for young infants; "crib gyms" are being created to stimulate infants' interest in touching, pushing, and exploring a variety of objects. These and other toys reflect a growing concern with providing infants (and older children) with sensory stimulation and opportunity for physical manipulation of objects. While there is little evidence for or against specific toys, the general importance of such stimulation cannot be denied.

It is much too early in the state of research on early cognitive development to prescribe specific practices for parents and other caretakers. Wach's study (1976), described above, suggests that regularity, stimulus change, and verbal stimulation facilitate cognitive development, while crowding and too intense stimulation interfere with intellectual growth. It sounds very much as if he is recommending conditions which are supposed to be characteristic of middle- and upper-socioeconomic status families. But, we do not yet know enough about the factors which lead to advanced cognitive development in children of lower-socioeconomic status families. These factors may include the social–emotional climate of the home as an important variable, in interaction with physical stimulus characteristics. We cannot simply use Wach's study, excellent as it is, to advocate middle-class practices for all.

In the many vignettes describing sensorimotor development, Piaget as an experimenter provides an interesting model of both scientist and parent. The clinical method allows for involved stimulation and experimentation by adults, but it also allows for times of observation without interference in the child's active experimentation. Parents who are attempting to understand their children may be ambivalent about sitting back and letting the child explore. They may be excited to see their child attempting to find out how things work, but especially in the fifth and sixth Sensorimotor substages, the child's exploration may lead in many unpredictable directions. Barriers such as gates and closed doors are challenges to be overcome. Pots, pans, dishes, clocks, important papers, cupboards and their contents are all part of the young child's natural laboratory. The cognitive benefits of manipulating the environment may have costs in materials and parental peace of mind. As in Piaget's own studies, it will be necessary for the adult to provide many environments which are safe to explore and to make some objects and environments at least temporarily off limits (by removing the objects, locking doors, etc.). It seems to me that the parent must somehow find a balance between encouraging the child to explore and assimilate, while at the same time providing and enforcing limits to which the child must accommodate. In that balance, especially if it is geared appropriately to the child's cognitive level, the disequilibration process in the child should operate in the direction of developmental growth.

This discussion has focused on both objects and people as important stimulators of cognitive development. Watson (1972) has developed an intriguing hypothesis about the related function of people and physical events in the young infant's cognitive and emotional life.

> Briefly, he notes that infants become very interested in the contingency relations between stimuli and responses. For example, an apparatus is rigged so that the infant's head movements set a mobile in motion. Not only do eight-to-ten-week-old infants begin to make increasing number of head motions, but they also begin to smile and coo as long as the contingency between head movements and mobile movements is maintained; the smiles disappear if the contingency is disrupted by the experimenter. It is as if the infants become emotionally attached to the game-like

contingency between action and mobile. Watson suggests that as adults begin to play with infants, they establish similar contingencies between their actions and the infant's actions.

Watson's hypothesis, then, is: " 'The Game' is NOT important to the infant because people play it, but rather, people become important to the infant because they play 'The Game' " (p. 338). In this hypothesis, he suggests specific ways in which both people and objects, separately and together, provide the stimulation for both intellectual and emotional development in the young infant.

Sensorimotor functioning at later stages

Symbols and concepts before language. Piaget's description of Sensorimotor development helps to establish clearly that concepts are not to be equated with words. Months before the first word, infant symbolic schemes have taken a great leap forward with the development of object permanence. Cognitive maps, mental trial and error, deferred imitations, and symbolic play are all symbolic activities which develop and occur prior to language. Further, symbolic concepts at all stages have roots in sensorimotor action. with the child's particular experiences and emotions included as part of the schemas and schemes. Even when words do appear, there will continue to be nonverbal, private, and emotional aspects of conceptual meaning.

What is conveyed in language by parent and teacher will not be conceptually received in exactly the same form by the child, nor will the child's meanings ever be completely conveyed to the adult. Communication with peers at each age level also faces the gap between the sending and receiving of spoken messages.

Value problems in play and imitation. The involvement of infants and young children in imitation and play is valued, encouraged, and applauded by most adults. Children are rewarded with parental pleasure when they act just like Daddy or Mommy, or when they talk just like Aunt Sara or Uncle Joe. When they play dress up, or let's pretend, wagging their finger scornfully at a doll, parents tend to be amused and to approve their children's activities. However, by the time children are ready to enter elementary school, imitation and play are both beginning to be devalued as part of "real" learning. Though children are required to copy graphemes, words, letters, and so on, they are advised never to copy answers or even to copy paintings during an art lesson. Play begins to take on secondary value when it is treated as what one does to blow off steam during recess, before settling down to work in class.

In Piaget's approach, the sensorimotor aspects of imitation and play are still involved in the growth of symbols long after the Sensorimotor period ends. Not only does imitation facilitate cognitive representation, but it is also an essential aspect of social learning of roles. Play, too, facilitates cognitive and role learning and also provides unlimited vistas for trying out, rearranging, and creatively transforming physical, social, and emotional input. These two aspects of intelligence continue over the lifespan, though the symbols that emerge may be quite unlike the original Sensorimotor schemas and schemes.

Microgenetic development. Heinz Werner (1948), a cognitive developmental theorist with an approach having some similarities with Piaget, suggests that in each new stimulus situation, we go through a rapid developmental progression. For example, microgenetic development occurs when we are presented a series of pictures in a tachistoscope with very short exposure times; there is a developmental increase in the quality of performance from early to late in the series. It is likely that sensorimotor functioning is involved, microgenetically, in approaches to new problems at every stage. Adults who are capable of formal thought still begin by making abstract problems concrete, building real models, groping, engaging in assimilative circular reactions and accommodative imitations before gradually internalizing and interiorizing a symbolic understanding. Changes which take months and years in infants may occur in seconds or minutes in adults but can also extend over a longer time period. Sensorimotor learning can play an important role in education at any developmental stage.

CHAPTER 6

Preoperations

The Preconceptual Substage

The stage of Preoperations is so named because it precedes operational thought, as if nothing of importance in its own right transpires in the age range from two to seven years. And yet, in two substages—Preconceptual (two to four years) and Intuitive (four to seven years)—language develops, stable concepts are formed, mental reasoning is established, psychological egocentrism begins to decline, far-reaching mythologies and magical belief systems are constructed. Spanning the earliest formal education from preschool through kindergarten to the early primary grades of elementary school, it is a time of tremendous intellectual, social, emotional, and educational change.

The Preconceptual substage of Preoperations is an underresearched developmental period by Piaget and, until very recently, by almost everyone else. Potential subjects are at an in-between age, no longer in cribs and playpens a good part of their days, not easily available for daily observations at home or in schools, and too young for many of the tests and interviews used extensively with older children. In Piaget's various investigations of conceptual development (conservation, number, space, time, geometry, etc.), three- and four-year-olds are given difficult tasks and always perform at the low end of the developmental scale. More detailed and useful information comes primarily from Piaget's accounts of his own children in *Play, Dreams and Imitation* (1946a) and from Inhelder and Piaget's *The Early Growth of Logic* (1959); in this latter work, special tasks were designed to observe the nonverbal classification and seriation behavior of Preconceptual children.

The first section of this chapter focuses on cognitive development. Like many other chapters to come, it will be followed by sections on social and emotional development, and by a discussion of how Piagetian theory and research can be applied to the education of children at this substage of intellectual development.

COGNITIVE DEVELOPMENT

Sensorimotor symbols can be described as concepts-in-action. By the sixth Sensorimotor substage, children represent and assimilate new objects into general schemes and demonstrate a fairly flexible behavioral concept of permanent objects, space, time, and causality. However, Sensorimotor symbolic concepts are tied directly to concrete events; in addition, they are slow-motion, private and fluctuating and are greatly affected by shifts in the child's attention to different aspects of perceived events. For example, many city-raised two-year-olds call almost all four-legged animals "doggie," but they may call a particular dog "horsie" because its brown color reminds them of a horse that they rode on the merry-go-round last week. Children usually center on the legs in grouping together all animals as dogs, but sometimes a child's concentration (focus of attention) shifts to color and size, or some completely idiosyncratic characteristic of objects or events. The stable, generalized concepts evident in overt behavior during the Sensorimotor period have not yet been transformed into stable, organizing dimensions in the realms of mental symbols. This reconstruction on the level of thought of what has already been established in behavior is the primary cognitive task of the Preconceptual substage.

Some definitions

In order to define what it is that leads Piaget to call "doggie" a preconcept, we must first know how he defines concepts. His terminology comes from the language of logic and mathematics.

Classes. In a defined class (logic) or set (mathematics), the smallest units of analysis are called elements. Like the psychological scheme, the size of an element is a relative matter. A single point, an object, a collection of objects, a category, or a statement can all be considered elements, depending on what we are classifying.

Elements can be grouped together in classes or sets on the basis of some defined similarity in physical properties (squares, large objects), functional properties (moving parts, reinforcers), connotations (religious objects, horror movies), and so on. Elements can also be described in terms of their difference from others (not long, not square). Consistent application of defining properties will determine the list of potential elements to be included in the class. If we know that a class is composed of square elements, we can determine which of the potential shapes to be classified will be included and which will be rejected.

Classes can be divided and redivided into subclasses. Within the class of squares are large squares and small squares. All of the elements are square: some are small; some are large; none is round. For adults, classes are based not only on the specification of similarities and differences, but also on the mastery of class inclusion—the concepts of "all," "some," and "none."

Relations. Within the smallest subclass under discussion, each element is interchangeable. No distinctions are made among the small squares or the large squares. However, within the subclass, or between subclasses, it is always possible to order each pair of elements on the basis of spatial position (to the left or right), temporal position (before, after), equivalence, identity, or class inclusion (B is a subset of A). The relation between elements or classes is defined by an ordering between pairs.

In many languages, including English, it is not always clear when we are referring to class membership and when to relational properties. Developmentally, this distinction is confused or ignored until children reach the stage of Concrete operations (at about age seven).

> A six-year-old boy is asked "How many brothers have you?" He replies: *One. His name is Paul.* How many brothers does Paul have?—*None.* Brother is treated only as a class membership property of a given person, not as a relation between the two boys.

Preconcepts. In adult logic, classes have (or should have) consistent, defining properties and can be structured into stable hierarchies of class inclusions (e.g., living things, vertebrates and invertebrates; the vertebrates can be further subdivided into mammals and nonmammals, etc.). While adults are never entirely consistent, their concepts of space, time, number, causality, identity, are based upon complex rules for grouping elements together and on rules for establishing relations among elements and classes. By contrast, as we shall see in the next several sections, preconcepts are mental combinations of elements which do *not* have stable defining properties, stable hierarchies of relationships, or clear distinctions between classes and relational properties.

And yet, preconcepts are very useful schemes. From Sensorimotor classification by overt action, the child can now sort objects and events by mental action. Representational symbols now go beyond deferred imitation of specific events to truly internalized images (e.g., daydreams); conceptualization goes beyond symbolic play to interiorized schemes (e.g., language meanings). Unlike Sensorimotor symbols, mental symbols in the Preconceptual substage become partly detached from their direct ties to experience. They extend to the future as well as the past, to fanciful concepts as well as real events. However fluctuating these preconcepts may be, they are achieved quickly by mental combination and are not just slow playbacks of perceived events. And preconcepts enable the child to emerge from the private symbols of sensorimotor action to the public and communicable symbols of spoken language.

Preoperations. At the end of the Preconceptual period (at about age four), concepts are achieving some degree of stability and consistency. Still, the child is Preoperational because mental concepts are not yet integrated in a coordinated system of mental operations.

> For example, near the end of the Preoperational stage, children can focus sequentially on classes and relations but cannot coordinate these dimensions simultaneously. In one experiment (Piaget, 1948), a six-year-old child is presented with twenty wooden beads, seventeen of which are brown, three of which are white. The child is easily able to demonstrate to the interviewer that he or she knows the meaning of the classes "all" and "some" and the relations "more than" and "less than." The interviewer asks, "Are there more brown beads or more white beads?" The child correctly answers that there are more brown beads. "Now are there more wooden beads or brown beads?"—*More brown beads.*—How do you know?—*Because there are more brown ones than white ones.*—But if I took away all the wooden ones, how many would be left?—*None.*—If I took away all the brown beads, how many would be left?—*Three.*—So, are there more wooden ones or brown ones?—*More brown ones.*

In the Intuitive substage of Preoperations (four to seven years), children develop the capacity to combine concepts mentally, but each mental combining operation is uncoordinated with others, and the system of operations is not reversible. Children cannot divide the whole into parts and mentally return to compare the parts with the whole. It is the fact that logic-based systems of mental operations are not yet in use that gives the Preoperational period its somewhat misleading name.

Piagetian research on preconcepts

Nonverbal classification. The private, fluctuating nature of preconcepts is not simply an inaccuracy in the use of words, but is characteristic of all conceptual activity. In "tests" created from the observation of spontaneous play, Inhelder and Piaget (1959) gave young children circles, squares, triangles, shapes, and objects of different colors and asked them to "put things together that are alike" or to "put them so they're all the same." Even two- and three-year-olds understood the instructions in the sense that certain objects were placed together and others were not.

The Preconceptual child's first "classifications" are what Piaget calls graphic collections. Children tend to arrange the objects in the shape of houses, trees, trains, and so on. Piaget interprets these collections as indicating that the first preconcepts are private and tend to emphasize figurative rather than operative properties of symbolic activity.

Three- and four-year-olds begin to make nongraphic "alignments," but the basis of the classification shifts in much the same way as the "horsie" example above.

> A child of three years and eleven months "places a blue triangle next to another and then continues with a blue square. The blue square is followed by a yellow square (a change from the criterion of color to that of form), and then by red, yellow, and blue squares. Since the last square is preceded by a yellow one, the child places a yellow triangle after it (probably guided by symmetry). This induced him to choose six more triangles—first two red, then two yellow, and finally two blue" (Inhelder and Piaget, 1959 p. 23).

In another task, children are asked to group together a set of pictures—flowers of different colors, fruits, articles of clothing. A four-year-old in a typical example makes three piles: 1) flowers, 4 yellow and 2 blue; 2) pink ones, 2 flowers and 1 cherry; 3) a flower and a hat, the flower is to go on the hat. Preconceptual children define separate piles of objects, but there is no notion of a set of (exhaustive) classes into which all the objects can be categorized; some objects are simply left over and are not in any of the piles. There is no coordination between classes; each pile is based on a different criterion (flowers, color, functional relation). Not surprisingly, children at this substage give random answers to questions about the relations between all and some and completely fail to understand questions about whether there are more flowers or more blue flowers, and so on. For Preconceptual children, then, there are neither consistent classes nor a hierarchically organized series of class inclusions.

Seriation (ordered relations). Two simple tasks involving seriation have been extensively discussed (Inhelder and Piaget, 1959; Piaget and Szeminska, 1941).

> First, children are asked to place in serial order ten sticks ranging in length from 9 cm. to 16 cm. The difference between each pair of sticks is quite small. Second, to investigate the child's concept of analogous series, he or she is given ten dolls of different height and (smaller) walking sticks. The task is to arrange the dolls and sticks so that "each doll can easily find the stick that belongs to it." This task examines the child's understanding that objects of different sizes can be equivalent in terms of their relative position (the midsize doll goes with the midsize walking stick). The child must coordinate two series along a single dimension (height).

In the Preconceptual stage, children do not form consistent ordering of a long series, unless the materials, like stacking boxes which fit one inside the other, provide an abundance of cues. They place the ten sticks in random orders or in several clumps by size. Some children line up the tops in a "staircase," but neglect variations in the bottoms. They can correctly compare any two sticks, but transitive orderings (A>B>C>D, etc.) are beyond them. Arranging one series of objects is difficult enough. Matching two series (sticks and dolls) is impossible.

Nonverbal preconcepts then, are fluctuating, private, and unidimensional. Neither classification nor relationship properties of objects are consistently and coherently combined. This same pattern is evident in the Preconceptual child's use of words.

Verbal preconcepts

Fluctuating. The symbol system of adult spoken language can be used for communication, in part, because the meaning of words has relative stability over time and relative stability in the transmission from one person to another. As you might expect, Piaget shows that the arbitrary symbols of adult language are not simply tacked on the fluctuating Sensorimotor symbols that came before. There is a long process in which words are simply one aspect of the development of conceptual schemes. The Sensorimotor achievement of object permanence must be paralleled by a Preconceptual achievement of permanence in the meaning of words.

> At about three years and two months, Piaget's daughter Jacqueline vascillated between applying a class-name to a collection of objects and to a single object. She could correctly indicate that the town of Lausanne was "all the houses in an area," but she also called her grandmother's house "Lausanne." Similarly, she referred to slugs which she saw on a walk with her father as slugs (a general class) and also as "the slug," as if she kept seeing the same one over and over again. (Piaget, 1946a)

Private. Even when words and concepts are used consistently over time, their meaning is based upon the specifics of personal experience.

> When children begin to say "mama" and "dada" the words are applied inconsistently, sometimes to one parent, sometimes to the other, sometimes to total strangers. After this period there can be some interesting consistencies. Friends of mine are parents of a very verbal fourteen-month-old girl. They alternate child care and employment so that one parent is home with the baby. This little girl always calls "dada" to the parent who goes out or comes in the door. Dada is the person-who-leaves-home-and-doesn't-stay-with-me. Since in most traditional households this person is the male, other children's use of "dada" may be consistent and correct, but may be based on an entirely different concept (the leaver) than the one generally understood by the parents.

Without extensive supporting evidence, Piaget uses anecdotes like these to suggest that *all* verbal preconcepts have private and idiosyncratic meanings. This claim appears to be overstated when we listen to three- and four-year-olds talk, noting the consistency and correctness with which language is used. But this correctness, from an adult point of view, does not rule out the possibility that unique and private meanings are also embedded in concepts underlying their words. In fact, Piaget's analysis indicates that, despite adult abilities to adopt and use arbitrary word meanings, words always carry private connotations, in part because symbols never lose their connections with their sensorimotor roots.

Confusion between symbols and things. Another salient characteristic of words and other symbols in the Preconceptual stage is that they are treated as central aspects of the things which they symbolize.

A four-year-old is questioned about the arbitrary properties of words. —Could you call this table a cup and that cup a table? —*No.* —Why not? —*Because you can't drink out of a table!*

The direct link between a symbol and its referent cannot be altered. This same principle holds when names or labels are applied to people.

Hartley and Hartley (1948), as a prelude to a study on ethnic identity, asked children about their conception of their mother as a working person. —Well, tell me. Is she still your mommy when she's working? —(Boy, 3 years, 3 months) *No.* —When she comes home at night and plays with you and talks to you, what is she? —*Mother.* —Is she still a sales girl [sic] when she's your mother at night? —*No.*

Though the experimenter never asked, it is likely that fathers do not remain fathers when they are at work either. In any case, a parent cannot have two labels, because that would imply two different people. Conversely, perceived changes in another person can lead the Preconceptual child to change the verbal name.

At two years, seven months, "Jacqueline seeing her sister Lucienne in a new bathing suit with a cap asked: '*What's the baby's name?*' Her mother replied that it was a bathing costume, but Jacqueline pointed to Lucienne herself and said, '*But what's the name of that?*' (indicating Lucienne's face) and repeated the question several times. As soon as Lucienne had her dress on again, Jacqueline exclaimed very seriously, '*It's Lucienne again*' as if her sister had changed her identity in changing her clothes.' (1946a, p. 224)

When Preconceptual children ask their endless "What's that?" questions, they are, in effect, asking for both the name of the object and its place in the class to which it belongs. But at first, the name, the thing, and the class are indistinguishable. Each changes when the other changes. The fusion of symbols and their referents contributes to the private, fluctuating aspects of concepts already described above. However, the communicative interaction resulting from asking the questions eventually challenges the children to correct their private concepts and to move toward socialized, agreed-upon verbal meanings.

One dimension at a time. The fluctuation of concepts and the confusion between words and things are both reflections of the fact that conceptual dimensions can be mentally manipulated only one at a time until late in the Preoperational stage.

The main focus of the Hartley and Hartley (1948) study was on young children's concepts of multiple class membership—religion and nationality. One child, three and a half years old replied to the question, "Are you American?" with, "*No, I'm a cowboy.*" Another child (4 years, 5 months) when asked, "Are you Catholic?" replied, "*No, I'm Richie.*" A third, the same age to, "Are you Jewish?" said, "*No, I'm only four. I'll get Jewish.*" Still another faced with "Are you American?" replied, "*No, my father is American, I'm a girl*" (from Hartley and Hartley, 1955).

The verbal symbols of the Preoperational child certainly expand his or her conceptual range, especially by enlarging the possibility of communicating about events which are no longer present or by sharing ideas. Late in the Preconceptual substage word-concepts develop some stability, permanence, and separation from the changing properties of objects, but they still do not meet the adult formal definition of classes. Flavell (1963), in summarizing Piaget's theory, points out that verbal preconcepts "refer neither to *individuals* who possess stable identity over time and in different contexts, nor to genuine *classes* or collectivities of similar individuals" (p. 160). Instead, the preconcept is a scheme lying part way between an action–symbol and a verbal sign, part way between an individual instance and a general class. Even when we use the same words as the two-to-four-year-old, adult words and preconceptual words have very different conceptual meanings. For example, children and adults can agree that "we'll do it soon" means "not now," but for the adult the action is postponed indefinitely, while the child expects that the action can happen later in the day.

Verbal reasoning

Like adults, young children are constantly involved in making inferences from specific experiences to general conclusions (induction) and from general categories and rules to specific experiences (deduction). I have already indicated in Chapter 2 that the reasoning of Mark, a late Preoperational child, follows highly consistent principles even when he arrives at "incorrect answers." Some more examples from Piaget's description of Jacqueline:

> Piaget usually carried hot water from the stove to prepare for his daily shaving. Every time two-year-old Jacqueline saw him carrying hot water, she would say "Daddy shave."
>
> In a neighboring house, lived a little boy who had a hunch back. "*Poor boy*", Jacqueline used to say. "*He's ill. He has a hump.*" One day she learned that he had the flu, which Jacqueline called "*being ill in bed.*" A few days later, she asked her father, "*Is he still ill in bed?* —No, I saw him this morning. He isn't in bed now. —*He hasn't a big hump now.* (1946a, p. 231)

Naturally, reasoning built on the unstable classification system described above will have its difficulties. But Piaget shows that there are certain predictable properties and principles which he summarizes in his label "transductive reasoning."

1. If A is like B in one respect, it is like B in all respects. (Father is getting the water again, so it must be for shaving.) This reasoning by analogy with past sequences is very useful in organizing experiences, even though it sometimes leads to incorrect conclusions.

2. The young child confuses particular and general cases and in the process reasons without regard for the precise meaning of "all" and "some." In effect,

the child makes inferences from one particular example to another but states the conclusion in general terms. When *this* event (water) is *sometimes* followed by that event (shaving) Jacqueline reasons as if shaving *always* follows from getting water.

3. Reasoning is frequently "backwards" from effects to causes. Hump implies illness; if not-illness, then not-hump. This logical slippage is reinforced by the use of different word-concepts with the same names—illness as influenza, and illness as hump are very different concepts, but because they are given the same name, they are treated as identical. In this example, the Preconceptual child shows reversibility in reasoning in the sense that events are conceptualized in a sequence opposite to the way in which they happened. However, this is not operational reversibility, in which the journey back and forth leaves the concepts undistorted.

4. Reasoning is one-dimensional. Like preconcepts which only focus on one attribute at a time, reasoning only operates on one conceptual dimension at a time. Preconceptual children expect taller people to be older, and empirically this is often the case for growing individuals. However, the Preconceptual child is unable to conceive of two independent dimensions—age and height—which could change at different rates.

As adults, we frequently make mistakes in our reasoning in ways that are similar to the examples above. However, we are capable of using more complex systems of logical rules, and so, in Piaget's emphasis on the highest level of performance, we are classified at a different cognitive stage. By contrast, Preconceptual children are limited to preconcepts and to transductive rules for forming and combining classes and relations.

The focus on what is missing in young children's cognitive structures, should not draw attention away from the fact that transductive reasoning is adaptive. It provides a powerful beginning link between inferences based on data (induction) and inferences based on other premises (deduction). And, transductive reasoning is often correct; Daddy usually *is* about to shave when he carries the hot water. Langer (1977) suggests that this ability of younger children to make correct inferences "may well account for much of what we may call the 'anything you can find, I can find it earlier' research literature" (p. 78). Given simple enough tasks, transductive reasoning is quite adequate to reach a conclusion which adults may arrive at in more complex ways.

Preconcepts of quantity, number, space, and time

Quantity. Around the age of two, children begin to develop a working notion of quantity as expressed in words: "want some," "gimme more," "all gone," "big dog." By the age of four, they use "more," "less," "the same amount," "all," "some," "none" in apparently consistent and correct sentences. Although they are not able to use number concepts to specify exactly how many or how big, late Preconceptual children seem to have well-established ordinal concepts of quantity. But in Piaget and Inhelder's (1941) famous experiments with conservation of clay and water, it is claimed that quantity concepts as understood by adults may be three or more years away.

> In a number of different tasks, the child is shown or asked to produce two equal amounts of substance—two equal amounts of water in identical containers, two equal balls of clay, (both continuous quantities), or two equal containers of beads (discontinuous quantity). One of the substances is transformed (e.g., poured into a taller, thinner container; changed into a longer, thinner piece of clay). With many different kinds of questions, in different orders, using the child's own vocabulary, the experimenter asks the child for a comparison of the two substances at the beginning and at the end of the transformation. The experimenter also asks for an explanation of the answer ("What leads you to say it's the same?" "How do you know it's different?"). Children were questioned about the amount of clay, water, or beads (substance), the comparative weights of the two substances, or the volume.

Conservation is said to be achieved when the child disregards the physical–perceptual transformations and responds that the amount of material remains unchanged. Typical reasons for conservation judgments include: "Nothing was added or taken away"; "It's taller, but it's thinner, so it's the same"; "If you change it back the way it was, it would be the same".[1] Adults are quite surprised that even very bright and verbal four-year-olds rarely demonstrate conservation of quantity. Almost inevitably, Preconceptual children interpret every perceived alteration as a change in amount. "It's more because it's taller." "This one's less because it's squished."

Number. Despite the use of quantity words, and even a few names of numbers, two-to-four-year-olds are described by Piaget as using only preconcepts of "How many?" They may be able to identify two rows of beads, checkers, eggs, sticks, or pennies lined up in one-to-one correspondence as "the same" number. But any perceptual arrangement of the objects leads the child to believe that the number of things has changed. Usually, but not always in the four-to-seven-year-olds tested (Piaget and Szeminska, 1941), the longer row is judged as having more objects.

On the topic of number conservation, Mehler and Bever (1967), in an article in *Science,* touched off a heated controversy with replies by Beilin (1968), Achenbach (1969), Siegel and Goldstein (1969), and Piaget himself (1968a); there were, in addition, replies to the replies by Bever, Mehler, and Epstein (1968), and Mehler and Bever (1968).

[1]This answer does not adequately demonstrate conservation. Many qualities of objects which *do* change as a result of pouring (e.g., height of water) also would return to the original quantity if the transformation were reversed. Piaget distinguished between this empirical *renversibilité* and conceptual reversibility, but most other researchers do not make the distinction and Piaget does not always make it consistently.

In the original study, Mehler and Bever tested 200 children between two years, four months and four years, seven months. Using either clay pellets or M & M's, they showed children two equal rows of four objects and asked if the rows were "the same" (Figure 5a). The experimenters then transformed the rows as in Figure 5b so that

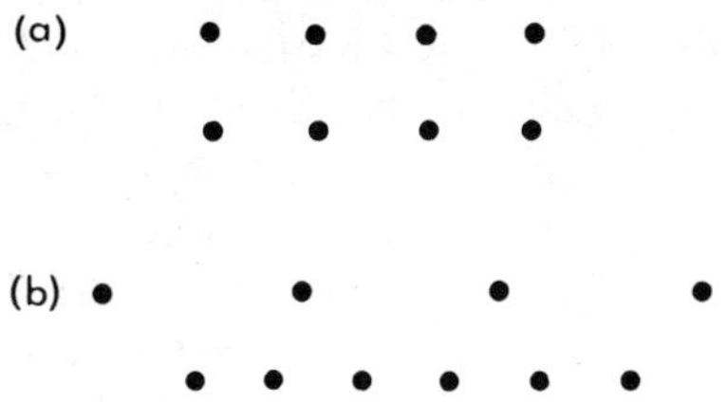

(a)

(b)

there were now four objects in the top row and six objects compressed in a shorter bottom row; children were asked, "Which row has more?" (clay) or, "Take the row you want to eat" (M & M's).

Children between two years, four months and two years, seven months were very accurate in choosing the row with more objects despite its transformation into a shorter array. There was a *decrease* in correct responses from two years, seven months to three years, eleven months and then an increase with age to four years, seven months. The authors concluded that conservation does not emerge between five and seven years but rather is reacquired ". . . nonconservation behavior is a temporary exception to human cognition, not a basic characteristic of man's native endowment."

Beilen (1968) and especially Piaget (1968a) pointed out that this task did not replicate the original conservation experiments and that Mehler and Bever had misused the term "conservation." Piaget applies it to a preservation of sameness despite transformations, but Mehler and Bever not only rearranged the objects, they increased the amount in one row. Mehler and Bever subsequently agreed that they had misused the term but did not agree that their findings were open to question. However, controlling for young children's tendencies to answer with the last concept mentioned by the experimenter (Is this row less, the same, or *more?*) and correcting for chance levels of responding substantially reduced the success rates of very young children (Siegel and Goldstein, 1969; Achenbach, 1969). Piaget produced new evidence and arguments to show that two-year-olds correctly judged the row of six objects as "more":

1. on the basis of the fact that the experimenter added an object to that row, not on a comparison between rows;
2. on the basis of the inference that the row which the experimenter manipulated (shortened and added to) has more;
3. on the basis of crowding (i.e., very young children tend to consider crowded heaps as more, while three-to-four-year-olds used length as a cue and were more often incorrect).

Thus, as Langer (1977) suggests, Preconceptual reasoning is adequate to solve some tasks; we need not assume a higher level of logical structure just because children obtain correct answers. Further, there are serious interpretational difficulties when experimenters change the nature of the task and continue to claim to refute Piaget's findings.

Almost inevitably, students who read about or observe conservation of quantity and number tasks raise the question of verbal understanding. They argue that "younger children fail because they just don't know the meaning of more, less, or the same." But children as young as two or three can correctly make those comparisons before the transformations begin. When the experimenter adds clay, water, or M & M's, the child knows there is more. Maybe, argue students, "more" means "taller" or "longer" to a young child. In a sense, that is true, but the problems cannot be dismissed as "merely verbal." First, we must explain how the relational term "more" shifts in meaning from one dimension to another in young children. Second, we must explain the fact that younger children conceptualize transformations in one dimension at a time (height or weight, length of row, or number of units), while older children coordinate and compensate for changes in two dimensions. Finally, the lack of conservation in Preconceptual children is part of a general cognitive pattern in which they classify, seriate, and reason in similar ways in many nonverbal and verbal tasks. Thus, the child's problem of understanding conservation is not limited to the verbal meaning of several quantity relations; conservation rests on a set of cognitive structures which cannot be equated with the meaning of specific words.

Space. If quantity and number concepts provide answers to the questions, "How much?" and "How many?" then spatial concepts answer the question "Where?" As we shall see in later chapters, the concepts come together logically and developmentally in concepts of measurement—the answer to "How far from here to there?" Without the ability to locate objects in space, we would have no way of understanding the causal relations between them. A ball (A) hits another ball (B), which then moves. Did A cause B's motion? It is impossible to know, unless we have some conceptual method of organizing our experience of events in space, whether A ever came into contact with B. In considering space as adults, we organize it in Euclidian concepts of straight lines, shapes, and measurements of equivalence. The world, as we look out on it, seems to be organized in a three-dimensional coordinate system, with two horizontal dimensions (left–right; toward–away) and one vertical dimension. Somehow (it seems "self-evident") these dimensions exist as perpendicular to each other, and the center of the coordinate system seems to be some fixed point outside our own bodies. When we give directions to guests who are coming to our home, we do not tell them to turn right or left until we know the direction they are coming from. If we fail to make this distinction, they will usually ask for clarification. When they want to know how far it is, we give them an estimate for the most direct route, not the route which we took on a day when we detoured to do several errands. Spatial coordinates and distances are (or can be) independent of our own actions and point of view. Length is unaffected by the direction of movement; a Sunday drive from A to B and back by the same route from B to A covers the same distance. A short ruler and a long ruler will each yield the same measurements of a room, even though one ruler will be placed and moved more often than the other.

In two important volumes on the concepts of space and geometry (Piaget and Inhelder 1948; Piaget, Inhelder, and Szeminska 1948), it is shown that none of the above assumptions about space is true for the Preconceptual child. Further, not until mid-Concrete operations (at about age ten) do children develop consistent, three-dimensional conceptions and measurements of space. Two brief examples:

In a simple conservation of length task, pairs of sticks of 5 cm. or 10 cm. are lined up as in Figure 6. Young children judge them to be equally long. Then, one stick is displaced 1 cm. to the right or left and the child is questioned again about the relative length.

———————

——————— – – →

Preconceptual children follow the stick with their eyes, clearly centering on the end point without regarding the beginning. The ordering of the end points determines the judgment of length; change of position leads to nonconservation.

In a measurement task, a tower made of blocks, 80 cm. in height, stands on a table. The child is asked to make a tower of the same height on another table 2 m. away, the surface of which is 90 cm. lower than the first. Between the two tables is a large screen; the child cannot look directly, but can walk from one table to the other at any time. The child's task is to construct a tower the same height (length) as the first, on the lower table. He or she is given many more blocks than are necessary to build an equivalent tower and is also given paper strips and sticks which can be used as an intermediate measuring instrument. Only when the child's spontaneous efforts have been exhausted and the child has not already done so, is it suggested that the paper and sticks can be used as "helpers." Preconceptual children build their towers by guess and by visual comparison. They obviously attempt to make their tower the same height *from the floor* as the model; no intermediate measures (hands, body, rulers) are used.

Time. Piaget began his foreword to two related volumes on the concept of time (1946), movement and speed (1947) with a very casual throwaway line. "This work was promoted by a number of questions kindly suggested by Albert Einstein more than fifteen years ago when he presided over the first international course of lectures on philosophy and psychology at Davos" (Piaget, 1946, p. vii). Apparently Einstein was much taken with Piaget's work, specifically the possibility of establishing a developmental answer to a puzzle in the circular definitions of time and speed. In traditional physics, there is a law stating the relations among time, distance, and speed of movement of objects:

$$\text{Time} = \text{Distance moved} \times 1/\text{speed}$$

Time increases with longer distance and slower speed. But there is a circularity in this law, because speed is defined in terms of time; for example 55 miles per hour as a measure of speed is calculated as the time-per-unit-distance. It was hoped that studies of young children could disentangle the concepts of time, speed, and distance traveled, to show whether any of them were basic to the development of the others.

Time is the second of two basic organizing dimensions of experience. Just as adult conceptions of space are not given in the Preconceptual child's experience, so preconcepts of time are quite different from adult notions. In the development of time, the child seems to face an additional obstacle in the path of arriving at inferences about "How long?" "How far?" and "How fast?" In simple space concepts, all the data necessary to make inferences about distance or length may be in plain view. However, at the instant we are perceiving one event in a time series, the preceding events may have disappeared. According to Piaget, the first three essential ingredients in the development of time, distance, and speed concepts are: (a) the ability to represent and remember the order of events; (b) the ability to conceptualize intervals between events; (c) the avoidance of confusions between time and space. Preconceptual children have great difficulty with all three.

(a) Remembering order. As adults, we are accustomed to perceiving and remembering a sequence of events—first we get up, then we get washed, dressed, then eat breakfast, and so on. Despite my familiarity with much Piaget material, I was still surprised when I first learned that young children cannot represent novel sequences.

> In an experiment on spatial order (Piaget, 1946c), Preconceptual children see three balls—red, blue, yellow—roll along a track into a "tunnel" beginning at A and ending at B. They can predict which colored ball will emerge at B when rolled in direction AB but cannot predict which will emerge first from the tunnel when the balls are rolled in direction BA. After several trials, they begin to predict that the middle ball will come out of the tunnel first "because it's the blue one's turn."

For Preconceptual stage children,[2] a sequence of perceptions does not establish the perception (and representional memory) of a sequence (Piaget, 1946, p. 15).

The ordering of a young child's world is not always as fluctuating as these examples imply. In each case, the child was asked to represent and remember novel events. But sequences of events in life tend to recur, so that memory and representation become less important in establishing order in many specific areas (e.g., Mommy or Daddy comes home, then dinner, then play, then bed). However, in new events, the Preconceptual child has no stable schemes of temporal and spatial order. As hard as it is for adults to imagine, an event that just happened may be no more salient to a three-year old than one that hap-

[2]and Intuitive stage children, too.

pened last week or last month. The concept of future events will be equally idiosyncratic. And adult concepts of causality, which depend so much on temporal order (causes come *before* effects), will not be possible. Piaget mentions in passing the connection between time and causality (1946b, p. 4) and also briefly notes that disturbance in temporal ordering should be important in the study of psychopathology at any age; individuals diagnosed as psychotic often confuse and distort past, present, and future.

(b) Intervals in time and space. Between the beginning and end of each event there is a time interval (a duration), between the beginning and end of each object movement there is a space interval (a distance). Longer intervals imply longer times or distances.

Adult conceptions of time and space intervals have three properties, none of which is present in children's thought *until mid-Concrete operations* (ages nine to ten).

1. The amount of time between the beginning and end of an event, or the distance from start to finish, is independent of how the intervals are filled. However, for very young children, the more activity in a given time, the longer the interval is judged to be; the more trips (stops and starts) in a given space, the longer the distance is thought to be.
2. Intervals are independent of order: the time from beginning to end of an event is the same as the time from end to beginning; the distance travelled in direction AB equals the distance BA. But young children believe that a return journey takes a different amount of time and covers a different distance from the original trip.
3. Time and space intervals form a series of inclusions. If A, B, and C are in a straight line, it is longer and farther from A to C than it is from A to B. Young children cannot use this property as a cue to place events in order from beginning to end.

Now, adults make all of the mistakes I have been attributing to young children. We cannot be absolutely accurate judges of time when we are involved in an activity; sometimes return journeys do seem shorter or longer than the original trips. But adults have metric and other conceptual means for adjusting their estimates; they are aware of the subjective properties of "lived time." Preoperational children lack this awareness and have no way of adjusting for their privately determined judgments of time intervals.

(c) Confusion between time and space. In an intricate series of experiments, Piaget shows how spatial ordering dominates judgments of temporal ordering for the Preconceptual child. The primary research task involves a pair of tracks, mounted on a table, with trains (I and II) moving along each track. The experimenter can vary which train starts first and can also vary the speed of each train.

In one experiment (1946b), train (I) moves from the beginning to the end of the first track (left to right), while (II) moves more slowly and stops part way. After (I) has stopped, (II) continues but not to the end of the second track. All children testify that (II) was still moving while (I) was at rest. To avoid the ambiguity of "before," which can mean "in front of" or "earlier,"[3] Piaget tells the child that (I) stopped for lunch and asks whether (II) stopped before or after lunch.

> (age 4;6) Did they stop at the same time? —*No, the yellow one (I) stopped before II.* —Which stopped first? —*The blue one (II).* —Which one stopped earlier? —*(II)* —If (I) stops at lunch, when does (II) stop? —*Before lunch.* —See for yourself (the experiment is repeated). —*Yes (I) stopped first; it went on longer* (the beginning of recognition). —and the other one? (II) —*It stopped before lunch.* —Look carefully (the experiment is repeated yet again.) —*Yes, (I) went on longer; it stopped here* (indicating the end of the track) *so it stopped first.* —But, when it stopped, wasn't the other one still moving? —*Yes.* —So, which one stopped first? —*The blue one* (II). (Adapted from Piaget, 1946b, p. 93)

This sounds very much like the brown beads–wooden beads problem, with the child vacillating between different meanings of "first." In order to show that this is not simply a verbal misunderstanding, Piaget repeats the experiment with both tracks stretched out in one straight line. From a common beginning, the trains travel in opposite directions. Without the strong pull of spatial cues as before (where (I) remains farther to the right than (II) even though it stopped first), Preconceptual children have little difficulty in stating that (I) stopped first and that (II) stopped after lunch. Piaget also cites other examples in which children at this stage do make verbal distinctions: "It goes on longer because it finishes farther." Thus, they combine a verbal differentiation with a conceptual confusion between time and space when the cues conflict. The meaning of a word in and of itself is not the issue; errors involving time and space are logical and inferential.

These examples, and others in quite different experimental tasks, all indicate that the Preconceptual child confuses space and time; final spatial order dominates judgments of simultaneity, succession, and distance. Further, the examples indicate that order and duration are themselves confused; the objects that finish second do not necessarily take longer time, according to children in the Preoperational stage.

Even before the precise experiments with moving objects and tracks, Piaget investigated the child's concept of age as a dimension of lived time. Focusing on order and duration concepts, Piaget asked children about the order of birth of members of their family and whether the duration between the ages is preserved. In general, he found exactly the same stages in these verbal interviews as he did in the interviews directed to observation of moving objects. In the Preconceptual substage, height (space) and age (time) are inseparable; taller children are thought to be older; adults who are no longer growing in height are deemed not to increase in age. And children assume that it is possible to catch

[3]French and English languages both mix spatial and temporal metaphors.

up. "I'm two years younger than my brother, but two years from now we'll be the same age." They may be younger than siblings, but egocentrically, they believe that they were born first. Time starts with their own birth; nothing much happens before that.

A note on speed brings us back to Einstein's initial questions about whether time and speed or distance concepts are developmentally prior. Piaget's experiments show that early time concepts are always affected by the speed of objects but that speed is judged independent of time *or* distance. At first it is equated with the perception of overtaking. If one object passes another it is judged to be moving more quickly; if it does not, the two are perceived as moving at the same speed, regardless of their actual velocities and regardless of where and when the objects began their journeys. Piaget's response to Einstein then, was that speed as judged by overtaking is a prior concept to time and distance. However, as an adult-level concept, speed is not achieved until Formal operations. Piaget's documentation of the developmentally inseparable nature of time, movement, and speed provide data consistent with the space–time concepts of relativity theory. In fact, two physicists have reconstructed the theory of relativity based on postulates derived from Piaget's developmental theory.

The preconcept: A summary

Everywhere Piaget looks at the two-to-four-year-old child, the findings have a similar pattern.[4] In both nonverbal and verbal classifications and orderings, preconcepts are fluctuating, private, one-attribute-at-a-time groupings of elements. Reasoning is transductive, from particular to particular, though it sounds as if conclusions are general. Given this conceptual system, it is evident that Preconceptual children do not conserve quantities, number, length, or time.

In the experiments and tests described above, Piaget is focusing on cognitive conceptions, not perceptual understandings. When young children are looking at objects, they can discriminate among them using multidimensional criteria; they can locate objects in time and space; they use language which recognizes more than one aspect of a situation. However, Preconceptual children have great difficulty representing and mentally coordinating simultaneous transformations of two or more dimensions. The child's conception of a series of events in a conservation task is dominated by the perceived end states of a set of transformations. The beginnings and the transformations themselves tend to be ignored. The Preconceptual child's conception of world is determined by how it looks and how it looks right now, with the likelihood that it will change at any moment. We should remember that Preconceptual children are not usually

[4]To what extent these similarities are dictated by the facts and to what extent they represent Piaget's own structuring of the facts is an issue I will return to in Part IV.

bothered by the resulting fluctuations and inconsistencies; from their point of view, that's just the way the world is arranged.

Piaget is often rebuked for focusing so much on what the child hasn't got and can't do. But his work provides a much-needed antidote to our tendencies to assume that children are just inexperienced versions of adults who think the way we do, though not as well. All of Piaget's work in the Preconceptual substage (and subsequent substages) demonstrates that experience is filtered and organized through a set of conceptual structures. These structures have regularities and stabilities of their own, even when they lead to fluctuating conceptions of a changing world.

Except in his discussions of symbolic development, Piaget himself sometimes forgets to emphasize the advances of Preconceptual thought over the Sensorimotor stage. Picture a six-month-old in the initial phases of constructing object permanence and a four-year-and six-month-old earnestly discussing the relative speed of two trains. First and foremost, concepts are now internalized and interiorized *mental* schemes, not so directly and inextricably linked with specific experienced events. Preconceptual children think *about* events, arranging and rearranging them, even if not in the correct order. The ability to fantasize, so evident in symbolic play, is a part of all cognitive activity. As a symbolic medium, language is just one of the ways in which events can be represented and understood, but it is especially important in facilitating social interaction and the exchange of points of view. It allows two or more people to learn about events which are not present to the senses and increases the content of what children can think about. In widening the cognitive and social world, language also increases the possibility that the child will be presented with disequilibrating events which can stimulate intellectual and interpersonal development.

COGNITIVE AND SOCIAL DEVELOPMENT

In his first book-length psychological publication—*Language and Thought of the Child* (1923)—and in *The Moral Judgment of the Child* (1932), Piaget explored the relation between cognitive and social development. However, it was not until the 1960s, with strong stimulation from Kohlberg (1963) and Flavell (1968), that theorists and researchers in significant numbers, began to follow up the social development issues raised in Piaget's early works. Here are three examples relevant to the Preconceptual stage: egocentrism, identity, and causality. Moral judgments have not usually been studied until the Intuitive substage (four to seven years).

Physical and social egocentrism

Piaget (1923) originally studied egocentrism in the young child's tendency to use language without taking into account the requirements of the listener;

egocentric speech is private and full of unspecified referents. Later, Piaget and Inhelder (1948) extended the concept to describe children's inability, until age nine or ten, to coordinate spatial perspectives concerning physical objects in the Three Mountains Task. Although some early writers (e.g., McCarthy, 1930) wrongly assumed that egocentric means selfish rather than centered on one's own point of view, others have found it a useful notion to bridge the domains of cognitive perspective-taking and social interaction.

In Piaget's own work there are two milestones in the decline of egocentrism (or, the development of perspective). First, there is the eighteen-month-to-two-year-old child's separation of physical self from objects during Substage 6 of the Sensorimotor stage. For the first time, the child is able to conceptualize the location of his or her own body as an object among other objects. Second, there is the achievement of three mountains perspective, in which nine- and ten-year-olds are able to conceptualize their own psychological perspective as one among many possible ways of seeing and understanding events. When the Three Mountains Task is treated as the prototypic measure of egocentrism, there is almost an eight-year gap between the two milestones. Some children younger than four cannot even comprehend the Three Mountains Task well enough to be tested; the conclusion at first was that psychological egocentrism is rampant in the Preconceptual stage.

One approach to the analysis of perspective development is the by-now-familiar strategy of constructing a different kind of task with a different response measure. Shantz and Watson (1970) had children view a "landscape" in a covered box and then move to the opposite side to view it again. On some trials the landscape also rotated 180° so that the child looked in to see the same view again. Nearly half of the three-to-five-year-olds in the study showed some surprise or startle on these trials, indicating a violation of some already-established expectancies about points of view.

Rather than claiming that egocentrism declines much earlier than Piaget suggests, Flavell (1974) and his colleagues (Lempers, Flavell, and Flavell, 1977) argue that there are two levels in the development of perspective after the Sensorimotor stage, with each level identified by a different kind of task.

> At Level 2 the child can represent the fact that an object or array of objects has different appearances when a person views it from different perspectives. At Level 1, the child does not yet represent such object perspectives but only whether the person sees the object qua object at all. . . . The Level 1 child only represents what whole object is seen, or whether someone is presently looking at it. The Level 2 child may also represent *how* it appears from a particular position and certainly knows *that* it presents *some* particular appearance determined by the viewer's location in relation to it (Lempers, Flavell, and Flavell, p. 6).

Administering 24 Level 1 tasks to 60 children, they showed that by three years of age the children developed high levels of skill in pointing out objects to others, showing pictures of objects to another person so that he or she sees it right side up, removing obstacles from others' eyes so that they can see a given object, hiding an object so that others can see it, and so on. These Preconceptual children are quite aware that others *have* another point of view, but they cannot represent how objects and events will appear to other people.

Shantz (1975), in an outstanding review of social cognitive development, categorizes the above studies as concerned with the child's knowledge of what someone else is seeing. Other studies indicate that Preconceptual children develop a beginning awareness of what others are feeling (e.g., Borke, 1973). American and Chinese three-year-olds recognize situations which produce happiness in others but have more difficulty with fear, sadness, and anger. And still other studies (e.g., DeVries, 1970) show that three- and four-year-olds are just beginning to have a notion of what someone else is thinking. When asked to fool an observer by hiding a penny in either hand, they sometimes alternate hands, indicating some need for a strategy to outwit another person. They do not, however, as most seven-year-olds do, attempt to be unpredictable to their opponent (i.e., to have a specific idea such as, "He's thinking 'this one,' so I'll hide it on the other side.") These examples again illustrate an awareness of other points of view, without the Level 2 perspective-taking[5] that allows older children to begin to see the world through others' eyes.

As Piaget noted initially (1923), Preconceptual egocentrism is particularly evident in verbal communication. When explaining to another child how a toy works, the youngster at this substage uses many indefinite terms and leaves out important information (Elkind, 1967b). Although this observation is sometimes explained by saying that the speaker fails to take the listener's point of view, it can also be explained as an outgrowth of the child's assumption that words carry much more information than they actually do. The child says, "I gave it to him" as if the words "it" and "him" convey the specific figurative properties of the thing and person which they represent. In short, the assumption of correspondence between symbols and referents is another example of both cognitive and social egocentrism. Elkind's analysis of egocentric communication emphasizes the fact that all of the characteristics of the Preoperational period are intertwined. Fluctuating classifications, uncoordinated operations, idiosyncratic verbal symbols, single-dimensional reasoning, and egocentrism (one point of view at a time) are all part of the same structural orientation toward the world. When two- and three-year-olds get together, very often there is parallel play in which each child engages in symbolic play beside the other one. When conversations begin, the egocentric quality is evident.

> Child 1: "I have a dog.
> Child 2: "I went to my grandma's yesterday" (which may actually have been last week or month).
> Child 1: "It's brown and white."
> Child 2: "We had fun there."
> Child 1: "I wash him sometimes." . . . and so on.

[5]Counting the achievement of physical perspective during the Sensorimotor stage as one level, this should really be labelled as Level 3.

Physical and social identity

In an invited lecture at Clark University, Piaget (1968b) described important distinctions between concepts of conservation and concepts of identity. For example, the six-year-olds who deny that there is the same *amount* of water when one of two beakers is poured into another of different shape, are quite clear that it is the *same water*. While conservation deals with quantitative aspects of objects which change in appearance, yet remain the same (height, weight, volume, number), identity refers to an essential quality of an object which makes it identifiable as particular or unique.

Piaget investigates the child's concept of physical identity in experiments with pouring water from one beaker to another (Is it the same water?), and bending a wire into an arc (Is it still the same wire?). Piaget and Voyat (1968) also ask children about the identity of plants in the process of growth (actually a chemical solution which looks like a growing plant). The task is to decide whether the "seed" and various other stages are part of the same plant. These questions begin to draw on conceptions of time and order as well as qualitative similarity. In an extension to the area of social cognition, Piaget asks about the identity of the experimenter (Does a picture of the experimenter at a younger age show the same person as the one with whom the child is now talking?). Preconceptual children generally do not see things or people as having a core and consistent identity over time. Remember Jacqueline's confusion about Lucienne in different clothes, and Hartley and Hartley's examples of perception of multiple parent roles. Changing a salient perceptual or role characteristic seems to make an important difference in how the Preconceptual child regards another person.

> Parents often note that their four-year-olds become quite jealous when the other parent comes home and the partners embrace. Usually some form of Oedipal interpretation is placed on the event; little boys are jealous of their father's sexual role with mother; little girls are outraged by the fact that mother is taking a fantasied but forbidden place with father. Perhaps, though, the child's upset is related to the fact that mother or father, in becoming wife or husband, has changed roles and is therefore not available at that moment, conceptually and literally, as a parent.

Piaget extends his investigation of the relation between physical and social identity to the area of personal identity—whether children have a sense of themselves as unique individuals, existing through time from birth.[6] He asks children to draw pictures of themselves or shows a series of pictures of them taken at yearly intervals. Preconceptual children cannot arrange the pictures in sequence. They seem to have little idea that their "self" of a few days ago is relevant to what is happening now, today. As parents we way in exasperation,

[6]This notion of personal identity precedes Erikson's notion of ego identity (1968) which I will discuss in connection with adolescence and Formal operations (Chapter 11).

"But I explained that to you yesterday!" In some sense, the child of yesterday may be someone else. Children may also see themselves as different people when they are in different places. As a three-year-old, our oldest daughter was certain that she would be a different person with another name when she attended preschool for the first time.

The Preconceptual child's notion of plasticity in identity extends to concepts of gender. Until the recent publicity about sex-change operations, it has been a fundamental assumption of adults that boys grow up to be men and girls grow up to be women. Kohlberg (1966a, 1967) indicates that four-year-olds have no such expectation; some of them are not clear that people remain people and cannot turn into animals and back again, as fairy tales sometimes suggest.

These examples imply that there are similarities in the developmental sequence and timing of physical, social, and personal identity. Evidence for such a conclusion comes only from studies of children at the next (Intuitive) substage of Preoperations.

Physical and social causality

Anne Bernstein and I (1975) became interested in the parallels between physical and social concepts in children's ideas about how babies come to be born. In all of the polemic about sex education (e.g., Breasted, 1971), we could find only three studies, all of a narrow age range, which investigated what children actually think (Conn, 1947; Kreitler and Kreitler, 1966; Moore and Kendall, 1971). It seemed to us that children's notions about the origins of babies ought to be related to their general ideas about the origins or causes of physical events. The general assumption of sex education literature is that children's strange ideas about where babies come from are a matter of misinformation. If Piaget's general approach is relevant, then ideas about babies should emerge in a regular sequence in which children *make up* their own answers and assimilate what they are told to their general cognitive level. Twenty boys and girls at each of three age levels (three to four, seven to eight, eleven to twelve) were interviewed and tested. Some results from the youngest subjects are presented here; the older children will be described in Chapters 7, 9, and 11.

Concepts of physical causality were assessed with an adaptation of Laurendeau and Pinard's (1962) standardized version of Piaget's interviews (1927). All children were asked to tell the interviewer what night is; why it is dark; where the dark comes from; and what makes it night. They were also asked if "we can make night in this room," if putting down the blinds would make it dark, and to explain where the dark comes from.

The first three levels of Laurendeau and Pinard's seven-level scale, apply to children in the Preconceptual period.

Level 0: No understanding of the question; refusal to answer.
Level 1: Absolute finalism. The end result is the cause (e.g., it becomes dark so we may go to sleep).

Level 2: Artificialism mixed with finalism. Like a manufactured product, some maker produces the result, but the process is still dominated by the effect (e.g., it becomes dark because God calls the dark in, or Mother puts the light out so we can sleep.

These levels and the subsequent ones in Laurendeau and Pinard's scale apply not only to the cause of night, but also to the apparent movement of the sun, the formation of clouds, the origin of the wind, and so on.

In an analogous interview constructed and administered by Anne Bernstein, the same children were asked about the origin of babies. Each interview included the following questions: "How do people get babies?" "What does the word 'born' mean?" "What does it mean to say someone [e.g., you] was born?" "How do mothers get to be mothers?" "How did your mother get to be your mother?" "When did she start being your mother?" "How do fathers get to be fathers?" "When did he start being your father?" "How was it that (name of younger sibling) came to live in your family and be your sister/brother?"

A scale was developed which followed the structural outline of Laurendeau and Pinard.

Level 0: No understanding, refusal to answer.

Level 1: No causality principle is needed because babies have always existed. The question, "How do people get babies?" is understood as spatial, not causal; it becomes "Where do people get babies?" (e.g., You go to the baby store and buy one (three years, eight months)). —How did the baby happen to be in your Mommy's tummy? —*It just grows inside.* —How did it get there? —*It's there all the time. Mommy doesn't have to do anything. She waits until she feels it.* —You said that the baby wasn't in there when you were there. —*Yeah, then he was in the other place in . . . in America.* —In America? —*Yeah, in somebody else's tummy.* —In somebody else's tummy? —*Yeah, and then he went through somebody's vagina, then he went in, um, my mommy's tummy.* —In whose tummy was he before? —*Um, the, I don't know, who his, her name is. It's a her.* (three years, six months).

At Level 1, children appear to be assimilating directly from their own experience. There is no "first cause." If something comes out, it can go back in.

Level 2: Artificialism mixed with finalism. —How does the baby get in the tummy? —*Just make it first.* —How? —*Well, you just make it. You put some eyes on it. . . . Put the head on, and hair, some hair all curls.* —With? —*You make it with head stuff.* —How? —*You find it at a store that makes it. . . . Well, they get it and then they put it in the tummy and then it goes quickly out.* (ages three years, seven months).

A few children at Level 2 connect a father with the birth process, but assimilate what they have been told to a mechanical process. A girl responds: —If the seed is in the Daddy, how does it get on the egg? —*I don't know. Cause he can't really open up all his tummies.* —Then how? —*It rolls out.* —How does it get to the egg? —*Well, I think that the Daddy gets it.* —How? —*Puts his hand in the tummy.* —Whose? —*His tummy.* —Then?

—He puts it on the bottom of Mommy and the Mommy gets the, gets the egg out of her tummy, and puts the egg on top of the seed. And then they close their tummies . . . and the baby is born. . . .

The same children were also administered a task involving concepts of social identity, which required them to locate the same person in pictures taken over a span of twenty years (Lemke, 1973) and a task assessing physical conservation of water. Over the whole age range of the study, there were consistently high correlations (ranging from .73–.83) among physical and social causality, social identity, and conservation measures. Within the Preconceptual period (three to four-year-olds) responses to the origin of babies (social causality) were correlated significantly with physical causality (r = .50) and even more highly with conservation of water (r = .68). The social identity task was too difficult for children at this level. We concluded that children's concepts concerning the origin of babies follow a developmental sequence and are embedded in a matrix of physical and social concepts. In this research, and in the studies of egocentrism and identity, we have some beginning indications of parallel development across three domains: cognition of physical objects; cognition of social objects; and in the case of egocentrism, social behavior as well.

COGNITIVE AND EMOTIONAL DEVELOPMENT

People tend to think of emotional and social development synonymously, but Piaget suggests that it may be important to maintain the distinction: we should not forget the importance of emotional factors in the child's interaction with the *physical* world. Unfortunately we do not yet have a body of empirical data concerning the interrelations among cognitive, social, and emotional development in the young child. Animal research and psychoanalytic theory both indicate that social–emotional factors affect the organism's tendency to learn about the physical world. Harlow's extensive studies (1958) show that monkeys deprived of the early social–emotional security, stemming from contact with real or "cloth" mothers, do not develop much curiosity in exploring their physical surroundings. Freud and Burlingham (1944), Erikson (1950), Spitz (1946) also indicate that early disruptions of emotional attachment have serious consequences for the child's engagement in seeking knowledge.

Piaget's findings emphasize the possibility that cognitive factors critically affect emotional development. In both social and physical arenas, cognitive structure places limits on the child's interpretation of the world and therefore influences his or her appraisal (Lazarus, 1966) of what is pleasurable, what is threatening, and so on. Consistent with this structure, the feelings of the Preconceptual child are generally fluctuating, centered on a particular event, changing when events change.

A particularly salient example of the cognitive generation gap in the interpretation of feeling-words occurs in the Preconceptual child's expression of angry feelings toward parents or siblings. "I hate you," they may shout as they slam the door to their room. Adults interpret this statement as if the child has a clear conception of "I," a clear conception of a separate other, and a notion of an enduring negative relation between the two. But the Preconceptual child is probably using words like "hate" to convey the feeling, "You are really making me mad right now." Because of this difference in meanings, children often recover their spirits quickly, while adults take much longer to get over the hurt. Five minutes after a tantrum, a three-year-old can come back cheerfully and ask a still-upset parent, "What's for dinner?"

For the Preconceptual child, feelings, like concepts, are one-at-a-time: either–or, love or hate. Adult notions of ambivalence (two simultaneous and conflicting feelings about the same person or thing) are beyond their understanding. So are adult ideas such as, "I'm angry at what you are doing, I'm not angry at you." Although this distinction will not be understood as intended for some years to come, it is useful for the adult to make and for the young child to hear.

Just as the verbal symbol is not fully separated from the action or object in the Preconceptual and Intuitive substages, so there is still no clear separation between internal feelings and overt behavior. Children who get so angry that they wish their parents dead, may feel as if they have taken some action against them. And, children who experience great affection for parents also believe that their feelings have somehow been conveyed; a young child is often surprised to the point of disbelief to find that others are unaware of his or her emotional states. This egocentrism is sometimes augmented when parents demonstrate uncanny ability to "read the mind" of young children who are more expressive than they realize.

The ability of Preconceptual children to view themselves as physical objects and Piaget's claim that thoughts and feelings are always part of cognition, indicate that children in the Preconceptual substage are beginning to develop explicit feelings about themselves. There are no data on this topic within the Piagetian tradition and so I will provide a few speculations. First, the Preconceptual child's concept of self is a preconcept, focusing on idiosyncratic details. While adults may view the child as competent, resourceful, and so on, the child may be focusing on less positive incidents. Conversely, adults may assume that the child is feeling badly about himself or herself, while the child has another view. Second, the fluctuating nature of preconcepts and lack of enduring self-identity suggests that feelings about the self are fleeting and changing. While an ongoing set of negative experiences may have a cumulative negative effect on the child's self-evaluation, no single event, unless it is highly traumatic, is likely to affect the natural resilience of young children. Third, psychoanalysts tend to make much of the tie between thought and action and assume that three- and four-year-olds often have guilt for what they have felt but never expressed. If guilt is a feeling that internalized standards of behavior have been violated and we learn that such standards have not even begun to be constructed until the Intuitive substage (see below), then Preconceptual children may not yet have such a feeling in their repertoires. They may feel bad; they may feel shame; but guilt as a self-evaluation may require a higher level of cognitive structuring than many two-to-four-year-olds have achieved.

Fourth, the development of mental symbols in the Preconceptual substage increases the range of children's fantasies and the use of fantasies for competence and mastery in the real world. Along with this bonus, as with every developmental advance, comes a new set of difficulties for the child. For example, the results of research from more than four decades ago (Jersild and Holmes, 1935) suggest that during the early Preconceptual period, there is a substantial increase in children's fears. As the child explores the recesses of his or her mind, finding superheroes, magicians, and good fairies, he or she may also discover fearful and terrible monsters or anticipated disasters (What if my parents never come back for me? What if there is a fire? etc.). Under relatively safe conditions, most children enjoy the scariness of thinking about monsters and disasters or hearing about them in fairy tales (Bettelheim, 1976). Sometimes however, the assimilative fantasies do not trigger realistic accommodation to the world, so Preconceptual children become frightened by their own creations. It may be difficult for parents attempting to deal with a frightened child to rejoice in the fact that this fear may also be signaling new and adaptive conceptual advances!

Most Preconceptual children are propelled further into the arena of social interaction by all of the emotional and social developments which I have been discussing. As they attempt to try out their new-found social, communicational, intellectual, and physical skills, they often become increasingly involved in a struggle for autonomy from parental restrictions. Freud and Erikson tend to see this struggle for autonomy as related specifically to anal functions and toilet training of eighteen-month-to-three-year-olds, but it is also possible to interpret the struggle as an inevitable and expectable outcome of the child's developing intellectual competence (White, 1959; Kohlberg, 1969).

EDUCATIONAL IMPLICATIONS FOR PRESCHOOLS

Differing theoretical assumptions

Preschools often look very similar to one another and very different from elementary classrooms beyond the kindergarten level.[7] Blocks, toys, arts and crafts materials, dress-up clothes, and sometimes pets, are available in every corner. The rooms usually open on outdoor areas with swings, slides, wagons, tricycles, and sandboxes. These environments reflect increasingly wider recog-

[7]We will see that British Infant schools (grades 1–3) are an exception; in general physical organization and materials they appear to be more like preschools.

nition of the idea that the child's "work" is play and that preschool is a place where play constitutes a major approach to learning.

Despite similarities in learning environments and agreements concerning the importance of play, there are important differences among preschool programs, based primarily on differing conceptions of intellectual development. Many preschools operate on flowering-seed assumptions. The school is a safe physical and social environment in which young children will develop if left to explore on their own. Beyond the purchase of equipment and materials there is very little specification by adults of what each child should be learning. By contrast, the clean-slate approach to preschool education adopts a very structured curriculum. There are designated periods during the day for the direct teaching of specific facts and skills. An extreme example is the DISTAR approach developed by Bereiter and Engelman (1966) which includes daily drills on verbal concepts and definitions. In the interactive generator–transformer conception of learning, the teacher is very active in selecting and organizing the content of the curriculum, but the focus in the classroom is on general structural concepts to be learned in whatever activities are chosen by the child.

I am aware of only one study which systematically compares a Piaget-based curriculum with other approaches. Lenrow (1968) contrasted three types of preschools; all of them emphasized the child's active role in learning, but only one focused specifically on Piagetian cognitive dimensions. Over the summer of the preschool program and into the next kindergarten year, there was significant intellectual and social growth in children from all three programs, with few differences attributable to a specific curriculum. It is too early to tell whether basic similarities among preschool environments override the effects of a curriculum based on theory. An outstanding study by Miller and Dyer (1975), which does not include a Piagetian curriculum, indicates that in the short run, at least, there *are* differential effects of curriculum on the cognitive development of preschoolers. However, in the long run (four years), the differential effects were primarily on "noncognitive" variables such as curiosity and inventiveness. More research is obviously needed to establish what kind of preschool program works best in which developmental domain for what kinds of children.

At this point I will simply describe in more detail the features which would be emphasized in a Piagetian preschool. The examples are taken primarily from the writings of Kamii (1970, 1972), an American educator who has worked with Piaget in Geneva.

Curriculum

In my description of Sensorimotor and Preconceptual development I have described only a small fraction of the natural learning activities which children are engaged in every day. In the cognitive domain, they have been working on: knowledge of physical objects; logico-mathematical knowledge such as classification, seriation, and transductive reasoning; and above all, on the development of representational symbols. In the social–emotional domain, they have been involved in: expanding their intrinsic motivation to explore the world; coming to know themselves and others as social objects; learning social rules and self control; establishing relationships with family members and other adults and peers. These natural learning activities are precisely the ones specified by Kamii as the curriculum for a Piagetian preschool.

In recent decades, educational curricula at all levels have begun to focus on teaching concepts as well as facts. One of Piaget's most important messages is that *words are not to be equated with concepts*. The conceptual notions underlying the Preconceptual child's use of words have very different structures from the same words used by adults. Concept learning, especially classification and seriation, involves logico-mathematical experience with actions on objects, not simply the learning of an appropriate verbal label or name.

Despite adults' and children's own fascination with language and communication, Piaget's description of development suggests that basic learning in the Preconceptual substage has strong nonverbal action-oriented components. The child who is playing with sand, pouring it into different containers is having fun, but is at the same time also strengthening his or her conceptual knowledge of empty, full, reversibility, identity, and so on. Arranging things and putting them in piles, experimenting with how things work, feel, smell, and taste are all ways of enriching both schemas and schemes. In Piaget's view, as we have seen, accommodative and assimilative activities are equally necessary for cognitive development. While every material and medium can be used in either way, some materials and activities tend to emphasize one side of the equilibration process. Sand, water, and paints tend to be used in assimilative ways. Pretend games like dress-up, shopping, cooking, tend to foster imitative accommodative functioning. Musical activities in the preschool tend to include both assimilative and accommodative functions—the child's own music-making may be assimilative, while the learning of songs involves accommodations to pitch, rhythm, and words. In the process of learning songs, the child is working on sequence, pattern, and meaning. And, at least on the verbal level, songs and rhymes familiarize children with numerical and causal ideas which they will return to later in a more action-oriented way ("Three Little Kittens," "The Alphabet Song," etc.).

The role of the teacher

What the teacher does in a preschool, or in any school, should be based primarily on his or her conception of the child's intellectual functioning. First and foremost the teacher must pay attention to the active assimilative aspects of the child.

> The role of the teacher in a Piagetian preschool . . . cannot be one of simply transmitting all types of knowledge to children. Her function is to help the child

> construct his own knowledge directly from feedback from objects and through his own reasoning with objects. In physical knowledge, for example, if the child believes that a block will sink, she encourages him to prove the correctness of his statement. If he predicts that chocolate pudding will turn into chocolate, she says, "Let's leave it here until tomorrow and find out what happens." Most four-year-olds predict, before a marble is placed in one pan of a balance, that that side will go down and that the other side will go up. When this prediction is given, the teacher does not say, "You are right," but instead says, "Let's find out"; she lets the objects give the feedback from the child's own action on objects. This is how she indirectly builds the child's initiative, curiosity, and confidence in his own ability to figure things out [i.e., cognitive learning is an arena for social–emotional learning as well] (Kamii, 1972, p. 117).

While the emphasis in these examples is on the child's activity, we should not ignore the active, stimulating part played by the teacher's questions and comments.

Because learning is also accommodative, there are some times where the teachers must play a direct teaching role. Kamii emphasizes this approach in the transmitting of social knowledge, which she defines as factual information about arbitrary conventions. For example, the teacher should feel free to tell the child that something is called a "pendulum" or a "tape recorder" and that we have to pay pretend money to buy things from a play store, and that a child cannot have birthday celebrations two days in a row. It seems to me that the teacher also has an active role to play in the statement and enforcement of rules about social interaction. But here, efforts to promote accommodation, especially when stated in the form of verbal rules, may run into the assimilative tendencies of the child.

> As we shall see, adult moral or value principles may have little meaning to the child. Even patient lectures or reasoning are unlikely to be successful if the concepts are far beyond the child's reach. I once heard two preschool children in an argument. One was saying angrily, "I'll hit you. I'll knock your head off. I'll kill you." Then, searching for an even stronger punishment, "I'll—I'll *reason* with you!"

It *is* possible for the adult to teach children to share—by making and enforcing an arbitrary rule of taking turns, or by physically removing objects when the child is not, at that moment, able to share. Thinking about sharing requires that we adults take time to find out how the child interprets things and to anticipate potential problems. If a parent takes a two-year-old child to visit another child, the almost inevitable confrontation about sharing toys can be avoided if the visitor brings along a few toys of his or her own.

The teacher in a Piagetian preschool is not always presenting tasks and asking questions. Most of the time a teacher grounded in the theory simply takes special note of the child's activities which are relevant to the development of operational schemes.

> One day in water play, for example, a child was surprised to find out that a fairly

> heavy block floated. She got up to get a larger block, thinking that a larger one would sink. Upon finding that the larger one also floated, she went to get another still larger one in an attempt to find one that would be heavy enough to sink in water. This spirit of generating a graduated order in a question raised by the child himself seems much more important than memorizing the generalization that wooden objects float regardless of size. In an intuitive way, this child learned that the phenomenon of sinking depends on something other than absolute weight and size (Kamii, 1972, p. 109).

In this example, the teacher did not interact with the child at all. Rather, the theoretical orientation influenced what to watch for and helped to provide an interpretation of the potential significance of the child's explorations for intellectual development.

A final related point. Children in Piagetian preschools do not spend all their time classifying and sorting objects and doing experiments. They are engaged in many of the same activities that all preconceptual children do, both in and out of the school setting. Sometimes, though, the theory provides a different interpretation of the function of these activities. For example, pretend play and arts and crafts are important not only because they are fun and creative, but also because they serve to develop and extend the child's construction of images and other representational symbols.

Cognitive, social, and emotional learning

In analyses of curricula and teaching methods, great pains are usually taken to distinguish cognitive, social, and emotional domains of development. While Piaget, too, defines them in different ways, his structural theory emphasizes the potential interrelationship and interaction among them. How a child feels in school may affect both quantity and quality of learning. Conversely, how a child learns can affect feelings about the materials and about the self.

In discussions with preschool teachers and parents, I have found that the greatest area of concern seems to be the frequent and intense emotional–social behaviors such as crying at separation from parent, tantrums, fighting, lack of sharing and at the other extreme of intensity, withdrawal, and shyness. I have no general prescription for these issues, but I do find that an approach to understanding the child's view of events can be helpful. Is the child actually disconsolate about a parent leaving? Often when parents leave without prolonged goodbyes, the child cries briefly and then proceeds happily on to play. Does fighting mean that two children will hate each other forever? Again, the children may be cooperating in a game two minutes after a fight. In these and other situations, adults may have to step in and set limits; what I am attempting to convey here is that adult interpretations of child feelings are not necessarily applicable to preschoolers. Further, I believe that some applications of the clinical method may be necessary to find out how the child's interpretation is affecting his or her behavior. Simply asking questions may help. But a brief experiment (e.g., having a parent leave quickly) may also serve to verify an interpretation.

Finally, while the opportunity for social interaction among children in a preschool has value in its own right, it also may serve as an important experience for stimulating intellectual and emotional development. And, as the child's cognitive world enlarges, there may be increased ability and motivation for communication and other forms of interaction with other people.

CHAPTER 7

Preoperations:
Early and Late Intuitive Periods

In the last chapter, I described the Preoperational child in transition from a system of Sensorimotor symbols to a new system of mental symbols. These symbols took the form of Preconceptual schemes of classes and relationships. Now, during the Intuitive substage (ages four to seven), the child constructs more stable and less private classes and relations, and then coordinates them in an overt trial and error fashion. Despite the rapid growth in the power and flexibility of mental symbols, children in the Intuitive substage of Preoperations do not achieve the mental *coordinations* of classes and relations necessary for the development of operational intelligence.

Philosophers and mathematicians sometimes use the term "intuition" to describe a faculty of the mind which directly grasps self-evident truths (see Chapter 14). Piaget adopts this term as a metaphor to describe four-to-seven-year olds' certainty about their knowledge on one hand, and the almost complete lack of awareness about how they know what they know, on the other. The lack of awareness can be seen in the Intuitive child's inattention to the details of justifying a conclusion.

> Given a pair of clay balls in which A has more clay than B, and another pair in which B has more clay than C, children near the end of the Intuitive substage do not have to look in order to respond that A has more clay than C. But if they are asked what leads to this conclusion, they may shrug and say, "You told me" or, "Because A had more than B" (which is correct but incomplete). Often, the look in the child's eye implies, "It's *obvious* that A has more, why are you asking?"

Generally, Piaget's descriptions of development between the ages of four and seven divide the Intuitive substage into Early and Late periods, which he numbers I or II, or letters A and B, but does not name. In some cases, especially in the work on numbers, classes, and relations, the Early Intuitive period overlaps in age (four to five), and structural level, the Preconceptual substage described in Chapter 6. In other cases, especially in Piaget's work on time and space, he locates the Early Intuitive period slightly later in age (five to six) and clearly differentiates it from Preconceptual performance. Since Piaget in his own research did not use the same subjects in his different investigations, we do not know whether stages occur at slightly varying times for the different major conceptual content categories. More recently, normative studies are beginning to provide answers to questions about individual consistencies and inconsistencies in developmental levels of performance (See Chapter 12). But what is central for Piaget's own work is the demonstration of similarity in the sequence of structural development across all tasks.

COGNITIVE DEVELOPMENT

Classification

The Intuitive child's approach to classification has been extensively studied as a topic of interest in its own right (Inhelder and Piaget, 1959) and also as a conceptual component of number development (Piaget, 1942; Piaget and Szeminska, 1941). As in every Piagetian investigation, a large number of tasks have been created in an attempt to converge on a diagnosis of the general cognitive structure underlying the child's specific responses. Here are two representative examples from *The Early Growth of Logic* (Inhelder and Piaget, 1959). The first assesses additive classification of flowers (primulas + other flowers = flowers), and the second assesses multiplicative classifications of geometrical shapes (red shapes × red square shapes = red squares).

I have briefly described the first task in Chapter 6. Children were asked to group twenty pictures: eight primulas (four yellow, four other); eight other flowers; four objects. From an adult point of view the pictures can be classified in a four-level hierarchy; yellow and other primulas; primulas + other flowers; flowers + other objects; things (see Figure 7). After observing children's spontaneous classifications, Piaget questions them about the relations of part to whole classes ("Can I place this primula in the pile with the other flowers?") and about the quantitative relations among different parts of the hierarchy ("Are there more flowers or more primulas?"). This rather complex task assesses the child's ability to combine classes additively, to understand the relations between all and some (class inclusion), and to understand the structure of a nested hierarchy of classes.

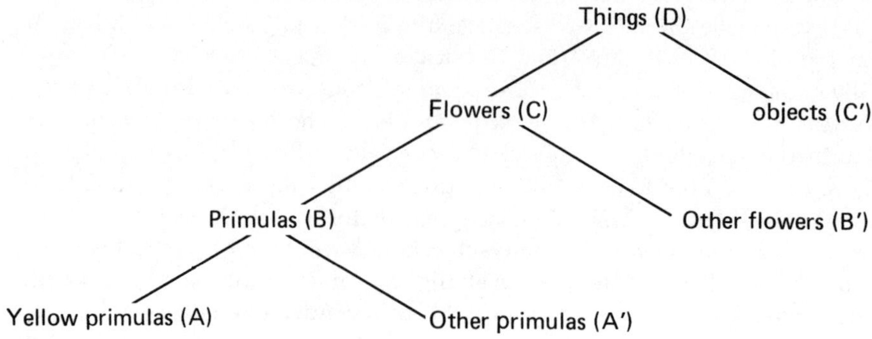

Figure 7. A class inclusion hierarchy

In another task, children are given a set of sixteen geometrical shapes: four blue squares, four red squares, four blue circles, and four red circles (other versions of this task use pictures of animals or people). First, children group together the "pieces that go together." Then, whatever they have done spontaneously, they are asked to divide the shapes into four piles and to place each pile in one of four compartments in an open box. Finally, either the horizontal or vertical compartment divider is removed; children are asked to make only two piles and to justify the resulting rearrangement. This task examines the child's ability to understand that one object may be classified on the basis of two different attributes. Like additive classification, this ability is essential to making sense of the physical world, as well as to general strategies of reasoning about the relations between classes or concepts.

For readers unfamiliar with the conventions of logic, a note about the notion of adding and multiplying classes. From formal logic, Piaget is borrowing the idea that the operation of combining classes in logic is equivalent to the operation of combining sets or numbers in mathematics. Addition and multiplication are both combining operations, but they function in different ways. Addition occurs in a sequence. Yellow primulas are taken as a group and then combined with other primulas to make a large class of flowers; the larger class contains either primulas, or other flowers, or both. By contrast, the operation of multiplication proceeds simultaneously. Each red element is paired with a square element to produce a smaller class of red squares; each element in the new class *must* have both characteristics to be included. While these two operations proceed by different rules, Piaget shows how they develop together.

Early Intuitive period (four to five years) We have seen that children in the Preconceptual stage deal with the twenty pictures by creating graphic collections (e.g., arrangements of the pictures to form a cross) or partial alignments in which unrelated principles may be used for each pile and all the objects may not be classified. The performance of the Early Intuitive child is quite different.

One child (five years, eight months) first groups pictures by their color, but soon makes three piles using all the pictures: primulas (B), other flowers (B′), other objects (C′). Piaget takes one of the (B′) flowers and places it in the (B) pile of primulas. —Can I put this here? —*Yes, it's a flower* [i.e., both B and B′ are included in C] —And is that pink flower (a rose) one of the primulas? [i.e., is the larger class included in the smaller class?] —*Yes, you can put all the flowers together.* (Adapted from Inhelder and Piaget, 1959, p. 102).

Early Intuitive children have constructed stable, consistent collections and behave as if they have some idea that there can be a set of categories into which all elements can be grouped. They are also able to combine part classes (yellow primulas and other primulas) into a whole (flowers). However, they do not yet understand the asymmetrical relation between all and some (in adult logic, B is included in C, but C is not included in B).

In the multiplication of classes task, these same children have gone beyond the Preconceptual stage in which only two piles are made (reds and blues or circles and squares). Now the children make two collections and divide one of them (reds, blue circles, blue squares), or they make four piles "correctly" but still focus only on one variable at a time.

One girl (five years, ten months) places blue squares in the top left compartment of the box, blue circles top right, red squares bottom left, red circles bottom right (Figure 8). The horizontal partition between top and bottom is removed. Piaget asks

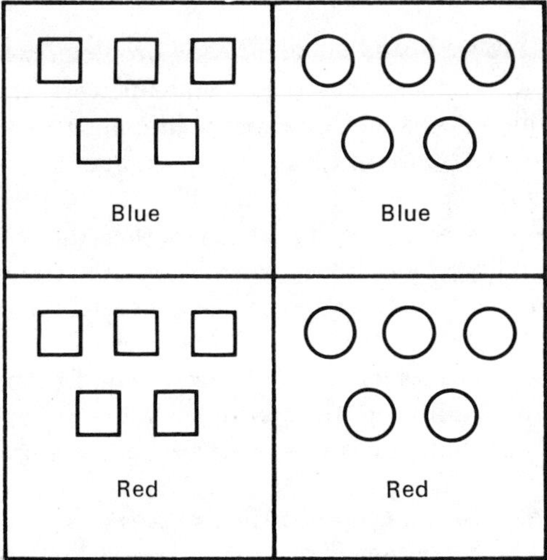

Figure 8. Classification

whether the top two piles (blue squares and circles) can be combined. —If we put them together what are they like? —*Squares.* —Is that all? —*And circles too.* —Can one put them together? —*Yes.* —Why? —*I don't know.* (They are all blue, but she does not see this possibility of classification even though she herself used it in the beginning.) (Adapted from Inhelder and Piaget, 1959, p. 168).

As in additive classification, the Early Intuitive child can combine classes using two-dimensional principles but cannot yet reason about their relationship.

Late Intuitive period (six to seven). After some trial-and-error rearranging, six-to-seven-year-old children often spontaneously lay out the twenty pictures in the four-level hierarchy shown in Figure 7. Also, they now are aware of a basic principle of class inclusion.

> (six years, six months) —Can I put a primula (B) in this pile (B′)? —*Yes, a primula is a flower too.* —Can I put one of these (other flowers) in here (with the primulas)? —*No, it isn't a primula.*

But none of these children can make a genuine quantitative comparison of the part and the whole.

> . . . How would I be making a bigger bunch, by taking the primulas or by taking the yellow primulas? —*They're both the same.* [The child is comparing four yellow primulas and four of other colors.] —And which is more, a bunch of flowers or a bunch of primulas? —*It's the same.* (Adapted from Inhelder and Piaget, 1959, p. 103).

Similar to the brown beads/wooden beads problem, when Late Intuitive children focus on the parts (primulas and other flowers) it is as if the whole ceases to exist, while a focus on the whole obliterates the parts. According to Piaget, this occurs because there is, as yet, no mental reversibility of additive operations. For adults, if $B + B' = C$, then $B = C - B'$; the whole is greater than either of two parts, while each part is less than the whole. Without this conceptual reversibility, Late Intuitive children still cannot master a class hierarchy *conceptually*, even though they can construct it in their classification *behavior*.

In the multiplication problem, Late Intuitive children begin to pay attention to two variables simultaneously, but they succeed in combining and conceptualizing them only after extensive overt trial and error.

> One child (five years, eleven months[1]) puts squares on one side and circles on the other, with red and blue counters alternating in each collection. Thus, the two collections are still not divided into red and blue subcollections. This graphic arrangement, which is a relic from the Preconceptual substage, is relinquished very gradually, but in the end he accepts a division into four subcollections. However, as soon as these are constructed, he places them correctly into the box. (One of the

[1]This child is younger than most of the examples for the Later Intuitive period. Again, ages may vary; it is the stage sequence which is important to Piaget.

partitions is removed.) What is this a box of? —*Circles and squares* (correct). —And like this (removing the other partitions and jumbling the elements on one side)? —*That doesn't make any difference* (mixing squares and circles) *because they're both red.* —And in the other side? *They're blue; squares and circles.* (Adapted from Inhelder and Piaget, 1959, p. 169).

In the Late Intuitive period, children do begin to understand simple class inclusions (all–some, and simple multiple classification. Multiple classifications and four-level hierarchies are only constructed after extensive trial-and-error behavior. We will not see children who begin with a spontaneous and accurate classification scheme until Concrete operations (seven to eight years).

Some new research by Rosch, Mervis, Gray, Johnson, and Boyes-Braem (1976) indicates that we need to make an important distinction when studying classification in young children. Most previous work, including Piaget's, has examined the child's skill in relating subordinate to superordinate categories (e.g., cats and dogs are both animals; cars and trains are both vehicles). However, Rosch, *et al.* also focus on the development of the classifications "cats" and "dogs," or "cars" and "trains," or "shoes" and "shirts," or "pianos" and "guitars." They argue that these are basic categories because, within each class, members share many attributes, including similar motor patterns in their use and similar perceptual features (e.g., shapes). Yet, they are not as similar as many finer category distinctions, for example, tabbies or persians, beagles or Airedales, and so on. In one of many excellent studies reported in their paper, Rosch, *et al.* gave children three and four years of age and older, two types of oddity problems. In the first, "basic level" sort, children were presented with three pictures, two different cats and one train (for example), and asked to put together or point to "the two that are alike, that are the same kind of thing." In a second type of oddity problem, the children were presented with a cat, dog, and train; this time, in order to indicate similarity, the child would be using a superordinate category (cat + dog = animal). Basic level sorts were virtually perfect for three- and four-year-olds. Correct pair-up in the superordinate sorts occurred only slightly more than half the time for three-year-olds, while four-year-olds were highly skilled. In both age groups, correct verbal labels for the categories were given much less often than the correct nonverbal responses. Thus, while Piaget's work emphasizes the difficulties which Intuitive children have in reasoning *about* classification hierarchies, even younger children are quite successful in making consistent classifications, especially of basic categories.

Seriation

Piaget has spent more time and effort investigating classification, but seriation is equally important in the development of both logic and number. One major difference between classification and seriation is that a class as such is not perceived (we do not *see* the class "dogs," only the individual instances), while an ordered relation does have perceptual characteristics (we *do* see size, location, etc.). Even though perceptual cues may be more salient in seriation, concepts in this area develop at the same time, in the same sequence, as classification.

Two seriation tasks have already been described. In the first, the child is asked to place ten sticks in order of size. In the second, he or she matches ten dolls of different sizes to ten walking sticks. There are two series to be constructed in this task but they vary along a common dimension (height). A third task examines multiplicative seriation of two different dimensions. Children are shown 49 leaves of different sizes and shadings. Inhelder and Piaget (1959) arrange a column of the seven darkest leaves in order from smallest to largest (Figure 9). Then he constructs the outline of a matrix by filling in the top row (of smallest leaves) in a sequence from darkest to lightest. Children are asked to complete the 7 × 7 matrix, which requires them to consider ordinal relations of two attributes (size, shading) simultaneously.

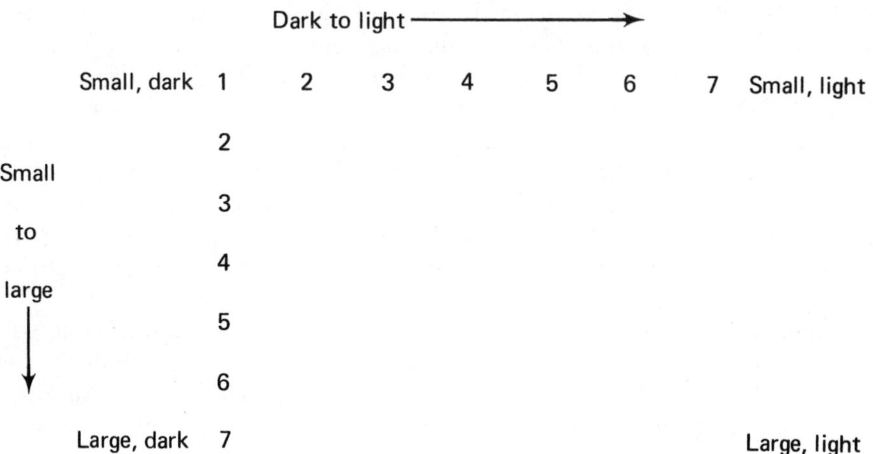

Figure 9. A schematic representation of the multiplication of relations task. (Adapted from Piaget and Inhelder, 1959, Chapter 10.)

Early Intuitive period (four to five years). Like children in the Preconceptual substage, four- and five-year-olds arrange the sticks in random order or in small groups by size, but there is no visible sequence from smallest to largest. Dolls and walking sticks are not accurately matched. Focusing either on size or shading of the leaves, children fail to complete the series in either dimension.

Late Intuitive period (six to seven years). The single row of sticks and the dolls with walking sticks are correctly placed in order of height after extensive rearrangement. Again by trial and error, the correct stick can be found for each doll if the two rows are matched in one-to-one correspondence, with each walking stick adjacent to a doll. However, if either the dolls or the walking sticks are moved closer together, the child loses the power to compare relative positions.

For example, the third doll is now matched with the closest stick, not with the stick that is third in size; seriation is easily destroyed by perceived transformations. In the 49 leaves problem, leaves are arranged either by size or by shading, but not by both. Like the children who create hierarchies but do not understand the whole system of class inclusion, Late Intuitive children create order, but not stable order, in a process of trial and error. Perceptual factors (e.g., number of flowers in parts B and B′, location of sticks) still dominate both classification and seriation.

Number as a synthesis of classification and seriation

We tend to believe that children have concepts of number when they begin to count correctly in sequence or to answer the question "How many?" In *The Child's Conception of Number*, Piaget and Szeminska[2] (1941) specify a more complex version of what "having" the concept of number means to them. First, the child should be able to equalize two small sets of objects by the scheme or strategy of one-to-one correspondence. Given a row of six egg cups, the child should be able to select six, and only six, eggs. Or, given a row of six pennies, the child should be able to match it with another row of six pennies. Second, if an experimenter modifies the spatial arrangement of one row without adding or taking away any of the objects, the child should still judge the rows as equal in quantity (he or she would conserve the equivalence). Third, the child should be able to conceptualize both *cardinal* and *ordinal* properties of number.

> The cardinal property refers to the quantity of elements in a set, for example, "How many candies in the bag?" The ordinal property refers to the ordered relation between sets; bags can be arranged in order from least to most candies. A complete concept of number requires a coordination of the two properties, for example, the knowledge that there are more candies in the bags with higher number labels. These last two skills are more elusive than they seem. Many children who can count the number of elements in a set do not really know that "seven" has more elements than "five."

Fourth, for an adult-level concept of number, children must have developed a system of cognitive operations to add and multiply units; further, they must be able to reverse each addition by a subtraction and to reverse each multiplication by a division.

Concepts of number seem to be quite different from concepts of classes and relations. However, in Piaget's analysis (Beth and Piaget, 1961) one-to-one correspondence, conservation, ordination, and reversible addition and multiplication must involve a coordination of classification and seriation schemes. The argument is based on empirical similarities between number and logic activities as well as on conceptual correspondence between the two disciplines.

[2]Inexplicably, Aline Szeminska has not been credited as coauthor in English translations of this important work, though she is frequently cited by Piaget.

When objects are grouped together in a class, many of their unique characteristics are ignored. For example, dogs of all colors and shapes are included in the class "dogs." Similarly, in order to count months of the year, trees in a forest, or children on a playground, we must ignore differences between individuals and focus only on the number of members in the set. Piaget also argues that there are similar intellectual structures required for adding or multiplying classes and numbers (Chapter 8). Classification and class logic, then, seem to be centrally involved in determining the answer to "How many?"—the cardinal property of number.

What if we eliminate all empirical differences between objects? (Suppose, for example, we consider a row of identical pennies.) How can we count the members of a set unless we identify them in some way, so that we make certain of counting every one, with each counted only once? Piaget suggests that we do this by arranging elements in a spatial order (a line, a circle) or a temporal order based on our actions of counting (first "this one," then "this one," etc.). Having counted all the elements in a set, we may also want to compare sets, to know whether one is larger than another. Again, we must arrange sets in a spatial or temporal series; 5 is less than 6, 6 is less than 7, and so on. Thus, seriation is centrally involved in counting and in understanding the ordinal property of number. Beth and Piaget go on to argue, on theoretical grounds, that not only cardination–ordination and multiplication–addition, but also one-to-one correspondence and number conservation are based on a synthesis of classification and seriation.

This conceptual analysis suggests that classification, seriation, and number should develop in the same sequence at the same time. We have already seen that in the Intuitive substage, classification and seriation emerge only after extensive trial and error but are not yet coordinated in mental constructs of class and relational hierarchies. We shall now see that while an early form of one-to-one correspondence appears during the Late Intuitive period, number conservation, cardination and ordination, and addition–multiplication fail to emerge until the next stage. Since the Intuitive substage tends to end when the child is around seven, in grade 2, the findings should have special importance for the teaching of mathematics in kindergarten and the earliest elementary grades.

Piaget's research usually suffers from summarization. When we write about his work, we present one or two examples from each area, and it sometimes seems as if important general conclusions are based upon one or two tasks worded in peculiar ways. With the exception of Flavell (1963), most summarizers do not recount the extensive selection of procedures, the cross-checking within the data gathering, and the converging methods of coming to a particular conclusion. In each topical area, a number of structurally equivalent tasks are presented to children of a given age and the same sequence must hold in all cases if the theory is to be supported. The *Child's Conception of Number* is a particularly elegant book on the systematic exploration of the number concept.

In reporting the results of these studies, Piaget and Szeminska described three stages: I, corresponding to Preconceptual; II, corresponding to Intuitive; and III, corresponding to Concrete Operations. There are no clear divisions of substage II into Early or Late Intuitive periods.

One-to-one correspondence and conservation. Here, a Preconceptual four-year-old is given six little bottles (about 1″ high) and twelve little glasses. He is asked to select one glass (to drink from) for each bottle.

> Gol (4;0) began by pouring the contents of each bottle into a glass. When he came to the fourth bottle he suddenly saw that he could not make the 6 bottles correspond to the 12 glasses, and cried: —*There aren't many bottles.* —Then you can take some glasses away. (He left 7 glasses for 6 bottles, putting the glasses rather closer together.) —Is there the same number of glasses and bottles? —*Yes.* (One glass was then put in front of each bottle, so that one could be seen to have no corresponding bottle.) *We'll have to have another bottle.* (He was given one.) —Is it right now? (He so arranged them that the first bottle corresponded to the second glass, and so on up to the seventh bottle, for which there was thus no glass.) —*No, here there's a glass missing, and there there's a glass that hasn't a bottle.* —What do we need then? —*One bottle and one glass.* (He was given them, but he put them opposite one another and never made the correct correspondence.) (Piaget and Szeminska, 1941, p. 128)

By contrast, Intuitive six-year-olds quickly place one glass in front of the six bottles. They can count each row accurately. However, if the row of bottles or glasses is spread out or bunched together, Intuitive children assert that there is no longer the same number in each row. In sum, a fragile form of one-to-one correspondence is established, but conservation of number is not achieved until the next stage.

One application of one-to-one correspondence is the activity of counting—pairing a numeral with each object in a series. The above results suggest that counting is possible in the Intuitive substage, but visual rearrangements will alter judgments of quantity; children who can count have not necessarily mastered adult-level concepts of number. The interpretation that counting in the Late Intuitive period is still tied to action rather than mental operations is supported by something our six-year-old son once asked me.

> —*Do you want to see me add seven and seven in my head?* —Sure. —*Seven* (and then he nodded his head with each numeral) *eight, nine, ten, eleven, twelve, thirteen, fourteen.*

Cardination and ordination. The developmental correspondence between concepts of cardination and ordination was explored in an ingenious experimental task.

> The child is presented with ten paper strips (A–J) of equal width. The first piece (A) is one unit in height, the second two units, the third three units, and so on. After children arrange the strips in sequence, they are shown, with a unit card, that A is one

unit, B can be cut in two, and so on. The experimenter asks, "If we cut up this one (B-J), how many little ones like A can we make?" If children can systematically deduce the cardinal value (e.g., 6) from the ordinal value (e.g., F is the 6th) without measuring the height each time, it is clear that they have grasped the relation between cardinal quantity and ordinal position.

Results show the same three stages as above. Preconceptual children cannot construct the series to begin with. Intuitive children construct the series by trial and error. However, unless the questions go in strict sequence, the child becomes confused.

> One five-year-old, after an early error, is correct all the way from C to J. He knows how many units in each strip without counting. However, Piaget asks about J again. —If we cut J up, how many little ones like A can we make? —*Nine.* —And out of H [the ninth one]? —*Ten.* —And out of G [the eighth one]? —*Eleven.* And out of F? —*Twelve.* Thus when the series was reversed [the child] began correctly by going down to 9, but went on with 10, 11, 12 . . . and only saw the absurdity of it when he came to B [which was only two units tall] (p. 136).

Only in Concrete operations do children relate ordinal and cardinal numbers successfully and systematically. This is true despite the fact that Intuitive children can count both ordinal and cardinal numbers correctly.

Multiplication. Piaget and Szeminska (1941) show that in the Intuitive substage, simultaneous combination of numbers (multiplication) is not yet possible. Children who know that they can place one set of ten flowers (x) in a set of ten vases (y) and then another set of ten flowers (z) in the vases, understand that $x = y$ and $z = y$, but they may deny that $x = z$. Nor can they deduce that if there are two equal sets of ten flowers, there will be two in every one of ten vases. Just as the Intuitive child has not established additive and multiplicative classes and relations, so the strategies for reversible mental addition and multiplication of numbers are beyond their reach.

The failure of classification, seriation, and number to emerge as mental constructs during the Intuitive substage, supports Piaget's claim that they are inseparably interrelated. However, there is some evidence that they do not all finally develop at the same time (Dimitrovsky and Almy, 1975). Number conservation tends to occur slightly before class inclusion and multiple classification. I will explore the meaning of observed departures from Piaget's structural model in Chapters 8 and 12. Here, I will simply comment on the fact that the schemes do not emerge simultaneously, but they do tend to develop around the same general period of time in the child's life.

Quantity

The concept of number involves a precise comparison between sets of objects (e.g., how much more in one set than another?). There is also a global concept of quantity which simply requires a judgment of more, less, or the same (e.g., conservation of water or clay). Piaget and Inhelder (1941) indicate that while number and quantity concepts emerge at similar times, conservation of number develops slightly earlier than conservation of quantity. As in the studies of number, three stages are described. Preconceptual children fail to conserve water and clay. Children in the Late Intuitive stage also fail to conserve but their judgments tend to vacillate. First they focus on the height of the water, then on the width of the glass. There is still a tendency to focus on perceived end states rather than on the transformations from beginning to end; figurative aspects dominate conceptual judgments. But, in their vacillation from one dimension to another, Intuitive children discover what begins to be regarded as conflicting data. The fact that the water level is higher suggests that the amount is more, but the fact that it is narrower suggests that the amount is less. According to Piaget and Inhelder, these kinds of disequilibrating conclusions eventually lead to the restructuring of the whole cognitive apparatus.

Piaget and Inhelder describe water and clay as *continuous* quantities; there are no observable units in the substances unless we apply a calibrated measuring instrument. In contrast, discontinuous quantities have observable units.

> In one task, beads are poured into two equal containers, and children are asked to judge, without counting, the equivalence of the amounts. Then, the contents of one container are poured into a taller, narrower container, as in the conservation of water and clay experiments.

Children consistently conserve discontinuous quantities at a slightly younger age than they do water and clay. This is one of many examples cited by Piaget whenever he discusses the fact that not all logically equivalent tasks elicit the same level of responses. The specific characteristics of the task interact with the child's cognitive structure in determining the child's cognitive level.

Space

Along with number and time, adult concepts of space involve conservations of quantity, and numerical measurements of the distances between points. Unlike number and time, there is a perceived coordinate system of up–down, right–left, toward–away dimensions. Here are some examples which describe the Intuitive child's approach to conservation and measurement of length and to the understanding of horizontal and vertical spatial coordinates.

Early Intuitive period (four to five years). As described in Chapter 6, a child's conservation of length is assessed by the experimenter's placing two identical sticks on a table, parallel to each other, and then moving one of the sticks to the right or left. Children are asked in various ways to judge whether the lengths remain the same. Like Preconceptual children, Early Intuitive children simply fail to conserve length; any movement of one stick results in a change in the child's judgment of how long it is.

The measurement of length task was also described above. Children attempted to construct a tower, equal in height to a model on a lower table in another part of the room. Early Intuitive children have advanced beyond the guessing typical of the Preconceptual stage. Sticks or hands are now used as an aid to visual estimates, but the child is still attempting to create a second tower the same height from the floor as the model; differences in table heights are ignored. Both conservation and measurement tasks demonstrate the emphasis on one salient dimension to the exclusion of others, so characteristic of children at this stage.

If you were given a picture or map and asked to locate a particular object, you would probably describe it in a two-dimensional, coordinate system. "It's in the top right corner," you might say, specifying a position in both vertical (bottom–top) and horizontal (left–right) dimensions at right angles to each other. To adults, it is obvious that the world is organized in Euclidean spatial coordinates. Piaget shows that despite the Intuitive child's use of dimensional words (up, down), a two-dimensional coordinate system does not emerge until mid-Concrete operations (at about age nine or ten).

The two tasks to be described are part of an even more complex experimental procedure (Piaget and Inhelder, 1948, Ch. 13). First, a rectangular bottle with a narrow neck is partly filled with water, and is placed on a table. The child is asked to guess, and then to draw, the position that the water will assume when the bottle is tilted at different angles or rotated upside down. (The water level will always be horizontal relative to the table.) Second, children are shown a small hill of sand and asked to draw what it looks like when sticks are placed upright in the sand (the vertical is defined by the experimenter in relation to the floor and walls of the room).

Before the Early Intuitive period (four to five years), children are unable to represent water or mountains as entities with an outer surface. Water is indicated by scribbles which cross the boundaries of the bottle. Figures are placed *inside* a schematic representation of the mountain (see Figure 10).

Now, in the Early Intuitive substage (IIA in Figure 10) children do represent surfaces. When the bottle is tilted, they recognize that the water comes closer to the mouth of the bottle; however, this change is represented as an increase in water amount, not a slant of the surface relative to the bottle sides. Defying gravity, the water level is stuck to the bottom of the bottle even when the container is upside down. Houses and flowers likewise are perpendicular to the sides of the mountain, not to the table. In both cases spatial orientation of horizontal and vertical is determined by the configuration of the salient figure—bottle or mountain—and not by the spatial coordinates of the table, the paper edge, or the child's own body.[4] These drawings occur in spite of the fact that children have observed and described what actually happens to the water.

[4]Here is an example where *failure* to use one's own perspective leads to an egocentric error. The concept refers to an inability to coordinate self and other points of view, not solely to a choice of one's own viewpoint.

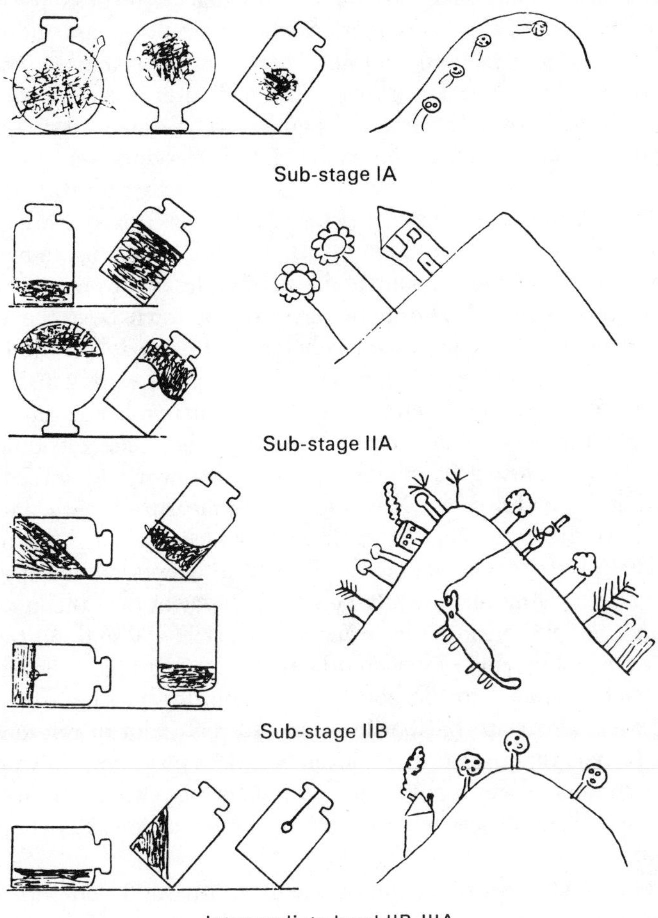

Figure 10. Stages in the development of horizontal and vertical axes. (From Piaget and Inhelder, 1948.)

Late Intuitive period (six to seven years). Piaget's description of the development of space concepts seems to pay more attention to the transitions between stages than some of his other works. For example, the Early Intuitive child's nonconservation of length is followed by a number of increasingly differentiated responses during the Late Intuitive period. First, the child conserves length when two 10 cm sticks are presented, but fails to conserve when the two sticks are only 5 cm long. Piaget suggests that this occurs because the relative movement increases with the shorter sticks. Second, the child judges the stick to be equal after one has been moved but believes that both sticks are now longer. Third, children recognize conservation when both sticks are moved simultaneously in opposite directions, but not when only one is moved. Fourth, some children appear to be puzzled (disequilibrated?) after one stick is moved, and they move the stick back to verify the equality. This demonstrates a reversibility in action. Fifth, children begin by not conserving, but after some experimentation, they finally conclude, "It looks larger, but it's the same after all" (Piaget, Inhelder and Szeminska, 1948, pp. 100–101). It is exciting to watch the child discover a concept right before your eyes and it happens in many of these geometry tasks. However, in none of these examples is conservation considered to be logically necessary ("It *has* to be the same") as it will be in the next stage.

In constructing the tower equal in height to the model on the lower table, Late Intuitive children begin to use their bodies as measuring instruments in a special way. First, the child climbs on a small chair, placing one hand at the bottom of the first tower and another at the top. Then, she gets down from the chair, drops her arms, goes over to the second tower and spreads her arms again. Similarly, children use hands or feet to measure length, but disregard the variability of the rulers. In addition to conceptualizing the need for an intermediate measure, children in the Late Intuitive period become aware that the top of the tower on the lower table should be lower than the model. Length is beginning to have meaning in terms of both start and endpoints.

When conceptualizing spatial coordinates, Late Intuitive children no longer draw the water parallel to the bottom of the bottle, but they still ignore the table surface underneath the bottle as an external point of reference (Figure 10). With respect to the vertical, children can place posts upright when they are working with the real sand, but in their drawings the posts are perpendicular to the slope. Children always seem to know more in action than they do in the area of symbols.

Piaget notes a further transition between Intuitive and Concrete operations. At the end of the Late Intuitive period, the child can accurately predict water level when the rectangular bottle is lying on its side, but not when it is tilted at an oblique angle (IIB–IIIA in Figure 10). Like the description of conservation above, the child's progress through the Late Intuitive period is not an all-or-none affair. Rather, there is a series of events, with the child gradually overcoming the perceptual pull of the material to make more adequate conceptual judgments.

Time

Chapter 6 documented the Preconceptual child's confusion between order of events and duration and between concepts of time and space. During the Intuitive period, there is a beginning independence of time and space, with the child hesitantly making correct answers to the problems of trains moving on two tracks. The correct answers occur after recognitions of initial errors and contradictions.

Early Intuitive period (five to six years).[5] In this period, children manage to separate the temporal order of events (seriation) from spatial cues, or they separate the temporal duration between events from spatial cues. Whichever one is separated, the other temporal dimension is still bound up with the location of objects in space.

> The train on track (I) moves along and stops at the end of the track. On track (II), the train moves slowly, stopping after (I) in time, but before (I) in space.
>
> (Age five to six years)—If (I) stopped at lunch, did (II) stop before or after lunch? —*After lunch because it arrived later* (order correct).—So which one moved for a longer time —*(I)* (incorrect duration: Piaget, 1946b, p. 97).
>
> (Age five to six years)—Which one went on longer? —*(II) because it went at medium speed.*—Which moved for a shorter time? —*(I)* because it went at great speed (correct duration).—If (I) stopped at lunch, when did (II) stop? —*Before lunch* (incorrect order) (p. 98).

Children in this substage are most puzzling. They seem to have correct answers and then they make incorrect ones. Piaget's analysis shows that in some cases at least, the inconsistency lies in *our* failure to recognize the different aspects of a problem; the child may focus on one aspect correctly and another incorrectly.

Children in the Early Intuitive substage often begin with both order and duration judgments incorrect, discover a new fact (e.g., that (II) was still moving), and correct one of their judgments. At this substage, the new fact has a specific application and does not lead to a general reconsideration of the confusion between time and space.

Late Intuitive period (six to seven years). The most salient advance during this period can be seen in what happens when the child discovers an error. In contrast with the five-to-six-year-old child, Late Intuitive children discover a contradiction in their answers and begin to consider the general principle behind the specific fact.

> Train (I) travels faster than (II) and goes farther; they stop simultaneously. At first, a six-year-old began by denying simultaneity. —*(II) stopped first, but (I) took a longer time because it went further.* Then Piaget administered some tasks involving temporal order of events during which the child finally arrived at the correct response that (II) stopped after (I) even though the distance was shorter. When Piaget

[5]Note the later age.

returned to the simultaneity tasks, he found that the child correctly distinguished duration and simultaneity from the spatial cues (p. 115).

Thus, a new specific fact is transformed into a principle which can be applied in comparable situations.

Early versus Late Intuitive periods: Structural and functional principles

Stage definition. The early period of the Intuitive substage has been defined primarily by tasks in which children do not succeed. They fail to achieve concepts of: class inclusion; one-dimensional seriation; one-to-one number correspondence; conservation of number, quantity, and length; measurement; horizontal and vertical coordinates; complete separation of time concepts from spatial cues. Nevertheless, they show important advances over Preconceptual children in their ability to form stable classes (Piagetian classification tasks; Rosch, *et al.*). The primary difficulty seems to be in coordinating different levels of classification and overcoming the pull of perceived transformations of objects within classes or sets.

In the Late Intuitive period, similar new achievements are noted in each of the conceptual areas: all–some class inclusion; one-dimensional seriation, one-to-one correspondence; vacillation between dimensions in conservation of number, quantity, and length; beginning "rubber" measurement (e.g., hands); beginning conception of horizontal and vertical; and, separation of spatial and temporal cues. Children of six and seven years do not seem to enter tasks with mental schemes of two-way classification, seriation, conservation, time, and space, but they tend to discover correct answers after an extensive period of trial-and-error manipulation of objects. It is as if coordinations of the classes established in the Early Intuitive period are now accomplished by sensorimotor mechanisms which are still heavily influenced by perceptual cues. Not until Concrete operations are these coordinations carried out internally. Then, for example, children "know" immediately that the number of checkers remains the same when the row is rearranged; they do not have to rearrange the checkers to reproduce the original one-to-one correspondence.

The existence of similarities in development across so many conceptual areas lends weight to Piaget's argument that the child is not simply acquiring a collection of separate facts, but rather is developing a new stage of cognitive organization. Other evidence for this argument comes from demonstrations that variations in the interviewer's questions or in the kinds of tasks do not materially affect the developmental sequence of the child's answers, even when they make it easier or harder to solve a specific task. Additional evidence for a stage interpretation comes from the child's strong resistance to the experimenter's attempts to change his or her answers.

The tenacity of the young child in maintaining his position can be illustrated by the five-year-old son of a friend of mine. The father had apparently made repeated attempts to drill the child on the conservation of water problem. One day the father proudly demonstrated the child's skill. On the first two trials the boy said, "There's more in this glass; it's higher." The father's face fell. Given a third try, his son said, "Oh, it's the same, it's still the same amount of water." The father beamed proudly while the son added in a tiny whisper, "but it really isn't!"

Piaget does not claim that it is impossible to change the child's stage, but he believes that each single response is symptomatic of a pervasive underlying organization of thought. For Piaget, resistance to change is one index of support for that hypothesis.

Intuitive regulations and the process of development. Piaget accounts for the Late Intuitive discoveries of correct answers after trial-and-error manipulation with a mechanism called "Intuitive regulations." Normally, in an interactive, equilibrated cognitive system, the child's attempts to bend the world to fit (assimilate) are met with resistance from the physical and social world; this leads to accommodative changes in schemes. Accommodations, in turn, always meet assimilative resistance and are transformed by existing schemes. Thus, there is a self-correcting process by which feedback from external events produces some, but not total, reorganization. This process is called a regulation (i.e., a self-regulation).

Early in life it is the child's perception (not just vision) of the physical world which provides the feedback necessary to correct maladaptive responses. In the Late Intuitive period, a new kind of regulation emerges.

For example, in the development of time concepts, seven-year-olds begin to shift focus from the speed of trains to the end points of the track, to distances, to movements, and back to endpoints, and so on. One set of data suggests that train (I) stopped second; another set suggests that (I) stopped first. Speeds seem faster from one point of view, slower from another. Conflicting conclusions.

The Intuitive child has begun to decenter and flexibly shift his or her focus of attention. In the Early Intuitive period this shifting among viewpoints sometimes leads to a recognition of an error and a correction during a particular task. However, in the Late Intuitive period, the conflict among conclusions leads to more vacillation, more experimentation, and to an ultimate reorganization of general principles.

Piaget argues that Intuitive regulations are not simply a product of perceptual feedback. If feedback from the physical world and from other people were sufficient to produce cognitive change, then Intuitive children would be giving conservation responses earlier or more frequently. Instead, Piaget interprets Intuitive regulations as *coordinations* of present perceptions with symbolic representations of past and present events. In the conservation of liquid task, there appears to be more water in the taller glass, but the Late Intuitive child is able to think back and remember that they were equal to begin with, nothing was added or taken away, and so on. The self-correcting feedback then is not simply an interaction between child and event, but also an interaction among representations. Regulations are now interiorized—not just internalized—perceptual cues. However, at this stage, they are still "incomplete or approximate compensations, in contrast to operations which entail complete (reversible) operations" (Inhelder and Piaget, 1955, p. 246).

SOCIAL DEVELOPMENT

In the Intuitive substage, there are advances in physical and social aspects of identity, causality, and egocentrism, all of which have implications for social interaction. This is also the stage at which studies of moral development begin (Piaget, 1932; Kohlberg, 1963, 1964, 1969).

Identity

Physical identity. In Piaget's short English summary of his work on identity (1968b), there is the ever-present theme that Preoperational identity concepts are basd on Preoperational, nonreversible logic structures. When a necklace is broken down into single beads and arranged in a circle, Intuitive children say that it's still the same necklace. But when beads are taken singly and formed into a necklace, children at this substage no longer believe that they are observing the same beads. The direction of the transformation affects the judgment; it is not yet possible for children to compensate for the observed change with a mental operation which enables them to consider the beginning state of the beads.

Piaget's studies indicate that qualitative identity tends to develop before quantitative conservation. In one clear example, Late Intuitive children state that a wire bent into an arc is still the same wire, but they also state clearly that its length has been altered by the transformation. Piaget concluded that the task of distinguishing between a permanent quality (wire) and a variable quality (shape) is easier than the operational composition of quantities required in the judgment of length. Recently, Brainerd and Hooper (1975) have questioned whether in fact identity always precedes conservation; the answer is complicated by the discrepancies in methods and materials used in the investigation of each concept.

Personal and social identity. The wire arc is an example of a reversible change. In human identity, however, changes resulting from growth are irreversible.

> An experiment briefly described in Chapter 6 focuses on the child's notion that growing things or people retain an essential sameness despite irreversible changes in appearance. Piaget (1968b) has children draw a picture sequence representing a

"flower" which they have seen growing in water. Then they examine pictures of themselves and of the experimenter at different ages.

At the beginning of the Early Intuitive period, four-year-olds respond to their old pictures with, "It's still me"; however, they are not convinced that they will be the same person in the future as adults. These children fail to recognize the continuity of identity in the experimenter or the flower. Five-year-olds in the Early Intuitive period, tend to apply identity concepts to themselves and to the experimenter. In a series of four pictures showing the growth of the flower from a "seed," they recognize identity between adjacent pictures but deny that the beginning and end of the sequence show the same flower. It seems as if the perceptual differences at the extremes overpower the conceptual judgments.

At the beginning of the late Intuitive period, six-year-olds who at first deny identity to the end pictures of the seed and the flower often accept identity after having been shown pictures of themselves and of the experimenter. Like the Intuitive regulations described above, experience with one task can now be used to create general principles applying to another area. Immediate recognition of identity in all the tasks does not occur until the end of the Intuitive substage or the beginning of Concrete operations.

More research on this topic is needed, but it seems that first the child discovers identity of his or her own body; then another person's identity over time is understood; finally, the child conceptualizes identity despite irreversible changes in nonhuman objects. Piaget recalls that the first permanent object in the Sensorimotor period is usually the parent, which suggests that there is something in the richness of social interaction leading to the earlier emergence of human identity concepts.

Gender identity, sex role identity, and identification. The explanation of how boys grow up to be like their fathers and girls grow up to be like their mothers is a central task for any theory of personality development. In Freud's formulations, four conceptually separable aspects of sexual identity are assumed to develop as a package: gender identity (labelling of self as male or female); sex-role identity (choice of behaviors or tasks considered appropriate for one sex and not the other); identification (wanting to be similar to the same-sexed parent); sexual orientation (choice of same- or opposite-sexed partner for sexual activity). Another theoretical approach, social learning theory (e.g., Bandura and Walters, 1963: Bandura, 1969a), while disagreeing with Freud's assumptions about the process of identification, still tends to treat these four aspects of identity as inextricably interrelated. Following a Piagetian framework, Kohlberg (1966) has questioned this package approach to identity development and sparked renewed research interest in the topic of personal identity. The interest has come partly because there are such clear contrasts among Freudian, social learning, and cognitive developmental explanations of identity development. But in another respect, the women's movement has helped to raise questions about the stereotyped relation between gender identity and traditional sex-role definitions (e.g., whether women and men should share more of the responsibility for child and home care and have similar opportunities to pursue careers).

Kohlberg provides a helpful schematic diagram (see Figure 11) of the contrasts among Freudian, social learning, and cognitive developmental perspectives. All of them focus on the four-to-eight-year-old Intuitive stage child.

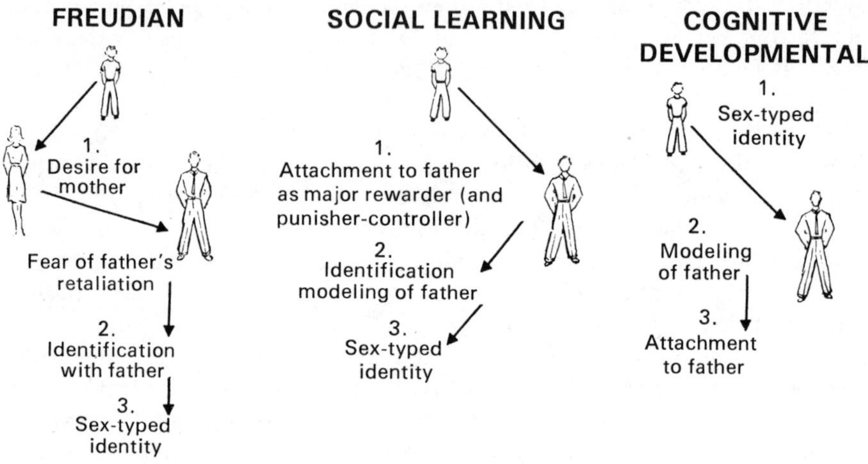

Figure 11. Theoretical sequences in psychosexual identification. (From Kohlberg, 1966 a, p. 128.)

Freud and social learning theory view sex-typed identity as a product of a sequence that begins with emotional attachment. For Freud, the four-year-old boy's sexual desire for the mother leads to fear of father's retaliation (e.g., by castration), which in turn leads to identification with father and results in sex-typed identity. By the age of six or seven the boy actively wants to become a man like daddy, doing the kinds of things daddies do. (The sequence for women has some similarities, but the account is negatively biased and much less clear.) In most psychoanalytic approaches the major feature of gender definition is the genital difference between males and females.[6] Social learning theory for both boys and girls assumes an initial attachment to the same-sexed parent, who is a powerful giver and receiver of reinforcements. This attachment, in combination with differential adult examples of sex-role behaviors and differential reward for "sex appropriate" child behaviors, encourages the child to imitate the same-sexed parent. This sequence, it is argued, establishes a behaviorally defined sex-role identity.

[6]One example of psychoanalytic sex bias is the assumption that all women have penis envy while there is very rarely a discussion of possible breast or vagina envy by the male.

By contrast, Kohlberg suggests that the sequence *begins* with a cognitively determined gender identity in the Intuitive substage. The child notes the similarity of his classification with the same-sexed parent ("We're both boys"; "We're both girls"), and this similarity of classification promotes imitation and modeling. At the end of this sequence, the child who was initially attached to both parents may develop a special emotional bond with the parent of the same sex.

The evidence for Kohlberg's views comes from a number of sources including his own research. While Freud describes gender identity, sex-role identity, identification, sexuality, and morality emerging simultaneously in the same Oedipal crucible, DeVries (1969) and Kohlberg find an interesting developmental sequence. Verbal self-labelling of gender ("I'm a boy"; "I'm a girl") begins along with other classifications made by two-to-three-year-old Preconceptual children. During the Early Intuitive period (four to five years) these labels are gradually applied correctly to boys and girls and to men and women outside the family. But gender labels still have some of the fluctuating qualities common to other classifications, conservations, and identity concepts.

In a study of identity development (Kohlberg, 1967), four-to-eight-year-olds were "asked whether a pictured girl could be a boy if she wanted to, or if she played boy games, or if she wore a boy's haircut or clothes. Most four-year-olds said she could be a boy if she wanted to, or if she wore the appropriate haircut or clothes."[7] Kohlberg (1966a) gives some additional anecdotal results, including an overheard argument between two four-year-old boys, one of whom thinks he will "grow up to be a mommy" and a three-year-old boy who told his mother, "When you grow up to be a daddy, you can have a bicycle too" [like his father]. By the Late Intuitive period (six to seven years) most children were quite certain that a girl could not be a boy regardless of changes in appearance or behavior.

DeVries and Kohlberg show how the development of gender identity is part of the general development of cognitive organization in the Intuitive substage. It is correlated with constancy of species identity in animals (cats do not grow up to be dogs) and with performance in Piaget-type conservation tasks. Without correlational data, they note the similarity of gender classification to other kinds of classification development during the Intuitive substage. Some support for these findings comes from studies of identity development by Guardo and Bohan (1971).

Kohlberg emphasizes the developmental primacy of self-classificatory gender identity. His description implies that it acts as a filter through which other sex-related aspects of behavior and identity are assimilated. Boys and girls, aware of their own gender identity, become interested in what things in their world are "boy things" and what are "girl things." They begin to try out sex-role behaviors, not at first to be like adults, but rather to do things that are consistent with themselves. Similar to other either–or views of the world, Early

[7] I don't know if he asked whether boys can become girls.

Intuitive children soon become very clear about sex role stereotypes ("This is for boys; that's for girls."). Like California children who draw snowy winter scenes even when they have never seen snow, these children may adopt more rigid and traditional sex-role stereotypes than the examples in their own homes.

So far, no mention of genital differences. Kohlberg cites convincing evidence that both gender and sex-role identity emerge long before children are clear about anatomical differences between the sexes. In contrast with Freud, Kohlberg's data indicate that children notice genital differences, but these differences do not seem to be the key early definers of gender and sex-role identity; and choice of a sexual object may not provide the primary motivating force for identification with the same-sexed parent. Perhaps the Oedipal castration anxiety is an adult-constructed metaphor for the real competitions for affection that exist in every family.

In Kohlberg's view, the sequence goes from cognitive gender identity to stereotypic sex-roles, to imitation of adults, to a special attachment to same-sexed parent. Knowledge of genital differences comes after both gender and sex-role identity. This view not only argues against Freud, but also against the social-learning hypothesis that it is imitation of adult sex-role behavior which produces gender and sex-role identity. In any case, he provides some important evidence that sex-linked identities do not emerge in one neatly wrapped package.

Causality

This section on cognitive and social development continues with the report of the study done by Anne Bernstein and me (1975) to investigate the relation between physical causality (origin of night—Laurendau and Pinard, 1962) and social causality (origin of babies). In the Preconceptual period, the first three levels (0, 1, 2) of causal explanations describe a lack of understanding of the question, a view of a finalistic universe (it gets dark so we can sleep), and an artificial personal "causer" (mother puts the light out). In the Late Intuitive stage there is a new explanation of how night is caused.

> Level 3: Physical causes transformed into animistic causes. In this stage, the mother as a cause of night is replaced by a natural agent, but one which has person-like qualities.—*The moon opens his eyes; he blows the sun away and he blows the night in.*

Animism is also evident in Early Intuitive conceptions of babies.

> Level 3: Mixture of physical, psychological and artificial causes (age four years, six months). —Where does the egg come from? —*From the daddy.* —Then what happens? —*It swims in; into the penis and then it . . . I think it makes a little hole and then it swims into the vagina.* —How? —*It has a little mouth and it bites a hole.*

Most Late Intuitive children (70 percent) were at Level 3 or below in their concepts of how babies are created. Generally, they focused on one of three causal ingredients: the social relationship between parents; the external mechanics of intercourse (imperfectly understood); the fusion of biological-genetic materials. They were not yet able to coordinate these variables into a coherent system.

> A girl (six years, two months) has described that the father *puts his penis right in the place where the baby comes out. . . . It seems like magic sort of, cause somehow it just comes out.* [Here she is assimilating the facts of conception to the facts about birth. Then she is asked why the father's contribution is necessary] *If he didn't, then a baby wouldn't come.* —Why? —*Because it would need the stuff that the father gives.* —Why? —*I don't know.* —What does it do? —*Helps it to grow. . . I think that stuff* [the egg] *has the food part, maybe, and maybe it helps protect it . . . I think he gives the shell part and the shell part of the skin.* [Here she assimilates the female "egg" to the concept of chicken eggs with shells; in addition, she may be assimilating the role of the male sperm to the culturally stereotyped role of protector.]

Despite the assimilative quality, this girl does have some idea about the role of genitals in intercourse. However, many of the older Intuitive children seem to make no such connection.

From Piaget's own research we know that animistic explanations of the world are not limited to explanations of night and dramatic accounts of sperm which swim and bite their way to their goal.

> The wind (age 6). —Where does the wind come from? —*They blow up in the sky.* —How? —*The things are full and then they lay down and then they blow. It comes at the end.* —What thing is it? —*It's for blowing* [a bicycle pump, as the child eventually tells Piaget] (1927, p. 36).

> The sun (age 8). —Is the sun alive? —*Yes.* —Why? —*It gives light.* —Is a candle alive? [Note the choice of example to test the generality of the child's explanation] —*No.* —Why not? [Child changes his mind] —*Yes because it gives light. It is alive when it is giving light, but it isn't alive when it is not giving light.* —Is a bicycle alive? —*No when it doesn't go it isn't alive. When it goes it is alive.* —Is a mountain alive? —*No.* —Why not? —*Because it does not do anything* (!) —Is a tree alive? —*No; when it has fruit it's alive when it hasn't any, it isn't alive.* —Is a watch alive? —*Yes.* —Why? —*Because it goes . . .* (1927, p. 196).

These children are at the limits of the Intuitive stage. We shall follow them later into the Concrete operations stage, but a few general principles are clear at this point. First, there is a strong relation between concepts of physical and social causality (e.g., night, babies). Second, during the Intuitive stage, there is still a confusion between physical and personal causality; the physical world appears to operate much the way people do. Third, all of these examples suggest that Intuitive children have already developed elaborate mythologies about cosmic questions such as the nature of life (and death) and the cause of wind. Further, these mythologies show many similarities from child to child across cultures and do not seem to have been directly taught by adults. Jung (1917, 1969) has attributed the cross-cultural universality of mythologies to social archetypes, memories stored in the collective unconscious of humankind. Piaget's explanation focuses instead on the structural characteristics of thought common to young children living in a universe with common physical characteristics. Transductive reasoning by analogy creates many explanations based on human activity—a bicycle pump "lies down" and a man blows the sun away. Children's cognitive egocentrism at this stage reinforces their tendency to assume that the rest of the world is like themselves—filled with living things which move and have thoughts and feelings of their own.

Egocentrism

Social interaction in play. In Chapters 5 and 6, I described the child's shift from the function–pleasure play of the Sensorimotor stage to the symbolic play of the Preconceptual substage. With the coming of the Intuitive substage, Piaget notes another qualitative change in the child's play behavior. In addition to the solitary fantasy involvement of symbolic play, and the largely parallel social play of the two-to-four-year-old, the Intuitive child becomes very much involved in truly interactive, rule-regulated games with peers. But the way in which the interaction occurs, according to Piaget, reflects the egocentrism of the cognitive apparatus of both participants.

As a prelude to his studies of morality and justice, Piaget (1932) conducted an observation and interview study of the game of marbles.

> First he familiarized himself with the game, with the countless numbers of variations in and around Geneva, so that he would know what to look for and what to ask about. Then Piaget approached pairs of players, interviewing one and then the other. He would ask them to show him how to play, claiming he had forgotten. Occasionally he would make intentional mistakes so that the child could counter with the correct rule. Then he asked who had won, and why (the criteria for winning). After interviewing both children individually, he would watch them play to find out whether their descriptions corresponded with their actual behavior in a game with a peer. In another part of the study, Piaget asked children to invent new rules and to speculate about the origins of existing rules for marble games.

Piaget describes four stages of marble play. The first stage is an idiosyncratic, motor manipulation of the marbles with no verbalized rules. The second stage, characteristic of what came to be called the Early Intuitive period, is called egocentric play.

In this stage, children seem to imitate the example of older children, but they assimilate the rules to their own point of view. A game for two players may be played alone; when played with someone else, each child operates according to different sets of rules and little or no attempt is made to recognize and reconcile the differences. Early Intuitive children can take turns and respond to each other's actions, but as often as not they fail to watch each other, and new turns have little relation to whatever came before. Games have no beginning and no end. Everyone can win; winning does not mean being better than others according to agreed upon criteria, but rather, playing on one's own and achieving one's own goals. In this period, then, there is neither true competition (to be best) nor true cooperation in which the interactions imply a system of mutual regulation and responsiveness. Further, there is a paradoxical discrepancy in the child's conceptions of rules. In practice, rules are often invented spontaneously, changed abruptly, and discarded. At the same time, rules are believed to be eternal and immutable. They are invented by fathers or grandfathers, the town council, or God. Many children assume that as far back as they can think (e.g., in Biblical times), people have played marbles in exactly the same way.

Piaget notes the similar structure of egocentrism in games and in children's conversations with each other. Like Preconceptual children, there is a preponderance of "pseudo-conversation" or "collective monologue" during which Early Intuitive children take turns in speaking what is on their minds without responding much to the other's content.

> A third stage appears between 7 and 8 [Late Intuitive, Early Concrete] which we shall call the stage of incipient *cooperation*. Each player now tries to win, and all therefore begin to concern themselves with the question of mutual control and the unification of the rules. But while a certain agreement may be reached in the course of one game, ideas about the rules in general are still rather vague. In other words, children of 7–8, who belong to the same class at school and are therefore constantly playing with each other, give, when they are questioned separately, disparate and often entirely contradictory accounts of the rules . . . (p. 27) [A fourth stage will be described in Chapter 9.]

Laboratory studies of egocentrism and communication. Stimulated primarily by an important book on the topic of role-taking and communication (Flavell, Botkin, Fry, Wright, and Jarvis, 1968), there has been a flurry of research on cognitive and social egocentrism during the Intuitive and Concrete stages. At this point, unfortunately, there seems to be more confusion than enlightenment on this topic, but a number of distinctions are gradually becoming clear. While investigators initially treated Piaget's concept of egocentrism as a unitary developmental dimension or variable, it is now evident that there are several theoretically defined types of egocentrism, with different tasks purporting to measure each type, and different cognitive components assumed to be relevant to each task.

a) Spatial perspective. Here the prototype is the Three Mountains Task in which the child must indicate what someone else sees from another physical vantage point. In its initial form, children have difficulty with this task until at least mid-Concrete operations. Many early adolescents are still not able to take another spatial perspective (Laurendeau and Pinard, 1970; Chandler and Greenspan, 1972). This should not be surprising, considering the difficulty that Intuitive children have with horizontals, verticals, and with coordinating two conceptual dimensions. However, when the display and the required responses are simplified, and the child has extensive opportunity to move from one position to another (e.g., Shantz and Watson, 1971; Borke, 1971, 1972, 1975), Intuitive children have at least some success in recognizing and predicting different spatial viewpoints.

Other versions of spatial perspective tasks have been created in which Intuitive children also demonstrate at least some ability to coordinate perspectives. Flavell, *et al.* describes a simple task which examines whether young children orient their pictures upside down when pointing out the location of an object ("Where is the doll?") to an experimenter seated opposite them. Still other versions assess the child's ability to construct a design or pattern which has been rotated 90° or 180° (Pufall, 1975).

b) Verbal communication accuracy. Glucksberg, Krauss, and Weisberg (1966) created one prototype of a task used by other investigators. Pairs of four- and five-year-olds were visually separated by a screen and given identical sets of blocks with nonsense figures or with pictures of familiar objects on them. The speaker in each pair had to describe a chosen block so that the listener could select the correct one from his set. When the stimuli were nonsense figures, these (presumably[8]) Intuitive stage speakers could not communicate effectively enough to direct the listener to make correct choices. However, when pictures of familiar objects were used, performance was quite good. The problem with the nonsense figures seemed to be located in the children's idiosyncratic encoding of verbal messages. When an experimenter read back the speaker's cryptic descriptions, the speaker himself could select the correct block almost every time, but to others the message was unintelligible.

c) Social perspective/role-taking. In a recent article, Marvin, Greenberg, and Mossler (1976) distinguish what they call perceptual perspective-taking as in the Three Mountains Task, from what they call conceptual perspective-taking. Since the Three Mountains Task *is* highly conceptual, their term might be misleading, but they are referring to an important phenomenon—"the inference a child makes regarding these less tangible aspects of another's internal experience such as his thoughts, desires, attitudes, plans" (p. 511). Shantz (1975) describes the same issue in terms of the child's ability to answer four related questions—what is another person seeing, thinking, feeling, or intending? Flavell, *et al.* (1968) and Selman (1971b, 1976) use the term "role-taking" to describe the general ability to understand another person's perspective. They also assume that role-taking underlies all abilities to coordinate perspectives, including the Three Mountains Task and the verbal communication tasks described above (i.e., the child takes speaker and listener roles).

[8]One problem in these studies is that stage is generally defined by age and not by some independent criterion of structure.

Unfortunately, it is difficult to design a task which will independently assess role-taking as a specific skill. The general approach, which overlaps with verbal communication tasks, is to investigate whether the child's communication is sensitive to special circumstances of the listener or observer. DeVries' (1970) guessing task, described in Chapter 6, shows considerable shift in the five- and six-year-olds' strategy of hiding pennies in an attempt to fool an adult observer. Selman (1971) in a much more complicated task, asked four-to-six-year-olds to predict what a peer would guess in a choice situation. Four-year-olds knew that there were two points of view but did not see how they could know what others were thinking. By contrast, five-year-olds tended to assume complete similarity between self and others' thoughts, while six-year-olds were aware of the possibility of both similarities and differences in guessing strategy. Yet, these six-year-olds were not skilled at predicting precisely what another person might understand. DeVries concluded that six-year-olds were doing relatively well, while Selman indicated that they were just at the beginning of coordinating perspectives. Shantz (1975) suggests that this discrepancy results from the fact that DeVries inferred cognitive strategies from behavior, while Selman posed questions to the child and used the verbal response to infer representations.

Another format for investigating role-taking was developed by Flavell *et al.* (1968) and also used by Chandler and Greenspan (1972). For example, children are shown seven pictures which tell a story of a man out walking. He meets an angry dog and climbs a tree to protect himself. The middle four pictures, including all reference to the dog, are removed. A new person comes into the room and the child is asked to tell the story that the new person would tell—that is, with the four pictures removed from the sequence. The Intuitive child's stories to the new person are still full of dogs. In other less direct measures of sensitivities to the requirements of the observer, the salient observer characteristics are varied on dimensions of age (a young child vs. an adult; Shatz and Gelman, 1973) or ability to see (sighted vs. blindfolded; Meissner and Apthorp, 1976). Variation in the child's response to different third persons is taken as an index of the recognition of perspectives. Generally, in these tasks, Intuitive children cannot always communicate accurately, but their communication does show some sensitivity to the particular requirements of the listener.

Two central questions emerge as dominant themes in this research: is egocentrism a unidimensional construct and does it decline much earlier than Piaget's writings suggest?

1. Unidimensional? Evidence for and against the notion of egocentrism as a unidimensional variable comes from studies which intercorrelate or factor analyze a number of different egocentrism tasks. Rubin (1973) found significant correlations (.65–.73) among communication, role-taking, and spatial perspective tasks in Intuitive and older children. Layton (1975) found a significant relation between Glucksberg-Krauss-type communications and role-taking in five- and six-year-olds. A study by Hollos and Cowan (1973) and another by Cowan (Chapter 9) also found correlations between spatial, role-taking, and communication ability in older children.

However, other studies of Intuitive children suggest that there are distinct components of egocentrism ability in different tasks. Urberg and Docherty (1976) focus on structural differences in tasks requiring sequential or simultaneous decentering. Salatas and Flavell (1976) suggest that the child's idea that the observer has one unique point of view comes long before the idea that one view cannot be seen from more than one position.

2. How early? Piaget and Inhelder (1948) tend to characterize Preoperational children as egocentric without much qualification. But many studies cited above indicate that Intuitive children do in fact show some ability to coordinate points of view (see Chapter 6). Trying to sort out the confusion, Harris and Bassett (1976) conclude: "Recent studies have generally confirmed [Piaget and Inhelder's] findings with the qualification that accurate reproduction of another's perspective varies with the nature of the display, the number of choice items and the mode of response" (p. 514). The research suggests, then, that egocentrism cannot be treated as a unidimensional concept. I suspect that further studies will begin to specify both the general and the specific cognitive skills involved in the solution of egocentrism problems and in the coordination of spatial, communicational, and social perspectives.

Moral development

The field of moral development arose in psychology in an attempt to answer several interrelated questions. 1) How do we explain the fact that children resist temptation—that they act against their own immediate self-interest or obey laws even when no parents, police, and so on are around? 2) How do we explain the fact that children come to make judgments concerning the "oughts" of behavior—to distinguish between good and bad, right and wrong, just and unjust? 3) How do we account for the emergence of moral feelings, especially the feelings of guilt which accompany violation of one's own moral judgments? The first of these questions focuses on the acquisition of moral behavior and has been studied extensively by social-learning theorists (e.g., Bandura and Walters, 1963; Aronfreed, 1968; Sears *et al.*, 1965; Ray and Alpert, 1965). The third focuses on the development of moral feelings and has been dominant in psychoanalytic and neopsychoanalytic writings (e.g., Erikson, A Freud). The second question, bridging the gap between feelings and behavior, is concerned with the development of moral judgments, and that is the territory of most interest to Piaget. His impact on the study of moral development is remarkable, because since he wrote *The Moral Judgment of the Child* (1932), he has never returned to study this topic. However, research and theory in the Piagetian tradition by Kohlberg (1963, 1969, 1976) and by Turiel (1969, 1978) has helped to keep current and vital the cognitive approach to moral development.

"All morality consists in a system of rules and the essence of all morality is to be sought in the respect which the individual acquires for those rules." This is why Piaget's book begins with a study of games with rules and then goes on to note a developmental sequence in the child's formulation of rules about good and bad, right and wrong, and so on. In general, he finds two different moral orientations, one typical of Intuitive age children and one typical of children in the late Concrete substage (ten to twelve years). At the lower end of the scale, children tend to focus on observed consequences of actions and believe in absolute, unchanging rules handed down by outside authorities. At the upper end children focus on the inferred intentions behind the act and conceive of relative rules constructed and changed by social agreement. "Though we could not point to any stages properly so-called which followed one another in a necessary order, we were able to define processes whose final terms were quite distinct from one another. These processes might mingle and overlap more or less in the life of each child, but they marked nevertheless the broad division of moral development" (p. 175). We shall return later to the issue of why moral development does not show the definite stage sequence characteristic of the other areas of cognitive development conceptualized by Piaget.

In Piaget's studies of morality, the typical format is the verbal interview in which stories are told about two children and the subject must choose which of the two is naughtier or which of two alternatives was more correct or more just.

> A. A little boy who is called John is in his room. He is called to dinner. He goes into the dining room. But behind the door there was a chair, and on the chair there was a tray with fifteen cups on it. John couldn't have known that there was all this behind the door. He goes in, the door knocks against the tray, bang go the fifteen cups and they all get broken!
>
> B. Once there was a little boy whose name was Henry. One day when his mother was out he tried to get some jam out of the cupboard. He climbed up on to a chair and stretched out his arm. But the jam was too high up and he couldn't reach it and have any. But while he was trying to get it he knocked over a cup. The cup fell down and broke. (p. 122)

This story pair and four others were designed to assess the child's evaluation of the relative importance of intention and consequences in judging the morality of an act; intentionality is only one of eleven dimensions of moral judgment described by Piaget. Here is a typical response by a six-year-old, presumably Intuitive substage child.

> —Have you understood the stories? —*Yes.* —What did the first boy do? —*He broke eleven cups.* —And the second one? —*He broke a cup by moving roughly.* —Why did the first one break the cups? —*Because the door knocked them.* —And the second? —*He was clumsy. When he was getting the jam the cup fell down.* —Is one of the boys naughtier than the other? —*The first is because he knocked over twelve cups.* —If you were the daddy, which one would you punish most? —*The one who broke twelve cups.* —Why did he break them? —*The door shut too hard and knocked them. He didn't do it on purpose.* —And why did the other boy break a cup? —*He wanted to get the jam. He moved too far. The cup got broken.* —Why did he want to get the jam? —*Because he was all alone. Because his mother wasn't there.* —Have you got a brother? —*No, a little sister.* —Well, if it was you who had broken

the twelve cups when you went into the room and your little sister who had broken one cup while she was trying to get the jam, which of you would be punished most severely? —*Me, because I broke more than one cup* (pp. 124–125).

Contrary to some interpretations (e.g., Costanzo, Coie, Grument, and Farnill, 1973), it is not that the young child fails to understand intentionality. Rather, the intentions of the actor are judged to be less important than consequences in determining the goodness or badness of an act. By contrast, older children tend to focus on the intent and minimize the consequences of the action.

In many ways, this verbal method of Piaget's leads to some confusion in understanding the application of moral judgment to everyday life. Adults do not always pay attention to intent; when a young child breaks a precious vase, the fact that it happened by accident does not always reduce the adult's anger. And, there are many occasions when moral judgments and behavior do not coincide; guilt often occurs in the situation where we have behaved inconsistently with our own moral standards. However, when we wish to explain rules to children, or to give them reasons why they should or should not perform a particular act, then our knowledge of Piagetian moral development becomes important in assessing what will be assimilated from the message that we intend to convey.

In two summary reviews of research on Piaget's conception of morality, Kohlberg (1963, 1964) finds that six of Piaget's dimensions have proved to define measurable developmental dimensions in the elementary school years.

1. Consequence versus Intentionality (see above).
2. Absolute versus Relative judgments. The Intuitive child tends to evaluate an act as totally right or wrong, or to assume that in a disagreement, adults have the correct point of view; they do not assume that morality may be relative to the context or point of view of the person judging an act.
3. Tied-to versus Independent-of sanctions. Older children assume that acts defined as bad may be followed by sanctions (e.g., If I'm bad, I'll get punished). Intuitive children tend to define an act by the sanctions (If I was punished, I must have been bad). This dimension is similar to 1.
4. Retribution versus reciprocity. Early Intuitive children do not usually use reciprocity as a reason for considering others. I have described Kohlberg's finding that even for ten-year-olds the Golden Rule is translated: "Do to others what they do to you."
5. Punishment versus Reform or restitution. For Intuitive children, misdeeds should be severely and painfully punished (see the morality of fairy tales). Older children favor treatments involving restitution to the victim (returning stolen money) and leading to reform of the "criminal."
6. Immanent versus Distributive justice. Younger children assume that physical accidents and natural misfortunes are punishments willed by God or by natural objects (justice is immanent in the physical world, "so watch out"): older children look upon justice as a social system of decisions.

There are a number of obvious similarities between moral judgments and other cognitive structural conceptions. Children focus on the perceptible (consequences) rather than the inferable (intentions); responses are either–or; reasoning is transductive, so if bad behavior leads to punishment, then punishment must have followed bad behavior; other points of view are not considered; God and natural objects are active as human causal forces in the universe. Surprisingly, there have been few empirical studies in the Intuitive stage which examine the intercorrelations among cognitive and moral tasks. Damon's excellent study (1975) of four-to-eight-year-olds showed high stage correspondence among concepts of justice and multiple classification, class inclusion, seriation, spatial perspective, and proportionality. His account is enhanced by a detailed analysis of the logical structural components of each of the tasks.

Kohlberg's summary of research on Piaget's judgment dimensions indicates that five dimensions of moral judgment described by Piaget do *not* show consistent age trends. These are the dimensions emphasizing moral feelings (e.g., the development of mutual respect for others). The fact that feelings and judgments come together in the area of morality may be one reason why Piaget found that there were no clear stage divisions even though there are consistent sequences of moral reasoning and the apparent limitation of the questions in revealing more important and work against the generality of structural stages. Kohlberg also points out the limitations of Piaget's two-story method in providing a range of moral reasoning and the apparent limitation of the questions in revealing developmental trends past the age of ten. In response, Kohlberg constructed a new interview which yields six stages of moral judgment, in a necessary sequence. The early interviews were done with ten-to-sixteen-year-olds and so the scale will be described in the chapters on Concrete and Formal operations.

Both Piaget and Kohlberg reject the view that children learn moral principles solely through adult teaching and example. They argue that children are active in constructing views of good and bad and that these views show at least some regularity in changes over time. Researchers and theorists investigating this topic tend to focus on how adult-level judgments are acquired. To me the most convincing support for Piaget and Kohlberg's view is found in the apparent universality of lower-level answers in younger children. Certainly, as Bandura suggests (1969a), parents stress consequences rather than intention in talking to younger children, but can parental teaching account for the fact that almost all five-year-olds in almost all moral interviews focus on consequences (e.g., Bandura and McDonald, 1963; Cowan, Langer, Heavenrich, and Nathanson, 1969)? And in Kohlberg interviews, ten-year-olds from the United States, Mexico, and Taiwan give almost half their responses at his stage 1, which also stresses consequences and obedience to external rules (reported in Kohlberg, 1969).

While moral judgments may not be directly attributable to adult teaching, there is still something inherently social in their development. Piaget speculated that as long as the young child was oriented to obeying adult authority, relativistic moral judgments were not possible. Only when the child entered the reciprocal, egalitarian world of peer interaction would higher level moral development be stimulated. Kohlberg (1969) cites evidence suggesting that there is no correlation between amount of peer interaction and moral development, but I am not certain that Piaget believes that amount is the critical variable. Kohlberg himself tends to attribute moral judgment advances to general intellectual growth (as would Piaget) and to the development of role-taking. Turiel (1977) has begun to argue that role-taking is not itself a developmental structural dimension. At this point, then, we know that moral judgments show developmental trends, but there is no agreed-upon explanation of the specific factors responsible for generating the developmental changes.

One final note. In all of this discussion of moral judgment, we should not forget that Intuitive children are capable of what we would label as moral behavior. They do, often, obey rules. They resist temptations even when they know they will not be caught. And they can apply consistent judgments to others and to themselves about the goodness or badness of actions, even though the criteria may differ from adult-level definitions. By the age of seven or eight, children have already learned a great deal about the shoulds and oughts of behavior, feelings, and judgments.

EMOTIONAL DEVELOPMENT

The structure of values

For adults, moral values and other values concerning what is better or more important are often ranked in some sort of hierarchy which helps to determine choices when values conflict. Should someone steal an expensive drug to save his dying wife (one of Kohlberg's moral dilemmas)? The answer depends to some extent on a judgment about the relative importance of preserving human life and obeying social rules, as well as a decision concerning whether ends ever justify means. In what may be a nonmoral situation, should one pursue a career as a doctor or as a poet, if we assume that the two cannot be combined? Again, the decision many be based in part on our judgment of the relative value of these activities.

According to Piaget, values are the products of our interests, projected onto the object or activity. The practice of medicine is not intrinsically better than the writing of poetry; one's interest (in the broad sense of emotional investment) makes one activity appear to be more valuable than the other. If Piaget's view is correct, then the person's value hierarchy is largely a product of his or her own feelings *and the cognitive organization which structures any series of events.* We have seen that until very late in the Intuitive stage there are no stable class-inclusion hierarchies, so we would expect an absence of a consistent rank-ordered set of values in children of this age. I am aware of no systematic research on this point, but casual observations suggest that it is correct. In fact, judging from the prevalence of adult-level inconsistencies (e.g., constantly shifting, vaguely specified sets of priorities), I wonder what *prevents* consistent value hierarchies from being organized long after the prerequisite cognitive apparatus has emerged. Is it, again, the intrusion of feelings into a cognitive organizational task? Or are values inherently resistant to logical classification hierarchies—for instance, if I like rock music better than instumental jazz, and jazz better than opera, do I *necessarily* like rock better than opera? Piaget's general discussions simply point to the relevance of cognitive organization in the organization of a value hierarchy. It is not clear on either theoretical or empirical grounds how close a correspondence between cognitive and value structures we should expect.

Self-evaluation

Usually, moral values are studied in the context of how children describe the actions of others. I believe that the emergence of moral values during the Intuitive substage should have some important implications for children's evaluations of themselves. Just as Intuitive concepts are present-oriented, non-conservational, either–or, we would expect feelings about the self to be based on inconsistent, fluctuating feelings of the moment. And, just as moral judgments focus on obedience to rules and on consequences, so the child's judgments of self should focus on the same things. Children described as "bad" by parents or teachers tend to get punished. But in the child's view there are two important corollaries: "If I am punished, then I must have been bad"; "If I haven't been caught, then what I did was not wrong."

It seems to me that the Intuitive stage may be a particularly vulnerable period for the learning of self-evaluative feelings. Freud's location of the Oedipal struggle during this period is one way of accounting for the emergence of moral ideologies concerning others and the self; however, in a Piagetian approach, the problem is more general and more related to cognitive structural factors (of course). By the end of the Intuitive stage, children have established a sense of self—of personal identity—being the same person in past, present, and future. This means that for the first time they are able to contemplate themselves as living, thinking, feeling beings, not just as physical objects. At the same time, their egocentric view of the universe limits their social interaction and limits their recognition of the multiplicity of points of view. In judgments of good and bad, their cognitive structures dictate a focus on the judgments of adults and on the adult behavior which follows their actions (consequences). Internal standards of self and judgments do not emerge for quite some time. Therefore, the time when the psychological self is emerging is the time when children are most at the mercy of external factors in forming their evaluative self-image.

EDUCATIONAL IMPLICATIONS FOR EARLY PRIMARY GRADES: KINDERGARTEN TO BEGINNING SECOND GRADE

It is probably necessary to remind readers at this point that there are no definitive prescriptions for curriculum and methods which come directly from Piaget's view (Duckworth, 1972; Case, 1973). And yet, there is an extensive and growing literature, ranging from simple ideas to whole curricula based upon general principles derived from Piaget's cognitive developmental approach. In this section I will describe some of the applications of Piaget's theory relevant to single subject areas in early elementary grades (reading, mathematics, science). The section continues with some implications of social–emotional development for education and concludes with a brief exploration of how Piaget's approach broadens current definitions of classroom learning.

Reading

In most schools, the centrally important activity of the primary grades is learning to read. Because many six-year-olds have great difficulty in this endeavor, there are an increasing number of "reading readiness programs" introduced in kindergarten and even some prereading activities in preschools. This emphasis on reading reflects the fact that personal experience is necessarily limited and that reading can expand the range of our knowledge. It also reflects a value that reading and writing are somehow *better* vehicles for conveying knowledge than speaking and acting. Finally, the cumulative sequence of education tends to give reading a built-in importance; in later grades the curriculum tends to be based increasingly on reading activities and on information which is derived from reading. And so a child who has reading difficulty in the early grades tends to find himself or herself farther and farther behind.

Reading involves a number of complex, conceptual, coordination skills. First, the child must learn to establish figurative correspondence between two modalities—words on the page and sounds as spoken. Unfortunately, in many languages including English, there is regularity, but no absolute consistency in the relation between the printed letter and the spoken sound (e.g., the "a" in papa, bad, gave). Second, written and spoken words must be matched with some figurative representation of the object or event ("house" refers to structures with certain physical characteristics). A third coordinational skill that a child must develop is the establishment of connection between symbolic representations (printed word, sounds, objects) and conceptual meaning—between the figurative and operative aspect of symbols.

In the teaching and test-evaluations of reading there is repeatedly expressed concern about meaning or comprehension. But in my experience, early reading classes spend most of their time on the decoding and figural identification of symbols: "m = a = n is pronounced *man*." Primary school textbooks are brightly illustrated as if the meaning of the words can be fully conveyed by the pictures. The idea that reading is primarily taught as a perceptual rather than conceptual skill can be inferred from the often-parodied content of the first grade reading texts. Few six-year-olds are conceptually challenged by deciphering the sentence "See Spot run." Most classroom teachers are aware of this discrepancy between conceptual level and perceptual difficulty, but they feel locked in by the state guidelines and curriculum requirements. Piaget's approach suggests that the figurative emphasis must be supplemented by conceptual development inherent in the child's action. In a sense, reading as an aspect of symbolic meaning may be as much affected by sorting and piling objects, as it is by poring over printed page. Studies of the relation between performance on Piaget tasks and reading readiness (Scott, 1969; Brekke, Williams, and Harlow, 1973) are beginning to find a correlation between operative development and reading skills. However, we do not yet know whether this relation is an artifact resulting from the fact that children who show advanced cognitive development will be readier to read at an earlier age.

Furth (1970), writing from a Piagetian point of view, makes the most extreme indictment I have seen of the tendency to overemphasize reading in the early grades. First, he argues that the *early* motivation for reading is often extrinsic—to please parents and to imitate older peers—in contrast with the intrinsic motivation to explore classification, space, time, and so on. Second, he points out that deciphering of the written code requires, at most, the intellectual level of a four-year-old. Many early reading programs are successful in that they can get very young children to say accurately what is printed on a page. Furth's most impassioned criticism is reserved for the notion that emphasis on reading at early ages can actually serve to impair the development of thinking.

"Assuming that many children who come to school are intellectually impoverished but still have enough internal motivation to grow intellectually—as is shown by the fact that their intellects will continue to grow with or without school—what, in effect, is the school offering the child? This is the message he gets: 'Forget your intellect for a while, come and learn to read and write; in five to seven years time, if you are successful, your reading will catch up with the capacity of your intellect which you are developing in spite of what we offer you.'

"Mark well these twin conditions: learn reading and forget your intellect. These two things go hand in hand. The average five-to-nine-year-old child from any environment is unlikely, when busy with reading or writing, to engage his intellectual powers to any substantial degree. Neither the process of reading itself nor the comprehension of its easy content can be considered an activity well suited to developing the mind of the young child." (p. 4)

Furth labels most schools as "reading schools" in contrast with the "thinking schools," which could be, must be, established by focusing on the development of operative intelligence. It is essential that we not lose the main point in the heat of the rhetoric. Furth is not against teaching reading, but against teaching it so early, with so much emphasis. The discrepancy between the intellectual content of early books and the intellectual level of the child, compounds the motivational problem which is at the heart of teaching reading—how to get children to *want* to take the trouble to crack the code.

Within a Piagetian framework, Elkind (1969, 1970) attempts to find structural analogies between perceptual and cognitive skills in reading with a set of three tasks involving "perceptual logic."

1. Perceptual reorganization. In a set of ambiguous figures, the black space appears as one object (e.g., a tree), the surrounding white space as another (e.g., a duck, see Figure 12a). Children must combine and reorganize different perceptual cues in order to see both objects, and this ability increases with age from the Early to Late Intuitive substage. Elkind argues that the ability to arrange and rearrange letters into words requires similar reorganization skills.

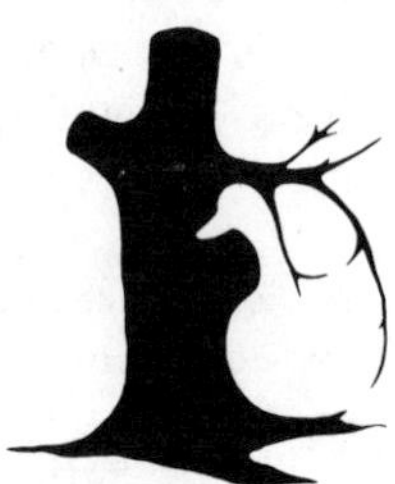

Figure 12. From Elkind, 1969

2. Perceptual schematization. In another set of drawings, whole figures (e.g., a person) are made of parts with independent meanings (e.g., fruits, Figure 12b). When these drawings were presented to children at different age levels, preschool children (age four) tended to see only parts, kindergarteners (age five) tended to describe only wholes, while second-graders and beyond (age seven+) said, "a man made out of fruit." Elkind argues that this perceptual–logical double classification is especially necessary for children to understand the idea that the same letters are paired with different sounds, while the same sound can be represented by different letters.
3. Perceptual exploration (decentering). Pictures of objects familiar to young children were pasted on a card, either in disordered array or in the form of a triangle. Children were asked to name every picture. In the age range from four to eight the number of errors of omission and commission declined (e.g., naming the same object twice). Also, there was an increase with age in children's ability to scan the arrays systematically from left to right and from top to bottom (an essential skill in reading).

In two studies, Elkind and his colleagues (Elkind, Horn, and Schneider, 1965; Elkind, Larson, and Van Doorninck, 1965) demonstrated a strong interrelationship among these tasks and reading ability, beyond the correlations attributable to general intelligence.

While Furth argues for a delay in the emphasis on reading, Elkind (1969) suggests that an analysis of reading skills into perceptual–logical–structural components and that training in these components may facilitate the development of meaningful reading skills in the early primary grades. However, his data indicate that the skills which he designates as important for reading do not emerge, on the average, until the second grade level. My own conclusion is that we would do well to consider a delay in the introduction of formal reading instruction until the second grade, but this represents a very radical shift in current conceptions of teaching. For guidance, we may look to the experience of the British Infant Schools (e.g., Featherstone, 1971), where books are available, but reading is not formally taught to young children. At the very least, we should establish some of the specific cognitive or perceptual skills necessary for reading and introduce formal instruction on the basis of individually determined developmental levels.

Mathematics

The Nuffield Mathematics program in England (e.g., 1967, 1970) is an attractive program of mathematics learning based on "Piagetian" activities (e.g., sorting, classifying). It provides teachers with both concrete examples and conceptual principles from which to generate a series of mathematics *activities* in the early years. Counting and numerals used as arbitrary symbols come only after long involvement in these overt activities.

The program places great emphasis on the use of available classroom materials. Children can gain experience with size relations by discussing belt sizes, ribbon lengths, and height. They can gain classification experience by sorting out junk drawers, as well as engaging in more goal-oriented classification activities such as dividing a pile of objects into "things which sink and things which float." After a single classification principle is mastered, double classification can be tried (children in the class who are boys or girls, right- or left-handed). Experiential activities relevant to mathematics can be seen in the child's play with containers of sand or water, "Lego" bricks, drawings, music and body movement (e.g., skipping ropes can be used to explore lengths). For explorations in one-to-one correspondence, the Nuffield program suggests Piaget's own examples of eggs and egg cups, flowers and vases, but also paint bottles and brushes, and so on. Ordering can be done by following instructions ("Put the box to the right or behind the table"), drawing pictures of family members, or playing with stacking boxes. Class inclusion begins with investigating the number of objects in subsets. With each activity, the Nuffield program suggests some ways in which children can record their observations. drawing pictures, using buttons as counters, bar-type graphs of number of objects in each category, and so on. Only after much experience with all these activities is the abstract notion of numerals finally explored.[9]

[9]Remember that classification, seriation, and number concepts may not fully develop in many children until second grade.

Is there anything basically new about this program? Yes and no. Teachers have always known that number must be taught concretely before it is taught in abstract form. What the Nuffield program does is to suggest specific kinds of concrete teaching, some of which seem unrelated to number (sorting junk drawers), but which Piaget's analysis suggests are necessary for the development of numerical conservation. Secondly, American programs in the "new math" (e.g., Greater Cleveland Mathematics Program, 1962) primarily present concrete examples to be completed in textbooks and workbooks. In the Nuffield program the children use both large and small muscles to manipulate objects in the real world. Again, the emphasis is on operative rather than figurative activity. Also, the program suggests the necessity of rearranging space in the classroom and abandoning the notion that every child be involved in the same activity at the same moment. Teachers who have not been involved in such a program tend to fear that such an arrangement will produce chaos. And without careful preparation and structuring of materials, without individual contracts for each student, chaos can result. The Nuffield program is a good example of the futility of the debate concerning whether or not classroom structure is necessary; the issue is, clearly, what *kind* of structure promotes optimal learning?

I am afraid that my optimism about the Nuffield program is neither supported nor negated by empirical evidence of its effectiveness. I am aware of no studies which directly assess the outcome of a Nuffield approach and compare it to more traditional programs. We are still a long way from knowing how much we can influence children's development of cognitive structures by direct experience with Piaget-type activities and materials (see Chapter 12). Still, it appears to me that some ideas from such a program, if not the whole program itself, can ultimately prove helpful to math teachers in meeting their central challenge—reaching children at their developmental level and interesting them in mathematical explorations and learning.

Science

The Science Curriculum Improvement Study (Karplus and Thier, 1967) has developed a number of study units, some of which are applicable to the earliest elementary grades. The approach of this program is much like Nuffield; in fact, many of the early science "lessons" overlap with the suggestions made by Nuffield for the teaching of mathematics. For example, in the "material objects unit," first-graders: sort objects by properties, not by use; classify objects into collections; note similarities and differences; make observations and inferences; manipulate objects (do "experiments" in order to gain information and make a decision).

Some specific activities:

> Children arrange leaves in different shapes and sizes both in classes and in serial order. They compare pictures of animals, such as tigers and zebras. Some teachers get children to sort words as well as objects (e.g., color words, shape words, size words, etc.), facilitating reading and meaning as well as science.
>
> One teacher asked children to examine which materials make sounds when

struck. When one boy said that he had found an object that didn't make a noise (balsa wood), the whole class stopped to listen; when everything was quiet the noise could be heard. In another activity, the teacher asked children about the materials themselves.—Is this [a bowling pin] made of steel? —*No.* —[Holding up a jar of paste] Is this made of steel? —*No.* —[Pen] Is this made of steel? —*Yes.* —Well, what is steel? —*It is made out of hard.* —[Gives him hardened paste] Is this steel? —*No, but it's hard. I guess everything that is hard isn't steel.*

One SCIS evaluation study (Stafford and Renner, 1971) indicates that the SCIS material objects unit enhances first-graders' ability to use simple class logic. Presumably this in turn enhances the child's scientific knowledge and increases the resources by which knowledge can be acquired. A study of another science program also showed that the curriculum enriched kindergartner's ability to conserve number in five of six conservation tasks (Science: A process approach, Ayers and Ayers, 1973).

Causal explanations

We have seen that children in the early primary grades are still struggling with notions of causality. They tend to see a universe peopled with lifelike beings, or physical forces with human characteristics. Magical explanations such as those found in fairy tales are no more fantastic than scientific metaphors such as force or gravity. If adults can hold in reserve their strong allegiance to "the truth" and focus on the quality of the explanations, children may be helped to grow intellectually in both fantasy and reality directions.

Teachers often ask children for explanations of their own and others' behavior. Inevitably, when two Intuitive children are fighting and the teacher asks, "Who started it?" the answer from both children is "he did" or "she did." We have seen enough to know that even Late Intuitive children have difficulty with reconstructing sequences and tend to focus only on salient events. And what is more salient than someone else's insult or punch in the arm?

Gender and sex-role identity

A continuing theme of Piaget's theory is that the child is always filtering material through the structure of his or her cognitive level. One implication of Kohlberg's analysis is that from the earliest self-classifications of gender, children begin to filter their understandings and interests through their gender and sex-role categories. His approach suggests that gender identity begins to be established early and does not depend upon participation in sex-roles. Children know clearly that they are boys or girls before they are consistently aware of sex-role stereotypes.

Boys and girls then seek out those activities "appropriate" to their own gender and tend to reject activities identified as characteristic of the opposite sex. I have no systematic evidence for this observation, but it seems to me that many children restrict their sex-role behaviors fairly early. In contrast with other areas of development in the Late Intuitive period, where children are engaged in much experimentation, the choice of activities "appropriate" to sex-roles seems to become more and more limited. Some adults give strong negative messages to both boys and girls who depart from clear sex-typed choices. Perhaps adults are acting on an implicit assumption that sex-role behaviors are intimately tied to the creation of a clear gender identity. Perhaps, they fear, a boy who plays with dolls may be confused about whether he is a boy; a girl who takes physical risks may not grow up to be feminine.

If sex-role is an important aspect of the self, and if, as Piaget suggests, growth occurs through action and experimentation, teachers and parents of Intuitive stage children should consider encouraging more experimentation with a wide range of behaviors previously reserved either for boys or for girls. It would certainly mean rethinking all those messages which we give to children, for example, about which sex is "good in math" and which sex should take cooking classes. It would also mean actively encouraging children to experiment with a wide variety of activities without framing these activities in the context of sex-related choices. Given that peers may also exert stereotypic pressure, parents and teachers might provide examples and extra support for a more open attitude to sex-role definition. I confess that my own values lead me to suggest making sex-roles less rigidly separate. I think that even those who believe in a clearer distinction between boy and girl activities, can allow opportunity for some role experimentation; I believe this experience will contribute to the development in the child of a firm sense of self. Then, perhaps, children will not need to use their sex-role identity filters to screen out some areas of knowledge as inappropriate.

Moral values

Schools transmit moral values along with academic subjects. Teachers expect to have impact on discipline, citizenship, and attitudes as well as on reading, arithmetic, and science. Although the particular values of teachers and the school systems may vary, no classrooms are value-free. Beyond the specific arbitration of what is good and what is bad, schools, as systems, have rules and ways of treating students, and it is in the children's contact with these rules and discipline policies that they begin to form moral judgments of their own.

Piaget's emphasis on the necessity of accommodation in development suggests that the presence of at least some clear, adult-enforced rules may facilitate the process of equilibration. We also know that the assimilation function operates in such a way that children and adults understand the rules quite differently. One very common bone of contention for children is the idea of "fairness." For Intuitive age children, fairness is often defined in terms of sameness. Only if everyone receives the same treatment is it "fair." Teachers are often caught in a dilemma; some children seem to require different treatment, but the rest of the class could regard special treatment as unfair. Sometimes, in fact, teachers seem to adopt the children's view as if differential treatment has become unjust in their own eyes. Moral influence does not only work in the direction from adult to child.

Broadening the definition of learning activities

In the process of defining what are appropriate learning activities in schools, teachers have a tendency to make unnecessarily rigid distinctions. Classrooms are for work; recess is for play. Mathematics train the mind; athletics strengthen the body. Reading and writing are intellectual, discussing is social. Piagetian concepts help to tie together what have been treated as separate activities, with a resulting expansion of the definition of school learning.

Classification and seriation are centrally relevant to number. The same concepts can be seen in quantity and measurement of number, space, and time. Physical and social causality, egocentrism, identity, and morality may be examined as part of a structure of cognitive–social–emotional understanding.

> Putting objects in piles or in order of size is not "simply" free play. It is a learning activity. With increasing efforts to improve on academic learning, "art" periods have usually been reduced or eliminated. But in art, the child is working on the creation of representational symbols. In physical education, the child is not just "running off energy." He or she is learning about the physics of objects (e.g., bouncing balls), coordinating muscles, as well as coordinating perspectives. In the game of dodgeball, for example, the thrower tries to anticipate the moves of children inside the circle, while those children are trying to anticipate the moves of the thrower.
>
> Also, as we have seen, while children are learning about words, numbers, and objects, they are learning about themselves. A more differentiated ability to conceptualize the self may lead to expansions in motivation and ability to think about other things and other people. Social interaction is necessary, not only as a break from school learning; it is also a context in which social and cognitive structural development can occur.
>
> Even daydreaming has its possibilities. Children solve important problems in daydreams, and also develop their symbolic capacities. One teacher asked me about a seven-year-old who was "always daydreaming." When we observed together, it became evident that he was not "always" off in his own thoughts; he managed to do all his work and then appeared to turn inward. The teacher made an agreement with the child that as long as he continued to do good work, she would stop interrupting his daydreams. The quantity *and* quality of his work improved.

Of course, there are limits to what is acceptable and productive in a school context. These examples are not meant to suggest that anything goes and that everything the child does is in the service of cognitive development. They do, I hope, raise the possibility that we consider each of the child's activities in their structural relation with others before we rule them imperiously out of the classroom. By broadening the definition of learning to include the wide range of activities described for children at every stage, Piaget's approach can provide the teacher with many more roads to travel and still arrive at the hoped-for destination.

CHAPTER 8

A Structural Analysis of Beginning Concrete Operations

In the previous two chapters, I have described the child's progress through the Preoperational stage. From the first formation of private mental symbols, the child constructs Preconceptual classes, relations, and general strategies of transductive reasoning. By the end of the Intuitive substage, children are coordinating classes and relations in two dimensions, but only after a period of overt trial and error. At the beginning of the Concrete Operational stage (at around seven or eight years), a number of new achievements are observed in a relatively short period of time. They give evidence that children have now developed a reversible system of mental operations, enabling them to construct stable hierarchies of classes and relations and to conserve quantity, number, and some aspect of space and time. According to Piaget, a whole new cognitive organization underlies the child's new conceptualizations across many different limited areas.

First, some of the new achievements will be briefly described. Then, there will be a presentation of the "grouping"—the logic structure proposed by Piaget as a model of cognitive organization underlying the Concrete Operational stage (ages seven to twelve). The final section will describe how mental symbols developed during the previous stage are restructured by the new logical grouping with its system of reversible mental operations. Because the focus is primarily on the logic model, I will postpone the usual sections on emotional and social development and applications to education until the next chapter.

NEW ACHIEVEMENTS AT THE CONCRETE OPERATIONS STAGE

Classification

When seven- and eight-year-old children are given the twenty pictures of primulas, other flowers and objects (Inhelder and Piaget, 1959), they go through a planning phase. They look at all the pictures, sit and think for a moment, and then lay them out in a four-level hierarchy with only minor adjustments. It is as if their behavior is guided by the notion of hierarchy, in contrast with Late Intuitive children who achieve it only after trial and error.

What is more, the children clearly recognize that there are more primulas (B) than yellow primulas (A) in a bunch. In a series of questions, Piaget and Inhelder demonstrate that children at this stage are also aware that B (yellow primulas) and B′ (other-colored primulas) can be combined to make up C (primulas) and that B is the result of subtracting B′ (other colored) from C (primulas). These simultaneous, reversible combinations without distortion of whole or parts give evidence of conservations of classes as well as a coordination of a system of mental operations.

In other classification experiments, Piaget shows that achievement of a system of class inclusions is accompanied by an ability to form consistent two-way classifications or matrices, for example, of color and shape (big–red, small–red, big–blue, small–blue), or height and age (taller–older, shorter–older, taller–younger, shorter–younger).

Seriation

Here, too, the child of seven or eight begins with a plan. In the single line of sticks the child looks over the array and first selects the largest (or smallest), then the next in size, then the next, and so on. The same strategy is applied to the dolls and the walking sticks so that the child quickly lays out two series ordered along a single dimension.

It is as if the child possesses a scheme of a *potential* series, and the objects are fitted into a prearranged order. This "planfulness" suggests that the child has some prior understanding that each element is smaller than one neighbor and larger than another, depending on its relative position. Quantity has shifted from a property of a thing (tall, short) to a property of a relation between things.

Just as Concrete operations brings an organized series of class inclusions, so it brings an organized transitivity rule. At this stage, if the child knows that A is longer than B and that B is longer than C, he or she can *deduce* the A–C relation without empirically checking it.

Finally, in the classification of 49 leaves, the child produces a matrix of seven rows increasing in size and seven columns increasing in color intensity. Both classes and relations are now conceptualized in two simultaneous dimensions.

Number

The Concrete child easily and quickly produces one-to-one correspondence between a row of eggs and a row of egg cups, flowers and vases, and between rows of checkers. (Piaget and Szeminska, 1941). The judgment of correspondence is not destroyed when one of the rows is rearranged. Numbers of objects can be arranged and rearranged without altering the total; the division of sweets between elevenses and tea time can be 4 + 4, or 1 + 7, or 2 + 6, or 3 + 5. Conservation is not all-or-none. At first the child conserves small numbers, but transformations of a large number of objects still leads to a nonconservation response. Gradually the concept is applied over the whole number range.

Mental reversibility can be seen in children's ability to consider initial states of the objects, final states, and the transformation between them.

> "Nothing was added or taken away."
> "If you change it back the way it was, it would be the same."
> "The row is longer, but it still has the same number;"
> "This pile has more, but this one has less."

The ability to add and subtract small numbers, or to multiply and redivide small sets, develops at approximately the same time as the child's achievements in adding and multiplying classes and relations.

If all of this activity is performed mentally, abstracted from overt actions, why is this stage still called *Concrete* operations? Because at this time the child's mental reversibility is limited to concepts with which the child has already had some experience, and it is limited to the perceived world rather than some hypothetical state of affairs. For example, the nine-year-old in Concrete operations can multiply 6 × 5 = 30, but cannot solve this problem: If dogs have 6 heads and there are 5 dogs in my yard, how many heads will there be? The reply: *You can't do that. Dogs don't have 6 heads.*

Quantity

In the conservation of water and clay tasks, the child asserts that the quantities are the same; at first this is asserted with small transformations, later with extensive transformation (e.g., one water glass divided into six smaller containers; clay divided into very small pieces). At this stage, children also conserve inequalities. Even though a smaller amount of water transferred to a tall, thin jar has a higher water level, children know that there is less to drink. Just as five-year-olds were so certain that the amount changes when the water or clay is transformed, now children are convinced that changes in appearance do not alter the quantity. The experimenter's countersuggestions are resisted.

> I told one seven-year-old, who insisted that there was still the same amount of water in the taller glass—But a girl your age was here yesterday and she said that there was more water because it's higher. —[The girl's eyes widened] *Well, she was just silly, that's all.*

In the quantity and number tasks, the child conveys a feeling of logical necessity: "They must be the same." It is no longer important to examine the two objects closely; a casual look during the transformation assures the child that nothing was added or taken away.[1]

Space

Length. When two sticks are placed one over the other, and one is moved, children respond firmly that the lengths are still equal (Piaget, Inhelder, and Szeminska, 1948). In constructing the tower, children begin to use a neutral measuring instrument such as a stick or a piece of paper, but can only solve the problem correctly when the stick is the same size as the tower. Then, they can infer, in effect, that Tower A = stick; stick = Tower B; therefore, Tower A = Tower B. Not until age nine or ten (Late Concrete) will any stick or small piece of paper be used repeatedly on one tower and again on the other. Thus, while conservation of number, quantity, and length occur at around ages seven or eight, measurement in which a line can be broken arbitrarily into units and then recombined does not occur for two or three years. The comparison of lengths (sticks) seems to be simpler than the establishment of a reference marker independent of the child's own body and actions.

Area. When a rectangular figure is cut into pieces, the conservation of area is now clear: "You're putting the same amount in different places." In comparing a triangle with an irregular figure, Concrete children spontaneously use the intermediate pieces of paper to cover the two figures. They can recognize transitivity immediately: A = M (intermediate pieces); M is greater than B; A is greater than B. But they often justify their answer by counting the number of pieces that it takes to cover the figures, forgetting that some of the pieces are different in size. There are as yet no arbitrary, equal-unit measures.

Horizontal and vertical. In the problems with the tilted bottle and the sticks in the "mountain" of sand (Piaget and Inhelder, 1948), children gradually apply principles of horizontal and vertical to all cases, but only after trial and error. (This sounds more like Intuitive level performance in other areas.)

Piaget discusses the child's Early Concrete performance when the jar is tilted.

> [One child (7;3) says in wonder], "There's something I don't understand; the water stays still and the jar moves!" It is evident that without the experiment the child would not succeed in discovering that the liquid remains horizontal, for this is given empirically and not deduced *a priori*. But why is this experiment not effective until stage III [i.e., why does it not induce children to conserve before the stage of Concrete operations]? . . . It is at this point that one realizes the indispensable role

[1]Children's nonverbal behavior becomes an important criterion for stage diagnosis. If you ask a child whether glass A now has more, less, and so on, and he or she peers intently at the glasses, even if the answer is correct, the child is in Late Intuitive rather than the Early Concrete substage.

of a frame of reference. In order to recognize that the water is permanently horizontal . . . regardless of the tilt of the jar, it is necessary . . . to establish a relationship between the water and a set of objects external to the jar (Piaget and Inhelder, 1948, p. 409).

Not until Late Concrete (at about ten years) does the child, in both water jar and mountain problems, *begin* to use the external horizontal and vertical reference points as a system of coordinates to solve the problem. This means that Early Concrete children can coordinate two surface dimensions in an area problem but have not yet fully established a system of spatial coordinates.

Time

We would expect, correctly, that changes in the mental coordination of quantity and space would be reflected in the Concrete child's conception of time (Piaget, 1946b, 1946c). First, children can now remember or anticipate an order of events, arranging a sequence of pictures to correspond with previously observed events, or predicting what will happen to colored balls which reverse their direction of travel through a tunnel. Second, time and space intervals are now judged to be independent of events within them; the train travels the same distance from A to B no matter how quickly or slowly; the amount of time taken is independent of the space travelled (in a given time, faster trains go farther). Third, no longer is there automatic confusion between time and space. And fourth, there is a beginning conceptual reversibility of both time and distance. If a train is still travelling at the same speed, a return journey is judged to take the same time as the original trip; the distance of a trip from A through B, C, and D is expected to be the same as the distance from D back through C and B to A. Like length and space, the Early Concrete child can reverse and conserve time units but has not yet developed unitized measuring instruments to measure time. While he or she may be able to "tell the time" on the clock, the precise measurement of hours and minutes may be several years away.

Many of Piaget's experiments involve trains moving on track, so that he can systematically control the variables involved, but the findings apply to many real-life judgments of time. Like seriation of sticks or lengths, the child appears to have a conceptual notion of the order in which events occur and can mentally consider this order without distorting the perceptions of present events. In part, it is the conceptual reversibility of temporal ordering which allows the child to return in thought to consider initial states and transformations of objects in many different content areas.

These accounts of classification, seriation, number, quantity, space, and time suggest a great uniformity in the child's new world-view. We shall see below that empirical studies indicate that seven- or eight-year-olds don't always show as consistent a picture as Piaget has painted. While there are general correlations among tasks, children are in the Intuitive substage in some tasks, in Early Concrete in others, and in Late Concrete in still others. Sometimes, changing the content changes the level—children who conserve water may not conserve melted butter, or ice. The problem in describing development at this point has the quality of the choice between optimistic and pessimistic interpretations—is the glass half empty or half full? In this case, does the child show unitary and coherent cognitive structure, or are there wide variations in level as the child attempts to understand different events? The answer is "both." At this point, I will focus on Piaget's attempt to account for broad general similarities in achievements at the Concrete operational stage. Later, I will explore the facts and implications for the logic model of heterogeneous levels of performance in the same child.

OPERATIONAL LOGIC AS A STRUCTURAL MODEL OF MENTAL OPERATIONS

How do we account for the fact that similar shifts in logic and conservation concepts occur across so many content areas within such a relatively short period of time? For Piaget, the answer must lie in the fact that these changes are all "symptoms" of an important reorganization of intellectual structure—the emergence of a system of reversible mental operations. The system properties cannot be stressed too strongly. The Preoperational child may well be able to make isolated mental combinations of symbols ($1 + 2 = 3$; this truck and that wagon are both toys). But not until the stage of Concrete operations is there a set of rules for combining and recombining *any* two numbers or classes without distorting the parts or the whole. A logical model called a grouping has been developed by Piaget (1942, 1949; Beth and Piaget, 1961) and formalized by Grize (1960). Based on a synthesis of mathematical groups and logical lattices, it attempts to provide an explanation for the coherence and consistency of mental combinations in the Concrete operational stage.

Before presenting the model in some detail, I think that it is necessary to make clear a distinction which is often implicit in Piaget's work. Formal logic, the union of mathematical and logical theory, describes a set of rules for combining written symbols. These rules have no reference to behavior or to perceived events. When Piaget applies the concepts of formal logic to mathematical or logical reasoning, he is really making an extension by simile—it is *as if* the child uses rules in this way. Thus, there should always be a differentiation between formal logic, which is a model of inference applied to the relations among symbols, and Piaget's use of *operational logic*, a model of organization applied to the relations among overt or covert behaviors.

For those readers not familiar with logic and mathematics, the concepts contained in the logical model of cognition are difficult to grasp in one or even two readings. I suggest that you first try to follow the general argument without becoming too concerned about the details. These details become important only later on, when you attempt to specify precisely the cognitive structure of a particular child or to examine the structural interconnections among different content areas of a curriculum. Later on you will also find that the structure of the group and grouping is essential for an adult understanding of the foundations of the "new math" in elementary and high schools and for the discipline of formal logic at whatever level it is taught.

The grouping structure of Concrete operations

In mathematics, a "group" is defined as a set of elements and a combination rule with the following four properties: combinativity, associativity, general identity, and reversibility. To construct a grouping, Piaget adds a fifth property, special identity, which deals with some unique properties of logical classes.

The two basic combination rules with which Piaget is most concerned are addition (one element joined successively with another) and multiplication (one element joined simultaneously with another). When children use these combination rules, or *operations*, all five properties must be present before Piaget will say that the structure can be described as a grouping. In describing each property, I will usually give four concrete examples: additive and multiplicative operations on both numbers and classes. Sometimes I will also illustrate with examples of combining relations.

1. *Combinativity.* Any two elements in the set may be combined and the resulting product is a third element within the set.

> The set of positive whole numbers, 1, 2, 3, 4, 5 does not have combinative properties under the operation of addition because, for example, 3 + 4 produces an element outside the set. By contrast, the set of all positive and negative numbers (including 0 and infinity) under the operation of addition is combinative, because each pairing of elements produces another element within the set (1 + 2 = 3; 1,000,000 + 2 = 1,000,002).
>
> In the logic of classes and relations there is also a combinative property when two classes are added to form a third (mothers + fathers = parents) or multiplied to form a third (male × friends = male friends). Relations can also be combined by addition (A is older than B; B is older than C; A is older than C), or by multiplication (taller kids × stronger kids = taller, stronger kids).[2]

First and foremost, the combinativity property asserts that the relation holds between every pair of elements in a group. Preoperational children are able to coordinate adjacent quantities or form classes with some of the objects in

[2]There is a restriction on combinativity in classification hierarchies. Combining the classes *necessarily* produces a new class within the hierarchy only when the two classes are at the same level. For example, superordinate class C includes B + B′; class B′ includes A + A′. While B + B′ = C and A + A′ = B, there is no class *in the hierarchy* which is formed from A′ + B′. Whole numbers have unrestricted combinativity; to describe limits on combinativity for classification, Piaget uses the special identity property of classes (below).

a collection, but other elements are completely ignored; there are gaps in the coherence of the system. Of course, no human mind can encompass the relations among all elements simultaneously. Rather, the combinative property implies that each separate operative act is an example of a set of potential combinations which can be performed. This extension from the actual to the potential is one of the hallmarks of operational thought.

Second, the ability to produce mental combinations begins to free the child from the one-at-a-time quality of perceived events. By uniting categories, the child quickly jumps beyond immediate experience. By combining relations to reach a conclusion (A *must* be older than C), the child avoids the necessity of step-by-step comparisons.

Third, the combinativity property, in its emphasis on remaining within a defined set, focuses on the "staying on topic" aspect of reasoning. Combinativity is lacking when reasoning leaps to a conclusion in one domain from a premise in another (e.g., explaining that physical bodies fall "because they want to"). Combinativity is also lacking when the young child shifts classification principles within the set—from type of object, to color, to function. With the property of combinativity there emerges a clear distinction between what is "inside" and what is "outside" the system and a corresponding ability to judge what is relevant and what is not relevant to a particular problem.

2. *Associativity.* By the rules of logic and mathematics, elements, classes, and relations can only be combined two at a time. If three or more elements are to be combined by addition or multiplication, then they must somehow be clustered; for example, $6 + 3 + 4$ can be arranged $6 + (3 + 4)$ so that 6 is added to the result of combining $3 + 4$. The operation is said to be associative if the arrangement does not affect the results, e.g., $6 + (3 + 4) = (6 + 3) + 4$. Associativity is a quality of between-pair (between 6 and $(3 + 4)$) combinations.

Within each pair, (e.g., $3 + 4$), some operations on elements have an additional property of commutativity if the order of combination is irrelevant to the results: addition and multiplication are commutative ($2 + 1 = 1 + 2$, $6 \times 3 = 3 \times 6$); subtraction and division are not commutative ($6 - 3$ does not $= 3 - 6$; $6 \div 3$ does not $= 3 \div 6$).

Logical combinations *may* also be associative and commutative.[3]

boys + girls + women + men = people

One way of combining the classes would be:

(boys + girls) + (women + men) = people
(children) + (adults) = people

Another combination would be:

(boys + men) + (girls + women) = people
(males) + (females) = people

[3]Again, logical hierarchies are not fully associative; special identity properties are needed to describe combinations across levels of classification.

In either case the combination of subclasses produces the same end result. Furthermore, the order within pairs (boys + men, or men + boys) is irrelevant to the outcome.

Like combinativity, the property of associativity binds separate actions together in a coherent system. The multiplication table becomes more than an assemblage of collected facts; it begins to function as an organizer of the possibilities involved in working with numbers.

Associativity and commutativity are relevant to the capacity for mental detours or taking alternative routes to the same goal. The order in which concepts are considered or hypotheses are made is logically independent of the conclusion, but for young children (and sometimes for older ones) the order in which ideas or events occur may strongly influence the outcome. For example, in the conservation of water experiment, the Concrete operations child conserves the amount of water regardless of the order of transformations—from a tall-narrow glass to a short-wide one, to several small glasses, to the original glass, and so on.

For people of any age, perceptual systems often lack the associative property. The order in which two events are perceived, especially when they occur in quick succession (hot–cold; cold–hot), alters one's perception of the next event (lukewarm water).

3. *General identity.* A crucial property of groupings and groups is that there is one element which can be combined with all other elements without producing any change whatsoever.

In mathematics:

under the operation of addition, the identity element is 0:

$$2 + 0 = 2; 6 + 0 = 6$$

under the operation of multiplication, the identity element is 1:

$$2 \times 1 = 2; 6 \times 1 = 6$$

In the logic of classes:

under the operation of addition, the identity element is the null class:

boys + [no one] = boys; flowers + [nothing] = flowers

The identity property is not readily understood by young children, who assume that any action on an object or class alters it in some fundamental way. For the Concrete operational child, at least one combination of elements produces no change. The identity property is cited in the general conclusion: "If nothing is added or taken away, then the object or class remains unchanged."

4. *Reversibility.* In general terms, reversibility is the opposite of combinativity; that is, if two elements can always be combined to produce a third within the set, then the third can always be decomposed to reproduce the first two. Part of the flexibility of groupings and groups rests with the fact that operations can be "undone" without disrupting the system. For young chil-

dren, thought is reversible in the sense that reasoning goes backwards from effects to causes. But the *system* is not reversible because this backward reasoning causes distortion of the original categories (e.g., all the brown beads are wooden, but *not* all the wooden beads are brown).

Piaget shows that there are two kinds of reversibility, one for classes (negation or inversion) and one for relations (reciprocity).

a) *Negation.* Given a particular operation, every element has an inverse which cancels it when the two are combined.

In mathematics:

Addition: Start with 3. Add 6 [3 + 6]. Now add the inverse of 6 [3 + 6 + (−6)]. This cancels the adding of 6 and returns you to the start (3).
In arithmetic addition, the combination of an element with its inverse, [6 + (−6)] is always 0 (the identity element).

Multiplication: Start with 3. Multiply by 6 [3 × 6]. The total is 18. Now divide by 6, which cancels the multiplication and returns you to the start (3).
In multiplication, the combination of an element and its inverse (6 ÷ 6) is always 1 (the identity element).

In the logic of classes:

Addition: Start with primulas. Add other types of flowers to make the class "flowers." Take away all the other flowers. This leaves you with primulas, back at the start. In addition, the combination of a class (A) with its inverse (−A) produces a null class.

Multiplication: Start with a set of "pieces of paper." Now partition it (by multiplicative classification) into four piles: red–square, red–circle, blue–square, blue–circle. The undoing of multiplication is the *elimination* of partitions. As in Piaget's experiment with the four-compartment box, removing one of the partitions results in a classification only by shape or by color. Removing both partitions returns you to the whole set—"pieces of paper." When you come to think of it, that's what arithmetic division does too. To divide 18 units by 3, you break down 18 small partitions and leave 6 larger ones.

The undoing of an operation by negation always creates an identity element. Thus, in conservation experiments when the child mentally returns to the start, he or she can say, "It's the same because if you pour it back to this glass, the water level will be just the same as it was".[4]

b) *Reciprocity.* For classes and numbers, the combination of elements and the negation of the original combination returns you precisely to the start. The number or class at the end is *exactly the same* as the one at the beginning. But relations do not work in the same way (Beth and Piaget, 1961). For one thing, when we say, "A is taller than B," we are referring to a relative position which

[4]This reason is neither necessary nor sufficient to justify conservation, but it demonstrates the formation of a reversible system, and so Piaget accepts it as evidence for the presence of Concrete operations.

holds over many different values of A and B. In cancelling a comparison, what we are really searching for is a return to something equivalent to, but not identical with the start.

Reciprocity can be seen in two forms.

> The simplest form of reciprocity is reversing the standard and the comparison. We can say that A is taller than B or that B is shorter than A.
>
> In a second form of reciprocity, after changing a relation in one aspect, we introduce another change which exactly compensates for it.
>
> > Area of a rectangle = Length × Width. If we double the length (2L) and halve the width 1/2 W), the area remains equivalent but the figure does not look the same as it did, i.e., it does not return *exactly* to the beginning. The reciprocal of 2/1 is 1/2. It is this numerical property which tells us that doubling one dimension of a rectangle (2 × length) can be exactly compensated for by halving the other (1/2 × width). In the conservation experiments, reciprocity arguments can be seen in the child's claim, "It's taller but narrow, or longer but thinner."

To emphasize the psycho-logic of these logical operations, Piaget traces their roots back to Sensorimotor behavior and then up the path we have so far traversed. For example:

> Negation has its origins in the most primitive forms of behavior: a baby can put an object in front of himself, then push it away; when he starts to talk, he is able to say "no" before he says "yes." At the level of the first preoperatory classifications he is able to add an object to others, or take it away. The generalization and particularly the exact structuration of such behavior patterns of inversion characterize the first operations and their strict reversibility. . . . Reciprocity is the form of reversibility which characterizes relational groupings, but it also has its source in early behavior patterns of a symmetrical nature. There are spatial symmetries, perceptive symmetries, representative symmetries, motor symmetries, etc. At the level of the preoperatory representative regulations, a child will say that when a ball of dough is rolled into a sausage it contains more dough because it is longer. If you keep making the sausage longer, however, he will change his opinion, by regulatory and not operatory reciprocity, and he will say that the sausage contains less dough because it is so thin. *Both kinds of reversibility* exist at the level of concrete operations. Lengthening can be negated by shortening or compensated for by thinning (Piaget and Inhelder, 1966a, pp. 126–137).

Piaget's general discussion of operational thought often cites its reversible quality as the major attribute of higher level functioning. However, reversibility is just one property, embedded within a set of properties, which enables a child at the level of Concrete operational thought to conserve objects and classes despite changes in appearance.

5. *Special identities*. The properties of combinativity, associativity, general identity, and reversibility define a mathematical group and also apply to the logic of classes and relations. But there are two characteristics of classes which are *not* applicable to numbers and require the creation of special rules.

With the exception of the identity element (0), adding a number to itself always produces a new number.[5]

$$1 + 1 = 2 \qquad 2 + 2 = 4$$

By contrast, adding a set of class members to the class does *not* produce a new category.

$$A + A = A \qquad \text{toys} + \text{toys} = \text{toys}$$

Every class, then, is an identity element when added to itself. This special identity property is called *tautology* by Piaget.

A second special identity property called *resorption* functions in a similar way with the multiplicative combination of classes. When a superordinate class is combined simultaneously with a subordinate class, the result is identical with the larger class. For example, if all the brown beads are wooden and we consider all the wooden beads and all the brown beads as well, we will have to examine all the wooden beads, but no more. This contrasts with property of numbers: with the exception of 1 (the identity element), when a smaller number is multiplied by a larger number, the total is larger still: $2 \times 4 = 8$, $3 \times 7 = 21$. It is the resorption property of classes which functions in the child's ability to compare parts and wholes without distorting either in the process of comparison.

In sum, the five grouping properties of numbers and classes all focus on rules for combining elements. Combinativity is the property of staying within the set ($1 + 1 = 2$; $3 + 3 = 6$). Associativity allows different orders of combination to produce the same result ($1 + [7 + 6] = [1 + 7] + 6$). General Identity describes an element which produces no change when combined with another ($6 + 0 = 6$; $6 \times 1 = 6$). Reversibility by negation or reciprocity decomposes combinations to return to the start or to establish equivalence ($6 + [-6] = 0$; $2 \times 6 = 24 \times \frac{1}{2}$). And, special identities provide rules for adding more members to a class ($A + A = A$) or combining superordinate and subordinate classes ($A \times B = B$). Together, these rules define the structure or organization of mental operations in the stage of Concrete operations.

Lattice properties in the grouping

The special identities are rules which are added to the mathematical group structure in order to provide a more adequate model of mental operations on classes and relations. These rules are actually derived from a symbolic logic structure called a lattice. With all of Piaget's emphasis on groups, the lattice tends to get pushed into the background.

Lattices are systematic classification networks in which all possible sets and subsets are arranged in a hierarchy from most to least inclusive. The most common example of a partial lattice is the genus–species classification hierarchy

[5] This is called an *iterative* property.

at the heart of traditional biology (see Figure 13). For example: Living things; Mammals and all other living things; as subclasses of mammals, dogs and all other mammals; as a subclass of all other living things, plants and all living things except mammals and plants. In a complete lattice, two classes at the same level of the hierarchy can always be combined to produce a more inclusive class.[6] And there is always a less inclusive class which is included in two higher level classes.[7] However, the classification system of biology and most other class hierarchies are incomplete lattice structures. Although two classes can always be included in a higher order class, at the bottom of the hierarchy are empty sets, not less inclusive classes. For example, there are no creatures which can be included in the joint class of dogs and plants.[8]

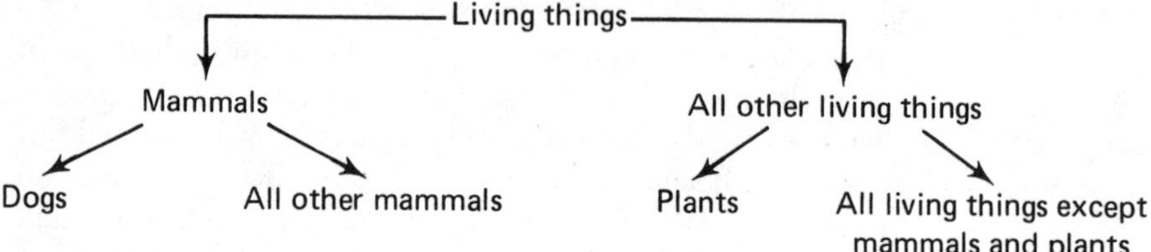

Figure 13. A partial lattice: Genus-species classification.

All lattice classifications systems, whether partial or complete, have at least three properties:

1. At a given level of the hierarchy, all classes are mutually exclusive. A living thing is either a mammal or a nonmammal, but not both.

2. Combining a subclass with a primary class results in the primary class (dogs and mammals = mammals).

3. Combining a subclass with itself leaves the class unchanged (A + A = A; dogs + more dogs = dogs). Thus, the special identities of the grouping stem from the lattice properties of class inclusion. The resulting structural model of thought is part way between a group and a lattice with some properties of each.

The grouping as a systematic structure

Combinativity, associativity, general identity, reversibility, and special identities are not simply five separate properties of operations. Each is related both logically and functionally to the others and that is why they are said to form a grouping structure.

> We can begin with an additive combination 2 + 2. Negating this combination results in the identity element 0. This fact would only be true if numbers are associative (if the order of combination does not affect the result).

[6]In formal logic terms, the two classes always *join* at the *least upper bound.*

[7]Two classes always meet at the *greatest lower bound.*

[8]The lattice is incomplete because there are always least upper bounds but not always greatest lower bounds.

Similarly with classification. Take some younger boys. Add some older boys, younger girls, and older girls (in any order—associatively). The superordinate class is children. Make them taller—the logical class is unchanged (general identity). Add more younger girls. The class is still unchanged (special identity). Negate the additions by taking away older boys, younger and older girls (in any order), and we return to the class of younger boys.

What may seem like a comparatively simple judgment of conservation across many areas, actually requires the systematic mental coordination of all of these operations before perceptual changes are minimized in favor of conceptual consistencies. At the Concrete operational stage, children who are trying to explain why numbers or amounts are conserved, tend to restate at least one of the grouping properties.

Identity: *"You didn't add anything or take anything away."*
Negation: *"If you pour it back to the first glass, it would still be the same."*
Reciprocity: *"It's larger but it's thinner."*

Thus, mental symbols created to represent and coordinate events are now combined in a system which does not distort the meaning with each separate transformation.

Because the grouping specifies the rules by which elements of thought (symbols) are combined, we can say that Piaget's grouping model defines the structural properties of the Concrete operational stage. In this definition, stage and structure are synonymous. There will be no stage change until the system of rules is modified (Kessen, 1962).

Functional properties of groupings

Structural principles describe the way in which parts in a system are related to each other. Functional principles describe how the system works. What makes Piaget's operational logic unique is that it not only defines a cognitive structure, but also has implications for how cognition functions when an individual attempts to make sense of the world. Specifically, like all cognitive organizations, groupings have three functional properties—assimilation, accommodation, and equilibration.

Assimilation. In a general sense, the system of mental operations acts as a "mold" for organizing observations, expectation, and actions; that is, it imposes organization on the world.

The child observes equal water levels in glasses A and B. When B is poured into C, the water level changes. However, the fact of apparent change is integrated into a structure which can mentally reverse the pouring of C back into B, or note the initial stages, or calculate that the higher water level is compensated by the narrower glass. All of these observations now lead to the conclusion that the amount of water in C equals A.

Within the logic and reasoning structure itself, three of the five major properties are predominantly assimilative in nature because they function so as to preserve stability and incorporate new information without changing present schemes. Reversibility and identity are logically related; we saw how the negation of an operation produces the identity element $(6 + [-6] = 0)$. Psychologically we can see these properties as functioning to ensure and verify stability. In reversibility, the child is able to keep track of initial and final states to evaluate identity. In identity operations the concern is with understanding transformations which do *not* distort the properties of elements, classes, and relations.

Accommodation. The structure of operational logic may function as a mold, but it is a flexible mold. As a general formal model it can be adapted to an almost infinite variety of situations and problems. Piaget claims that it is because the operations are initially based upon sensorimotor action on the world, even the most abstract of logic systems may be applied to configurations of real events.

Within the logic structure, combinativity and associativity function accommodatively to create new elements and to rearrange elements into different pathways. The Concrete operations child can create new combinations and arrive at conclusions in more than one way, adjusting mental operations to the demands of the particular problem.

Equilibration. For Piaget, the most important aspect of a grouping is that it describes an equilibrated system. Reasoning is flexible and reversible so that there is a way of returning to the start or to any other place in the reasoning chain. Imagine what would happen if, in our conception of space, the end point varied with the path taken to reach it, or if, having returned by the same path we traveled earlier, we found that the beginning was no longer in the same place.[9] Chaos would reign in our manipulation of ideas and symbols. In logical groupings, when there is the possibility of returning to the start and attaining a goal by alternate routes, the system is governed by a self-regulating set of rules. These self-regulations compensate for potential or actual perturbations or changes. Any addition of elements can be nullified by an inverse operation. If one path is blocked or unproductive, another can be used. Thus, the grouping represents an equilibrated system, with a self-regulating or homeostatic mechanism.

A grouping is the first equilibrated system of mental operations in which there is a balance between accommodative and assimilative intellectual functioning. Since figurative schemas (e.g., images) are primarily accommodative, and operative schemes (e.g., seriation strategies) are primarily assimilative, we should expect a greater figurative–operative balance once the grouping appears. In fact, we do find in the stage of Concrete operations that the perceptual

[9]Alice in Wonderland explores some of these problems; Lewis Carroll was a mathematician and logician.

appearance of an object no longer dominates the child's interpretation of states and transformations. The emergence of an equilibrated grouping in a child's cognitive structure signals that figurative and operative intelligence have progressed beyond object permanence, word-symbol permanence, and class permanence, to stable schemes of class inclusion and conservation of number, quantity, space, and time.

The process by which the grouping structure develops is just like that described for meaningful symbols in Chapter 3. Along the figurative dimension, children internalize the results of experience. By abstracting from perceived states, they create figurative schemas which expand their representation of specific events in the world. Along the operative dimension, there has been extensive progress in interiorization. Abstracting from the results of their actions on things (classifying, seriating, arranging, and rearranging), children organize separate overt actions into a *system* of internal, reversible mental operations. Thus, mental combinations are not the same as actions, but arise from an interior structuring of actions. Just how this abstraction occurs has not been specified. But, assuming that it does occur, Piaget argues that the emergence of interiorized operative schemes increases the child's ability to transform figurative information so that the world can now be interpreted in new ways.

This presentation of groupings summarizes the general features but omits Piaget's exhaustive classification of grouping types (Piaget, 1942; Inhelder and Piaget, 1955). Briefly, he distinguishes first between *logical* and *infralogical* groupings applied to physical events.

> Logical groupings occur when the objects are discrete items (foods, cities). The items have no intrinsic spatial or temporal relation with each other (e.g., combining New York and San Francisco as cities does not depend on their location or the distance between them). Also, the characteristics of the items are not modified by the combining operations (placing sticks in a series does not alter the properties of the sticks). Simple classification and seriation are the primary examples of logical groupings.
>
> By contrast, infralogical groupings of physical objects are those in which a whole object or a whole series of events is the largest unit. There are no perceivable divisions into units unless a measuring instrument is applied (e.g., a glass of water, a series of moments in time). In this case there *are* unique intrinsic relations among the parts, so that the whole is perceptually modified when the parts are rearranged. The primary examples here are quantity conservation (clay, water), space, and time concepts.

The properties of logical and infralogical groups are formally identical, but the part–whole characteristics of the problem are different. While the sequence of development is assumed to be identical, it is possible that Concrete operations may not occur at exactly the same time for each kind of grouping.

Furthermore, there are actually nine types of groupings applied either to logical or infralogical elements, though each one has the general principles described above. Some groupings describe operations on classes, some focus on relations. Within each category there are additive operations (symmetrical and asymmetrical) and multiplicative operations (one-to-one; one-to-many). Flavell (1963) provides an excellent description of each separate grouping. In some cases there are no psychological examples to go with the grouping, but it is a logically possible structure. Piaget's writings on logic illustrate that his interests as a philosopher extend beyond his concern with cognitive development.

Limitations of Concrete operational groupings

Given such a complicated model of intellectual organization, it seems as though nothing would be beyond the Concrete child's intellectual grasp. But Piaget is attributing this model to seven and eight-year-old children whose thinking, when compared with that of adults, still shows many cognitive generation gaps.

1. *The grouping may not be applied correctly.* Operational logic describes a set of rules which children are capable of using; it does not explain whether and when the rules are correctly applied. For example, the identity property is maintained for the *amount* of water poured into another glass, but the rule, "If nothing is added or taken away, then the object remains unchanged" does not apply to *surface area* of the same water in the same experiment. Thus, above and beyond the grouping, there is specific learning which determines the correctness of inference in many tasks.

2. *Groupings are applied to concrete events.* A Concrete operational child can use mental operations only on problems or events with which he or she has had some experience. There is no sustained concern with the hypothetical case, as exemplified by the child who rejects the problem of dogs with six heads. In going beyond immediate perceptual experience, Concrete operational children do not stray too far away.

3. *The grouping has structural limitations.* The child can classify observations and see what goes together with what." But causal relations can be inferred only if the child locates these observations in a system of *all possible* occurrences.

> A child who has observed that when he does something wrong (e.g., breaks a family rule), his parents become angry, sees that his parents are angry. Did he do something wrong? In order to disentangle the causal relations, the child would have to consider, at first, four possibilities: (a) breaking a rule and parents' anger; (b) not breaking a rule and parents' anger; (c) breaking a rule and no parental anger; (d) not breaking a rule and no parental anger.

The Concrete operational child is perfectly capable of noting whether (a) or (b) or (c) or (d) occurs. But these are only four possible outcomes. It could happen that (a) and (b) occur, but not (c) and (d); or (a) and (c), but not (b) and (d). All in all, there are sixteen possible sets of observations. As we shall see in the chapter on Formal operations, each outcome leads to a different inference about the relation between child and parent behavior. And, the calculation of outcomes and possibilities is far beyond the capability of the Concrete operational child.

4. *The grouping structure does not emerge simultaneously for all tasks (the issue of horizontal décalages).* The elaborate grouping model seems to imply that at one fell swoop, children should be able to conserve quantity, number, space, time, and so on, in a wide variety of situations—as if Concrete operations is an all-or-none structural event. But Piaget himself repeatedly refers to what he calls horizontal (within-stage) *décalages* (developmental lags in the application of structure to particular tasks). Some horizontal décalages appear to be idiosyncratic, attributable to individual differences in interest, motivation, or opportunity; some children are more interested in exploring sand than water, or vice versa. There are, however, many systematic sequences in conceptual development within a stage.

a. Amount of deformation. In a conservation of water or clay or number task, children conserve small changes before demonstrating reversible mental operations on large perceptual quantities or large transformations of the material (Piaget and Inhelder 1941).

b. Material content. Piaget and Szeminska (1941) indicate that conservation of discontinuous quantity (beads poured into jars) emerges before continuous quantity (liquid). Macready and Macready (1974) find a consistent sequence in which children conserve their own and another person's weight before achieving conservation of object weights. This corresponds with the developmental trend from mastery of personal concepts to mastery of object concepts found in the area of identity.

c. Grouping type. Each one of the nine grouping types (Flavell, 1963) supports a different conceptual achievement within concrete operations: one for conservation, one for transitivity, one for class inclusion, and so on. The logical grouping model implies that all of these achievements should appear at the same time because they share an identical formal structure. However, given the same material content, there are some regular sequences in which the grouping types emerge; for instance, conservation is almost always found to precede transitivity (Smedslund, 1963; but see Brainerd, 1973). Pinard and Laurendeau (1969) refer to these as intraconcept differences in performance.

d. Interconcept differences. Some systematic décalages can be seen in children's ability to transform different conceptual dimensions. Beginning with Elkind (1967a), a number of investigators attempted to evaluate Piaget's claim that identity concepts emerge before conservation of the same materials. Brainerd and Hooper (1975) conclude in their review of many claims and counterclaims that the findings support Piaget's conclusion when method variance and age of the subjects are taken into account. The best-documented of all décalages is the developmental sequence of conservation of amount (at about seven years), weight (at nine or ten years) and volume (at about twelve years).

While the grouping structure is equally applicable to number, quantity, classification, space time, and so on, studies find that conceptual categories tend to emerge in a regular order. Number conservation seems to be the first to appear; it is prior to liquid quantity (Brainerd and Brainerd, 1972; Inhelder,

Sinclair, and Bovet, 1974), and also prior to class inclusion, multiplicative classification, and transitivity of length (Dimitrovsky and Almy, 1975).

Thus, Concrete operational groupings are limited by factors determining when the rules should and should not be applied. These groupings are further limited by their application to concrete events and by the lack of extension to a calculation of all possible observations. Finally, Concrete operations do not emerge in one all-or-none flash, but instead become consolidated in one task and across tasks over a period of time. The grouping, therefore, is a general logical model of structure, while the organization of behavior shows much specificity as the child moves from one task to another.

THE IMPACT OF LOGICAL GROUPINGS ON SYMBOLIC THOUGHT

In the above section, I have focused on the rules for combining mental symbols, but I have ignored the symbols themselves. Piaget's research indicates that as children come into the Concrete operational stage, there are significant changes in mental imagery, drawing, memory, and language—the symbolic media used by children to represent objects and events.

Mental imagery

Throughout the previous chapters I have repeated Piaget's claim that the Preoperational child conceptualizes static states and disregards transformations. When *Mental Imagery in the Child* is examined directly (Piaget and Inhelder, 1966) it becomes apparent that before Concrete operations, the child's mental images are like static snapshots rather than smoothly moving pictures. Then with Concrete operations comes a qualitative change in the child's use of mental images. Again, operative development seems to result in a restructuring of figurative representations.

Piaget and Inhelder devised tasks which investigate reproductive imagery of the present and past and others which focus on anticipations of what will happen in the future. Within each category they examined imagery of static states, imagery of moving objects, and imagery of transformations.

In a task involving static reproduction, children are presented with two blocks; the top one is offset over the bottom (See "Model A," Figure 14). Children are asked to recreate with blocks or to draw the model. Another version of this task, assessing static anticipation, presents children with one block directly on top of the other (model B); children draw what they imagine the model would look like if the top block were moved slightly to the right.

A movement reproduction task is created by placing a stick perpendicular to a table, fastened at its base by a nail, so that it can rotate from upright to horizontal (Model C). The experimenter lets the stick fall and the child draws a series showing the stick at various in-between points. In an anticipatory version of the task, the stick is kept upright and the child draws what he or she imagines will happen when it falls.

Reproduction of a transformation is examined in a task in which an arc of curved wire is slowly straightened (Model D). Again, the child draws a series of pictures showing the arc's in-between and final points. In the anticipatory version, the child draws what will happen when the bent wire is straightened.[10]

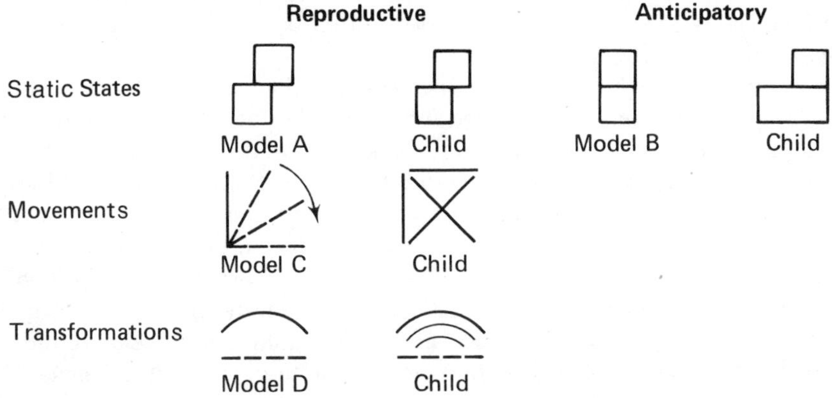

Figure 14. Imagery tasks and examples of Preoperational performance.

Five-year-old (Intuitive stage) children are able to copy the two blocks in their offset position (static reproduction, Model A) but cannot anticipate the end result of moving the top block (static anticipation, Model B). Generally the children recognize that there will be some change in the top block, but they keep the edge of the top and bottom blocks aligned.

No such discrepancy between reproduction and anticipation is found in movement and transformation images. Despite the experimenter's emphasis that the upright rod is nailed at the base, Intuitive children draw and imagine the stick falling at right angles near the top, or randomly. As in the time experiments, the series of events is not remembered in order. In the transformation of a wire arc, five-year-olds tend to keep the straight wire between the bounds of the arc, even though they have seen and described the straight wire as longer (in identity and conservation experiments with the same material). Children in Concrete operations, by contrast, draw the falling stick correctly and also accurately reproduce or anticipate the transformation of the wire arc.

In sum, before the stage of Concrete operations, imaginal representation as seen in drawings is static and focuses on initial or final states; children at this stage are apparently unable to represent a series of perceived events. While one might expect reproductions of events to be easier than anticipations, the two develop together for both movement and transformational images. Piaget concludes that reproduction of changes always involves transformations and vice versa.

[10]Note how the same apparatus is used for different purposes.

Except for the reproductive copy of a static image (and even here, other experiments show marked distortions), the Intuitive child's coordination of images does not follow a reversible, sequential system typical of operational grouping. The full development of figurative imagery seems to await the emergence of logical grouping; figurative development is not determined solely by the development of perception. These conclusions have been verified with many "imagery" versions of tasks already described as logic, conservation, space, and time tasks.

An interesting switch on a traditional conservation of water task also illustrates the change in imagery between Intuitive and Concrete stages. Given the two equal glasses of water, children are asked to predict (imagine) what will happen if the water from one is poured into a taller, thinner container. Early Intuitive children claim that there will be the same amount of water (apparent conservation, or at least identity).[11] However, with an elastic band on their finger, they indicate that they expect the water to be at the same height as it was in the original container. Once they observe the water being poured, they quickly deny conservation of amount. A few older children in the Late Intuitive period (six to seven years) anticipate correctly that the water will change level, but from this they conclude that the amount will not be the same. Not until Concrete operations do their images and the judgments correspond. For Piaget, this is one more bit of evidence to support his hypothesis that mental images do not give rise to operational coordinations; rather, it is the logical grouping which finally promotes accurate and meaningful imaginal representations.

Drawings

The relation between imagery and symbolic representation of space in child art was further explored by Piaget and Inhelder (1948). When Intuitive children attempt to draw pictures of people and scenes, they simply place related elements near each other. For example, legs come out of the head, or buttons are arranged beside the body in human figure drawing. Early Concrete operational children organize their pictures, but they tend to put into their drawings what they know to be there, rather than what they see; for instance, human figures drawn in profile still have two eyes and two ears. This drawing style (also typical of so-called "primitive" art) appears to be a juxtaposition of many perspectives rather than simple elements. Not until age nine or ten, when the coordinate system is established, do children's drawings adopt one perspective, with objects inside opaque containers no longer portrayed. At this point we also see the use of receding lines to represent three-dimensional spatial perspective on a two-dimensional page. While children vary tremendously in their ability to produce "photographic" drawings, their ability to reproduce relational and

[11]Some writers (e.g., Bruner, 1966) interpret this as evidence of early conservation. But for Piaget, once the perceptual "contradiction" is removed, it is no longer a problem requiring conservation concepts for a correct answer.

perspective aspects of people and objects is one index of intellectual maturity (e.g., Harris, 1963). "Art" is not an activity outside the realm of cognition, especially in the child's representation of space and objects.

Memory

In most common-sense theories of memory and most psychological theories as well, the process of memory is described as a sequence of coding of an event, of storage, retrieval, and decoding in which memory "decays" over time. Piaget investigates whether the rules for coding, storage, retrieval, and so on, are constant over time, or whether the codes depend upon the subject's level of cognitive operations.

I have already described the memory for seriated sticks experiment in which children were shown a series of ten sticks and then asked to draw what they had seen—a week later and six months later. The drawings corresponded to their level of operations in seriation tasks. What is more, 74 percent of the subjects had a more accurate memory after six months than they did after a week. Whatever else happens, memories do not always decay and fade over time.

In another experiment (Inhelder, 1969), children were shown eight matches, arranged as in Figure 15 with four in a row on top and four in a zigzag pattern on the bottom. Once again, children were tested immediately, after a week, and after six months.

Figure 15. Two rows of matches.

Before the stage of Concrete operations, children tended to make the rows the same length. Early Intuitive children added more matches; Late Intuitive children preserved the number of matches but drew longer matches in the zigzag row. There was little improvement in memory over six months, and in some cases there was a decline. Piaget suggests that this is a case in which two Preoperational schemes are in conflict: numerical equivalence should produce the same length, but if two lines are the same length they should have the same terminal points. This conflict results in some (temporary) developmental regression of memory images over time.

Piaget (1968b) varied the responses required in the task. When children were asked to draw from memory (evoke an image) they found it most difficult. When asked to recognize the correct answer in a range of choices, they found the task much easier. This corresponds to an age-old distinction between recognition and recall in memory research. In between these two types of memory, Piaget locates what he calls a reconstruction task, in which the child is given the materials (partly recognition) but must arrange the materials to match the original display (partly evocation).

In an experiment similar to the one with matchsticks, Piaget found that after six months, 61 percent of the subjects from four to eight years of age regressed in their memory ability if tested by free recall or evocation. A reconstruction test showed regression in four-to-five-year-olds, but 48 percent *progression* among six-to-eight-year-olds. Piaget suggests that the order of response difficulty—from recognition as easiest to reconstruction and evocation as most difficult—is based on the fact that recognition is perceptual, that reconstruction involves internalized imitation, and that evocation involves mental images. Each of these figurative mechanisms emerges successively later in development.

But the memories are not purely figurative. Each experiment reveals that the pattern of accuracy, improvement, and regression is determined by initial conceptual understandings and is altered by new understandings. Duckworth (1973) cites an example. In a variant of the brown beads, wooden beads problem by an associate of Piaget's, the child is asked, in effect, "Are there more wooden beads than brown beads?" The child answers, "More brown." The experimenter says, "What did I just ask?" The child: "Are there more brown beads than white beads." No amount of repetition improves the child's "memory"; he is convinced that the experimenter has asked for a brown–white comparison. Duckworth comments that parents and teachers often interpret young children's instant memory lapses as inattention. Piaget suggests that sometimes the child is transforming the stimulus to fit the present structure, and if it does not fit—then it is instantly "forgotten."

Memory for Piaget is not a matter of copy, storage, and decay, but an active transformational process like the rest of the symbolic function. His findings emphasize the fact that whether and what children remember depend in part upon their operational level and in part on how they are tested (recognition, reconstruction, or recall).

Language

Piaget's discussion of language development during the Preoperational to Concrete operations stages repeatedly seeks answers to two questions: Is language the major medium for achieving symbolic meaning? and Is language the source of logic and the coordinator of mental operations?

Language as a symbolic medium. Piaget is quick to agree that linguistic symbols represent an important advance over sensorimotor symbols. Verbal narration and evocation can represent a long chain of actions rapidly, liberating thought from immediate events and allowing cognition to range over vast stretches of time and space. As a consequence, verbal symbols transcend the step-by-step of Sensorimotor intelligence and facilitate simultaneous representations of many elements in an organized structure (Piaget and Inhelder, 1966a). But, as we have seen in the discussion of the Preconceptual stage, language is only one of the semiotic instruments and is subject to the same organizational laws as symbolic play, deferred imitation and imagination. Rather than providing the major impetus for symbolic development, language itself must be assimilated to a symbol system that has been developing since the achievement of the first object permanence (at age six months).

Language and coordination of symbols. Piaget (1971a) and Inhelder, Sinclair, and Bovet (1974) cite four sources of evidence, all of which support the hypothesis that the construction of logic is prior to language; language does *not*, they believe, provide the organization for logical thought. First, studies of deaf mutes by Olèron (1957) and by Furth (1966) indicate that with a delay of only a year or two, children without *spoken words* develop logical structures in the same sequences and of the same kinds as normal children. Second, Sinclair de Zwart (1969) indicates that the achievement of logical groupings has a marked effect on the use of language.

> For example, she gave children two pencils, one of which was longer and thicker than the other. In one phase of the experiment she simply asked for verbal descriptions of the pair. Each child was also tested for operatory level on a liquid conservation problem.

Children who conserved liquids used comparatives (longer, thinner) in describing the pencils, while nonconservers used undifferentiated terms, with the same word indicating length in one situation and thickness in another (big/little, thick/little). Finally, the conservers used this sentence: "This pencil is long but thin, the other is short but fat." Nonconservers tended to say, "This pencil is long; that one is short; this one is thin; that one is fat," if they referred at all to both differences.

Third, as part of the same set of experiments, the experimenters demonstrated that while the achievement of logical grouping affects language, the achievement of more differentiated language does not appreciably affect the child's logical grouping.

We will be looking more closely at studies which attempt to accelerate cognitive development. At this point, one brief summary. After a number of pretests like the one above, children were given two long training sessions on different days. The training was directed toward increasing the use of verbal comparatives and expanding the meaning of more and less, by providing examples of the more complex syntactic structure (longer but thinner, etc.). A posttest of conservation was administered immediately after and two weeks later.

Only three of 28 nonconservers became conservers as a result of this training. Another seven children shifted from nonconservation to an intermediate stage. The remaining eighteen children showed no stage change, though some gave evidence of using the new level language in explaining their (nonconservation) answers. Thus, "the hypothesis that a child needs only to understand to use correctly certain expressions to allow conservation, should be discarded" (Inhelder, Sinclair and Bovet, 1974, p. 115).

Piaget has taken great pains to make certain that failures to conserve, and so on, are not simply verbal misunderstandings. This experiment suggests that new verbal acquisitions are not sufficient for the attainment of the grouping structure. But grouping structures do affect the use of language and the egocentrism, or lack of it, in the communication process. While language is an important symbolic medium and may even be necessary to reach Formal operational stage, it is definitely not the primary organizing factor in intellectual development. The hypothesis of Whorf (1956) and Vygotsky (1962) that language shapes thought is rejected in favor of the hypothesis that logic (e.g., the grouping) structures linguistic concepts. During the transition to Concrete operations the figurative aspects of symbols (mental imagery, drawing, memory, *and* language) are enriched, extended, and restructured by the operative system of the grouping. I will proceed in the next chapter to describe a few cognitive advances during Late Concrete operations, and especially to describe social–emotional aspects of development during the whole Concrete operational stage.

CHAPTER 9
Early and Late Concrete Operations

Within the general limits of the Concrete operational logic structure, children change a great deal as they progress from age seven (about grade 2) to age twelve (junior high school and the beginning of adolescence). Cognitive characteristics of the Early Concrete substage have been described in Chapter 8. The first section of this chapter continues with the Late Concrete substage, another transitional period which has not received the attention it deserves. It is a time when the grouping structure is applied to an ever-widening array of content areas and to measurement—of number, space, and time. It is also a time when children construct two- and three-dimensional, spatial coordinate systems (up–down, right–left, toward–away). This shift in mental coordination and spatial perspective is accompanied by a quantum leap in the social–emotional functioning of the child. The remaining sections of this chapter focus on social and emotional developments during the entire Concrete operational stage.

COGNITIVE DEVELOPMENTS IN LATE CONCRETE OPERATIONS

While the basic construction of class hierarchies and class inclusions was well begun in the Early Concrete substage, there are several important advances which do not appear until children are about nine or ten (Inhelder and Piaget, 1959). First, children begin to operate on more complex hierarchies. Given pictures or objects, they go beyond simple class inclusion to produce additional levels of classification in the array: for example, a set of pictures is divided into living versus nonliving things; within the class of "living things" are animals that do not fly and animals that do; within the class of flying animals are insects and birds; within the class of birds are ducks and other birds, and so on.

Second, in contrast with Early Concrete children who are just beginning to quantify class inclusion (more wooden beads than brown beads) but still switch answers from moment to moment, nine- and ten-year olds show less vacillation; they frequently give correct answers right from the start.[1] Third, the child's conception of mutually exclusive alternatives becomes a reality. A particular object is either animal or mineral, but not both; an event can occur or can fail to occur, but not both. This truth of adult logic is not a stable part of children's assumption systems until the Late Concrete substage. An integral part of this truth is the concept of the null class—a class that is conceptually meaningful, but has no members. For example, there are no members of the joint class animal-*and*-mineral, or the class possible-*and*-impossible.

> In a simple experiment children were asked to classify square, round, and rectangular cards, some of which had pictures on them and some of which were blank. Early Concrete children readily grouped cards on the basis of shape, but never spontaneously created two piles—pictures versus blank. They strenuously resisted both hints and direct suggestions that this categorization was possible. Not until the age of nine or ten did "blank cards" constitute a real or meaningful category.

This experiment in itself is inconclusive, but in the context of related experiments reported by Inhelder and Piaget, it seems likely that the full conceptual use of the null class is a Late Concrete operational achievement.

Conservation

To my knowledge, Piaget has not written in detail about number conservation or about other aspects of number development beyond the Early Concrete substage. In the primary report on number, Piaget and Szeminska (1941) focused on the correspondence between logic and quantity concepts in the *emergence* of number conservation. While all the basic numerical operations appear around the age of seven, full use of multiplication, division, and so on, is acquired gradually throughout the Concrete operational stage.

Conservation of number and amount of clay or liquid seem to emerge near the beginning of Concrete operations, while conservation of the weight of clay balls does not occur for another two or three years. Inhelder and Piaget (1941) speculate about the reasons for this décalage (developmental lag). Conservation of amount of clay in seven- and eight-year-olds is facilitated by their ability to

[1]The average age is not precisely specified. Presumably, this is one of the many times when the "emergence" of a new skill means that 75 percent of the children at that age pass a specified test.

conceptualize two balls of clay as wholes which can each be divided into a number of small parts; that is, they conceptually convert the problem into a number conservation task in which parts change location but not numerical quantity. The same children believe that a change in location of (conceptual) parts *does* affect weight, possibly because weight is still a preconceptual notion referring to the sensation of pressure on the hands.

It seems to me that a simpler explanation of the décalage lies in the number of dimensions to be isolated and treated as conceptually independent. Conservation of amount is a two-dimensional problem—separating number of units from the location of units. Conservation of weight involves the additional separation of a weight dimension from number and location. We shall see that volume conservation, another apparently similar task, requires an even more complex mental structure and does not emerge until Formal operations.

Space and time measurement

Back to the child struggling to build a tower at the same height as a model (Piaget, Inhelder, and Szeminska, 1948). In Early Concrete operations, he or she could use a neutral measuring instrument as a ruler only if the instrument were the same size as the tower. With smaller sticks or pieces of paper, children did not consistently divide the length of the model into units and create a new tower with the same number of units. The act of measuring distorted their conceptions of beginning and end points. Now, in the Late Concrete substage, children easily solve the problem, using commercial rulers, or creating unit rulers from sticks, cardboard, or paper. The equilibrated grouping, applied several years ago to judgments about length conservation, can now be applied to the measurement of length.

Similarly, Late Concrete children can use two-dimensional units in the measurement of area. In comparing dissimilar figures (A and B), they make certain that the intermediate (M) measuring pieces are the same size (A=M; M>B; A>B). Again, children at this stage now have the concept of *arbitrary*, equal units which can be applied to determine the length of a one-dimensional line, or the area of a two-dimensional surface.

In the development of time concepts (1946b, 1946c), the major achievement of the child in Late Concrete operations is also the understanding of unit measurement. Using stopwatches and hour glasses full of sand, Piaget demonstrates just how difficult it is for children to measure time. First, they must be able to conceptualize time as independent of their activities; young children egocentrically assume that sand flows faster and clock hands move faster when they themselves are very involved in activities. Second, children must be able to judge intervals as equal if stops and starts occur simultaneously; when equal amounts of water are poured simultaneously into unequal containers, even Early Concrete children assume that the visually smaller amount takes less time to pour. Third, children must be able to judge intervals as equal when they occur successively. (This minute equals the minute just past.) And fourth, they must be able to divide duration into arbitrary, equal-sized units which can then be added and subtracted numerically; equal spatial divisions on the clock face represent equal units of time.

Time conservation and the operational grouping of time emerge in Early Concrete operations. Time measurement, however, requires the further coordination of time and space and the arbitrary division of time and space dimensions into units. Time measurement, then, like space measurement, occurs in Late Concrete operations, several years after the first conceptual conservations.

A new spatial coordinate system

Two-dimensional coordinates. In the experiments with the tilting bottle (horizontal) and poles on the mountain of sand (vertical), Early Concrete children arrive at correct drawings of horizontal and vertical only after extensive trial and error (Piaget and Inhelder, 1948). By the end of the experiment, many children infer from this observation that the water is permanently horizontal and the poles can be permanently vertical despite the jar position or the mountain slope.

By contrast, Late Concrete children "know" the answer to what will happen to the water before the jar is tilted. They also use external reference points (the table, the paper edge) to line up their drawings and rulers to make certain that the lines which they draw are parallel or perpendicular to these reference points. Thus, they begin with the implicit assumption that there are horizontal and vertical coordinates at right angles to each other. These coordinates appear to be conceptual constructions which the child can use to evaluate the spatial orientation of the water and the poles. Another experiment (Piaget, Inhelder, and Szeminska, 1948) shows the same results. Children are given a page with a single dot placed off-center and a blank page on which they are to draw a dot in exactly the same position. Not until the Late Concrete substage do children locate the dot at the intersection of lines drawn perpendicular to the top and side of the page. While even very young children use words like "up," "down," "sideways," "flat," children do not organize space into a two-dimensional coordinate system until about nine or ten years of age.

Three-dimensional coordinates—the development of perspective and point of view. The above experiments focus on the relationship among objects and reference points external to the child. In the Three Mountain Task, Piaget and Inhelder (1948) examined the child's conceptual grasp of two dimensions (mountains are to the right or left, in front or behind) with reference to a third dimension—the child's own body versus the viewpoint of a doll at another compass point of the display.

Until the age of about seven, children who are asked what the doll sees from behind the display consistently draw or choose a picture very similar to the arrangement as *they* view it. In Early Concrete operations, they recognize differences in point of view, but they cannot coordinate perspectives accurately. The pictures they choose are different from their own view but do not consistently represent the view taken by the doll (the "other"). It is important to remember that this task can be solved mentally by rotating the display in one's mind, or by systematically reversing near–far, right–left relations to infer the other perspective. It is not dependent on the child's having seen the other side of the mountains. Finally, in Late Concrete operations, children begin to coordinate three-dimensional perspectives and to solve the problem successfully. It is at this same age that they begin to represent three-dimensional space in their drawings on a two-dimensional surface (using converging lines).

Piaget and Inhelder suggest that the solution to the Three Mountains Task does not come all at once. Children may be more successful in thinking about how the mountain looks from the opposite side than they are in conceptualizing left–right reversals. Minnigerode and Carey (1974) obtained results supporting this hypothesis in a study of third and fifth grade children (ages eight and ten). Inevitably there are methodological variations which influence the results. For example, Garner and Plant (1972) demonstrate that if children are asked to find their own viewpoint first, they commit more egocentric errors than children who select other views first.

Piaget's research indicates that the logical groupings underlying time and space conservation are not applied to measurement and coordinations of spatial viewpoints until relatively late in the child's development. Not until the fourth or fifth grade does the child conceptualize time and space as containers within which events occur and can be measured.[2] These results led Piaget to return to the argument concerning the perceptual origins of intelligence. If space *concepts* are derived directly from perception of events, it is difficult to understand why their development should take so many years. Piaget argues that the role of cognitive structuring in the conception of space makes this delay understandable. A mental coordination of two or three spatial dimensions involves (1) logical multiplication, and (2) seriation; and these abilities only emerge with the general grouping structures described above. To my knowledge, Piaget has not yet discussed why there seem to be new advances in space and time measurement and perspective during the Late Concrete operational substage. The answer may lie in the increased number of dimensions that can now be isolated and conceptualized as independent factors.

SOCIAL DEVELOPMENT

Egocentrism–perspectivism

Social perspective/role-taking. We have seen that children in the early Intuitive substage of Preoperations have made substantial progress in overcoming their own egocentrism and in becoming aware of other people's points of view.

[2]This is a Newtonian view of space and time. Einstein's theory reconsiders the notion that these are separate dimensions and that they are containers, independent of events.

They can observe themselves and others and tell whether another person sees an object. They can identify *what* another sees but cannot conceptualize *how* objects appear from other perspectives. They are becoming sensitive to special characteristics of the observer (age, blindfolded status) but are not able to interpret the world through others' eyes. In other words, while Early Intuitive children know *about* other points of view, they are not yet able to take the role of the other, if taking the role of the other is measured in a task in which self and other have significantly different points of view.

Selman (1976; Selman and Byrne, 1974) describes three structural levels of role-taking occurring between Late Intuitive and Late Concrete operations. The descriptions here are modified slightly from the originals.

Level 1[3]. *Social informational role-taking (about ages six to eight).* Children at this level (presumably Late Intuitive) realize that differences in how people feel or think can be caused by their different situations or different information. The children can infer correctly what others are thinking and feeling, as long as the other's situation is not very different from their own (Chandler and Greenspan, 1972; Shantz, 1975). At this level, children do not coordinate perspectives—for example, to consider that their views of others are influenced by their conception of how others view them.

Level 2. *Self-reflective role-taking (about ages eight to ten).* At this level (presumably Early Concrete), children are aware that people think and feel differently because each person has a uniquely ordered set of values or purposes (i.e., children don't think in these words, but they are now aware that there are internal psychological processes which affect others' interpretations). Children are able to reflect on the self's behavior and *motivation*, as seen from the others' point of view, or to anticipate others' reactions to their own motives. Thus, they realize that their own inner workings can be objects of speculation by others. In contrast with Preconceptual children, who assume that parents always know what children think, Level 2 children begin to realize that parents, teachers, and peers may be able to figure out what they think and feel. These reflections about self and others occur sequentially, not simultaneously; the child cannot "get outside" the two-person situation to view the inner states of self and other from a third perspective.

Level 3. *Mutual role-taking (about ages ten to twelve).* Children differentiate their own perspective from the point of view taken by an "average member" of a group (that is, they adopt a generalized perspective). In a two-person interaction, children can distinguish each party's point of view from that of a third person. They can be impartial spectators and maintain a point of view in which their own ideas and feelings do not intrude. (They *can* do this, but we don't know how often or under which circumstances they *do*.) At this level each participant can conceptually place the self in the other's shoes and view the self

[3]In the earlier article they refer to "levels" and in the later article to "stages." I think that "levels" is a better label until structural characteristics of the child at each level can be thoroughly investigated.

from that vantage point before deciding how to act (e.g., the golden rule is now conceptualized correctly.)

> Trust, friendship, and mutual respect and expectations are viewed as dyadic or mutual. At [Level] 2 the concept of friend is defined from only one perspective: A friend is someone who does the self a favor and acts kindly from the self's perspective. At [Level] 3, the concept of friend is defined in interpersonal or mutual terms which go beyond simple reciprocity. A temporal component also emerges as the child begins to perceive consistency of actions by each member of the relationship over time as necessary to the definition of mutual relations. (Selman, 1976, p. 306)

When children at ages four, six, eight, and ten were interviewed about relationships between people in a story, Selman and Byrne (1974) showed a high correlation between chronological age and role-taking ($r = .80$). Selman (1971a) also reported a substantial relationship between role-taking levels and Kohlberg's moral judgment stages (see below). As far as I know, the correspondence between role-taking and logical operations has not been assessed; my estimates of the presumed Piagetian stage associated with the levels described above were based simply on general correspondence in chronological ages. While all of the aspects of Selman's account have not yet been investigated, he has developed the most comprehensive, structural model of role-taking to date.

The extensive advances in role-taking during middle childhood (seven to twelve years) have been documented in a number of studies which do not use Selman's stage model, but which obtain results consistent with its general outline. Feffer (1971; Feffer and Gourevitch, 1960) asked children to retell stories from the point of view of each protagonist and found ages and levels of perspective-taking quite similar to Selman's. Chandler and Greenspan (1972) assessed children's ability to adopt two different informational perspectives, by asking children to respond to a set of cartoons that tell a story.

> In one story, for example, a boy is saddened when he accidentally drops his coin down a sewer grating. He is then joined by a companion who is perplexed by the hero's refusal to join him in a ball game. The subjects were first asked to relate the story from their own point of view and then to reinterpret the same events from the limited perspective of the late-arriving bystander. Egocentrism was indexed in this procedure by the intrusion of privileged information offered as descriptive of the point of view of the bystander.

An earlier study by Borke (1971) used picture stories and found that three-year-olds were able to identify what the story child was feeling. She claimed that this required role-taking ability and that the finding raised serious questions for Piaget's theory of egocentrism. Chandler and Greenspan agreed that young children could identify another's feelings, but indicated that six-year-olds had extreme difficulty in adopting a point of view significantly different from their own; when the pictures were removed even ten and eleven-years-olds were still not able to maintain the two perspectives consistently.

As we know from research at other stages, progress in developing perspective during Concrete operations is not an all-or-none affair. Coie, Costanzo, and Farnill (1973) indicate that children first learn to discriminate what objects in a landscape are visible from a given perspective. Then they begin to conceptualize the aspects of the object that can be seen, and finally, they corate the objects in terms of relative left-right dimensions. This sequence appears similar to that found by Lempers, Flavell, and Flavell (1977) for much younger children in much simpler tasks.

Livesley and Bromley (1973) focused on the development of psychological conceptions of others. Between seven and fifteen years of age, English children showed an increase in the proportion of psychological statements about self and others in written descriptions. The only statistically significant increase between adjacent ages occurred between seven-and-a-half and eight-and-a-half years of age; possibly, the emergence of Concrete structures affected the change in social cognition. In another study of conceptions of others, Miller, Kessel, and Flavell (1970) examined children's understanding of "recursive thinking" in a set of cartoons which showed a person (1) thinking about two people; (2) thinking about talking occurring between two people; (3) thinking about the thinking of another person; and (4) thinking about thinking about thinking. Item 1 was understood by all first grade children, but not until fourth grade (ages nine to ten) did 75 percent of the children understand (2). Only about half the fifth and sixth graders understood (3), while one-third could conceptualize Level 4. Thus, evidence supports Selman's claim of significant advances in social cognition during the middle childhood period. The evidence also suggests that some role-taking skills have not yet reached a peak by the time children are about twelve years of age.

The ability to conceptualize different social perspectives may have important implications for social interaction. Using Miller, et al.'s task, Rubin (1973) found a correlation of about .70 with communication skills. Chaplin and Keller (1974) assessed role-taking and social interaction with peers and found that poor social interactors (as rated by observers) at the third grade level tended to be less skilled in a role-taking task than "good" social interactors; however, the relationship was not found in sixth graders. Rubin (1972) also seems to find relationships between cognitive egocentrism and social interactions in younger, but not older children. It could be, as Hollos and I suggest (1973), that there is a minimum developmental level of perspective-taking necessary for advances in social interaction. Once this threshold level has been passed, other variables (e.g., motivation) begin to affect the quality of a child's interaction with peers.

Spatial perspective and communication. A previously reported, unpublished study of mine (Cowan, 1966) suggests that there is a strong relationship between the achievement of perspective in the Three Mountains Task and the Late Concrete child's ability to overcome egocentrism in communication.

> Boys eight, nine, and ten years of age were tested on a version of the Three-Mountains Task. At each age level, children who were primarily egocentric (Lo) and primarily nonegocentric (Hi) were selected for further study.

Pairs of children were seated back to back in front of identical boards marked off with sixteen squares (four columns × four rows). The top eight squares were all yellow and the bottom eight were all red. Each child was given a set of sixteen objects. The task for each pair was to agree where to place each object so that the boards would look the same when the game was finished.

Children were paired on the basis of their previously assessed spatial perspective scores. At each of the three age levels there were three Hi–Hi pairs, three Lo–Lo pairs, and three Hi–Lo pairs, for a total of 27 pairs of children.

a. Egocentric vs. perspectivistic pairs. It is apparently not self-evident to the children that the only way to solve this problem is to talk to each other. Only 50 percent of the Lo–Lo pairs realized this without the experimenter's help, compared with 67 percent of the Hi–Lo pairs and 100 percent of the Hi–Hi pairs.

Here is a Lo–Lo pair of eight-year-olds:

Experimenter: I want you to decide between you where to put each thing.
Child 1: I did . . .
E: (Repeats instructions)
C 1: How can we decide when we can't see the other guy's board?
E: Exactly. How can you?
C 1: We can't.
E: What would you do if you wanted to know what he was doing?
C 1: Turn around.
E: How else could you do it if you couldn't turn around?
C 1: Get a walkie-talkie.
E: OK. And what would that mean you'd be doing?
C 1: Talking.
E: OK. Why don't you try talking?
C 1: What through? . . . .

After about 30 seconds they began to talk to each other.

On the average, it took Lo–Lo pairs four times as long to understand and begin communicating with each other as the Hi–Hi pairs. The Lo–Lo pair continued:

C 2: OK, put the pan on the first one, the first red one (places it bottom *left* relative to his body).
C 1: (Interrupts) What?
C 2: Put the pan on the first red one.
C 1: The badge?
C 2: No, the pan.
C 1: The pan?
C 2: Yeah.
C 1: Oh, great. (Places it bottom *right* relative to his body.)

In talking about where the object should be placed, the spatially egocentric children often gestured although their partners could not see them, or said,

"Put it over there." Often they located a piece in only one spatial dimension, for instance, "Put it in the bottom corner," when there were two bottom corners. What makes this an egocentric *interaction* is that, in the Lo–Lo pairs, the other member assumed he knew what this command meant and failed to question it. In only 25 percent of the Lo–Lo pairs did children locate the first object placement in two spatial dimensions (up–down; right–left) while 78 percent of the Hi–Lo and 100 percent of the Hi–Hi pairs did so.

Here is a Hi–Hi pair of eight-year-olds:

E: (Gives the instructions)
C 1: We can't turn around?
E: No, don't turn around.
C 1: Lorin?
C 2: Yeah?
C 1: I'll do it, and then you do it, and then I'll do it, okay?

In very few cases did the children engage in metacommunication, that is, talk about how they were going to talk to each other. This was much more common in a group of adults I tested later and emphasizes that the high and low spatial perspective designations in the study were only relative ones.

C 1: See the line that isn't touching the red?
C 2: Yes.
C 1: And if the red is closest to you on the table, put it in the last-out square, right?
C 2: Of the red or the yellow?
C 1: Of the yellow. The furthest-out left square, but if the yellow is right next to you, then put it on the out-square that's closest to you on the right. (Puts it bottom right relative to his body.)
C 2: Okay. (Also puts it bottom right.)

This last part of the exchange, however unclear, represents a specific recognition, by at least one child in the pair, that the other child might be seeing something different and that it is necessary to be clear about both spatial dimensions. The explicit attempt to check both the location of the object and the orientation of the board relative to the other's body occurred in only 13 percent of the Lo–Lo pairs, 33 percent of the Hi–Lo pairs, but in 100 percent of the Hi–Hi pairs.[4]

b. Mismatch conditions. The above results refer only to the first, agreed-upon placement of objects. In order to see what happened over the course of the task, each remark made by each child was rated on a three-point communication egocentrism scale by a rater unaware of the child's age and Three Mountains Task performance. A score of three was given for a remark clearly taking into account the listener's point of view (e.g., "If the yellow squares are on top of your board, put the blue circle in the top right yellow corner.") Two points were given for a remark which showed that differences in viewpoint were recognized but not adequately dealt with (e.g., "Put it in the first square

[4]This and most of the differences reported here were statistically significant.

on your left."). One point was given for a relatively egocentric statement (e.g., "Put it there.").[5]

Hi–Lo pairs at each age level were examined separately. The language used by Hi children was consistently less egocentric than that used by Lo children at the beginning of the task. However, in the eight- and nine-year-old Hi–Lo pairs, the communication of the Hi became more egocentric, while in the ten-year-old pairs, the Lo child began to sound more like the Hi's. Intensive analysis of the interaction suggests that the eight-year-old Hi gives fairly precise directions, but when mistakes are made, or when he receives negative feedback from his partner, his performance deteriorates. In the ten-year-old Hi–Lo, pairs, a potentially disequilibrating situation becomes a spur for the Hi to ask questions, recheck, and provide a model for the Lo, who begins to follow it.

Three conclusions may be drawn from these results so far:

1. Spatially egocentric pairs of children talk to each other on a different level than spatially nonegocentric pairs. Using a similar version of the Three Mountains Task, Coie and Dorvall (1973) also found a relationship between spatial perspective and communication. They indicate that conventional intelligence tests predict communication level about as well as Inhelder and Piaget's spatial perspective task.

2. The cognitive level of the partner, as measured by both the Three Mountains Task and verbal communication, influences a child's level of egocentric language. (In eight- and nine-year-olds, communication becomes more egocentric when a Hi child is paired with a Lo, while in ten-year-old Lo's, communication becomes less egocentric when the child is paired with a Hi.) This conclusion is based on a total of nine pairs and should be examined further. It suggests, nevertheless, that cognitive performance is not completely determined by individual characteristics; it may be affected by social context.

3. The results of this study also suggest that children who develop spatial perspective at ages eight or nine have not yet attained a stable perspective structure. They tend not to maintain their level in communication with a Lo. And, the eight-year-old Hi–Hi pairs who communicate less egocentrically than Lo–Lo's at the beginning of the task, are no more effective in matching their boards by the end of the task. Thus, a child with the ability to take another point of view in spatial perspective is not immediately or fully able to translate the ability into skills of interpersonal communication.

c. Cognitive development and social stucture. Although the partners were roughly matched for egocentrism level, in each pair of children, one child usually had a slightly higher spatial perspective score than the other. Over all 27 pairs, in the first event and throughout the task, children of higher spatial perspective ability significantly more often determined where objects should be placed. Miller and Brownell (1975) paired conservers and nonconservers of length and weight and asked them to arrive at one answer between them. The conservers' answers prevailed significantly more often. Cognitive level, then, may play some role in determining leadership relations, especially in a task requiring a great deal of intellectual activity.

[5]Not all of the egocentric communications were shorter.

The interaction of the eight- and nine-year-old Hi–Lo pairs was quite unlike that of pairs in the other cells. For example, communication was most often one-way for long periods of time, while both Hi–Hi and Lo–Lo pairs took regular turns. There was a definite quality of what Piaget refers to as cooperation in the Hi–Hi pairs at all age levels. These children often checked whether they were "in the same stimulus universe" (e.g., "Do you have a red and yellow board? Do you have a red star?"); they showed reversibility in being able to recheck object placements; and they most often established an implicit or explicit strategy for procedure, for instance, moving row by row from left to right. It seems as though the cognitive level and level of language expression of the pair leads to the building of a social communication system with a common framework. Further research and analysis should be directed to the question of whether a notion of "conservation of roles" (maintenance of roles despite transformations) can be usefully applied to this kind of social organization.

Self-image. Children's ability to adopt more than one perspective on the physical and social world should be related to their perspective on themselves. In a very interesting study, Leahy and Huard (1976) examined the relations among role-taking (seven pictures–four pictures), Glucksberg-Krauss communication (communication about nonsense shapes), and the discrepancy between real self-image ("This statement is true of me.") and ideal self-image ("I would like this statement to be true of me").

In this fourth-to-sixth grade sample, Glucksberg-Krauss communication was unrelated either to role-taking or to self-ideal discrepancies. The authors conclude, again, that egocentrism may not be a unitary variable. Interestingly, better role-takers had a *larger* self-ideal discrepancy than poorer role-takers; children who could more accurately adopt the viewpoint of a new observer in the room tended to perceive more difference between themselves as they were and as they wanted to be. The increased self-ideal discrepancy can be interpreted as a more differentiated self-concept, but it can also be interpreted as a decrease in self-esteem (moving farther from one's ideal). What would be important to know is the set of conditions under which differentiated self-perceptions lead, or do not lead, to self criticism.

Physical and social causality

With the coming of Concrete operations, children's explanations of physical causes (Laurendeau and Pinard, 1962) begin to shift from finalism (it becomes dark so we can sleep) and artificialism (someone makes it dark) to primarily physical causes. However, there are still various colorings of the previous stages. In the Bernstein and Cowan study, there were two Concrete stages of physical causality.

Level 4. Physical explanations with strong overtones of previous stages (e.g., when the sun turns the other way, it's real dark, when the moon comes). These seem to be Early Concrete explanations.

Level 5. Physical explanations with faint overtones of previous stages (e.g., it becomes dark because we need rest and the sun goes over to the other side of the world). These seem to be Late Concrete explanations.

These two levels come before what may be a Formal operations response with purely physical explanations (e.g., Level 6: it becomes dark because the sun is shining on the other side of the world).

In other Piagetian investigations (1927) there are other versions of level 5 physical explanations. At this level, things sometimes contain their own causes.

[A nine year old] —What is the wind made of? —*Dust* —Does it stand still? —*It blows.* —Does it move? —*Yes.* —Where does the dust of the wind come from? —*From old rags.* —Do you really think so? —*Yes.* —On the Mont-Blanc there is nothing but snow, no dust. What is the wind made of up there? —*Dust.* —Where does it come from? —*From here.* —Does the wind move? —*Yes.* —How? —*By itself* (p. 40).

In another example at this stage, causality is physical, but circular.

[A ten-year-old] —And what makes the waves? —*It's the air.* —And what makes the wind? —*The waves.* —What makes the waves? —*It's the air* (p. 91).

Again, there are parallel stages in children's ideas about the origins of babies (Bernstein and Cowan, 1975).

Level 4. Physical explanation with strong overtones of previous stages. In this area children reject finalism and artificialism in their ideas about conception; though they recognize the parent's role, they fail to see why the participation of both parents is necessary.

[Age seven years, nine months] —Why do the seed and the egg *have* to come together? —*Or else the baby, the egg, won't really get hatched very well.* —How does the baby come from the egg and the seed? —*The seed makes the egg grow. It's just like plants; if you plant a seed a flower will grow.* —There's no egg with plants. —*No, it's just a special kind of seed that makes an egg hatch.* —Why must the seed touch the egg for the baby to grow? —*The egg won't hatch.* —What about its coming together makes a baby? —*I don't know. Well, I don't think . . . I don't know.* —Can the egg grow into a baby without the seed? —*I don't think so.* —Can the seed grow into a baby without the egg? —*I don't know.*

Level 5. Preformation. Causes are physical, but the baby exists preformed *either* in sperm or egg.

At this level all children refer to sexual intercourse as the beginning of fertilization. But when questioned about fertilization they reveal their Preformation ideas.

[Eleven-year-old] —What does fertilize mean? —*Kind of give it food and things like that.* —Can the egg grow if no sperm goes into it? —*I don't think so.* —Can sperm grow with no egg? —*No, that doesn't have the baby; it's the egg that would have the baby in it.* Responding to the question, "How do fathers get to be fathers?" another eleven-year old said: —*Well, if they're the man that made love to your mother, then they're your father because you really originally came out of him and then went into your mother.* —Say more. —*Well, you were a sperm inside of him there. So that you're really his daughter or son. 'Cause he was the one that really had you first.* —Why must the egg be there for the sperm to develop into a baby? —*'Cause otherwise the sperm will have, uh, nothing to nourish it, or sort of keep it warm or, you know, able to move or something. Just has, it's not, just has to have the egg to be able to do something, develop. It just dies if it doesn't have the egg.*

The Preformist notion of causality in social objects seems to be parallel with the Level 5 explanations in physical causality: things have their own causal forces within them. In the quoted examples, these eleven-year-olds are stating that the baby exists inside somewhere, just as the three- and four-year-olds assumed that babies always exist somewhere, but their belief is part of a much more sophisticated and complicated causal theory. This is one of many times that we see children spiral back to an earlier issue but at a much more differentiated and integrated level.

In our article, Bernstein and I also pointed out that children's development of ideas about babies may recapitulate part of the history of the field of embryology, in which scientists originally believed in preformed foetuses existing either in sperm or egg. Like the development of science itself, children will later reach another level in which the genetic material is believed to be furnished by both parents and in which the foetus is an interactive product of both parents' contributions.

In our sample, only 10 percent of the seven- to-eight-year-olds, but 90 percent of the eleven- to-twelve-year-olds gave Level 5 responses or above. This fact, and the general correlation between physical and social causality concepts, supports the interpretation that Level 5 is a Late Concrete operational achievement. Children's ideas about babies, like their ideas about other "objects" and situations, are shaped by their current cognitive structural levels.

Moral and conventional judgment

In Chapter 7, I described Piaget's (1932) only investigation of conventional rules (the marble game) and moral principles. This work contrasted Preoperational children with children somewhere in the middle of the Concrete stage. Because Piaget never returned to research in this area, we have no information directly from him concerning the details of moral development from mid- to late Concrete operations and beyond. Leadership in the cognitive developmental approach to this topic has been assumed by Lawrence Kohlberg and by Elliot Turiel. While these two investigators initially collaborated on theory and research, they have more recently followed somewhat different paths. Kohlberg has continued with the exploration of moral issues, while Turiel has begun to view the development of social conventional thinking as a partially separate conceptual domain.

Moral development. In an impressive set of studies and theoretical articles, Kohlberg has proposed a six-stage structural sequence in the development of moral judgments. His own initial studies focused on children between ten and sixteen years of age (1963), but now we have data from five-year-old (Kuhn, 1976b) all the way to fifty-year-old subjects (Kuhn, Langer, Kohlberg, and Hahn, 1977).

Kohlberg presents subjects with three to nine moral dilemmas like this one:

> In Europe, a woman was near death from cancer. One drug might save her, a form of radium that a druggist was charging $2,000, ten times what the drug cost him to make. The sick woman's husband, Heinz, went to everyone he knew to borrow the money, but he could only get together about half of what it cost. He told the druggist that his wife was dying and asked him to sell it cheaper or let him pay later. But the druggist said, "No." The husband got desperate and broke into the man's store to steal the drug for his wife. Should the husband have done that? Why?

Kohlberg's moral dilemmas differ from Piaget's stories which contrast the behaviors of two children. First, in the Piaget stories, the choice of a particular child as naughtier leads to a particular reasoning level; the child who does the most damage always does it unintentionally. In Kohlberg's dilemmas, the answer can be either "yes" or "no." The scorer is not interested in whether Heinz should or should not steal the dug, but in the structural level of the reasons given to justify the answer. Second, these stories are constructed so that any one of a number of dimensions of moral reasoning can be made relevant to the story, in contrast with Piaget's stories, which focus on one dimension at a time (e.g., intentions vs. consequences), or which confuse several dimensions in a single choice. Kohlberg (1969) lists 25 aspects of morality on which responses to each story could focus, including: intention–consequences; guilt; responsibility of actor and victim; orientation to rules; conformity; punishment; reciprocity and justice, and so on. Presumably, the six-stage sequence holds up no matter which aspects are spontaneously used by the subjects.

a. *Definition of stages.* Kohlberg groups the six stages into three levels: Preconventional, Conventional, and Postconventional. Here are the definitions of the levels and the descriptions of the two stages within each level (taken from Kohlberg, 1969; Turiel, 1973). Also included are pro and con responses to Heinz's dilemma quoted by Kohlberg from research by Rest (1968). All of these examples focus on the intention-consequences aspect of judgment, but other examples would illustrate the developmental sequence. I am including the first *four* stages in this chapter, even though stages 4 through 6 are associated primarily with Formal operational stage reasoning (Black, 1976), when they are found at all (Kuhn, et al., 1977).

I. Preconventional level.

The child judges good and bad, right and wrong, on the basis of actions and transactions, not on the basis of conventional agreements or personal standards.

Stage 1. *Punishment and obedience orientation.* Like Piaget's definition of early morality, what is good or bad depends on the consequences of an act, not on intent or on context (e.g., mitigating circumstances). The avoidance of punishment and the promotion of obedience are valued in their own right, not because they represent respect for a moral order supported by punishment and authority (this latter is Stage 4).

Pro: He should steal the drug. It isn't really bad to take it. It isn't like he didn't ask to pay for it first. The drug he'd take is only worth $200, he's not really taking a $2,000 drug.

Con: He shouldn't steal the drug, it's a big crime. He didn't get permission, he used force and broke and entered. He did a lot of damage, stealing a very expensive drug and breaking up the store, too.

Stage 2. *Instrumental relativist orientation.* Good or bad, right or wrong is determined by actions which satisfy one's own needs and sometimes the needs of others. Fairness, sharing, and reciprocity are present, not as principles, but as a marketplace *quid pro quo:* I'll do what you want in order to get you to do what I want.

Pro: It's all right to steal the drug because she needs it and he wants her to live. It isn't that he wants to steal, but it's the way he has to use to get the drug to save her.

Con: He shouldn't steal it. The druggist isn't wrong or bad, he just wants to make a profit. That's what you're in business for, to make money.

II. Conventional level.

Moral value resides in performing good or right roles regardless of immediate consequences. One conforms to family, group, or national expectations out of loyalty, actively maintaining the social order and identifying with the people or groups involved.

Stage 3. *Interpersonal concordance or "good boy–nice girl" orientation.* It is good to please and help others, to meet their expectations. At this stage, people develop a stereotype of what the majority does, and whatever that is becomes normal and natural. Intention to do right becomes important for the first time.

Pro: He should steal the drug. He was only doing something that was natural for a good husband to do. You can't blame him for doing something out of love for his wife, you'd blame him if he didn't love his wife enough to save her.

Con: He shouldn't steal. If his wife dies, he can't be blamed. It isn't because he's heartless or that he doesn't love her enough to do everything that he legally can. The druggist is the selfish or heartless one.

For purposes of comparison, I will describe Kohlberg's fourth stage, though there is evidence that this level does not emerge without some other evidence of Formal operational reasoning.

Stage 4. *Authority and social order maintaining orientation.* Authority and rules must be obeyed because they maintain the social order. For this reason, doing one's duty and showing respect for authority are also highly valued.

Pro: You should steal it. If you did nothing you'd be letting your wife die, it's your responsibility if she dies. You have to take it with the idea of paying the druggist.

Con: It is a natural thing for Heinz to want to save his wife but it's always wrong to steal. He still knows he's stealing and taking a valuable drug from the man who made it.

b. *Stage and Structures*. When all nine dilemmas are administered it is evident that Kohlberg's method can produce a richly detailed set of responses. Each of the many possible responses to a dilemma can be given a separate stage-level score. In fact, the scoring procedure is so complex that application of it requires training—in Kohlberg's own laboratory or by someone very familiar with the system.

Kohlberg reports that there is a modal response-level to each dilemma, with a few responses at stages one or two above or below the mode. Generally, he gives the subject a single modal score or a more global score, for each item; this seems a waste of such detailed scoring. Kurtines and Greif (1974), in a critical review of Kohlberg's work, point out that there have never been systematic tests of the psychometric reliability and validity properties of Kohlberg's instrument. Although these critics are factually correct, they miss the point that Kohlberg has not created an IQ test, but rather a clinical instrument to explore the nature of moral stages. Despite reservations such as these, there is evidence from a number of sources, which suggest that Kohlberg's stages form a developmental cognitive structural sequence.

1. With increasing age there is increasing use of higher stages. In a sample of 25 children, kindergarten through grade two, almost all were at Stage 1. Only one showed clear use of Stage 2 responses without a high proportion of Stage 1 (Kuhn, 1976b). Kohlberg's own results (1969) for an American sample show ten-year-olds primarily in the first three stages, with a few at Stage 4, and none at Stages 5 or 6. By age sixteen, use of lower stages is declining and use of higher stages is increasing. However, these data and others (e.g., Kuhn, et al., 1977; Black, 1976) find a majority of college-level adults in Stage 4, with very few people of any age at Stage 6.

2. An incomplete longitudinal study by Kohlberg (1971) indicates that subjects tend to progress over time to the next stage in the sequence. Ultimately, longitudinal results will be crucial to the establishment of a sequence.

3. Beginning evidence suggests that attainment of Concrete operations (as measured in physical tasks) is necessary, but not sufficient, for the achievement of Stage 3 and that attainment of Formal operations is necessary for Stages 4 through 6 (Black, 1976; Keasey, 1975). These findings suggest that cognitive structures may provide the foundation for moral development, but that moral judgment advances do not automatically accompany cognitive change.

4. An ingenious study by Rest, Turiel, and Kohlberg (1969) examined the child's understanding of, and preference for, reasoning at various moral stages. After the predominant stage was assessed, the child was presented with statements at each of the six stages and asked (1) to "put each statement in his

own words" and (2) to choose the statement which he thought "best" or "smartest." All children could correctly rephrase statements at their dominant stage or below. Very few were able to understand statements at two stages above their own (+2). Some, who had shown a substantial use of the stage just above their modal response (+1), could correctly rephrase the +1 reasoning. And, finally, whatever their initial stage, children seemed to *prefer* higher level responses, whether or not they fully understood them.

5. Turiel (1966) attempted to influence children to respond at +2, +1, and −1 levels, relative to their predominant stage. Consistent with the preference data, the +1 condition produced the most change and the −1 condition produced the least change in children's responses.

Thus, cross-sectional age data, longitudinal trends, correspondence between cognitive and moral stages, children's understanding and preferences for higher levels, and a social influence study all suggest that Kohlberg's stages form a regular, structurally based sequence.

c. *Role-taking and moral judgment.* Kohlberg has argued that it is not social interaction *per se,* but rather the development of role-taking ability which is a key factor in moral judgment progression. Selman (1976) extends the argument: cognitive stage indicates level of physical and logical understanding; role-taking level indicates understanding of social relations; moral judgment stages indicate the manner in which the child resolves social conflicts between people with different points of view. When a child is incapable of coordinating perspectives of self and others, he or she will likely have difficulty with moral judgments of reciprocal rights or duties, and so on. In a study of 60 eight-to-ten-year-olds (Selman, 1971a), the association between a Flavell role-taking task and Kohlberg's moral stages was statistically significant over the whole sample and in each age group. The major finding was that children low on role-taking ability (low role-takers) tended to respond at Stages 1 and 2, while high role-takers' responses were at Stages 3 or 4. The author interprets role-taking as being a mediator between purely cognitive skills and the moral domain. Moir (1972) extends this finding, obtaining similar results, using several role-taking measures. It is certainly too early to go beyond the weak statement that there is a relation between role-taking and moral judgment; there is as yet, no strong evidence for or against Kohlberg's assertion that role-taking is a *central* variable in moral development.

Games with rules. In Chapter 7, I described the first three Piagetian stages in the development of children's conceptions and use of rules in marble games. Following Sensorimotor regularities and egocentric imitations, Early Concrete children adopt a general approach to rules in which winning is defined as getting the better of others.

> [But] mere competition is not what constitutes the affective motive power of the game. In seeking to win, the child is trying above all to contend with his partner *while* observing common rules. The specific pleasure of the game thus ceases to be muscular and egocentric and becomes social (Piaget, 1932, p. 42).

Games become, in action, what discussions have become in words—a mutual and reciprocal exchange, according to a shared set of procedures.

In later writings (1948), Piaget suggests that this mutuality is possible only when the individual's operative system permits him or her to enter into a cooperative system; social exchanges can occur reversibly without distorting the perception of the event or task. In the Early Concrete substage, cooperation is more an attitude than an achievement. Agreements on rules are fleeting. There is not yet a machinery for negotiation of differences, so each participant is left with a perceived opinion about the value of shared rules. Consistent with other findings of Early Concrete operations, the new structure is still particular and not extended to all cases or to hypotheticals.

Beginning in Late Concrete operations, a fourth stage of rule-related conceptions emerges, which will be actualized only in the Formal stage. Children of eleven or twelve years become interested not only in knowing "correct" rules, but also in thinking and talking about the rules themselves. Piaget gives an example of the emerging legalistic turn of mind.

> The fact that the child enjoys complicating things at will proves that what he is after is rules for their own sake. We have described elsewhere [Piaget, 1924] the extraordinary behavior of eight boys of 10 to 11 who, in order to throw snow-balls at each other, began by wasting a good quarter-of-an-hour in electing a president, fixing the rules of voting, then in dividing themselves into two camps, in deciding upon the distances of the shots, and finally in foreseeing what would be the sanctions to be applied in case of infringement of these laws. Many other facts analogous to this could be culled from studies that have been made on children's societies (1932, p. 50).

Turiel's analysis of conventional rules. Piaget included a study of marble games as introductory to his moral judgment research because he believed that the understanding of rules was the essense of moral development. In some exciting new studies and theoretical analyses, Turiel (1975, 1977, 1978) has demonstrated that rules of games, moral judgments, and social conventions may not form a unified structure; instead he conceptualizes them as different domains governed by a set of interrelated, but still independent, cognitive structures.

> *Games with rules.* Here, Turiel and Piaget both emphasize games with rules, not solitary play or social fantasy games. In contrast with moral and conventional rules, game rules are specific to that activity and are not meant to apply to behavior across situations (e.g., "If you pass 'Go' collect $200.").
>
> *Moral rules.* Issues in this domain include: the value of life; the welfare of individuals and groups; avoidance of physical or psychological harm; protection of human and property rights; fairness, equality of treatment, and justice. These issues are believed by most people to be universally applicable. Even if there is a group or society that condones random killing or stealing, the acts would still be considered immoral by most observers outside that society. In this domain, laws follow from already-established moral principles.

Social–conventional rules. Issues in this domain include: forms of address (use of Mr., Ms., Dr., titles); dress codes; sex-role stereotypes (can men take jobs as nurses?); sexual mores; national and religious customs. These issues are not considered to be universally applicable; as long as a relevant social collective agrees, then the rule can be changed.[6] In contrast with morality (where goodness or badness of an act leads to rules), here rules and laws determine what is good or bad. There is nothing inherently wrong with the act of calling teachers by their first names unless teachers forbid it. Thus, what is right in the social–conventional domain is determined by the social system in which the rule is formed. As we shall see, the development of conventional rule concepts is intimately tied to the child's conception of the social system.

Studies of distinctions among these domains. In a study of six-to-seventeen-year-olds, Turiel (1977) constructed a long and detailed clinical interview which asked children to give examples of rules of games, rules at home, rules at school, and legal rules. Children were also asked to discuss some issues raised by the interviewer: rules about stealing, about addressing teachers by title and not by first name, about men wearing jackets in business offices, and so on. The home and school rules were classified as either moral or conventional on the basis of the criteria described above. Stealing rules were classified in the moral category.

When asked to rate the importance of the rules they had generated (1–4), or to rank the importance of rules, children at every age level gave the highest rankings to moral rules (first stealing, then moral rules at school and home); conventional rules were consistently considered to be less important. While it is only at adolescence that children begin to verbalize the distinction between moral and conventional rules, it is evident that children from six to seventeen years of age can verbalize their views about the relative importance of rules within different domains. Children as young as six years old showed as much differentiation in the ratings of importance as did the late adolescents.

Children were also asked a number of questions about each rule: whether it could be changed; whether they and their friends or another family could change it; whether, if a whole country agreed, the violation of a rule would be all right (i.e., are rules absolute or relative?). At all ages, the majority stated that stealing rules could not be changed; about half stated that specific moral rules about persons or property at home could not be changed. However, beginning with an almost even split in the six-to-seven-year-olds, an increasing number of children over the age range suggested that conventional home rules and game rules could be changed if others agreed. Children at all ages rated game rules as very important, but a majority felt that the rules could be changed. Turiel interprets this result as indicating that game rules are important to children in the context of playing the game, but over time, the rules

[6]In specific instances, there may be disagreements on whether a rule is universally applicable. Especially in the area of sexuality, some individuals believe that standards are relative, while some believe that there are absolute criteria (see current legal controversies over obscenity and pornography laws).

come to have increasingly less intrinsic importance and thus a change in rules can be considered. By contrast, rules regarding stealing *have* intrinsic importance, and most children at every age believe that they cannot be altered.

Referring to previously puzzling findings in others' research, Turiel makes a case for the usefulness of his distinction between moral, conventional, and game domains.

1. By tabulating and classifying some of Piaget's own results, Turiel demonstrates that children's judgments of game rule violations are quite different from their judgments of unfairness or inequality. He cites other studies which indicate that young children's judgments of intentions and consequences in situations involving material damage are different from their judgments in situations involving lying or physical harm to persons. Thus, Piaget's (1932) equation of game rules and moral rules may be incorrect.

2. A study by Gilligan, Kohlberg, Lerner, and Belensky (1971) and a longitudinal follow-up by Stein (1973), attempted to apply Kohlberg's moral judgment scoring to middle and late adolescents' responses to sexual dilemmas (e.g., unmarried high school couples engaging in sexual intercourse). Gilligan, et al. found more Stage 2 scores on sexual stories and more Stage 4 scores on the original Kohlberg moral dilemmas. The stage scores for the sexual stories were more variable. One possible interpretation of these data is that moral judgment is simply less developed in the sexual (personal?) area, but Turiel argues otherwise. In Stein's follow-up of the original subjects two years later, stage changes in Kohlberg items followed Kohlberg's developmental sequence, but changes in the sexuality interview did not follow that same sequence. These results, according to Turiel, support the interpretation that consenting sexual behavior is primarily a matter of social convention (not justice) and, again, that social concepts develop independently from moral concepts.[7]

3. Turiel's latest article (1978) performs a valuable service by reanalyzing much of the earlier work in moral development within the framework of his moral–conventional distinction. For example, he takes a new look at Hartshorne and May's (1928–1930) classic studies of moral behavior. Their general conclusion was that many children violate rules and that moral behavior is primarily a function of environmental context and opportunity. There was no consistent tendency for children to obey or to violate rules across many situations. Turiel points to this previously unnoticed fact: when children were provided with opportunities to be dishonest in game and classroom test situations, 50–75 percent of them "cheated"; but only 15 percent did so in situations providing an opportunity to steal money.

Turiel also reexamines the social learning research on resistance to temptation in which young children are asked not to touch a certain object; after they

[7]This analysis reminds us that cognitive developmentalists are often more interested in competence than in performance. Adolescents for the first time are *able* to separate moral and conventional aspects of sexuality, but this does not mean that they and adults always do so. There are many instances where conventional infractions are treated as moral violations.

have opportunity to watch a model violate the rule, the experimenter leaves the child unattended. Since the rule is arbitrarily set by the experimenter, Turiel argues that these studies are instances of conventional rather than moral violation (he calls them "quasi conventions of the social structure of the experimental situation"). In one set of studies (Sears, Rau, and Alpert, 1965), greater "transgressions" were observed in the forbidden toy situation than in a situation where children could steal another child's candy. And so, the children themselves seem to be responding in a way that is consistent with Turiel's distinction.

Developmental sequence of conventional judgments. Both Piaget and Kohlberg assume that younger children confuse social–conventional and moral judgments. As children grow older, they begin to distinguish the two, so that judgments of good and bad based on social conventions are *replaced* by an autonomous, principled morality (Piaget's heteronomous stage, Kohlberg's Stages 5 and 6). Turiel's analysis (1977) indicates that even six-year-olds *do* distinguish the two domains and that these two domains remain separate over time, so that conventional judgment develops side by side with moral development—through adolescence and beyond. Turiel argues that it is their failure to keep moral and conventional items separate which has led to Piaget's and Kohlberg's erroneous conclusions about sequence.

Approximately 140 subjects from ages six to twenty-five were presented with a series of hypothetical stories about conventional rules (Turiel, 1977, 1978). Subjects were asked probing questions in order to obtain information about the ways in which they conceptualized convention. Two of the interview stories dealt with social–conventional issues already discussed: forms of address and styles of formal and informal dress. Other stories dealt with (a) sex-appropriate occupations (a boy who wants to become a nurse caring for infants when he grows up); (b) use of titles (a boy who is brought up to address people by first names comes into conflict with teachers who insist on formal titles); (c) patterns of living arrangements in different cultures (fathers living apart from the rest of the family); and (d) modes of eating (with hands, knife, or fork).

In this preliminary study, Turiel finds a sequence of seven levels, but they have not yet been established as stage sequences à la Kohlberg. He notes three general trends. First, there is a progression toward viewing conventional rules in relation to social systems with rules serving the function of coordinating social interaction. Second, the levels reflect changes in the child's conception of social systems and how they operate. Third, the course of development is not straightforward or linear. Rather, the child oscillates between accepting the convention and negating it, with different grounds for affirmation or negation at each level.

1. Level 1. *Conventions describe social uniformity* (ages six to seven).[8] Con-

[8]All ages are approximate.

ventional rules describe uniformities in behaviors—not just what is observed, but what is assumed to be the case.

> [A girl (about six) was asked about a man who wanted to be a nurse; his father objected:]—Should he become a nurse? —*Well, no because he could easily be a doctor and he could take care of babies in the hospital.* —Why shouldn't he be a nurse? —*Well because a nurse is a lady and the boys, the other men would just laugh at them.* —Why shouldn't a man be a nurse? —*Well, because it would be sort of silly because ladies wear those kind of dresses and those kind of shoes and hats.* —What is the difference between doctors and nurses? —*Doctors take care of them most and nurses just hand them things.* —Do you think his father was right? —*Yes. Because, well, a nurse, she typewrites and stuff and all that.* —The man should not do that? —*No. Because he would look silly in a dress.* (Turiel, 1978, in press)

At this stage the child accepts common practice as a rule. Once the rule is made it should not be violated, even though the child would agree that without the rule, the act would be permitted. The only sanctions for violations of the rule would be social—ridicule by others. While children perceive, quite accurately, some products of the social power hierarchy (teacher–students; doctors–nurses), their answers show no explicit recognition of the social system origins of the rule.

2. Level 2. *Negation of convention as description of social uniformity* (ages eight to nine). The fact that most people behave in a given manner is no longer accepted as the basis of social convention. Perceived exceptions[9] are cited as justification for the reaction to social rules as binding.

> [A girl of eight:] —*It doesn't matter. There are men nurses in the hospitals.* —Why do you think his parents think he should not take care of little kids? —*Because his father might be old-fashioned and he would think that men could not take care of babies.* —Why do you think he thinks that? —*Because it is a lady's job, because ladies know what babies are because they have them.* —You don't think that is true? —*No. Because ladies are the same and men might know a lot about babies too.* (1978, in press)

There is no intrinsic basis for acting one way or another. Conventional acts are arbitrary, and because they are arbitrary there is no reason to go along. At this level children do not recognize the coordination function which conventional rules may have.

3. Level 3. *Convention as affirmation of a rule system; Early Concrete views of a social system* (ages ten to eleven). At this level, conventions are still viewed as arbitrary and changeable, but now they *should* be obeyed because they are authoritative expressions of people in power.

> [A boy of eleven was asked:] —Do you think Peter was right or wrong to continue

[9]The fact that younger children ignore exceptions, even in their own families, is puzzling. Do they not *perceive* instances when women are doctors, and so on, or do they discount exceptions when they are discussing the general topic?

calling his teachers by their first name? —*Wrong, because the principal told him not to. Because it was a rule. It was one of the rules of the school.* —And why does that make it wrong to call a teacher by his first name? —*Because you should follow the rules.* —Do you think if there weren't a rule, that it would be wrong, or would it be right to call teachers by their first names? —*Right. Because if there wasn't a rule, it wouldn't matter. . . .* —What about the rule makes it wrong? —*They made the rule because if there wasn't any rules, everybody would just be doing things they wanted to do. If they didn't have any rules everybody would, like, be running in the corridor and knocking over people!* (1978, in press)

Rules come out of the relationship between individuals in a system, in which some individuals hold more power and authority. The act itself is variable and arbitrary, but the rule applying to the act is not.

4. Level 4. *Negation of convention as a rule system* (ages twelve to thirteen). Children at the beginning of adolescence go one step further. Because conventional acts are seen as arbitrary, these children argue that the rules regulating such acts are invalid.

[A boy of twelve is asked:] —Do you think Peter was right or wrong to continue calling his teachers by their first names? —*I think it is up to him what he calls them because a name is just like a symbol or something and it doesn't really matter, just as long as the teacher knows or everybody else knows who you are talking about.* —What about the rule, do you think it would be wrong to disobey it in the school? —*No. . . .* —Some people might argue that it shows a lack of consideration and respect to call a teacher by their first name. What would you say to that? —*I think that is stupid. There is nothing wrong with a name no matter which you say. It doesn't really matter.*

Early adolescents dispute the constraining effects of social rules without recognizing the adult view that there is a social system which requires some stability-maintaining rules—a system that has legitimacy beyond the sheer power or authority of adult leaders.

The last three levels of social–conventional morality will be presented in Chapter 11 in a discussion of social–personality aspects of Formal operations. One general point of Turiel's analysis applies to all of the levels: in contrast with Piaget's emphasis on the generality of cognitive systems, Turiel's work is directed to exploring the potential separateness of cognitive and social domains.

EMOTIONAL DEVELOPMENT

Potential impact of the grouping structure

Once the logical grouping appears, the same structure which is applied to the stable hierarchy of class inclusions in the physical world can also be applied to the field of values. Beyond the feelings of the moment, the Concrete child begins to make reference to an implicit "list." At the top of the list is what is best, most important, most exciting, fairest, and so on, with other things or situations ranked in descending order. At the beginning, of course, the child may hardly be aware of the list and the rankings may fluctuate; but over time, children develop a sense that some activities are consistently more desirable, some values inherently more salient, some transgressions definitely more serious. References to this hierarchy will come to have increasing importance in the making of choices and decisions.

Piaget (1962) uses the term "will" to describe the regulating mechanism which brings values (feelings) into the child's decisions. "Will power" is applied when a weak sense of duty or obligation is about to be overcome by a stronger pull of desire (e.g., for a forbidden activity). Will is a product of the grouping structure in that it is a reversible conceptual mechanism; just as the child overcomes the visual salience of the water level to return to the initial state of the containers, so the child overcomes the perceived temptations of the moment to reassert the value hierarchy. In this way, the child develops a code of ethics—Piaget views this code as a logic of feelings and values.

Logical classification and time perspective seem to be important cognitive organizational dimensions of the child's emotional states. I have described Pre-operational children as very "either–or" in their feelings about people and things. But with the development of a continuum of preferences, Concrete children may now be less upset if they lose a piece of candy than if they misplace their favorite toy; all tragedies are not equally serious, nor are all satisfactions equally gratifying. And, with increased time perspective, children may begin to transcend the "always–never" perceptions of their own feelings; they know in some sense that even if they or someone else is upset now, the feelings will pass and the relationship will probably continue.

Now, it may be possible for Concrete operational children to adopt this more differentiated perspective, yet many adults who become upset or depressed seem unable to maintain it consistently. Piaget's discussion of the relation between cognitive and affective hierarchies is speculative, not based on the kinds of investigations described above. From a few similarities in the two hierarchies (e.g., rank ordering, ability to overcome the pull of immediate perceptual stimulation), he concludes that there is an identical organizing principle (the logical grouping). I think that Piaget's cognitive structural model may help to specify the child's potential for relatively stable structures of feelings and values; but, as is the case in many areas of emotional–social development, we need more detailed research to specify the situations in which these structures operate and the situations in which they do not. Presumably, the intensity of a person's involvement in a specific content area may either facilitate or hinder the application of the grouping to emotional–social situations.

Feelings and relationships

The emergence of a value hierarchy, even if not perfectly stable, suggests that Concrete operational children may be developing what Piaget (1964) has called "conservation of feelings" (1964). Feelings about what is important do not always change in response to situational demands. Children can understand that the parent who is angry at the moment may still love them (and vice versa). And peer relationships begin to develop on a long-term basis, in part because feelings about the person in general are not totally transformed by day-to-day fluctuations in the interaction.

Piaget has always claimed, and Turiel's work makes it even clearer, that moral–conventional–game judgments about rules are also feelings and that changes in the child's conception of rules will inevitably be accompanied by alterations in the child's feeling and relationship life. Younger children believe that "lying is bad because you'll get caught," while mid- to Late Concrete children believe, in effect, that lying is bad because it violates trust (Piaget, 1964, p. 56).

Piaget also explores the implications of developmental change in the source of the child's feelings of duty or obligation. Preoperational children's respect for adult authority provides the emotional foundation for lower-level moral judgments based on getting caught and consequences. By Late Concrete operations, this unilateral respect for adult authority has given way to respect for peers as the foundation for judgments of justice and moral autonomy. The primary source of moral obligation, Piaget argues, has shifted from parents to peers. I am not aware of any careful documentation of this claim, and I am not at all certain that peers *replace* parents as the primary source of duty. However, the Late Concrete child's changing conception of rules is certainly accompanied, in Western industrialized societies, by a new investment in peer relationships and the formation of a peer culture[10] (e.g., Mussen, Conger, and Kagan, 1974).

As children begin to move away from judgments and values solely based upon parental (or other adult) authority, the potential for conflict between generations increases. Typically, it is the adolescent who is pictured as the rebel against societal values. But in Turiel's studies we see the first of several periods of rejecting social conventions in the eight-to nine-year-old children at Level 2. Beyond the content of particular value disputes, the fact that the child is engaged in constructing his or her own conception of the world is bound to create stress in families which value uniformity of beliefs.

Self-evaluation

Late Preoperational children were just beginning to look at themselves as social objects. With the decline in egocentrism of the Late Concrete substage (e.g., Three Mountains Task), children can now view themselves as active subjects as well. When they become aware that they *have* a point of view, they are increasingly able to examine how their own activities play a role in their situations. They may also begin to examine their own feelings more closely. Up

[10]Presumably in other societies, peer cultures formed by younger children would show different structures of social interaction.

until Concrete operations, children tend to assume, when they think about it at all, that their feelings are always caused by external events (they are happy because they are having a birthday, sad because they can't stay up late, etc.). Inhelder (in Piaget, 1954) describes this stance as "affective realism" and notes that it passes sometime in mid-Concrete operations. From that point on, children become more aware that they produce feelings and have moods, sometimes independent of what is occurring around them.

Concrete operations may be a particularly important time for the development of guilt. Essentially, guilt is a self-judgment, based on violation of some internally held standards, whether or not the standards "come from" outside. Psychoanalytically oriented writings (A. Freud, 1946; S. Freud, 1917; Erikson, 1950) tend to attribute guilt feeling, to the child in the Oedipal period as early as four or five years of age. Of course, it is true that before Concrete operations children may feel badly when they have not lived up to others' expectations, but the feeling may not necessarily have the characteristics of guilt. Preoperational children, for example, believe that they are bad when they are caught violating rules, or when their actions lead to negative consequences; their definition of bad comes from external sources and external events. But the capacity to make a *self* judgment, it seems to me, does not occur until a child can adopt a perspective on the self, and until he or she can evaluate the discrepancy between actual and ideal self. A number of factors may combine to establish guilt as a Late Concrete development: increases in the discrepancy between actual and ideal self; the increase in perspective-taking; the new view of self as subject and cause; and the emergence of autonomous moral standards. If this speculation is verified in later research, it will underline the ever-present possibility that adult interpretations of child feelings, based on adult-level cognitive structures, may distort feelings as they are expressed and interpreted by the younger child.

Late Concrete operations as a substage

The data presented in this chapter suggest a consistent and general increase in the complexity of cognitive, social, and emotional organization as the child progresses from Early to Late Concrete operational substages. As a consequence of this general structural progression, there may be an important cluster of changes occurring in children when they reach nine or ten years of age.

In the cognitive domain, the Early Concrete substage is marked by the emergence of the logical grouping, conservation, and the reversible mental coordination of two spatial or temporal dimensions. A few years later, when a child has demonstrated the use of arbitrary measurement units, horizontal and vertical spatial coordinates, and the representation of spatial perspectives (in the Three Mountains Task), he or she is described as having reached the Late Concrete substage. It seems to me that all of these Late Concrete abilities require mastery of the mental coordination of at least *three* dimensions—two dimensions of objects (e.g., length, width) and one dimension describing the relation between the observer and the event. In the case of measurement units, for example, the child is able to use a measuring instrument independent of his or her body (one dimension) and is able to apply it to two dimensions of the object. In the Three Mountains Task, the child coordinates right–left, back–front, with a clear conception of how the observation point affects the way in which the display will be viewed.

Social–emotional changes at about ages nine or ten also seem to involve a third perspective. We have seen above that the Three-Mountains perspective level is related to the child's language level and to the social structure created by two participants in the back-to-back task. Selman's role-taking model describes the development of a third perspective (Level 3) at around the age of ten. Piaget's fourth stage of game interaction is said to occur at about the same time. Turiel's third stage of conventional judgments (ages ten to eleven) locates the first conceptualization of rules within the context of the social system. And, I have suggested that "true" guilt emerges only in Late Concrete operations, when children are able to make explicit judgments about the discrepancies between actual and ideal self. The numbering of stages and levels across these domains is very confusing. Little research has been done to establish whether this multitude of social–emotional achievements is, in fact, related to cognitive stage, and whether the changes in many domains tend to occur at the same time in the same child. There is sufficient evidence, however, to indicate the importance of further investigation of a possible qualitative change in cognitive organization leading to change in many domains for children in the middle of the Concrete operations stage.

EDUCATIONAL IMPLICATIONS OF CONCRETE OPERATIONS

Structural unity of curricula

The arrangement of curriculum in most schools is based on subject content: reading in one period; language, math, history, social studies, science, art, physical education, in others. Obvious overlaps are sometimes arranged—art in connection with a history project, language composition in combination with social studies, and so on.

One approach, not entirely new, is to teach by the project method, in which a number of different content areas are combined. Here, a Piagetian analysis would emphasize the separate conceptual realms that can be taught together if the teacher systematically explores more than one subject matter per period.

> The making of maps is an enterprise which calls for a number of different cognitive skills. In an effort to breathe life into maps and map-making, teachers are beginning to abandon the traditional memorization of existing geopolitical and topographical maps. Instead they begin by having students draw a map of their desk and

their classroom (perceptual representation) and then maps of the school (in which all the parts can't be perceived at the same time, so that map-making requires conceptual skills). The production of some maps requires accurate scale drawings. Students become actively involved in measuring (rulers, scale representation) and in using conservation of length or area skills in the service of solving a problem. The structural cohesion of knowledge in children may be promoted when they learn mathematics and map-making at the same time, as well as in separate lessons.

When children work in groups on a project, the learning may extend beyond social studies, art, and mathematics to language development and egocentrism reduction. In Piaget's terms this is not just a fortuitous by-product, but a necessary consequence of the structural unity of cognitive development.

In examples such as these, the teacher "keeps an eye out" for opportunities to teach the content of two or more subjects simultaneously. Bruner (1961) has suggested that the most elegant arrangement of instructional material is based upon similarities in structures and sequences. It is not easy or obvious, however, to come up with workable examples. We are just at the beginning of knowing how to analyze the content of a particular subject and how to determine the cognitive structures that are necessary for the child to understand it.

An account of new methods for teaching poetry (Koch, 1970) suggested to me an outline for a combined course in poetry and science. Rather than begin with the study of poetry written by established authors, the first activity is observation (of a leaf, a rock, a fingerprint, etc.). Then children report their observations in discussion or in written form. After doing something with the material—rearranging it, tearing it, and so on— the children report additional observations. In these class discussions, children gain opportunities to coordinate and combine observations, to compare and contrast differences in initial descriptions. Then the students are asked to create similies. "What does it look like?" "It looks like an eye." "It's as big as a house." They create metaphors: "A leaf is a home for a ladybug."[11] Soon the children begin writing their own poetry in a structure given by the teacher; next they begin to share their poems with others. Only at the end of the course does the teacher bring to the classroom the poetry of established authors, by which time the children have a conceptual base and some active experience to help them appreciate and enjoy the poems.

To me, it seems that all these activities, in the same sequence, are basic to the empirical sciences as well. Science rests on observation and reporting of events in situations where more than one observer can arrive at the same report. Scientific models and concepts (e.g., force, weight) are usually metaphors or analogies in which some abstract principle is represented in some concrete physical or mechanical form or model. Fresh poetic metaphors relate previously unrelated events; scientific metaphors serve the same function. It is not necessary, then, to separate all language and science teaching; some principles common to both areas may be better understood when presented in this complementary style.

[11]Preconceptual children unconsciously create metaphors all the time in reporting their observations. Our older daughter, as a three-year-old, described the feeling of her foot "falling asleep" when it was curved under her by saying, "I've got stars in my shoes."

Many teachers today make some effort to combine subject materials across the arbitrarily defined periods of the classroom day. Where Piaget's approach may be especially helpful to teachers is in the task of identifying structural similarities in what appear to be very different content areas: poetry and science; physics and physical education (properties of physical objects, such as balls); debating and drawing (representing points of view); music and measurement (properties of note values); spelling and drawing (figurative representation).

Because each child presents structural variations in performance, a structurally unified curriculum will not match the child's cognitive level in all areas. And it *should* not. Only with some areas of mismatch will there be the disequilibrating child-environment interactions necessary for cognitive growth. The specification of curriculum in terms of stage-structures could help teachers to adjust their general teaching level to provide more optimal match/mismatch with the cognitive levels of specific pupils.

Developmental sequences in curriculum

The natural sequence of stages and the spiral curriculum. There is evidence throughout Piaget's work of a natural and inevitable stage sequence of cognitive development; it makes sense that this developmental sequence should determine curriculum sequencing over the child's formal education career. Curricula based on enhancing the skills of each stage—Sensorimotor, then Preoperational, then Concrete, then Formal—are planned and presented to children as they progress through these developmental stages. Although new stages require new materials, children in each new stage come back to some of the same old problems, returning each time at a more differentiated and integrated level. Attempts to establish object permanence give way to efforts toward symbol permanence; in turn, the child focuses on identity, then conservation, until finally there is a stability of formal schemes. Conceptual coordination first occurs within one dimension, then between two, then among three. Like the child, the curriculum should follow a spiral course, returning every few years to similar problem areas, but each time requiring different structural levels of thought and action. While similar problems may be addressed, the disequilibrating questions should occur at even higher levels of development.

Most school curricula contain frequent pauses for review. Unfortunately, review often means repetition; many children are accustomed to learning addition facts, reviewing them midway through the first grade, at the beginning of second grade, and then at the beginning of each succeeding grades for the next seven or eight years. For those students who have acquired beginning number principles, it may be more profitable to proceed to a new level of the spiral (reversible addition–subtraction, multiplication–division of larger numbers). For those who have not mastered the basic number principles, simple repetition of earlier lessons may not be more effective than they were originally.

These children may require a curriculum at a much lower point on the spiral, one that would be closer to their current level of functioning, regardless of their age or the number of times they have been exposed to the lesson (e.g., they might require more practice with simple classification and seriation).

Sequences within stages. I will explore in detail the systematic sequence in which the grouping is applied to different tasks (e.g., conservation of amount, weight, volume). Here I wish to emphasize the more general sequences that seem to be present in every stage: overt action to internal organization; present to past to future; personal–egocentric to general–perspectivistic.

I share Elkind's (1976) despair whenever I see teachers in the early elementary grades expecting children to comprehend history and geography lessons about other peoples who live at different times or places, who exist within a different social, geographical, or political context. Even at the Early Concrete operations stage, children are having difficulty with space and time concepts. Their fundamental egocentrism makes it difficult for them to understand that people lived in different historical periods under different conditions. It is true that constructing a model of Columbus's ship may make the "discovery" of America more vivid (figurative), but the meaning of the voyage in an historical context will elude most children until Late Concrete or Early Formal operations.[12]

> One possible approach for teaching history would begin with experienced events in the present. Children can describe what is happening now in the classroom (again, emphasis on active observation). In a second "lesson," children would be asked to describe an event that happened five minutes ago; this activity would begin to involve them in the problems of knowing *what* happened in the past. Gradually, the activities of these young historians could be extended to a reconstruction of events earlier in the day, then last week, last month, last year.
>
> As a second major step, the children could begin to trace their own history and the history of their families. In the process they would begin to confront questions about geography (e.g., immigration from *where*) and the existence of family members in other times and places. Only then, in a third phase, would other peoples and events be studied.

Because this approach to history promotes movement from action to contemplation, from present to past, and from personal to general, children are engaging in operations concerning time-sequencing, causal explanations, perspective-taking, communication, and so on. By using students' own experiences and observations as reference points, this curriculum approach capitalizes on the child's inherent egocentric views and slowly encourages some historical and cross-cultural perspective-taking. The program I have described here is not

[12]I am not suggesting here that there is anything wrong with presenting historical material or unfamiliar peoples. I am saying that children may not understand the data *as* history or appreciate other cultures in their own terms until Late Concrete operations.

stage specific. Personal history could be relevant to any age or stage. The details of such a curriculum would be filled in as teachers assess the child's current cognitive organization and attempt to determine the kinds of issues and questions appropriate to a particular stage or substage.

The Nuffield Mathematics Program

In Chapter 7, I described some ideas from the Nuffield mathematics curriculum for teaching the precursors of number. Piaget indicates that children at about the age of six or seven begin to act as if they have use of a set of operations on elements with the grouping properties of combinativity, associativity, general identity, reversibility, and special identities. The rules are not always explicit or conscious, but they seem to work together. In the teaching of mathematics, and later in the teaching of logic, the goal is to facilitate the child's *explicit* acquaintance with the grouping properties of number sets and logical classes. In two general texts for teachers, the Nuffield curriculum (1970, 1972) describes both Early and Late Concrete operational concepts. Here are some examples from the teaching of specific properties of the grouping.

Mapping of operations. After the first few number facts have been acquired, the Nuffield curriculum begins to focus on the properties of the operations. It recommends that before using the traditional symbols (+, −, ×, ÷, =), teachers introduce a partly figurative technique called mapping. It is a pictorial representation in which every element in Set 1 is connected by an arrow to one, and only one, element in Set 2. Figure 16a illustrates a simple one-to-one mapping, in which the arrows chart the connection between individual children (Set 1) and the color of paper they choose for an art project (Set 2). Figure 16b is a many-to-one mapping, in which several children choose one of the paper colors. The same mapping procedures can be used to describe the operative relationship between sets of numbers (Figure 16c); Set 1 contains three ordered pairs and Set 2 contains some combinations. In adult language, the arrow describes the operation of addition. Children understand the arrow as telling them what to do—in this case, to start with the numbers 2 and 3, put them together, and show the result. Using figurative mapping as a recording and organizing device, children can discover the properties of operations and the relations among numbers, for example, that (2, 4) and (5, 1) both map onto 6 under the operation of addition. The children do not yet need the operational terms or the abstract concepts and symbols.

Early Concrete addition and subtraction. In the Nuffield approach, children are often presented with problems to solve, as in Figure 16d. To the question about whether any pairs are missing from the set, the child may respond that all pairs map onto 10, and may then arrange all pairs in order (Figure 16e).

> "When I tried to put these pairs in order I found that some pairs were missing. The first numbers of each pair go like this: 1,2,3,4,5,6,9 so I think 7 and 8 are missing. The second numbers of each pair go like this: 9,8,7,6,5,4,1 so I think 3 and 2 are missing. All the pairs add to 10 so the missing parts must be (7, 3) and (8, 2)."

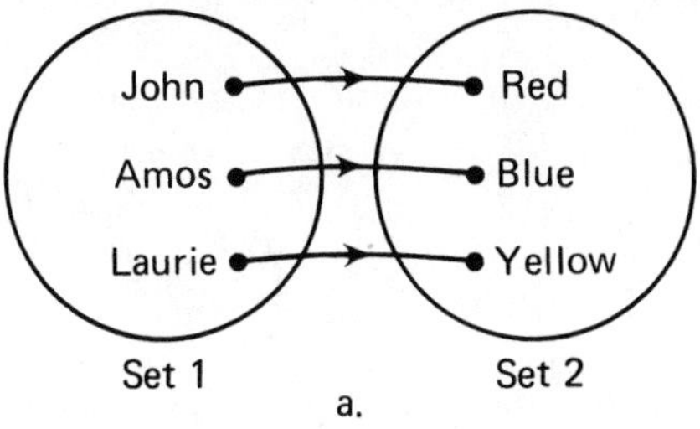

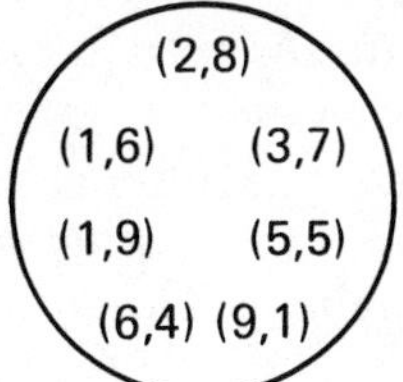

d. Problem: Are there any pairs missing from this set?

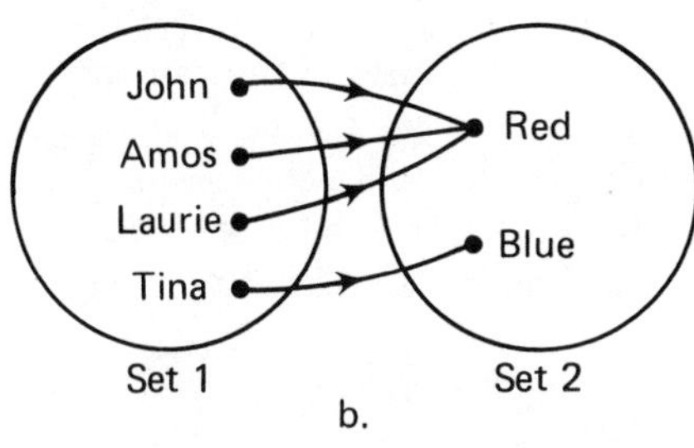

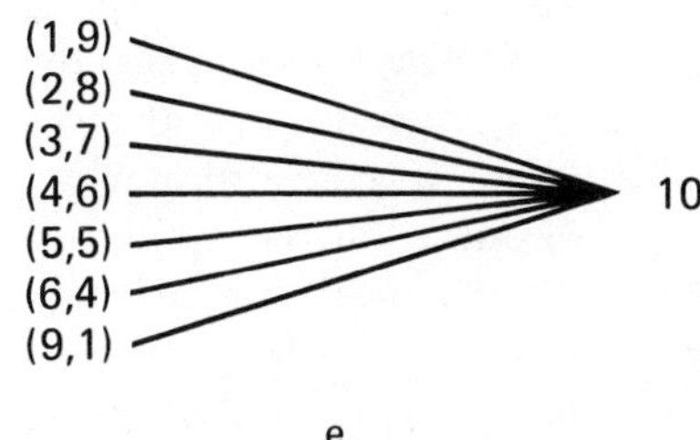

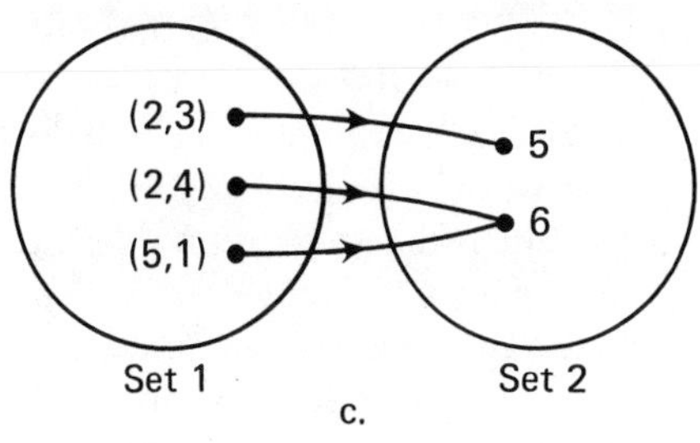

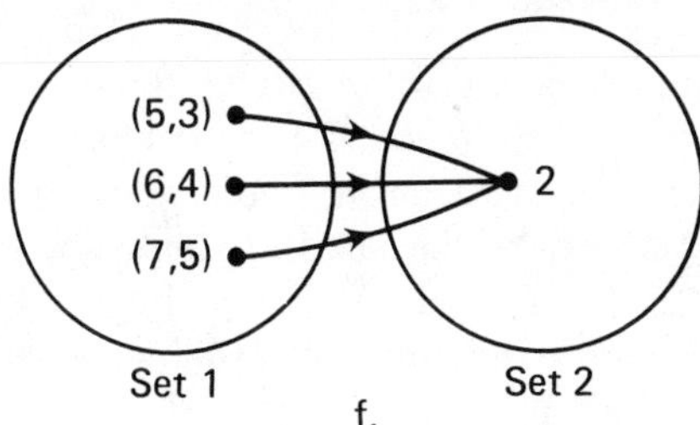

Figure 16. Mapping.

> Here, a child was finding out about 10. In order to do so, it was necessary that he should be able to: (i) understand the cardinal aspect of number (this enabled him to see, after a few preliminary experiments, that his problem concerned the number 10); (ii) understand the ordinal aspect of number (this enabled him to see a possible pattern in the arrangement of the pairs. He saw that the first numbers of the pairs were 1,2,3,4,5,6,9 and knew that 7 and 8 were missing) (Nuffield, 1970, pp. 47–48).

In the Preoperational stage, children were experimenting with classifying and ordering objects and general quantities (more, less). Now, at a higher level of the developmental spiral, they are performing the same classifying and ordering operations directly on the numerals.

One new and potentially confusing fact about subtraction is that in combining numbers, the order of the pairs makes a difference; subtraction is *not* commutative. In Figure 16f are three ordered pairs (5, 3) (6, 4) (7, 5) all mapped onto the number 2. The arrow signifies either that the second number has been subtracted from the first or that we must search for what must be added to the second number so that it equals the first. In Early Concrete operations, children can experiment with counters to find that they cannot "take" 5 from 3 or 6 from 4 or that they cannot add anything to the second number to equal the first. Not until Late Concrete operations will "negative 2" be defined by the teacher in a Nuffield program.

Once children find out through experimentation and manipulation that order makes a difference in subtraction (a disequilibrating event?), they can be encouraged to go back and test the hypothesis that the order of the pairs does *not* make a difference in addition. They can also have some fun in discussions and experiments concerning whether order matters in other activities, for instance, "I put on my socks and then my shoes" does not have the same outcome as the reverse order. "What happens if we eat dinner starting with dessert?" and so on.

Measures of length. Length measures can be created from ropes and ribbons. First, children can compare ribbons with each other; then they can experiment, using ribbons to measure such things as their waists, the size of their desks, the length of the room. After some time it may be useful for children to find out what happens when two different units are applied to the same space, for example, the table is three ribbon lengths, eight cardboards, eighteen chalk pieces, and so forth. Use of hand spans as a measure may help to stimulate discussion of the need for some standard units, but if the suggestion doesn't work this time, it may in the future. Finally (the time isn't specified), children become acquainted with rulers and units of feet, yards, etc.[13] New problems are then prescribed to provide continual challenge to the child's imagination.

Chosen from many in the Nuffield series, these examples are designed for Early Concrete stage children coming to know the properties of numerical operations; they provide opportunities for placing objects and numerals in sets, for ordering and commuting relations, for mapping, combining, reversing, associating, and so on.

The authors of the Nuffield program make an explicit distinction between the logic of mathematics and its computational aspects. In the examples they advise teachers not to concentrate on the correct answers, but to help children focus on the operations and general principles. After these principles are established, computation, drill, and practice can be profitable, if they are not overdone.

[13]This learning sequence parallels the historical development of measurement from arbitrary personalized units to formalization in a metric system.

The Nuffield program shows that the activities involved in early mathematical and scientific learning overlap a great deal. Further, the Nuffield math curriculum encourages a scientific, experimental approach to numbers in which experiments are performed, observations are made, and inferences are discussed.

Science

The Science Curriculum Improvement Study (SCIS), headed by Berkeley physicist Robert Karplus (Karplus and Thier, 1967), has already been described. In the SCIS elementary school science curriculum, the preferred teacher role is so close to that already proposed by Nuffield and by other Piagetian curriculum builders, I will not repeat it all here (see their pages 80–97).

Not only does SCIS encourage teachers to act as stimulators and questioners, the program also provides some guidelines to help teachers avoid difficulties when they assume the questioning role.

> 1. Try not to ask questions which are too broad or too far removed from the child's experience.
> 2. Questions should not be asked only when teachers are displeased with the child's responses. "One nice way to prevent this from happening is to ask the same kinds of questions of good students who have given perfectly acceptable answers. This technique has the added advantage of encouraging children to have confidence in their ideas. By attempting to support the position they have taken, they will rethink their own ideas and so develop a deeper understanding of the subject under discussion."
> 3. "A child's direct observations should not be evaluated as right or wrong. Instead, a question, such as What is your evidence? can be used to focus the child's attention on what has actually happened (Karplus and Thier, pp. 90–92)."

One of my favorite SCIS units is Relativity, in which children of the third, fourth, and fifth grades become acquainted with the necessity of establishing a frame of reference. How fast is a motor boat travelling? The answer depends on a decision concerning the reference point—because it is moving up-river against a strong current, it travels 10 miles per hour when measured relative to the water surface, but only 1 mile per hour relative to the river bank. One of the devices used to convey the notion of relativity is a character named Mr. O (observer), who is totally egocentric. Mr. O always describes events from his own viewpoint. In one picture where he is flying, face down, over the earth's surface, he reports the earth as above him and the sky below. Mid-Concrete operational children are beginning to overcome their own egocentrism to the point where sometimes they are amused at his "stupidity" and sometimes they share his outlook. But they do learn throughout this unit, that when people view events from different perspectives, contradictory reports may both be correct.

After exploring Mr. O's point of view, children go on to investigate frames of reference; here, they gradually learn about coordinates which will help to describe relative positions precisely. While some of the exercises focus on the conceptual aspects of relative position, others encourage the use of rulers, protractors, and so forth, in an exploration of measurement. Again, the materials provide a link between mathematics and science.

SCIS materials encourage teachers to feel free to follow the basic ideas of the curriculum, rather than to use it rigidly or mechanically. In order to capitalize on the spontaneous happenings in the classroom, however, teachers must become very familiar with the underlying conceptions.

> I observed one trial of the SCIS program in a school where the teacher was discussing Mr. O with a third grade class, and all were making progress in understanding the need to specify a frame of reference. In the middle of the lesson, one boy gave an example which was unintelligible to the rest of the class because it was so egocentrically conveyed. The teacher, intent on doing justice to the lesson, went right on instead of spending time exploring the live "Mr. O" problem right there in the classroom.

Social–emotional implications of Late Concrete operations

A number of observations lead me to suspect that the social–emotional difference between Early and Late Preoperational children is implicitly recognized by teachers and school systems.

1. In the United States there is a conceptual break between primary (kindergarten to grade 3) and intermediate (grades 4 to 6)[14] elementary school curricula. Somehow the K to 3 period has been seen as a preparation; teachers of fourth graders (ages about nine to ten) convey a feeling that learning is now "more serious."

2. My reading of Piaget's work suggests that the first few years of Concrete operations *can*, in some sense, be considered a preparation. The beginning grouping framework is only gradually filled in and extended to a wide range of content areas. In Late Concrete operations, egocentrism declines markedly, spatial and social perspectives increase, value hierarchies begin to achieve stability, social conventions are reconceptualized, and moral judgments begin to reject consequences and power as a foundation for defining what is good and bad. What we have, then, is a ten-year-old (approximately) with new-found intellectual powers and a newly forming sense of standards which are not simply handed down from others.

3. My impression is that "discipline" becomes more of a problem in the intermediate grades, both in terms of classroom "control" and in terms of passive or direct defiance of teachers by a few students. These difficulties that are real from the teachers' point of view, may be stemming in part from the real

[14]If this division implicitly recognizes a stage transition, then, by the same logic, the early primary grades fail to recognize a stage transition between Intuitive and Early Concrete operational substages at around six or seven.

developmental advances shown by the children as they become more peer-oriented and more able to analyze and criticize adult-controlled social conventions. This interpretation does not immediately eliminate the classroom difficulty. But it does provide the teacher with a way of reconceptualizing the problem; he or she can work toward eliminating the disruptive aspects without at the same time disparaging the child's new skills. Teachers can and do provide legitimate vehicles for expression of the child's new interests; time for small group discussions, debate, or other formats for social interaction; opportunities to determine *some* of the classroom rules and conventions. These opportunities are not merely "outlets" for social–emotional tension; they are important and necessary avenues for development in all domains.

4. It is my impression, though I don't know where to get the data, that many more referrals for learning disorders or emotional problems seem to spring up early in the fourth grade than at other times. If this is a fact, it may be due in part to teachers' attitudes which differ from grade 3, and it may reflect, in part, some real changes in children.

Not every child enters the transition to Late Concrete operations at the same time. If the curriculum, in its new seriousness, is based more closely on Late concrete operational structures, children who develop more slowly may be seriously mismatched. On the other hand, children who develop quickly may be able to handle the academic material, but some of them may be creating social disturbances by virtue of their new emotional and judgmental criticism of adult authority.

The emerging self-criticalness of Late Concrete children may also contribute to feelings of distress experienced both by quiet children and disruptive children in the class. In this formulation, students and teachers may be out of synchronization during a period of cognitive developmental transition. We shall see an amplification of these between-peer and cross-generational difficulties in the transition to Formal operations and the more familiar "stormy period" of adolescence.

It is, I think, an accurate reflection of current school practices that social and emotional factors are considered integral to the curriculum in preschools and early elementary grades, but are considered to be "problems" when children grow older. My hope is that we can continue to pay attention to these important aspects of personal development at all levels of the educational system.

CHAPTER 10

Early and Late Formal Operations

Cognitive Aspects

In the period between approximately twelve and eighteen years of age, the structural advance of cognition is completed with the development of Early (twelve to fourteen years) and Late (fifteen+) Formal operations. This does not mean that we are over the intellectual hill as we enter our twenties or that we are doomed to an adult life of intellectual stagnation. We can always learn more, create new theories, attempt to come to a more sophisticated understanding of events and ideas. But according to Piaget, the organization of our basic equipment generally reaches its highest level of equilibration by the end of adolescence. Whenever I repeat Piaget's claim to a group of college students, they are challenged to find examples illustrating a stage beyond Formal operations, as if there must always be something better and higher than adolescent thought. It is possible, of course, that as human evolution continues, some higher stage will emerge. It is also possible that Piaget is overlooking some existing examples of a more differentiated and integrated stage. But, a cognitive system of Formal operations which can apply equilibrated operations to both observed events and statements is a very flexible tool. The form can be applied over time to an incredibly vast number of content areas. So, I do not see Formal operations as a very low ceiling on intellectual development. As we shall see, it is a level which many adults do not attain in most areas of their cognitive life.

Formal operations begin when children are about twelve years old, just at the start of biological, psychological, and social adolescence in Western industrialized countries. Most theories of development view adolescence as a time of inner stress and overt conflict, resulting from intense preoccupation with emerging sexuality and identity. As the reader may expect by now, Inhelder and Piaget (1955) state clearly in *The Growth of Logical Thinking from Childhood to Adolescence*, that our understanding "would be muddled before we started if we wished to reduce adolescence to the manifestations of puberty" (p. 336). In fact, Inhelder and Piaget *do* have some important ideas about the relation between intelligence and emotion in adolescence, but they correctly point out that in the many works on adolescence over the decades, from G. Stanley Hall to Anna Freud and Margaret Mead, very little attention has been paid to adolescent thought.

Because Piaget is mainly concerned with accounting for the emergence of adult scientific and philosophical theories, most of his studies of intelligence in persons between the ages of twelve and eighteen present adolescents with situations in which they can perform experiments to discover physical principles or laws. The major conclusion of these studies is that in the adolescent's development of systematic hypothesis testing, we can see a transformation from the Concrete operational groupings (mental combinations of classes, relations, and number) to new and more equilibrated Formal operational systems (mental combinations of relations among propositions). The logical structure of Formal cognitive development will be described in this chapter, while the implication for social–emotional–personality development will be explored in Chapter 11.

COGNITIVE DEVELOPMENTS IN ADOLESCENCE

In a series of sixteen experiments with children from four to eighteen years of age (Inhelder and Piaget, 1955), I can find five interrelated achievements which mark the emergence of Formal operations. First, adolescents discover the world of the hypothetical, in which each observation is considered in relation to the set of all logically possible outcomes. Second, adolescents create experiments in an attempt to examine the relation between hypotheses and data. Third, they develop a new and sophisticated pattern of deductive inference which Piaget describes as "the sixteen binary operations." Fourth, Piaget shows that the adolescent's reasoning goes beyond the Concrete grouping to a new "structural whole" with both group (INRC group) and lattice properties. And, fifth, there are new formal schemes in adolescent reasoning—proportion, equilibrated systems, probability, volume, speed, and the development of four simultaneous perspectives. If one of the major achievements of the Concrete operations stage is the mental coordination of three dimensions, then the Formal operations stage can be characterized as a four- (or more) dimensional outlook on the world. Much of this chapter will demonstrate how the addition of just one more dimension makes such a profound difference in the adolescent's world view, both inside and outside the scientific laboratory.

Logical possibilities

Here is one of Inhelder and Piaget's experimental problems requiring Formal operations for a complete solution:

> A child is presented with four large flasks labeled 1 through 4, and one small flask labelled g. Each flask contains a colorless liquid: (1) diluted sulphuric acid; (2) oxygenated water; (3) tap water; (4) thiosulphate; (g) potassium iodide. Two glasses are placed in front of the child; one contains an *already prepared* mixture of (1 × 2) and one contains tap water (3). The experimenter demonstrates that when g is combined with (1 × 2) the liquid turns yellow, but g × water remains colorless. The child is asked to produce the yellow color using any or all of the five flasks.
>
> The solution to this task does not require a knowledge of chemistry. It is a logical problem of testing 1–4 mixed with g in order to find those combinations which produce the effect and those which do not. If the tests are systematic, subjects will discover that it is necessary to combine 1 and 2 with g in order to produce yellow and that 3 is an "identity element," leaving the product unchanged. They will also discover the presence of a complicating factor; when 4 is combined with g × 1 × 2, the mixture is bleached and appears colorless again. Unless this complicating factor is discovered and isolated, the child may be quite puzzled. Sometimes, the combination of liquids produces a yellow color but sometimes the yellow fails to appear. Only when all the flasks (variables) are treated separately and combined systemically can the problem be solved.

Inhelder and Piaget describe how this task is approached by children from Intuitive to Late Formal substages. Children in the Intuitive substage (four to seven years) tend to combine flasks randomly, rarely more than two at a time. If the color is accidentally produced and then cancelled (by the addition of 4), they believe that the "syrup went away" or became invisible. Children offer no physical explanations to account for these mysterious comings and goings, even when they begin their answers with "maybe it's because." At this stage they do not attempt to verify their conclusions by performing the experiment again (checking results).

In the Early Concrete stage (seven to nine years), children are quite ready to speculate and to begin a systematic manipulation of materials. But, they generally combine g with each flask separately and then stop. When Piaget encourages them, they try several more combinations but they forget which ones have already been tested. Some children become aware that flask 4 is "a kind of water which takes away color" but in the process of combination, fail to *isolate* it as a variable which excludes color. At this stage the color is not attributed to a combination of elements but rather is still believed to be *in* one of the flasks.

By the Late Concrete stage (ten to twelve years), children have established conservation and measurement of quantity, time, and space, but they have made only moderate progress as scientific investigators. In the chemical combination task, the major innovation of this substage is that the child spontaneously begins to combine flasks two at a time, three at a time, and so on. Since the combinations are still not systematic, all possible pairings are not yet tested.

In Early Formal operations (twelve to fourteen years), after a period of trial and error, adolescents begin to realize that all possible combinations of flasks must be tried. They often pause to write down each trial so as not to forget which ones have already been completed. Even after the g × 1 × 2 combination producing yellow has been found, they go on to investigate other possibilities. They seem to be interested not only in the correct answer, but also in understanding the role which this combination plays among the total number of possible combinations (Inhelder and Piaget, p. 118). When the bleaching occurs, Early Formal adolescents systematically isolate the possible cause (4) and arrive at the conclusion that some kind of chemical inhibitor is present. This conclusion is then tested with each combination of flasks. The cause of the color and the bleaching is attributed not to a single flask, but to an interactive combination of elements.

In Late Formal operations (fourteen to fifteen + years,) the major advance over the previous substage is that adolescents *begin* with a plan and organize the experiment with an eye to proving or disproving an initial hypothesis. It is *as if* adolescents at this stage have a notion that they can investigate all possible combinations of 1–4 with g and that they can conduct a hypothetico-deductive scientific experiment. Whether or not they are aware of such notions, their behavior certainly suggests that a new cognitive structure has been achieved.

The shift between Early and Late Formal stages recalls some characteristics of the Intuitive to Concrete transition. In this earlier period, Intuitive children discover correct answers about conservation as they experiment with the materials, while Concrete children are correct from the beginning. In Formal operations, Early adolescents experiment with many different strategies, while Late adolescents seem to have a systematic strategy right from the start. This is another example of Piaget's spiral development model in which the Formal child faces an earlier problem, but this time it is posed at a more differentiated and integrated level.

Along with the general approach to solving a problem, the chemical combinations task illustrates one of the specific ingredients of Formal operations—the adolescent's emerging ability to determine all logically possible outcomes.

> Consider two hypothetical sets of findings. In the first, as above, when g × 1 × 2 is combined, yellow appears; when g × 1 × 2 is not combined, the color is absent. In a different experiment g × 1 × 2 also produces color, but so does every combination of two flasks with g. The same fact (g × 1 × 2 is associated with yellow) would be interpreted quite differently in the two cases. In the first experiment, there is beginning evidence of a specific causal connection between g × 1 × 2 and color. But in the second experiment, color is not attributable to any specific combination of flasks; it might be that the act of combining liquids (shaking, stirring, etc.) rather than the contents of the flasks is responsible for the appearance of the color.

If Concrete operational children try out g × 1 × 2 early enough, they are likely to stop and conclude that they have found the cause of the color. But this example suggests that no single observation is sufficient to establish the nature of causal or other kinds of relationship between variables. Rather, it is the pattern of actual and possible outcomes, available to Formal operational children, which provides the key to interpreting any specific observed event. If there are two variables (flask combination, color), each with two values (flask present or absent; color present or absent), then there are four possible combinations of variables; in the general case, the number of combinations is n × n—the number of variables multiplied by the number of values of each variable.

The emergence of n × n combinations marks a new attitude toward "data" in the Formal operations stage. Adolescents are not satisfied with regarding events as givens. Nothing is accepted for what it appears to be until after it has been analyzed. With this opening up of the world of possibilities, adolescents become permanent skeptics concerning what they observe. While parents and teachers may have difficulty with this healthy but constant questioning ("Why not *this* way?"), skepticism about existing conclusions challenges adolescents to become involved idealistically with the world as it could be, in contrast with the way it is now.

Systematic inferences from data: the logic of experiments

In the chemical combination task, inferences about the relations among flasks follow from the observations. While children at all ages draw conclusions from data, the adolescent may be capable of determining that all possible combinations have been observed and recorded before the conclusion is stated. Other tasks used by Inhelder and Piaget illustrate a different sequence. Hypotheses about relations between variables are created, an experiment is designed, and observations are made to determine whether the hypothesis is correct. This sequence describing the so-called hypothetico–deductive method of science emerges only in Formal operations and is not firmly established until the Late Formal substage.

The changing relation between observations and hypotheses. The notion that empirical experiments can be helpful in testing hypotheses and making inferences seems obvious to adults in this age of science. But it was not accepted by sophisticated adults in early Greece, who were convinced that the road to knowledge lay in the direction of deductive logic and philosophy, rather than in the direction of inductive principles derived from the particulars of scientific investigation (see Part IV). And, Early Concrete children, as practiced as they have become in manipulating materials, do not tend to conduct systematic experiments to clarify an explanation or to verify a conclusion. Furthermore, after they have been exposed to experimental demonstration, children at this substage are sometimes more confused than when they began.

> In one simple task, Inhelder and Piaget give children a set of objects varying in size, material, and density (wood, nails, needles, candles, corks, hollow metal tubing, keys, stones); they are asked to predict which objects will float and which will sink. After a demonstration to test their predictions, Early Concrete operational children tend to show more chaotically organized reasoning than they displayed before the demonstration. It is as if the Early Concrete operations child is saying "don't confuse me with the facts."

In a pendulum problem, Inhelder and Piaget describe significant shifts in the relation between experimental observations and hypotheses, as children enter the Formal stage.

> A weight is suspended from a string fastened at the top to a rod. Subjects are to find out what makes the "pendulum" swing faster or slower (oscillations per unit time). They can vary the length of the string, the weight on the end, the height of the dropping point (amplitude), and the force of a push. Only the length of the string actually affects the speed of oscillation.

By the end of the Concrete operational stage, children discover that string length is an important variable, but they assume that other concomitant factors are also involved. For example, string length and weight are simultaneously varied (long string, heavy weight compared with short string, light weight). The child concludes that *both* length and weight are involved in the speed of the pendulum motion.

Early Formal stage adolescents go beyond summarizing observations to search for a general factor which will explain the results. They may develop a preliminary hypothesis that string length affects speed, and test its merit. They rarely are concerned, however, with testing hypotheses about factors that do *not* affect the pendulum, so they still fail to separate length from some of the other variables.

In the Late Formal substage, hypotheses function quite differently. First, they do not always arise from the data as given, but are sometimes formulated at the beginning as a guide to further observations. Hypotheses, then, do not function as end products of observations, but rather as the starting points for new experimental investigations. Second, the adolescent in Late Formal operations is not content with a description of a general factor common to cause and effect; he or she seeks the factor which is *necessary* and *sufficient* to account for an observed effect. This stimulates the further separation of length and weight variables to see whether one of them acting alone may be adequate to account for the oscillation. Now the mid-adolescent's conclusions begin to take on the sound of certainty: "*It must be,*" "*It has to be.*" In contrast with the self-assurance of the Concrete operations child, this certainty is based not on what is experienced as true, but on what is *known* to be true by a combination of experimental induction and logical deduction.

Third, the Late Formal adolescent begins to create hypotheses which might help to clarify a problem; these hypotheses are not directly given in experience but are based solely on abstract suppositions.

> The adolescent propels billiard balls against one edge of a billiard table in an attempt to hit objects on the rebound. In the course of this task, Early Formal adolescents discover the principle that the angle of incidence is equal to the angle of reflection. Late Formal operations subjects come to account for this law by *supposing the existence of an imaginary line* at right angles to the edge of the table, from which the angle of incidence and the angle of reflection can be measured.

Isolation of variables and logical reversibility. In nature and in the laboratory, more than one aspect of a situation varies at a given moment. How do we isolate variables in order to determine which ones produce the effects we observe? Inhelder and Piaget describe three strategies which, taken together, constitute the cornerstone of scientific method; all of them rely on some form of logical or physical reversibility, and all of them emerge as a coordinated set of strategies in Formal operations. If any two variables *are* related, then at the very least we must establish that x (the cause) is present or tends to be present when y (the effect) is present, and that x is absent or tends to be absent when y is absent.[1] The observer, then, must coordinate two statements concerning observations made at different times; thinking about one statement must not distort or transform the meaning of the other. This reversible coordination can occur by negation, by reciprocity or by a simultaneous use of both operations.

a. Reversibility by negation. Inhelder and Piaget argue that there are two forms of logical negation which allow Concrete operational children to separate variables; one is purely observational and one is experimental–manipulative. In the observational approach children can note whether the presence of a factor is followed by the presence of an effect, while the absence of that factor is followed by the absence of the effect (e.g., observations of correlations in nature—between lightning and thunder, wind and the motion of trees, and so on). In the experimental approach, children can introduce or eliminate, increase or decrease a variable in order to see if it plays an active role (add flask 4 to g × 1 × 2 on one trial, not another). A factor is introduced, eliminated, introduced and eliminated, and the reversible activity clarifies rather than distorts the results. In each case, Piaget points out, the reversibility is analogous to the logical operation of negation. If x is added, then y appears. The cancellation of x results in the cancellation of y. This form of reversibility is within the capacity of the Concrete operational child (Chapter 8).

b. Reversibility by reciprocity—holding factors constant. What happens when a single factor cannot be eliminated through observational or experimental negation?

[1]This is necessary, but not sufficient, to establish a correlation or causal connection between them. In the following discussion I will be referring to both absolute causality (x always precedes y, and only x precedes y) and probabilistic causality. The logical issues are similar, but not identical (see Piaget and Inhelder, 1951).

In one experiment, Inhelder and Piaget give children a set of rods varying in material (brass or steel), length (long or short), thickness (thin or thick), shape or cross-section (round or square). Rods can be fastened on one end to a stand, so that they extend in space horizontally. Objects of different weights can be placed on the end of the rod, some of which cause the rod to bend. The task is to find out what variables affect flexibility of the rods. In fact, all five variables (material, length, thickness, cross-section, and weight) are relevant; however, to *prove* the involvement of each, the variables must be isolated and examined separately.

The negation strategy of withdrawing a variable is not possible here, because material, weight, length, and so on, cannot be physically eliminated from a rod. Instead, two complementary strategies are necessary to neutralize the effects of one variable while another is being examined.

1. Material, as a factor, can be "held constant," for example, by choosing two brass rods which differ only in length.
2. All other variables can be held constant while the effect of material is studied; for example, by comparing two short, thin, square-ended rods with heavy weights—one made of brass, the other of steel.

In the terminology of logical operations, the action of holding a variable constant does not negate it. Rather, the Formal operations adolescent is able to introduce a *compensation* which makes two rods equivalent; he or she does not eliminate the variable itself but equalizes its impact on other comparisons. This can be done either by taking two same-material rods of different lengths or two same-length rods of different materials; Piaget describes this compensation as a reversibility by reciprocity.

An example of how reversibility by reciprocity is more difficult than negation: In the chemical experiment, the Concrete child examines the effect of variable x by introducing or removing it to see if it plays an active role. By contrast, in the rods experiment the adolescent at the Formal operations stage neutralizes x *in order to examine variations in y* without interference and then neutralizes y in order to examine variations in x.

Thus the two discoveries found at the beginning of the formal level are (1) that factors can be separated out by neutralization as well as by exclusion, and (2) that a factor can be eliminated not only for the purpose of analyzing its own role but, even more important, with a view toward analyzing the variations of other associated factors (p. 285).

With these two discoveries, Formal operations adolescents can look separately at each of the five variables in the rods problem. In the Early Formal stage the experiments are still not completely systematic, but by the Late Formal stage, experiments often begin with an organized, reversible, analytic approach.

c. The mastery of both negation and reciprocity.

In Chapter 8, we saw that one of the limitations of the Concrete grouping was that logical operations were reversible by negation or reciprocity, but not both. An experiment with a balance scale demonstrates how in the Formal stage the two reversibilities function together as parts of an integrated structure.

Balanced on a fulcrum is a simple crossbar with holes at equal intervals (see Figure 17). Weights of different amounts can be hooked and hung in the holes. In one of many variations, unequal weights are placed at distances which allow the arms to balance—a lighter weight is placed on arm A, relatively farther from the fulcrum, while a heavier weight is placed on arm B, relatively closer to the fulcrum. The arms balance because the weight × distance units on arm A equals the weight × distance units on arm B (e.g., 5 gms × 12 holes = 60; 12 gms × 5 holes = 60). An additional weight is placed on the left arm A, in the same hole as the first. The arm tips down to the left and the child is asked to restore the balance. More generally he or she is asked to experiment and discover what makes the scale balance (return to equilibrium).

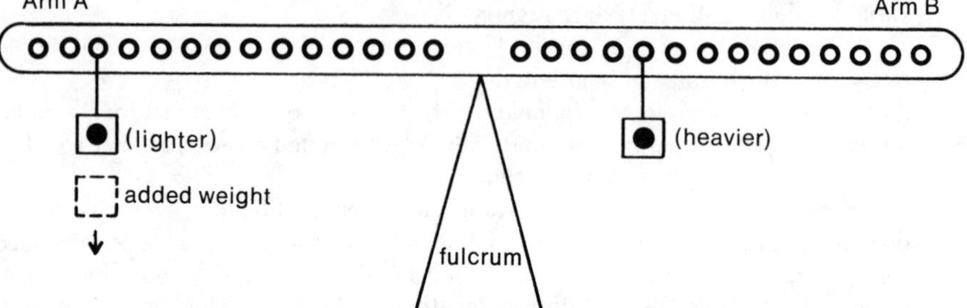

Figure 17. The balance problem, in which weights are hanging on hooks from a balance.

In reversing the state of disequilibrium, the subjects have two sets of choices. Focusing on side A (left), where the additional weight was placed, they can:

1. decrease the weight on A (−w);
2. decrease the distance on A by moving one or both weights toward the center (−d);
3. decrease a combination of weight and distance on A (e.g., by substituting a weight lighter than the two combined, and placing it nearer the fulcrum; −[w × d]).

All of these reversals of disequilibrium, if made with the correct weights and distances, can *negate* the addition of a second weight to A.

There is, however, another set of alternatives. After the experimenter places the additional weight on A, subjects can focus on B, and:

4. increase the weight on B;
5. increase the distance from the fulcrum of the existing weight, (+d);
6. increase a combination of weight and distance (e.g., with a weight heavier than the original on B, farther from the center; +[w × d]).

While changes 1 to 3 *restore the balance as it was*, with one weight on each side, changes 4 to 6 if made with the correct weights and distances, all provide *equal and opposite forces which exactly compensate* for the addition of weight to A. Each decrease on B by negation (−w, −d, −[w × d]) can be equivalent to a *reciprocal* increase on B (+w, +d, +[w + d]). There are, then, two coordinated strategies, negation and reciprocity, for reversing the initial change and returning the balance to equilibrium.

Inhelder and Piaget's research with the balance clearly shows that in the Concrete operational stage, only one of the strategies is used at a time. Primarily, the children experiment with negation, adding and subtracting weights on the same side of the balance. Occasionally, equal weights are placed at equal distances on the other arm, but the task of balancing unequal weights and unequal distances is very confusing. Not until Formal operations do subjects consistently balance the scale in both ways using negation and reciprocity in a single system.

This discussion emphasizes the developmental correspondence between strategies of isolating variables in experiments and the emergence of a coordinated system of reversibility (by negation and reciprocity). It is not possible to say which comes first. Logical reasoning affects experimental manipulations, but the adolescent's engagement in systematic experiments fosters the development of logical inference. The same can be said for all the topics discussed in Formal operations. For example, the emergence of the notion of possibilities certainly facilitates the development of hypotheses and the design of experiments. Conversely, the adolescent's involvement in the puzzles of experimentation induces disequilibration, which stimulates thinking about possibilities and about the inferences that can be drawn from observations of events.

Systematic inference from propositions: the sixteen binary operations

Neither children nor adults are limited to inferences concerning the relation between specific data and general hypotheses. Often, we are given or we create one or more verbally stated premises, and we attempt to deduce a conclusion; or we are given a conclusion which someone claims is true, and we attempt to examine the premises. In either case we are making inferences about the relations among sentences, and some of these sentences have the form of logical propositions.

> In the field of logic, a proposition is a statement containing two terms (elements, classes) with the assertion that a relation holds between them: John loves Mary; this chemical solution neutralizes another; Socrates is a man. One form of propositional reasoning is the Aristotelian syllogism:
>
> Socrates is a man (A included in B)
> All men are mortal (B included in C)
> ___
> Therefore Socrates is mortal (A included in C)
>
> In logic, each proposition has a truth value—it is either true (T) or false (F). In most traditional theories of logic, the truth value of the premises, as well as the form of the argument, determine what is accepted as a valid conclusion.

Proposition	Truth Value
A included in B	T
B included in C	T
A included in C?	F

but:

Proposition	Truth Value
A included in B	F
B included in C	T
A included in C?	F or indeterminate

Propositional statements, then, are sentences which: relate two, and only two, terms; assert that the statement is either true or false, but not both; define truth by assumption and not by correspondence with empirical observations. Propositional reasoning can be concerned with arbitrary symbols, pink elephants, frogs playing banjos, or any content of interest to the logician. What is of chief concern is the form of the reasoning—whether a conclusion derived from a set of premises is logically valid.

It has always been the case that when I
left my umbrella at home, it rained.
I left my umbrella at home.
Therefore, I can conclude that it rained.

This conclusion is logically valid or true, even if none of the statements is empirically true.

In Chapter 8, the account of the logical groupings at the Concrete stage indicates that seven-to-twelve-year-olds have great difficulty following the form of an argument when they cannot accept the premises. Piaget (1942; Inhelder and Piaget, 1955) attempts to demonstrate that the new ability to master formal reasoning emerging in adolescence stems from a new inference structure based on what he calls the sixteen binary operations. In contrast with the Aristotelian reasoning of the syllogism, this set of operations is concerned with drawing conclusions from premises describing the relation between two variables. I will begin with a concrete example, because it is difficult for most of us to follow the form of new ideas when they are expressed entirely in abstract symbols. Please note that although the example refers to observable events, the task is to arrive at a conclusion deductively, not to determine the relation between variables as they occur in the real world.

A common task for all of us is to determine what can logically be inferred from a statement made by someone else. Young children are often told by teachers that if they work hard, they will receive good grades. Regardless of the empirical truth of this claim, the children may believe that good grades are attributable to hard work, and that if they do not receive good grades, they did not work hard enough. (Establishing the direction of the relationship between variables is an important issue.)

Children in Late Concrete operations, too, are concerned with understanding the relation between their behavior and their teachers' grading practices. However, they are beginning to question the "truths" of their childhood. First, they now know that there are four possible combinations if two variables are dichotomized (work hard—not work hard; good grades—not good grades).

Behavior	*Consequences*
1. work hard	good grades
2. work hard	not good grades
3. not work hard	good grades
4. not work hard	not good grades

Two combinations are consistent with the hypothesis that student hard work is necessarily related to good grades: (1) they work hard and receive good grades; (4) they do not work hard and do not receive good grades. When the presumed "cause" is present, the effect is present; when the cause is absent, the effect is absent. There are also two combinations that do not fit the hypothesis of a direct relation between hard work and good grades: (2) they work hard without receiving good grades, and (3) they receive good grades without working hard.

The adolescent's notion of possibility allows him or her to take this analysis of combination one very important step further. Each of the four basic combinations of binary variables may be true or it may not. If 1, 2, 3, or 4 are true alone or in combination, there are sixteen possible patterns of truth values. The list is critically important because each pattern leads to a different conclusion about the possible relation between two variables.

The sixteen patterns

1, or 2, or 3, or 4 are true	4 patterns
12, or 13, or 14, or 23, or 24, or 34 are true	6 patterns
123, or 124, or 134, or 234 are true	4 patterns
All are true (1234)	1 pattern
All are false[2]	1 pattern
Total =	16 patterns

With the ability to consider all possible outcomes, the adolescent has moved to a four-factor conceptual system. There are (i) two variables, (ii) each with two values formed into 4 propositions; (iii) each of the propositions can be true or false, and (iv) from each one of the sixteen patterns a different inference must be drawn. For example,

Pattern A. All four combinations are true. Grades are good whether or not the student works hard; working hard is followed by good grades in some instances, not

[2]This pattern is logically possible, but it is difficult to know what it means. *If* the universe is limited to two mutually exclusive values of two variables, it would seem that *one* combination would have to occur. Perhaps this refers to a case where no instances of the two occurring together could (hypothetically) be observed, for instance, with a student on leave from school.

good grades in others. Overall, it can be deduced that grades are not necessarily related to student working hard.

Pattern B. Combinations 1 and 4 are true. Working hard is always followed by good grades, never by "not good" grades. Not good grades follow from a lack of hard work. If we know what the student does (p), we can infer the grades (q). Conversely, if we know the grades, we can infer what the student has done (p implies q, and q implies p).

Pattern C. Combinations 1, 3, and 4 are true. As above, working hard is never followed by not good grades (2 is false). But it does sometimes happen that not working hard leads to good grades. So, the correct inference is that working hard implies good grades (p implies q) as above, but good grades do not necessarily imply having worked hard—there is no reciprocal implication.

The contrast between patterns B and C is one example of an important difference in inferences which can be drawn from the relations among propositions. In pattern B, working hard (variable p) always leads to good grades (variable q) and q is always preceded by p. If we know the student's behavior, we know the grades and vice versa; in logic, this is the relation of reciprocal implication. By contrast, in pattern C, we can make valid inferences from work to grades, but not from grades to work. The implication holds from p to q, but not in the reverse direction. Establishing the direction in which valid inferences can be made can have important applications to daily life. Advertisers assert that beautiful and successful people use Brand X, hoping to convey the (invalid) conclusion that people who use Brand X will be beautiful and successful. In the area of moral reasoning, young children not only believe that if they are "bad" they will be punished; they also conclude that if they are punished, they must have been bad. In adolescence, with Formal operations comes the possibility of analyzing such relationships systematically.

In sum, we began with two variables—work and grades—each expressed in binary form (work hard, not work hard; good grades, not good grades). The possible combinations of these variables were described in a set of four "simple" propositions (1, 2, 3, 4). Each proposition is created as a product of a logical combining operation on two binary variables. So far this cognitive task is within the capacity of a Late Concrete operational child. Formal operations is a new structural level, defined in part by adolescents' ability to combine systematically these simple propositions and their truth values; patterns A, B, and C represent only three of sixteen possible outcomes, and in each case a different conclusion follows from the arrangement of propositions and truth values. Each conclusion, then, is a product of an operation on the results of an operation, variously called by Piaget "a second order operation," "an interpropositional operation," or "a logical operation." In all cases he is referring to a *formal* operation because the original variables have already been transformed into symbolic statements.

Because each inference is a product of an intellectual operation on the four basic binary combinations, Piaget calls this deductive inference structure "the sixteen binary operations."[3] No adolescent or adult unfamiliar with logic rules could diagram all sixteen binary operations or keep them in mind while solving a problem. However, each of the binary operations is said to be available for use during the Late Formal substage. In one case, Inhelder and Piaget (1955) claim that all sixteen are explicitly considered by an adolescent in the course of a single intellectual task (pp. 103–104).

According to Piaget, it is the deductive use of the sixteen binary operations which enables adolescents to reason from one verbal statement to another without referring to observed events. If "p implies q" is true, and "q implies r" is true, then it necessarily follows that p implies r, even if we do not know the content of p, q, and r. Thus, a central quality of Formal operational reasoning is the ability to draw valid conclusions from the form of an argument regardless of whether the premises are empirically true or believed. As we shall see later in this chapter, the fact that it may be possible to do this does not guarantee the appearance of Formal operations in all tasks or in all adolescents.

When the sixteen binary operations are used, they add a significant dimension to adolescent intelligence. The ability to operate (make mental combinations) on the products of operations means that for the first time adolescents can think systematically about their own thoughts and evaluate the consistency of their inferences. Formal thought, then, is in a literal sense, self-conscious, reflective, and introspective.

Structural characteristics of Formal operations

For Piaget, it is no coincidence that the achievements I have catalogued do not emerge until adolescence. The shift from mental operations on observable events to operations on possibilities, the $n \times n$ combinations, the creation of experiments, the isolation of variables, and the sixteen binary operations all go beyond the limits of Concrete operational groupings. Piaget argues that these new achievements reflect the emergence of a new cognitive structure with both INRC group and lattice properties.

Group properties. What Piaget calls the INRC group structure of reasoning concerns the interrelation of Identity. Negation, Reciprocity, and Correlation operations. Perhaps the clearest of the many complex examples can be seen in another variation of the balance problem (Figure 18 a, b, c).

[3]There are also ternary combinations (three variables) and quaternary combinations (four variables) resulting in 256 or 65,536 patterns, respectively. Though more numerous, the logic and the psycho-logic involved in their use is the same as above. The rapidly accelerating number of possibilities illustrates one reason why computers are often necessary to handle problems involving complex combinations of variables.

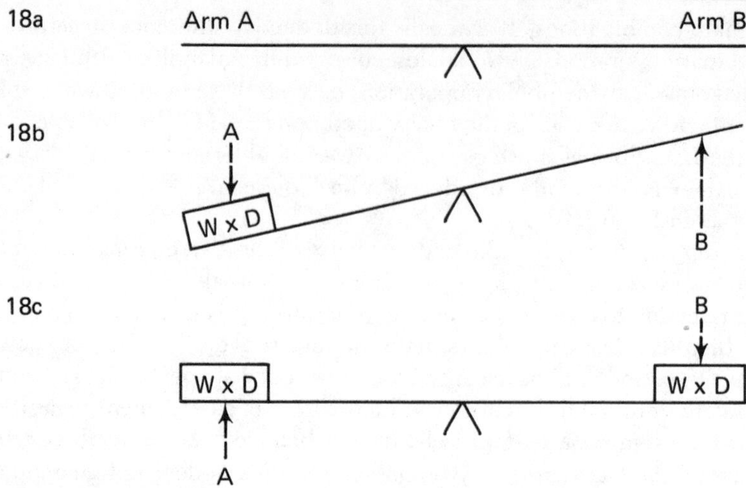

Figure 18. A three-phase balance problem. First (18a), a scale is placed so that the arms balance without any weights on either side (A or B). In 18b, a weight is added to the end of the left arm (w × d), which then tilts downward. 18c shows the result of placing an equal weight at the end of the right arm, bringing the balance into equilibrium.

Again, I advise the reader to follow the general drift of the analysis and to avoid becoming enmeshed in the details.

Identity (I). Consider the change from 18a to b. Having placed one weight on the left, any additional weight or distance simply increases the combined force pressing down on arm A, but it does not alter the result; the arm stays down. In this sense, any *increased* weight and distance on the same side is an identity operation.

Negation (N). Focusing on the left arm only, we can see that the increase of weight and distance from 18a to 18b has been cancelled by a relative decrease in weight and distance from b to c; the arm is again horizontal. Negation coordinates the successive actions—doing and undoing—resulting in a return to the starting point. Note that the same result could be attained by a decrease in weight *or* distance of force from the balance point or by a decrease in weight *and* distance from the fulcrum.

Reciprocity (R). The relative decrease from b to c in weight and distance on the left can be viewed as a reciprocal increase in weight and distance from b to c on the right.

Correlation (C). The previous comparisons were concerned with successive transformations. Now, focus only on 18b. The force of weight × distance pushing down on the left, from another point of view is exactly equal to a simultaneous force of weight × distance pushing up on the right. This example considers only one of three correlates—an equal and opposite force on the other side. Two additional possibilities would be an increase in weight and a decrease in distance of an object on the balance, *or* a decrease in weight and an increase in distance. All three transformations could be perfectly correlated with the initial addition of weight to the balance.

Piaget's theory of logic (1942) led him to a discovery. Taken together, the four general operations of identity, negation, reciprocity, and correlation go beyond the properties of the grouping to constitute a logical group (INRC). The relationship among the four second-order operations is depicted in Figure 19.

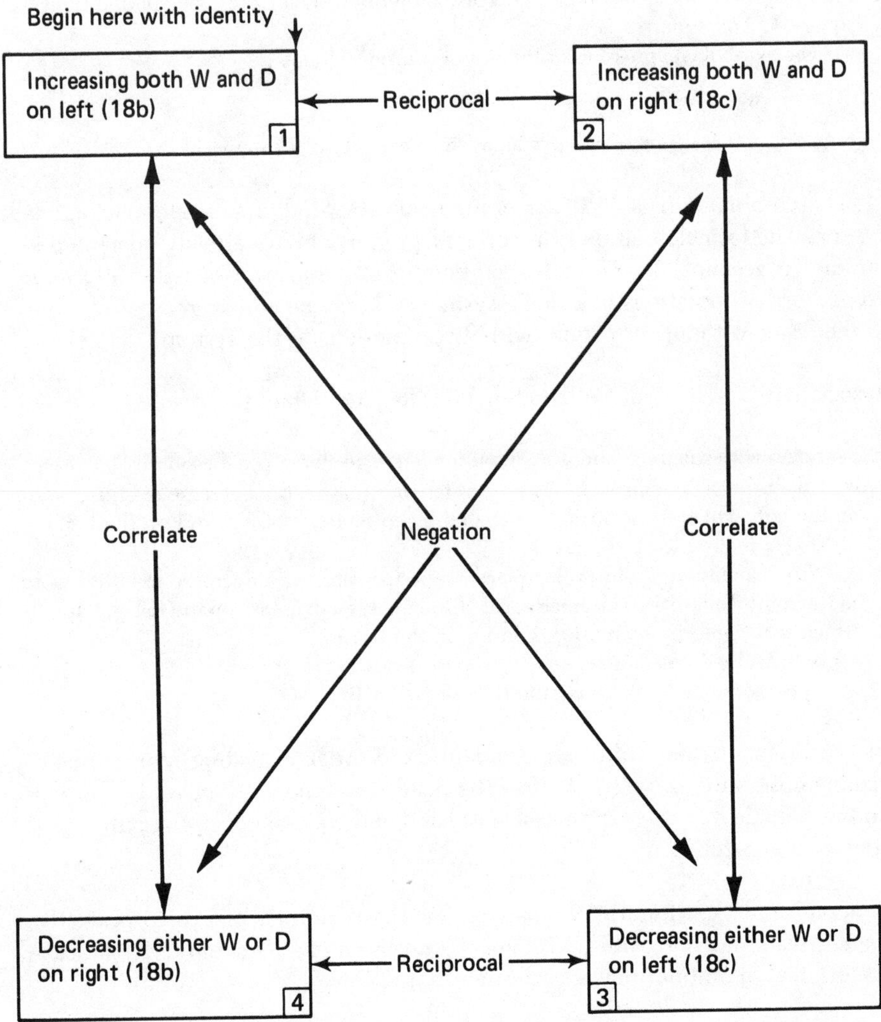

Figure 19. The INRC group of four operations applied to the balance problem.

Each square contains one first-order operation—increasing weights or distances on either side of the balance.

Combinativity. Each square is an element in the system and can be mentally combined with another square to produce a third element in the system. The diagram shows that each square participates in three relationships—it is a reciprocal of one, a negation of another, and a correlate of a third.

Begin with square 1 (adding a weight at a given distance on the left); this is the Identity operation. Its Reciprocal (adding a weight on the right) is square 2. Negating the Reciprocal would result in a decrease either of weight or distance on the right—square 4. And square 4 is a Correlate of 1.

The symbolic expression of this set of transformations is

$$NR = C.$$

Negating the Reciprocal of I produces the Correlate of I. Similarly, NC = R, etc.

The combination of INRC operations always produces an element in the system. The formal notation summarizes a property I have already presented in the above account. In Formal operations, the adolescent can use all of the second-order operations in a single system and may be able to reason from one to the other without distortion (without going outside the system).

Associativity. The order of combination does not affect the result.

Begin with square 1 (add w × d) on the left. The Reciprocal of square 1 increases w × d on the right (square 2). The Correlate of square 2 is a decrease of either word on the left, which in turn can be negated by an increase of w and d on the left.

(RC)N leads back to square 1.

Now, beginning again from square 1, the Correlate is a decrease of either word on the right (square 4). The Reciprocal of square 4 is a decrease on the left (square 3), which is negated by increasing 2 and d on the left.

(CR)N also leads back to square 1.

The operations are also commutative—NR = RN.

In the balance scale and other problems, the order of testing hypotheses or making observations does not affect the results, as long as all possible observations are made and the variables are isolated and controlled so that only one is operating at a time.

General Identity. Figure 19 indicates that the reciprocal of a reciprocal (RR), the correlate of a correlate (CC), and the negation of a negation (NN) all leave the original operation unchanged (identity).

RR = CC = NN = I.

Begin with square 1, increasing weight and distance on the left. Its reciprocal is a decrease in both weight and distance on the right. And the reciprocal of *that* brings us back to the start.

Like the balance scale itself, Formal operational identity suggests that operating on the results of operations produces an equilibrated, balanced system.

Reversibility. The examples of combinativity and associativity demonstrate one significant advance of the INRC group over Concrete operations—reversibility by negation and by reciprocity is integrated into a single system.

The operations of identity, negation, reciprocity, and correlation have formal properties which are present in a mathematical group (combinativity, associativity, identity, and reversibility). This is one of Piaget's unique contributions to the overlapping fields of cognitive structure and formal logic. In Piaget's view, it is this group structure which underlies the new intellectual status of the Formal operations adolescent. So far, the INRC group has been described as if it deals only with combinations of physical events, but as I will show in the next section, it also applies to inferences within and between the sixteen binary operations on propositions.

Lattice properties. In describing the adolescent's ability to enumerate all possibilities, I repeated Piaget's claim that in a two-variable problem, all sixteen binary operations are available to function as a coordinated system. But why does such a system emerge at the Formal operational stage? Part of the answer lies in the above analysis of the INRC group. The INRC group structure enables the adolescent to combine one or more of the binary operations with another. The resulting organization, Piaget demonstrates, is a lattice in which the sixteen binary operations are organized from most to least inclusive. Like a complete logical classification system (and unlike the grouping), the lattice property indicates that formal reasoning provides rules relating each single element of the system (each proposition) to every other element in the system.

The discussion of sixteen binary operations began with an example of inferring the relations between working hard and good grades. In Figure 20, all sixteen possible combinations are arranged in order from least inclusive (no combinations occur) to most inclusive. It is not necessary to work out the logic of each combination in order to understand the general thrust of Piaget's analysis (if you adopt a Formal operational stance).

Each box is numbered underneath so we do not have to refer to the contents every time. Box 1 is the case where no combinations are true. We cannot infer anything about the relation or lack of relation between two variables. Boxes 2 through 5 are the four simple propositional combinations of working and grades. In each of these boxes, I have labelled the logical inference that can be made; for example, in box 2 we can say that there is conjunction between the variables because both are true. In 3 we can say that there is nonimplication; working hard does not imply good grades.

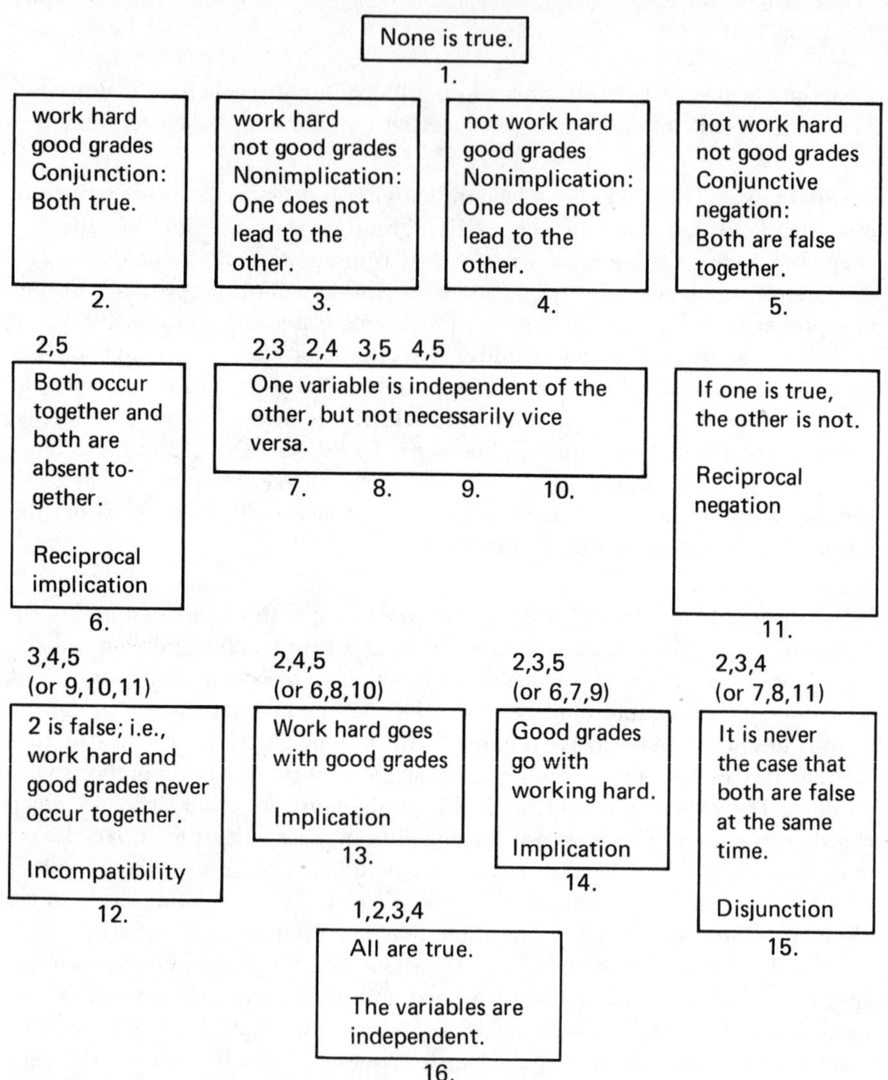

Figure 20. The lattice of sixteen binary operations.

Now, each of the basic four combinations can be combined two at a time, three at a time, or four at a time. One practical consequence of this fact is that when we see one occurrence (e.g., box 2—working hard and good grades), it could be part of any one of eight binary operations (2, 6, 7, 8, 13, 14, 15, 16). In order to arrive at a valid conclusion about the relation between two variables, it will be necessary to make further inferences—in effect, to locate the relevant binary operation box from which an inference can be made.

Several conclusions follow from arranging the boxes in this hierarchy from least to most inclusive. First, *every* binary operation can be included in a more complex combination, and in a less complex combination (down to the empty set). Second, every binary operation has a definable relationship with every other.

> For example, the relation between 2 and 12: Box 12 states that working hard never implies good grades (all the other possibilities occur). But box 2 states that working hard and good grades go together; therefore 2 is a negation of 12, and vice versa. In the same way it could be seen that 3 and 13, 4 and 14, 5 and 15 are pairs in which, if one is true, the other is false.

Each box summarizes a particular pattern of relationships and represents a logical truth table.

The sixteen binary operations, then, are structured as a lattice arrangement of truth tables, which the adolescent can actually use (though not necessarily specify explicitly) in the solution of problems. This lattice structure of operational logic is formally identical to the structure of Boolean algebra—a formal logic of propositions invented by George Boole in 1849.

It is also possible to demonstrate that the sixteen binary operations in Figure 20 are subject to the INRC group structure—some boxes are negations of others, some are reciprocals, some are correlates, and some are identity operations. Thus, the crowning achievement of Formal cognitive organization is a set of operations on propositions with both group and lattice properties. It is a structure more equilibrated, more flexible, and more comprehensive than the Concrete operational grouping. It enables adolescents to adopt a hypothetical attitude, to explore all possible combinations, to formulate and verify hypotheses, and to conduct experiments using several strategies of isolating variables. Conversely, all of these activities create the kind of disequilibration which stimulates the adolescent's structural development.

The Formal operational structure is equilibrated in a number of senses. It represents the most comprehensive system of operations in which all elements of sixteen binary operations are accessible to a consistent set of transformations. It is the most general structure, in that the form of reasoning is now liberated from a specific content. It represents a final structure in the sense that there are no further structural modifications (though "simple" Formal operations can be integrated into more complex forms; e.g., polyvalent logic).

Formal operations is the structure which produces the greatest self-regulating balance between assimilation and accommodation. The mental transformation system at this stage is capable of assimilating evidence to hypotheses and accommodating conclusions to the evidence. Internally, the assimilative properties of the INRC group facilitate stable patterns of reasoning while at the same time they provide flexibility in adapting to new problems. Here, at the highest level of cognitive structure, we have Piaget's answer to one of his earliest questions: How can we account for the structure of adult-level scientific and philosophical thought? The answer lies in the emergence of the INRC group and lattice structure of Formal operations.

Formal operational schemes

As a consequence of the group and lattice structure of the INRC operations, adolescents develop a set of what Piaget calls formal schemes. These general operational strategies govern their approach to achieving and understanding in a variety of content areas. We have already seen two formal schemes—the strategy of holding one variable constant and the n × n combinatorial system.

When the adolescent holds one variable constant in an experiment, he or she makes things equal in variable z (by the operation of reciprocity) and then examines the relation between variables x and y (by the operation of negation). In the n × n combinatorial system, actual combinations are examined in the light of possible combinations. By contrast with the Concrete operational child, who coordinates two variables, the Formal operational adolescent coordinates two operational systems. It is now possible for him or her to think about the relationship between sets of relationships.

One important outcome of the structural ability to coordinate two operations is the development of formal schemes of proportional relationships. For example,

$$\frac{1}{2} = \frac{2}{4} = \frac{3}{6} = \frac{4}{8}, \text{ etc.}$$

In mathematical terms, proportional comparisons involve the operations of division (1 ÷ 2; 2 ÷ 4) and multiplication (1/2 × 2/2 = 2/4). The fraction 1/2 is not exactly the same as 2/4; the numbers are obviously different. What is the same is the relation between two relationships: 1 and 2; and 2 and 4. Just like the isolation-of-variables strategy, the adolescent can examine the relation between two variables (numerator and denominator) at different values of a third variable (multiplication by a constant).

Concepts of systems in equilibrium. One example of proportional relationships has already been explored—the coordination of weight and distance (x and y variables) on both arms of a balance scale (the z variable).

> To balance an increase of w × d on the left, it is possible to decrease w × d on the left (negation), or increase a proportional amount on the right (reciprocity). Furthermore, there are many proportional changes in the relationships between w and d which would leave the balance unchanged (identity).

The balance scale example demonstrates three important properties of the Formal scheme of proportionality. First, the scheme allows the observer to make judgments based not on identity, but on equivalence (variables which have the same relation to each other are equivalent). Second, the proportionality scheme enables the adolescent to master the idea of a system in equilibrium—a balance scale, a hydraulic system, a piston system, and so on. While Piaget and other adult observers have been building a model of the child's cognitive structure as an equilibrated system, this is the first time that the child himself or herself applies such concepts to understanding the world. Typically, equilibrium concepts are first applied to external events like balance scales. Only later, if at all, can adolescents apply the equilibrium notion to themselves.

Probability. Piaget and Inhelder (1951) have investigated the adolescent's notion of probability.

> What is the chance that one red ball will be chosen from ten red and five black balls? These familiar problems in high school algebra texts are, of course, relevant to much that we do in human life. The world is rarely arranged in a binary system—"yes or no," "it will happen or it will not." More usually, we want to know what the probabilities are. And of course, in scientific experiments statistical probabilities are essential for estimating the possibility that a given observation could have occurred "by chance."

Few of us ever master the exact formulas for calculating probabilities, but at around the age of twelve, adolescents begin to adopt a rough notion of estimating the odds. Estimates and actual calculations have two features in common. First there is a comparison of the number of ways in which the described event can occur (10 red balls) with the total number of possibilities (15 balls). Second, no matter what the absolute number of possibilities, it is the *proportion* of favorable instances to the total number of instances which determines probability (10 in 15, or 2 in 3).

Volume. In Chapters 8 and 9 it was stated that concepts of volume conservation do not appear until Formal operations. Now it should be evident why that is so; volume concepts require schemes of proportion. The relation between length and width must form a constant ratio with a given height. Or, reciprocal changes between two variables (length and width) will leave the volume unchanged, as long as a third variable (height) remains constant.

> Children are presented with a solid block 4 cm in height on a square base 3 cm × 3 cm. The volume is 36 cubic centimeters (4 × 3 × 3). This block is described as a house on an island. Then, on other bases (2 × 2; 2 × 3; 1 × 2; 1 × 1; 3 × 4), the child is asked to build a house which has "as much room," using blocks which are 1 cubic cm in size. (Piaget, Inhelder, and Szeminska, 1948.)

When the new base is smaller than the model base, Preoperational children build the house as tall as the model. Late Concrete operational children build the house taller, but do not make exact compensations. Only in Formal operations does the adolescent explicitly state that there is an exact mathematical relation between area and volume.

In a variation of this experiment, the "houses" are built in a bowl of water. Late Concrete operational children (ten to twelve years) believe that no matter how the blocks are rearranged, there will still be the same amount of room inside (interior volume). But not until the Formal operations stage do they believe that the amount of water displaced by the blocks is equal to the interior volume. That is, Formal operations children come to realize that the amount of space contained inside the edges of the block is equal to the amount of space occupied by the external surface of the block. The distinction is important in arriving at laws of floating bodies—objects will only float if their weight is less than the weight of the water volume which they displace.

Again the emphasis in Formal schemes is on the coordination of two transformational systems. Not only can adolescents observe and reason about changes in the interior of the house, they can also be concerned with reciprocal changes in the surrounding environment. Only then, for example, will they be able to conceptualize an ecological system in which changes in one aspect may lead to a whole system of changes in the *balance* between other aspects of nature.

Time and Speed. We return to the issues of the relation between time, distance, and speed, raised by Einstein and studied by Piaget. What is perplexing about speed is that an object may travel a long distance in a long time, or a short distance in a short time, and still be moving at the same speed. The absolute values of time and distance are not relevant; speed is determined by the proportional relationship between distance travelled and time elapsed. And so, true concepts and measurement of speed do not occur until Formal operations. You may recall that judgments of time represent coordinations of order and duration; judgments of distance represent coordinations of order and length. Speed, then, represents a coordination of these two coordinations, an achievement of Formal operations.

Piaget also demonstrates that Formal operations are necessary for the coordination of two different time systems (1946c). In a set of experiments, a snail moves along a board, which itself is moving along a table. Only children at the Formal operations stage can calculate the distance which the snail travels relative to the board *and* to the table. Here we find the intellectual equipment necessary for conceptions of relativity—that time taken or space travelled cannot be absolute, but must be measured relative to some arbitrary, fixed point.

The development of four perspectives. I have described in Chapter 9 how the Late Concrete child's ability to master the Three Mountains Task involves a coordination of three perspectives—self-doll, right–left, behind–in front. With the adolescent's Formal operational skill, it seems to me that there comes a mental ability to coordinate four or more dimensions, factors or perspectives.

For example, in the snail and board experiment above, there are four simultaneous points of reference: the snail, the board, the table, and the observer. In the volume problem, the adolescent conceptualizes length, width, and height with reference to both the inside and the outside of the cube. More formally, they coordinate four different transformations (I, N, R, C) into a single structure. As we shall see in the next chapter, this added conceptual dimension may enable adolescents to go beyond the third perspective in a social interaction, to conceptualize the relationship between individuals and social systems. And, an increasingly complex view of the physical and social world should be accompanied by an increasingly differentiated perspective on the self.

LIMITS OF THE FORMAL OPERATIONS MODEL

In describing the flexibility and mobility of Formal operations, I have reflected Piaget's tendency to highlight new achievements and advances. The adolescent in the Formal operations stage can conceptualize all possibilities and n × n combinations, design hypothetico–deductive experiments, make deductive inferences using sixteen binary operations, and arrive at formal schemes of proportion, probability, equilibrium, volume, and speed. However, Piaget's own writings and other analyses indicate that there are limitations and qualifications to the implicit claim that the INRC group and lattice account for all Formal-level thought. Three types of questions have been raised: (1) Does the model describe what adolescents actually do when they deal with formal problems? (2) How widespread is the use of Formal operations in adolescents, young adults, and aged populations? and (3) What are the conceptual limitations of the model—namely, the inconsistencies or inadequacies, and the instances where it should not be expected to apply.

Does the model describe what people do?

The Concrete–Formal sequence. A number of researchers have attempted to convert Inhelder and Piaget's more leisurely clinical method investigations of Formal reasoning into standardized tasks for assessment of stage level. Bart (1972) and Rowell and Hoffman (1975) review a number of group tests of Formal thinking, while individually administered tests are also being developed: pendulum (Somerville, 1974); proportionality (Brainerd, 1971; Chapman, 1975); probability (Hoemann and Ross, 1971), and horizontality (Thomas and Jamison, 1975). When these tasks are administered to eight-to-seventeen-year-olds, there is a predominance of Concrete level reasoning in the younger samples and an increase in Formal operational performance as children grow older.

Cross-task consistency. Because Formal operations is defined, in part, by the ability to follow the form of an argument without reference to content, it might be expected that adolescents who show Formal reasoning in one task would show it in all. Keating and Schaefer (1975) report on two studies in which water displacement, balance, and pendulum problems were administered to 52 boys and 40 girls between the ages of ten and thirteen. They found an average correlation of .63 among the tasks in the boys and .84 in the girls. Lawson (1976) found a correlation of .92 between a bending rods problem and a balance problem. Berzonsky, Weiner, and Raphael (1975) found *no* significant correlation between two different formal tasks, but it is questionable whether one of them (a psychological identity task) conforms to the kind of reasoning Piaget had in mind.

These very preliminary results suggest that there is some cross-situational consistency in Piagetian Formal tasks, but levels of performance here, as in other stages, are influenced partly by the content of the problem. When Piaget is discussing cognitive structures, he tends to emphasize the consistency and coherence, but his equilibration theory of function always suggests that performance is a product of person-situation interaction. He recognizes this aspect when he cautions teachers (1972) that Formal operations are logically independent of reality content, but for best results, adolescents should be tested in fields which are relevant to their career interests.

The use of binary operations. A serious empirical challenge to Piaget's model of Formal operations comes from a group of studies which question whether adolescents in fact master all sixteen binary operations. Airasion, Bart, and Greaney (1975) and Benefield and Capie (1976) found that there is a systematic hierarchy of difficulty within the set of sixteen binary operations, so that some are consistently easier than others. Even more serious criticism comes from another group of researchers (Bynum, Thomas, and Weitz, 1972; Weitz, Bynum, Thomas, and Steger, 1973). Documentation for the claim that adolescents can use all sixteen binary operations rests on the analysis of only one protocol from one subject in Inhelder and Piaget's studies (1955). Bynum, et al. found evidence for only eight of the sixteen operations, and Weitz, et al. found that not one of 57 subjects (nine to sixteen years of age) used more than five binary operations in the solution of any formal problem.

I believe that these criticisms are important, but premature. Piaget has never claimed that Formal operations structures emerge in an all-or-none fashion. Inhelder and he have carefully distinguished Early from Late Formal substages; so far, very few studies have assessed Formal operations performance in the Late adolescence and early adulthood range in which Formal operations first become integrated and stabilized. And, finally, it is not entirely clear what behaviors *ought* to follow from mastery of Formal operations.

> A Piaget nearer to one's heart's desire would no doubt have gone far beyond a simple assertion that the logico-mathematical structures are intended to model thought structures. He would have indicated clearly and unambiguously how each model component is translated isomorphically into a specific behavior component.

> He would certainly have made clear how the model is supposed to function, not just in organizing and explaining certain known cognitive facts and relationships, but also in suggesting the existence of facts and relationships not yet discovered. And he would spell out, in good theory-of-theory fashion, just what sort of a model it is, what recalcitrant facts would require what sorts of changes in the model, and so on (Flavell, 1963, p. 188).

How widespread is the use of Formal operations?

The above studies are concerned with the consistency and coherence of Formal operations once they appear. But there is a question of whether, in fact, some adolescents and adults tend to use Formal operations at all. There is also some question about whether this stage disappears in an adult's later years.

Adolescents and young adults. It is expected, and seems to be the case, that all normal adults in industrialized societies will display Concrete operational structures. Inhelder and Piaget's book about Formal operations seems to imply that most, if not all adolescents, by the end of their teen years would have mastered the INRC group. But empirical studies indicate that Formal operations reasoning does not come automatically with adolescent and adult years. Tomlinson-Keasey (1972), Elkind (1961), and Nodel and Schoeppe (1973) obtain consistent findings. Only 29–33 percent of their thirteen-year-old subjects display Formal structures on pendulum, balance, rods, and volume problems. Tomlinson-Keasey and Elkind, along with Towler and Wheatley (1971), and Schwebel (1975) also obtain consistent findings in a sample of college subjects; from 58–67 percent show Formal reasoning, but only about 17–20 percent are in the Late Formal stage.

These studies suggest that Formal operations are not at all common in early adolescence and are certainly not universal in adults. Given Piaget's equilibration theory, it seems surprising that the best equilibrated cognitive system fails to occur in a substantial number of people. Several considerations should temper this very pessimistic interpretation until more research has been done. First, in contrast with the extensive research on Concrete operations, empirical work on the Formal stage is relatively sparse, the range of tasks so far is very narrow. *If* we can find formal tasks which deal with everyday problems and not chemicals, pendulums, and floating bodies, it is possible that more adults may demonstrate Formal structures. Second, it is possible that everyday life does not always demand the use of Formal structures; thus, opportunities for disequilibration are less here than they are when children are in transition from Preoperations to Concrete operations. It may be that Formal operations are not inevitable unless the individual is involved in situations for which Concrete operations prove to be inadequate.

Cognitive development and aging. Partly because of a growing interest in developmental studies of aging, and partly because researchers are interested in knowing whether there are regressions in Piaget's stages, a number of studies of older populations have begun to appear. A review by Papalia and Bielby (1974) describes some general trends and also notes the difficulties in interpreting the results.

In general, before and after that review, researchers find lower-level performance in "elderly" subjects (65 to 80 years) than they do in "middle-aged" subjects (35 to 55 years). The decline may be specific to the particular task. Papalia (1972) found that conservation of number and substance held up over the cross-sectionally chosen age groups, but that conservation of weight and volume (Formal) were lower in the over-65's than in college student and general adult groups. Denny and Cornelius (1975) found a decline in class inclusion, but Storck, Leoft, and Hooper (1972) did not. Rubin (1974) found greater spatial and communicative egocentrism in his older sample.

Research on problems of aging is a complex enterprise (Birren, 1964). The cross-sectional studies have not examined the possibility of cohort effects—systematic differences between younger and older samples.

Papalia and Bielby note that studies so far do not allow us to conclude that the lower levels of functioning, when found, are attributable to neural degeneration. Several studies find that elderly subjects living in the community perform much better than institutionalized subjects of the same age. While it is possible, of course, that there are real differences between those inside and outside the institution, it is also possible that social isolation and lack of motivation in the testing situation lower the performance of some older people. Because many of their elderly subjects responded very quickly to a simple training procedure, Hornblum and Overton (1976) suggest that older subjects may decline in performance, but have not lost the competence for Concrete or Formal thought. Rubin (1976) argued against this interpretation in his study of resistance to extinction after training. It will take both cross-sectional and longitudinal studies to begin to isolate the variables which determine the stage level of older subjects and to distinguish among environmental, neurological, and task factors which appear to influence performance. Only then will we know whether individuals who develop Formal operations may lose this structure as a consequence of complex cognitive, social, and motivational factors involved in aging.

The conceptual limitations of the Formal model

Logical aspects. Bynum, et al. (1972) argue that in Inhelder and Piaget's presentation of sixteen binary operations, eight of the analyses are faulty; they also claim that six of these eight cases show no day-to-day examples of reasoning outside technical logic books. Parsons (1960), a logician, also criticizes some logical inconsistencies in the Formal model. In general, his criticisms center around the adolescents' applications of the formal deductive model to a set of empirical data. As a psychologist, I am not in a position to evaluate the merits of their criticisms. I believe that there may be some difficulties when a logical model based on combinatorical operations on propositions is applied to inferences from observable events. Perhaps the model is more directly applicable to deductive than inductive inference.

Where the model does not apply. Piaget's INRC group and lattice model is an attempt to account for the way in which scientific knowledge is gathered and organized, but it does not account for the emergence of new and creative ideas. It describes how hypotheses are tested, but it does not reveal precisely how the hypotheses and formulations are derived. In other words, the structural model focuses on intellectual organization; inspiration and creativity are described as active constructions, but few details are given. Inhelder and Piaget (1955) are quite aware of this limitation. They quote the philosopher Brunschvicg to the effect that logic is like literary criticism, which codifies the laws of already-written poetry but is not present at its creation. "There is more to thinking than logic" (p. 385).

One final area in which the Formal operations model may not apply. While some of the researchers described above are interested in the fact that young and old adults may not achieve Formal operations, or may decline from this level, a few authors wonder whether there is a stage beyond Formal operations as described by Piaget. Piaget's Formal operations stage is considered to be a problem-solving stage (Arlin, 1976), adequate to deal with scientific problems presented by the experimenter. But beyond this stage are the truly creative scientists and thinkers who define important problems and ask important questions (Arlin, 1976); Gruber, 1963; Gruber and Barret, 1973). Their argument suggests that while Piaget's Formal model is adequate to describe the cognitive structures of bright adolescents and competent adults, it is not adequate to describe the towering intellect of Nobel laureates, great statesmen and stateswomen, poets, and so on.

This argument is appealing to me, but there are three difficulties in deciding whether it has merit. First, we need to investigate Formal operations in more detail, to decide which new ideas represent a décalage, and which might stem from a more differentiated and integrated structure with the same basic rules. A second and related difficulty is that few of us are at a cognitive level which would enable us to describe and understand the dimensions and properties of such a structure. While Piaget, Freud, and Skinner, to name only three psychological theorists, may have achieved a more advanced cognitive level, it may require someone even more advanced than they to create a model of a beyond-Formal-operations stage. Third, the problem may not be that we need a person intelligent enough to formulate a new stage. Consistent with Gödel's incompleteness theorum (see Part IV), there are always aspects of a theory which cannot be formalized within the rules specified by the theory itself. Only when we step to another theoretical viewpoint can we begin to specify those aspects, at which time there will be still other aspects of the new viewpoint which cannot be described and formalized, and so on, in infinite regress. Therefore, it may not be that we need to search for a stage *beyond* Formal operations, but rather, that we must search for a new vantage point from which to interpret the as-yet-unspecified aspects of the Formal operational stage.

This chapter on Formal operations feels to me like the beginning of a ride on a roller coaster. First we have ascended to a dizzying summit, as we explored all of the advantages of the new structural organization. Then, suddenly, in this last section we have descended rapidly in a series of qualifications, limitations, and criticisms of the formal model. My guess is that the ride will end at a point somewhere in between the heights and the depths. I believe that we will find the model useful in describing a very important new aspect of intellectual functioning, occurring in the vast majority of normal adolescents. They tend to develop a "formal attitude," they are willing and able to deal with hypotheticals, to explore possibilities, and to reason from one proposition to another. At the same time there may be wide individual differences in the extent to which each individual develops a coherent and consistent Formal structure as the INRC group or the sixteen binary operations.

EDUCATIONAL IMPLICATIONS

In contrast with the almost daily appearance of new articles applying Piagetian principles to preschool and elementary education, there are very few attempts, so far, to examine high school and college education in a cognitive developmental framework. Most of the research describes variation on a single theme: many high school and college students do not achieve or use Formal operations, so teaching strategies relying on Concrete operations must be devised to reach them.

The relative neglect of cognitive developmental principles after the beginning of adolescence may stem from at least two sources. First, those adolescents who do arrive at Formal operations function at a level similar to their teachers and the authors of textbooks; it no longer seems necessary to pay attention to qualitative differences in intellectual structure. But, the fact that the Formal operations stage is divided into Early and Late substages indicates that there are noticeable differences between the first applications of Formal structures and the subsequent completion of INRC and sixteen binary operations equilibrium. Second, the structure of education itself undergoes a marked change between elementary and secondary levels. In preschools, kindergartens, and grades one through six, the basic focus of education is the child in a classroom; children may be involved with, at most, several teachers during the day. In secondary schools and colleges, the focus shifts to subject matter divisions of curriculum. Each teacher sees a student for 45 to 60 minutes only in connection with a particular content area (English, history, math, philosophy, etc.) Thus, both teachers and texts may become more focused on the development of curriculum and less on the developmental characteristics of the students. And when they *are* concerned with the developmental level of the students, teachers may pay more attention to individual differences in personality-social-emotional characteristics than to variations in the structure of adolescent thought. These are some of my speculations about causes, but the fact remains that applications of Piaget's cognitive developmental principles to post-elementary education are just beginning to emerge.

Secondary education

In the United States it is the usual practice to divide secondary education into two levels, junior high and high school. Children in grades seven, eight, and sometimes nine (twelve-to-fifteen-year olds) attend junior high while fifteen-to-eighteen-year-olds are enrolled in high school. This division represents an implicit recognition of the qualitative differences inherent in Piaget's distinction between Early and Late Formal operations.

In stage-structural terms, there are both advantages and disadvantages to be gained from attempts to keep children of the same stage in one school. Junior high schools, usually larger than elementary schools but smaller than high schools, are meant to serve as a transition between the two—a middle ground between the child-in-the-classroom focus and the independent-student subject-matter orientation of later education. It is hoped that the narrow age range will reduce the social and intellectual heterogeneity of the student population and facilitate the creation of a more coherent educational program. In fact, within the twelve-to-fifteen-year age span, normal children range from Early Concrete to Late Formal structures. Teaching to the "average" in this range is virtually impossible given current classrooms, and so junior high programs usually begin the controversial practice of separating children into as many as nine educational tracks.[4] Even when the age restriction does reduce heterogeneity, it tends to gather together adolescents who are in the Early Formal stage—the more egocentric phase of Formal operations (see Chapter 11). There are fewer older students available to provide the social disequilibration which encourages progress to the next cognitive developmental stage.

Formal operations and academic learning

Correlation between stage and achievement scores. Two studies suggest that students with Formal operational skills demonstrate higher levels of academic achievement. Sayre and Ball (1975), testing over 400 junior high and high school students, showed that science students capable of Formal operational

[4]Children in elementary schools are also grouped on the basis of reading ability, and sometimes math, but most still spend the rest of the day in a heterogeneous classroom.

logic tended to receive higher grades than non-Formal operational students. Lawson, Nordland, and DeVito (975) found, in college education majors, that scores on Piaget tests were correlated significantly (though far from perfectly) with College Entrance science, math, and English scores, with rank in high school graduating class, and even with scores on a test measuring positive attitudes toward science and science teaching. This last result illustrates the familiar finding that students tend to demonstrate more interest in areas where they are more skilled and tend to be more skilled in areas which interest them.

Nonachievement of Formal operations. I expect that further studies will corroborate the findings of Sayre and Ball, and Lawson, et al. Formal structures make a difference to academic achievement. Most courses in secondary schools and colleges are taught in formal modes, but as I have shown above only about one-third of the young adolescent population and, *at most,* two-thirds of a college population give consistent evidence of Formal operations and Formal reasoning skills. The potential consequences of this mismatch between teaching and learning structures in the area of biology have been summarized by Lawson and Renner (1975).

> . . . as expected on the basis of Piaget's theoretical discussions, those students who demonstrate that they have not acquired Formal reasoning patterns are severely limited in their ability to comprehend concepts such as photosynthesis, ecosystem, respiration, density, and enzymatic activity when the concepts are introduced at a Formal level (p. 342).

More generally, for all of science teaching, Lawson and Renner observe,

> Science teaching should promote Formal thought, but it cannot do so if Concrete operational thinkers are asked to interact with science on a purely verbal level and their teachers teaches them as though they think formally. Concrete operational learners must interact with science at that level; they *cannot* do otherwise (p 342).

Most junior high and high schools have at least some laboratory equipment which provides for students' active involvement in scientific experimentation. However, the fact that students perform experiments is no guarantee that they have operated on the material; too often science experiments are used to demonstrate correct answers rather than to acquaint students with the process of scientific investigation. Further, we have seen that the very notion of designing experiments and testing hypotheses is a central developing aspect of Formal cognitive structures; the relation between experiments, facts, and hypotheses, "self-evident" to the teacher, does not become clear to students until the later phase of Formal operations. This means that some of the effort directed toward conveying scientific results could be focused more profitably on the teaching of scientific method.

In *Teaching Science in the Secondary School*, Renner and Stafford (1972) describe a number of ways in which scientific method can be taught. Their approach, adjusted for the developmental level of high school students, still bears a strong resemblance to Piagetian approaches to children of younger stages. For example, in a biology course, students are not taught the traditional taxonomy of classifying organisms. Instead, the students observe and collect organisms in their natural habitats and then sort them into subsets. They invent a taxonomic system of their own and in the process make discoveries about the nature of taxonomic systems. Renner and Stafford's discussion stresses "inquiry" and "discovery" methods of teaching, trying to make clear that students' discovery learning must go beyond the discovery of answers which teachers know at the beginning of the lesson. In the taxonomy example, the goal is not to recreate the classification system of traditional biology, but rather to *construct* a scheme for organizing scientific observations.

Studies of biology learning at the junior high, high school, and college levels by Lawson and Wollman (1975), McKinnon and Renner (1971), and Stafford and Renner (1972) showed that significant gains can be made in students' understanding of scientific concepts by beginning with the assumption that most of the students are Concrete thinkers. In "laboratory" experiments which did not always involve extensive equipment, students collected data, discussed ideas, and tested hypotheses. Textbooks were regarded as minimally useful and direct manipulation of materials was maximally useful in helping students to arrive at their *own* understanding of the scientific discipline and the concepts within it.

This discussion has focused on the teaching of science, but I believe that similar conclusions will be found in all areas of secondary and college educations. Because many students have not yet reached Formal operational thought, provision must be made for Concrete operational teaching and learning. High schools and colleges need not repeat the Early Concrete approach found in elementary schools, but experimentation with Late Concrete principles may be helpful as an introduction to more formal classroom learning. No matter what their level of intellectual sophistication, new subject matter will probably be learned better by the majority of students if they are given an opportunity to manipulate concrete examples and models and to operate mentally on the material to be learned.

We shall see in Chapter 12 that a great many studies attempt to teach Concrete operation to Preoperational children, but only a very few deal with the teaching of Formal operations. And yet, most adults in Western cultures apparently achieve Concrete structures, while a sizable number *may* not reach the Formal stage. If we accept the premise that Formal operational reasoning is important and valuable, we will have to find ways of creating conditions which challenge and help adolescents and adults to reach that stage. Increases in general Formal structures may lead to higher levels of accomplishment in science and many other intellectual endeavors. Conversely it is quite possible that gains in specific academic learning might be reflected in more differentiated and integrated cognitive structures (Karplus and Thier, 1967).

CHAPTER 11

Cognitive Aspects of Adolescent Personality

This chapter explores significant changes occurring in social, emotional, and personality characteristics as children enter and pass through adolescence. Piaget assumes that shifts in cognitive organization occurring during adolescence cause many of these changes. Beginning evidence supports the conclusion that there is a close relation between logical structures and social cognition. In the area of personality development, there are some interesting parallels between cognitive and personal traits, but the nature of the relation between the two domains has yet to be examined empirically.

SOCIAL JUDGMENTS: CAUSALITY, MORALITY, AND CONVENTIONALITY

Social and physical causality

A final report follows on the Bernstein and Cowan study of children's conceptions of conception. It seems likely that the sixth level of response to both the origin of Night task and the origin of Babies task requires Formal operational reasoning (assessed in this study by a volume conservation task.)

Night. In their explanation of how night comes to be, Level 6 children give responses which exclude any taint of finalism or animism. Instead, they offer physical explanations which describe interactions between variables; for instance:

> *—It is dark here because the sun is shining on the other side of the world. That happens when the earth turns, making it light over there and dark here. When the earth turns more, it will be dark there and light here.*

In this explanation the child goes beyond the Concrete stage ability to describe the relation between two bodies, to a Formal level description of an interacting system.

Babies. Children attaining Level 6 scores explain that the embryo begins its biological existence at the moment of conception and that it is a product of genetic materials from both parents. Unlike Level 5 ideas, the baby is not considered to be preformed either in sperm or egg; for example:

> *—Well, it just, it starts it off I guess. You know, well . . . mixes something or you know (?). Mixes the genes or, well, puts particles or something into the egg to make it, you know, fertilized. And so it will, you know, have genes and different kind of blood and stuff like that, I guess. Because if it didn't it would be more like the mother, I guess.* —What do genes have to do with it? *—Well genes are the things from the father and the mother, you know, and they put a little bit of each into the baby so the baby turns out to be a little bit like the mother or father or something. Not always, but a little bit.*

While the responses of eleven-to-twelve-year-olds would not be mistaken for explanations made by adult scientists, they do have some of the same qualities that we have come to expect of a Formal operational outlook on the world. In the Night task, Level 6 children are able to coordinate sunlight with the relative position of sun and earth.

In the Babies task, the same children are able to operate on a number of separate and distinct factors—parental relationship, biological conception, genetic interaction, and uterine development. In contrast with Concrete stage children, who also know that "both parents are involved," these children focus on an interactive, necessary, and sufficient explanation of conception.

In the Origin of Babies task, only one of twenty seven-to-eight-year-olds received a Level 6 score, while eight of twenty eleven-to-twelve-year-olds did so. It was not really possible to examine the correlation between social and physical concepts in the eleven-to-twelve-year-olds because there was so little variability in responses to the physical tasks. Over the whole sample, there were *no* children who reached the Concrete level (Levels 4 to 6) in the Babies task and who failed to reach that level on the Night task; all 27 children with Concrete reasoning in the Babies task showed the same level of conceptualization about Night.

Finally, especially at the higher levels, children's own explanations tended to make direct use of principles derived from physical causality, conservation, and social identity when accounting for the origin of babies. These concepts appear to be part of a cohesive cognitive structural network of ideas for explaining how events come to pass.

Moral judgment

In Chapter 9, I left Kohlberg's approach to moral development at the fourth stage, a conventional outlook in which authority and rules must be obeyed because the rules maintain social order. I indicated that stage 4 moral orientation seemed to require Formal operational structures, perhaps because this is the first level of moral judgment with an articulated view of the social *system*. (Turiel, 1978)

Now we proceed with the third general level and last two stages which Kohlberg found in response to moral dilemmas like the story of Heinz and the drug.

Post-conventional autonomous, or principled level In the highest two stages, moral values are considered valid *apart from* the authority of groups or other people. The emphasis here is on standards which are created and voluntarily adopted on the basis of individual choice.

Stage 5. *Social contract, legalistic orientation.* In stage 4, morality came down from adult authorities. In stage 5, morality is a matter of individuals freely entering into agreement. Personal values and opinions are seen as relative, depending upon context and point of view; some individual rights are important and are not to be violated. Laws are products of agreed-upon procedures and can be changed, rather than frozen as in stage 4. Duties and obligations result from binding contracts arrived at by mutual agreement. Turiel (1973) notes that this is the "official" morality of the American government and Constitution. Concrete examples, again, are quoted from Kohlberg (1969).

Pro: The law wasn't set up for these circumstances. Taking the drug in this situation isn't really right, but it's justified to do it.

Con: You can't completely blame someone for stealing but extreme circumstances don't really justify taking the law in your own hands. You can't have everyone stealing whenever they get desperate. The end may be good, but the ends don't justify the means.

Stage 6. *Universal ethical principle orientation.* Right is defined by self-chosen ethical principles. These principles are assumed to hold comprehensively, universally, and consistently. Not concrete moral rules such as the Ten Commandments, but more abstract statements, these principles of justice, reciprocity, and equality are based on respect for individuality and the dictates of individual conscience.

Pro: This is a situation which forces him to choose between stealing and letting his wife die. In a situation where the choice must be made, it is morally right to steal. He has to act in terms of the principle of preserving and respecting life.

Con: Heinz is faced with the decision of whether to consider the other people who need the drug just as badly as his wife. Heinz ought to act not according to his particular feelings toward his wife, but considering the value of all the lives involved.

Even in these brief examples, it is evident that not everything the subject says would be scored at the same cognitive level; rather, each subject receives one score based on the predominant stage of the response.

In Kohlberg's examples it is not easy to see how each moral stage represents a different structure of reasoning. This kind of structural analysis is described in a new study by Kuhn, Langer, Kohlberg, and Haan (1977). They provide some important evidence concerning the interrelation between the development of logical operations and Kohlberg moral stages in adolescents and adults. From the longitudinal samples of The Institute of Human Development, University of California, Berkeley, 265 subjects were selected. The sample contained 130 of the parent-generation (aged 30 to 50) and 135 of their children (age 10 to 30). Each person was tested on two logical problems (the pendulum and correlation task adopted from Inhelder and Piaget, 1955, Chapter 15) and also given a Kohlberg moral judgment interview.

Using very careful and differentiated scoring procedures for the logical operations tasks, Kuhn, et al. found that 85 percent of the total sample showed *some* use of Formal operations, but only 30 percent were at a consolidated Formal stage (from mid- to Late Formal in all their responses). This result, and the earlier-quoted findings that Stage 4 moral judgments seem to require Formal operations, would lead us to expect that high level moral responses would not be prevalent in the sample. Fewer than 10 percent of the ten-to-fifteen-year-olds showed consistent Stage 4 moral reasoning or above, while about 35 percent of the sixteen-to-fifty-year-olds did so. (None in the Kuhn sample reached Stage 6.)

Comparing the performance of subjects on tasks from both logical and moral domains, the researchers found that only four of 35 subjects clearly at the Concrete level in logical tasks showed solid Stage 4 moral reasoning. By contrast, 46 of 104 subjects clearly at beginning Formal operations gave predominantly Stage 4 or 5 responses to the Kohlberg stories. These results suggest that consistent Formal reasoning in either logical or moral domains may not be typical of most adults. In addition, Formal logical structures seem to be necessary but not sufficient for Stage 4 moral reasoning. Without Formal operations, very few people attain that moral stage; with Formal operations they may or may not attain it. Lee (1971), Keasey (1975), and Black (1976) came to similar conclusions in earlier studies of samples with a much smaller age range. Finally, moral reasoning tended to occur at lower structural stages for each subject than their level of logical reasoning would suggest. The reason for this décalage between domains remains to be investigated. The authors conclude:

> . . . moral development may entail a somewhat (but not completely) different set of organism–environment interactions than does logical development . . . . [It may be that] there are actually two kinds of interactions which are sources of developmental change. One is the interaction of the individual's structures with the structures comprising the environment. The other is the internal interaction among the structures themselves. In other words, the discrepancy between the level of development of the individuals' operational structures in one domain and their level of development in another may itself be a source of disequilibrium and hence change. [We] would suggest the further hypothesis, as have Inhelder and Sinclair (1969), that purely logical operations hold the most central position in the organization of operational structures. . . . mental operations in the purely logical domain should influence operations in more peripheral domains more so than the reverse (pp. 177–178).

That there is a relation and yet a difference between logical and moral domains is beginning to be established. However, though the above results are consistent with the hypothesis that cognitive structure is somehow more fundamental, I believe that the claim of cognitive primacy is still a wide-open question.

Social conventional judgment

Chapter 9 also ended with Turiel's Level 4 responses—the twelve-to-thirteen-year-olds' rejection of conventional rules on the ground that if rules are arbitrary, they must be invalid. Turiel's account of Level 5 shows that mid-adolescents are beginning to examine the social system as a frame of reference for evaluating whether or not conventional rules should be obeyed.

Level 5. *Convention as mediated by a social system* (fourteen to sixteen years). For the first time, mid-adolescents begin to form systematic concepts of a social organization to which individuals must be subordinate. This system provides a context for understanding and accepting some rules, even if one doesn't agree with them.

> (A fifteen-year-old boy)—Do you think Peter was right or wrong to continue calling his teachers by their first names? —*I think he was wrong, because you have to realize that you should have respect for your elders and that respect is shown by addressing them by their last names.* —Why do you think that shows respect? —*Informally, you just call any of your friends by their first names, but you really don't have that relation with a teacher. Whereas with parents too, you call them Mom and Dad and it's a different relation than the other two.* —What if Peter thought it didn't make any difference what you called people, that you could still respect them no matter what you called them? —*I think he'd have to realize that you have to go along with the ways of other people in your society.* —Why do you have to go along with the societal part of it in this case? —*I think in society when you talk to an elder or teacher you*

[1]Turiel refers to his developmental divisions as levels, not stages, but his criteria for the divisions are similar to Kohlberg's.

have a more formal—you do it more formally, whereas a first name basis would be informal and it would be just ordinary, really. As if it was just anybody. (Turiel, 1978, in press)

At first, this fifteen-year-old talks about respect for adults, then about Peter's point of view; he finally coordinates them in one general principle. Individuals in the social system are described clearly in role and status dimensions. Mid-adolescents, potentially skilled as physical scientists, are becoming social scientists as well.

At Level 5, adolescents believe that the group can legitimately make demands of individuals who wish to be included. The primary punishment for deviation, they believe, is exclusion from the group. Later in the Level 5 period, there evolves a new idea about the nature of social systems. Mid-adolescents come to believe that some uniform requirements at the societal level may be necessary in order to maintain the system. Some societal rules may be enforced whether or not individuals wish to be included in the group.

(A boy, aged fifteen and a half.) —*I think it was wrong.* —Why? —*His parents said it was all right for him to do it, and I think that was fine in his house, but I don't think that he should. What he's able to do at home, I don't think he should be able to think what he's able to do there he can do anywhere else. He should follow the rules of where he is and act accordingly.* —Why should he follow the rules of where he is? —*I don't know, I guess if nobody ever followed the rules of what they were supposed to do, we'd have chaos. Nobody would do anything that anybody else would want to do, everybody would do everything that they wanted to do. You'd just have chaos.*

As in the Kohlberg examples, not all statements seem to be made at the same level. And not all statements demonstrate the entire range of Formal operations—for example, the use of all logical possibilities. Yet, we can see the "Formal attitude" emerging in statements about what would happen if nobody ever followed the rules.

Level 6. *Negation of convention as societal standards (seventeen to eighteen years.* At about ages twelve and thirteen, adolescents were rejecting conventions as arbitrary expectations made by particular people (teachers, parents, etc.). Now, conventions are rejected once again, this time because the *social system* is perceived as setting up arbitrary expectations. We can see here one reason why parents and teachers find adolescents unpredictable.

Do you think Peter was right or wrong to continue calling his teachers by their first names? —*Well, obviously he was right. Just the fact that teachers in schools have to be called Mr. and Mrs. is no valid reason for that. And also they simply refuse to acknowledge the fact that he's used to calling people by their first names, which is a natural thing to do.* —Why is there no valid reason for calling teachers by? . . . —*Well, there is no good reason for it, the reason is to give the teacher in the classroom respect and give him a feeling of power and authority over the kids in the class.* —And why don't you think that's a good reason? —*Well because classroom situations don't turn into learning situations, they turn into situations where there is one person in the class who has all the knowledge and has all the controlling force over the class. And*

> *you have a bunch of students who are supposed to play a role which is subservient to him. And it's a different situation when one person obviously has more knowledge than the other people but he doesn't require them to be subservient to him.*

This is the third major cycle of acceptance and rejection of social conventional rules (see Chapter 9). In six-to-ten-year-olds, uniform actions are at first enough to justify conventions (e.g., men aren't usually nurses). Later, the arbitrariness of a practice constitutes grounds for rejection ("It's done that way, but it doesn't *have* be be."). Next, with ten-to-fourteen-year-olds, an arbitrary rule is accepted because it is a rule (calling teachers by their first names), but the rule is later rejected *because* it is arbitrary ("I think it's up to him what he calls them, because a name is just like a symbol."). And, in a third cycle, from mid-adolescence to adulthood, the legitimate needs of a social system are at first accepted, but then complete conformity may no longer be regarded as necessary to the functioning of that system.

Level 7. *Convention as a coordination of social interaction (eighteen to twenty-five years).*

In this seventh level, the focus shifts from society back to individual relationships. Conventions are seen as helping to regulate the way in which people interact with each other. Conventions are seen as arbitrary, with many alternatives considered to be equally valid, but some uniformity (even if it is arbitrary) is viewed as necessary.

> (A nineteen-year-old.) —Do you think Peter was right or wrong to continue calling his teachers by their first names? —*He was wrong.* —Why? —*Because the teacher didn't like to be called by his first name, and I think this was right, if that was how he wanted to be addressed. . . .* —Why shouldn't the teacher just change for him? Why should he change for the teacher? —*Well, I'd say the teacher has to make a general—rules have to be a accepted between teacher and student. If it was a tutorial then the student would probably be able to convince the teacher that it would be all right to do that, as long as the student is not showing any lack of respect by addressing the teacher by his first name. . . .* —Do you think it is ever wrong to go against conventions? —*It is wrong if quickness of communication is of great importance. Then obviously doing things that are unconventional or communicating things in an unconventional manner slows up the thing which is communicated.*

Not only are individual and societal perspectives coordinated, but there is a value priority given to the rules from one perspective. As adults, we have trouble believing that young children consider morality and conventionality separately because we have come to the point where we integrate them and even confuse them in a simple structure. However, Turiel's theoretical scheme and his empirical results indicate that children aged six and seven see them as quite separate domains. Piaget and Kohlberg, he asserts clearly, are wrong in their assumption that the two domains are gradually differentiated from each other over the course of development. Rather, stage-structural differentiation over time occurs *within* each of the domains; in his assumption of stage and sequence, Turiel remains firmly in the cognitive developmental tradition.

How is it possible for moral and social conventions to develop separately? Consistent with the general Piagetian assumption that concepts are formed in the child's interactions with objects and events, Turiel believes that different types of interactions in each domain produce different kinds of concepts. Experience with retribution, sharing, and inflicting harm should be relevant to moral development, while experience with commands, disobedience, and being different from the group should be relevant to developing ideas of social conventions. A new observational study of young children by Nucci and Turiel (1978) indicates that in a nursery school setting, young children differentiate between moral and conventional incidents and that there are different adult reactions to their behavior, depending on whether moral rules or conventional rules are violated.

It is too early to evalute the stage-like properties of Turiel's seven-level scheme of conventional development; it seems likely that the notion of separate domains and partial structures will prove to be useful in both theoretical work and in the day-to-day understanding of the adolescent. Particularly intriguing is the notion that adolescents swing through phases of accepting and rejecting social conventions. These swings are not simply cycles, but represent developmental progressions, with each acceptance and rejection symptomatic of a more sophisticated conception of the social system in which conventions arise.

Those who use Piaget's formulations as points of departure for new explorations seem to be involved in making more precise distinctions and discriminations within the general guidelines of the structural model. In the case of Turiel's work, I would suggest three further distinctions which might prove to be important. The conventional rules studied to date seem to deal with abstract principles of dress codes, and so on. Home and school rules were mentioned in one study (Turiel, 1977), but no detailed information about these rules was reported. It seems to me that it would be instructive to investigate rules about conventions with which the child is directly concerned (e.g., bedtimes, requirements about going to school). Second, so far, both Kohlberg and Turiel have focused on rules about the propriety of an individual's actions. We need to explore further whether conceptions of rules about social relationships (friendships, love relationships, parent–child relationships) follow the same set of developmental principles. Finally, in both moral and conventional development, it is time to explore the correspondence and the discrepancies, if any, between judgments about what is right and wrong for others and judgments about what is right and wrong for oneself.

ADOLESCENT PERSONALITY

We have seen that the Formal operational stage expands the adolescent's world by allowing him or her to consider possibilities, to conduct experiments and test hypotheses, to think about thoughts, to coordinate several transformations and perspectives, and to construct individual moral or conventional principles. These cognitive achievements provide the impetus for a potentially dramatic restructuring of the personality—the adolescent's self-concept and identity, interactions with peers, relations with parents and other adult representatives of society (Elkind, 1967b; Inhelder and Piaget, 1955; Piaget, 1964). In contrast with past chapters, I will describe cognitive, social, and emotional developments in the same section because they are so obviously and inseparably intertwined.

Books, movies, and TV tend to portray adolescence as a period of extreme internal and interpersonal stress and strain. Parents and teachers seem to have special difficulty in coping with teenagers; teenagers have difficulty coping with their parents, other teenagers, and themselves. I believe that a consideration of the cognitive structural factors which are emerging in adolescence can help us to answer two important questions: Why is it that twelve-to-twenty-year-olds are particularly susceptible to *"sturm und drang"*? Why is it that the adolescent stereotype does *not* apply to all people in this age range?

Introspection

The ability to coordinate four dimensions and operate on the results of operations means that adolescents can (1) think about (2) their thoughts about a complex combination of variables (3, 4). For example, they can criticize their own ability to understand the relation between what they do and how others react. The presence of these second-order and third-order operations allows them to be introspective in an analytic mode, to think critically about themselves and about the way that they think and behave.

As both Piaget (1964) and Elkind (1967b) point out, this widening of perspectives brings with it a new and strong form of egocentrism. Like a child with a new toy, the adolescent may frequently use this emerging ability to introspect and become preoccupied with himself or herself. How one is thinking and feeling at a given moment, and what one will do based on those thoughts and feelings, become the primary topics—more salient, for example, than coping with the expectations conveyed by parents and teachers.

Identity and identity crisis

I have described in Chapter 7 Piaget's account of how six-or seven-year-olds begin to develop a concept of self-identity; they realize that there is a continuity to their concept of themselves in the past, present, and future. If they are asked about what career-identity they will choose, they give firm, and often sex-stereotyped choices—doctor, nurse, fireman, pilot, and so on. With the coming of adolescence, children have the more serious dilemma of choosing a career. They become aware of the array of career alternatives; at the same time they may also be considering the new question of what kind of person they want to become. This is one case in which new abilities to create complex classifications make the choices even more complex (e.g., there are different kinds of doctors and different kinds of artists; within each group are people I admire and people I do not, etc.)

Erik Erikson, a psychoanalyst who has made the topic of identity his own (1950, 1968), writes with great insight and compassion about the adolescent's struggle with what he calls the questions of ego identity, "Who am I, and who will I be?" Erikson suggests that most adolescents, when faced with the overwhelming array of alternatives, enter a period of "moratorium" in which they try out many roles and personalities before making hard-and-fast decisions. Erikson's account of the moratorium period of exploring roles and personalities recalls Piaget's account of the general experimental attitude adopted by adolescents in relation to physical events. The tendency to take up and abandon new food, styles of dress, or music, and the tendency to be belligerent one moment and charming the next, may be part of a deliberate trying-on of *personas* (masks, roles, outer images) to see how they fit. Unfortunately, adults often react quickly and negatively to young people's experiments, before the adolescent has a chance to use his or her own judgment about a particular style.[2]

Decisions about self and career are very difficult to arrive at, especially if adults keep pushing for a choice, and so adolescents are prone to experience what Erikson calls an identity crisis. By the end of adolescence, if this crisis is not resolved with some provisional career choice or life plan, there may be a difficult period of identity diffusion—roles and personalities continue to be tried on without a feeling of center or solidity to the self. Piaget, in a discussion with Erikson (Tanner and Inhelder, 1958), remarks on the fact that the onset of identity crisis seems to coincide with Formal operations. He implies that the appearance of Formal operations may be necessary if the ego identity questions are to be raised at all. Not until a person can consider the self in the context of an almost infinite variety of possibilities does it become necessary to ask, "Who am I and who will I be?" Not until an introspective, self-critical capacity develops does the question, "What kind of person do I want to be?" become a matter of some urgency. Piaget's comments imply that it is the emergence of Formal operations which makes possible this crisis of identity. Cognitive developments may initially *create* new problems as we confront major issues in our lives.

Adolescents as political and moral theorists

On one cognitive pole is the adolescent's growing conception of self in relation to society—on the other, a developing conception of society in relation to the self. Adolescents are using their skills to consider possibilities and test hypoth-

[2]I am not suggesting here that all adults need to do is wait; adolescents also need and even seek adult opinions and limits. What I am emphasizing here is that we cannot always assume that a given behavior or attitude has been incorporated as a permanent part of the adolescent's identity, just because we witness a "trying-on."

eses in order to build systematic theories about their political and social environments. For the first time in adolescence, they become adept at generating ideas about the world as it *could* be. With the emergence of higher levels of moral judgment, they quickly make the leap from how it could be to how it *should* be (Piaget, 1964; Kohlberg, 1971). Along with a preoccupation with themselves and their identity goes an equally strong concern with transforming society in the direction of some utopian ideal.

As a result of the young adolescent's overassimilative assumptions about the force and power of ideas, there is an egocentrism implicit in this new role as a political–moral theorist. The unlimited capacity of the mind to transform hypotheses is somehow assumed to correspond with great flexibility in manipulations of the physical and social world. The reversible flow from actuality to possibility in the world of ideas is accepted as a model of change in the real world. What should be, and could be, *can* be.

An unrealistic belief in the power of ideas, of proof, or of science itself may trigger many adolescent crises of faith. Religious beliefs are sometimes abandoned during this period because there are logical gaps or empirical impossibilities discovered in Biblical accounts; faith is not sufficient as a justification for belief, and metaphor is not accepted in lieu of literal truth. The basic skepticism of adolescents, coupled with their strong proof-orientation, means that many childhood beliefs, values, and current parental pronouncements may also be rejected out of hand. Along with a fervent theory of how to change the world, comes a view of oneself as fulfilling a special, unique role in achieving that change. Here is Piaget's somewhat patronizing description:

> . . . the adolescent's systems of life plans are at the same time filled with generous sentiments and altruistic or mystically fervent projects and with disquieting megalomania and conscious egocentricity. In a discreet and anonymous inquiry into the daydreams of a class of fifteen-year-olds, a French teacher found future marshalls of France or presidents of the Republic, great men of all kinds, among the most timid and serious boys, some of whom already saw their statues in the squares of Paris. In short, these were individuals who, had they been thinking out loud, would have been suspected of paranoia (1964, p. 66).

Despite the fact that Piaget uses words like paranoia and megalomania, he acknowledges that the disequilibrium engendered by the utopian view may have significant positive effects on later development.

> In general, individuals who between the ages of fifteen and seventeen never constructed systems in which their life plans formed part of a vast dream of reform or who at first contact with the material world sacrificed their chimeric ideals to new adult interests are not the most productive [in later careers]. The metaphysics particular to the adolescent, as well as his passions and his megalomania, are thus real preparation for personal creativity, and examples of genius show that there is always continuity between the formulation of personality, as of eleven to twelve years, and the subsequent work of the man (1964, p. 69).

Piaget's hypothesis, then, which could be tested longitudinally, is that the egocentrism of adolescence may provide that disequilibrating force which leads to, and is necessary for, later more equilibrated creative growth.[3]

Interaction with peers

Piaget notes, as have others before and since, that adolescents tend to swing from being withdrawn uncommunicative loners to being gregarious participants in large peer groups, and back again. Even in their withdrawn phases, there tends to be an emphasis on social concerns—the state of their relationships and the state of society (or at least some of the institutions within it). The ability to adopt several perspectives noticeably broadens the adolescent's social world.

However, Elkind (1967b) suggests that this new perspective is also the source of a new egocentrism. Although early adolescents understand perfectly well that other people have different points of view, they assume that these points of view are focused on issues with which *they* are most concerned. Because of many important physical and psychological changes, adolescents become concerned with their appearance and often believe that others are as obsessed with their behavior and appearance as they are themselves (1976, p. 1030). Thus, even though they are quite capable of seeing the world through others' eyes, adolescents may appear to be self-centered and unaware of others' real concerns.

Elkind sees the adolescent as continually constructing or reacting to an imaginary audience. "It is an audience because the adolescent believes that he will be the focus of attention; and it is imaginary because in actual social situations this is not usually the case unless he continues to make it so" (p. 1030). This imaginary audience increases self-consciousness and self-criticalness, increases the felt need for privacy, and, for some, may make feelings of shame the central torment of the adolescent years.

Let us now follow the adolescent into a social situation with peers. Each one appears to have several different mental tracks operating at the same time, a picture of him or herself as the focus of an imaginary audience, a feeling of being unique—an internal image of self as hero or heroine, hoping that others will be able to see it. Social interaction may take place through several mental filters constructed by the participants. "When these young people meet, each is more concerned with being observed than with being the observer . . . each is simultaneously an actor to himself and an audience to others"[4] (Elkind, p. 1030). With all this mental activity going on, it is a wonder that authentic relationships do in fact begin to grow.

Piaget comments on adolescent love relationships, primarily in the context of distinguishing his approach from the psychoanalytic focus on genital-libidinal

[3]As Michael Maratsos points out (personal communication), an alternative hypothesis would be that the imaginative power necessary for adolescent dreaming might later lead to more interesting careers. Thus early and later behaviors may result from the same underlying tendencies, rather than events at one stage causing events later on.

[4]This phenomenon is not unique to adolescence.

aspects of sexuality. Certainly adolescents fall in love, intensely and passionately. But, consistent with other aspects of the personality, each participant may be trying things out, watching her or himself as an actor in a romance, and assuming that, because of her or his uniqueness, no one else could possibly know how it feels to be in love.

Feelings, ideas, and intergenerational conflict

At earlier stages, children have feelings about people, things, and events; the Formal stage adolescent also has feelings about ideas and ideals. We have seen that adolescents are constructing a more differentiated system of values as evidenced by their judgments of conventional and moral issues. Based, presumably, on a more sophisticated structuring of classes, relations, and logical hierarchies, this newly organized value system is accompanied by increasingly differentiated feelings and attitudes. There is some evidence that patriotic ("love of country") feelings emerge at this time. A heightened intellectual awareness of issues of ideology and morality, coupled with a sharpened ability to disprove thoughtless or inconsistent statements, leads many adolescents to state their strong feelings in moralistic judgments and criticisms of hypocrisy.

With this Piagetian analysis, it becomes clearer why many adolescents tend to clash with parents and others in positions of authority. Using their new Formal operational skills, adolescents meet the adults in their world as cognitive equals (and sometimes superiors) for the first time. The child who at the Concrete operation stage could say to a parent or teacher, "I think you're wrong" can say as an adolescent, "I know you're wrong and I can prove it!" Many adolescents and young adults begin to use their intellectual resources in attempts to change their world. These attempts to improve political or moral conditions are implicitly or explicitly a rejection of some part of the adult world as it exists. Adults who appear to tolerate or condone practices considered unjust by newly idealistic young people are especially subject to scorn. Adults react with hurt, anger, and criticism of the critics. So begins a period of mutual disillusionment.

Parents and teachers often struggle to find satisfying or comfortable relationships with their teenagers. Where adults have little tolerance for intellectual or actual experimentation with new ideas, the potential for conflict seems inevitable. But the conflict is generated in the interaction between generations. Adolescents begin to experiment with new styles of dress and behavior, to criticize the ideas of adults, or to attempt to help create a more ideal world. Adults often find themselves unprepared for the resulting disequilibrium which *they* experience. Reactions of both generations can contribute equally to the tension between them. At this point, sadly, many parents and teachers begin to feel that they have "lost control" of their youngsters; more unfortunately, some adults relinguish their attempts to provide guidance, as if their children *are* already lost to them. Turiel's account of the adolescent's swing between acceptance and rejection of conventions has led him to conclude that conventional and moral issues which are clarified or resolved will be replaced by new issues for the young adult to cope with. If, as adults, we can use the notion of developmental progression to help us tolerate and appreciate some of the experimentation of young people as they undertake the critical task of deciding who they will be, in what kind of world, perhaps we can begin to provide an environment in which both generations can interact and grow.

Is this a portrait of all adolescents?

No, of course not. There are at least several reasons why a significant number of adolescents do not fit the description above.

1. Piaget's theory of development is an *interaction* theory. Cognitive structures provide only one set of developmental ingredients; the social context provides another. What occurs when a critical, moralizing adolescent confronts the adults in his or her world can have an important effect on the degree of conflict in subsequent adult–adolescent interactions. And societal conditions in the larger world may also play a role in the formation of individual personality. For example, we have seen that adolescents often engage in social criticism; but it took a compelling combination of civil rights issues and the war in Vietnam in the 1960s, to create a public mobilization of American youth. Even then, of course, not all youth held the same beliefs or became involved in the same actions (Haan, Block, and Smith, 1968).
2. There are individual differences in the rate of development. While some people enter Formal operations early in adolescence, others may not progress to this stage until late adolescence or sometime in later adulthood. We should expect to see the characteristics of the "adolescent personality," emerging at different ages in different people.
3. Not all adolescents or adults reach Formal operations. While most people actively choose or follow some kind of life course, some do not seem to grapple seriously with issues of identity, perhaps because they never arrive at the Formal stage that opens up the array of possibilities.

These speculations about why adolescents may differ rest on cognitive structural assumptions. We should not forget that there *are* other factors in personality development. Rapid physical development has important effects on self-image and social development (Mussen and Jones, 1961). Sexual drive and opportunity for sexual expression may influence self-concept and social role development. And individual differences in families, neighborhoods, and institutions can have a powerful impact on the course of development shown by each individual adolescent.

EDUCATIONAL IMPLICATIONS

Moral and conventional values

Until the early twentieth century in American schools, moral education was an integral part of the academic curriculum. McGuffey's reader is one example of how moral–conventional homilies are contained in the first sentences which young children were taught to read. Teachers and principals today are still very much involved in transmitting and shaping values—by deciding what is acceptable school behavior. But explicit teaching about right and wrong is rarely seen in the modern curriculum. Contributing to this lack of direct classroom focus on moral and social issues is what seems to be increasing disagreement among parents and educators about which values should be conveyed. I suspect that the reluctance to let teachers present material about moral values is based primarily on a content view of moral and conventional judgment in which a particular answer is regarded as a statement of moral value. With a Piaget-Kohlberg-Turiel framework, it is possible for teachers to consider conventional and moral situations in which they encourage students to focus on reasoning structures without taking positions for or against a given issue. Based on the notion that Formal operational judgments will be possible only when students are able to adopt perspectives on a situation, this manner of examining content has much to recommend it.

One arena considered acceptable for the teaching of moral values is the religious school associated with church or synagogue. Blatt and Kohlberg (1975) Kohlberg stages 2 to 4. Over twelve weeks, children discussed moral dilemmas studied 11 twelve-year old children in a Sunday school class, who ranged from with each other and with an experimenter; the experimenter helped to highlight the reasoning of students at higher stages and to clarify arguments one stage above the majority of the children, regardless of the side of the argument adopted by each student. In a posttest immediately after the series of discussions, four of the eleven children progressed slightly, while four showed an advance of *more* than one stage. In a posttest a year later, however, the four with a small amount of change maintained their gains, while those with greater initial change were back at pretest levels. Turiel (1977) interprets these results as indicating that long-term stable changes require small steps; much higher levels cannot be assimilated on a permanent basis. So, we might expect that in moral judgment, as in any other cognitive structural domain, classroom teaching can produce change, but the change is not rapid, and long-term structural alteration is difficult to achieve in a brief set of lessons.

For the past several years, Kohlberg has been involved in several large-scale projects attempting to influence the moral judgment of prisoners while they are in prison. Although I am aware of no written reports presenting the results, I am interested in one central premise of this endeavor.[5] The way to influence moral reasoning, Kohlberg feels, is to enhance role-taking; the major way to enhance role-taking in prisons is to restructure the society so that prisoners participate in *creating and enforcing* the moral–conventional rules which they are attempting to understand. My interpretation of this premise is that moral–conventional growth occurs in a social context in which individual participants can *operate* on at least some of the rules which govern their lives.[6]

[5]Discussed in a talk by Kohlberg at the University of California, Berkeley, in 1975.

[6]Perhaps it is the lack of opportunity for most of us to participate directly in rule making which leads to the finding that so few adults in our society advance beyond Kohlberg's stage 4.

I realize that in the last paragraph, I may have scared off teachers who want to bring value-learning back into the classroom. Most high schools are not likely to restructure in a way that permits student participation in social and moral judgments. Even though, during the late 1960s, some American colleges and universities began such a restructuring in the wake of civil rights and anti-war activism (e.g., Cowan and Cowan, 1970), my impression is that the most dramatic of these changes were short-lived. And yet, I believe that it is both possible and necessary to focus on moral and social issues in the classroom. I believe that it is possible with minimal restructuring of the curriculum and the classroom. I believe that it is necessary because these issues are of central concern in the lives of many students. To exclude the content of these issues from the classroom is to communicate to students that the central concerns of life are not part of the process of education.

Students' social judgment horizons may be expanded within the existing course structures. For example, some new history curricula are suggesting that students reenact controversial decision-making processes, such as the debates at the American Constitutional convention; the decisions to rebel against British rule, and so on. These reenactments do more than motivate students to become interested in history and to learn historical facts; they also involve students in operating upon, rather than memorizing, the moral–ethical principles at issue. Moral and ethical dilemmas can also be raised as part of the curriculum in other areas (e.g., the uses of science; new biological issues of genetic engineering; the role of servants as portrayed in plays and novels, etc.)

A second possibility of introducing moral–conventional concerns into the curriculum is the creation of new courses focusing explicitly on the law, within departments of social science at the high school level or within liberal arts at the college level. These courses would encourage students to come to their own conclusions about the process by which laws are created, enacted, administered, and obeyed or disobeyed.

So far, my examples are relatively "safe" ones because they focus mainly on past issues, or upon issues in the world far beyond the classroom in which teacher and students are conversing. But what about contemporary political issues (e.g., poverty, racism, sexism)? And what about school rules affecting the behavior of both student and teacher in the classroom? What about the "hot" issues of the day in the community, nation, and world? I believe that important learning could take place, and the schools would not be perceived as divorced from society, if such issues could be discussed within the classroom. People fear that the teacher's views will bias the students' conclusions. It seems to me that if adolescents are given the opportunity to explore important contemporary ideas, and if teachers are focusing on the reasoning and justification for a given position, the risk that students will adopt teacher bias may be decreased rather than increased.

In California, schools have become directly involved in some moral–legal–conventional issues—education about venereal disease prevention (though usually without discussions of sex) and education directed against drug abuse.

However, it is rare for any more open-ended discussion of sexual mores or the personal social issues surrounding drug use and abuse to be discussed officially in classrooms. I have not yet stated one of the prime reasons that such discussions do not occur in classrooms. Parents do not want their children involved in them. The implicit theory seems to be that such discussions "give kids ideas." It seems to me that kids already have these ideas and that explicit discussion might in fact help students to arrive at more defensible foundations for moral decisions.

There are always issues of rules and regulations within the school. I believe that it is inevitable, with or without active staff encouragement of discussions of moral–conventional issues, that adolescents will begin to question the content of school rules and the processes by which rules are created and enforced. Some high schools and colleges have dealt with this issue by including student representatives in the decision-making process. Usually this proves to be less than satisfying when students realize that they have little input and power on important issues. More realistic may be a clear and explicit set of guidelines which delineate those issues in which students may be involved and those issues are not open for student participation. But, even if students are not included in the process of rule formation and enforcement, it may be desirable to incorporate a place for discussion of these issues. It is, I think, important to recognize and validate within the institution, that concerns about these issues exist. Values and other social judgments can become an explicit part of what schools define as central areas of knowledge.

Personality and education

The suggestion that moral conventional issues be made an explicit aspect of school curricula is part of a more general outlook on educating adolescents. I have described how many of the new cognitive achievements of adolescence contribute to clashes with parents and other adult members of society. Mostly, however, these characteristics (skepticism, idealism, individually determined principles, independence, hypothesis testing, experimenting with roles and identity, values, and aesthetic orientations) are traits which many parents and teachers value and hope that their children or students will ultimately possess. It seems to me that we need to find ways of incorporating adolescent strengths into adolescent education. We dare not shut off the inquiring minds which challenge our rules, for they may well be the minds which find new scientific, political, or artistic discoveries to enrich their future and ours.

Although there are exceptions, my impression is that most high schools and colleges have maintained a verbal-scholastic-Platonic approach to education; many preschools and elementary schools seem to be changing more quickly in the direction of a curriculum emphasizing operative skills. Older children and adolescents can and do learn through verbal symbolic transmission; that is one of the great advantages of attaining the Formal cognitive operations stage. However, I believe that in a frantic attempt to convey subject matter answers to prepare students to meet a world of rapidly expanding knowledge, secondary and college education have given short shrift to meaningful opportunities for students to construct ideas, to discover facts, to create theories, to test hypotheses, and to exchange viewpoints. This is not to say that schools must become student-centered learning-by-discovering assimilative institutions. Rather, we must create a better balance at the older age levels, between the flowering seed and the clean-slate approaches, so that students may emerge as true interactive generators of knowledge.

It is difficult for teachers to encourage student challenges of academic ideas, while discouraging student challenges of their role and their authority in the classroom. Perhaps, taking their cue from Nuffield and other Piaget-based curricula for younger children, high school and college teachers can begin to change their roles, so that they are not central arbiters of knowledge in each classroom. New teacher roles must capitalize not only on what the teacher and the curriculum bring to the learning situation, but also on the substantial contribution to be made by the cognitive and personality characteristics of the (potentially) Formal operational student.

PART III

Individual Differences

CHAPTER 12 *Normal Differences in the Consistency and Rate of Development*

In the psychological study of the child, two seemingly contradictory questions dominate the field: "How is it that children are so much the same?" and "How is it that they can be so different?" Teachers and parents are aware of both realities. There appear to be enough regularities so that we can generalize about children of a given age or stage. "Two-year-olds tend to be negativistic." "Concrete operational children approach tasks with mental grouping strategies." However, there is also a wide and sometimes puzzling array of stage-level differences between children of the same age and inconsistencies in level when the same child is followed across situations or over time. Not *all* two-year-olds are negativistic, and none of the most negativistic two-year-olds resist every adult command or suggestion. Not all Concrete operational children display their predominant structural level at all times in all tasks.

Developmental theorists and researchers must somehow incorporate both regularity and uniqueness in their understanding of children, but most of them devote their primary efforts to the investigation of one aspect or the other. As we have seen, Piaget emphasizes universalities, consistencies, and similarities in the sequence of development and in the cross-situational coherence of a given stage. This emphasis stems from the fact that he is mainly interested in how newborns eventually become scientific and philosophical thinkers. He acknowledges that two children may show different patterns of cognitive skills or that one may reach Formal operations before the other, but this information is simply not relevant to the task of explaining how adult knowledge is possible.

As soon as we depart from Piaget's interest in the cognitive precursors of adult thought and focus instead on the question of how children generally think and behave, we immediately begin to be concerned with variations from one child to another or from one situation to another. For example, we know that no matter how homogeneously we attempt to group children for the purposes of instruction, there will be many cognitive, social, and emotional variables which make each child in the learning group unique. Before we can predict what will happen to each one in new situations, we must develop a more differentiated description which pays attention to specific individual attributes as well as to general developmental characteristics. Only if we can provide a precise description of the child's current status will it be possible to design situations with the optimal mismatch most likely to facilitate developmental growth. In the planning of interventions, then, the assessment of both universal and unique characteristics is a necessary first step.

After a brief presentation of Piaget's criteria for defining and assessing cognitive stage, this chapter examines two aspects of individual differences in the cognitive structure of normal children.[1] First, the very nature of a structural model of cognitive organization implies that each child should show some cross-situational consistencies in cognitive level. Empirical data concerning the extent of this consistency tells us a great deal about the correspondence between the hypothetical model and the real child. Second, Piaget's description of structure implies that there is some degree of stability in a child's level of performance over short periods of time and at least *some* resistance to the impact of specific environmental stimulation (i.e., the child's stage isn't easy to change). By examining research on the effects of natural environmental variations (e.g., cross-cultural studies) and the effect of laboratory attempts to accelerate developmental progress, we will arrive at a more differentiated picture of the factors affecting differences between individuals in their rate of cognitive development. These studies of differences in consistency and rate of development will help us to see how the assimilative stage structures operate when faced with environmental pressures for accommodation.

DEFINING AND ASSESSING COGNITIVE STAGE

Logically, prior to the evaluation of cross-situational consistencies and environmental influences on rate of change and necessary sequences, is the set of issues concerning how stages are to be defined and measured. When we move from the level of the theoretical model to the observation of a single child, what constitutes a cognitive stage and what constitutes a change in stage? It seems obvious in retrospect, but too many claims that Piaget's model does not fit the data are based on definitions or measurements of stage which the theory does not accept.

[1]Children with developmental disturbances are discussed in the next chapter.

Conceptual criteria for developmental stages

1. Qualitative changes. As Flavell (1971) points out, there is often a quantitative contrast when Piaget compares stages. Each one is *more* equilibrated, *more* mobile, and *more* flexible than the one before. However, his main emphasis in comparing stages is on qualitative differences between them. In general terms, the qualitative differences can be seen in the kind of response strategies adopted by the child. A Concrete conserver gives answers, reasons, and even uses his or her eyes in a different way from the Intuitive nonconserver. More specifically and centrally, the qualitative difference between stages is defined by the set of logical rules used by the child to combine symbols (Kessen, 1962). The transductive reasoning of the Preoperational stage is followed by the grouping rules of Concrete operations. And still later, the grouping is superseded by the INRC group and the set of sixteen binary operations.

One formulation of qualitative stage change requires an abrupt rather than gradual shift from one stage to another. While some of Piaget's writings seem to imply a sequence of sudden changes, a careful review of his work indicates a belief that there is always a period of transition, followed by a period of new stage formation which is still quite unstable. Only after some time (often several years) is there a period of consolidation (Langer, 1977).

There is something elusive about the controversy concerning whether development proceeds incrementally and quantitatively (as learning theorists would have it) or by qualitative stages as Piaget suggests. A number of psychologists and philosophers of science have pointed out that the distinction between quantitative and qualitative is partly determined by the time periods under consideration and by the concepts and measuring units involved in the observations. A minute-by-minute analysis of response content may reveal what appears to be quantitative change. A more formal look at the beginning and end of the process may reveal what is described as a qualitative structural transformation.

2. Hierarchical integration. Each new stage does not simply replace the old one. Rather, the old stage is transformed, reorganized, and coordinated into a new stage—both more differentiated and more integrated than the one before. For example, the fluctuating one-to-one correspondence of the Intuitive stage is succeeded by stable one-to-one correspondence when Concrete operations emerge. And, with each new stage comes an increased range and scope of application, increased generality of concepts, increased consciousness of the rules, and a greater resistance to extinction of concepts by means of perceptual tricks or misinformation from the teachings of others.[2]

[2]"Hierarchical integration" means different things to different theorists. Piaget tends to assume that old structures are reorganized. Werner (1948) suggests that old structures may be embedded in their original state within new structures. This second view makes it easier to account for regression.

This is, of course, a very optimistic picture of development. Since Piaget is not dealing directly with psychopathology or with the normal crises of personality development, he usually ignores the possibility that a more differentiated and integrated intellectual structure is also open to more complexity, more problems, more gray between the blacks and whites, and therefore, more difficult choices among what used to be simpler alternatives.

*3. **Structured wholes.*** Piaget developed the grouping and INRC models to account for the possibility that many single bits of behavior are integrated in a coherent cognitive structure.

> As a first approximation, we may say that a structure is a system of transformations. Inasmuch as it is a system and not a mere collection of elements and their properties—these transformations involve laws: the structure is preserved or enriched by the interplay of its transformational laws which never [in their ideal form] yield results external to the system nor employ elements that are external to it. In short, the notion of structure is comprised of three key ideas: the idea of wholeness, the idea of transformation, and the idea of self-regulation (1968c, p. 5).

In this and subsequent passages from the book, we see Piaget's by now-familiar ideas: (i) structures are systems of rules relating parts to wholes without distorting either; (ii) mental structures shape the interpretation of the world (i.e., structure is an active verb, not just a noun); (iii) because mental structures transform input, they can deal with change as well as static states; (iv) psychological structures are self-regulating in the equilibrated sense of self-motivating–self-correcting; (v) attempts at self-correction often fail, producing disequilibrium which ultimately leads to cognitive reorganization at a higher level.

*4. **Invariant sequence.*** In a general way this criterion is easiest to understand. For every child, each of Piaget's qualitative stages must appear in order and none can be skipped. It is possible that higher stages may not appear, but once they do, they must have been preceded by all the earlier ones. Serious questions about the theory would be raised if we found a number of examples in which behavior typical of Concrete operations were to come before Preconceptual, or Intuitive preceded Late Sensorimotor. However, Wohlwill (1966) points out that Piaget's stages are so widely spaced that it is difficult to conceive of radical departures from the sequence, such as Formal before Intuitive.

One part of Flavell's (1971) excellent discussion of stages makes clear that the notion of necessary sequence refers to the onset of each stage. It is tempting to think of a child as *in* a developmental stage for a time, and then *in* another one, as if each stage ends just as the next one begins. This is simply not the case. To take an example of a single concept: there is a sequence from Early to Late Concrete operations in which conservation of length comes before measurement of length. But this does not mean that conservation of length is completely consolidated when measurement begins. Rather, it is still being organized, integrated, generalized to new materials, even while early forms of measurement are beginning. The most critical test of necessary sequence is this: on the same task, in the same conceptual domain, using the same criteria of measurement, we should expect children to pass through each of the Piagetian stages in order.

Criteria (1) and (2)—asserting that stages are qualitative, hierarchically integrated organizations—appear to be general principles or definitions, not subject to empirical test. By contrast, empirical tests seem very relevant to the central implications of (3) and (4)—stages are structured wholes occurring in a necessary sequence. Specifically, we can examine children on two or more tasks, noting consistencies and inconsistencies in performance, and we can see whether children, given the same tasks at different periods of time, tend to follow the developmental sequence described by Piaget. But before we examine this evidence, we should consider some methodological issues involved in applying Piaget's model to the stage-level assessment of a specific child.

Method variance in the assessment of stage levels

Because there are a number of unresolved issues in stage definition, I will restrict this discussion to the diagnosis of a child's stage level on a single task. I will not be concerned here with the possibility or the usefulness of assigning the child an over-all stage label.

The clinical method (Chapter 4) provides some general guidelines for approaching the assessment of children; it also suggests that methodological decisions made by the experimenter may have a marked effect of the results.

There is ample evidence that the way the task is administered may influence our estimate of whether a child has the characteristics of a given stage. For example, Rothenberg (1969) found that the number of conservers identified in a sample of 210 preschool and kindergarten children depends on the nature of the questions and the number of task transformations presented. Rose and Blank (1974) found that if first grade children are not asked to make a judgment of equality before the conservation task, there is more frequent conservation after the transformations. Hunt (1975) showed that the experimenter's expectancy concerning the child's success influenced the conservation performance of very young children.

The experimenter's criterion of successful performance will obviously affect his or her conclusion concerning the child's developmental level. This rather simple point seems to be forgotten in some of the "anything you can find, I can find it earlier" studies (Langer, 1977). For example, Piagetians almost always diagnose stage level using verbal explanations as well as correct answers; they not only want to know whether the child believes the two balls of clay to be the same amount, they also want to know how the child explains his or her answer. Other examples throughout this book (e.g., Mehler and Bever's (1967) controversy with Piaget) provide illustrations of the principle that different "facts" can arise from different diagnostic criteria.

Inhelder and Sinclair (1969) show clearly how the criteria accepted for diagnosing stage change can alter the conclusions to be drawn from an experiment. Kohnstamm (1967) used a verbal teaching procedure for class inclusion concepts and claimed that it was relatively easy to produce stage change (see below). With his methods and criteria, Inhelder and Sinclair obtained identical results; nine of eleven children "succeeded" in achieving class inclusion (e.g., they correctly answered in the posttest that there were more animals than dogs when shown pictures of dogs and cats).

However,

> If we demand that for success at least one three-stage item should be solved (terriers, dogs, animals), only six of these nine succeed; if, in addition we take into account the arguments these six subjects give for their correct answers, only three of them satisfy our criteria; and if, finally, we demand that they should be able to solve problems where the answer has a different form (for example, the subject is shown a group of terriers and other dogs and he is asked: "Are there more dogs or more animals?"), only two of our subjects succeed (p. 14).

The conclusion here is *not* that Inhelder and Sinclair are right and Kohnstamm is wrong. It is possible to argue, as does Brainerd (1977), that the Inhelder-Sinclair criteria are too restrictive and make it difficult to demonstrate short-term stage change. However, before we accept an author's interpretation of results, we need to be very clear about the data gathering and scoring methods that were used, especially if the study claims either to support or reject Piaget's hypotheses.

EVIDENCE CONCERNING CROSS-SITUATIONAL CONSISTENCIES

The horizontal décalage

In Chapter 8, I summarized a number of studies which showed that there are systematic developmental lags in the achievement of concepts within a stage (horizontal décalages). The evidence is particularly focused on the Concrete stage, but the principle presumably applies at all levels. It was shown that amount of deformation makes a difference to the child's achievement; small quantities are conserved before large ones. Material content also makes a difference; conservation of discontinuous quantity (beads) emerges before continuous quantity (liquid). Grouping types do not appear at the same time (e.g., conservation precedes transitivity). And there are many systematic interconcept sequences (identity before conservation, number conservation before liquid, etc.). The presence of décalages is one source of evidence that individual children do not perform at the same logical level on all tasks.

Correlational analyses

When Piaget describes the results of his studies of quantity, space, time, and number, he reports that the same kinds of performance occur at about the same chronological ages. But we rarely have information about the same child's cognitive level on different tasks. Given the existence of method variance and the presence of décalages, we should not expect perfect correlations between a child's level on one task and his or her level on another. Yet, Piaget's model surely suggests that there should be significant intercorrelations among tasks which are assumed to require similar logical operations for successful performance. Low correlations would indicate that there is very little cross-situational consistency as the child moves from one task to another.

Simple intercorrelational studies of Concrete operations, such as those done by Tuddenham (1971) and Dodwell (1960, 1963) suggest that the degree of correlation among number tasks and among spatial tasks is not impressively high. Unfortunately, in these and other studies, the performance criteria emphasize correct responses and do not record children's explanations of the responses. Two Formal operations studies (Keating and Schaefer, 1975; Lawson, 1976) find higher correlations between tasks than those found by Tuddenham and Dodwell, but studies at this level have barely begun.

Factor analytic studies, in which the tendency of many responses to cluster together can be statistically evaluated, have also produced mixed results. Children generally show similar performance levels on quite similar tasks but display wide intraindividual variation on tasks in different conceptual areas. Goldschmidt and Bentler (1968), for example, found that seven conservation of length items clustered together and that six conservation of distance items clustered together, but that there was no significant correlation between the two clusters. Similarly, Winkelman (1974) found four factors in 31 conservation tasks: (1) conservation of substance equality or identity; (2) conservation of substance inequalities; (3) conservation of number equality; and (4) conservation of number inequality. Berzonsky (1971) isolated five factors in tests of conservation and logical thinking. Hollos and Cowan (1973) found two factors—logical operations and role-taking—in a group of nine tasks administered to Norwegian children.

Does this tendency to find independent (uncorrelated) clusters of items represent a serious blow to the criterion of structured wholes in Piaget's stage theory? Some investigators think so (e.g., Berzonsky, 1971; Winkelman, 1974). Toussaint (1974) suggests another approach to this question. Using four tasks (multiplication of classes, multiplication of relations, seriation, and transitivity), he carefully equated the amount of information in each task (e.g., number of stimulus dimensions). Further, he administered each task in three formats; two required figurative responses and one required operative transformations. Toussaint found one clear operative factor for all tasks and another figurative factor for all tasks. He found much higher cross-task consistency in operative performance (correlation ranging from .72 to .86) than in figurative responses *to the same tasks.* This suggests, again, that we must pay attention to the method used. When investigators attempt to be faithful to Piaget's own formulations, the results of their studies are often more consistent with his theoretical orientation.

Another important attempt to interpret the inconsistencies between tasks was made by Keller and Hunter (1973) in a study of conservation of length, conservation of continuous quantity, and transitivity of length, each assessed separately on three tasks. They concluded that children in stage transitions were quite inconsistent, while children in the initial and final phases of stage formation tended to show considerable synchrony (correspondence of levels).

The research on synchrony suggests two conclusions; one is specific to Piaget's theory, while the other is applicable to the whole enterprise of testing theories. The issue of cross-task consistency appears to be much like an earlier issue in the history of intelligence—is intelligence a general factor or is it composed of a number of specific abilities? The answer appears to be "both." There is a statistical tendency for children to be at similar levels in two or more tasks, but we do not see the monolithic, unified cognitive structure implied by the logical model. It appears that children develop grouping structures at different rates in different areas with performance affected in part by the way in which the task is administered and scored.

The meaning of stage mixture

Some writers point to variations within individuals as evidence against Piaget's theoretical model. Others, however, suggest that stage mixture is not an indication that something is wrong with the theory, but rather a natural and critical aspect of every child's cognitive organization (e.g., Turiel, 1969). Piaget and his colleagues generally make the point that for children in periods of stage transition one should expect both vacillation and inconsistencies in levels of responding. Given the fact that substages are always in a period of formation and consolidation, it could be argued that stage mixture should be more of a rule than an exception.

Piaget does not make this distinction clearly, but Flavell (1971; Flavell and Wohlwill, 1969) borrows from Chomsky's psycholinguistic theory (1965) the contrast between competence and performance. Competence refers to the potential capacity of the structure, while performance is the ability or disposition to use the structure effectively in a given situation. One child may be completely unable to adopt another point of view, while another can do it but chooses not to. When children are given a large number of tasks, factors leading to performance differences would lead to stage mixtures in responses, even if the competence levels across task were identical.

In sum, empirical facts and theoretical assertions apparently lead in two directions at once. It is a fact that most children (at least from about four to fourteen years) show both consistency and variation in their level of response to logically equivalent tasks. It is also true that the logical model emphasizes stability and consistency, while the functional and dynamic aspects of the theory (transition, competence, performance) emphasize change, inconsistencies, and stage mixture. My own view is that readers of Piaget should adopt a multiple structural–functional perspective which Piaget himself often forgets when he focuses on one or another aspect of his approach. Turiel's (1975) notion of partial structures may be helpful in this endeavor. He was referring to differences between moral and conventional domains of social judgment, but perhaps we can generalize the approach to conceive of a set of parallel, upward-pointing spiral tracks. Within each narrowly defined domain, structural sequences may be maintained, but progress may occur at different rates on each "developmental track." Thus, Piaget's logical model serves as a general guide to describing a child. Inhelder (1969) is clear that the Piagetian model is a logical construction; we would expect that psychological coherence and consistency in the real world will not be nearly as equilibrated as the model.

SOCIAL SETTING INFLUENCES ON RATE OF DEVELOPMENT

There are two basic strategies for examining the possible influences of environmental events on the development of cognitive structures: the first, a "naturalistic approach," compares children who grow up in different social settings (countries, socioeconomic milieus) or who have had long exposure to different kinds of experiences (schooling versus no schooling; social isolation versus peer interaction); the second is a laboratory experimental approach which explores various techniques for "training" children to accelerate their progress through the stages. The naturalistic approach is discussed in this section, and the laboratory approach is discussed in the next.

Geographical locations

Using Piagetian tasks, primarily in the Preoperations to Concrete range, investigators in an awesome array of continents and countries have replicated Piaget's experiments and findings.

1. Europe and the Middle East: Switzerland and France (Piaget and Inhelder, 1966a); Germany (Aebli, 1970); Italy (Peluffo, 1962); Norway (Hollos and Cowan, 1973); Sweden (Bergling, 1974); Hungary (Hollos, 1975); England (Vernon, 1965a); Israel (Strauss and Liberman, 1974); Iran (Mosheni, 1966).
2. North America: English-speaking Canada (Dodwell, 1960); French-speaking

Canada (Laurendeau and Pinard, 1962); United States (hundreds of studies including Elkind, 1961a); Mexico (Kohlberg, 1969; Price-Williams, et al., 1969).
3. West Indies (Vernon, 1965a,b);
4. Costa Rica (Youniss and Dean, 1974).
5. Asia: India (Bergling, 1974); Korea (Youniss and Dean, 1974); Hong Kong (Goodnow and Bethon, 1966).
6. African peoples: Tiv (Price Williams, 1961); Woloff (Greenfield, 1966), Mende (Ohuche, 1971); Yoruba (Lloyd, 1971), Ruwandese (Pinard and Lavoie, 1974).
7. Australia: Caucasians (Tenezakes, 1975); Aborigines (De Lemos, 1966; Dasen, 1972).

All of these studies support Piaget's general statements about age progression and sequence. Many of them show that Concrete operations seem to emerge surprisingly near the age of seven, even in children from disparate environments—for example, children from cities such as Geneva, from rural Tiv in West Africa, and Greek-born urban white children living in Australia.

There are some reports of different rates of development when children of two countries or cultures are compared (e.g., Bergling's (1974) comparison of Swedish and Indian children; Kohlberg's (1969) comparison of Mexican, American, and Taiwanese children). Some writers (e.g., Kohlberg, 1968) conclude that there may be somewhat slower development in children of non-Western cultures who have not gone to school (see below).

Unfortunately, few researchers are as differentiated in their reports as Vernon (1965a, b) who compared West Indian and English children a variety of Piagetian tasks. He found large differences in number concepts and conservation of water, area, and length (with English children more often at higher levels); small differences in time concepts and representational imagery; no differences in conservation of clay and class inclusion. Again, concept-type and task-type variables affect performance. Still, we do not know whether the samples of children from the two countries are directly comparable, and we do not know what it is about the two cultures that might lead to this particular array of results.

Socioeconomic status

Within the United States and within other countries there are studies which compare infants and Concrete operational children who differ in socioeconomic status. They generally indicate that children who grow up in poorer environments appear to develop at a slower pace in Piaget-related tasks (Kohlberg, 1969; Carlson, 1969; Baker and Sullivan, 1970; Tam, et al., 1971; Case, 1975; Hunt, 1976; Wachs, 1976). Of course, the distributions overlap, demonstrating that many children from lower SES areas perform very well, while many higher SES children have difficulty. And, a few studies do not reveal these general trends at all (e.g., Haney and Hooper, 1973). The authors of this last paper suggest that previous studies fail to distinguish between SES variables *per se* and the underlying differences in verbal skills associated with social class groups.

Comparisons of groups within countries, then, suggest that there may be some differences in performance, presumably attributable to experience, but we do not yet know what differences associated with relative poverty produce slower development in what kinds of tasks, with what kinds of children. We do not even know whether the differences are in cognitive competence or in performance (motivation, use of middle-class language, effect of testing in school by middle-class examiners, etc.).

Specific experience differences

Schooling. Greenfield and Bruner (1971) claim that it is the spoken and written language environment which stimulates and provides the necessary tools for conceptual growth. Thus, a long-term lack of schooling may result in lower developmental scores. Mermelstein and Shulman (1967) compared six-to-nine-year-old children in Prince Edward County, Virginia (the schools had been closed for years during controversies over integration) with northern urban black children of the same age. Overall, no differences in Concrete operational levels were observed.

Most studies suggest that some tasks are affected more than others by a lack of schooling. Goodnow and Bethon (1966) in a study of Hong Kong children and Vernon's (1965a,b) studies of Jamaican children indicate that tasks which require children to work out the problem in their heads (i.e., require them to create images) seem to be more difficult for nonschool children. This does not support Greenfield's and Bruner's interpretation that schooling has greatest effects on verbal–conceptual development. Greenfield (1966) found some delay of liquid conservation in nonschooled Woloff children, but the results were much better when the child poured the water than when the pouring was done by the experimenter. Goodnow (1969) suggests that tasks are less vulnerable to environmental circumstance if the child has an action strategy for dealing with them.

Goodnow goes on to speculate that schooling and other forms of teaching by adults may have three different effects on children's experience. Adults may influence familiarity with certain *objects*, familiarity with certain *operations*, and familiarity with certain *operations applied to certain objects*. In some cases, children may show delays in development because they have not had physical experience with object-contents, while in other cases, children may be suffering from a much more serious lack of logicomathematical operational experience which would affect the development of structures.

Some of the above authors suggest that in some non-Western, rural tribes, Formal operations do not emerge. However, as we have seen, consistent application of Formal operations is not universal in Western college populations, either. It may also be that researchers are confusing the content of beliefs with the structure of thought. Kohlberg (1969) reports a fascinating study.

> Studies of Canadian and American children (Pinard and Laurendeau, 1964; Kohlberg, 1966b) suggest that four-year-olds are beginning to give up the notion that dreams are real and to proceed through a three-year sequence of steps in which they believe that dreams are: invisible, created internally, located inside the person, composed of thoughts, and, at the end of the sequence, self-caused. Interviews with Atayal children (a Malaysian aboriginal group on Formosa) reveal that they go through the identical sequence, though somewhat more slowly, abandoning their early childhood belief in the external reality of dreams to acknowledge the internal psychological origin. After the age of eleven, however, they adopt the prevalent beliefs of adults in their culture, that dreams are real and caused by ghosts.

In early development of Atayal children, there is evidence for the operation of cognitive developmental principles of constructing beliefs. In later development, there is evidence for the powerful effect of environmental influence. Turiel (1969) suggests that, as they become adults, Atayal adolescents begin to superimpose the content of an old belief on a new and mature cognitive structure. That is, he does not interpret the new belief as a stage-structural regression.

Life experience with materials. In a novel study, Price-Williams, Gordon, and Ramirez (1969) compared Mexican children who grew up in families of potters with other children. It was predicted that their life experience with clay might facilitate the development of conservation. The study found that these children were indeed significantly better at conservation of substance (clay), but no differences were evident in tasks assessing conservation of number, liquid, weight, and volume. Thus, a specific, long-term, life experience seemed to have a specific accelerating effect.

Social isolation. Marida Hollos and I (1973) described a study of logical operations and role-taking development in seven-to-nine-year-olds from farm, village, and town communities in Norway. As studied ethnographically by Hollos (1974), these communities were remarkably similar in social class, family size, and child-rearing practices. They differed primarily in the opportunity for children to be involved in verbal and social interaction with peers. The farm children were isolated from peers, though not from family, while village children had frequent access and town children had constant access to peers. The results indicated that social setting did not affect logical operations development; isolated farm children performed as well or better than their village and town age-mates. In fact, preschool farm children (seven-year-olds) were superior to children in the other two groups. However, the social isolation of farm children was associated with much lower role-taking scores than village and town children, who did not differ from each other.

We concluded that our data are consistent with a threshold hypothesis:

> We are not arguing that speech and language experience of some kind is unnecessary for cognitive development. Without exposure to communication the child will fail to show normal cognitive growth. . . . [But] some minimal level of experience in verbal–social interaction appears to be sufficient for the development of logical operations reasoning. The lower role-taking scores of the farm children suggest that the threshold in this area is higher than the one required for logical operations development. Beyond this threshold, the sheer amount of interaction does not affect the development of role-taking skills (p. 640).

We were also led to reconsider the tendency to treat isolation as deprivation. The farm children were isolated from peers but had endless opportunities to be with parents and siblings during the daily routine of farm life. No single label (including socioeconomic status) provides an adequate description of the essential features of a social milieu. The findings from this study were replicated by Hollos in a similar comparison of environments in Hungary (1975).

In summary, cross-cultural studies suggest that Piaget's age-progessions are verified everywhere. Concrete operations tend to emerge around the age of seven, even in very different settings, but socioeconomic factors, cultural features, and schooling circumstances may alter the precise age of emergence. When specific naturalistic differences in social settings are identified (e.g., clay experience, social isolation), they seem to be related to specific effects. However, we need much more research with more attention paid to early years and adolescence to establish the details of the relation between environmental features and cognitive stages at all developmental levels.

LABORATORY TRAINING EFFECTS ON RATE OF DEVELOPMENT

Until recently, the research question in both naturalistic and laboratory studies of developmental change has been, in effect, "Is environmentally induced acceleration or retardation possible?" The answer in both approaches seems to be "yes." Unfortunately, a number of researchers interpret this result as evidence that Piaget's theory is in error. In fairness, Piaget himself must take some responsibility for this inference. For example, in an interview in *Psychology Today* (1970a), Piaget says, "As for teaching children concepts that they have not attained in their spontaneous development, it is completely useless." (p. 30) But in the same year (1970b), he writes in detail about the Genevan learning experiments, to argue that learning *can* occur in laboratory settings, but that it is affected by the developmental stage of the child (pp. 713–717). The equilibration aspect of Piaget's theory *must* accept some influence of external events on existing structures, as long as these events occur at an appropriate level in relation to the child's cognitive organization. My aim in this section is to go beyond the question of whether laboratory training influences children's response, to the more differentiated question of how various types of training conditions produce different effects on different kinds of subjects.

Laboratory training studies usually adopt the following experimental format. First, a pretest identifies subjects unable to produce a given level of response. Some of these subjects are selected for one or more varieties of training, while another untrained group serves as a control. Subjects are then given a posttest immediately after the training; in some studies posttests are repeated several weeks or occasionally several months later, to test for longer term maintenance of training effects. Except for the area of moral development, almost all of the studies focus on the transition from Preoperations to Concrete operations. I will not attempt to provide a detailed account of each experiment (for other reviews see Brainerd, 1977; Kuhn, 1974; Langer, 1974; Strauss, 1972). Instead, I will summarize the findings for Concrete operational training under the general headings of teaching methods and subject variables, with a brief final section on Formal operations training.

Teaching methods

Simple feedback. A series of early studies by Smedslund (1959, 1961a, 1961b) suggested that telling or showing Preoperational children whether their answers were correct did not lead to their achieving conservation of amount or weight. The procedure, referred to as "reinforcement," was actually a verbal feedback or knowledge of results technique. Smedslund's findings have often been quoted by Piaget and his colleagues to illustrate the hypothesis that simple procedures do not lead to stage changes. This conclusion has been questioned by Brainerd (1977) on two grounds. First, the feedback to children took the form of weighing two clay balls on a balance scale; perhaps the children did not understand the information. Second, while simple feedback may not affect children's responses, there is no reason why it *could* not produce disequilibration and a resulting structural reorganization. In one of Brainerd's own studies (1974), simple feedback was sufficient to produce significant pretest to posttest gains in correct answers *and reasoning* in conservation of length, transitivity of length, and class inclusion. There was also some generalization to concepts which were not part of the training for each child.

Verbal rule training. Challenged by Smedslund's early results, a number of researchers have attempted more complex studies designed to teach verbal rules to nonconservers. Beilin (1965) claimed to replicate Smedslund's procedure, but actually added rule training to simple feedback procedures[3]. He found significant effects of training on the specific conservation tasks, although the effects did not generalize to a related task.

[3]As did Brainerd (1974) on some trials.

One of the most elaborate sets of teaching techniques was developed by Kohnstamm (1967). The teaching included simple feedback (correct or incorrect), child manipulation of materials, experimenter demonstrations, *and* didactic teaching of the rules of class inclusion. He managed to accelerate development in many of the children, but note Inhelder and Sinclair's comments (above) that the criteria of success affect one's interpretation of the results. This study also demonstrates that it is difficult to know precisely what the "active ingredients" of training may be. Kohnstamm himself refers to his approach as "verbal rule training," but other teaching techniques were also involved.

Training on components of the problem. A number of researchers assume that the way to help children achieve a complex concept is to help them acquire the necessary components. These components may include verbal labels such as "the same" (Gruen, 1965), or operational concepts such as the results of adding or taking away (Smedslund, 1961). Kingsley and Hall (1967), in a very elaborate training procedure isolating the components of conservation, combined almost all the techniques above and below, and managed to stimulate progress in conservation. However, training on conservation of number did little to increase children's ability to conserve length and substance.

Discrimination training. In what is still one of the best studies of acceleration, Gelman (1969) began by assuming that five-year-olds have difficulty in conservation because they pay attention to irrelevant dimensions of the stimulus (e.g., the length of the line of objects in a conservation of number task). As a training method, she created an intricate set of "oddity problems," in which children had to indicate which two of three elements were the same or which one was different; because of the systematic arrangement of examples in these problems, children learned to focus on some cues and disregard others in judging number of checkers or length of sticks. With appropriate control conditions and pretest/posttest comparisons, Gelman found that the training produced over 90 percent correct responses and explanations in number and length conservation tasks, both in immediate and delayed posttests (two to three weeks later). There was also substantial generalization (over 50 percent correct responses and explanation) to nontrained conservation of liquid and amount.

It seems to me that Gelman's training procedures focus on a variable of central importance to Piaget's approach. He notes emphatically that in the Intuitive substage, the figurative function (perception, images) still dominates operative thought. Gelman's training procedures appear to reduce figurative influence and allow the child to use operative transformations to make judgments of conservation.

Observational learning (modelling effects). A number of studies indicate that nonconservers can acquire conservation simply by observing adult models (Botvin and Murray, 1975; Charbonneau, et al. 1976; Kuhn, 1972; Rosenthal and Zimmerman, 1972; Zimmerman and Lanaro, 1974). Other studies indicate that moral judgments can also be affected by adult models (Bandura and McDonald, 1963; Cowan, et al., 1969; Turiel, 1966). We shall see that the learning theorist authors in the above list interpret the results as supporting their emphasis on environmental determinants of cognition. In response, cognitive developmentalists point to the fact that the model's impact depends upon an interaction between the cognitive level of the model's response and the cognitive level of the child (see below).

Social interaction. Botvin and Murray (1975), Murray (1972), and Silverman and Geiringer (1973) show that when two or more peers must discuss and decide on one conservation response, and at least one of them is a conserver, the nonconservers improve on posttests.

Almost all of the studies outside the cognitive developmental tradition report data in terms of statistically significant mean differences between pretest and posttest or between treatment groups and controls. When we read about a statistically significant training effect on a group of children, we may erroneously conclude that most subjects changed a great deal. Gruen's study (1965) is not unusual; in his attempt to train for conservation, there were statistically significant effects of training, but over half the subjects did not give one single conservation response or explanation in pre- or posttest performance. It is evident that many children are partially affected and many are not at all affected by training conditions. By contrast, cognitive developmentalists tend to report their results in terms of number of subjects reaching a given criterion, instead of comparing numbers of correct responses. In so doing, they convey more of an emphasis on children's resistance to training.

In spite of methodological differences in point of view between cognitive developmentalists and others, it is no longer possible to ignore the evidence that laboratory training, even of short duration, may produce at least some significant alterations in cognitive level in at least some subjects. Since Smedslund's initial failures, simple feedback, verbal rule training, focus on components of the problem, discrimination training, observational learning, and social interaction have all been shown to produce changes in children's performance. Most of the studies also demonstrate generalization of training to some other tasks. But, before proceeding to an examination of subject variables in learning, we must take a closer look at the disequilibration model of training used by investigators within the Piagetian tradition.

Disequilibration training. Inhelder, Sinclair, and Bovet (1974), introducing a beautifully executed and reported series of training studies,[4] describe the gen-

[4]These studies will be criticized by traditional experimentalists for their lack of standardization and small number of cases, but they provide excellent examples of the systematic use of the clinical method to investigate a complex problem.

eral principles which they followed in creating learning experiences for Preoperational and Early Concrete children. These principles were implicit in many earlier studies within the Piagetian tradition. (1) Training sessions should resemble conditions under which progress takes place outside the laboratory. (2) Since development results from equilibrative interaction, the more active a subject is, the more successful his or her learning is likely to be. "However, being cognitively active does not mean that the child merely manipulates a given type of test material; he can be mentally active without physical manipulation just as he can be mentally passive while actually manipulating objects" (p. 25). (3) In training procedures, confusing factors should not be washed out, because true developmental change occurs only when these factors are recognized and compensated for. (4) New structures are formed through the integration and coordination of already existing schemes. Developmentally prior schemes are not errors to be eliminated; for example, the idea that quantity of liquid increases from smaller wider glasses to taller narrower glasses is a legitimate inference based on the fact that increases in quantity do raise water levels. Children should not be told that their response is wrong. (5) In training, the adult should help the child use his or her present developmental schemes to recognize the need for new information or organization; this disequilibration should lead toward attempts to resolve the new problems. (6) Training must be matched to the level of the child and proceed in the natural sequence. Thus, for a child at a given level, training should be aimed toward the level directly above (optimal mismatch). (7) The implication of the first six guidelines is that all of the techniques described above may be employed in attempts to accelerate children, but the focus of these techniques should be on inducing disequilibrative conflict and developing cognitive operations in the child, not on conveying more facts or new and specific rules.

There are three major differences between the disequilibration approach described by Inhelder, et al. and the approach used in most of the other training methods above. First, children generally tend to be more active in manipulating materials. Second, they are challenged by the experimenter but rarely informed of the correctness of their response. And third, the cognitive developmentalists are usually not content with a simple pass–fail criterion of pretest performance; it is the interaction between training method and subject variables that is expected to determine the results.

Subject variables

Stage transition and consolidation. It seems reasonable to assume that children who are "transitional"—between consolidated stages—might be more influenced by laboratory training. At first the diagnosis of transition was based primarily on the child's inconsistency of performance on one or two tasks requiring the same logical level for a correct answer. Inhelder and Sinclair (1969), in an early report of a training experiment, described just two groups—"frankly Preoperational" and "in transition." Frankly Preoperational children consistently gave nonconservation-of-liquid responses; intermediate or transitional subjects frequently oscillated between judgments of conservation and nonconservation. After training, only 12.5 percent of the frankly Preoperational children showed any progress; they advanced to an intermediate level, but none achieved conservation. Of the children who began in the transitional phase, however, 75 percent benefited from the training in varying degrees. About half of the improvers were able to give better but still intermediate responses, while the other half seemed to attain Concrete operations, at least with reference to liquid. Similar results favoring transitional subjects (defined by passing one task and failing another) over consolidated subjects (failing both tasks) have been obtained by Strauss and Langer (1970).

In a later report of the Inhelder and Sinclair study (in Inhelder, et al., 1974) the experimenters had begun to use a more differentiated diagnosis of transition. They selected thirty-four subjects from ages 5–1 to 7–0 on the basis of pretests in both conservation of liquid and clay tasks.

> Fifteen were clearly at the preconservation level (I);
> Six gave only incorrect answers on one task and a few correct on the other (II);
> Nine gave some correct and some incorrect answers (including reasoning) in both tasks (III);
> Four gave correct answers to clay and not to liquid (IV);
> An additional eight children were chosen as consistent conservers (V).

Data were presented for *each subject* on the pretest, posttest 1 (immediate), and posttest 2 (three weeks after training). There was a striking relation between pretest level and the effects of training. Thirteen of fifteen level I children made no changes. None of the level II children attained conservation, while some level III and all level IV children did so. Intermediate stages were relatively unstable over time. Children at levels I and V on posttest 1 all stayed at the same level on posttest 2; but children in the intermediate stages tended to progress or to "regress."

Stage mixture. The above definition of transition emphasizes the amount of vacillation between one stage and another. Other studies indicate that the presence of at least two stable levels within a stage has even more important implications for the effect of training. Inhelder, Sinclair, and Bovet's studies (1974) taken as a group, suggest that when children have *no* conservation concepts of any kind, it is very difficult to produce conservation in the laboratory.[5] However, if children have mastered conservation of number, then it is possible to produce some progress in concepts of liquid, length, or weight conservation. Bearison (1969) and Curcio, et al. (1971, 1972) also show that children who have some, but not all, of the components of conservation im-

[5]Though Gelman's subjects seem to fit this description and she did produce change, she did not compare "frankly" preoperational children with others in transition.

prove with training, while children with no mixture of levels are generally unaffected. Training may not create new structures (at least not quickly in the laboratory), but may be effective in promoting generalization or partial advances once the structure has emerged.

Pretest level and training level. By assessing stages in a more detailed step-sequence than Intuitive, Concrete, Formal, it is possible to design studies which examine the effect of a discrepancy between the structure of material to be learned and the child's predominant stage. Turiel's (1966) study of moral development and Kuhn's (1972) study of classification development use the same format. After defining subjects' cognitive stage, and experimenter presents the child with examples of moral reasoning (Turiel) or classification behavior and reasoning (Kuhn): in different groups the model's examples are two stages above (+2), one stage above (+1), and one stage below (−1) the predominant stage of the child. Both studies find that training which is one stage above the child is most effective; +2 is less effective; −1 has minimal effect. There is an optimal mismatch between the structure of training and the level of development of the child.

Pretest level and posttest generalization. Three important facts about generalization are revealed in Inhelder, Sinclair, and Bovet's training studies. First, the extent of generalization may depend on the pretest level of the child. The more consolidated and consistent the lower-level stage, the less will training effects be generalized to new tasks. Conversely, the more transition and stage mixture revealed in the pretest, the more likely will training generalize to related concepts by the time of the second posttest. Second, in contrast with what one might expect, these researchers found that very quick change during training was associated with less generalization; there tended to be much greater generalization if the child showed struggles and slow progress from one training session to another. Turiel (1977) and Blatt and Kohlberg (1975) also find that slower learning may be associated with longer maintenance. Third, there are important order effects in the impact of training. Children who benefit from training in logical classification tend to show substantial increases in conservation, but the reverse is not true. Similarly, as I have already reported, children who progress in conservation tend to show an increase in the area of vocabulary (taller, thinner), but vocabulary training does not facilitate conservation. The authors conclude that logic and analytical development rather than language learning is the basis of "true" developmental change.

Direction of influence. With the exception of the studies by Kuhn and Turiel which included training condition at a stage below the child's pretest scores, all of the studies I have described so far attempt to influence children to respond at a developmentally higher level. In order to explore the limits of laboratory training, some investigators have explored what happens when children and adults are influenced to respond at a lower stage. An extreme and simple version of a clean-slate learning approach would assume that concepts are habits which can be altered in any direction by judicious application of stimuli. More sophisticated learning theories might predict that reversal of an already-learned habit would be more difficult than acquisition of a new habit. Cognitive developmentalists believe that disequilibration should promote change in the direction of natural development much more easily than in the reverse sequence; the child's initial level is expected to be a factor in the outcome of training.

Studies which have attempted to influence children and adults to respond at a lower stage provided "counter-evidence" (apparently contradicting the facts of conservation), or used other persons as models of higher or lower cognitive stages.

Counter-evidence. In an attempt to refute the theoretical interpretations that laboratory training studies produce simple learning, simplistic learning theories were attacked by Smedslund (1961b). He devised a procedure which provided children with empirical "evidence" of nonconservation of weight. Two clay balls were weighed, and one of them was then transformed in shape. Surreptitiously, a bit of clay was removed so that when the clay pieces were again placed on a scale, the weights were unequal. Smedslund reported that all subjects who had acquired conservation of weight through laboratory training "extinguished" their responses when faced with the trick demonstration. By contrast, half of the group of natural conservers maintained their orginal judgments despite the counter-evidence.

Subsequent studies of children (Miller, 1971, 1973; Miller and Lipps, 1973; Strauss and Liberman, 1974) and college students (Chiseri, 1975; Hall and Kingsley, 1968) have produced evidence both for and against the proposition that conservation can easily be extinguished by empirical disconfirmation. This is one of many areas where the differences in criteria for stage diagnosis (e.g., the use of explanations in assessment of stage) may seriously affect the conclusions.

Modeling influences. A study by Bandura and McDonald (1963) claimed that adult models have strong effects on five-to-ten-year-olds' moral reasoning. After a pretest on Piaget-type moral judgment stories, children were classified as predominantly high (intent) or low (consequences) in moral orientation. In a training session, children were exposed to an adult model making choices (Who was naughtier?) and giving reasons (Why do you think so?) at a developmental level opposite from that shown by the child in the pretest. In a posttest administered immediately after training, there seemed to be an equal and significant effect on initially low subjects influenced in a developmentally upward direction and initially high subjects influenced to respond at a lower level.

In a later study, three collaborators and I (Cowan, Langer, Heavenrich, and Nathanson, 1969) noted a number of difficulties with the Bandura and

McDonald experiment. First, each group (high and low) changed from a pretest average of 20 percent responses in the to-be-influenced direction to about 50 percent responses in that direction—not a convincing demonstration of a new stage. There was no clear evidence that moral judgments were altered, because the child's reasoning in the posttest was not reported. Bandura and McDonald gave an immediate posttest and did not test for maintenance over time. Finally, they did not assess whether children solidly in high or low moral orientations were affected differently from children in transition. We replicated the Bandura-McDonald study with an eye to correcting some of these ambiguities. Using the same items and the same format, we found approximately the same pretest to immediate posttest changes in responses to who was naughtier *and* in the children's explanations of their answers. Although we replicated the experiment successfully, we obtained a number of results which did not support the strict social-learning-imitation theory of moral development and the initial interpretation that laboratory training works equally well in either developmental direction. In our study:

1. Children's reasoning was much harder to score at posttest than at pretest. While the format of the experiment required a classification of explanations as high or low, children's responses after exposure to models were not always so clear.

2. "Pure cases"—children *consistently* responding at one level or the other—showed much smaller effects of exposure to adult models. The more the children showed a mixed pretest level of responding, the more susceptible to social influence they seemed to be.

3. In the immediate posttest, the effect of the model on initially low children was equal to the effect on initially high children, as Bandura and McDonald had found. However, children influenced in a developmentally upward direction showed *even more* imitation after two weeks than a comparable group posttested immediately. This "snowball" effect, in which performance continues to develop in the direction of natural growth without further training, is present in a number of cognitive developmental studies (Kuhn, 1972; Lasry and Laurendeau, 1969; Shepard, 1973). By contrast, children who shifted down at posttest 1 began to return to their initially high level of responding on posttest 2, especially on new items.[6] The trend was seen primarily in posttest explanation data, not in the simpler responses to "Who was naughtier?" LeFurgy and Woloshin (1969) found the same trend in their study of modelling and moral judgments; by the end of fourteen weeks the modelling effect on initially high children had disappeared.

Studies using empirical counter-evidence do achieve a downward shift, but they do not provide evidence from delayed posttests which might reveal a tendency to return to higher levels of functioning. The modelling studies described here, and the +1, +2, −1 studies described above, indicate that while

[6]Bandura's response to our study (1969c) erroneously stated that this result was not statistically tested.

models do have an effect, it does *not* seem to be equally easy to alter moral judgments in either developmental direction.

Formal operations training.

In contrast with the vast literature on accelerating development from Preconceptual to Concrete operational stages, only a few studies have tried to speed up the transition from Concrete to Formal structures. One set of studies selects children in the ten-to-twelve-year age range who would not ordinarily be expected to show Formal reasoning. Brainerd and Allen (1971) and Siegler, Liebert, and Liebert (1973) have shown that training can increase children's ability to predict and explain the results of experiments. Siegler and Liebert (1975) have also constructed an ingenious apparatus for investigating a problem with the same structure as the chemical combination experiment: teaching children a conceptual framework about factors of experiments (using logic tree diagrams) and giving them practice with analog problems, influenced their ability to "design" and conduct experiments.

Several other studies choose adolescent and adult subjects who have not achieved formal operations in a particular problem area; they also demonstrate significant gains after training (Hammond and Raven, 1973; Leina and Williamsen, 1976; Ross, Hubbell, Ross, and Thompson, 1976). One study demonstrates that administration of a pretest, without intervening treatment, can itself increase posttest scores (Lawson, Anton, Nordland, Floyd, and Devito, 1974).

In an excellent example of a Genevan approach to disequilibration training carried out in the United States, Kuhn and Angelev (1976) successfully induced advances in stage-level responses to pendulum and chemical problems. They trained fourth and fifth graders either once or twice a week for fifteen weeks, with children having an opportunity to experiment with materials and isolate variables. Significant advances occurred in both tasks at immediate and fourth-month posttests. The child's pretest level affected the final scores in two ways. First, the lower the pretest level, the lower the post-training score. Second, only three of 82 subjects made the transitions from Concrete to clear Formal operation; most of the changes occurred within Concrete substages.

Conclusions from the laboratory studies

It is very tempting to enter into the endless polemic between learning theorists and cognitive developmentalists over the meaning of the training studies. But since my own venture into the fray (Cowan, et al., 1969), I have begun to have some second thoughts. First, I have already stated above that the results of the various teaching methods leave no doubt that training has some effect on responses—an effect which often generalizes to other tasks. It seems to me that children do in fact accommodate to well-designed stimulus conditions which help them focus on relevant aspects of the task. In itself, this finding does no violence to Piaget's theory, especially since there is ample evidence that structural assimilative characteristics of the subject play an important role in what is learned. Children in stage transition, or showing stage mixtures, tend to make within-stage advances more easily than "pure cases." There seem to be optimal discrepancies between pretest and training levels, if the goal is to raise the child's cognitive stage. Pretest levels also seem to be related to posttest generalizations, and at least in the area of moral judgment, strongly affect the direction in which laboratory influences can occur; change occurs more easily in the direction of the developmental sequence described by Piaget than against it.

Thus, both assimilative and accommodative factors are interacting in the laboratory as they are presumably interacting in real life. I think that learning theorists who tend to emphasize stimulus events in changing response can benefit from considering the structural characteristics of the child. And I think that cognitive developmentalists could well pay more attention to the specific stimulus conditions which produce specific effects in children at a given structural level. Piaget (1970b) prefers to believe that the laws of learning (at least in their simple stimulus–response formulation) are subordinate to the laws of development. My reading of current research suggests that these laws provide information about accommodation, but not until assimilation is also taken into account do we have a full picture of the factors affecting individual differences in the rate of development.

INDIVIDUAL DIFFERENCES IN SOCIAL AND EMOTIONAL DEVELOPMENT

In other chapters, I have presented evidence and speculation about "structured wholeness" across cognitive, social, and emotional domains. In the present chapter, evidence suggests that there are both cross-situational consistencies and variations in cognitive development, and so we should expect the same when we view social and emotional domains. Further, the data suggest that both natural and laboratory settings affect the rate of cognitive structural progression. To the extent that there is cross-domain consistency, we should also expect these external factors to affect social–emotional development. And, we should expect that changes occurring in one domain may have a developmental impact on changes in another (e.g., Kuhn, Langer, Kohlberg, and Haan, 1977).

There is much more documentation of cross-domain consistency in the area of cognitive and social development. Here I would like to present some speculation by Anthony (1970) which suggests that there may be very specific correspondence between individual development characteristics in cognitive and affective domains. In a complex table (Table 2) he compares the sequence and age of emergence of Piagetian stages, with the affective stages proposed by Freud (1950), Erikson (1950), and Jersild and Holmes (1935). The table is presented with very little discussion (one brief paragraph in a 97-page article), so it is not clear what conclusions Anthony would like us to draw.

Table 2: Cognitive, Educational, and Emotional Stages (from Anthony, 1970)

Ages	*Educational Status*	*Psychosexual Stages (Freud)*	*Psychosocial Stages (Erikson)*	*Psychocognitive Stages (Piaget)*	*Psychoaffective Stages (Jersild)*
0–18m	(Infancy)	Oral	Basic trust vs. Mistrust	Sensori-motor	Fears of dark, strangers, aloneness, sudden noise, loss of support.
18m–3	(Nursery)	Anal	Autonomy vs. Doubt, Shame	Symbolic	Fears of separation, desertion, sudden movements.
3–5	Preschool and Kindergarten	Genital Oedipal	Initiative vs. Guilt	Intuition, Representational	Animals; Imaginary creatures; Injury.

6–11	Elementary School	Latency	Industry vs. Inferiority	Concrete operational	School failure; Ridicule; Loss of possessions; Disfigurement; Disease; Death.
12–17	Junior and Senior High School	Adolescent recapitulation	Identity vs. Role confusion	Formal operational	Being different physically, socially, intellectually; Sexual fears; Loss of face.

It is no accident that Freud's psychosexual stages and Erikson's psycho–social–emotional stages go together. Erikson explicitly set out to describe the interpersonal tasks associated with Freud's libidinal stages and to find the dominant feeling-themes associated with the successful or unsuccessful completion of each task. For the infant, when pleasure is initially centered on oral activities (e.g., eating), the major emotional task is the establishment of interpersonal trust; failure to establish a relationship in which oral needs are gratified leads to mistrust. In the interaction over bowel training and other forms of social control, two-year-old children attempt to achieve feelings of autonomy; if they fail, the pervasive feelings are shame and doubt. Along with genital-oedipal strivings in the four-year-old, issues of initiative arise; if the Oedipal struggle is unsuccessfully resolved there will be guilt associated with real or imagined transgressions. In the period of sexual latency before puberty, children struggle with intellectual learning; the enjoyment of work (industry) accompanies success, while failure brings feelings of inferiority. And with adolescence and genital sexuality comes the task of integrating the self-concept and social roles into an enduring ego identity; failure to do so leads to a sense of identity diffusion.[7]

To Freud's and Erikson's developmental sequences, Anthony adds the results of Jersild's studies of developmental changes in typical fears. Children in the oral-trust stage seem to be most afraid of the dark or strangers. In the anal-autonomy stages, children tend to fear separation and desertion. The phallic-initiative period is the time of greatest fears of animals and imaginary creatures, and so on.

Anthony's table suggests that developmental shifts in biological pleasure zones, interpersonal feelings, and characteristic fears seem to occur at the same ages as the transitions in Piaget's cognitive stages. There does indeed seem to be an interesting correspondence. We have seen in Chapter 5 how cognitive schemes, attachments, and fear of strangers are interrelated in the Sensorimotor stage. It seems reasonable that in the Preconceptual substage, the child's new symbolic representation equipment may contribute to strivings for autonomy and also to fears of separation and loss. In the Intuitive substage the child's ability to manufacture realistic images independent of perceived events may contribute to the fear of animals and imaginary creatures; and these creatures just might be seeking to punish the child for Oedipal or other forbidden fantasies concerning parents. Concrete operational structures, new conceptions of life and living things in the early school years, may set the stage for industry and inferiority feelings, fear of school failure, and fears of death. Finally, Formal operations does seem to raise issues of identity, sexuality, and being similar to or different from one's peers.

Implicit in Anthony's comparison of these stage sequences is the hypothesis that in normal children, cognitive and affective stages develop in synchrony. Individual differences in one area should be accompanied by similar

[7]Erikson posits three more stages after the completion of Freud's.

individual differences in the others. However, the conceptual correspondences are only approximate and have not been established empirically; we do not know whether these cognitive and affective sequences vary together in the same child. I suspect that moderate correlations will be found, but this means that there will also be unique patterns in the level of cognitive and emotional development shown by each child.

EDUCATIONAL IMPLICATIONS

In my view, two very hopeful conclusions can be drawn from the above data concerning cross-situational consistencies and individual differences in rate of structural development. First, each child in a classroom is most likely to display a mixture of cognitive levels; while there are always tasks and situations which present difficulty for him or her, there will almost always be some areas of relatively higher-level performance. Both the teacher and the child will benefit from focusing on areas of intellectual competence not only on areas of difficulty. Second, children from different settings may display different levels of cognitive skill; however, laboratory training studies suggest that it is possible to develop techniques which will increase a child's cognitive competence, at least on the kinds of tasks which have been examined so far. We do not yet know whether these increases will result in higher-level academic performance, but it is reasonable to expect that they might.

The role of the teacher.

Because I have referred a number of times to the Piagetian teacher as a questioner, it is important to clarify what kind of questions are suggested by the theory. The questions which facilitate development are more likely to be those which raise disequilibrating possibilities—which help children to consider alternatives, see things in a new way, generate contradictions within the child, and so on. Beyond the asking of questions, I believe that laboratory training studies do suggest some techniques which can be and are applied in the classroom.

1. For children in the range of beginning Concrete operations, simply informing children about the correctness of their responses or teaching them a single operation (addition–subtraction) seems to have little effect on their development.
2. Teaching techniques which break complex concepts into components are more likely to be successful than techniques which focus immediately on a correct answer to the final problem.
3. Both observational learning and social interaction with peers can be valuable teaching tools.
4. A combination of techniques is generally more successful than any one

technique by itself. Teachers really know this, but the point tends to get lost in the rhetoric which urges us to take sides and choose the one best approach. In my view, multiple techniques not only provide variety, but also maximize the possibility of provoking the particular disequilibrating experience which would be productive for a particular child.

5. Concepts and structures are formed over a period of time. The further along the child may be in the development of a concept, the more generalization can be expected from specific teaching. This finding, and the fact that transitional states are less stable, suggests that intensive training may be optimal in the middle-to-late phases of stage development rather than at the beginning. Since the child is at different levels in different concepts, it will not be difficult to find an area in which the child may be ready for intensive teaching.

6. The choice of specific teaching techniques and materials must be governed by the teacher's assessment of the child's current cognitive level. This adds the role of diagnostician to the already overburdened teacher. However, the information gained by the relationship fostered in a brief Piagetian clinical exploration may more than compensate for the added burden in time and effort.

7. The natural developmental sequence frames the broad general outline of the order in which curriculum should be presented to the child. If children are not learning a concept at a given level, it may be necessary to back up to the developmental level just before the child's present structure. In some tasks there may be a surprising amount of backing up before the child's level is located (e.g., third graders who function with numbers at the Preconceptual level).

8. The assessment of teaching effectiveness must also pay attention to the criteria by which the child's learning is to be measured. It does not make sense to introduce a Piagetian curriculum and then to assess its effectiveness by current standardized tests, just as it would be futile to assess a behavior modification program solely with Piagetian tasks. If the specific training is designed to produce structural change, then adequate measures of structural change must be adopted.

Optimal mismatch

In almost every modern educational approach, there is an effort to design curricula which will "reach children where they are." A Piagetian approach to "where they are" lies in a careful assessment of predominant stage and an assessment of stage transition and stage mixture. The results of the studies by Turiel (1966) and Kuhn (1972) in particular suggest that if materials are structured *exactly* where the children are, or below, there will be little developmental change. Instead, there must be an optimal degree of mismatch, just one stage above the child's predominant structural level. In less technical terms, children respond to material which is challenging, but not too challenging, and do not progress in response to material below their stage level.

When teachers are frustrated in their attempts to explain a concept or idea, they often find that there are some students who can convey it more effectively to others in the class; the explainers may be communicating at a structural level closer to their peers. Teachers who recognize this general principle often select the best students in the class to help others. The optimal mismatch hypothesis implies that the "best" students may be more than one stage level above the children whom they are attempting to teach, so "average" students, or even students not generally doing well, may prove to be more effective teachers for some classmates who are having academic difficulties.

I have mentioned above that teachers and parents are frequently faced with a dilemma when considering the principle that the structure of materials is most effective at one step above the child's current level. When children are young, the next step above does not always represent the correct or most desirable answer. But young children do not always require, and cannot always use, knowledge of the highest-level correct answer. In teaching mathematics to Preoperational children, it is easy for us to focus on one-to-one correspondence and to ignore conservation for the time being. But what about physical causality, when children are convinced that the sun moves and no amount of telling will shift their opinion? Or, in moral development where Concrete operational children believe that they shouldn't do things that produce large negative consequences. In Kohlberg's stage system, the next level would emphasize morality as defined by the good opinions of others. What do adults at Stage V do, if they believe that moral principles should be determined by voluntary contracts or by one's own internal standards? In discussions of moral issues with young children, should they maintain their own point of view or should they present reasoning closer to the level of the child? In part, this is itself a moral choice and the answer will depend upon the adult's judgments. In part, some knowledge of a child's current ability to conceptualize inner standards should help adults decide how far to reach.

The question can be reconceptualized in line with general statements I have made about the role of the teachers and parents in a Piagetian approach. The adults' role in accelerating development is not simply to provide right answers, but rather to raise questions and to encourage the child to become involved in optimally disequilibrating situations. Adults *can* present their own moral views, even though children at very discrepant levels may not understand or appreciate them yet. In addition, adults can raise questions about, or suggest alternatives that "other people believe," which are closer to the child's own level. I should add that in the area of physical concepts the results suggest that direct teaching of correct answers may have significant effects.

Emotional and social aspects of educational change.

To the extent that cognitive, social, and emotional stages develop in synchrony, we should find that interventions which affect one area may have impact on others. Increasing the child's or adolescent's cognitive structural level may result in important social or emotional changes. And, conversely, altering social or emotional levels may have a significant impact on intellectual performance. Again, the evidence suggests that the structured whole is not a cohesive unit, but it may be that there are enough linkages among domains for the kind of system-wide effects I am describing.

In schools and families, applications of this general principle are being made all the time. Children with learning problems are sometimes referred to therapists to remove "emotional blocks" to learning. Some low achievers in school are provided with opportunities for success in sports or social activities in hopes that a rise in self-esteem may result in an increase in academic achievement. What Piaget's approach adds is a potential for examining the *level* of experience in different domains that might be appropriate as a training device.

> For example, children who are described as antisocial—who don't get along with peers—may benefit from training in cognitive communication tasks as a way of decreasing their communicative egocentrism. (See Chandler's (1973) study of perspective training for delinquent children.) Or, children who are intimidated by mathematics and the manipulation of numerals may be provided with more experience in the manipulation, classification, and seriation of objects.

I want to advise the reader here that there is, as yet, little specific evidence that interventions will generalize across domains. But I believe that the idea is certainly worth investigating in some detail.

The issue of optimal speed

In all of the debate concerning whether or not we can accelerate the development of a specific cognitive concept, Piaget reminds us that we often forget to ask whether we *should* attempt to accelerate the child's cognitive growth (Piaget, 1970a). Though good evidence is hard to find, Piaget raises the possibility that an emphasis on acceleration of isolated skills might in the long run interfere with natural developmental progression. He suggests that a strategy which encourages horizontal breadth of application of structures (horizontal décalage) may ultimately prove to be more beneficial to the child in the long run. Perhaps it produces a better, broader foundation for the creation of an intellectual pyramid.

Piaget also wonders whether there is a developmental progression that is too slow. Is there a critical period for the acquisition of structures? It is possible that if environmental or congenital difficulties prevent a child from reaching a point by a given age, it will be too late for future learning? These questions are important to consider but are impossible to investigate experimentally in human beings. The questions themselves, however, may stimulate a search for ways to conceptualize and maintain an optimal developmental rate—not too fast, not too slow—which will facilitate the widest possible application of the child's newly emerging cognitive structures.

CHAPTER 13

Developmental Dysfunction: Diagnosis and Intervention[1]

Piaget was well acquainted with the beginnings of modern abnormal psychology. He worked in Bleuler's clinic in 1917, only six years after Bleuler renamed *dementia praecox* as schizophrenia, reconceptualizing it as a treatable disease. He had indirect contact with the ideas of Freud and Jung and direct contact with Binet's collaborator, Henri Simon. As we have seen, he chose to adopt the clinical method from psychiatric investigations while virtually ignoring content areas to which the method had been applied. We are free, however, to determine whether principles derived from this theory of normal development are helpful in understanding and treating developmental dysfunction.

The definition of dysfunction always begins with an implicit or explicit evaluation of individual differences; people whose behavior deviates markedly from the central tendency of a population or subpopulation are more likely to be diagnosed as dysfunctional, emotionally disturbed, abnormal, and so on. However, symptoms of what has been diagnosed as developmental dysfunction appear to be relatively common in children. Epidemiological studies in the United States and in England (Lapousse and Monk, 1958; Shepherd, Op-

[1]The formulation of this chapter began during a three-year period in which I was a consultant to the East Bay Activities Center, Oakland, California. I wish to thank the dedicated staff of this day-treatment center for children and to extend special thanks to Frankie Lemon, Head Teacher and to Dr. Joel Saldinger, Director.

penheim, and Mitchell, 1966) suggest that as many as 50 percent of the children at every age between six and twelve years have symptoms which psychotherapists tend to evaluate as pathological (such as fears and worries, frequent temper tantrums, nightmares, stammering, enuresis, tics, thumbsucking, nail biting). As many as 20 percent of a random sample of children seen by professional diagnosticians may be described as having a serious degree of emotional–intellectual disturbance (Stennet, 1966; Rutter and Graham, 1965). Thus, unless we are prepared to label a large segment of the population as abnormal, the frequency of occurrence of symptoms should be considered as only one of the criteria involved in the diagnosis of developmental dysfunction.

Children are rarely described as abnormal or disturbed on the basis of a single behavior. Traditional diagnostic categories (retardation, organic dysfunction, psychosis, neurosis, character disorders, delinquency, learning disorders) are based on *patterns* of symptoms, with each pattern assumed to represent an underlying, unitary disease-like state. Unfortunately, this diagnostic system has been appropriated directly from adult psychopathology (see the Diagnostic and Statistical Manual—"DSM-II", 1968). There is very little recognition of the fact that there may be less similarity between a child and adult schizophrenic than between two children or two adults in different diagnostic categories. The traditional system also fails to pay attention to the possibility that symptom patterns change systematically with age or stage. In brief, it is a classification system for children which often ignores principles of development[2] (see Achenbach, 1974).

Controversies surrounding the conceptual distinctions between normal and abnormal development have increased rather than decreased over the years. There is, as yet, little consensus concerning the diagnostic criteria considered central to each diagnostic category. There tends to be low agreement between clinicians classifying the same child. The interpretation of each category as an illness or disease has been strongly questioned, as has the medical model of mental illness, diagnosis, and treatment. And a relatively new issue has extended the controversy still further. Given the fact that there can be severe social stigma attached to anyone labeled as mentally ill or disturbed (Goffman, 1961; Rosenhan, 1973), many laymen and professionals are questioning the whole diagnostic enterprise. If labeling may harm children, should we attempt to distinguish between normality and abnormality?

The position I will take in this chapter is that there is an alternative to the choice between total acceptance of traditional categories and total rejection of diagnosis. While it may not be useful to differentiate between normality and abnormality as mutually exclusive labels implying health or illness, it is essential to explore a continuum ranging from adaptive to dysfunctional patterns of individual differences. Toward the adaptive end are patterns of structural, functional, and behavioral variation in combination with situational contexts,

[2]In contrast with *DSM–II*, psychoanalytic diagnosticians *do* attempt to provide developmental stage and structural descriptions for each of the categories.

which lead to further developmental change without special interventions. Near the midpoint, interventions are not necessary, but they would be effective in stimulating optimal developmental growth. Toward the dysfunctional end of the continuum are patterns of person-environment match/mismatch in which developmental progress will not occur without specially designed conditions. Dysfunctional patterns may be frequent or infrequent and may cut across traditional diagnostic categories. Diagnosis becomes not merely a labeling or categorization, but rather a differentiated description of person-in-context; I see this as a first step in evaluating the need for intervention and the form such intervention should take if it is to stimulate developmental growth.

In the following sections of this chapter, I will show that Piagetian principles can help us to take a new look at children in existing diagnostic categories and lead us to new ideas in creating therapeutic treatment and special education. I will begin with an extended discussion of childhood psychosis as one of the most extreme forms of developmental dysfunction. Principles developed in this discussion will be applied to retardation, to organic dysfunctions and "specific learning disabilities," and to internalizing–externalizing disturbances (including neurosis and delinquency).

CHILDHOOD PSYCHOSIS

Schizophrenia and autism are the two most common labels for serious psychotic disturbance in childhood. Compared with other diagnostic categories, the prevalence in young children is very low (from one to nine per 100,000 in one-to-fourteen-year-olds); it is only slightly higher in adolescence (17 to 23 per 100,000 in fifteen-to-seventeen-year-olds; Clarizio and McCoy, 1976). Yet, children diagnosed as schizophrenic or autistic are so puzzling and so challenging that a great many theorists, researchers, and therapists have attempted to understand them. Each writer paints a slightly different picture of the psychotic child (Anthony, 1958; Bender, 1947; Bettelheim, 1966; Escalona. 1948; Ekstein, 1966; Goldfarb, 1970; Kanner, 1942; Lovaas, 1976; Mahler, 1952; Rimland, 1964; Boatman and Szurek, 1960).

A British group led by Creak (1963) outlined a set of nine diagnostic criteria which seem to provide a consensus description of "the schizophrenic syndrome in childhood":

1. Severe, sustained impairment of relationships with people (e.g., treating people as objects).
2. Serious general retardation, with islands of near-normal to exceptional skills (e.g., drawing, computation, reading).
3. Pathological preoccupation with particular objects or parts of objects (e.g., light switches).
4. Sustained resistance to change in the environment and a striving to maintain or restore sameness.

5. Abnormal perceptual experience in the absence of discernible organic abnormality (e.g., hallucinations).
6. Acute, excessive, and seemingly illogical anxiety.
7. Speech disturbance (e.g., absence of speech, or echoing what has just been said).
8. Distortion in motility (e.g., bizarre postures, repetitive banging and rocking).
9. Apparent unawareness of personal identity to a degree inappropriate to their age (apparent lack of self-environment differentiation).

In a comprehensive review, Goldfarb (1970) concludes that there is a common core of agreement between Creak's nine criteria and 52 other published descriptions of childhood schizophrenia. He cautions that no single symptom is sufficient to establish the diagnosis; each one may be found in other disorders,[3] so a consideration of the total constellation is essential.

There has been some debate about whether a subgroup of psychotic children with a disorder labeled by Kanner (1942) as Early Infantile Autism should be regarded as a separate category from childhood schizophrenia. Autistic children show an aloneness (1), fascination with objects (3), obsessive insistence on sameness (4), impaired communication (7), and motility distortion (8), either immediately or very soon after birth. Studies indicate that these children cannot be reliably discriminated from other psychotic children (Goldfarb, 1970). However, I believe that there is some usefulness in the category because it describes children who appear to be almost unreachable, in contrast with children who are relating to others but in very bizarre ways.

As in almost all of the literature on childhood difficulties, the emphasis has been placed on what these children cannot do. And yet, within the pathology-oriented descriptions themselves are glimmers of strengths: islands of exceptional talent; ability to mimic others; sensitivity to stimulation. R. D. Laing (1967), a controversial critic of traditional definitions of schizophrenia, points out that psychosis may represent an adaptive response to very bizarre family or societal situations. There may be special sensitivity shown by psychotic children: what seems like "excessive anxiety" may represent a reaction to very real but subtly masked parental rejection or marital breakdown. Finally, no child or adult is psychotic all of the time. Many of their behaviors, fears, requests, and so on represent perfectly natural responses to situations. It is a serious mistake to interpret every action and statement as part of some developmental disturbance.

In the past twenty years, and particularly in the past decade, schizophrenic children have been given Piagetian tasks and their behavior has been described in Piagetian terms. The emphasis has been focused primarily on structural retardation and cross-situational inconsistencies. Investigators in the Genevan group have done some of the studies (particularly de Ajuriaguerra, Inhelder, Jaeggi, Roth, and Stirlin, 1970; Schmid-Kitsikis, 1969, 1973, 1976), while other schizophrenic populations have been assessed in Australia, England, Canada,

[3]And in younger normal children.

and the United States. I will use data from all of these sources to convey a description of psychosis as a developmental dysfunction in Piagetian structural and functional categories.

Structural retardation

Schizophrenic children and adults consistently show severe structural retardation in at least four important conceptual schemes or abilities: object permanence; symbol formation; conservation; egocentrism.

Object permanence. Woodward (1963) has observed severely retarded children and described their behavior using Piagetian concepts. Her observations may apply to severely psychotic children as well; the rigid, stereotyped behaviors of older retarded children, including repetitive eye rolling or hand flicking, are very similar to the normal primary and secondary circular reactions characteristic of the first three Sensorimotor substages. Is it possible that schizophrenic children have not successfully completed the Sensorimotor stage? Preliminary evidence comes from Serafica (1971), who used Uzgiris and Hunt's (1975) Piagetian infant scale with four-to-eight-year-old schizophrenic children. Some children were not able to find an object when it was moved behind a screen (i.e., they failed to reach Substage 4, beginning object permanence). Other children who could find an object hidden at one location, could not find it again when it was visibly moved to another hiding place (i.e., they failed Substage 5). Still others had reached Substage 6, following invisible displacements with familiar objects, but not with unfamiliar ones.

Symbol formation. As we have seen, around the age of two, normal children begin to establish internal symbolic schemes which ultimately become independent of their own actions. Anthony (1956) notes that there is a frequent failure of schizophrenic children and even adults to separate symbols from things they represent. Pictures and words may be treated as real; ideas and wishes may be indistinguishable from deeds. For these children, symbols retain their private, fluctuating, one-dimension-at-a-time meaning long after most children have moved to the Intuitive stage or to Concrete operations.

Conservation. Several studies suggest that conservation schemes come very late to psychotic children and adults, if they develop at all. Marks (1972) tested 25 psychotic five-to-fourteen-year-olds on five tasks and found that: conservation did not begin until about age nine; between ages nine and twelve, children showed extensive scatter on all five tasks; not until age twelve did some children pass them all. This study seemed optimistic about the eventual achievement of Concrete operations. However, in one of Schmid-Kitsikis' reports, only three of fiteen schizophrenic adolescents were found to have achieved any degree of conservation. Goldfarb and Mintz (1961), Halpern (1966), Lovell and

Slater (1960), and Berger, et al. (1969) obtained similar results for conservation of quantity, space, and time in psychotic children. Other studies indicate that some adult schizophrenics cannot conserve at all, while those with higher IQ's may conserve and seriate number but not volume (Bearison, 1974; Hamilton, 1972; Lerner, Bie, and Lehrer, 1972).

Egocentrism. Not surprisingly, Anthony (1956) and de Ajuriaguerra, et al. (1970) describe psychotic children as egocentric. Neal (1966) compared normal and hospitalized eight-to-eleven-year-old children; they were matched for age and IQ and given a version of Piaget's Three Mountains Task. The psychotic children were more egocentric at each age. Further, there were no developmental increases in perspective scores for older psychotic children as there were in the normal group: "emotional disturbances in children are strong enough to override the strong developmental trend in overcoming egocentricism noted by Piaget and Inhelder (1956)" (Neal, p. 101).

Two studies found that schizophrenic adults communicate more egocentrically than normal controls (Cohen and Camhi, 1968; Suchotliff, 1970). The task was a "Password" game in which one player attempts to communicate a (hidden) referent word to another using a succession of one-word clues, for instance, to get the listener to think of "king" by saying "crown." Cohen and Camhi found that the performance decrement occurred when schizophrenics were speakers, but not when they were listeners. Suchotliff also found that egocentric errors on the communication task were correlated with difficulties in using the abstract thinking necessary to define proverbs (e.g., a rolling stone gathers no moss). He concludes that an important component of what has been called thought disorder can be described as a disorder of decentering—an inability to coordinate two points of view so as to enrich the limited understanding available from a single frame of reference. The data also suggest that the schizophrenic's level of understanding may be higher than his or her level of expressing ideas.

De Ajuriaguerra, et al. note the Preconceptual centrations which lead to unstable, tangential, personal concepts with potentially rapid fluctuations in meaning. Failures to differentiate between words and referents are accompanied by failures to differentiate between self and others and between fantasy and reality. These investigators interpret all of these failures as resulting from general conceptual egocentrism in which the child cannot decenter well enough to "take a position outside himself and to situate himself in an objective world."

On the basis of the tasks so far described, psychotic children and adults have difficulty all along the developmental range from Sensorimotor to Formal operations, consistently performing less well than their age peers. This intuitively obvious result is nevertheless difficult to interpret because no longitudinal assessments have been made, and different tasks have been used with people of different ages. Without longitudinal data we do not know whether structures are retarded or regressed. Without a common set of tasks for all ages, we do not know whether lower level difficulties eventually are resolved. For example, as far as I know, no object permanence tasks have been administered to psychotic children older than age eight. Do at least some of them eventually emerge from the Sensorimotor stage? If so, then there is a developmental–structural progression within the category of psychosis; that is, psychosis can occur at different structural levels. If not, then we will have great difficulty explaining how older psychotic children and adults achieve beginning conservations without having established schemes of object permanence. This would force us to reexamine the notion of necessary sequence, at least in cases of severe dysfunction. My own guess is that the answer lies somewhere in between. There *is* a developmental structural sequence within specific conceptual domains, but partial structures may exist so that conservation in some areas could exist side by side with Sensorimotor functioning in others (see structural-functional asynchronies, p. 341). The details of how such a structure operates remain to be worked out.

Functional imbalance

In Piaget's work with normal children, he describes short-term imbalances between assimilation and accommodation and some long-term imbalances which ultimately lead to new developmental stages. While disequilibration is a general fact of life, there usually seems to be movement in the direction of some equilibrated state. Evidence from the Genevan group and from my own observations lead me to suggest that in children labeled as severely dysfunctional, there may be permanent or at least very long lasting assimilation–accommodation imbalances, with a resulting imbalance in figurative and operative functions.

Assimilation–accommodation. Descriptions of schizophrenic children as "lost in fantasy, out of touch with reality, resistant to change, obsessively and repetitively preoccupied with a limited range of objects," all suggest an overassimilative aspect to psychosis. The children seem to bend the world to fit their own inner meanings and needs. In Creak's list of symptoms, however, and in the Genevan accounts of schizophrenic children, there is a number of overaccommodative aspects as well. These children are often very reactive to stimulation, sensitive to what seems to be very low intensity of light, sound, touch.[4] They are usually highly distractible; in testing sessions, the examiner must repeatedly entice the child from a long chain of ideas or actions back to the task at hand. Many schizophrenic children spend much of the day imitating TV characters and mimicking other people. Like chameleons they merge with surrounding personalities, apparently lacking a central core and a solid sense of self.

[4]Though they also may be underreactive.

While a few psychotic children seem to be permanently stuck on one side of the assimilation–accommodation imbalance, most seem to fluctuate between the two extremes, with only rare and brief flashes of equilibration.

> For half an hour in a day-treatment classroom, a six-year-old boy has been attempting to assimilate each new object to a set of banging and throwing actions; he stops only when physically restrained by the teacher. The next minute, he can be seen and heard in an uncanny copy of the teacher's mannerisms and voice. Then, after a quick insightful glance to gauge the exact moment before the teacher loses his temper, the child returns to assimilative banging of the objects.

All children display assimilation–accommodation imbalances. However, in the course of developing an assimilative–accommodative behavior-rating scale, Leonard Breslow and I (1977) shared three strong clinical impressions about differences between psychotic and normal children:

1. The imbalances in psychotic children are more extreme, fluctuate more quickly, occur across a wider range of situations, and last developmentally longer than in an equivalent population of normal children. (We are in the process of testing this impression empirically.)

2. In schizophrenic children there is often very limited generalization of newly learned schemes from one situation to another. Children may quickly become familiar with the sequences of activities in their treatment center but may never learn other sequences of events. Or, they may acquire conservation with respect to one set of materials but not generalize the scheme to other tasks. While overassimilation in normal children may imply an ever-wider incorporation of events into schemes, in schizophrenic children there may be a more restricted, repetitive assimilation from one occasion to another.

3. In trying to decide what behaviors signal the operation of assimilation or accommodation, we found it necessary to pay attention to a contrast between present and past. Schizophrenic children, it seems to us, very often accommodate to a past event (e.g., they run away in appropriate fear of a stranger) and then overassimilate new events to that response in the present (by running away from everyone). Other examples: a specific word ("gum," "cookie," "milk") may be used for all food items; accidental dropping of a lunch box beside the school gate becomes a ritual which must be repeated every morning.

Static figurative dominance over operative transformations. As described in Chapter 3, the normal symbolic function integrates figurative, static schemas of specific events with operative, transformational general schemes. The figurative function, closely allied with accommodation, includes perception, deferred imitation, and imagery. In normal children, figurative schemas end their domination of operative schemes in Early Concrete operations. In the Genevan research on schizophrenia, there are many examples which indicate that between the ages of nine and fifteen these children still show a dominance of static figurative functioning over operative transformational schemes. The difficulties reported above with object permanence, symbol-referent differentiation, conservation, and perspective taking can all be seen as cases in which static schemas are dominant; children are swayed by what they see right now rather than what they know. To these examples, we may add: a tendency to focus on details; to be distracted; to have difficulty anticipating future events or representing spatial transformations.

Tai at age 9–5 achieved at his age level on verbal IQ tests, but could not anticipate or even copy the water level in a rotating bottle (a Later Concrete achievement in normal children). It was apparent that he also could not imagine the displacement of one block on top of another, or picture the outcome of a 180° rotation of three beads on a wire [correct performance is an Early Concrete achievement]. Tai was also highly inaccurate in copying Bender Gestalt designs, but much better in tasks which did not require the visual representation of spatial transformations and relationships (Schmid-Kitsikis, 1969).

Beyond this general hypothesis of figurative dominance, I would like to suggest the possibility that figurative schemas tend to be primary determinants of symbolic meaning, even when higher-level operational coordinations occur. For example:

A schizophrenic girl experiences the adult asking "Do you want some . . ." with many different kinds of food. She selects a particular representational image of one time when she was asked "Do you want some milk?" This figurative schema is used to refer to the general class food, so that "Do you want some milk" is what she says whenever she is hungry. This is understandable to adults as a general request, but because it is based on a static image, it lacks the true generality of conceptual schemes and is of relatively little use in conceptualizing transformation of food-related objects and events.

Another example: Breslow (personal communication) relates a set of incidents with one eight-year-old boy. A television commercial saturating the air waves at the time advertised the softness of Charmin toilet paper in a series of "playlets" with the concluding refrain, "Please don't squeeze the Charmin." In the day-treatment classroom where Breslow was a once-a-week volunteer, he asked the child to squeeze some clay; the response was, "Please don't squeeze the Charmin." The next week when Breslow was absent from the classroom, the child said to the regular teacher, "Please don't squeeze the Charmin bye-bye" (i.e., Breslow's gone away).

Thus, we as adults can construct general conceptual schemes from the children's language, but they seem to be using figurative schemas as general concepts. And they generalize these concepts on the basis of specific, partial, figurative characteristics, much like Preconceptual children's classification.

Fluctuations in centering. As one would expect from children with figurative dominance and fluctuating uncoordinated centrations, schizophrenic children have a strong tendency to change answers quickly and to give almost simultaneous, inconsistent, or contradictory responses.

> In the familiar conservation of clay task, children will point to the clay ball and then to the sausage, saying, "This one has more *and* this one has more." Sometimes they will attribute different quantities to the same object, "There is more clay in the sausage, there is less clay in it." And often they will demonstrate simultaneous beliefs at different cognitive levels, "There's the same amount, there's less, there's the same." (Schmid-Kitsikis, 1976)

Normal children, especially those in stage transition, change their minds frequently during Piagetian testing. The Genevan investigators seem to be saying that in schizophrenic children these fluctuations occur within the same judgments, rather than varying over the course of an interview. The children do not present their new answers as corrections of previous ones; there is no overt recognition of the fact that conflicting responses have been given.

Avoidance of further disequilibration. I do not know how schizophrenic children experience the above-described chronic disequilibrations and fluctuations. I do know that they tend to be very active in attempting to avoid further disequilibration, especially in the form of surprise. At the lowest developmental level we find the obsessive insistence on sameness noted in autistic children, in which they attempt to avoid changes in the environment. At higher levels, Schmid-Kitsikis and de Ajuriaguerra describe children who transform the reality of tasks in order to avoid conceptual–perceptual conflict. For example, in a conservation of clay task, they transform the unchanged ball into a sausage so that they can compare two identical objects. In a classification task they simplify the problem by rearranging the material to reduce the number of classification criteria. At the highest developmental levels tested by de Ajuriaguerra, et al. there is a strong tendency to avoid uncertainty. They find that even when Schizophrenic children demonstrate beginning Formal operations, they do not accept concepts of chance or probability.

> Thierry, a precocious Formal-operational thirteen-year-old psychotic child, insists that the same color will always turn up in a random series of cards if you have the necessary manual skill to act the same way each time. He is finally led to admit that if you cannot act so skillfully "it will happen differently each time" (p. 340), but he will not guess according to probabilities. Pierre, a precocious ten-year-old at the beginning of Formal operations considers every coin toss to be deducible. He is unable to distinguish a "fixed" toss of a handful of coins (all came out heads) from a "true" toss; he assumes that the fixed toss is due to the tester's skill. (de Ajuriaguerra, et al., p. 340)

Not all of the above examples necessarily demonstrate avoidance of disequilibration as Inhelder and Schmid-Kitsikis claim. Children who physically transform problems to make them simpler, probably know something about what it is they are avoiding. In some schizophrenic children, then, cognitive structures and functions may be working well, but the child may be avoiding the demands of the experiment and possibly attempting to provoke the experimenter. Ultimately, whatever the motivation, continued avoidance of disequilibrating situations almost inevitably results in structural retardation and further functional imbalance.

Structural-functional asynchronies

In the section on structural retardation, I stated that there are consistent tendencies for schizophrenic children to perform at a lower level; but if all of their behaviors revealed a consistently low level of performance, they would probably have been diagnosed as retarded. In discussing functional imbalance, I emphasized inconsistency and fluctuation in assimilative or accommodative approaches to the world. There is, in addition, a characteristic which makes schizophrenic children especially puzzling; their behavior shows a stable but extreme *mixture* of intellectual–emotional–social levels. We cannot simply describe this mix as structural inconsistency or asynchrony, for in these children every time there is a discrepancy between levels, there also seems to be an imbalance between figurative and operative functioning. At the extremes of developmental dysfunction, it becomes clear that functional and structural aspects of development are intimately interrelated.

Logical versus physical concepts. Results reported by Schmid-Kitsikis (1973, 1976) suggest that there are consistent décalages between logical and physical tasks within the stage of Concrete operations. Class inclusion (more flowers than pink flowers) tends to be solved earlier than two-dimensional classification (red or round, circles or squares); and two-dimensional classification seems[5] to be easier than seriation. Children whose judgments are dominated by figurative schemas should have increasing difficulty because the salience of perceptual cues increases from class inclusion to classification to seriation. Similarly, nine-to-fifteen-year-old schizophrenic children tend to achieve class inclusion, but not conservation of liquid or weight. Logical concepts with less emphasis on perceptual characteristics are at a higher structural level than conceptions of physical events. This structural décalage may result from the functional imbalances between figurative schemas and operative schemes.

IQ versus cognitive stage discrepancies. The correspondence between IQ or mental age scores and Piagetian stage levels is never perfect. However, Schmid-Kitsikis implies that in her case studies of children in various diagnostic categories there are very large discrepancies between the two kinds of cognitive level assessments. Schizophrenic children seem to show a much *lower* Piagetian stage level than their scores on at least some WISC IQ subtests would suggest. This finding may help to make sense of a pervasive impression that schizophrenic children are bright "but just don't show it." They seem to have

[5]No data are given for group trends.

acquired some specific skills and information at a precocious or average level, but this information is processed (combined and transformed) by lower-level cognitive structures.

> A twelve year old boy diagnosed as schizophrenic gives the meaning of words on an IQ test at the fifteen-year age level, but his logical thinking is Preoperational—he cannot conserve water, number, and so on. In the IQ test he defines "knife" correctly, but first he falls on the floor in fear. Further testing reveals that he does not separate the word meaning from the potentially harmful effect of the object; it is dangerous even to *say* the word "knife."

His specific verbal definition attained a high score on an IQ subtest, but his Preconceptual operations contributed to a confusion between symbol and object.

Thought disorder and its emotional-social implications

In definitions of adult and child psychosis, a common assumption is that underlying specific symptoms, there is a general condition of "thought disorder." In sometimes circular fashion, this condition is used to explain the presence of bizarre ideas and actions ("Why does she do that?" "She has thought disorder." "How do you know she has thought disorder?" "Look at what she does."). In a less circular approach, traditional IQ tests have been used to define patterns of disordered cognition (e.g., Rapaport, Gill and Schafer, 1968), but the extensive clinical lore surrounding these patterns has been difficult to validate in systematic empirical studies.

From the above list of cognitive difficulties, it seems to me that four are central in providing a Piagetian definition of thought disorder: (1) the static figurative emphasis in the symbolic function used by children to represent external and internal events; (2) the structural asynchronies in the rules by which symbols are transformed and combined to arrive at inferences; (3) the lack of integration between structures, functions, or contents, leading to fragmented, centered, seemingly fragile constructions of the world; and (4) the self-protective avoidance in which schizophrenic children seem to defy the human tendency to seek information and challenge. Functional imbalance, structural asynchrony, integration, and motivation are interrelated characteristics and yet they can vary independently. This means that we should expect to find schizophrenic children at different general developmental levels, with different patterns of skills in different situations. What tends to set schizophrenic children apart is the extent to which the characteristics interact synergistically to produce *severe* disruptions in social and emotional behavior.

It is not possible to conclude that the symptoms of thought disorder are *explained* by cognitive structural and functional categories. But there are enough points of correspondence to indicate that these individual-difference dimensions will be relevant to the description and understanding of childhood schizophrenia. I should point out that most of these Piagetian descriptions have focused entirely on the child and not on his or her social and physical environment. Not until we develop better ways of assessing structural or functional mismatches can we truly claim to be applying Piagetian principles to developmental diagnosis. Then these environmental assessments may be able to help us see how understandable and systematic the puzzling, unpredictable behavior of schizophrenic children can be.

Implications for treatment of schizophrenic children

Once we have created a conceptual system for evaluating the current status of a schizophrenic child, we can begin to plan optimal match/mismatch conditions to facilitate structural progress and functional equilibration. But how do we turn this abstract principle into a concrete reality? I have stated that there is, as yet, no Piagetian therapy for schizophrenic children or for children in any of the other categories of developmental dysfunction. What follows, then, is a set of suggestions for intervention, based on the cognitive developmental diagnostic model. You will find that these suggestions only begin to deal with the complexities of alleviating severe dysfunction. I offer them in hopes of providing some disequilibration to stimulate your further thinking and exploration.

Structural considerations. The most obvious advantage of structural diagnosis is that it helps us to place the child's behavior in the context of a necessary sequence of development. It identifies the next stage or substage just beyond the child's current level, and this suggests tasks or situations which may stimulate the disequilibration necessary to facilitate progress toward that goal.

> People who work with schizophrenic children have special difficulty adjusting their expectations and providing interventions relevant to a variety of (asynchronous) levels. They are often surprised that a ten-year-old, verbally bright child could have difficulty with object permanence. But they are also surprised when they find that the child's temper tantrums and avoidance of change have hidden the fact that he or she is now ready to move on to more challenging, higher-level teaching and learning.

The general principle, more easily said than done, is to provide situations one step above the child's current level *in a given area.* For example, to play peek-a-boo and other games of object-finding with children, no matter how old, at the third Sensorimotor substage in the conception of permanent objects.

More specifically, Piaget's stage-structural formulation helps us discover the interrelated components of many intellectual skills.

> If we want to teach a child to anticipate the consequences of his or her actions, not only do we need to reduce impulsivity. We must also provide experiences in spatial

and temporal seriation, in transformation of imagery, and in general cognitive activities which stimulate the development of groupings underlying more differentiated notions of causality.

Another closely related advantage of structural analysis is that it can help us to identify situations which are formally similar to those which cause the child great difficulty, but which have less emotionally loaded content. It may be easier to learn about perspective in Three Mountains Tasks than in interpersonal situations. Or, about consequences of actions in scientific experiments rather than family interactions. Or, about sequence in strings of beads before understanding and accepting the sequence of daily routines.

We know that for normal children, learning in one situation does not necessarily transfer to a structurally similar task. We also know that schizophrenic children have a great difficulty with scheme generalizations. Therefore we must discover conditions which facilitate the transfer of learning from less-threatening to more-threatening situations.

Functional considerations. In the dimensions of functional imbalance, too, the therapist's dictum to "meet the child where he or she is" must be modified to read "meet the child where he or she almost is." With children who temporarily or permanently emphasize one side of the assimilation-accommodation balance, we must start with that emphasis and move gradually in the opposite direction.

a. Overassimilators. Autistic children can create so much disruption when parents, teachers, and therapists attempt to impose controls, that the adults characteristically back off, leaving the child free to overemphasize assimilation. Play therapy (e.g., Axline, 1969; A. Freud, 1946), with its assimilative emphasis is a good beginning, but very quickly the therapist must begin to shift from low to higher adult controls and to engage in other disequilibrative acts.

In play therapy, children are usually left free to select materials and choose themes to explore; the expectation is that they will project inner conflicts on the objects and situations, experiencing more actively what was experienced passively in real life (Erikson, 1950). External restraints (pressures toward accommodation) are provided only in the form of limits on destruction of materials or on physical aggression toward the therapist. Especially with overassimilative psychotic children, it seems to me that long-term traditional play therapy provides very little disequilibrative stimulation. While it can help the child to build a positive relationship with the therapist, even that has disadvantages if the therapist never makes demands and never deals with the typical crises concerning what happens when pressures to accommodate are instituted in the child's daily life. Early in play therapy, therapists can begin, gradually, to take an active role: directing the children toward certain materials; departing from ritualistic roles in a puppet play to provide unexpected events; introducing issues relevant to the difficulties experienced by children outside the therapy hour, even if the child is unwilling to raise them first.

Another general class of interventions for overassimilators, emphasizes the imitative and copy aspects of accommodation. Games such as "Simon says" require children to imitate the leader's actions. Accommodation can also be encouraged when children attempt to match perceptual figures (put a red circle on top of a printed red circle) or copy others' drawings. In these activities it is helpful to the child if feedback for correct answers can be gained from the materials and not from adult evaluations (e.g., form board puzzles in which pieces do not fit within the frame unless the puzzle is correctly put together).

Although practitioners do not use the word accommodation, behavior modification approaches based on operant conditioning attempt to alter the child's behavior in response to specific stimulation.

> Autistic children have responded well to reinforcement for self care, language and social behaviors (Lovaas, 1976). At first, a specific response criterion is selected and reinforcement is given for responses remotely resembling it. Gradually, rewards are given for responses more closely approximating the criterion (shaping). After some time, reinforcements are given less consistently and may eventually be withdrawn entirely (fading).

b. Overaccommodators. It is more difficult to conceptualize situations which will move the child away from accommodation in the direction of assimilation. As we have seen, some schizophrenic children imitate and copy almost all of the time: they tend to resist opportunities to impose their own structure on events. Imitation games may be the place to start, but variations must soon be introduced which encourage more playful participation. For example, if the adult is involved with the child in acting the part of a TV character, he or she can begin to vary the role in order to stimulate the child to produce new responses. Any interventions which help to create an interpersonal feeling of safety may reduce avoidance and facilitate active, self-directed contact with materials.

The difficult task of "weaning" children away from overaccommodation may require some form of paradoxical prescriptions (Haley, 1976) in which therapists use active controls to provoke children to take control of their own and others' actions.

> I have noticed that schizophrenic children who emphasize imitation of others are very startled when adults imitate them. Sometimes, after a double-take, they continue to respond with imitation. If the adult continues to imitate, an interesting reversal begins to occur. The child's actions are transformed from a passive response to an active stimulus; what the child does begins to shape the adult's behavior. This turns the child into an assimilative structurer, and the adult into an accommodative responder.

My impression is that an overaccommodating child who invariably changes in response to external stimulation has no stable concept of self. One goal of therapy for these children is to divert their attention from the characteristics of physical objects to focus on their own actions. Physical sensorimotor activities (exercises, climbing, carrying, etc.) may be helpful in this regard. The intent is to encourage interiorization, which is an operative, assimilative process, and to discourage the exclusive emphasis on the internalization involved in figurative, accommodative functioning. One environmental way to discourage figurative emphasis is to conduct some activities in spaces with very few visual or auditory distractions.

c. Active disequilibration. Like newborns, psychotic children are unpredictable and often unable to communicate their own needs. As adults, we often have the feeling that their actions, words, and sounds would be meaningful if only we had the key to the code. In order to look after these children and to avoid tantrums, outbursts, and physical aggression, adults become adept at figuring out what the children mean and what they want, anticipating the consequences of most actions. The more skilled adults become in this endeavor, the more peace there is likely to be, but the less opportunity there will be for the child to grapple with the results of disequilibration.

One way of approaching this issue is through the relatively benign (for adults at least) task of helping the child to specify expectations or predictions. We can ask verbal psychotic children in the course of many activities, "What will happen next?" "If I throw the ball, where will it land?" "If I pour the juice how high will it go?" "What activity comes after this one?" "If you hit him what will happen?", We can help nonverbal children to set goals; for example, to set up a bowl before throwing bean bags into it, or to run to a spot where a ball will land. These predictions serve several purposes at once. First, they give the child experience with event sequences. Second, they stimulate the use of transformational images. And third, they get the child actively involved in stating an expectation and then verifying whether the expectation is fulfilled; if the unexpected occurs, then the child's own behavior has created a potentially disequilibrating set of events which may stimulate further exploration.

Integration. How do we bring together the fragmented aspects of the schizophrenic child's intellectual apparatus? The only answer that I have so far is very general: present the child with tasks or situations which emphasize the relation between dimensions. For example, a simple "feely box" can be very useful in exploring the interrelations between vision, touch, language concepts, and imagery.

> Children place one hand inside a box to explore a collection of objects which they can't see. They are asked to (1) select an object that matches one placed in front of them, or (2) name the object on the basis of touch alone. The complexity of the task can be varied by altering the number, complexity, and similarity of the objects placed in the feely box.

Almost all therapies attempt to integrate or reintegrate feeling and thinking. Unfortunately, treatment centers tend to separate the two domains, reserving feelings for "therapy" and intellectual development for "school."[6] As all teachers know, there is no way to compartmentalize these two aspects of children. Therapists must learn how to pay more attention to the development of cognitive skills, and teachers must be given the support and resources to explore the emotional and social issues involved in intellectual development.

The social milieu of treatment. Much of the discussion so far has emphasized treatment approaches in which one adult therapist or teacher works with one psychotic child. In these situations, distractions attributable to other people may be avoided, but there are compelling reasons to consider additional treatment in the context of the peer group and the family. Since these considerations apply to treatment of children in all categories of dysfunction, I will present them at the end of this chapter.

The role of the therapist/change agent. The general task faced by the person working with psychotic children is no different from that faced by parents and teachers of normal children—to provide a setting with optimum levels of disequilibration for each individual child. The primary difference in the realm of developmental dysfunction is the presumption that some major interventions will be necessary in order to "unstick" the child's current retardations, imbalances, and asynchronies, and to facilitate further structural and functional progression.

The therapist/change agent begins as a disequilibration monitor, attempting to make certain that there is neither too much nor too little mismatch between child and environmental context. This requires a careful initial assessment and frequent ongoing assessments of where the child is, and it requires creative resourcefulness to design specific interventions in relation to the needs of the child. Many of the current therapeutic approaches can be useful. Play therapy, behavior modification, individual group and family work—whether in the home, the school, or the treatment institution—may all be relevant to the treatment of some psychotic children in some circumstances. We need to go beyond this already-established array, however, to construct new guidelines for a therapist/change agent who can function as an interactive generator–transformer; this person's main goal is to find ways of starting or restarting, the interactive generator–transformer functioning of the psychotic child.

MENTAL RETARDATION

Like the classification of schizophrenia, the diagnosis of mental retardation encompasses a heterogeneous group of children and adults, with a variety of presumed causes of dysfunction. The central defining characteristic is a

[6]Since very few children identified as psychotic are accepted in public schools, even in special classes, I am referring here to schools within day-treatment or hospital settings.

significantly lowered level of intellectual functioning in comparison with one's peers. While assessment criteria generally include family history, social competence, personality characteristics, language functioning, and ability to learn academic material, the primary emphasis is placed on results from standardized IQ tests. The proportion of the population classified as retarded depends, of course, on the cut-off score. About 2 percent of the population achieve an IQ score of 50 or less (depending on the test), but some school systems consider children with IQ's as high as 80 eligible for special classes for the retarded, this cut off score would include as many as 10 percent of the school population.

Cognitive developmental diagnosis of retardation

A number of investigators have verified the rather obvious expectation that children diagnosed as retarded develop more slowly on Piagetian tests and reach a lower structural ceiling. In addition, the research consistently makes the point that the cognitive structures and sequences found in retarded children and adults are almost identical to those found in children who develop at an average or above average rate.

Woodward (1959) observed and tested 147 severely retarded children from seven to sixteen years of age who had no identifiable sensory or motor disability. All of them failed to pass the two-year-old basal tests on the Terman-Merrill IQ scale. Three different Piagetian measures of the six Sensorimotor substages were obtained in a combination of free play and test situations: means–end problem solving (using strings or sticks to bring an object closer); object permanence (e.g., search for hidden objects); level of hand gestures or manipulation (e.g., primary, secondary, and tertiary circular reactions). There was a remarkable correspondence between Piaget's hypothesized sequence of normal development and the level of task difficulty in this sample of retarded children. Children with abnormal patterns of scores tended to be those who also showed signs of severe emotional disturbance or epilepsy.

Inhelder's (1943, 1966) fine study continues up the developmental scale with children and adults from ten to 36 years of age who were much less retarded than the children in Woodward's sample. There were six physical tasks (conservation of amount, weight, and volume of clay balls and of sugar dissolved in water), and three logical transitivity tasks (variants of the format "given bar A = bar B in weight, and B = C, what about A and C?"). Inhelder found that 90 percent of her subjects could be classified in three recognizable stage levels.

1. Preoperational. All tasks failed. Difficulties were attributable to reasoning rather than memory because subjects could easily recall initial events, even when they did not conserve.
2. Early Concrete operational. Conservation of substance passed with reversible reasoning. A simple version of logical transitivity passed by overt trial and error. Weight and volume conservation not passed; neither were more difficult transitivity problems (e.g., A + B = C + D = ?; or Bar A weighs the same as lead ball B, ball B = Bar C, what about A and C?).

3. Late Concrete operational. Conservation of substance and weight with clay and sugar, and logical tasks also passed. However, there were *no* instances of Formal reasoning. In fact, when formal problems were presented, the children often fell back on Early Concrete strategies, as if they had given up the idea of thinking the problem through to a conclusion.

Thus, development in a retarded population is formally parallel to the normal sequence, but it occurs more slowly, with a ceiling that cuts off before Formal operations. In addition to these findings, Inhelder notes seven important qualitative differences between normal children and retarded children at the same stage levels. First, despite the fact that their answers are very similar (e.g., it's more because it's wider), retarded children are described as less interested and less dynamic in the way they make use of information during the tasks. Second, unlike normal children, they frequently make correct answers on the basis of nondeductive, nonperceptual cues (e.g., if A = B and B = C, then "A = C because it's always supposed to be the same weight.")[7] Third, Inhelder suggests that retarded children may be *less* susceptible than normals to perceptual illusion and the figurative emphasis which produces wrong answers in physical conservation tasks. Fourth, at the upper limits, retarded children maintain previous lower level strategies. Fifth, in retarded populations, development in older subjects seems to be slowing down, while in normal populations there is an acceleration of knowledge growth with increasingly mobile structures. Sixth, the upper levels of retarded structures are described as representing a "false equilibrium."

> In the mentally retarded child . . . access to certain [Concrete operational] structures seems to be an end in itself, without hope of subsequent evolution. Ceiling and closure are terms that suggest themselves, rather than completion or fulfillment. And this closure cannot really be said to lead to a state of equilibrium, since only a passive stability is attained. It does not seem exaggerated to us, therefore, to speak of a false equilibrium when we are talking about states that reach an apparent stability but which are subject to a certain viscosity. (Inhelder 1966, p. 313)

And seventh, in 90 percent of her sample, there seemed to be great homogeneity and consistency in levels of responding across tasks. In the remaining 10 percent of the subjects she found several different kinds of fluctuation.

> A very few subjects consistently improved in responding over the course of the assessment. Inhelder assumed that they were "slow learners" misdiagnosed as retarded. Some subjects exhibited the quick oscillations between levels described above for schizophrenic children. And, especially in severe retardates, some subjects seemed to deteriorate over the course of the task, as if the clinical interview gradually burrowed beneath rote answers at the surface to find the retarded structural core.

[7] I have found many normal young children who do this.

A number of studies lend credence to the claim that retarded children develop more slowly than normal children but that structural stage sequences are similar in the two groups. In five different samples, retarded children identified by IQ test scores showed lower scores but recognizable stage levels in various Piagetian tasks—conservation of weight (Boland, 1973), conservation of number (Woodward, 1961), seriation (Broadley, 1973), class inclusion (Stephens, Menhaney, and McLaughlin, 1972), and moral judgment (Taylor and Achenbach, 1975). In most of these samples, only a small number of children and adolescents gave evidence of Concrete operations; none reached the Formal stage.

Implications for intervention

Because IQ has been interpreted as an inborn, fixed characteristic of an individual, there has been little hope that interventions could alter the child's intellectual level; this belief has often mistakenly led to pessimism that any new skills can be acquired by retarded children and adults. To a large extent, the emphasis in the study of retardation remains where it began, with Binet and Simon's (1905) attempt to *identify* retarded children, to remove them from regular classrooms, and to provide the best possible educational conditions consistent with their low level of intellectual functioning.

And yet, retarded children do learn new skills, and IQ's do change. Follow-up studies reveal that 50 to 80 percent of children in the 50–70 IQ range become at least marginally self-supporting adults, with higher adult level IQ's (Baller, Charles, and Miller, 1967; Kennedy, 1966; Skaarbrevik, 1971). These data can be interpreted two ways. On one hand, a substantial number attain less than marginal adult adjustment, and even the successes tend to be in low-paying jobs with low job stability and status (e.g., Peckham, 1951). On the other, there has indeed been substantial progress by many retarded individuals in the learning of both social and intellectual skills.

Traditionally, three forms of intervention have been available for retarded children—institutionalization, special classes, and psychotherapy. The results for the first two are not encouraging. Children at the lowest end of the IQ continuum may have to be hospitalized because even the most devoted parents cannot look after them as well as their normal siblings. However, there is ample evidence that at higher IQ levels, institutionalization can have a long-term, negative impact on the retarded child (Blatt and Kaplan, 1966). Special classes, in or outside of local public schools, have been a fixture of the educational scene for decades. The rationale is that smaller classes with special teachers are required to provide for special needs. There is no good evidence, however, that special classes are more effective than regular classes in providing a developmental climate for intellectual growth (see Sarason and Doris, 1969). Psychotherapy can be effective in promoting behavioral change, adjustment, and even IQ increases in retarded children (Bialer, 1967), but it is a time-consuming, costly process and is usually recommended only for those retarded children for whom emotional disturbance is also a primary issue.

Two relatively new approaches have been directed toward children in both institutions and special classes. The first, behavior modification, accepts the social system as it is and helps adults to teach retarded children both self-help and academic skills in step-by-step, concrete fashion. The second, advocated by Sarason and his associates (Sarason, et al., 1966; Sarason and Doris, 1969; Sarason, 1974), has focused on providing consultation to families, community) agencies, and schools, to maintain children in their communities and in regular classrooms. The emphasis here is on intervention to *change systems* so that previously excluded "deviants" can now be incorporated. In the process, less isolation and greater stimulation (disequilibration) may be provided for the children and for their parents and teachers as well.

From my limited experience with retarded children, I can only begin to suggest how a Piagetian developmental approach may be relevant for treatment and education. First, in contrast with IQ numbers which do not specify absolute intellectual levels (e.g., both a two-year-old and a twelve-year-old may have an IQ of 60), the use of Piagetian measures helps to locate children's structural levels and to suggest what must come next. Just possibly, this descriptive labeling may reduce the stigma associated with "retarded," taking the focus off speed and placing it on skill.

Second, there have been a few laboratory training studies which suggest that, especially at higher mental age (MA)[8] levels, retarded children and adults can benefit from specific experience with Piaget tasks (e.g., Vitello, 1973). Barnes and McManis (1973) found that two one-hour training sessions produced significant gains in relational thinking in a group of adults at MA levels below five and eight years. However, after one month, higher MA subjects (seven to eight years) maintained their gain, while lower MA (five to six years) adults lost their advantage over nontreated controls. And, Bovet (1976) reports briefly on a pilot study in which ten retarded children between the ages of seven and eleven were given two training sessions per week for an entire academic year. One child with the lowest initial IQ performed at a homogeneous pretest level (failed all tasks) and failed to show any change over the year. Six children in initial tests showed some asynchrony, with at least one skill (logic, spatial relationships, etc.) at a higher level than others; at the end of the year they showed a homogeneous level corresponding to their best performance in the initial tests. Two other children, with only one area impaired at the beginning (language or motor) progressed to an "almost normal level." And one child simply varied the task on which he showed asynchrony. All in all, Bovet concludes, "Well-designed [training] exercises can have a beneficial effect in certain cases of mental retardation."

[8]On an IQ test, the mental age is the score attained by the average child at a given chronological age; for example, the score attained by the average eight-year-old is designated MA = 8.

Third, in schools, the focus on education for retarded individuals has remained on intellectual and vocational skills; yet they experience many serious problems in their social relationships. Perhaps both cognitive and social training in perspective-taking would facilitate day-to-day communication and other aspects of social interaction.

Finally, a theme in Bovat's and many other studies is that more homogeneity of intellectual skill is associated with less change. If this homogeneity implies that there is reduced internal disequilibration (necessary for cognitive growth), it may be that more intense and focused *external* disequilibration is required. Perhaps it is the lack of such disequilibration that leads to the negative effects of many institutions and the lack of positive effects in many special classes. And, perhaps the success of behavior modification and of Sarason's system intervention lies in the provision of dynamic, high impact and responsive environments which promote more optimal disequilibration in retarded children.

ORGANIC DYSFUNCTIONS AND "SPECIFIC LEARNING DISABILITIES"

Children who cannot see or cannot hear—and who therefore have great difficulty with language development—clearly suffer from some form of organic (neurobiological) impairment. For children who show "specific learning disabilities" in a single academic skill (reading, writing, speaking, figural copying, numerical calculation), the etiology is not as clear. Psychological causes have sometimes been proposed, but, even when there are no gross signs of organic damage, "minimal brain dysfunction" is often used to account for the difficulty. Children with sensory impairment and with "specific learning disabilities" share a set of diagnostic characteristics: they are neither retarded nor psychotic; the dysfunction is serious and long-lasting; dysfunction is revealed primarily in perceptual–cognitive symbolic activities, though it has emotional–social ramifications; dysfunction seems to be localized in one or two areas of symbolic function, with other areas at age-appropriate developmental levels. There is an enormous research and theoretical literature on the topic of organic dysfunction in children. Here I will focus on the studies which use a Piagetian approach.

Sensory impairment

Studies of blind children by Hatwell (1966), Gottesman (1971, 1973), and Brekke, Williams, and Tait (1974) indicate that there may be differences in rate of development between young blind and sighted children on visually oriented tasks. However, (1) the differences may disappear with age; (2) the differences depend on the kind of task; (3) the differences may depend on general life circumstances (such as institutionalization vs. living at home—Brekke, Williams, and Tait); and (4) the Piagetian stage sequence is identical in both blind and sighted groups.

Furth (1966) and Youniss (1974) have contributed to our understanding of deafness and language deficiency in cognitive development. They find that younger deaf children show one or two years' retardation in Piagetian stage levels, but older children often catch up, *or* brief training is sufficient to bring their performance to age-appropriate levels. The Piagetian stage sequence is apparently maintained in spite of severe sensory deficit. Since this development occurs in the absence of spoken language, they also conclude that logical development can occur when there is no direct internalization of a societal language. Evidence that language disorders do not interfere with logical development also comes from studies of aphasia and other language difficulties (Tissot, et al., 1963; de Ajuriaguerra, et al., quoted by Schmid-Kitsikis, 1973).

"*Specific learning disabilities.*" About 10 percent of the student population, or more in many schools, have great difficulty learning new skills in one specific academic area—reading, hearing, speaking (no deafness involved), figural copying, and computing. These students have no gross perceptual or motor malfunctions, no obvious thought disorder, and they give every evidence of having adequate skills for the tasks. Sometimes, but not always, this condition is accompanied by what adults call hyperactivity and by social maladjustment or emotional disturbance. The hyperactivity and social–emotional difficulties are presumed to be secondary to the difficulties the child is having in processing or using information.

There is a pervasive tendency to give this combination of symptoms a name—specific learning disability—as if by naming it, we have completed our diagnostic task. As I have argued elsewhere (Cowan, 1970), the learning disability terminology implies that there is some kind of learning sickness or disease located in the child, whether or not the cause is assumed to be organic. Then, in line with the medical model of illness, the child's treatment begins with quarantine or isolation (special classes) in which there are attempts to change the child rather than to reexamine the physical and social system in which the dysfunction originated and was maintained.

Unfortunately, the two major Piagetian studies of specific learning difficulties also focus on the children without describing their learning context. Schmid-Kitsikis (1973) describes seven-to-twelve-year-old children with "dyspraxia." They have no gross physical or perceptual handicap, no psychosis, and no general intellectual retardation. They have no problems with spoken language, but they do have great difficulty with perceptual motor integration. Each child was assessed with three main tasks: class inclusion (colored beads, wooden beads), classification (of geometric shapes), and seriation (of sticks). In both classification and seriation tasks, the child was first asked to observe the materials and to tell how to solve the problem; then the child was asked to manipulate the materials, placing them in piles or arranging the sticks in order. The results were similar in some respects to the profile of schizophrenic children. Class inclusion was achieved fairly easily. Classification was relatively well done when the child observed the objects and named the classes, but placing the objects in piles seemed to cause great confusion. And, insuperable difficulties were experienced with seriation in the object manipulation activity. As in the schizophrenic sample (above), logical tasks were solved more easily than physical tasks, with the difficulty centering on symbolic representation or physical transformations, especially in spatial relationships. Other tasks showed that the children also have great difficulty in using visual schematic models to solve problems or in drawing copies of simple geometric shapes, even though they can recognize and name them. The problem, then, seems to be located in the realm of figurative integration rather than in operative intellectual functioning.

There are two important differences between the children with perceptual–motor integration difficulties and the psychotic children studied by Schmid-Kitsikis. First, unlike the psychotic children, the dyspraxic children *demonstrated* high-level understanding of principles, even when they couldn't apply them. For example, at the beginning of the seriation task, they were able to state that "one must put from smallest to biggest," but when they actually tried it, their responses were random. Thus, figurative representation was more disrupted during sensorimotor activity than during contemplation of objects and future action. Second, while the psychotic children were apparently unaware of contradiction and resisted testing, dyspraxic children were painfully aware of their inadequate answers and highly motivated to compensate for their figurative difficulties. Unfortunately, the compensation often did not work. In most accounts of specific learning disabilities, it is assumed that something is wrong with some aspect of sensory or motor functioning. These studies suggest that at least some children perceive and even represent events accurately (e.g., in contemplating the task). However, they cannot seem to integrate sensory representation with their own motor activities and thus have great difficulty operating on stimulus transformations.

Implications for treatment

Cause and locus of the problem. A great deal of time has been wasted in trying to decide whether specific learning disabilities have psychological–emotional origins or are traceable to dysfunction within the brain or central nervous system. Unless the impairment obviously disrupts one area of sensory or motor function (blindness, cerebral palsy), diagnosis is a tricky business at best. In most cases, there is no hard neurological evidence at all; neurologists turn to psychologists to provide evidence of "minimal brain damage." The circular explanation is perpetuated. (What causes the child's learning disability?

Some form of minimal brain dysfunction. How do you know there is minimal brain dysfunction? Look at the learning disability.)

If the cause of the learning difficulty is indeed organic, it does not follow that neurobiological treatments are the only ones that will work. What may amount to a national scandal in this country has occurred in the public schools, where thousands of "hyperactive" children with specific learning problems have been administered high doses of ritalin: in children, this amphetamine has the paradoxical effect of slowing the children down, but there is no consistent evidence of accompanying gains in cognitive skill (Schrag and Divoky, 1975). Even if the condition has an organic basis, providing different stimulus environments and different materials, making different demands, emphasizing different sensory modalities may go a long way toward improving the child's level of performance. And, if we assume that the causes are psychological, the same programs developed for so-called brain-injured children, with structured step-by-step interventions, may be equally effective in remedying long-term specific problems in learning. We do not need to assume that etiology and treatment are necessarily tied together.

Even with children who have major sensory impairment, it will be profitable to locate learning problems, not in the child, but in the child-environment mismatch. Instead of *naming* the difficulty (e.g., blindness, dyslexia), we must begin to describe tasks and situations which, in interaction with child characteristics, will provide a differentiated picture of learning strengths and weaknesses. Interventions can then be designed to compensate for the weaknesses and capitalize on the strengths.

Attentional problems. Two of the most common complaints about children with presumed organic dysfunctions are that they are hyperactive and that they do not pay attention to the learning task for very long. The descriptions above suggest that the children *do* pay attention—that in fact they are so busy paying attention to so many things, they become distracted from the tasks set by parents or teachers. While they are not as overaccommodative and centered as schizophrenic children to a point where they lose themselves and merge with a conceptually fragmented environment, their problems certainly seem to be located on the overaccommodative side of the equiliibration balance—they accommodate too quickly to environmental changes in stimulation.

One remedy is recommended by almost all writers in the area of organic dysfunction: reduce distractibility by reducing the amount and complexity of stimulation in the learning environment. Most elementary classrooms these days have walls covered with brightly colored pictures and samples of the children's work. Attractive to adult eyes, these visually busy rooms provide endless distractions for children with visual centering problems. Similarly, noises which are filtered out by most adults and children can dominate the field of a child with difficulties in the symbolic representation of sound. While special classrooms may occasionally be necessary to provide controlled environments, some teachers reduce stimulus impact by providing screened-off "booths" in which children can work for short periods of time. These booths may be more helpful for children with visual problems than for those with difficulties in sound or motor processing.

The learning difficulties experienced by children with attentional problems dramatically illustrate the general thesis that no single learning environment is right for all children all of the time. The increasing number of "open classrooms" may provide much relief for a self-motivated, self-stimulated, self-directed child. But the lack of structure and the increase in visual and noise disorganization may almost literally drive an already hyperactive distractible child "up the wall."

Training in the dysfunctional modality. A number of programs have been developed to provide training or retraining of the impaired sensory or motor system. Clarizio and McCoy (1976) list some of the major ones:

1. Motor development (Barsch, 1967; Kephart, 1971)
2. Perceptual training (Frostig, Lefever, and Whittlesey, 1961; Wepman, 1960; Getman, Kane, Halgren, and McKee, 1968)
3. Language (Dunn and Smith, 1966; Minskoff, Wiseman, and Minskoff, 1972)
4. Reading (Bond and Tinker, 1973; Harris, 1970)
5. More general surveys (Hewett and Furness, 1974; Kephart, 1971)

These approaches have in common attempts to remedy the deficit by: careful developmental diagnosis; provision of a sequence of tasks beginning at the appropriate level; partition of difficult tasks into smaller parts; extensive drill, but in short drill periods. They tend to operate on the assumption that the disorder will become less emotional if the learning environment is more sympathetic and individually tailored, and especially if the child experiences new successes in learning.

Shifting to other symbolic modalities. The programs listed above also attempt to work around learning deficits by providing materials which take advantage of the child's strengths.

> Children with visual difficulties in reading can be helped to learn letters or words by associating visual and sound cues with kinesthetic stimulation. For example, Montessori (1964) alphabet materials provide large letters made of distinctive materials; letters can be seen, touched, and traced while they are being sounded.

Schmid-Kitsikis' research suggests that in the area of specific learning problems we are not simply dealing with sensory or motor deficits. Rather, the child-focused part of the problem lies in the integration of the symbolic function—the way in which figurative aspects are combined with each other and coordinated with the operative aspects of the symbol. While every effort should be made to provide experiences which will reduce specific symbolic dysfunction, we must also consider the possibility of accepting and encouraging intellectual development in those symbolic modes which are working well.

> Children who have difficulties in reading, for whatever reason, are doubly handicapped in school. Not only do they receive low grades in reading, but since most of the curriculum in higher grades is based on information from books, they are also restricted in other areas. And they do not receive credit for what may be high-level operational thinking and learning in nonvisual modalities.

I am suggesting then, that for some children with visual–symbolic problems, we provide more experience in sound and kinesthetic learning. And most important, these children should *not* be required to demonstrate their knowledge in traditional-format exams which require reading of questions and written answers. Tape-recorded formats or other assessment procedures can be devised. This suggestion raises two issues: first, the issue of whether such a program will, in fact, provide for greater (higher and wider) intellectual growth; second, the issue of whether the de-emphasis on reading is acceptable on value grounds. Reading is important in school, not only because other aspects of the curriculum depend on it; it is also a valuable activity in its own right. Working with children who have specific learning disabilities reminds us that in our emphasis on reading skills, we may have neglected skills in other modalities which are essential to the development of symbolic thought.

COGNITIVE FACTORS IN INTERNALIZING–EXTERNALIZING DISTURBANCES

The proportion of a childhood population with psychotic, retarded, or presumed organic dysfunction varies from about 1 to 10 percent, depending on the category and inclusiveness of the diagnostic criteria. In contrast with these three categories is a much larger group of children, up to 40 percent or 50 percent of the population, whom some diagnosticians would label as emotionally disturbed. These children display a variety of symptoms, traits, and behaviors, singly or in combination, such as generalized anxiety, specific phobias, obsessive compulsive rituals, depression, hypochondria, physical symptoms, extreme dependence or independence, drug abuse, aggression, violations of the law. In traditional diagnostic practice, these symptoms are grouped in three general categories—neurosis, personality disorders, and character disorders (*DSM–II*, 1968). Achenbach (1966), however, has identified one bipolar dimension describing two types of children in treatment: Internalizers—who show anxiety, depression, obsessive–compulsive rituals or somatic (bodily) complaints—and Externalizers—who show aggressive or delinquent behavior. The bipolar factor was based on a 91-item symptom checklist applied to 300 boys and

300 girls, all clinic patients with no signs of organic problems. The study has since been replicated in other populations and settings (Achenbach and Lewis, 1971; Shechtman, 1970). To my knowledge, there are no Piaget-oriented studies of children that Achenbach would describe as Internalizers, and only a few concerned with the children he would call Externalizers. On the basis of these studies and other data, I will present some speculations concerning the role of cognitive developmental variables in the diagnosis and treatment of emotional disturbance.

Characteristics of Internalizers

Sigmund and Anna Freud developed and extended psychoanalytic theory with a primary focus on neurosis—a condition in which severe anxiety is described as creating structural conflicts (id vs. ego and superego), stage fixations and regressions (oral, anal, etc.), and conflicts between conscious and unconscious aspects of personality. These conflicts are expressed in the form of neurotic symptoms which are usually displayed in an inward-turning, inhibited withdrawal from engagement with the physical and social world; sometimes, however, the conflicts can be "acted out" (externalized). In a state of neurosis there is a relative absence of pleasure and a large measure of self-inflicted psychological pain. The primary treatment vehicle for children suffering from neurosis is play therapy—the child's equivalent of adult free association (A. Freud, 1946)—which allows the child to project internal conflicts onto the play materials, so that the therapist can help the child to "make the unconscious conscious."

Just as Piaget overemphasizes cognition at the expense of feeling and motivation, so the Freuds tend to overemphasize feeling and motivation at the expense of cognition. Bruner (1968) cites an example to show how a child's *interpretation* of events plays a large role in the creation of what may be called neurotic anxiety in a learning task.

> A bright boy of about eight was having great difficulty learning to divide numbers. Bruner's exploration determined that this child tended to restrict his classification of the world into potentially helpful and potentially harmful situations. Dividing numbers had been taught first by cutting paper "pies" into pieces. Cutting things up was considered potentially harmful. Assuming that cutting numbers was also potentially harmful, this child who did well in other school subjects, avoided the task. The presence of what may be labeled transductive reasoning in an otherwise Formal Concrete operational child indicates that strong emotional factors may combine with structural asynchronies to produce marked individual differences in the child's tendency to approach or avoid specific events.

Another example illustrates the central role of cognitive level in determining the child's feelings about a particularly traumatic event.

A five-year-old boy accidentally shot and killed a young friend while playing with a loaded gun. Several weeks later, taken by his parents to the grave of the dead child, he became very upset and began to have nightmares, which had not occurred immediately after the death. The parents and the therapist to whom the family was referred assumed that the boy was overcome with guilt. As a supervisor of the therapist, I raised the issue of how the boy understood death. In subsequent play and talk sessions it turned out that the boy believed that death, like sleep, was reversible, and that justice involved eye-for-an-eye retribution. When he went to the grave that day, he had expected the dead child to be waiting for him with a loaded gun. His dominant emotion was fear, not guilt. It was important that his treatment be directed toward an understanding of general concepts of life and death, as well as toward feelings about specific events.

Avoidance of learning is not a specific symptom discussed by Achenbach in his bipolar factor, but it fits within the general category of Internalizing disturbances. While the psychoanalytic approach looks to the unconscious motivation involved in such avoidance, I have found that there are many conscious reasons why children avoid learning or resist revealing what they have actually learned. These reasons again emphasize the cognitive–interpretational factors involved in emotional reactions to life situations.

In informal interviews with elementary school children identified by their teachers as underachievers (Cowan, 1970), I was surprised by the number of students who described active decisions to disengage from the learning process and who were very clear about their motivations. Some children wanted to win a battle with parents or teachers; since they had absolute control over nonlearning, it was a battle that they could win. Some wanted to avoid failure and so didn't want to risk trying (see also Horner 1972, for studies of fear of success in college women). A few children actively avoided learning because they actively rejected the adult models of what they might be like when they grew up. Other children wanted to avoid the jeers directed at the "class brain." Still others had a "Peter Pan" syndrome: with increased learning comes increased responsibilities and expectations; this cycle can be avoided by not learning or by deliberately giving wrong answers on tests.

Avoidance is a general theme in the maintenance of Internalizing disturbances. Children with phobias actively avoid the feared situation (school, high buildings) and never test the reality of their fears. Depressed people feel helpless and avoid taking the kind of actions on their own behalf which can alleviate depression. Physical symptoms may help people to avoid the experience of psychological conflicts. In each of these examples, a person's conscious or unconscious interpretations of the world are not subjected to the potential disequilibrations of experience, and so, in circular fashion, the interpretations and the feelings continue. The interactive generator, with its potential for searching for new levels of equilibration, is not given a chance to function.

Characteristics of Externalizers

Clinic children categorized as Externalizers on Achenbach's bipolar factor were compared with Internalizers; in test situations they were found to be more impulsive and less able to delay gratifications (Weintraub, 1968, cited in Achenbach, 1974). Externalizing boys were also rated by a psychiatrist as more impulsive and more aggressive (Achenbach and Lewis, 1971), tending to act quickly and without much forethought. In different subject populations, studies of delinquent preadolescents and adolescents find cognitive parallels to these emotional characteristics. Delinquents tend to be less future-oriented, have difficulty coordinating points of view (Chandler, 1973), and show less differentiated moral judgments (Kohlberg, 1964; Ruma and Mosher, 1967). There may be, then, a consistent pattern of cognitive difficulties operating in concert with an inability or unwillingness to exert internal controls on needs or wishes of the moment.

Of course, aggression appears very often without violations of the law. It tends to be regarded by parents and teachers as much more of a problem than Internalizing disturbances, and it may be much more difficult to treat with the traditional child-guidance play-therapy model of intervention. The aggressive child is often described as "out-of-control," as if the problem involves an inability to accommodate. More accurately, I think, these children should be described as highly accommodative in the sense that their behavior, like that of the delinquents above, is under control of present physical stimulation rather than verbal–symbolic re-presentation of past or future rules and demands.

Treatment for Internalizers and Externalizers

Play therapy and its limitations for Internalizers. A playroom with a few toys, art materials, dolls, and a sandbox has much to recommend it for the individual treatment of Internalizing children. When these children are young, they are not likely to sit down with adults and discuss their conflicts; without much introspection, they may not even be aware of the conflicts, though they may be aware of unhappiness or discomfort. Especially for the inhibited, somewhat withdrawn or avoidant Internalizing child who does not openly express thoughts and feelings, the playroom can be an enticing environment. Relatively unstructured, it places few demands on the child. It allows for expression of ideas and feelings. It fosters activity, not just talk. The activities here are a spontaneous and natural part of the child's life, used for amusement, for problem solving, and for communication.

In Piaget's analysis, play is more than an activity with expressive, problem-solving, and communication value. Beyond its role in symbolic exchange, play has an even more important role in the child's construction of meaningful representational symbols. Play therapy then can provide an important setting for cognitive intellectual growth. Assuming an intimate tie between cognitive and affective symbolic development, the therapist can be looking both ways. Cognitive changes in scheme organization (e.g., conceptions of death) may facilitate changes in feelings. And changes in feelings, especially if they reduce the tendency to avoid, can open up new areas to disequilibration and stimulate developmental progress.

But before these wonders can occur, it is necessary to take a closer look at play therapy. It is important to remember that symbolic play is primarily an assimilative activity, although it does include many deferred imitations. Therefore, just as in play therapy with schizophrenic children, treatment for Internalizing children must provide opportunity for accommodation and disequilibration, to insure that they will be able to use the play therapy experience for growth.

> A common problem, especially early in therapy, is that the child knowingly or unknowingly stays away from themes which the therapist knows (from parents and teachers) are involved in real-life difficulties. Direct questions may be answered with a shrug or with elaborate attention to the wheels on a truck. One alternative is a set of meetings with the child and the family or school personnel so that the issues can be raised in a constructive but direct way. Another alternative, not mutually exclusive, is for the therapist to begin to play a more active role in gently but firmly creating some disequilibration during the play session. Instead of asking questions, the therapist can make statements, introducing speculations about how a child in the patient's situation might be thinking or feeling. Adults are usually reluctant to do this for fear of imposing their views on the child, but I have found that if the adult is very far off the mark, the child will not hesitate to say so or to indicate his or her disagreement through play. Other disequilibrating activities include the therapist's choosing specific materials rather than letting the child always having free choice, or the therapist in puppet play deliberately departing from the role which the child expects, and so on.

When I talk to clinical psychology students about the introduction of disequilibration in play therapy, they resist because they are reluctant to frustrate the child who generally has a difficult enough life as it is. In my view, the *goal* is not frustration, though sometimes frustrations do occur. The goal is to provide an experience for children which will lead them to reorganize their patterns of interactions with the world. In the process, the child and the play therapist literally develop a new language and symbol system together. The hope is that this new language and the structure which supports it will be useful to the children in their struggles with both assimilative and accommodative demands and opportunities in daily life.

Cognitive and behavioral treatments for Externalizers. If delinquents are more egocentric and lower in moral judgment than their age peers, will treatments designed to raise cognitive level have any effect on the antisocial behavior? A study by Chandler (1973) indicates that training delinquents in role-taking with videotape feedback may be associated with a lowered rate of repeat offenses over a period of 18 months. It will, of course, take many more studies over longer periods of time to isolate role-taking as a causal variable. But it makes sense that increases in ability to take another's point of view will facilitate more differentiated understanding and help to increase participation in more socially acceptable interactions, although it would also increase the ability to avoid getting caught.

In a laboratory study, Prentice (1972) demonstrated that it was possible to raise the moral judgment level of delinquents, but it was not clear that this had any effect on their antisocial behavior. Kohlberg has publicly described pilot work with prisoners; his assumption is that an improvement in ability to make better moral judgments must be accompanied by changes in the whole social system of the prison before it would be expected to have an impact on moral behavior. I believe that at this time in our history, there are no grounds for expecting that a rise in moral judgment level will *inevitably* dissuade individuals from breaking laws; I do believe, however, that efforts toward cognitive and moral differentiation as part of a general societal intervention will *tend* to reduce the incidence of delinquency and other antisocial behavior.

Behavior modification has been selected as a treatment for aggressive children in both family and classroom settings (e.g., Patterson, 1971). The general strategy is to provide rewards for prosocial behavior and to arrange conditions as much as possible so that rewards for antisocial behavior are not provided. In my experience, these procedures can be effective from the point of view of both adult and child. The adult becomes able to impose reasonable limits on children with some degree of confidence. Once this occurs there is rarely a tendency for the adult to use the techniques as a weapon with the goal of total behavioral control. Both adults and children can then begin to relax.

But, just as play therapy tends to overemphasize assimilation, so behavior therapy tends to overemphasize accommodation in treatment. The goal is not only to bring some behavior under environmental control, but also to help the child establish a more assimilative stance in which he or she can choose to *resist* present environmental changes and to focus on past principles or future goals. Thus, an assimilative emphasis in the treatment of Externalizers must be provided. The child needs the active role of making choices—of really knowing what he or she wants—in order to resist temporary distractions. He or she can benefit from assimilative opportunities to grow in skills which will have an impact on the world (change it) without extremes of physical aggression or delinquency.

GENERAL PRINCIPLES OF DEVELOPMENTAL DYSFUNCTION AND INTERVENTION

From the above discussions of psychosis, retardation, presumed organic dysfunction and internalizing–externalizing disturbance, I have extracted ten general principles; each is considered necessary but not sufficient for an understanding of diagnosis and treatment. Taken together, they are offered as a beginning Piagetian model of developmental dysfunction and intervention.

1. Search for the logic of the child's illogic.

In a children's psychiatric hospital, a twelve-year-old girl diagnosed as schizophrenic was working on a two-headed clay figure; she had just finished painting one head green and the other head red. I asked her what she was making and she replied, *It's my parents. They're traffic lights. One always says "go, go, go," and the other says "stop, stop, stop."*

At another time, I tested a boy of six who could do complicated multiplication problems in his head, but when asked, "What's 2 + 3?" counted on his fingers. I asked him why he did this—*Well, your brain is made up of cells, right?* —Right. —*And cells die, right?* —Right —*For hard problems I use my brain, but for easy problems I can save the cells by counting on my fingers.*

A cognitive developmental point of view assumes that reality is always a transformation—a construction shaped in part by the observer—not merely a copy of external events. In searching for the logic of the child's illogic, the diagnostician arrives at his or her construction of the child's construction of the world.

2. Focus on structure and function.

In the study of normal development, the Piagetian theorist and researcher looks for structural and functional rules which make sense of the child's thoughts, feelings, and behavior. This remains as the task of the diagnostician in the study of developmental disturbance.

3. Describe the child's status on normal individual difference dimensions.

In an assessment of troubled or troubling children, we must begin with a description of the child's status on the individual difference dimensions of structure and function found in normal development. If we ask ourselves, "At what developmental level, in what context would we normally expect this behavior to occur?" the emphasis shifts from a labeling of pathology to a detailed account of the developmental structures and functions actually in use. We begin to know more about how far the child has come and what the next step is likely to be or about the current functional imbalance; then we are in a position to decide in what direction we should be heading to help the child reach equilibration.

As a working hypothesis, I propose that every individual difference in behavior structure and function—no matter how inappropriate it seems for a given child—is normal within some developmental context. Understanding this context (e.g., Sensorimotor function in a twelve-year-old) helps us to know at which level to intervene when the behavior is no longer age-appropriate or adaptive.

4. Dysfunction tends to be associated with long-term individual difference extremes.

Children are more likely to be referred for treatment when they show extremes of structural retardation or acceleration, functional imbalance, or structural–functional asynchrony. All people vary along these dimensions. I am assuming that as the variations approach the extremes, children are more likely to feel troubled, to be diagnosed as disturbed, and to need special interventions to help them progress developmentally.

5. Dysfunction occurs in departures from optimal person–environment match/mismatch.

While the above examples focus on individual differences in characteristics of children, it is ultimately the match/mismatch between these characteristics and external factors which determines the diagnosis of dysfunction. We must consider two kinds of match or mismatch: between structures or functions of the child and situational demands; and between the child's behavior and what is valued in the peer group, family, school, and community. It is not that the *child* is dysfunctional, but rather that his or her pattern is dysfunctional with reference to a particular set of demands or expectations and values. Redefining the locus of the problem has an extremely important consequence for our conceptions of abnormality, psychopathology, developmental disturbance, and so on. We cannot analogize psychological problems in development to medical diseases, as if children carry the problems with them from one situation to another; treatment is not to be conceptualized as a procedure designed to produce changes only within the child. Instead, in planning interventions, we must always consider the possibility that changes in the child's physical or social environment will be necessary; such changes in the environment contribute to that optimal level of mismatch which facilitates developmental change in the child.

I must emphasize the point that mismatch *per se* is not to be equated with dysfunction. Children who are different from their peers, who do not conform to prevailing demands and values, are not automatically to be regarded as in need of therapy or remedial education. Difference and mismatch bring with them the potential for disequilibration, and disequilibration is absolutely necessary for growth. It is only when match/mismatch departs from an as-yet-unspecified optimal level, that the tendency toward dysfunction increases.

6. Problems are inevitable and necessary in development.

Since mismatch and the accompanying disequilibration are both inevitable and necessary in development, it follows that conflicts, tensions, and problems are also inevitable and necessary as children grow up. In the cognitive developmental model, the optimal internal and interpersonal condition for growth is not a problem-free absence of tension. Success *and* failure, problem solutions *and* problem creations, satisfaction *and* frustration are all part of the normal course of development. Problems are not invariably reduced by developmental advances. With each new stage, there are new mismatches, new disequilibrations, and new problems to be faced.

I am not suggesting here that adults should rejoice when child problems arise, or that they should sit back and ignore them. To promote future development and to preserve the adult's sanity, interventions are often necessary. But if adults consider the possibility that some problems, struggles, and conflicts occur in the service of growth, attempts at intervention will not be made prematurely and adults may be able to be more supportive of the child's own strategies for coping with disequilibration.

Unfortunately, there are no precise guidelines for teachers and parents that will help to determine when and when not to intervene. Generally, the severe dysfunctions which require special education and psychological therapies occur for a very long time before formal assessment and planned treatment are sought. The approach I am presenting here must begin earlier in the process, when there is time for informal but careful assessment of the child in his or her environments. If the child appears to be actively involved in coping with disequilibration, there will be time to determine whether the activities are leading in the direction of adaptation. If not, we can begin with some modest plan for altering, but not ending, discrepancies between child characteristics and environmental demands.

7. Theories of intervention tend to correspond with theories of developmental change.

The multitude of specific alternatives for treatment of all categories of child may be reduced to three general types, similar to the three developmental models described in Chapter 3: the clean slate; the flowering seed; and the interactive generator–transformer. As I have indicated, these models represent differences in emphasis rather than mutually exclusive alternatives.

Clean slate. Theorists in this category generally expect to find the sources of developmental dysfunction in external events—past and present environmental stimuli, rewards, social modelling, and so on. Almost invariably, they recommend some form of behavioral treatment, in which alterations in the external stimulus are created to produce alterations in the response (Bandura, 1969b; Lovaas, 1976; Patterson, 1971). Especially in child treatment, the goal of therapy is generally conceptualized as an accommodative change in the child produced by changes in the physical and social environment.[9]

Flowering seed. There are various versions of the flowering seed model, but each focuses on dysfunction as an internal disruption. Psychoanalytic theories examine the conflict among various structural or dynamic aspects of the personality (e.g., id, ego, superego). Treatment is aimed at encouraging the internal reorganization necessary for the elimination of symptoms and the freeing of energy for progress toward higher developmental levels (A. Freud, 1965; Klein, 1952). Humanistic psychologists (e.g., Rogers, 1961) assume that dysfunction results from a blockage of one's inborn tendency to grow. Like a gardener, the therapist provides the water, light, and soil that allow the plant to realize its initial potential (Axline, 1969).

In both psychoanalytic and Rogerian treatment of children the primary therapeutic approach is play therapy.[10] The pairing of a minimally directive therapist with an active, assimilative child follows logically from the flowering-seed emphasis on internal origins of dysfunction and on internal factors in developmental change.

Interactive generator–transformer. In this view, external events are transformed by inner structures to produce various states of adaptation and dysfunction. The analysis goes beyond the simple assertion that both internal ("nature") and external ("nurture") factors are important, to the hypothesis that different factors may have different weights in different cases. For example, rather than searching for organic *or* genetic *or* familial factors as *the* primary causes of schizophrenia, investigators in the cognitive developmental tradition would assume that many combinations of factors could produce a given pattern of symptoms.

There is no existing "school" of cognitive developmental therapy in the same sense that internal and external approaches have stimulated well-defined treatments. It is clear, though, that a generator–transformer model would have two characteristics. First, treatment would be designed to correspond, not with past etiology, but with an assessment of the present developmental characteristics of the child and his or her environment. Second, the goal of therapy would be to promote optimal mismatch by focusing on the child, the environment, or both. Guidelines for achieving this optimal mismatch can be found in the training studies discussed in Chapter 12.

[9]Current versions of behavioral modification theory pay more attention to the patient's activity in changing his or her own behavior (Lazarus, 1977), but the general model still focuses on the relation between external stimulus and internal response.

[10]Parents (usually mothers) are usually seen separately, often by a different therapist.

8. The family context in etiology diagnosis and treatment must be reconceptualized

I realize that in this book, as in Piaget's own accounts, parents are usually treated as voices in the wings, rarely as characters with important roles in the child's cognitive, social, and emotional life. In this section, I will briefly consider the family at center stage.

Etiology. Studies of normal development tend to focus on the impact of parents on children rather than assessing the mutual interaction between the two generations. Exclusive credit for well-functioning children, and exclusive blame for childhood problems tend to rest squarely and somewhat heavily on parental shoulders. In addition, almost all of the parent–child research relates *maternal* characteristics to child outcome. (For a recent review see Martin, 1975.) A few studies do indicate that fathers' characteristics are important, but only a handful consider the possibility that it is the joint pattern formed by parents' interactions with one another and with the children that should have the greatest impact on the cognitive, emotional, and social adaptation of all the family members (e.g., Cowan, Cowan, Coie, and Coie, 1978).

While true interaction approaches are rare in the study of normal development, an interactional systems approach *has* emerged in the study and treatment of family dysfunction (Satir, 1964; Laing, 1971; Minuchin, 1974; Watzlawick, et al., 1967; Wynne and Singer, 1963). These theorists, therapists, and researchers have discovered the important role of the family communication system in defining symbolic meaning and shaping what individual members accept as reality. Unfortunately, their descriptions of family systems provide little information about ways in which adaptive and dysfunctional systems change over time, and very little consideration is given to the possibility that the developmental status of all the participants may influence the structure and function of family communication. For example, the system formed by the parents in their late twenties conversing with their Preconceptual two-year-old, will be quite different from that formed by those same parents in their forties, facing a mid-adolescent Formal operational child and a midlife crisis simultaneously.

Thus, in family theories so far, developmentalists tend to ignore interaction models of causation, while interaction theorists give short shrift to developmental principles which influence the degree of adaptation and dysfunction in the system and in the individual family members. Schematically we must work toward conceptualizing some kind of two-dimensional model of family development, to examine how the status of each family member affects the communication system and vice versa, in a given period of time.

Diagnosis. The family provides one of the most important environmental contexts for assessing dysfunction in a given child.

> A very passive, quiet child in an active, noisy family may be regarded as an oddity, just as a noisy child in a temperamentally quiet family may be labeled as a problem. In a very bright family, one child of average IQ may suffer by comparison. Or, there may be a mismatch of patterns. A child who emphasizes visual symbols, focusing on how things look, may appear strange to a highly verbal–conceptual family where words and ideas are the currency of intellectual and emotional exchange.

What family members usually do, and what they believe *ought* to be done, provide normative standards by which individual members can be assessed. This standard can be used in evaluating which individual differences are to be considered extreme, and which of the extremes are likely to be dysfunctional.

Change and treatment. By virtue of physical proximity, emotional salience and continuity over time, the family is one of the most comprehensive environments for the cognitive, affective, and social learning of each of its members. The family environment has both functional and structural implications for individual development. While social factors and personal relationships are an important part of this environment, the family also plays a key role in arranging the physical characteristics of the home as well (space, organization, materials, etc.). Each member, as a disequilibrator, affects others' functional balance or imbalance. Family conditions, then, contribute to individual differences in the rate, synchrony, and direction of structural development of its members.

In the literature on treatment of childhood dysfunction, almost everyone agrees that the therapist should see the child's parents. But there is no consensus about whether it is best to see family members separately (the child guidance model) or together (conjoint approach). The cognitive developmental model is probably closer to the systems position of the conjoint family therapists. However, if the family is truly an interactive system, then changes at any place (in any individual) may affect all the others. A multiple treatment approach to whole systems and to subsystems, then, is often most desirable, especially if the problem occurs in a family which actively organizes to maintain stability and to ward off disequilibrating events.

9. The role of the school in etiology, diagnosis, and intervention must also be reconceptualized

The themes raised in discussing the role of the family in etiology, diagnosis and treatment may be applied with minor variations to the school. Teachers sometimes say, "What can I do when the child comes from a home like that?" I believe strongly that the home contributes in important ways to children's strengths and weaknesses, but I have also indicated that there is no necessary relation between etiology and treatment. The child is in the classroom for as much as 25 hours per week, so there is time *and responsibility* for diagnosis and intervention within the school setting.

Diagnosis and intervention. The mismatch conception of diagnosis can be applied in both general and specific ways to children in classrooms. The general approach is based on the truism that children identified as learning or emotional problems in one classroom may not be so identified in another. This fact has often been used as evidence of teacher intolerance for certain kinds of behavior. However, we know that classroom environments differ markedly and it may be that different educational structures will provide more appropriate learning environments for different children.

In the field of education, the polemic surrounding competing educational questions suggests that there must be one correct answer: open classrooms, traditional 3 R's, programmed learning, and other solutions are presented as if we should reject one existing mold and substitute a new, equally monolithic classroom organization. However, if there is a range of structural and functional differences between and within children, then different classrooms with different formats must be an integral feature of each school. This variety might help to reduce substantially the number of children referred for therapy because they do not fit the existing classroom environment. And it may help to allow teachers to work in environments more suited to their particular learning and teaching styles.

I want to make clear that I am not recommending that teachers become diagnosticians and therapists for children with developmental dysfunction *in addition* to their already complex roles. Rather, I have been suggesting throughout this book that a general reconceptualization of the teacher's role is necessary and that developmental diagnosis and planning is essential for all children in the classroom. Since time and energy are finite and classrooms tend to be large (25–45), the teacher can only accomplish these tasks in a classroom where he or she is not the sole dispenser of information and discipline. In such a classroom, individual diagnostic work with 30 children for 20 minutes each, early in the year would take only ten hours of classroom time; during this time, most other children could be working on their own, or with teachers' aides, or with older children in the school.

But what about disturbed children who cannot work on their own? I have two, admittedly general, answers. First, a restructuring of the curriculum and classroom using principles of optimal mismatch could help to reduce the number of children now referred for special education because they just don't fit in. Second, there would have to be, in every school, some classrooms or spaces with more structure and more staff, so that for at least part of the day, specific children can receive education matched to their structural capabilities and functional styles.

Finally, I also wish to make it clear that the teacher alone is not responsible for making the changes required in individual classrooms. School principals, parents, and elected school board officials are all part of the system and must provide some of the support necessary to reconceptualize the teaching role and the educational environment. However, I question the individual educator who blames the system for his or her own inaction. "They won't let me do it," teachers often say.

In my experience consulting in schools, many well-planned requests for educational change are supported, or at least, not resisted. The role of all individuals in the educational system, then, must be double-edged—one edge directed toward disequilibration of children and other toward disequilibration of existing practices and patterns in the system. It is important to see that in both cases, only those actions creating optimal mismatch are likely to have a chance of success.

10. The study of developmental dysfunction has implications for understanding normal development.

The study of children diagnosed as dysfunctional or disturbed helps to expand our view of the normally developing child and to raise some questions about general developmental principles. First, it helps to expand our knowledge of individual differences in both structural and functional development. Second, a study of developmental dysfunction reinforces the general conclusion that cognitive, social, and emotional factors in development are interrelated. It is essential in the education of all children to pay more attention to bringing these aspects together. Third, work with dysfunctional children raises additional questions about whether progressive development is inevitable and challenges Piagetians to provide a more differentiated model of cross-situational consistencies and inconsistencies. And finally, a consideration of children at the extremes makes even more graphic the general principle that it is necessary for adults to understand the world as children do.

This completes the presentation of Piaget's psychological theory of development, with extensions and speculations by other researchers and theorists. Now, in a brief Part IV, we will see that Piaget's work is meant to provide a set of answers to some long-standing philosophical questions.

PART IV

Piaget's Theory of Knowledge

CHAPTER 14

Genetic Epistemology

The psychological study of the child has always been, for Piaget, part of a larger philosophical inquiry into the nature and origins of scientific knowledge. It was not until 1950, however, that he published the first full statement of his epistemological position in a three-volume work, *Introduction à l'épistémologie Génétique.* Shorter accounts have appeared in English in *Insights and Illusions of Philosophy* (1965), *Structuralism* (1968c), and *Genetic Epistemology* (1971a).

Just as Piaget's genetic (developmental) psychology emphasizes the activities of the child in coming to an understanding of the world, so his genetic epistemology draws our attention to the activities of philosophers and scientists in constructing their formal theories. In the process, we come to understand more about Piaget's own theoretical choices: why he stresses the balance between sensory experience and reason; why he rejects picture theory as a model of symbolic function; why he is so concerned with the topics of space, time, number, causality, and conservation; why he selects a biological model of function and a logical model of structure; and why he chooses clinical method as his major tool of scientific inquiry. As we begin to understand Piaget's approach to theory-making, we will be able to evaluate some general issues involved in the creation of a theory. As I present Piaget's genetic epistemology, then, I will be summarizing the major themes which have been presented throughout this book.

In order to provide a context for Piaget's approach, I will describe briefly some of the questions about knowledge raised by philosophers in all periods of

Western civilization; I will then present some of the conflicting answers offered by three major schools—Rationalism, Empiricism, and the Kantian tradition. After considering Piaget's critique of all three, I will proceed to an exploration of the subject matter and methods of genetic epistemology. The last section includes some final thoughts about the current status of Piaget's philosophical and psychological contributions.

TRADITIONAL EPISTEMOLOGICAL THEORIES

Professional philosophers are not the only ones who consider the nature of knowledge. If we think about it, all of us would realize that we have a set of more or less firmly held notions about knowledge and that these notions correspond to the issues raised over the centuries by epistemologists. Consider the following sets of statements and see whether you find that one of the claims in each set is obviously correct.

Set A: Best examples

Mathematics and geometry are the best examples of knowledge.
Physics and biology are the best examples of knowledge.
Art and poetry are the best examples of knowledge.
Common sense is the best example of knowledge.

Set B: Certainty

There are some facts we can know for certain.
No facts are certain.[1]

Set C: Stability

There are some permanent unchanging truths.
There are no permanent unchanging truths.

Set D: Truth

A true statement is one that is logically consistent and coherent with other statements.
A true statement is one that is verified when it corresponds with reality.
A true statement is one that is verified when it corresponds with our systematic observations.

Set E: The role of perception

Perceptions allow us to know what is truly out there in the world.
The external world can never be known directly and without distortion.

[1]Let's not get involved in the difficulty that if no facts are certain, then the statement itself is uncertain.

Set F: The role of reason
Rational analysis alone can lead to knowledge.
Rational analysis alone cannot lead to knowledge.

Set G: Sensory Experience versus Reason
Sensory experience is more important than reason in arriving at knowledge.
Reason is more important than sensory experience in arriving at knowledge.

When I present these examples to undergraduate classes, I find an approximately even split between those who choose mathematics and those who choose science as the best examples of knowledge. Poetry and common sense are usually ignored. About 80 to 85 percent of the class usually agrees on Sets B to F that: there are some facts we can know for certain; there are some permanent truths; a true statement is one that corresponds with our systematic observations; the external world can never be known directly; rational analysis alone cannot lead to knowledge; sensory experience is more important than reason. While a consensus favors these choices in every class, some students always endorse each of the remaining alternatives. As you may already be aware, each statement represents an answer to basic epistemological questions first raised by the Rationalists in early Greece (e.g., Plato) and then responded to by seventeenth-century Empiricists (e.g., Locke, Berkeley, Hume). If you felt frustrated by having to make a choice among alternatives, you might share Piaget's initial sympathy with the approach taken by Immanuel Kant in the eighteenth century. However, Piaget ultimately rejected Kant's attempt at a synthesis of the Rationalist-Empiricist alternatives and went on to develop one of his own.

Rationalism versus Empiricism

The definition of knowledge. Each theorist who defines knowledge has in mind a best possible example of what knowledge could or should be. The Rationalist's candidate has been mathematics (geometry, arithmetic, algebra); the Empiricist's ideal has been the physical sciences. The choice of either one as a prototype leads to a very specific characterization of knowledge.

Mathematics is a discipline concerned with consistencies in the relations between symbolic statements. As idealized, this discipline is capable of arriving at certain truths—not the psychological feeling of certainty, but the logical invulnerability of statements to doubt, question, contradiction, or refutation. The truths of mathematics are usually thought to be permanent or eternal; for example, Euclidian triangles always have three sides and three angles which sum to 180 degrees. Plato looked out on Greece in the fifth century B.C. and became acutely aware of the confusion resulting from the endless number of conflicting opinions in the Athenian marketplace of ideas. He believed that if he could discover absolute, universal ideas about Goodness, Beauty, and Truth which had the mathematical quality of certainty and permanence, then conflicting versions of reality would be resolved and political turmoil would disappear.[2] The search for certain and permanent knowledge remains a goal for Rationalists to the present day.

Scientific knowledge presents a contrast with mathematics at every point. The meaning and validity of scientific ideas rests on the correspondence between hypotheses and observed facts, not on the consistency or coherence among statements. Running through the history of epistemology is the theme that science, because it deals with a world of flux and change, cannot achieve certain and permanent truth. For the Rationalists, this resulted in the exclusion of science and all information based on sense experience from the realm of knowledge. While earlier British Empiricists had attempted to establish the certainty of knowledge based on perceptual data, Hume accepted the failure of science to reach certainty and instead, attempted to redefine knowledge as probabilistic.

Reason and sense data

a. *The Rationalist argument.* A central aspect of the controversy between Rationalism and Empiricism focused on the comparative effectiveness of the senses and of reason in the process of acquiring knowledge. Plato was highly skeptical about sense experience, even in what he believed to be its highest form—scientific investigation. He acknowledged contributions of science to practical affairs (e.g., navigation, farming), but he was part of a society in which practical affairs were not highly valued; a career devoted to the study of things was not nearly so respected as a life of the mind.[3] Plato marshalled more direct arguments leading him to choose the road of reason. Sense data, he claimed, have two major flaws. First, perceptions are often distorted and observers are always subject to illusions; what's worse, observers never know when their perceptions are distorted and when not. Second, even if no distortion occurs, it is a fact that things (objects) are always changing. It seemed obvious to Plato that a study of science and sense data could never lead to his goal of establishing certain and permanent truth.

Plato looked longingly at Greek achievements in mathematics—an area in which sense experience was excluded. Because rational analysis can come to such clear, certain, and permanent ideas in mathematics, it became self-evident to Plato that only this approach would allow him to make similar kinds of statements about the nature of Truth, Goodness, and Beauty. For the next 22

[2]If he was correct, we still need him.

[3]Values as well as facts determine the direction of a theory.

centuries, most of the influential philosophers (e.g., Plato, Aristotle,[4] Descartes) chose reason and excluded sense data in their quest for certainty and permanence.

b. *The Empiricist argument.* It was self-evident to Plato that knowledge could not originate in sense experience; it was equally self-evident to Locke that sense experience did provide the basic material for knowledge. Locke (1632–1704) adopted a version of the picture theory of symbolic functions in an attempt to show that knowledge based on sense data could be certain. Objects create sensations, which in turn lead to perceptions, which then lead to impressions, which finally lead to ideas. Not all perceptions and ideas are exact copies of external events, so not all ideas about the world are certain or true. Locke suggested that there are two kinds of ideas—simple and complex—and that complex ideas are nothing but associations of simple ideas. Further, there are two kinds of simple ideas—the primary or secondary qualities of objects. Primary qualities are those without which it would be impossible to think of objects at all—qualities of extension in space, number, shape. Other qualities such as color are secondary because they are not intrinsic aspects of the objects. Debate about whether some qualities are really primary or secondary tends to obscure Locke's general strategy—to show that there is *something* about the external world (primary qualities) which can be known directly through sensory experience because some ideas correspond exactly with the things they represent. The first philosopher to be called an Empiricist, Locke still had a foot in both Rationalist and Empiricist camps. Sense experience provided raw data, but the mind had two central roles in the attainment of knowledge. First, the mind somehow builds complex ideas from simple ones. Second, the mind applies intuition and logical analysis so that certain knowledge is finally attained.

Berkeley (1685–1753) carried Empiricism a step beyond Locke. It is not simply that the materials for knowledge come from sense perception; all knowledge is founded on sense perception. Knowledge comes when we have direct, undistorted perceptions *of our ideas.* The problem never solved by Berkeley was to explain which of our ideas are directly and truly perceived and which are only products of imagination. In his attempts to speak to that issue, Berkeley came up against a dilemma faced by all theorists. Each attempt to remedy the impurities and inconsistencies of past theories contains within it the seeds of its own destruction.

In his analysis of causality, Hume (1711–1776) wanted to reexamine the distinction between logical relations among ideas (of interest to philosophers) and factual relations among events (of interest to scientists). As an Empiricist, he wondered how logical ideas about causality could be traced to sense experi-

[4]Aristotle is best remembered for his contributions to science, but as a philosopher, he believed that certainty was possible only in mathematics and logic.

ence. For example, if billiard ball A hits billiard ball B, which then moves, we describe this sequence as "A caused B to move." But, Hume pointed out, we can never observe a cause, only a sequence of events in space and time. Why, then, do we think that there must be some necessity in causal explanations? There can't be logical necessity, because causal relations refer to factual events. There can't be strictly empirical necessity, because we cannot observe causes. Hume attempted to explain how the general principle of causality is inferred from our knowledge of particular causal connections.

Hume argued that beliefs about causality are determined by repeated experiences which lead to perceptions, impressions, and then ideas. Thus, associations between external events function as the source of associations in the mind. In a new departure for an Empiricist, Hume did not provide a justification for logically certain ideas of causality. Rather, he provided a psychological explanation of how beliefs originate. In the process, he concluded that knowledge of the external world, based on our inferences about connections between events, can never be certain. In his attempt to be consistent with Empiricist principles, Hume reluctantly joined the ranks of epistemological skeptics who claimed that Rationalist ideals of certain knowledge were unattainable.

Kant's attempted synthesis

There are no absolute distinctions between opposing points of view. Rationalists became increasingly interested in the role of the empirical sciences in knowledge, while Empiricists were always concerned with the role of the mind in organizing the results of sense experiences. The two grand traditions cried out for some attempts at synthesis. Kant (1724–1804), both a scientist and a philosopher, rose to the challenge.

Kant re-examined the best examples of knowledge discussed by both. Rationalist and Empiricist philosophers. The Rationalists believed that in mathematics, certainty is achieved by avoiding the contamination of sense experience. But mathematics as described by the Rationalists achieves certainty without finding new information. In the equation $12 = 5 + 7$, the right side only tells what is already implicit in an analysis of the left side. Kant describes the statements of mathematics, as conceived by Rationalists, as *a priori* (prior to experience), and *analytic*. He notes that the Empiricists began to assume that the truths of mathematics rested on experience; $7 + 5$ equals 12 because that is how we find things in the world. In this case, mathematics would be characterized as *a posteriori* (after experience) and *synthetic*. It can tell us something new about the world, but it can never arrive at certainty. For the Empiricists this description applies to all statements from the physical sciences as well.

On one hand, then, Rationalist knowledge is *a priori* analytic, necessary, universal, certain, but never new. On the other, Empiricist knowledge is *a posteriori* synthetic, new but never certain. Is it possible, Kant wondered, to have knowledge which is prior to experience (therefore certain) *and* still have it tell us something new about the world? Stimulated by Empiricist arguments like Hume's, Kant decided to take another look at perception. When Hume said that causality is inferred from a sequence of events in space and time, Kant agreed. However, he did not accept Hume's view that inferences follow passively from observations of events. Kant argued that we cannot make inferences about causal relations, unless we already have prior notions of time and space in which to organize our perceptions. We would have no way of knowing, for example, whether the path of billiard ball A ever connects with B, and no way of making inferences about sequences in which events occur.

Through intuitions of space and time, the mind is active in structuring knowledge of experience. A similar kind of argument is used by Kant in his examination of intellectual concepts. In order for us to have the understandings that we do, judgments of experience and judgments of reason must be evaluated in light of formal principles, or rules, which he called categories. There are, he believed, twelve universal categories which are prior to all understanding of particular judgments:

Quantity: unity, plurality, totality
Quality: reality, negation, limitation
Relation: substance-and-accident, cause-and-effect, reciprocity
Modality: possibility, existence, necessity.

Despite Kant's emphasis on the *a priori* structuring aspects of intuitions and categories, it is evident that he wanted to reform Rationalism as thoroughly as he wanted to correct the excesses of Empiricism. His major work is entitled *Critique of Pure Reason*. For Kant, "pure" reason is *a priori* analytic. It enables us to break arguments into constituent parts and to reconstruct them. Principles of logic, however, are independent of experience and do not deal with empirical validity. These categories of the understanding go far beyond the limits of reason in allowing us an *a priori synthetic* approach to human judgments; this understanding is never independent of sense data. While understanding is not possible without prior categories, a category has no meaning without sensory input. Intuitions and categories are forms for which sense experience provides the content. Neither exists without the other. Kant's synthesis of Rationalism and Empiricism, then, reconsiders the previous choice between reason and sensation and argues that some important knowledge is a product of the interaction between them. Piaget, of course, is an intellectual descendant of Kant, as we can see from his interactional approach and his choice of categories of experience as a framework for analyzing the contribution of the mind to the structuring of reality.

PIAGET'S CRITIQUE OF TRADITIONAL EPISTEMOLOGY

Piaget argues that the rational methods inherent in philosophy are insufficient to synthesize Rationalism and Empiricism. He admired Kant's valiant attempt to justify both Rational and Empirical approaches to knowledge. He was especially sympathetic with Kant's hypothesis that some important knowledge is a joint product of empirical sense data and the structuring characteristics of the mind. But, like all epistemologists, Kant achieved his synthesis using the rational, analytic methods of philosophy. Even the Empiricists were empirical only in attitude; they too arrived at their conclusions through reason rather than through empirical research. What is needed, Piaget claims, is a new discipline which is a synthesis of epistemology and science.

Piaget argues that:

> For many philosophers and epistemologists, epistemology is the study of knowledge as it exists at the present moment; it is the analysis of knowledge for its own sake and within its own framework without regard for its development. For those persons, tracing the development of ideas or the development of operations may be of interest to historians or to psychologists, but is of no direct concern to epistemologists. . . . But it seems to me that we can make the following reply to this objection. Scientific knowledge is in perpetual evolution; it finds itself changed from one day to the next. As a result, we cannot say that on the one hand there is the history of knowledge and on the other its current state today, as if its current state were somehow definitive or even stable. The current state of knowledge is a moment in history, changing just as rapidly as knowledge in the past has changed, and, in many instances, more rapidly. Scientific thought, then, is not momentary; it is not a static instance; it is a process. More specifically, it is a process of continual construction and reorganization (1971, pp. 1–2).

Essentially, then, Piaget's objection to traditional epistemology centers around the fact that epistemologists have always examined scientific methods and changing conceptions of the world with nonscientific, nondevelopmental methods.

Arguments for including empirical–scientific data in a philosophical theory

Verifying implicit assumptions. Despite the strong opposition from most epistemologists to the inclusion of observational data,[5] implicit and untested assumptions about psychological characteristics of the knower usually underlie philosophical theories of knowledge. For example: Empiricists

[5]D. W. Hamlyn (1970), a philosopher at the University of London, ends a discussion of Piaget with the statement, "While empirical investigations may throw up suggestions for the philosopher and vice versa, and while these suggestions may be valuable, I am still inclined to think that a theory which rests directly upon both empirical and philosophical considerations must have a degree of incoherence (p. 23).

tended to see infants as clean slates with picture-copy perceptual abilities; Rationalists initially assumed the presence of innate ideas which, like flowering seeds, become clarified as adults engaged in philosophical discourse; Kant not only assumed that categories impose order on experience, but he also assumed that these categories were unchanging. Thus, no matter what epistemologists *say* about the use of data, we should pay attention to what they do and see if their assumptions can be tested more systematically.

Defining problems. Epistemologists tend to be attracted by significant questions which too often are vague and unanswerable. Piaget admires the strategy of scientists, logicians, and mathematicians who avoid the vast problems of understanding knowledge-in-general by dealing only with specified problems in a given area. They attempt to reduce the universe of possible questions to precisely formulated problems which conceivably can be solved. Piaget attempted to remain within the general territory of epistemology, but to reformulate it by asking a series of limited questions about the origins and developmental course of causality, number, space, time, and so on.

Choosing among competing theories. When philosophers create a hypothesis or reach a conclusion, they must ultimately persuade others that their statements should be accepted and that those of others must be rejected. Sometimes they can demonstrate a logical flaw in another position. Often, however, it is possible to derive at least two internally consistent theories which contradict each other. At that point, epistemologists can only claim that their conclusions are true if the premises are true; but they and we know nothing of the truth of the premises. Further, they can only demonstrate that the conclusions follow from the premises by presenting their rational reconstruction of the steps which, they believe, led to their conclusions. Because philosophers cannot fully describe the rules for their own reasoning—and may not even be aware of all the rules—their verifications are only partially available for public scrutiny. Theoretical stalemates are inevitable, because the method for choosing among theories is the same method by which theories were constructed in the first place.

Scientists often develop hypotheses in the same way as philosophers (through rational analysis and deduction), though they may also use intuition and hunch. However, the scientific experiment provides a partially independent strategy for assessing the merits of their ideas. In the experimental approach it is at least possible for others to repeat the operations used by the first experimenter and to arrive at the same conclusions. Of course, scientists' theories can distort their observations, but the verification approach is public; this increases the possibility of objectivity in the sense of coordinating at least two points of view.

The argument here is not meant to downgrade rational methods, especially in the creation of hypotheses or in the analysis of conclusions. Piaget wants to *add* empirical verification as a strategy in helping to make choices among alternatives, each of which may be logically coherent within itself. He implicitly argues that both logical consistency and correspondence with facts should be accepted as criteria for truth.

Combining "norms" and "facts." One important limitation of both rational philosophy and introspective psychology is that there is no systematic way for theorists to examine the nature of theory-making. Traditionally, epistemologists have claimed that this question is not relevant to the study of knowledge. Even Empiricists study how people ought to perceive and reason if they are to avoid error. Philosophical theories are concerned with *norms* in the sense that they prescribe what ought to be done—how knowledge should be attained, how experiments should be performed, how symbols should be used, how inferences should be made. By contrast, psychologists are concerned with *facts*—how people actually think.

Piaget acknowledged the necessity of keeping a clear conceptual distinction between norms and facts but went on to emphasize the interrelation between them. The psychologist cannot ask whether certain rules lead to logically valid statements; that is the normative task of the logician. However, he can and should ask how the rules are interpreted and used. Does the scientist who rests his claim to knowledge on empirical experiments actually reach his conclusion by guess and by hunch? Under what conditions does a theorist accept a statement as true? Is the philosopher who believes in certain knowledge different in important ways from the philosopher who champions skepticism? (That is, are conclusions determined by the logic of the material or are they influenced by the viewpoint of the observer?) Thus, Piaget's response to the epistemological rejection of psychology and the absolute distinction between norms and facts was to create a new area of study in between them. He argued that there is a special class of facts—he called them *normative facts*—which are concerned with the ways in which theorists create and use normative theories.

Normative facts are not merely interesting sidelights on the sometimes zany and idiosyncratic behavior of academicians. Rather, they represent crucial information which had been missing from descriptions of their theories. It was missing, claimed Piaget, because neither rational philosophy nor psychology allow for independent observations of the theory-maker's activities. Piaget's concept of normative facts defines a territory where epistemology and science meet. Not just any facts about behavior and thought are relevant to genetic epistemology, only those facts which are important in defining the theorist's active role as a generator–transformer, shaping the outcome of the theory.

And so, we return to the notion of triangulation—attempting to interpret a set of events from at least two points of view. Here we have: epistemology and science; philosophy and psychology; norms and facts; reason and empirical investigation. Knowledge, the elusive mountain peak, is located in the triangulated coordination of perspectives which have previously been regarded as incompatible.

Arguments for a developmental approach

We have seen that Rationalism, Empiricism, and Kant's theory were all concerned with the issue of whether knowledge changes and whether it can be considered permanent. This issue encompasses two major questions—whether there are any unchanging *aspects of things* and whether there are any *ideas about reality* which are true for all time. The rational methods of epistemology resulted in a variety of answers to both questions, with the overall issue unresolved.

Piaget approaches the problem from several different directions. From Darwin's evolutionary biology he draws some conclusions about changes in the physical world; from both history and child development, he considers the need for a developmental theory of ideas.

Darwin's biology. Piaget's early biological research on the evolution of molluscs and his interest in Bergson's philosophy made it inevitable that he would focus on change. In *Origin of Species* (1859), Darwin provided the intellectual justification for the direction taken by Piaget. He had argued strongly that minds as well as bodies were subject to evolutionary forces. That argument and Darwin's example in the form of the first systematic diary of a human infant, helped to make the study of changes in mental function scientifically acceptable. Further, the Darwinian tradition emphasized the importance of historical explanation in understanding present events; the present can be fully understood only in the context of a series of changes in the past.

Theories of evolution are not concerned with just any changes over time. They focus on a necessary sequence of qualitative rather than quantitative alterations (like the evolution from one species to a higher species). Evolutionary theorists tend to focus on changes in structure rather than content. They study those biological changes that result in an organism becoming more *differentiated* and more *integrated,* and therefore achieving a higher level of *adaptation* to the environment. As a product of this new biological tradition, Piaget believed that human intelligence should be studied from a developmental point of view. The search would be for a necessary sequence of changes (over history or over a lifetime) in which quantitatively new, increasingly differentiated and integrated mental structures would produce more adaptive means of dealing with self, with the world, and with the relations between them.

Historical changes in ideas. The relation between human beings and the physical universe is one aspect of the subject–object relationship so important to epistemologists. Piaget's historical survey indicated that conceptions of this relationship have changed markedly over the centuries.

When Greek philosophers regarded the heavens they must have experienced a grand and heady feeling of importance. In their view, earth was the king at the center of the universe, man was a special being, the crown of all living things, and the rational mind of the philosopher was the diamond in the center of the crown.

The Copernican revolution displaced the earth from its central position, although human beings were still considered central and special inhabitants of the natural world. Darwin's evolutionary theory, especially in the eyes of the theologians who interpreted the Bible literally, struck another blow at our relative importance; now human beings were one among many animals subject to the same mechanisms of natural selection and heredity. These and many other changes indicate that there have been important structural alterations in our conceptions of the relation between knower and known.

Many of the historical changes in ideas about knowledge represent a developmental increase in perspective-taking (a decline in egocentrism). Like pre-Copernican astronomers, early Rationalists and Empiricists tended to ignore the observer's role in constructing knowledge. In response to this egocentrism, one of Kant's major contribution was a demonstration of how both observers and objects play a role in determining what we know. Within philosophy and science, there has been increasing attention paid to both rational and empirical contributions to knowledge. From an emphasis either on subject (knower) or object (known), there has been a shift to a focus on the interaction between them.

In Piaget's view, these changes do not simply reflect the replacement of one belief with another. The observer becomes aware of his or her own point of view, differentiates subject from object more clearly, and also explicitly integrates them in a new conception. Because these changes occur in a sequence in which subject and object become more integrated, they result in a qualitatively different organization of the knower and known. In brief, they represent developmental changes in knowledge.

Parallels between child development and historical change. As Piaget became familiar with the history of epistemology and with the facts of child development (ontogenesis), he was struck by an apparent parallel between historical and ontogenetic changes in world view. He repeatedly compared the Copernican revolution to the modern eight-year-old's discovery that the sun moves around the earth. The argument is not that child development recapitulates history—pre-Copernican Plato is at a much higher cognitive level than the modern four-year-old, even though they share a particular belief in the sun's motion. Rather, Piaget's comparison between historical development and child development reveals a similarity in structural progression. At each stage of the history of ideas and of cognitive development, some egocentric assumptions are discovered, assessed, and rejected; current views of the world are held until still other egocentric assumptions are uncovered.

Traditional epistemology raised the issue of whether reality and knowledge change. A triangulated approach, which considers Darwin's evolutionary theory, historical analysis, and psychological studies, suggests that subject–object relations may in fact change structurally over time. At the same time, other aspects of the world and of knowledge may remain stable. A theory of knowledge, insists Piaget, must provide explanations of both stability and change in knowledge.

This analysis led to Piaget's basic reformulation of the central issues in epistemology. Instead of two cosmic questions, "What is knowledge?" and "How can we justify our claim to know something?" Piaget began to ask, "How does knowledge change and grow?" This question is open to scientific investigation historically and developmentally—any time we can examine a change from point A to point B. In this reformulation, epistemology turns from a study of knowledge to a study of the quest for knowledge.

THE SUBJECT MATTER OF GENETIC EPISTEMOLOGY

The area of intersection of knowledge

Newborn infants and philosopher kings, business people and school children, doctors and budding adolescents, plumbers and biologists, psychologists and politicians all travel different paths in the personal quest for knowledge. Piaget sets for himself the awesome task of establishing a theory broad enough to be relevant to all our quests, yet narrow enough so that empirically testable questions can be raised and answered. As a beginning strategy, he has ignored the particular concerns and approaches unique to each separate path and has tried to find or create questions, concepts, methods, and language common to all. In other words, Piaget has defined an area of study in which all paths intersect,[6] somewhere at a midpoint between the vagueness of "knowledge in general" on the one hand and the precise but limited content of any one approach on the other.

Epistemology, biology, and psychology

Piaget first searches for similarities among epistemology, biology, and psychology, the three academic disciplines involved in the study of knowledge. He finds that their foci converge on a basic issue—the relation between knower and known.

A comparison of epistemology and biology:

> All knowledge, in fact, whatever its nature, raises the problem of the relation between subject and object, knower and known. This problem gives rise to the multiple solutions of attributing the source of this knowledge to the subject only, to an action

[6]The area of intersection metaphor was suggested by Grize (1966).

> of the object, or to interactions of diverse kinds. Now, the subject being an aspect of the organism and the object being an aspect of the environment, the problem of knowledge from this point of view corresponds to the problem of the relations between organism and environment. It would be difficult to deny that this question is also the most general one raised by biology (1967, p. 65).

Further, the study of biology raises issues of concern to psychologists. While Darwin originally emphasized the evolution of physical structures, he was also directly concerned with the evolution of mental structures and functions. Piaget points to a central area in which biology and psychology overlap.

> Verbal or cognitive intelligence is based on practical or sensorimotor intelligence which in turn depends on acquired and recombined habits and associations.[7] . . . These presuppose . . . the system of reflexes whose connection with the organism's anatomical and morphological structure is apparent (1936, p. 1).

Piaget brings epistemology, psychology, and biology together by studying people who are searching for knowledge—a choice which permits him to examine the psychological behavior of a biological organism while it is in the process of constructing an epistemological theory.

The epistemic subject

The intersection of epistemology, biology, and psychology defines an extremely broad territory, far larger than the traditional focus on formal theories. The quest for knowledge is as much a part of the two-week-old's rooting for the nipple of breast or bottle as it is evident in Einstein's monumental theories of space, time, and energy. Piaget attempted to reduce the field to manageable proportions by confining his attention to what he called the epistemic subject. This is the person, at any age, who is posing questions and seeking answers relevant to the traditional epistemological issues described above. Thus, genetic epistemology is not responsible for the explanation of all aspects of psychological development.

To illustrate the difference in emphasis between genetic epistemology and psychology, let us examine an incident in which a five-year-old boy is about to touch a hot stove. The boy knows that the stove is hot and will burn him; he also remembers that he has been repeatedly told not to touch it. The child's mother, and most psychologists, would be interested in why the boy is defying the mother and how the defiance can be eliminated. This question is not one which Piaget would ask as an epistemologist. If it is assumed that the boy is trying to test empirically the meaning of the word "hot," trying to create classification of objects into hot things and not-hot things, then Piaget's interest would definitely be aroused because the origins of classification and the origins of the hypothetico–deductive scientific method are issues at the heart of science and

[7]Piaget reinterprets reflexes and habits, showing that they have the accommodative and assimilative properties of schemas and schemes.

epistemology.[8] Piaget's focus on the epistemic subject helps to redefine and limit the very general question, "How does knowledge grow?" Specifically, he is concerned with the set of normative facts about how human babies eventually come to be able to formulate theories like those in biology, psychology, epistemology, logic, mathematics, physics, chemistry, and other academic subjects.

The structural approach

The general need for a structural approach in the area of intersection can be conveyed quite simply. The various paths to knowledge are incredibly diverse: each has different specific goals, different language, different methods, different problems. It is unlikely that a unified theory of knowledge can be based on the study of the content of each path. Taking his cue from the biologists, Piaget focuses on the structure of knowledge—its form or organization—regardless of the particular content to which it refers.

Since structural concepts describe the form rather than the content of elements and relations, they can be applied to a wide variety of situations. What makes them particularly relevant to the area of intersection is that they can be used to describe and analyze normative facts about objects (atomic structures, living cells, social systems); they can also be applied to epistemic subjects (organization of behavior, intellectual structures, and categories in the mind). In addition, as the Rationalists pointed out, formal structural analysis is helpful in the understanding and evaluation of theories about subject–object relations. The logical consistency of theoretical propositions, the rules for relating symbols to concrete referents, even the language in which theories are expressed, can be clarified by analysis of formal structures. Thus a formal unity, at least of conceptual analysis, may be brought to both rational and empirical approaches to knowledge.

The functional approach

In philosophy and science there tends to be a division between those who adopt a structural analysis and those who adopt a functional point of view. Mathematicians and logicians are more structurally oriented, while psychologists are often functionalists. Biologists, however, generally adopt both approaches. By locating knowledge in the normative facts constructed by the epistemic subject, Piaget is attempting to create a synthesis of structural and functional approaches. Knowledge and intelligence exist in living organisms who have a

[8]This example makes two additional points. The first is the obvious but important fact that the same phenomenon can be examined validly in quite different ways, depending upon the interests of the observer. Secondly, it demonstrates that the analysis of an event from an epistemological point of view can also have direct relevance to the psychologist. If the child is seen as conducting experiments rather than defying authority, the strategies adopted for changing his behavior may be quite different.

history and who change and grow. Normative facts are derived from observations of the epistemic subject's behavior. All behavior has both structural and functional properties which are not separate facets of intelligence, but two sides of the same coin.

The functions of assimilation and accommodation bring the structures in contact with the physical world. The symbolic function extends the depth and range of intellectual operations to the possible as well as the real, to the past and future as well as the present. In the process of interaction, the adaptive function of intelligence is strengthened as the complexity of the structure is increased. Langer (1969a) suggests that we think of "functional structures" rather than becoming enmeshed in the artificial task of distinguishing these two aspects of the epistemic subject. Both functional and structural analysis are relevant to the double-edged task of genetic epistemology—the task of explaining stable and changing properties of intelligence and knowledge.

LOGIC: AT THE CENTER OF THE INTERSECTION AREA

The general boundaries of the intersection area have now been defined. Within biology, epistemology, and psychology, Piaget studies the structural and functional properties of the epistemic subject's quest for knowledge. This is still a very large territory in which to search for the holy grail. Piaget narrows the boundaries further by developing a new synthesis of formal logic and behavioral structures which he calls operational logic. If genetic epistemology focuses on the intersection of all knowledge quests, then operational logic, for Piaget, lies at the very center of this intersection.

Formal logic

Logic is usually discussed in the singular, as if there were one logic or one unitary academic discipline. In fact, there have been many logic systems, some with quite different sets of assumptions and conclusions. What is common to all of them is the idea that logic is a theory with rules for deciding whether one statement necessarily follows from another.

There are a number of reasons why logic is a particularly appropriate analytic tool in the intersection area of all knowledge. First, as a language, logical symbols and rules are more precise than common speech. Second, logical rules and transformations make it possible to assess the internal consistency of a set of statements. Third, formal logic is relatively content-free, and therefore provides a language which is generalizable across a very wide range of subject matter. Fourth, logic is a theory of elements, propositions, and relationships.

Structure is defined as a set of relations among elements. Logic, then, is by its very nature suited as a tool for the analysis of structures in both subjects and objects, knowers and what is known.

The need for Operational logic

Since formal logic theories and rules are used as tools of analysis by theorists in most academic disciplines, they are important for understanding the role of the knower in the quest for knowledge. The adequacy of formal logic as a model of human reasoning has always been an issue in traditional epistemology. Piaget takes a triangulated approach to the investigation of this issue, using historical perspective, psychological studies of child development, and rational analysis. He concludes that we need a new kind of logic—Operational logic—to serve as a model of the knower's structure and function.

In a detailed historical analysis, Beth and Piaget (1961) describe changing conceptions of the relation between logic and human reasoning. Until the eighteenth century, the two were generally assumed to coincide; the laws of logic could be used to describe the laws of thought. Since then, various theories have begun to provide differentiated, and then integrated, models of correspondence between the two domains.

As we have seen in Part II of this book, Piaget's psychological analysis indicates that the gap between formal logic and human reason changes over time. In the case of child development, there is a very close relationship between reasoning and the logic of a given stage, but not until adolescence is there any appreciable relationship between the structure of reasoning and the principles of *formal* logic. And even in the Formal operations stage, human reasoning is not identical with formal logic. Both systems share a set of formal properties—sixteen binary operations, lattices, and group structures. This correspondence of properties occurs despite the fact that adolescents and adults may never have conscious mastery over the theories of formal logic as constructed by logicians.

Finally, rational analysis triangulates on the same issue. Piaget often uses Gödel's incompleteness theorum in support of his own position. There is always at least one legitimate proposition in a system which is not provable within that system; no formal theory can prove its own consistency within the rules of that system. Most theory makers attempt to deal with the completeness of formal systems by moving to a new level of formal analysis. Piaget suggests that some of the gaps could be filled in by observations of what theorists do. In effect, Piaget is arguing that the incompleteness of formal logic can be increased by a psychological analysis of normative facts. In this realm, the study of developmental sequence may shed some light on the logical priority of axioms in a theory. Piaget does not assume either that logical priority or developmental priority provides a more "correct" solution, rather that we can learn from a comparison between the psychological and the logical sequence. If a correspondence is found, a genetic epistemologist should try to explain it; if there is no correspondence, the epistemologist must account for that too.

Everywhere Piaget looked, it seemed evident that there was a need for a model which could remain true to formal logic, but would also be adequate to explain the reasoning and inferences of the epistemic subject at any age—a system as relevant to overt behavior as it is to inner thought. A system such as this, encompassing norms and normative facts, would provide a new synthesis of rational and empirical models of human understanding. Operational logic, then, is a psycho-logic of intellectual function as well as structure. As a logic of behavioral interactions with the world, it can provide a model of the ongoing relations between the knower and what is known. It is a synthesis at the area of intersection because it encompasses theories and theorists as well as normative facts about epistemic subjects from newborns to adults—in times and places from ancient Greece to modern America.

Operational logic as a model of mind

Piaget's strategy of creating a theoretical model of thought is not, of course, a new one. Many theorists have developed pictorial, physical, electrical, mathematical, logical, or verbal representations of intellectual structures and functions. All of these models are analogies. They depict a system of concepts, metaphors, and rules which, *if* they were operating in the subject, would lead to the observed behavior. The immense effort devoted to constructing models is usually justified by the economy and clarity of communicating the theorists' ideas and by the fact that models are helpful in relating, explaining, and predicting previously unrelated, puzzling, or unforeseen events. In addition, I suspect that the pleasure which a child finds in constructing models of cars and airplanes continues into adulthood with the building of theoretical models.

However carefully related to empirical observations a model may be, it is evident that the "description" of underlying structures and functions are inferential creations of the theorist rather than direct empirical discoveries. No less than the creative artist, the epistemologist and the scientist are involved in the poetics of constructing effective metaphors and similes to make sense of the world and to convey their point of view to others. Even models which use physical or graphic representations imply the use of metaphor and simile. The investigator interested in the computer simulation of human thought is making the implicit statement, "I am going to assume for the moment that the human information processing system is organized as if it were a computer."

It should be recognized that the model itself and the language in which it is described have a number of built-in limitations. First, the metaphor focuses on those aspects of events in which the theorist is most interested. A model for explaining parent–child interaction is not likely to focus on the small muscle movements of each participant, even if the equipment were available to observe and measure them. Second, in relating observable events to the model, the observer must translate or transform the observations into a theory language. There are both gains and losses in the translation. It is currently fashionable for social scientists to translate as much of their data as possible into numerical form so that mathematical models can be applied to the analysis. Certainly a record of the number of times a response occurs represents precise information. What the numbers often ignore, however, is the fact that the responses occurred in a great variety of forms, even though the end result is the same.[9] Neither quantitative nor qualitative models and data languages have a monopoly on objectivity. The model and the language not only organize observations in a systematic way, they also shape the content and meaning of those observations.

Finally, one of the major problems in the use of models is the overwhelming tendency for theorists to forget that they are dealing with an analogy and to assume instead some kind of special insight into the actual inner workings of mental and physical events. Piaget, whose structural model stresses the centrality of logical organization, sometimes appears to be arguing that there "really is" a logic in the physical universe, in behavior, in psychological processes, and in the physiological structure of the central nervous system. We and he must remember that operational logic is a construction of a set of metaphors, not a true picture of the human mind.

CHOOSING AMONG ALTERNATIVE FORMULATIONS OF KNOWLEDGE

Piaget recognizes that his new epistemology represents one more alternative theory among the many already clamoring for allegiance. How can he claim that his view is any more valid or useful than other formulations? His general answer is to submit the alternatives to empirical study.

Biology, epistemology, and psychology are all concerned with how logic structures come to be in the epistemic subject, and whether this subject, as knower, plays a major role in structuring knowledge. Historical and contemporary views suggest that biologists, epistemologists, and psychologists have arrived at the same range of alternative answers to these questions. Some theorists assume that mental structures or knowledge structures are stable, others assume that they change, and still others assume that change is developmental—a necessary sequence of structural change in the direction of increasing differentiation and integration. Within each of these alternatives, some theorists emphasize the role of the knower (internal factors), some focus on the known (external factors), and some, like Piaget, focus on the interaction

[9]Piaget keeps reminding his readers that the recording of psychological behavior in numerical language does not imply that the event itself is numerical. So too, the recording of behavior in terms of concepts derived from formal logic does not imply that all behavior is in essence logical.

between the two. Combinations of three assumptions about change and three assumptions about the role of the knower lead to nine alternative possibilities to account for the structure of knowledge.[10]

Because the examples of these alternatives are spread across many books, I will briefly summarize them here. As you will see, included among the nine alternatives are the clean-slate, flowering-seed, and generator–transformer conceptions of knowledge and the knower. The choice of an epistemological position from this list may make an important difference to how we think about knowledge and what we do to provide the best possible education for children. You may find it challenging to read each alternative, to stop, and to think of an educational approach which matches that particular set of assumptions.

1. **Structures are stable: Emphasis on internal factors**
   Biological and mental structures are present at birth, fully formed or in some preformed state. Each person arrives at knowledge through the use of reasoning structures which already exist in the human mind.

2. **Structures are stable: Emphasis on external factors**
   Some philosophers and theologians look to God or other stable external sources as the ultimate source of certain and permanent knowledge. Some psychological theorists (e.g., Gibson) focus on external cues and yet emphasize perceptual or conceptual stability.

3. **Structures are stable: Emphasis on interaction**
   Pre-Darwinian biology studied the interactive adaptation between organisms and environment, but the hierarchical organization of the species was believed to be fixed. Kant's approach to *a priori* synthetic knowledge suggests that knowledge is a stable product of interaction between categories and sense experience.

4. **Structures change: Emphasis on internal factors**
   I am not aware of specific examples in this category. It is difficult to conceive of structures which change internally, relatively independent of external events, but which do *not* show a general developmental sequence.

5. **Structures change: Emphasis on external factors**
   Here we have the clean-slate theories of how structures originate and change. In this category is Lamark's evolutionary hypothesis that environmentally acquired characteristics of parents can be inherited. Locke and the Empiricists also belong here, as do their intellectual decendents, Watson, Skinner, and other psychological learning theorists who look to the environment to account for the organization of individual behavior and ideas.

6. **Structures change: Emphasis on interaction**
   Henri Bergson's philosophical treatment of evolution maintained that particular sets of organism–environment interactions create new structures which emerge unpre-

[10]Piaget only specifies six alternatives. He categorizes change and developmental theories together, but distinguishes them clearly in his analysis.

dictably from old ones. Therefore, structures change, but not in a necessary developmental sequence. The same principle is central in Köhler's Gestalt theory of intellectual structure and function; new insights are sudden, unpredictable emergents from reorganizations of stimuli or ideas.

7. **Structure is developmental: Emphasis on internal factors**
The key concept in this group of theories is biological maturation, and the key metaphor is the flowering seed. In this category are theories of evolution which focus on genetically determined aspects of structural growth. In psychology, this approach is shared by two very different theories: Gesell's account of development emphasized physical maturation, while Freud emphasized the biological unfolding of oral, anal, phallic latency, and genital stages. In both approaches, social factors in development are acknowledged, but only as interferences with the biologically determined sequence. Piaget classifies the philosophies summarized under the general heading of Pragmatism (Charles Peirce, William James, John Dewey) in this category as well, but I believe that they belong in the interactionist camp. One of Piaget's first philosophical papers was concerned with an attempt to create a neopragmatism; it is evident that this approach provided a stimulus for the creation of genetic epistemology.

8. **Structure is developmental: Emphasis on what is known**
In biology, epistemology, and psychology this category is represented in aspects of theories which emphasize social transmission. What we know is handed down through the behaviors and verbal teachings of adults. The emphasis on transmission from adults to children assumes a gradual but necessary series of changes in the direction of adult forms of knowledge.

9. **Structure is developmental: Emphasis on interaction**
Most current theories of evolution assume that the organization and development of structure result from an interaction between external and internal forces. It is not simply that both external and internal factors are involved, for according to this weak definition, all of the above theories are interactionist. It means, rather, that when one investigates the impact of external events, factors in the knower must always be considered; and when one investigates the knower, environmental conditions must always be considered. The operation of one factor cannot be understood without reference to the other. Piaget feels that the developmental interaction position, with the knower as a generator–transformer, has not been fairly represented in epistemology or in psychology.

If one is trying to be precise in classifying the above theories, few of them fit smoothly into one of the nine categories. Obviously there has been some rather arbitrary cutting and trimming so that minor qualifications, exceptions, and overlaps can be ignored. What is important for Piaget's purposes is that (1) in addition to the communality of concerns, nine clear differences in emphasis emerge when theorists try to explain how structures arise, and (2) that the same nine differences occur in the three academic fields most relevant to the study of knowledge.

According to Piaget, the major task facing genetic epistemologists is to determine which of these alternatives should be chosen. This must involve empirical examination of which alternative best fits the epistemic subject's quest. In order to avoid trivializing his investigations, Piaget focused his investigations on the structured concepts which Kant had described as categories into which all human experience *must* be organized—space, time, number, and so on. Within each category, Piaget examined the changes over the sweep of history and the child's progress from birth to maturity. Empirical evidence in support of any of the above alternatives (e.g., that structures develop in an interactive process) should be tested and retested in the intersection area which encompasses biology, psychology, and epistemology, past and present, young people and old, untutored seekers and professional academics.

Piaget's theory of psychological development, then, was a by-product of the empirical search for the one theoretical alternative that provides the best account of the normative facts of the epistemic subject's development. All that remains in this presentation of genetic epistemological principles is a description of the methods by which data must be gathered in order to make the choice.

TRIANGULATION AND THE CLINICAL–CRITICAL METHOD

The creation of an appropriate match between problem and method is one of the crucial issues in the construction of a theory. Actually there are very few definite guidelines; even the clearest statement of a problem does not automatically lead to a precise methodological prescription for a solution. In defining the subject matter of genetic epistemology, Piaget was able to establish a rich area of intersection from the similarities and overlaps among many different knowledge quests. In making the choice among nine theoretical interpretations of knowledge, epistemological methods should not be biased against any particular alternative before the investigation begins. Methods, too, must be located as syntheses in the area of intersection—a place where rational analysis, historical search, and empirical investigation come together.

The empirical aspect of genetic epistemological method has been described in Chapter 4. In the clinical approach to the epistemic subject, tests, observations, and experiments are combined in order to interpret an event from the point of view of both experimenter and subject. The present chapter indicates that the construction of an epistemology of science also requires a rational analysis of issues and, in addition, an historical perspective on changes in scientific ideas over the centuries. This approach has been called the "historico–critical method" (Piaget, 1965), a somewhat awkward phrase. Together these approaches form what might be called the clinical–critical method of genetic epistemological analysis.

Here is a brief and schematic outline of how the triangulations involved in such a method might occur. The specific problem, determined both by theoretical and empirical considerations, is to achieve a theoretical understanding of conservation (see figure 21). Child 1, about seven years of age, is

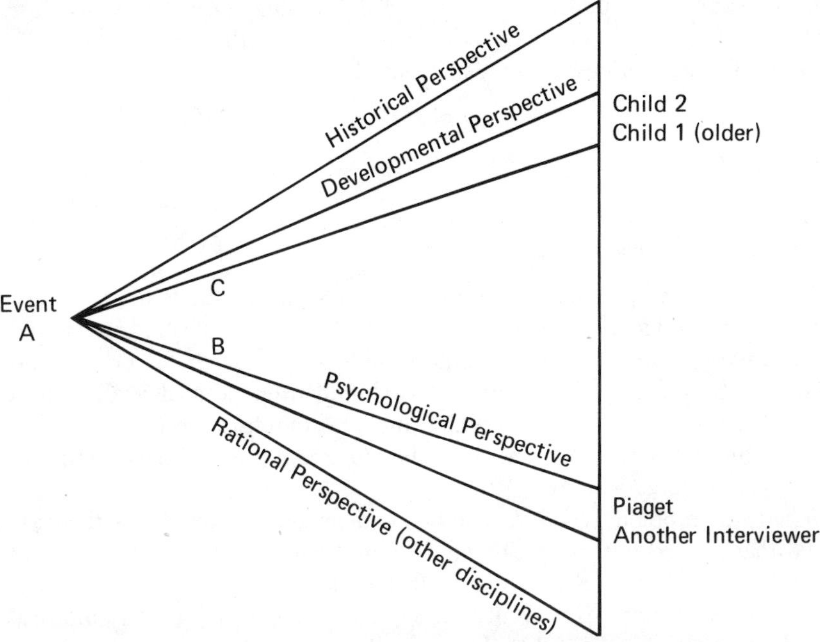

Figure 21. Piaget's methodological triangulations on a single event.

situated at point C, being interviewed by Piaget (at B) about a conservation of liquids task (at A). In the first triangulation, Piaget compares his own understanding of the clay problem with his understanding of the child's interpretation in order to arrive at a statement concerning the meaning of events at A, B, and C.

The principle of triangulation is extended in many complex ways. First, consistent with Behaviorist and other scientific approaches, the experiment is repeated with other subjects and other experimenters. Second, the experiment is repeated at different points in the child's lifespan, to provide a developmental perspective for the knower, who is attempting to understand an event. Third, the data concerning possible developmental trends in conservation are examined from an historical perspective. In this case, both ontogenetic and historical analysis reveal a similar sequence in people's conception of what can be done to things without changing their amount. Fourth, in addition to other psychologist-interviewers, Piaget invites scholars from other disciplines to examine the empirical experiments, the developmental trends, and the historical context with reference to a specific set of events. Thus the Center for

Epistemological Studies is not only an exciting place where intellectual cross-fertilization can occur, it is a logically necessary extension of Piaget's method.

Not all these perspectives converge on a single interpretation of facts. Rather, the triangulation strategy represents an attempt to search out and reconcile conflicting points of view. This strategy can lead to less egocentric interpretations of data and is one instance of the equilibration process which Piaget assumes underlies all cognitive growth.

CONCLUSIONS

The nature of epistemology

In Piaget's genetic epistemology,[11] the questions and methods of traditional theories of knowledge have been reformulated. The central question has shifted from an investigation of forms of understanding to a search for origins and changes in these forms. The method has shifted from rational analysis to a clinical–historical–critical method which includes empirical research. As you might imagine, philosophers have not rushed to accept this relative upstart into their own ranks (e.g., Hamlyn, 1971).

In part, the problem is one of definition and personal choice. Some theorists believe that an account of origins of structure can provide a necessary and sufficient explanation of the nature of that structure; other theorists do not accept this assumption. Almost all philosophers emphatically reject empirical research methods as irrelevant to the study of epistemological questions. If the question is asked, "Is genetic epistemology really an epistemology?" the answer depends upon how the practicing professionals define the field. This not very satisfactory answer still illustrates one of Piaget's central points: theorists exert an organizing force on the nature and scope of their theories.

Choices among theories

Assuming that we accept the central questions and methods of genetic epistemology, we are faced with a number of alternative interpretations of how conceptual structures originate and how, or even whether, they change. Piaget seems to enjoy the give and take of polemical argument. Many of his books are introduced or concluded by critical discussion of other points of view (selected from the nine alternatives), followed by historical and developmental evidence supporting the correctness of genetic epistemology.

For example, we can return to Figure 21 and the triangulation concerning the concept of conservation. A view of history and a longitudinal study of the child

[11]Piaget (1957) points out that there are other philosophers who have used the term "genetic epistemology"—most notably Baldwin (1901) and Cassirer (1950).

suggest that the structure of knowledge is not stable (eliminate alternatives I, II, and III above). Empirical studies of children and operational logic models suggest that there is a necessary developmental sequence to the changes (alternatives IV, V, and VI should be eliminated).

Conservation develops with one of three alternatives: as a function of internal factors, external factors, or an interaction. It is possible but difficult to conceive of a flowering-seed explanation of how a specific conceptual scheme—conservation—changes in both content and form as children grow older. What about external factors in change? Evidence from Piaget's analysis of perception suggests that we do not have, at any age, a perceptual copy mechanism which allows us to obtain information directly from external sources. And, finally, laboratory training studies suggest that there are both internal and external components of conservation, with the impact of one always dependent upon the characteristics of the other.

This brief summary does not do justice to the richness of detail with which Piaget presents his arguments; it is meant to convey a sense of the strategies by which he attempts to validate genetic epistemological hypotheses. Having verified a hypothesis in one conceptual area, Piaget does not then claim total vindication of his theory. Consistent with the approach of defining specific and testable questions, the weighing of alternatives occurs in one content area after another (space, time, and so on).

To me, Piaget's arguments and evidence in support of the interactive generator–transformer model of the knower are impressive. But I do not believe that genetic epistemology offers proof that other alternatives are incorrect. Certainly there are eminent philosophers, psychologists, biologists, and educators who believe or act as if these other alternatives have much to offer. Perhaps they are basing their conclusions on different examples of knowledge, or different situations, or different individuals. Perhaps, as suggested above, the alternatives do not represent mutually exclusive alternatives, but, rather, differences in relative emphasis. Some knowledge changes more, some less. Though change sometimes seems to result more from internal processes, and sometimes from external events, it actually results from a combination of the two. Piaget's formulation of the questions and methods relevant to the study of the quest for knowledge is unique. To the myriad alternatives he has added a steady focus on the importance of creating a theory that recognizes interaction between subject and object, knower and known.

A summary picture

Chapter 2 began with a "picture" of four-year-old Mark and his father discussing their differing interpretations of a sunset. For me, this picture holds images of many of Piaget's major themes.

1. There are qualitative differences between child and adult understandings.
2. There is a necessary sequence of cognitive stages in development from birth to maturity.

3. There are developmental, historical, epistemological, and logical aspects of the same event.
4. Knowledge about the world is not transmitted directly to children from external sources in the physical and social environment; children also assimilate events to their present structures.
5. Knowledge proceeds from overt action on objects and events to internalized symbolic transformation.
6. Facts are constructions, not copies or inventions.
7. There are many emotional and social ingredients of a cognitive task. (Father and son are conversing about the sunset. The fact that the two participants have feelings about the sunset and about each other will influence their attempts to share their points of view and to understand their different perspectives.)
8. In an equilibration theory of change, there must be individual differences in level of performance across situations and differences in the speed with which individuals progress through the stages. Equilibration theory also implies that for developmental progress, there must be some optimal degree of match and mismatch between environmental demands and individual structures.
9. Not mentioned by Piaget, but implicit in the Genevan work on developmental dysfunction, are two principles: (1) structural progress is not inevitable; and (2) assimilation–accommodation imbalances may be very long-lasting. Powerful interventions may be necessary in order to promote developmental growth.
10. Simple observation of the discussion between Mark and his father does not yield all the information needed to understand cognitive development. The clinical method with its synthesis of observation, tests, and experiments, provides a set of systematic procedures for gathering data. The method also suggests a new way of interacting with children in order that adults understand their understanding of the world

Future directions

Predictions about future trends in Piagetian theory and research are usually biased by the worst fears and best hopes of the forecaster; this final summing up is no exception. I have two worst fears. First, I am concerned about the negative tone of much recently emerging work. If some authors don't find results clearly predicted by Piaget, they tend to reject his whole theory. Instead, I see their research as providing a more differentiated account of the domains in which Piaget's theory provides a useful model, and of the domains in which it does not. I do not expect Piaget's theory to account for every single finding and phenomenon in development. I also have some concern about the pervasive, overly assimilative citation of Piaget's theory in support of each innovation in education. People rightly become skeptical of a theory when excessive and undifferentiated claims are made in its behalf.

I do have some hopes and expectations for cognitive developmental research over the next few years. I expect that more attention will be paid to the theoretical and empirical issues involved in defining and measuring stages. Second, I believe that more work will be done in the area of designing settings in classrooms and at home to provide the best levels of challenge (and support) for children's growth. Third, I hope that we can begin to explore in detail a Piagetian model for assessment and intervention with children whose developmental progress is less than it could be. Fourth, most people think that Piaget's theory deals only with cognition. It is my hope that this book has shown that it is a theory *with feeling* as well.

Beyond the specific content of the theory, I see an outstanding contribution made by Piaget. In his lifelong attempt to understand the nature of human intelligence, he has raised provocative questions about children and about knowledge. Piaget's disequilibrating questions, I believe, will prove to have the strongest impact on those of us concerned with child development, epistemology, and education.

References[1]

Achenbach, T. M. The classification of children's psychiatric symptoms: A factor analytic study. *Psychological Monographs*, 1966, *80*.

Achenbach, T. M. "Conservation" below age three: Fact or artifact? *Proceedings of the 77th Annual Convention of the American Psychological Association*, 1969, 275–276.

Achenbach, T. M. *Developmental psychopathology.* New York: Ronald Press, 1974.

Achenbach, T. M., & Lewis, M. A proposed model for clinical research and its application to encopresis and enuresis. *Journal for the American Academy of Child Psychiatry*, 1971, *10*, 1535–1554.

Aebli, H. Piaget, and beyond. *Interchange*, 1970, *1*, 12–24.

Ainsworth, M. D. S. Patterns of attachment behavior shown by the infant in interaction with his mother. *Merrill-Palmer Quarterly*, 1964, *10*, 51–58.

Ainsworth, M. D. S., & Bell, S. M. Attachment, exploration and separation: Illustrated by the behavior of one-year-olds in a strange situation. *Child Development*, 1970, *41*, 49–67.

Airasian, P. W., Bart, W. M., & Greaney, B. J. The analysis of a propositional logic game by ordering theory. *Child Study Journal*, 1975, *5*, 13–20.

[1]The original French publication date for works by Piaget and his colleagues, cited in the text, is included in parentheses after the English title.

Anthony, E. J. The significance of Jean Piaget for child psychiatry. *British Journal of Medical Psychology*, 1956, *29*, 20–34.

Anthony, E. J. An experimental approach to the diagnosis of psychosis in childhood. *British Journal of Medical Psychology*, 1958, *31*, 211–225.

Anthony, E. J. Behavior disorders. In P. Mussen (Ed.), *Carmichael's Manual of Child Psychology* (Vol. 2). New York: Wiley, 1970.

Arlin, P. Cognitive development in adulthood: A fifth stage. *Developmental Psychology*, 1975, *11*, 602–606.

Aronfreed, J. *Conduct and conscience: The socialization of internalized control over behavior.* New York: Academic Press, 1968.

Ausubel, D. P. *Educational psychology: A cognitive view.* New York: Holt, Rinehart and Winston, 1968.

Axline, V. *Play therapy* (Rev. ed.). New York: Ballantine Books, 1969.

Ayers, J. B., & Ayers, M. N. Influence of SAPA on kindergarten children's use of logic in problem solving. *School Science and Mathematics*, 1973, *73*, 768–771.

Baker, N. E., & Sullivan, E. V. The influence of some task variables and of socioeconomic class on the manifestation of conservation of number. *Journal of Genetic Psychology*, 1970, *116*, 21–30.

Baldwin, A. L. *Theories of Child Development.* New York: Wiley, 1967.

Baldwin, J. M. *Thought and things* (Vol. 1). London: Macmillan, 1906.

Baller, W. R., Charles, D. C., & Miller, E. L. Mid-life attainment of the mentally retarded: A longitudinal study. *Genetic Psychology Monographs*, 1967, *75*, 235–329.

Bandura, A. Social-learning theory of identificatory processes. In D. A. Goslin (Ed.), *Handbook of socialization theory and research.* Chicago: Rand McNally, 1969.(a)

Bandura, A. *Principles of behavior modification.* New York: Holt, Rinehart and Winston, 1969.(b)

Bandura, A. Social learning of moral judgments. *Journal of Personality and Social Psychology*, 1969, *11*, 275–279.(c)

Bandura, A., & McDonald, F. J. Influence of social reinforcement and the behavior of models in shaping children's moral judgments. *Journal of Abnormal and Social Psychology*, 1963, *67*, 274–281.

Bandura, A., & Walters, R. H. *Social learning and personality development.* New York: Holt, Rinehart and Winston, 1963.

Barnes, H. A., & McManis, D. J. Training of relative thinking in retardates. *Journal of Genetic Psychology*, 1973, *123*, 345–357.

Barsch, R. *Achieving perceptual–motor efficiency.* Seattle: Special Child Publications, 1967.

Bart, W. M. Construction and validation of formal reasoning instruments. *Psychological Reports*, 1972, *30*, 663–670.

Bart, W. M., & Airasian, P. W. Determination of the ordering among seven Piagetian tasks by an ordering–theoretic method. *Journal of Educational Psychology*, 1974, *66*, 277–284.

Bearison, D. J. Role of measurement operations in the acquisition of conservation. *Developmental Psychology*, 1969, *1*, 653–660.

Bearison, D. J. The construct of regression: A Piagetian approach. *Merrill-Palmer Quarterly*, 1974, *20*, 21–30.

Becker, J. A learning analysis of the development of peer oriented behavior in nine-month-old infants. *Developmental Psychology*, 1977, *13*, 481–491.

Beilin, H. Learning and operational convergence in logical thought development. *Journal of Experimental Child Psychology*, 1965, *2*, 317–339.

Beilin, H. Cognitive capacities of very young children: A replication. *Science*, 1968, *162*, 920–921.

Bender, L. Childhood schizophrenia: Clinical study of one hundred schizophrenic children. *American Journal of Orthopsychiatry*, 1947, *17*, 40–56.

Benefield, K. E., & Capie, W. An empirical derivation of hierarchies of propositions related to ten of Piaget's sixteen binary operations. *Journal of Research in Science Teaching*, 1976, *13*, 193–204.

Bereiter, C., & Engelman, S. *Teaching disadvantaged children in the preschool.* Englewood Cliffs, N.J.: Prentice-Hall, 1966.

Berger, E. T., Prentice, N., Hollenberg, C. K., Korstvedt, A. J., & Sperry, B. M. The development of causal thinking in children with severe psychogenic learning inhibitions. *Child Development*, 1969, *40*, 503–515.

Bergling, K. *The development of hypothetico-deductive thinking in children: A cross-cultural study of the validity of Piaget's model of the development of logical thinking.* International Association for the Evaluation of Educational Achievement, Monograph Studies, No. 3. New York: Wiley, 1974.

Bernstein, A. C., & Cowan, P. A. Children's concepts of how people get babies. *Child Development*, 1975, *46*, 77–91.

Berzonsky, M. D. The interdependence of Inhelder and Piaget's model of logical thinking. *Developmental Psychology*, 1971, *4*, 469–476.

Berzonsky, M. D., Weiner, A. S., & Raphael, D. Interdependence of formal reasoning. *Developmental Psychology*, 1975, *11*, 258.

Beth, E. W. & Piaget, J. *Mathematical epistemology and psychology.* Dordrecht, Holland: D. Reidel, 1966. (Originally published, 1961.)

Bettelheim, B. *The empty fortress.* New York: Macmillan, 1966.

Bettelheim, B. *The uses of enchantment: The meaning and importance of fairy tales.* New York: Knopf, 1976.

Bever, T. G., Mehler, J., & Epstein, J. What children do in spite of what they know. *Science*, 1968, *162*, 921–924.

Bexton, W. H., Heron, W., & Scott, T. H. Effects of decreased variation in the environment. *Canadian Journal of Psychology*, 1954, *8*, 70–76.

Bialer, I. Psychotherapy and other adjustment techniques with the mentally retarded. In A. A. Baumeister (Ed.), *Mental retardation: Appraisal, education and rehabilitation.* Chicago: Aldine, 1967.

Binet, A., & Simon, T. New methods for the diagnosis of the intellectual level of subnormals. *L'Année Psychologique*, 1905. Translated and reprinted in A. Binet & T. Simon, *The development of intelligence in children.* Baltimore: Williams & Wilkins, 1916, 9–36.

Birren, J. E. *The psychology of aging.* Englewood Cliffs, N.J.: Prentice-Hall, 1964.

Black, A. E. *Coordination of logical and moral reasoning in adolescence.* Unpublished doctoral dissertation, University of California, Berkeley, 1976.

Blatt, B., & Kaplan, F. *Christmas in purgatory.* Boston: Allyn & Bacon, 1966.

Blatt, M., & Kohlberg, L. The effects of classroom moral discussion upon children's level of moral judgment. *Journal of Moral Education*, 1975, *5*, 129–161.

Boatman, M. J., & Szurek, S. A clinical study of childhood schizophrenia. In D. D. Jackson (Ed.), *The etiology of schizophrenia.* New York: Basic Books, 1960, 389–440.

Boland, S. Conservation tasks with retarded and nonretarded children. *Exceptional Children*, 1973, *40*, 209–211.

Bond, G. F., & Tinker, M. A. *Reading difficulties: Their diagnosis and correction.* New York: Appleton-Century-Crofts, 1973.

Borke, H. Interpersonal perception of young children: Ego-centrism or empathy? *Developmental Psychology*, 1971, *5*, 263–269.

Borke, H. Chandler and Greenspan's "ersatz egocentrism": A rejoinder. *Developmental Psychology*, 1972, *7*, 107–109.

Borke, H. The development of empathy in Chinese and American children between three and six years of age: A cross cultural study. *Developmental Psychology*, 1973, *9*, 102–108.

Borke, H. Piaget's mountains revisited: Changes in the egocentric landscape. *Developmental Psychology*, 1975, *11*, 240–243.

Botvin, G. J., & Murray, F. B. The efficacy of peer modeling and social conflict in the acquisition of conservation. *Child Development*, 1975, *46*, 796–799.

Bovet, M. Piaget's theory of cognitive development and individual differences. In B. Inhelder & H. H. Chapman (Eds.), *Piaget and his school: A reader in developmental psychology.* New York: Springer-Verlag, 1976.

Bower, T. G. R. The visual world of infants. *Scientific American*, 1966, *215*, 80–92.

Bower, T. G. R. *Development in infancy.* San Francisco: W. H. Freeman, 1974.

Bower, T. G. R., & Wishart, J. G. The effects of motor skill on object permanence. *Cognition*, 1972, *1*, 165–172.

Bowlby, J. Separation anxiety. *International Journal of Psychoanalysis*, 1960, *41*, 89–113.

Bowlby, J. *Attachment (Vol. I of Attachment and loss).* New York: Basic Books, 1969.

Bowlby, J. *Separation: Anxiety and anger (Vol. II of Attachment and loss).* New York: Basic Books, 1973.

Brainerd, C. J. The development of the proportionality scheme in children and adolescents. *Developmental Psychology*, 1971, *5*, 469–476.

Brainerd, C. J. Order of acquisition of transitivity, conservation, and class inclusion of length and weight. *Developmental Psychology*, 1973, *8*, 105–116.

Brainerd, C. J. Training and transfer of transitivity, conservation, and class inclusion of length. *Child Development*, 1974, *45*, 324–334.

Brainerd, C. J. Learning research and Piagetian theory. In L. S. Siegel & C. J. Brainerd (Eds.), *Alternatives to Piaget: Critical essays on the theory.* New York: Academic Press, 1977.

Brainerd, C. J., & Allen, T. W. Experimental inductions of the conservation of "first-order" quantitative invariants. *Psychological Bulletin*, 1971, *75*, 128–144.

Brainerd, C. J., & Brainerd, S. H. Order of acquisition of number and quantity conservation. *Child Development*, 1972, *43*, 1401–1406.

Brainerd, C. J., & Hooper, F. H. A methodological analysis of developmental studies of identity conservation and equivalence conservation. *Psychological Bulletin*, 1975, *82*, 725–737.

Breasted, M. *Oh, sex education!* New York: New American Library, 1971.

Breger, L. The ideology of behaviorism. In L. Breger (Ed.), *Clinical-cognitive psychology: Models and integrations.* Englewood Cliffs, N.J.: Prentice-Hall, 1969, 25–55.

Brekke, B. W., Williams, J. D., & Harlow, S. Conservation and reading readiness. *Journal of Genetic Psychology*, 1973, *123*, 133–138.

Brekke, B. W., Williams, J. D., & Tait, P. The acquisition of conservation of weight by visually impaired children. *Journal of Genetic Psychology*, 1974, *125*, 89–97.

Bresson, F., & Montmollin, M. *Psychologie et épistémologie genétique: Thèmes Piagetians.* Paris: Dunod, 1966.

Broadley, D. L. *The use of Piaget's developmental psychology in a study of trainable mental retardation.* Honors thesis, University of California, Berkeley, 1973.

Bruner, J. S. *The process of education.* Cambridge, Mass.: Harvard University Press, 1961.

Bruner, J. S. The course of cognitive growth. *American Psychologist,* 1964, *19,* 1–15.

Bruner, J. S. On the conservation of liquids. In J. S. Bruner, R. R. Oliver, & P. M. Greenfield (Eds.), *Studies in cognitive growth.* New York: Wiley, 1966, 183–207.

Bruner, J. S. *Toward a theory of instruction.* New York: Norton, 1968.

Buhler, C. *Kindheit und jugend.* Genese des Bewusstseins (3rd ed.). Leipzig, Germany: Herzel, 1931.

Bynum, T. W., Thomas, J. A., & Weitz, L. J. Truth-functional logic in formal operational thinking: Inhelder and Piaget's evidence. *Developmental Psychology,* 1972, *7,* 129–132.

Carlson, J. S. Children's probability judgments as related to age, intelligence, socioeconomic level, and sex. *Human Development,* 1969, *12,* 192–203.

Case, R. Piaget' theory of child development and its implications. *Phi Delta Kappan,* 1973, *55,* 20–25.

Case, R. Social class differences in intellectual development: A neo-Piagetian investigation. *Canadian Journal of Behavioral Science,* 1975, *7.*

Cassirer, E. *The problem of knowledge* (Vol. IV). New Haven, Conn: Yale University Press, 1950.

Chandler, M. J. Egocentrism and antisocial behavior: The assessment and training of social perspective-taking skills. *Developmental Psychology,* 1973, *9,* 326–332.

Chandler, M., & Greenspan, D. Ersatz egocentrism: A reply to H. Borke. *Developmental Psychology,* 1972, *7,* 104–106.

Chaplin. M. V., & Keller, H. R. Decentering and social interaction. *Journal of Genetic Psychology,* 1974, *124,* 269–275.

Chapman, R. H. The development of children's understanding of proportions. *Child Development,* 1975, *46,* 141–148.

Charbonneau, C., Robert, M., Bourassa, G., & Gladu-Bisonnette, S. Observational learning of quantity conservation and Piagetian generalization tasks. *Developmental Psychology,* 1976, *12,* 211–217.

Charlesworth, W. R. Persistence of orienting and attending behavior in infants as a function of stimulus–locus uncertainty. *Child Development,* 1966, *37,* 473–491.

Chiseri, M. J. Amenability to incorrect hypotheses in the extinction of conservation of weight in college students. *Merrill-Palmer Quarterly,* 1975, *21,* 139–143.

Chomsky, N. *Aspects of the theory of syntax.* Cambridge, Mass.: M.I.T. Press, 1965.

Clarizio, H. F., & McCoy, G. F. *Behavior disorders in children* (2nd ed.). New York: Crowell, 1976.

Cohen, B. D., & Camhi, J. Schizophrenic performance in a word communication task. *Journal of Abnormal Psychology,* 1967, *72,* 240–246.

Coie, J. D., Costanzo, P. R., & Farnill, D. Specific transitions in the development of spatial perspective-taking ability. *Developmental Psychology,* 1973, *9,* 167–177.

Coie, J. D., & Dorval, B. Sex differences in the intellectual structure of social interaction skills. *Developmental Psychology,* 1973, *8,* 261–267.

Conn, J. M. Children's awareness of the origins of babies. *Journal of Child Psychiatry,* 1947, *1,* 140–176.

Corman, H. H., & Escalona, S. K. Stages of sensorimotor development: A replication study. *Merrill-Palmer Quarterly*, 1969, *15*, 351–361.

Costanzo, P. R., Coie, J. O., Grument, J. F., & Farnill, D. A reexamination of the effects of intent and consequences on children's moral judgment. *Child Development*, 1973, *44*, 154–161.

Cowan, P. A. Cognitive egocentrism and social interaction in children. *American Psychologist*, 1966, *21*, 623. (Abstract)

Cowan, P. A. The nature of psychological-educational diagnosis. In D. B. Carter (Ed.), *Interdisciplinary approaches to learning disorders*. Philadelphia: Chilton, 1970.

Cowan, P. A., & Breslow, L. A behavioral rating scale for assimilation–accommodation balance and imbalance. Work in progress, University of California, Berkeley, 1977.

Cowan, P. A., & Cowan, C. Six weeks in May: An academic reconstitution project and its significance for the psychology curriculum. In D. Adelson (Ed.), *Man as the measure: The crossroads* (Community Psychology Series, APA Division 27). New York: Behavioral Publications, 1970.

Cowan, C. P., Cowan, P. A., Coie, L., and Coie, J. Becoming a family: The impact of a first child's birth on the couple's relationship. In W. Miller and L. Newman, *The First Child and Family Formation*. Chapel Hill, N.C.: University of North Carolina Population Center, 1978.

Cowan, P. A., Langer, J., Heavenrich, J., & Nathanson, M. Social learning and Piaget's theory of moral development. *Journal of Personality and Social Psychology*, 1969, *2*, 261–274.

Creak, M. Childhood psychosis: A review of 100 cases. *British Journal of Psychiatry*, 1963, *109*, 84–89.

Curcio, F., Kattef, L., Levine, D., & Robbins, O. Compensation and susceptibility to conservation training. *Developmental Psychology*, 1972, *3*, 259–263.

Curcio, F., Robbins, O., & Ela, S. S. The role of body parts and readiness in acquisition of number conservation. *Child Development*, 1971, *42*, 1641–1646.

Damon, W. Conception of positive justice as related to the development of logical operations. *Child Development*, 1975, *46*, 301–312.

Darwin, C. R. *On the origin of species by means of natural selection or the preservation of favored races in the struggle for life*. New York: Modern Library, 1949. (Originally published, 1859.)

Dasen, P. R. The development of conservation in aboriginal children: A replication study. *International Journal of Psychology*, 1972, *7*, 75–85.

de Ajuriaguerra, J., Inhelder, B., Jaeggi, A., Roth, S., & Stirlin, M. Les troubles de l'organisation et la désorganization intellectuelle chez les enfants psychotiques. *La Psychiatrie de l'Enfant*, 1970, *12*, 309–412.

Décarie, T. G. *Intelligence and affectivity in early childhood*. New York: International Universities Press, 1965.

De Lemos, M. M. The development of conservation in aboriginal children. *International Journal of Psychology*, 1969, *4*, 255–269.

Denney, N. W., & Cornelius, S. W. Class inclusion and multiple classification in middle and old age. *Developmental Psychology*, 1975, *11*, 521–522.

Dennis, W. The effect of cradling practice on the onset of walking in Hopi children. *Journal of Genetic Psychology*, 1940, *56*, 77–86.

DeVries, R. Constancy of generic identity in the years three to six. *Monographs of the Society for Research in Child Development*, 1969, *34*, No. 3.

DeVries, R. The development of role-taking as reflected by the behavior of bright, average and retarded children in a social guessing game. *Child Development*, 1970, *41*, 759–770.

DeVries, R. Relationships among Piagetian, IQ and achievement assessments. *Child Development*, 1974, *45*, 746–756.

Diagnostic and statistical manual of mental disorders (DSM-1). Washington, D.C.: American Psychiatric Association, 1968.

Dimitrovsky, L., & Almy, M. Linkages among concrete operations. *Genetic Psychology Monographs*, 1975, *92*, 213–229.

Dodwell, P. C. Children's understanding of number and related concepts. *Canadian Journal of Psychology*, 1960, *14*, 191–205.

Dodwell, P. C. Children's understanding of spatial concepts. *Canadian Journal of Psychology*, 1963, *17*, 141–161.

Duchworth, E. The having of wonderful ideas. *Harvard Educational Review*, 1972, *42*, 217–231.

Duckworth, E. Language and thought. In M. Schwebel & J. Raph (Eds.), *Piaget in the classroom*. New York: Basic Books, 1973.

Dudek, S. Z., Lester, E. P., Goldberg, J. S., & Dyer, G. B. Relationship of Piaget measures to standard intelligence and motor scales. *Perceptual and Motor Skills*, 1969, *28*, 351–362.

Dunn, L., & Smith, J. *Peabody language development kits*. Circle Pines, Minn.: American Guidance Services, 1966.

Ekstein, R. *Children of space and time, of action and impulse*. New York: Appleton-Century-Crofts, 1966.

Elkind, D. Children's conceptions of right and left: Piaget replication study IV. *Journal of Genetic Psychology*, 1961, *69*, 269–276.(a)

Elkind, D. Quantity conceptions in junior and senior high school students. *Child Development*, 1961, *32*, 551–560.(b)

Elkind, D. Piaget's conservation problems. *Child Development*, 1967, *38*, 15–27.(a)

Elkind, D. Egocentrism in adolescence. *Child Development*, 1967, *38*, 1025–1034.(b)

Elkind, D. Reading logic and perception. *Educational Therapy*, 1969, *2*, 195–207.

Elkind, D. *Children and adolescents: Interpretive essays on Jean Piaget*. New York: Oxford University Press, 1970.

Elkind, D. *Child development and education: A Piagetian perspective*. New York: Oxford University Press, 1976.

Elkind, D., Horn, J., & Schneider, G. Modified word recognition, reading achievement and perceptual de-centration. *Journal of Genetic Psychology*, 1965, *107*, 235–251.

Elkind, D., Larson, M. E., & Van Doorninck, W. Perceptual learning and performance in slow and average readers. *Journal of Educational Psychology*, 1965, *56*, 50–56.

Erikson, E. H. *Childhood and society*. New York: Norton, 1950.

Erikson, E. H. *Identity: Youth and crisis*. New York: Norton, 1968.

Escalona, S. Some considerations regarding psychotherapy with psychotic children. *Bulletin of the Menninger Clinic*, 1948, *12*, 126–134.

Featherstone, J. *Schools where children learn*. New York: Liveright, 1971.

Feffer, M. Developmental analysis of interpersonal behavior. *Psychological Review*, 1970, *77*, 197–214.

Feffer, M., & Gourevitch, V. Cognitive aspects of role-taking in children. *Journal of Personality*, 1960, *28*, 383–396.

Festinger, L. *A theory of cognitive dissonance*. Evanston, Ill.: Row, Peterson, 1957.

Flavell, J. H. *The developmental psychology of Jean Piaget*. Princeton: Van Nostrand, 1963.

Flavell, J. Stage-related properties of cognitive development. *Cognitive Psychology*, 1971, *2*, 421–453.

Flavell, J. H. The development of inferences about others. In T. Mischel (Ed.), *Understanding other persons*. Oxford, Eng.: Blackwell, Basel & Mott, 1974.

Flavell, J. H., Botkin, P., Fry, C., Wright, J., & Jarvis, P. *The development of role-taking and communication skills in children*. New York: Wiley, 1968.

Flavell, J. H., & Wohlwill, J. F. Formal and functional aspects of cognitive development. In D. Elkind & J. H. Flavell (Eds.), *Studies in cognitive development*. New York: Oxford University Press, 1969.

Freud, A. *The ego and the mechanisms of defense*. New York: International Universities Press, 1946.

Freud, A. *Psychoanalytic treatment of children*. London: Imago, 1946.

Freud, A. *Normality and pathology in childhood*. New York: International Universities Press, 1965.

Freud, A., & Burlingham, D. T. *Infants without families*. New York: International Universities Press, 1944.

Freud, S. Three essays on the theory of sexuality. In *Standard edition of the complete psychological works of Sigmund Freud* (Vol. 7). London: Hogarth Press, 1953, 125–243. (Originally published, 1905.)

Freud, S. Introductory lectures on psychoanalysis, part III: General theory of neuroses. In *Standard edition of the complete psychological works of Sigmund Freud* (Vol. 16). London: Hogarth Press, 1963. (Originally Published, 1917.)

Frostig, M., Lefever, D. W., & Whittlesey, J. R. B. A developmental test of visual perception for evaluating normal and neurologically handicapped children. *Perceptual and Motor Skills*, 1961, *12*, 383–394.

Furth, H. *Thinking without language: Psychological implications of deafness*. New York: Free Press, 1966.

Furth, H. *Piaget and knowledge*. Englewood Cliffs, N.J.: Prentice-Hall, 1969.

Furth, H. *Piaget for teachers*. Englewood Cliffs, N.J.: Prentice-Hall, 1970,

Furth, H., & Wachs, H. *Thinking goes to school: Piaget's theory in practice*. New York: Oxford University Press, 1975.

Gardner, H. *The quest for mind: Piaget, Levi-Strauss, and the structuralist movement*. New York: Random House (Vintage), 1974.

Garner, J., & Plant, E. L. On the measurement of egocentrism: A replication and extension of Aebli's findings. *British Journal of Educational Psychology*, 1972, *42*, 79–83.

Gelman, R. Conservation acquisition: A problem of learning to attend to relevant attributes. *Journal of Experimental Child Psychology*, 1969, *7*, 167–187.

Getman, G. N., Kane, E. R., Halgren, M. R. , & McKee, G. W. *Developing learning readiness*. Manchester, Mo. McGraw-Hill Webster Division, 1968.

Gilligan, C., Kohlberg, L., Lerner, J., & Belenky, M. Moral reasoning about sexual dilemmas: The development of an interview and scoring system. Unpublished paper, Harvard University, 1970.

Ginsburg, H., & Opper, S. *Piaget's theory of intellectual development: An introduction*. Englewood Cliffs, N.J.: Prentice-Hall, 1969.

Glucksberg, S., Krauss, R. M., & Weisberg, R. Referential communication in nursery school children: Method and some preliminary findings. *Journal of Experimental Child Psychology*, 1966, *3*, 333–342.

Goffman, E. *Asylums: Essays on the social situation of mental patients and other inmates.* New York: Doubleday, 1961.

Goldfarb, W. Childhood psychosis. In P. Mussen (Ed.), *Carmichael's Manual of Child Psychology* (Vol. II). New York: Wiley, 1970, 765–830.

Goldfarb, W., & Mintz, I. Schizophrenic child's reactions: Time and space. *Archives of General Psychiatry,* 1961, *5,* 534–543.

Goldschmidt, M. L., & Bentler, P. M. The dimensions and measurement of conservation. *Child Development,* 1968, *39,* 787–802.

Goodman, P. *Growing up absurd: Problems of youth in the organized system.* New York: Random House, 1960.

Goodnow, J. Problems in research on culture and thought. In D. Elkind & J. H. Flavell (Eds.), *Studies in cognitive development.* New York: Oxford University Press, 1969.

Goodnow, J., & Bethon, G. Piaget's tasks: The effects of schooling and intelligence. *Child Development,* 1966, *37,* 573–582.

Gottesman, M. A comparative study of Piaget's developmental schema of sighted children with that of a group of blind children. *Child Development,* 1971, *42,* 573–580.

Gottesman, M. Conservation development in blind children. *Child Development,* 1973, *44,* 824–827.

Greater Cleveland mathematics program. Cleveland: Educational Research Council of Greater Cleveland, 1962.

Green, D. R., Ford, M. P., & Flamer, G. B. *Measurement and Piaget.* New York: McGraw-Hill, 1971.

Greenfield, P. M. On culture and conservation. In J. S. Bruner, R. Oliver, & P. M. Greenfield (Eds.), *Studies in cognitive growth.* New York: Wiley, 1966.

Greenfield, P. M., & Bruner, J. S. Learning and language. *Psychology Today,* 1971, 5, 40.

Grize, J. B. Du groupement au nombre, essai de formalisation. *Études d' épistémologie génétique, XI,* 1960.

Grize, J. B. Propos pour une methode. In F. Bresson & M. Montmollin (Eds.), *Psychologie et épistémologie génétique.* Paris: Dunod, 1966.

Gross, R. Two-year-olds are very smart. *New York Times Magazine,* Sept. 6, 1964 *1011,* 410.

Gruber, H. E. Courage and cognitive growth in children and scientists. In M. Schewebel & J. Raph (Eds.), *Piaget in the classroom.* New York: Basic Books, 1973.

Gruber, H. E., & Barret, P. H. *Darwin on man: A psychological study of creativity.* New York: Dalton, 1973.

Gruen, G. E. Experiences affecting the development of number conservation in children. *Child Development,* 1965, *36,* 963–979.

Guardo, C. J., & Bohan, J. B. Development of a sense of self-identity in children. *Child Development,* 1971, *42,* 1902–1921.

Haan, N., Smith, B., and Block, J. Moral reasoning of young adults. *Journal of Personality and Social Psychology.* 1968, *10,* 183–201.

Haley, J. *Problem-solving therapy: New strategies for effective family therapy.* San Francisco: Jossey-Bass, 1976.

Halpern, E. Conceptual development in a schizophrenic boy: The use of traditional scales and Piaget tasks. *Journal of the American Academy of Child Psychiatry,* 1966, 5, 66–74.

Hamilton, V. Deficits in primitive perceptual and thinking skills in schizophrenia. *Nature,* 1966, *211,* 389–392.

Hamlyn, D. W. Epistemology and conceptual development. In T. Mischel (Ed.), *Cognitive development and epistemology.* New York: Academic Press, 1971.

Hammond, J., & Raven, R. The effects of a structured learning sequence on the achievement of compensatory tasks. *Journal of Research in Science Teaching*, 1973, *10*, 257–262.

Haney, J. H., & Hooper, F. H. A developmental comparison of social class and verbal ability influences on Piagetian tasks. *Journal of Genetic Psychology*, 1973, *122*, 235–245.

Harlow, H. F. The nature of love. *American Psychologist*, 1958, *13*, 673–685.

Harris, D. B. *Children's drawings as measures of intellectual maturity.* New York: Harcourt, Brace and World, 1963.

Harris, P. L., & Basset, E. Reconstruction from the mental image. *Journal of Experimental Child Psychology*, 1976, *21*, 514–523.

Hartley, E. L., & Hartley, R. E. *Fundamentals of social psychology.* New York: Knopf, 1955.

Hartley, E. L., Rosenbaum, M., & Schwartz, S. Children's perceptions of ethnic group membership. *Journal of Psychology*, 1948, *26*, 387–398.

Hartshorn, H., & May, M. S. *Studies in the nature of character.* (3 vols.) New York: Macmillan, 1928–1930.

Hatwell, Y. *Privation sensorielle et intelligence.* Paris: Presses Universitaires de France, 1966.

Hewett, F. M., & Forness, S. R. *Education of exceptional learners.* Boston: Allyn & Bacon, 1974.

Hoeman, N. H., & Ross, B. M. Children's understanding of probability concepts. *Child Development*, 1971, *42*, 221–236.

Hollos, M. *Growing up in Flathill: Social environment and cognitive development.* Oslo: Universitetsforlaget, 1974.

Hollos, M. Logical operations and role-taking abilities in two cultures: Hungary and Norway. *Child Development*, 1975, *46*, 638–649.

Hollos, M., & Cowan, P. A. Social isolation and cognitive development: Logical operations and role-taking abilities in three Norwegian social settings. *Child Development*, 1973, *44*, 630–641.

Holt, J. *How children fail*, New York: Pitman, 1964.

Hornblum, J. N., & Overton, W. F. Area and volume conservation among the elderly: Assessment and training. *Developmental Psychology*, 1976, *12*, 68–74.

Horner, M. S. Toward an understanding of achievement-related conflicts in women. *Journal of Social Issues*, 1972, *28*, 157–175.

Hunt, J. McV. *Intelligence and experience.* New York: Ronald Press, 1961.

Hunt, J. McV. The utility of ordinal scales inspired by Piaget's observations. *Merrill-Palmer Quarterly*, 1976, *22*, 31–45.

Hunt, T. Early number "conservation" and experimenter expectancy. *Child Development*, 1975, *46*, 984–987.

Inhelder, B. *The diagnosis of reasoning in the mentally retarded child.* New York: John Day, 1968. (Originally published, 1943.)

Inhelder, B. Some aspects of Piaget's genetic approach to cognition. In W. Kessen & C. Kuhlman (Eds.), Thought in the young child. *Monographs of the Society for Research in Child Development*, 1962, 27, (Whole No. 2), 19–33.

Inhelder, B. Cognitive development and its contribution to the diagnosis of some phenomena of mental deficiency. *Merrill-Palmer Quarterly*, 1966, *12*, 311–319.

Inhelder, B. Memory and intelligence in the child. In D. Elkind & J. H. Flavell (Eds.), *Studies in cognitive development*. New York: Oxford University Press, 1969, 337.

Inhelder, B., & Piaget, J. *The growth of logical thinking from childhood to adolescence*. New York: Basic Books, 1958. (Originally published, 1955.)

Inhelder, B., & Piaget, J. *The early growth of logic in the child: Classification and seriation*. New York: Harper & Row, 1964. (Originally published, 1959.)

Inhelder, B., & Sinclair, H. Learning cognitive structures. In P. H. Mussen, J. Langer, & M. Covington (Eds.), *Trends and issues in developmental psychology*. New York: Holt, Rinehart and Winston, 1969.

Inhelder, B., Sinclair, H. & Bovet, M. *Thinking and the development of cognition*. Cambridge: Harvard University Press, 1974.

Jersild, A. T., & Holmes, F. B. Children's fears. *Child Development Monographs*. New York: Teachers College, Columbia University, 1935.

Jung, C. G. *Collected papers on analytical psychology*. New York: Moffat, Yard, 1917.

Jung, C. G. *Psychology and education*. Princeton, N.J.: Princeton University Press, 1969.

Kamii, C. Piaget's theory and specific instructions: A response to Bereiter and Kohlberg, *Interchange*, 1970, *1*, 33–39.

Kamii, C. An application of Piaget's theory to the conceptualization of a preschool curriculum. In R. F. Parker (Ed.), *The preschool in action: Exploring early childhood programs*. Boston: Allyn & Bacon, 1972.

Kanner, L. Autistic disturbances of affective contact. *Nervous Child*, 1942, 2, 217–250.

Karplus, R., & Thier, H. D. *A new look at elementary school science*. Science Curriculum Improvement Study. Chicago: Rand McNally, 1967.

Kaufman, A. S., & Kaufman, N. L. Tests built from Piaget's and Gesell's tasks as predictors of first-grade achievement. *Child Development*, 1972, *43*, 521–535.

Keasey, C. B. Implications of cognitive development. In D. J. De Palma & J. M. Foley (Eds.), *Moral development: Current theory and research*. Hillsdale, N.J.: Laurence Erlbaum Associates, 1975.

Keating, D. P., & Schaeffer, R. A. Ability and sex difference in the acquisition of formal operations. *Developmental Psychology*, 1975, *11*, 531–532.

Keller, H. R., & Hunter, M. L. Task differences on conservation and transitivity problems. *Journal of Experimental Child Psychology*, 1973, *15*, 287–301.

Kennedy, R. J. R. *A Connecticut community revisited: A study of the social adjustment of a group of mentally deficient adults in 1948 and 1960*. Hartford: Connecticut State Department of Health, Office of Mental Retardation, 1966.

Kephart, N. C. *The slow learner in the classroom* (2nd. ed.). Columbus, O.: Merrill, 1971.

Kessen, W. "Stage" and "structure" in the study of children. In W. Kessen & C. Kuhlman (Eds.), Thought in the young child. *Child Development Monographs*, 1962, *27*, 65–82.

King, W., & Seegmiller, B. Performance of 14-22-month-old black first born male infants on two tests of cognitive development: The Bayley Scale and the Infant Psychological Development Scale. *Developmental Psychology*, 1973, *8*, 317–326.

Kingsley, R. C., & Hall, V. G. Training conservation through the use of learning sets. *Child Development*, 1967, *38*, 1111–1125.

Klein, M. *The psychoanalysis of children.* London: International Psychoanalytic Library, 1932.

Koch, K. *Wishes, lies, and dreams.* New York: Random House, 1970.

Kohl, H. *Thirty-six children.* New York: New American Library, 1967.

Kohlberg, L. Moral development and identification. In H. Stevenson (Ed.), *Child Psychology* (62nd Yearbook of the National Society for the Study of Education). Chicago: University of Chicago Press, 1963, 277–332.

Kohlberg, L. Development of moral character and moral ideology. In M. L. Hoffman & L. W. Hoffman (Eds.), *Review of child development research* (Vol. I). New York: Russell Sage Foundation, 1964, 383–432.

Kohlberg, L. A cognitive-developmental analysis of children's sex-role concepts and attitudes. In E. Maccoby (Ed.), *The development of sex differences.* Stanford: Stanford University Press, 1966.(a)

Kohlberg, L. Cognitive stages and preschool education. *Human Development,* 1966, *9,* 5–17.(b)

Kohlberg, L. The impact of cognitive maturity on the development of sex role attitudes in the years four to eight. *Genetic Psychology Monographs,* 1967, *75,* 91–165.

Kohlberg, L. Early education: A cognitive-developmental view. *Child Development,* 1968, *39,* 1013–1062.

Kohlberg, L. Stage and sequence: The cognitive-developmental approach to socialization. In D. A. Goslin (Ed.), *Handbook of socialization theory and research.* Chicago: Rand McNally, 1969, 347–408.

Kohlberg, L. From is to ought: How to commit the naturalistic fallacy and get away with it in the study of moral development. In T. Mischel (Ed.), *Cognitive development and epistemology.* New York: Academic Press, 1971, 151–235.

Kohlberg, L. Moral stages and moralization: The cognitive-developmental approach. In T. Lickona (Ed.), *Moral development and behavior: Theory, research and social issues.* New York: Holt, Rinehart and Winston, 1976.

Kohlberg, L., & Mayer, R. Development as an aim of education. *Harvard Educational Review,* 1972, *42,* 449–498.

Köhler, W. *The mentality of apes.* New York: Harcourt, Brace, 1925.

Kohnstamm, G. A. *Piaget's analysis of class inclusion: Right or wrong?* New York: Humanities Press, 1967.

Kreitler, H., & Kreitler, S. Children's concepts of sexuality and birth. *Child Development,* 1966, *37,* 363–378.

Kuhn, D. Mechanisms of change in the development of cognitive structures. *Child Development,* 1972, *43,* 833–844.

Kuhn, D. Inducing development experimentally: Comments on a research paradigm. *Developmental Psychology,* 1974, *10,* 590–600.

Kuhn, D. Relation of two Piagetian stage transitions to IQ. *Developmental Psychology,* 1976, *12,* 157–161.(a)

Kuhn, D. Short-term longitudinal evidence for the sequentiality of Kohlberg's early stages of moral judgment. *Developmental Psychology,* 1976, *12,* 162–166.(b)

Kuhn, D., & Angelev, J. An experimental study of the development of formal operational thought. *Child Development,* 1976, *47,* 697–706.

Kuhn, D., Langer, J., Kohlberg, L., & Haan, N. S. The development of formal operation in logical and moral judgment. *Genetic psychology Monographs,* 1977, *95,* 97–188.

Kurtines, W., & Greif, E. B. The development of moral thought: Review and evaluation of Kohlberg's approach. *Psychological Bulletin*, 1974, *81*, 453–470.

Laing, R. D. *The politics of experience*. New York: Pantheon, 1967.

Laing, R. D. *The politics of the family, and other essays*. New York: Pantheon, 1971.

Langer, J. *Theories of development*. New York: Holt, Rinehart and Winston, 1969.(a)

Langer, J. Disequilibrium as a source of development. In P. Mussen, J. Langer, & M. Covington (Eds.), *New directions in developmental psychology*. New York: Holt, Rinehart and Winston, 1969.(b)

Langer, J. Interactional aspects of cognitive organization. *Cognition*, 1974, *3*, 9–28.

Langer, J. Cognitive development during and after the preconceptual period. In M. H. Appel & L. S. Goldberg (Eds.), *Topics in cognitive development*. New York: Plenum Press, 1977.

Lapouse, R., & Monk, M. An epidemiologic study of behavior characteristics in children. *American Journal of Public Health*, 1958, *48*, 1134–1144.

Lasry, J. C., & Laurendeau, M. Apprentissage empirique de la notion d'inclusion. *Human Development*, 1969, *12*, 141–153.

Laurendeau, M., & Pinard, A. *Causal thinking in the child*. New York: International Universities Press, 1962.

Laurendeau, M., & Pinard, A. *Development of the concept of space in the child*. New York: International Universities Press, 1970.

Lavin, D. E. *The prediction of academic performance* (Science edition). New York: Wiley, 1965.

Lawson, A. E. Formal operations and field independence in a heterogeneous sample. *Perceptual and Motor Skills*, 1976, *42*, 981–982.

Lawson, A. E., Nordland, F. H., & De Vito, A. Relationships of formal reasoning to achievement, aptitudes and attitudes in preservice teachers. *Journal of Research in Science Teaching*, 1975, *12*, 423–431.

Lawson, A. E., & Renner, J. W. Piagetian theory and biology teaching. *The American Biology Teacher*, 1975, *37*, 336–343.

Lawson, A. E., & Wollman, W. T. *Encouraging the transition from concrete to abstract cognitive functioning: An experiment*. Unpublished manuscript, University of California, Berkeley, 1975.

Layton, T. L. Role-taking, conservation and language usage of five- and six-year-old children. *Perceptual and Motor Skills*, 1975, *40*, 810.

Lazarus, A. A. Has behavior therapy outlived its usefulness? *American Psychologist*, 1977, *32*, 550–554.

Lazarus, R. *Psychological stress and the coping process*. New York: McGraw-Hill, 1966.

Leahy, H., & Huard, C. Role taking and self-image disparity in children. *Developmental Psychology*, 1976, *12*, 504–508.

Lee, L. C. The concomitant development of cognitive and moral modes of thought: A test of selected deductions from Piaget's theory. *Genetic Psychology Monographs*, 1971, *83*.

Le Furgy, W. G., & Woloshin, G. W. Immediate and long-term effects of experimentally induced social influence on the modification of adolescents' moral judgments. *Journal of Social Psychology*, 1969, *12*, 104–140.

Leino, V., & Willemsen, E. Use of a perceptually based apparatus to train adult women's performance on a Piagetian measure of the horizontality concept. *Perceptual and Motor Skills*, 1976, *42*, 363–369.

Lemke, S. Children's identity concepts. Unpublished doctoral dissertation, University of California, Berkeley, 1973.

Lempers, J. D., Flavell, E. R., & Flavell, J. H. The development in very young children of tacit knowledge concerning visual perception. *Genetic Psychology Monographs*, 1977, *95*, 3–54.

Lenrow, P. B. Preschool socialization and the development of competence: An exploratory research project. Project Summary, Institute of Human Development, University of California, Berkeley, 1968.

Lerner, S., Bie, I., & Lehrer, P. Concrete operational thinking in mentally ill adolescents. *Merrill-Palmer Quarterly*, 1972, *18*, 287–291.

Linn, M. L., & Thier, H. D. The effect of experiential science on development of logical thinking in children. *Journal of Research in Science Teaching*, 1975, *12*, 49–62.

Livesley, W. J., & Bromley, D. B. *Person perception in childhood and adolescence.* London: Wiley, 1973.

Lloyd, B. B. Studies of conservation with Yoruba children of differing ages and experience. *Child Development*, 1971, *42*, 415–428.

Lovaas, O. I. *The autistic child: Language development through behavior modification.* New York: Irvington, 1976.

Lovell, E., & Slater, A. The growth of the concept of time: A comparative study. *Child Psychology and Psychiatry*, 1960, *1*, 179–190.

Macready, C., & Macready, C. Conservation of weight in self, others and objects. *Journal of Experimental Psychology*, 1974, *103*, 372–374.

Mahler, M. S. On child psychosis and schizophrenia: Autistic and symbiotic infantile psychoses. *Psychoanalytic Studies of the Child*, 1952, *7*, 286–305.

Main, M. Avoidance of the mother in young children: Implications for day care. In R. Webb (Ed.), *Social development and daycare.* Baltimore: John Hopkins Press, 1976.

Markle, S. M. *Good frames and bad.* New York: Wiley, 1969.

Marks, E. Slow learning children. *Australian Journal on the Education of Backward Children*, 1972, *19*, 92–101.

Martin, B. Parent-child relations. In F. D. Horowitz (Ed.), *Review of child development research* (Vol. 4). Chicago: University of Chicago Press, 1975.

Marvin, R. S., Greenberg, M. T., & Mossler, D. G. The early development of conceptual perspective-taking: Distinguishing among multiple perspectives. *Child Development*, 1976, *47*, 511–514.

McCarthy, D. *The language development of the preschool child.* Minneapolis, Minn.: University of Minnesota Press, 1930.

McKinnon, J. W., & Renner, J. W. Are colleges concerned with intellectual development? *American Journal of Physics*, 1971, *39*, 1047–1052.

Meissner, J. A., & Apthorp, H. Nonegocentrism and communication mode switching in black preschool children. *Developmental Psychology*, 1976, *12*, 245–249.

Mehler, J., & Bever, T. G. Cognitive capacity of very young children. *Science*, 1967, *158*, 141–142.

Mehler, J., & Bever, T. G. Reply by J. Mehler and T. G. Bever. *Science*, 1968, *162*, 979–981.

Meltzoff, A. N., & Moore, M. K. Imitation of facial and manual gestures by human neonates. *Science*, 1977, *198*, 800–802.

Mermelstein, E., & Shulman, L. S. Lack of formal schooling and the acquisition of conservation. *Child Development*, 1967, *38*, 39–52.

Miller, D. H., Kessel, F. S., & Flavell, J. H. Thinking about people thinking about people thinking about . . . : A study of social cognitive development. *Child Development*, 1970, *41*, 613–623.

Miller, L. B., & Dyer, J. L. Four preschool programs: Their dimensions and effects. *Monographs of the Society for Research in Child Development*, 1975, *40*, 5–6.

Miller, S. A. Extinction of conservation: A methodological and theoretical analysis. *Merrill-Palmer Quarterly*, 1971, *17*, 319–334.

Miller, S. A. Contradiction, surprise and cognitive change: The effects of disconfirmation of belief on conservers and nonconservers. *Journal of Experimental Child Psychology*, 1973, *15*, 47–62.

Miller, S. A. Nonverbal assessment of Piagetian concepts. *Psychological Bulletin*, 1976, *83*, 405–430.

Miller, S. A., & Brownell, C. A. Peers, persuasion and Piaget: Dyadic interaction between conservers and nonconservers. *Child Development*, 1975, *46*, 992–997.

Miller, S. A., & Lipps, L. Extinction of conservation and transitivity of weight. *Journal of Experimental Child Psychology*, 1973, *16*, 388–402.

Minnigerode, F. A., & Carey, R. N. Development of mechanisms underlying spatial perspective. *Child Development*, 1974, *45*, 496–498.

Minskoff, E., Wiseman, D., & Minskoff, G. *The MWM program for development of language abilities*. Ridgefield, N.J.: Educational Performance Associates, 1972.

Minuchin, S. *Families and family therapy*. Cambridge: Harvard Univesity Press, 1974.

Moir, D. J. *Egocentrism and the emergence of conventional morality in preadolescent girls*. Master of Arts in Education thesis, University of Canterbury, Christ Church, New Zealand, cited in Selman (1976).

Montessori, M. *The Montessori method*. New York: Schocken Books, 1964.

Moore, J. E., & Kendall, D. C. Children's concepts of reproduction. *Journal of Sex Research*, 1971, *7*, 42–61.

Mosheni, C. Piagetian concepts in Iran. In H. Burton & D. Burton (Eds.), *Vistas*. Berkeley: Buena Vista Press, 1966.

Murray, F. B. Acquisition of conservation through social interaction. *Developmental Psychology*, 1972, *6*, 1–6.

Mussen, P., Conger, J. J., & Kagan, J. *Child development and personality* (4th ed.). New York: Harper & Row, 1974.

Mussen, P., & Jones, M. C. Self-conception motivations and interpersonal attitudes of late and early maturing boys. *Child Development*, 1957, *28*, 243–256.

Nadel, C., & Schoeppe, A. Conservation of mass weight and volume as evidenced by adolescent girls in eighth grade. *Journal of Genetic Psychology*, 1973, *122*, 309–313.

Neal, J. Egocentrism in institutionalized and noninstitutionalized children. *Child Development*, 1966, *37*, 97–101.

Neill, A. S. *Summerhill: A radical approach to child rearing*. New York: Hart, 1964.

Nocci, L., & Turiel, E. Social interactions and the development of social concepts in pre-school children. Unpublished manuscript. University of California, Santa Cruz, 1977.

Nuffield Mathematics Project. *I do, and I understand*. London: Newgate Press, 1967.

Nuffield Mathematics Project. *Mathematics: The first three years*. London: Newgate Press, 1970.

Nuffield Mathematics Project. *Mathematics: The later primary years*. New York: Wiley, 1972.

Ohuche, R. O. Piaget and the Mende of Sierra Leone. *Journal of Experimental Education*, 1971, *39*,

Oleron, P. *Récherches sur le développement mental des sourds-muets.* Paris: Centre Natural de Récherche Scientifique, 1957.

Osborn, J. Reading and language development. In *Summary of Proceedings of the Tenth Annual Reading Reform Foundation Conference.* New York: Reading Reform Foundation, 1971.

Papalia, D. E. The status of several conservation abilities across the life span. *Human Development*, 1972, *15*, 229–243.

Papalia, D. E., & Bielby, D. Del V. Cognitive functioning in middle and old age adults: A review of research based on Piaget's theory. *Human Development*, 1974, *17*, 424–443.

Paraskevopoulas, J., & Hunt, J. McV. Object construction and imitation under different conditions of rearing. *Journal of Genetic Psychology*, 1971, *119*, 301–321.

Parsons, C. Inhelder and Piaget's *The growth of logical thinking* (II): A logician's viewpoint. *British Journal of Psychology*, 1960, *51*, 75–84.

Patterson, G. R. *Families: Applications of social learning to family life.* Champaign, Ill.: Research Press, 1971.

Peckham, R. Problems in job adjustment of the mentally retarded. *American Journal of Mental Deficiency*, 1951, *56*, 448–453.

Peluffo, N. Les notions de conservation et de causalité chez les enfants prévenant de differentes milieux physiques et socioculturels. *Archives de Psychologie*, 1962, *38*, 75–90.

Piaget, J. *The language and thought of the child.* London: Routledge, 1960. (Originally published, 1923.)

Piaget, J. *Judgment and reasoning in the child.* New Jersey: Littlefield, Adams, 1964. (Originally published, 1924.)

Piaget, J. *The child's conception of the world.* New Jersey: Littlefield, Adams, 1960. (Originally published, 1926.)

Piaget, J. *The child's conception of physical causality.* New Jersey: Littlefield, Adams, 1960. (Originally published, 1927.)

Piaget, J. *The moral judgment of the child.* New York: Collier, 1962. (Originally published, 1932.)

Piaget, J. *The origins of intelligence in children.* New York: Norton, 1963. (Originally published, 1936.)

Piaget, J. *The construction of reality in the child.* New York: Ballantine, 1971. (Originally published, 1937.)

Piaget, J. Classes, rélations et nombres: Essai sur les groupements de la logistique et sur la réversibilité de la pensée. Paris: Vrin, 1942.

Piaget, J. *Play, dreams and imitation in childhood.* New York: Norton, 1962. (Originally published, 1946.)(a)

Piaget, J. *The child's conception of time.* New York: Ballantine, 1971. (Originally published, 1946.)(b)

Piaget, J. *The child's conception of movement and speech.* New York: Ballantine, 1971. (Originally published, 1946.)(c)

Piaget, J. *The psychology of intelligence.* London: Routledge, 1950. (Originally published, 1947.)

Piaget, J. *Introduction a l'épistémologie génétique* (Vols. I, II, & III). Paris: Presses Universitaires de France, 1950.

Piaget, J. Biography. In C. A. Murchison (Ed.), *A history of psychology in autobiography.* (Vol. 4) Worcester, Mass.: Clark University Press, 1952.

Piaget, J. Les relations entre l'intelligence en l'affectivité dans le developpement de l'enfant. *Bulletin Psychologique*, 1954, *7*, 143–150, 346–361, 522–535, 694–701.

Piaget, J. *Logic and psychology*. New York: Basic Books, 1957.(a)

Piaget, J. Programme et methods de l'épistémologie génétique. In E. W. Beth, W. Mays, & J. Piaget (Eds.), *Études d'épistémologie génétiques* (Vol. 1). Paris: Presses Universitaire de France, 1957, 2–84.(b)

Piaget, J. *The mechanisms of perception*. London: Routledge, 1969. (Originally published, 1961.)

Piaget, J. Will and action. *Bulletin of the Meninger Clinic*, 1962, *26*, 138–145.

Piaget, J. *Six psychological studies*. (D. Elkind, Ed.). New York: Random House, 1967. (Originally published, 1964.)

Piaget, J. *Insights and illusions of philosophy*. New York: Meridian Books, 1971. (Originally published, 1965.)

Piaget, J. *Biology and knowledge*. Chicago: University of Chicago Press, 1972. (Originally published, 1967.)

Piaget, J. Quantification, conservation and nativism. *Science*, 1968, *162*, 976–979.(a)

Piaget, J. *On the development of memory and identity*. Worcester, Mass.: Clark University Press, 1968.(b)

Piaget, J. *Structuralism*. New York: Basic Books, 1970. (Originally published, 1968.)(c)

Piaget, J. Interview with Elizabeth Hall. *Psychology Today*, 1970, *3*, 25–54.(a)

Piaget, J. Piaget's theory. In P. Mussen (Ed.), *Carmichael's manual of child psychology*. (Vol. I) New York: Wiley, 1970.(b)

Piaget, J. *Genetic epistemology*. New York: Norton, 1971.(a)

Piaget, J. *Science of education and the psychology of the child*. New York: Viking, 1971.(b)

Piaget, J. Intellectual evolution from adolescence to adulthood. *Human Development*, 1972, *15*, 1–12.

Piaget, J. *To understand is to invent: The future of education*. New York: Penguin, 1976.

Piaget, J., & Inhelder, B. *Le développement des quantités chez l'enfant: Conservation et atomisme*. Neuchâtel and Paris: Delachaux et Niestlé, 1941.

Piaget, J., & Inhelder, B. *The child's conception of space*. New York: Norton, 1967. (Originally published, 1948.)

Piaget, J., & Inhelder, B. *The origin of the idea of chance in children*. New York: Norton, 1976. (Originally published, 1951.)

Piaget, J., & Inhelder, B. *The psychology of the child*. New York: Basic Books, 1969, (Originally published, 1966.)(a)

Piaget, J., & Inhelder, B. *Mental imagery in the child: A study of the development of imaginal representation*. New York: Basic Books, 1971. (Originally published, 1966.)(b)

Piaget, J., & Inhelder, B. *Memory and intelligence*. New York: Basic Books, 1972. (Originally published, 1968.)

Piaget, J., Inhelder, B., & Szeminska, A. *The child's conception of geometry*. New York: Harper Torchbook, 1964. (Originally published, 1948.)

Piaget, J., & Lambercier, M. Transpositions perceptives et transitivité opératoire dans les comparaisons en profondeur. *Archives de Psychologie*, 1946, *31*, 325–368.

Piaget, J., Sinclair, H., & Vinh-Bang (Eds.). Épistémologie et psychologie de l'identité. *Études d'épistémologie génétique* (Vol. XXIV). Paris: Presses Universitaires de France, 1968.

Piaget, J., & Szeminska, A. *The child's conception of number*. New York: Norton, 1965. (Originally published, 1941.)

Piaget, J., & Voyat, G. Recherche sur l'identité d'un corps en development et sur celle du mouvement transitif. In J. Piaget, H. Sinclair, & Vinh-Bang (Eds.), Épistémologie et psychologie de l'identité. *Études d'épistémologie génétique* (Vol. XXIV). Paris: Presses Universitaires de France, 1968.

Pinard, A., & Laurendeau, M. "Stage" in Piaget's cognitive developmental theory: Exegesis of a concept. In D. Elkind & J. H. Flavell (Eds.), *Studies in cognitive development: Essays in honor of Jean Piaget.* New York: Oxford University Press, 1969.

Pinard, A., & Lavoie, G. Perception and conservation of length: Comparative study of Rwandese and French-Canadian children. *Perceptual and Motor Skills,* 1974, *39,* 363–368.

Pinneau, S. The infantile disorders of hospitalism and anaclitic depression. *Psychological Bulletin,* 1955, *52,* 429–452.

Prentice, N. M. The influence of live and symbolic modeling in promoting moral judgment of adolescent delinquents. *Journal of Abnormal Psychology,* 1972, *80,* 157–161.

Price-Williams, D. A. Study concerning concepts of conservation of quantity among primitive children. *Acta Psychologica,* 1961, *18,* 297–305.

Price-Williams, D. A., Gordon, W., & Ramirez, M. Skill and conservation: A study of pottery-making children. *Developmental Psychology,* 1969, *1,* 769.

Pufall, P. B. Egocentrism in spatial thinking: It depends on your point of view. *Developmental Psychology,* 1975, *11,* 297–303.

Rapaport, D., Gill, M. M., & Schafer, R. *Diagnostic psychological testing* (Revised and edited by R. R. Holt). New York: International Universities Press, 1968.

Renner, J. W., & Stafford, D. G. *Teaching science in the secondary school.* New York: Harper & Row, 1972.

Rest, J. Developmental hierarchy in preference and comprehension of moral judgment. Unpublished doctoral dissertation, University of Chicago, 1968.

Rest, J., Turiel, E., & Kohlberg, L. Level of moral development as a determinant of preference and comprehension of moral judgments by others. *Journal of Personality and Social Psychology,* 1969, *37,* 225–252.

Ribble, M. A. Infantile experience in relation to personality development. In J. McV. Hunt (Ed.), *Personality and the behavior disorders.* New York: Ronald, 1944.

Rimland, B. *Infantile autism: The syndrome and its implications for a neural theory.* New York: Appleton-Century-Crofts, 1964.

Rogers, C. R. *On becoming a person.* Boston: Houghton Mifflin, 1961.

Rosch, E., Mervis, C. B. Gray, W. D., Johnson, D. M., & Boyes-Braem. Basic objects in natural categories. *Cognitive Psychology,* 1976, *8,* 382–439.

Rose, S. A., & Blank, M. The potency of context in children's cognition: An illustration through conservation. *Child Development,* 1974, *45,* 499–502.

Rosenhan, D. On being sane in insane places. *Science,* 1973, *79,* 250–258.

Rosenthal, R., & Jacobson, L. *Pygmalion in the classroom.* New York: Holt, Rinehart and Winston, 1968.

Rosenthal, T. L., & Zimmerman, B. J. Modeling by exemplification and instruction in training conservation. *Developmental Psychology,* 1972, *6,* 392–401.

Ross, R. J., Hubbell, C., Ross, C. G., & Thompson, M. B. The training and transfer of formal thinking tasks in college students. *Genetic Psychology Monographs,* 1976, *93,* 171–187.

Rothenberg, B. R. Conservation of number among four- and five-year-old children: Some methodological considerations. *Child Development*, 1969, *40*, 383–406.

Rothenberg, B. R., & Orost, J. H. The training of conservation of number in young children. *Child Development*, 1969, *40*, 707–726.

Rowell, J. A., & Hoffman, P. J. Group tests for distinguishing formal from concrete thinkers. *Journal of Research in Science Teaching*, 1975, *12*, 157–164.

Rubin, K. H. Relationship between egocentric communication and popularity among peers. *Developmental Psychology*, 1972, *7*, 364.

Rubin, K. H. Egocentrism in childhood: A unitary construct? *Child Development*, 1973, *44*, 102–110.

Rubin, K. H. The relationship between spatial and communication egocentrism in children and young and old adults. *Journal of Genetic Psychology*, 1974, *125*, 295–301.

Rubin, K. H. Extinction of conservation: A life span investigation. *Developmental Psychology*, 1976, *12*, 51–56.

Ruma, E. H., & Mosher, D. L. Relationship between moral judgment and guilt in delinquent boys. *Journal of Abnormal Psychology*, 1967, *72*, 122–127.

Rutter, M., & Graham, P. Psychiatric disorders in 10- and 11-year-old children. *Proceedings of the Royal Society of Medicine*, 1965, *59*, 382–387.

Salatas, H., & Flavell, J. H. Perspective taking: The development of two components of knowledge. *Child Development*, 1976, *47*, 103–109.

Sarason, S. B. *The psychological sense of community. Prospects for a community psychology*. San Francisco: Jossey Bass, 1974.

Sarason, S. B., & Doris, J. Psychological problems in mental deficiency (4th ed.). New York: Harper & Row, 1968.

Sarason, S. B., Levine, M., Goldenberg, I., Cherlin, D., & Bennett, E. *Psychology in community settings: Clinical, educational, vocational, social aspects*. New York: Wiley, 1966.

Satir, V. *Conjoint family therapy*. Palo Alto: Science and Behavior Books, 1964.

Sattler, J. M., & Theye, F. Procedural, situational and interpersonal variables in individual intelligence testing. *Psychological Bulletin*, 1967, *68*, 347–360.

Sayre, S., & Ball, D. W. Piagetian cognitive development and achievement in science. *Journal of Research in Science Teaching*, 1975, *12*, 165–174.

Schaeffer, H. R., & Emerson, P. E. The development of social attachments in infancy. *Monographs of the Society for Research in Child Development*, No. 3, 1964, 29.

Schmid-Kitsikis, E. *L'Examen des operations de l'intelligence—psychopathologie de l'enfant*. Neuchâtel, Switzerland: Delachaux et Niestlé, 1969.

Schmid-Kitsikis, E. Piagetian theory and its approach to psychopathology. *American Journal of Mental Deficiency*, 1973, *77*, 694–705.

Schmid-Kitsikis, E. The cognitive mechanisms underlying problem-solving in psychotic and mentally retarded children. In B. Inhelder & H. H. Chapman (Eds.), *Piaget and his school: A reader in developmental psychology*. New York: Springer-Verlag, 1976.

Schrag, P., & Divoky, D. *The myth of the hyperactive child*. New York: Pantheon, 1975.

Schwebel, M. Formal operations in first year college students. *Journal of Psychology*, 1975, *91*, 133–141.

Scott, R. Social class, race, seriating and reading readiness: A study of their relationship at the kindergarten level. *Journal of Genetic Psychology*, 1969, *115*, 87–96.

Sears, R. R., Rau, L., & Alpert, R. *Identification and child rearing.* Palo Alto: Stanford University Press, 1965.

Selman, R. L. The relation of role-taking to the development of moral judgment in children. *Child Development*, 1971, *42*, 49–91.(a)

Selman, R. L. Taking another's perspective: Role-taking development in early childhood. *Child Development*, 1971, *42*, 1721–1734.(b)

Selman, R. L. Social-cognitive understanding: A guide to educational and clinical practice. In T. Lickona (Ed.), *Moral development and behavior: Theory, research, and social issues.* New York: Holt, Rinehart and Winston, 1976.

Selman, R. L., & Byrne, D. F. A structural-development analysis of levels of role-taking in middle childhood. *Child Development*, 1974, *45*, 803–806.

Serafica, F. C. Object concept in deviant children. *American Journal of Orthopsychiatry*, 1971, *41*, 473–482.

Shantz, C. U. The development of social cognition. In E. M. Hetherington (Ed.), *Review of child development research* (Vol. 5). Chicago: University of Chicago Press, 1975.

Shantz, C. U., & Watson, J. S. Assessment of spatial egocentrism through expectancy violation. *Psychonomic Science*, 1970, *18*, 93–94.

Shantz, C. U., & Watson, J. S. Spatial abilities and spatial egocentrism in the young child. *Child Development*, 1971, *42*, 171–181.

Shatz, M., & Gelman, R. The development of communication skills: Modifications in the speech of young children as a function of the listener. *Monographs of the Society for Research in Child Development*, No. 5, 1973, *38*.

Shechtman, A. Psychiatric symptoms in normal and disturbed children. *Journal of Clinical Psychology*, 1970, *26*, 38–41.

Shepard, J. L. Conservation of part and whole in the acquisition of class inclusion. *Child Development*, 1973, *44*, 380–383.

Shepherd, M., Oppenheim, A. N., & Mitchell, S. Childhood behavior disorders and the child guidance clinic: An epidemiological study. *Journal of Psychology and Psychiatry*, 1966, *7*, 39–52.

Siegel, L. S., & Goldstein, A. G. Conservation of number in young children: Recency versus relational response strategies. *Developmental Psychology*, 1969, *1*, 128–130.

Siegelman, E., & Block, J. Two parallel scalable sets of Piagetian tasks. *Child Development*, 1969, *40*, 951–956.

Siegler, R. S., & Liebert, R. M. Effects of presenting relevant rules and complete feedback on the conservation of liquid quantity task. *Developmental Psychology*, 1972, *7*, 133–138.

Siegler, R. S., & Liebert, R. M. Acquisition of formal scientific reasoning by 10- and 13-year-olds: Designing a factorial experiment. *Developmental Psychology*, 1975, *11*, 401–402.

Siegler, R. S., Liebert, D. E., & Liebert, R. M. Inhelder and Piaget's pendulum problem: Teaching preadolescents to act as scientists. *Developmental Psychology*, 1973, *9*, 97–101.

Silberman, C. E. (Ed.). *The open classroom reader.* New York: Random House (Vintage Books), 1973.

Silverman, I. W., & Geiringer, E. Dyadic interaction and conservation induction: A test of Piaget's equilibration model. *Child Development*, 1973, *44*, 815–820.

Sinclair-De Zwart, H. *Acquisition du language et développement de la pensée.* Paris: Dunod, 1967.

Sinclair-De Zwart, H. Developmental psycholinguistics. In D. Elkind & J. H. Flavell (Eds.), *Studies in cognitive development.* New York: Oxford University Press, 1969, 315–336.

Skaarbrevik, K. J. A follow-up study of educable mentally retarded in Norway. *American Journal of Mental Deficiency,* 1971, *75,* 560–565.

Skinner, B. F. *The technology of teaching.* New York: Appleton-Century-Crofts, 1968.

Smedslund, J. Apprentissage des notions de la conservation et de la transitivité du poids. *Études d'Épistémoligie Génétique,* 1959, *9,* 3–13.

Smedslund, J. The acquisition of conservation of substance and weight in children, II: External reinforcement of conservation of weight and the operations of addition and subtraction. *Scandinavian Journal of Psychology,* 1961, *2,* 71–84.(a)

Smedslund, J. The acquisition of conservation of substance and weight in children, III: Extinction of conservation of weight acquired "normally" and by means of empirical controls on a balance scale. *Scandinavian Journal of Psychology,* 1961, *2,* 85–87.(b)

Smedslund, J. Development of concrete transitivity of length in children. *Child Development,* 1963, *34,* 389–405.

Smedslund, J. Concrete reasoning: A study of intellectual development. *Monographs of the Society for Research in Child Development,* No. 2, 1964, *29.*

Somerville, S. C. The pendulum problem: Patterns of performance defining developmental stages. *British Journal of Educational Psychology,* 1974, *44,* 266–281.

Spitz, R. A. Hospitalism: A follow-up report on investigation described in Volume 1, 1945. *Psychoanalytic Studies of the Child,* 1946, *2,* 113–117.

Stafford, D. G., & Renner, J. W. SCIS helps the first grader to use simple logic in problem solving. *School Science and Mathematics,* 1971, *70,* 159–164.

Stein, J. L. Adolescents' reasoning about moral and sexual dilemmas: A longitudinal study. Unpublished doctoral dissertation, Harvard University, 1973.

Stennet, R. G. Emotional handicap in the elementary years: Phase or disease? *American Journal of Orthopsychiatry,* 1966, *36,* 444–449.

Stephens, B., McLaughlin, J. A., Miller, C. K., & Glass, G. V. Factorial structure of selected psycho-educational measures and Piagetian reasoning assessments. *Developmental Psychology,* 1972, *6,* 343–348.

Stephens, B., Manhaney, E. J., & McLaughlin, J. A. Mental ages for achievement of Piagetian reasoning assessments. *Education and Training of the Mentally Retarded,* 1972, *7,* 124–125.

Storck, P., Looft, W., & Hooper, F. Interrelationships among Piagetian tasks and traditional measures of cognitive abilities in mature and aged adults. *Journal of Gerontology,* 1972, *27,* 461–465.

Strauss, S. Inducing cognitive development and learning: A review of short-term training experiments, I: The organismic developmental approach. *Cognition,* 1972, *1,* 329–357.

Strauss, S., & Langer, J. Operational thought inducement. *Child Development,* 1970, *41,* 163–176.

Strauss, S., & Liberman, D. The empirical violation of conservation laws and its relation to structural change. *Journal of Experimental Child Psychology,* 1974, *18,* 464–479.

Suchotliff, L. C. Relation of formal thought disorder to the communication deficit in schizophrenia. *Journal of Abnormal Psychology,* 1970, *76,* 250–257.

Tam, W. T. D., Lavatelli, C. B., & Jones, R. S. Piaget's concept of classification: A comparative study of socially disadvantaged and middle-class young children. *Child Development*, 1971, *42*, 919–927.

Tanner, J. M., & Inhelder, B. (Eds.). *Discussions on child development* (Vol. II). New York: International Universities Press, 1954.

Tanner, J. M., & Inhelder, B. (Eds.). *Discussions on child development* (Vol. III). New York: International Universities Press, 1958.

Taylor, J. J., & Achenbach, T. M. Moral and cognitive development in retarded and non-retarded children. *American Journal of Mental Deficiency*, 1975, *80*, 43–50.

Tenezakis, M. D. Linguistic subsystems and concrete operations. *Child Development*, 1975, *46*, 430–436.

Thomas, H., & Jamison, W. On the acquisition of understanding that still water is horizontal. *Merrill-Palmer Quarterly*, 1975, *21*, 31–44.

Thompson, W. R., & Grusec, J. E. Studies of early experience. In P. E. Mussen (Ed.), *Carmichael's manual of child psychology* (Vol. I). New York: Wiley, 1977, 565–656.

Tisher, R. P. A Piagetian questionnaire applied to pupils in a secondary school. *Child Development*, 1971, *42*, 1633–1636.

Tomlinson-Keasey, C. Formal operations in females from eleven to fifty-four years of age. *Developmental Psychology*, 1972, *6*, 364.

Tolman, E. C. *Purposive behavior in animals and men*. New York: Appleton, 1932.

Toussaint, N. A. An analysis of synchrony between concrete-operational tasks in terms of structural and performance demands. *Child Development*, 1974, *45*, 922–1001.

Towler, J. O., & Wheatley, G. Conservation concepts in college students: A replication and critique. *Journal of Genetic Psychology*, 1971, *118*, 265–270.

Tuddenham, R. D. Theoretical regularities and individual idiosyncracies. In D. R. Green, M. P. Ford, & G. B. Flamer (Eds.), *Measurement and Piaget*. New York: McGraw-Hill, 1971.

Turiel, E. An experimental test of the sequentiality of developmental stages in the child's moral judgment. *Journal of Personality and Social Psychology*, 1966, *3*, 611–618.

Turiel, E. Developmental processes in the child's moral thinking. In P. Mussen, J. Langer, & M. Covington (Eds.), *New directions in developmental psychology*. New York: Holt, Rinehart and Winston, 1969, 92–133.

Turiel, E. Stage transition in moral development. In R. M. W. Travers (Ed.), *Second handbook of research on teaching*. Chicago: Rand McNally, 1973.

Turiel, E. Conflict and transition in adolescent moral development. *Child Development*, 1974, *45*, 14–29.

Turiel, E. The development of social concepts: Mores, customs, and conventions. In D. J. De Palma & J. M. Foley (Eds.), *Moral development: Current theory and research*. Hillsdale, N.J.: Lawrence Erlbaum Associates, 1975.

Turiel, E. Social convention and the development of societal concepts. Unpublished manuscript, University of California, Santa Cruz, 1977.

Turiel, E. The development of concepts of social structure: Social convention. In J. Glick & A. Clarke-Stuart (Eds.), *Personality and social development* (Vol. 1). New York: Gardner Press, 1978.

Urberg, K. A., & Docherty, E. M. Development of role-taking skills in young children. *Developmental Psychology*, 1976, *12*, 198–204.

Uzgiris, I. C. Patterns of cognitive development in infancy. *Merrill-Palmer Quarterly*,

1973, *19*, 181–204.

Uzgiris, I. C. Infant development from a Piagetian approach: Introduction to a symposium. *Merrill-Palmer Quarterly*, 1976, *22*, 3–10.

Uzgiris, I. C., & Hunt, J. McV. *Assessment in infancy: Ordinal scales of psychological development*. Urbana, Ill.: University of Illinois Press, 1975.

Vernon, P. E. Ability factors and environmental influences. *American Psychologist*, 1965, *20*, 723–733.(a)

Vernon, P. E. Environmental handicaps and intellectual development. *British Journal of Education Psychology*, 1965, *35*, 1–12 (Pt. 1), 13–22 (Pt. 2).(b)

Vinh-Bang. La méthode clinique et la récherche en psychologie de l'enfant. In F. Bresson and M. Montmollin (Eds.), *Psychologie et épistémologie génétiques: Thèmes Piagetiens*. Paris: Dunod, 1966.

Vitello, S. Facilitation of class inclusion among mentally retarded children. *American Journal of Mental Deficiency*, 1973, *28*, 158–162.

Vygotsky, L. S. *Thought and language*. Cambridge, Mass.: M.I.T. Press, 1962.

Wachs, T. D. Relation of infants' performance on Piaget scales between twelve and twenty-four months and their Stanford-Binet performance at thirty-one months. *Child Development*, 1975, *46*, 929–935.

Wachs, T. D. Utilization of a Piagetian approach in the investigation of early experience effects: A research strategy and some illustrative data. *Merrill-Palmer Quarterly*, 1976, *22*, 11–30.

Watson, J. B. *Behavior: An introduction to comparative psychology*. New York: Holt, 1914.

Watson, J. S. Smiling, cooing and "the game." *Merrill-Palmer Quarterly*, 1972, *18*, 323–339.

Watzlawick, P., Beavin, J. H., & Jackson, D. D. *Pragmatics of human communication*. New York: Norton, 1967.

Wechsler, D. *The measurement and appraisal of adult intelligence* (4th ed.). Baltimore: Williams and Wilkins, 1958.

Weschsler Intelligence Scale for Children. New York: The Psychological Corporation, 1974. (Originally published, 1949.) (Manual)

Weintraub, S. A. *Cognitive and behavioral impulsivity in internalizing, externalizing and normal children*. Unpublished doctoral dissertation, University of Minnesota, 1968.

Weitz, L. J., Bynum, T. W., Thomas, J. A., & Steger, J. A. Piaget's system of 10 binary operations: An empirical investigation. *Journal of Genetic Psychology*, 1973, *123*, 279–284.

Wepman, J. M. Auditory discrimination, speech, and reading. *Elementary School Journal*, 1960, *9*, 325–333.

Werner, H. *Comparative psychology of mental development*. New York: Follett, 1948.

Wheatley, G. H. A motion picture test of Piagetian concepts. *Psychology in the Schools*, 1975, *12*, 21–25.

White, R. W. Motivation reconsidered: The concept of competence. *Psychological Review*, 1959, *66*, 297–333.

Whorf, B. L. *Language, thought and reality* (J. B. Carroll, Ed.) Cambridge: M.I.T. Press, 1956.

Winkelmann, W. Factorial analysis of children's conservation task performance. *Child Development*, 1974, *45*, 843–848.

Wohlwill, J. F. Piaget's theory of the development of intelligence in the concrete operations period. *American Journal of Mental Deficiency Monograph Supplement*, No. 4, 1966, *70*.

Woodward, M. The behavior of idiots interpreted by Piaget's theory of sensorimotor development. *British Journal of Educational Psychology*, 1959, *29*, 60–71.

Woodward, M. Concepts of number in the mentally subnormal studied by Piaget's method. *Journal of Child Psychology and Psychiatry*, 1961, *2*, 249–259.

Woodward, M. The application of Piaget's theory to research in mental deficiency. In W. R. Ellis (Ed.), *Handbook of mental deficiency*. New York: McGraw-Hill, 1963.

Wynne, L., & Singer, M. Thought disorder and family relations of schizophrenics, II: A classification of forms of thinking. *Archives of General Psychiatry*, 1963, *9*, 199–206.

Youniss, J. Operational development in deaf Costa Rican subjects. *Child Development*, 1974, *45*, 212–216.

Youniss, J., & Dean, A. Judgment and imagining aspects of operations: A Piagetian study with Korean and Costa Rican children. *Child Development*, 1974, *45*, 1020–1031.

Zimmerman, B. J., & Lanaro, P. Acquiring and retaining conservation of length throught modeling cues and reversibility cues. *Merrill-Palmer Quarterly*, 1974, *20*, 145–161.

NAME INDEX

SUBJECT INDEX